From Hitler's Doorstep

FROM HITLER'S DOORSTEP

The Wartime Intelligence Reports of Allen Dulles, 1942–1945

Edited with Commentary by
Neal H. Petersen

The Pennsylvania State University Press
University Park, Pennsylvania

Library of Congress Cataloging-in-Publication Data

Dulles, Allen Welsh, 1893–1969.
From Hitler's doorstep : the wartime intelligence reports of Allen Dulles, 1942–1945 / edited with commentary by Neal H. Petersen.

p. cm.
Chiefly a collection of telegrams from Allen Welsh Dulles, as head of the Bern Office of the OSS, to headquarters in Washington; based on the operational records of the OSS (Record Group 226) in the U.S. National Archives.
Includes bibliographical references (p.) and index.
ISBN 0-271-01485-7
1. World War, 1939–1945—Secret service—United States. 2. World War, 1939–1945—Sources. 3. Dulles, Allen Welsh, 1893–1969. I. Petersen, Neal H. II. United States. Office of Strategic Services. Bern Office. III. Title.
D810.S7D78 1996
940.54'8673—dc20 95–34966
CIP

Printed in the United States of America
Published by The Pennsylvania State University Press,
University Park, PA 16802–1003

It is the policy of The Pennsylvania State University Press to use acid-free paper for the first printing of all clothbound books. Publications on uncoated stock satisfy the minimum requirements of American National Standard for Information Sciences—Permanence of Paper for Printed Library Materials, ANSI Z39.48—1992.

To those who fought the secret war
against twentieth-century totalitarianism

Contents

Preface

This volume is based primarily on the Operational Records of the Office of Strategic Services (Record Group 226) at the National Archives, Washington, D.C. The author is grateful for expert advice from John Taylor and Lawrence McDonald on the use of OSS records. I also appreciate the assistance I received from staff members at the Seeley G. Mudd Manuscript Library, Princeton University, repository of the Allen Dulles Papers; the U.S. Army Military History Institute, Carlisle Barracks, Pennsylvania, which houses the William J. Donovan Papers; and the Franklin D. Roosevelt Library, Hyde Park, New York. I was fortunate to have the editorial assistance of my wife, Nancy Petersen, and the computer guidance of Joseph Longo. Richard Breitman, Dean Rexford, and James Dacey helped me obtain photographs. Sandy Thatcher, Peggy Hoover, and Andrew Lewis of Penn State Press provided support, encouragement, and first-rate treatment of the manuscript in editorial review and other aspects of the publication process.

Most messages reproduced in this volume are telegrams from Bern to Washington, with information copies often sent to London and Algiers or Caserta. When the telegram is directed to a location other than Washington, the heading so indicates. Information copies of such telegrams were generally transmitted to Washington. Telegrams from Bern to OSS Washington were usually designated "SI" (Secret Intelligence Branch) for action, with information copies to Director William J. Donovan and the OSS secretariat. Distribution is not indicated unless it had particular significance. Transmittal to the White House or State Department is often noted.

When a telegram was slugged for special handling according to topic, for instance BREAKERS, KAPPA, or AZUSA, this designation is reproduced in the first line of the telegram. The times of transmittal and receipt are not indicated in the text or annotation unless they had special significance. Telegrams from Bern were sometimes classified "secret." This security classification is not reproduced. A second category of message sent by Allen Dulles from Bern were radiotelephone transmissions, or "flashes." Less secure than telegrams, they usually bore the classification "restricted," which is also not reproduced here.

When a document is not printed in its entirety, omissions are indicated by ellipses. Deletions were made in the interest of saving space, eliminating extraneous or repetitive material, or maintaining clarity and simplicity of presentation. No material was removed due to continuing security classification or sensitivity.

Similarly, when an individual or source is not fully identified it simply indicates that the matter defied my best efforts. Generally, punctuation, capitalization, and the spelling of place names have been reproduced from the original documents, although a number of obvious errors have been corrected.

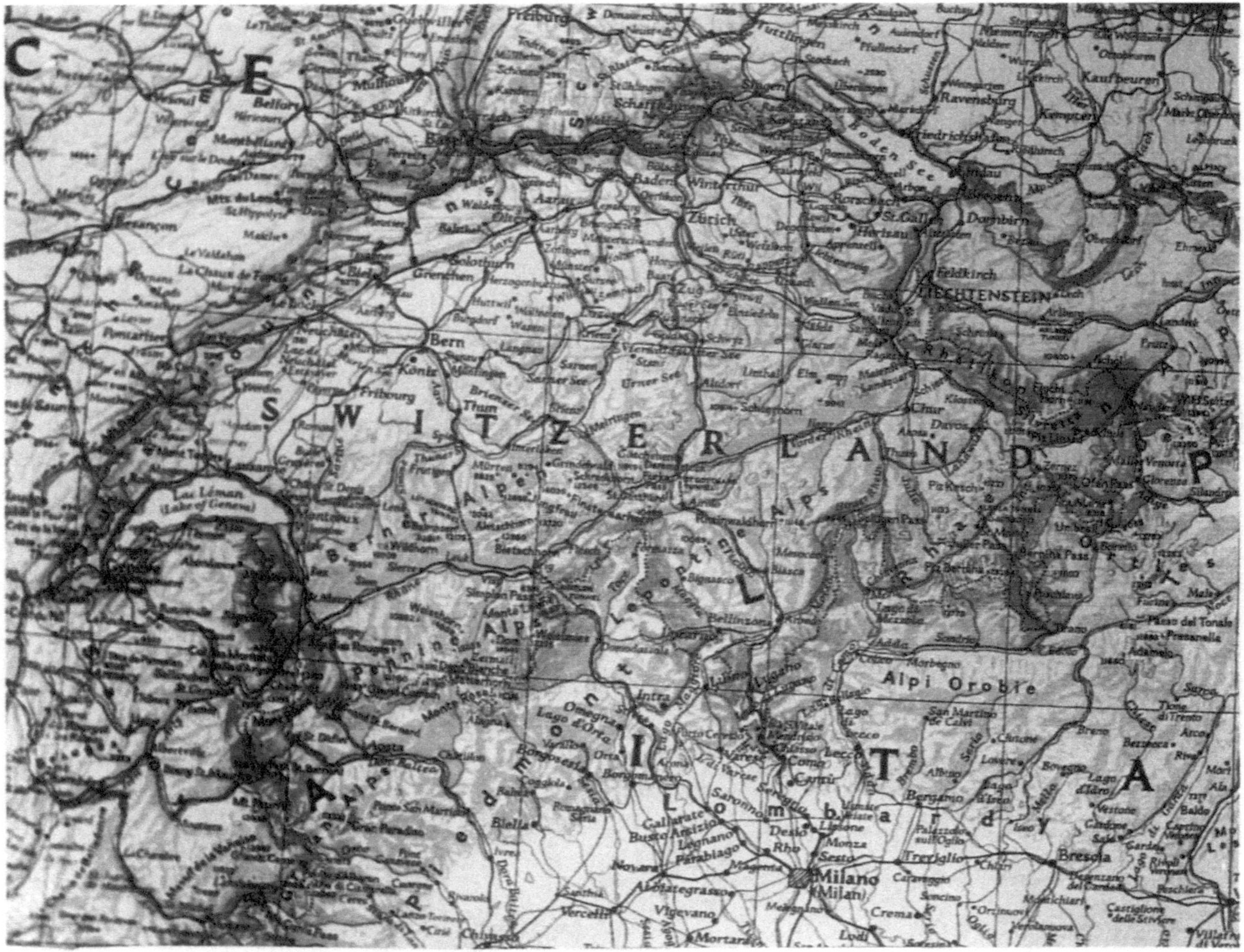

Wartime Switzerland (Courtesy, National Geographic Society)

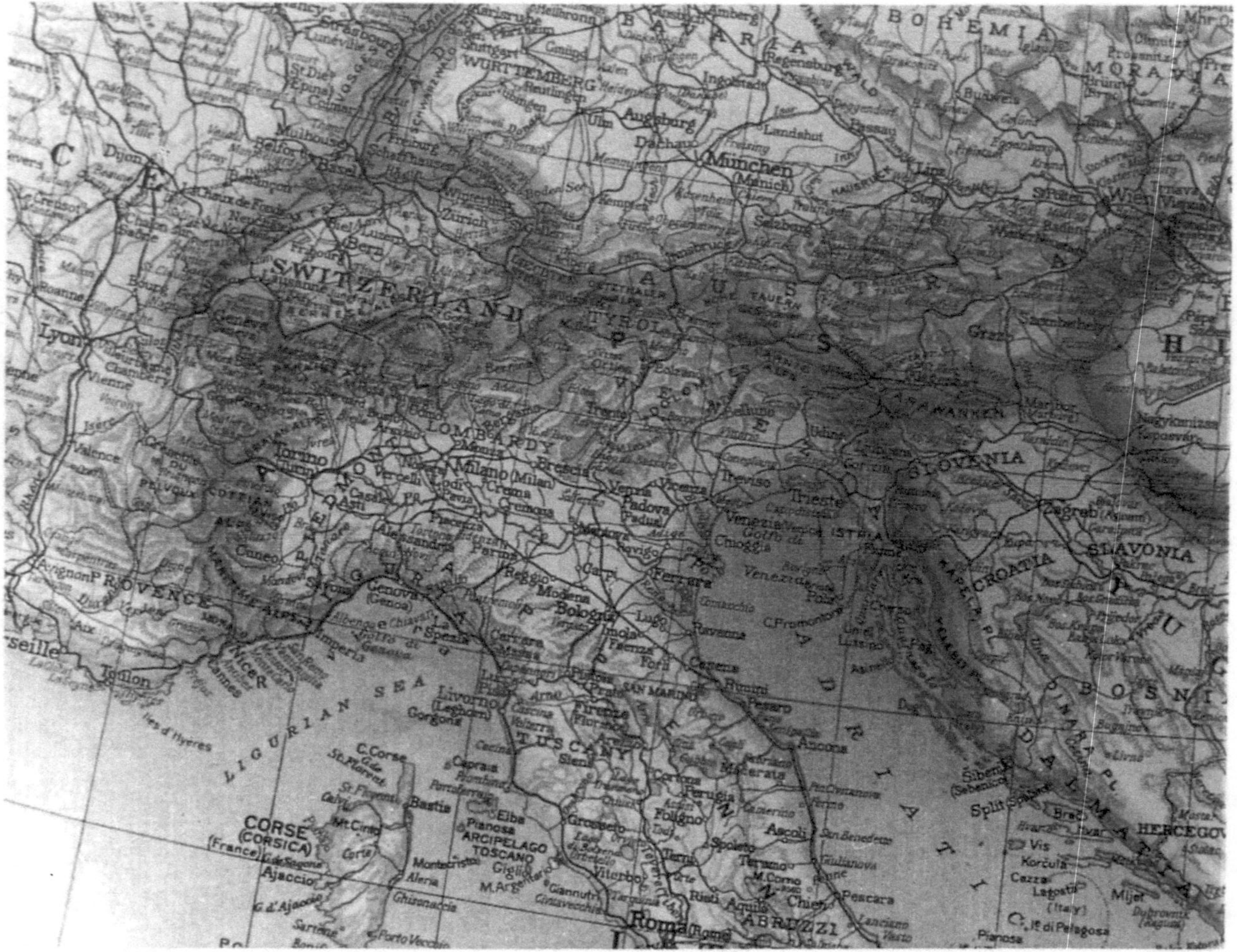

Switzerland and surrounding territory, 1943 (Courtesy, National Geographic Society)

Introduction

For thirty-two months during World War II, the mission of the Office of Strategic Services (OSS) in Bern, Switzerland, was an American observation post at Hitler's doorstep. It transmitted thousands of messages to Washington, many of them bearing evidence of the personal involvement of Allen Dulles, mission chief. OSS Bern constituted a virtual Central Intelligence Agency in itself, with operations ranging from the gathering of battle order information, to running espionage networks in enemy territory, to orchestrating unconventional military operations. Dulles ventured far beyond the usual domain of intelligence, offering his own views on grand strategy and psychological warfare.

The historical significance of the Bern episode is multifaceted. We see in action one of the important figures of twentieth-century American statecraft at the height of his powers. The messages also offer a new perspective on the history of World War II, providing rich detail and insight and a bridge between diplomacy and intelligence. The Bern operations and the views of Dulles deserve a place in the final analysis of the political/military course and outcome of the conflict. With regard to the evolution of American intelligence, the Bern documents indicate the emergence of institutional cohesiveness and proficiency in tradecraft. One stands at the moment of OSS transition from old-fashioned political intelligence-gathering to more sophisticated techniques of the modern era.

Background of a Spymaster

Early Years

By the age of fifty, Allen Dulles had accumulated impressive career accomplishments. Upon arrival in Switzerland in November 1942, hours before the Nazis sealed the French border, he was eminently qualified by experience and intellect for the task he was undertaking. Born in Watertown, New York, into an internationalist environment—his grandfather and uncle were Secretaries of State—he was soon exposed to foreign affairs and foreign dignitaries. The influence of his father, a liberal Presbyterian minister, left him at once deeply religious and broad-minded. He had the benefit of visits to highly placed relatives in Washington, and European travel and studies as a youth. Dulles developed an early confidence based on a belief that he belonged to an aristocracy of ability, intellectual accomplishment, connections, and service, rather than of wealth. Allen and his siblings, particularly older brother Foster (Princeton valedictorian of 1908) and younger sister Eleanor, provided powerful support for one another over the decades.

At Princeton, Allen Dulles established lifelong friendships with other future men-of-affairs. For example, his classmate John C. Hughes would head the OSS office in New York and later become Ambassador to NATO. After college, Dulles taught English at the Ewing Christian College in Allahabad, India, traveled in the Far East, and took a graduate degree in international relations before joining the diplomatic service in 1916 at the age of twenty-three.

Posted to Vienna and Bern during World War I, his duties included collecting intelligence, there being no centralized national intelligence service. Dulles later described his real activity as providing Washington with intelligence about affairs in Germany, Austria-Hungary, and the Balkans. He became familiar with the culture, politics, and ethnic divisions of Central Europe in the final days of the Austro-Hungarian Empire. His letters to his mother reveal the evolution of an awe-struck beginner to a self-assured and proficient young diplomat–intelligence-gatherer. His early assignments provided him with lifelong contacts in the Foreign Service—including Hugh Wilson, who administered the oath to Dulles when he became Third Secretary at Bern. Wilson rose to become Minister to Switzerland (1927–37) and Ambassador to Germany (1938) and served on the OSS Planning Board during World War II.

The Paris Peace Conference

The Paris Peace Conference of 1919 was crucial for Dulles's career. He served as a low-level adviser on the Central European settlements, while his brother Foster played a larger role on the economic provisions. The brothers had influence far beyond that accorded by their official positions, because their uncle was Secretary of State Robert Lansing ("Uncle Bert"). Allen made additional long-term friendships and associations at Paris. He reported to Leland Harrison, with whom he was soon on a first-name basis. Harrison became Minister to Switzerland in 1937 and cooperated intimately with Dulles during World War II. Dulles also had official contact with Joseph Grew, Secretary General of the American Commission to Negotiate the Peace. Grew, subsequent Ambassador to Japan and Undersecretary of State, eventually became a Dulles friend.

The Dulles brothers sat on an intelligence committee focusing on Germany that included Ellis Dresel of the State Department; Adolph A. Berle, destined to become State's focal point for intelligence in World War II; and Royall Tyler, later a League of Nations expert and a leading Allen Dulles collaborator in Switzerland two decades afterward. The experience of helping to draw borders and determine the fate of European peoples had a lasting effect on Allen and convinced him that the problem of Europe was essentially the problem of Germany. The Dulles brothers, supportive of the Wilsonian precepts of self-determination and peace through international law, left Paris partially dissatisfied with the conference results, and in particular with the stern provisions of the Versailles Treaty respecting Germany. Allen was also critical of the dismemberment of Hungary.

State Department Official, 1920–1926

After Paris, Dulles accompanied Dresel to open the U.S. mission in Berlin and witnessed the anarchy of 1920. He was then stationed in Constantinople, where he gained an appreciation of the Turkish perspective on international relations that would serve him later. He formed a new network of contacts, including Betty Carp, an Austrian-born linguist and scholar who was associated with the State Department for decades. One of his concerns was the fate of General Peter Wrangel, the White Russian leader. Back in Washington, he became Chief of the Division of Near Eastern Affairs in 1922. For the next four years he appeared to be the model young officer destined for high rank. However, he devoted his nights to obtaining a law degree and in 1926 resigned to accept a position in New York. His departure, ostensibly based on financial grounds, received wide notice. Dulles's ten years in the diplomatic service gave him an enormous advantage over other able and well-connected private citizens who rallied to the government standard in World War II. The State Department leaders of the war period had been his colleagues in the 1920s. His term of duty gave him an intimate understanding of the foreign policy process, from high-level diplomacy to the intricacies of protocol, consular affairs, networking, and intelligence-gathering.

New York, 1926–1941

From 1926 to 1941 Allen Dulles practiced law at Sullivan & Cromwell in New York, where his brother held a top management position. Here he interacted with the aristocracy of East Coast business and finance while establishing powerful international commercial connections. That his work often took him to Europe was of great value later. During the war, Max Shoop and Philippe Monod of Sullivan & Cromwell's Paris office were to manage critical espionage lines from Switzerland into France.

In this New York period, Dulles was a leading light in the Council on Foreign Relations, holding the position of Secretary from 1933 to 1941. He was to serve as Vice-President and then President of the organization after the war. His close friend Hamilton Fish Armstrong was editor of *Foreign Affairs*. Whitney Shepardson, later Chief of the OSS Secret Intelligence Branch, was Treasurer of the Council. Dulles further augmented his range of acquaintances through membership in the Century Club, the Lloyd Neck Bath Club, and the Piping Rock Country Club (which was to hound him about his delinquent dues during World War II). Dulles was active in Republican politics, running unsuccessfully for Congress in 1938 on a reform platform and working on the Willkie campaign of 1940.

Dulles also maintained his State Department ties in an advisory capacity in areas including disarmament. These activities frequently took him to Switzerland, where he renewed acquaintances and further developed sources of information. The election of a Democratic President, Franklin Roosevelt, in 1932 diminished Dulles's State Department advisory function, but he did continue to assist in the area of disarmament for a time. In the spring of 1933, Dulles accompanied arms-control expert Norman Davis on a tour of European capitals for meetings with leaders including Ramsay MacDonald, Neville Chamberlain, Leon Blum, and Paul Boncour. On April 8, 1933, Davis and Dulles met Adolf Hitler and his advisers in Berlin.

The Approach of World War II

From his first posting in 1916, to his final official duty as a representative of the President at the funeral of Konrad Adenauer in 1967, Germany remained among Dulles's foremost concerns. As officers of Sullivan & Cromwell, the Dulles brothers arranged massive loans for Germany, motivated in substantial measure by the belief that that nation's economic health was essential for international economic stability and world peace. Allen reacted vigorously to the rise of Hitler, and over the objections of Foster convinced Sullivan & Cromwell to close its Berlin office in 1935. Allen became a leader of the interventionist movement, heading organizations and writing books on the theme that U.S. interests were best served by helping the democracies of Western Europe resist Nazi revisionism.

William J. Donovan, President Roosevelt's personal intelligence adviser, reportedly approached Dulles about a position in his envisaged national organization at the Republican National Convention of 1940. Dulles himself later wrote that Donovan, an old friend whom he had known in Washington and in New York, had asked for his services shortly after Pearl Harbor. Yet the two men were not intimate associates, and the circumstances of Dulles's recruitment remain unclear. According to Dulles, Donovan had first wanted him to go to London to work with Donovan himself and David Bruce but he, Dulles, had opted for Switzerland. In any event, before the United States entered the war, Dulles became chief of the New York office of the Coordinator of Information (COI), forerunner to OSS. The COI offices were located in the same building as those of British Security Coordination headed by William Stephenson, "Intrepid." There Dulles honed his skills in the fine points of information-gathering, espionage, and psychological warfare. The fragmentary records of this period indicate that Dulles's office had a strong interest in enlisting foreign nationals in the United States and that he concentrated on French and Swiss matters. While in Bern from 1942 to 1945, Dulles maintained an intimate relationship with the New York OSS office, treating it almost as a personal home port and headquarters, as opposed to Washington.

By experience, intellect, and temperament, Dulles was superbly qualified for the Bern position. The man who went to Switzerland bore scant resemblance to the partially self-created avuncular buffoon image of later years. He was a figure of ability, shrewdness, and complexity. His power base rested not on personal ties to Donovan or the President or on institutional factors, but on twenty-five years of accumulated contacts, friends, and associates from the East Coast, international business, and finance, and especially the Department of State.

Assignment in Switzerland, 1942–1945

The Bern Environment

Dulles lived and worked at Herrengasse 23 in comfortable accommodations once occupied by his friend Hugh Wilson. Clover, Dulles's wife, remained in the United States. He bore the title of Special Assistant to the Minister, Leland Harrison, a State Department acquaintance of long standing, and drew on the Legation for staff and communications support. His small contingent consisted of a few true OSS officers and whatever help he could get from Americans trapped in Switzerland by the war, downed airmen, and foreign nationals. His top aide was Gero von Gaevernitz, a German-American businessman residing in Switzerland. He relied heavily as well on Gerald Mayer, the Legation's representative of the Office of War Information, and worked closely with Military Attaché Brigadier General Barnwell Legge. Late in the war, with the border again open, the staff was augmented by OSS operatives Paul Blum, Gerhard Van Arkel, Henry Hyde, and Tracy Barnes. Dulles friends resident in Switzerland included American Mary Bancroft, British scholar Elizabeth Wiskemann, and psychologist Carl Jung. OSS maintained posts at Geneva, Zurich, Basel, and Lugano.

Switzerland teemed with the spies of all nations, closely watched by the intelligence service of the neutrality-conscious local authorities. The OSS maintained satisfactory ties with Swiss intelligence, which improved as the outcome of the war became apparent. Dulles played by rules that allowed the Swiss to avoid German objections. The many refugees and exiles in Switzerland offered rich intelligence possibilities, as did the diplomats of neutral, Axis satellite, and indeed Axis nations. International business and religious connections survived amazingly well in wartime conditions; travelers regularly supplied reports for the Dulles operation.

With Switzerland entirely surrounded by enemy-controlled territory, written documents could be smuggled in and out only at great risk, and telegraphic and radio means provided the only reliable links to Washington, London, and Algiers. Operating under infrequent directives from Donovan and guidance from his old Council on Foreign Relations associate Whitney Shepardson, head of the OSS Secret Intelligence Branch, Dulles exploited the opportunity to develop a large measure of autonomy. He worked closely with the Legation and Minister Leland Harrison, but more as a respectful colleague than as a subordinate. It is important to note that, well before the arrival of Dulles, the Legation and its consular satellites in Geneva, Zurich, and Basel had established an elaborate intelligence network of its own reaching into enemy territory. Sources including "Ralph" and "Frank" reported regularly on conditions in France and Germany. The Dulles system, involving scores of sources with code and cover names, and intermediaries, was as much an extension of State Department practice as anything invented by the infant OSS or borrowed from the British.

Battle Order, Bombing Targets, Secret Weapons

Most OSS Bern reports concerned military subjects—enemy formations, troop movements, and bombing results. The present volume includes little of this information, except for illustrative purposes or in special circumstances. It remains for military historians to assemble the data and evaluate it in detail. Dulles's military intelligence information originated with courageous patriots (and occasionally swindlers) on beaches, in factories, at railway stations and highways, and in partisan bands. Reports, in French, Italian, or German, made their way to Switzerland through local resistance or OSS courier services. They were processed, usually by source 284, Max Shoop, in Geneva or by source 472, the remnants in Switzerland of prewar French intelligence, prior to transmittal. Dulles sometimes added a comment or caveat. Order of Battle information took a long time to get from the source through Bern to London or Washington and was not closely keyed to wartime developments of the moment. Events such as the Normandy invasion and the Battle of the Bulge scarcely caused a blip in the flow of reports. The value of this material was in its quantity and detail. Initial military reaction was scathing denunciation of Bern's inaccuracy. Ratings from Washington improved as the war progressed. Also, the Bern information was used to confirm and supplement Ultra intercepts. Bombing result reports and suggestions for targets also were valued highly. In some matters Ultra could not replace eyewitness accounts.

The Dulles organization contributed to the aggregate Allied effort to determine the state of Nazi progress in atomic energy ("Azusa" reports) and chemical and biological warfare ("Toledo" reports). The theater-wide message that emerged was reassuring: most Nazi secret weapons were not far advanced and were dangerous only as propaganda. Bern also made a great contribution to Allied knowledge of the German V-1 and V-2 programs, reporting on the progress of research and development and the location of scientific installations and deployed launching sites. Information transmitted by Dulles helped make bombing strikes effective and mitigated surprise and dismay in England when German rockets and missiles became operational. As in the case of battle order intelligence, the Bern contribution is difficult to assess in terms of its importance in the overall mosaic created from multiple sources, including Ultra and information from French agent/patriots reporting directly to London.

The French Resistance

Upon arrival in Switzerland, Dulles immediately addressed the question of support for the French resistance in the southern part of the country. His former Sullivan & Cromwell colleagues Shoop and Monod organized lines from Geneva to Lyons and established close contacts with resistance figures, including Henri Frenay of the Combat organization and the rightist Pierre de Benouville. League of Nations officials René Charron (code name "Boatman") and the American Royall Tyler also submitted frequent reports from sources within France. The role of Dulles and the OSS generally was minor in terms of arms and financial support, but it was enough to infuriate General Charles de Gaulle, who resented American interference and the British who legitimately claimed a violation of the OSS-SOE agreement of June 1942 that accorded London the leading role in Allied relations with European resistance movements. Dulles claimed that he was only gathering intelligence, but he clearly sought to provide direct American support to groups that were in desperate straits and whom the Free French abroad and the British could not or would not assist.

OSS Bern rendered important services to the resistance in the form of funds and encouragement. Source 328 in Switzerland maintained steady contact with "Eva" in New York through Bern, involving anti-Axis exiles in the United States such as Jacques Maritain. The Dulles organization within Switzerland included many French officers who had taken refuge there after the 1940 collapse. OSS Bern was quite willing to deal with General Giraud and quasi-Vichy types, further complicating U.S. relations with de Gaulle. At the same time, Dulles maintained relations with the extreme French left, both in Switzerland and in the occupied homeland. In the latter stages of the war, the OSS supported Maquis operations in southeastern France and used the area as a staging area for penetration of Germany. As a final insult to the proud and determined leader of the Free French abroad, Dulles provided a channel of communication to remnants of the centrist political parties of the Third Republic and implicitly supported their contention that the Anglo-American allies should not turn control of the country over to de Gaulle without an expression of national opinion.

The Italian Resistance

Geographical factors and imperfect German control made Italy a prime target for Dulles, both for intelligence-gathering and for resistance support. Dulles advised Washington on the twists and turns leading to Il Duce's fall, the Italian surrender, and the German retreat, constantly agitating for Allied support of partisan warfare in the north. OSS Bern worked closely with Magistrati, the Italian minister in Switzerland, and some military figures, but concentrated on contacts with the democratic left in northern Italy. The aging socialist exiles Ignazio Silone and Joseph Modigliani received support and were given a channel of communication to the outside world. Dulles doubtless spent too much effort on ineffectual intellectuals, British cast-off sources, and dangerous political renegades. Yet he also gained the confidence of many truly important Italians—including Ferruccio Parri, a future Premier—and laid the groundwork for successful late-war maneuvers, including the German surrender in North Italy. OSS Bern served as a mailbox for the resistance and exile figures, including Count Sforza, and for contact with Italian-American labor and liberal elements. Through Dulles, the Italian opposition received significant funding from U.S.-based sympathizers, such as Maestro Arturo Toscanini. This presaged the U.S. role in the Italian elections of 1948. In the last months of the war, Dulles waged a bitter struggle on behalf of direct U.S. aid to partisans, over British opposition.

The German Resistance

Throughout his career, Allen Dulles remained preoccupied with Germany. In Bern, his top priority was fulfillment of the complementary objectives of Nazi defeat and emergence of a democratic and pro-West Germany. His top assistants and sources were German expatriates, German-Americans, and German agents, including Gaevernitz, Hans Bernd Gisevius, and Eduard Waetjen of the Abwehr, businessman Eduard Schulte, and Fritz Kolbe of the German Foreign Ministry.

Kolbe, code name "George Wood," was among the most important agents in place of the war. An assistant to Karl Ritter who was responsible for liaison between the Foreign Ministry and the military, Kolbe had access to an incredible array of documents that were exchanged between the two entities. A passionate anti-Nazi, he arranged for official duties to take him to Switzerland, offered his services to the Allies as a walk-in, and then returned to his post. Beginning in August 1943 he smuggled hundreds of top German diplomatic and military documents to Dulles in Bern. Once Kolbe's good faith was established, the information he provided was circulated widely, probably too widely for the agent's safety. OSS Bern cabled the Wood Traffic to Washington with the designation "Kappa." At OSS headquarters, the take was reorganized by subject and distributed as the "Boston Series." The White House received this material on a regular basis. The Wood Traffic shed light on German policy, plans, activities, and problems around the world. It was particularly helpful on the Reich's relations with neutral Turkey and its difficulties with its satellites. The Germans spied constantly on their Japanese allies, often picking up information on Tokyo's relations with the Soviet Union, which in turn was intercepted by Kolbe for the West. The Wood Traffic contributed to the unmasking of Cicero, the German spy in the household of the British Ambassador in Turkey.

In large measure, Dulles established his credibility in Washington by reporting on the emergence of the German military opposition to Hitler, which culminated in the July 20, 1944, attempt on the Führer's life. He transmitted vital information from a variety of sources, including German intelligence agents, in the "Breakers" series. His foremost contact was Gisevius, an Abwehr officer stationed in Zurich, who was a member of the opposition's inner circle. Just before the failed putsch on July 20, 1944, Dulles was able to inform Washington of the imminent move against Hitler and to identify the major plotters.

Dulles also nurtured contacts with numerous German center-left exiles, including labor leaders and such Weimar-era politicians as former Chancellor Jozef Wirth. He began planning for postwar Germany in 1942, compiling lists of "useful Germans" who could serve in a new democratic regime by virtue of their anti-Nazi records. Dulles was the driving force behind the organizing of the OSS postwar mission in Germany, which he ultimately headed.

Throughout the war, Dulles promoted policies he deemed conducive to winning German hearts and minds for western democracy. While expressing support for the doctrine of "unconditional surrender" as good psychological warfare, he spoke out against any interpretation that could be viewed by the German people as meaning dismemberment, poverty, humiliation, and Soviet domination. Neither Dulles's espionage success through contacts in Germany nor his policy views had any appreciable impact on the conduct of the war by the Anglo-American high command. His efforts did contribute to an enlightened and effective postwar occupation policy.

The Balkans, Hungary, and Austria

Dulles developed close ties with influential representatives of the Balkan states and Hungary who sought to save their homelands from both German and Soviet control. He benefited tremendously from previous Foreign Service and business contacts. His top assistant with regard to Hungary and to some extent other East European nations was Royall Tyler, an American official of the League of Nations who had served in Budapest between the wars as a financial adviser to the Hungarian government. Tyler had the full confidence of Premier Nicholas Kallay and other Hungarian leaders. Information from Bakach-Bessenyey, the Hungarian minister in Bern, Gregoire Gafencu of Rumania, and Gheorghi Kiosseivanov, the Bulgarian minister (code name "Kiss") gave Dulles an excellent, up-to-date appreciation of the tumultuous three-way struggle for power in central and southeastern Europe. But neither OSS Bern nor the western allies generally could influence events. Some operations designed to link up with friendly elements, such as "Sparrow" in Hungary, ended in disaster.

Austrian resistance elements were slow to develop both within the country and in exile. Dulles did receive information from some businessmen and powerless left-leaning labor elements. Late in the war, he employed Fritz Molden, a courageous young resistance activist who was to become his son-in-law. Austria assumed substantial importance in 1945 from Allied apprehension that its mountainous regions might be the site of a Nazi last stand.

Psychological Warfare

In addition to his weighty responsibilities in traditional intelligence matters, Dulles devoted priority attention to psychological warfare and the more mundane area of information collection and dissemination. The importance he attached to ideas, perceptions, and the use of both sensitive and public information to influence events is central to understanding the man's performance in Bern and his career generally. From day one, he bludgeoned Washington and London with psychological warfare proposals designed to split the Axis peoples from their leaders and the satellites from the principal enemies.

Dulles pursued three interlocking psychological objectives: victory through the undermining of German morale; support for the German opposition; and the winning of the hearts and minds of the peoples of Europe for the West and for democracy, in competition with the Soviet Union. In January 1943, Roosevelt and Churchill enunciated the doctrine of "unconditional surrender" at the Casablanca Conference. Dulles initially supported the policy as sound psychological warfare. It underscored for the Nazis the inevitability of defeat, sapped their will to prolong the war in hope of a negotiated settlement, and dashed hopes for a separate peace with the Anglo-Saxons, who might have been expected to be amenable in order to prevent the spread of Bolshevism.

As the war progressed, Dulles became discouraged by the effect of the "unconditional surrender" policy on the German resistance. He relayed the laments of would-be opponents of Hitler who felt that the West offered them no hope for the future and no reason for risking death at the hands of the Gestapo. He urged explicit statements by Roosevelt and Churchill that unconditional surrender did not mean the destruction of the German nation and people. In August 1943 he cabled that psychological efforts of the West lagged behind military progress, and implied that the psychological war was being lost to both Goebbels and Stalin.

One recurring theme in Dulles's reports was the danger that the frustrated Germans might seek the Eastern Solution, a new accommodation with Russia. In his view, Soviet propaganda was busy and successful. He warned of such tendencies among military opponents to Hitler, including Count von Stauffenberg, the would-be assassin of July 20. He feared the effect of the Free Germany Committee, established in Moscow and headed by respected captured German generals, and lamented that the West had nothing comparable. By 1944 he was urging that OSS Morale Operations personnel be transferred to secret intelligence duties, because the United

States had no psychological strategy to implement. Dulles advocated a campaign to place the western allies in a favorable light vis-à-vis the Soviet Union in the eyes of Europeans. With regard to bombing, he wanted to plaster Berlin to break German morale, but he urged great caution in targeting non–German-occupied areas and regions of the Reich remote from the capital.

Press, Church, and Scholarly Contacts

Under Dulles, OSS Bern spared no effort in providing Washington with useful unclassified information, including press coverage. For most of the war, Dulles delivered extensive nightly radiotelephone transmissions, dealing in part with pure intelligence and his personal thoughts on the course of the war, but mainly on what Europeans were thinking and writing. Bern also sent a "Weekly Summary for Elmer," which was much valued by the OWI and its chief, Elmer Davis. Via a system patterned on that of the *New York Times*, Dulles sent copious quantities of press material to the OSS New York office. This material, called "Hugbear" after Dulles's friends John Hughes and Frederick Dolbeare of OSS New York, had a counterpart to satisfy Dulles's interest in U.S. press items ("reverse Hugbear"). The New York office's "Swiss Project" consisted of efforts to digest Dulles material and to respond to his requests.

Dulles recognized that the world of intellectual and religious pursuits offered additional potential networks for intelligence/information-gathering and possibilities for influencing international opinion-makers. With the war raging, Dulles found time to interest himself in publisher Emil Oprecht's ties to the U.S. market, Professor V. F. Wagner's Danubian studies (financed by the Carnegie Foundation through Dulles), the publication of Gisevius's manuscript on the German resistance, Italian resistance figure Ignazio Silone's search for a U.S. publisher, and the procurement of the Ciano diaries from the count's widow.

As a lifelong Presbyterian lay activist, Dulles cultivated clergymen and officials of religious organizations residing in wartime Switzerland. These included German Catholic and Protestant notables and Dr. W. A. Visser 't Hooft of the World Council of Churches. He also remained in close contact with Unitarian relief and the International Committee of the Red Cross.

The British Connection

Allen Dulles may have augmented his knowledge of intelligence tradecraft developed in the Foreign Service by association with British Security Coordination in New York in 1941–42. He cooperated extensively with the representatives of both the Secret Intelligence Service and the Special Operations Executive in Switzerland. The British (code name "Zulu," also known as "our friends" and "our cousins") and the Americans used numerous common sources and sent many combined reports ("Unison" sources). However, there was friction as well as cooperation in the relationship. While it may be unfair to assert that Dulles had an anti-British bias—he had many British friends—there is a pattern, from his publication at the age of eight of a book on the Boer War, through the Paris Peace Conference and the interwar years, that suggests Dulles was not the familiar eastern establishment Anglophile. For his part, Claude Dansey, SIS deputy with oversight for Swiss operations, was contemptuous of U.S. intelligence, if not outright anti-American. Dulles found the British jealous of their sources and hostile to U.S. participation in support for resistance movements. There was bitterness on both sides respecting overlapping contacts with the French Maquis, and Dulles's relations with the SOE broke down badly regarding air supply of partisans in northern Italy. He sometimes criticized the BBC for the content of its broadcasts to occupied Europe. Dulles was less than forthright when he wrote in 1943 in response to criticism of his security procedures: "Broadway's [British intelligence in London] comments for my guidance are always welcome." British intelligence in Bern turned away Fritz Kolbe as a Nazi plant before he contacted Dulles. For many months thereafter, London refused to accept the authenticity of the Wood (Kolbe) Traffic or Dulles's Breakers reports. Dulles once commented that the British were mistrustful of all purported German sources because they had been burned early in the war, presumably a reference to the Venlo incident, in which the Nazis lured and captured British agents in Holland.

British intelligence in London tended to disparage Dulles's information and sources. Kim Philby, the Soviet spy within MI-6 (SIS), was involved in checking OSS Bern material against Ultra. There were a variety of causes for resentment and recrimination. Zulu pointed out that certain codes of the U.S. Legation in Bern used by Dulles were not secure, while Dulles, through Kolbe, helped to unravel the Cicero episode—an egregious British security failure.

The Soviet Union and Communism

Although his views appear to have had little effect in influencing top-level U.S. strategy, Dulles was outspoken in the belief that preventing the domination of Europe by Soviet communism was a paramount war aim. Again and again, he urged that the war be conducted in a way that would convince the peoples of Europe that they would not be abandoned and that their future lay with the West. He worried that Germany would again come to terms with Stalin or that the dissident German generals who might displace Hitler would seize the Eastern option for a separate peace. The Free Germany Committee set up in Moscow caused him great concern.

At the same time, Dulles advocated full cooperation with communist resistance forces, often to the dismay of fiercely anti-communist elements of the democratic left in Italy and France. He courted sources regardless of far-left proclivities. Dulles dealt regularly with Noel Field, a communist who, it later developed, had spied for the Russians at the State Department and the League of Nations. Field discriminated in favor of communists in his relief activities, yet Dulles vouched for the man's nonpolitical outlook, and even went along with him in dealing with the Paris branch of the Soviets' Free Germany front. Did Dulles base his approach on wartime expediency, a desire to plant information, a penetrate-to-coopt-or-destroy strategy, or a belief that he could not have too wide a range of contacts? Perhaps all factors were involved.

Questions remain about Dulles and Soviet communism that the available documents do not answer. What did he know about Soviet spy rings in Switzerland, and what did they know about him? Some experts believe that the Soviets gave some of the information they obtained through espionage against the Germans to Swiss intelligence for transmittal to the Western allies, and that, conversely, the British provided Moscow with disguised information about German military intentions gleaned through Ultra. OSS Bern had intimate ties with Swiss and British intelligence. Was Dulles involved in or aware of any such exchanges? Was information gathered by OSS Bern passed on to Moscow by the Swiss through Soviet agents, inadvertently or intentionally? Did Dulles, and the Western allies through him, use channels in Switzerland to inform or mislead the Soviets? The existing declassified documentary record does not say. It is known that, in London, Soviet spy Kim Philby had access to Dulles's Wood Traffic and Breakers material (as well as to some categories of Ultra). It is not known whether Philby was able to communicate this information to Moscow, or what use his masters made of it.

Late 1944 and Early 1945

The arrival of Allied troops at the Swiss border in September 1944 transformed the situation of OSS Bern. Many intelligence reports from the field were now transmitted directly to Washington and London, without being processed by Dulles and his staff. Access to the outside world made it easier for U.S. intelligence to operate, but only to a degree. In view of Switzerland's continued defense of its neutrality, constraints remained on the size and freedom of movement of the OSS staff. There was great relief, of course, that the outcome of the war was no longer in doubt, only its duration.

For the first time in twenty-two months, Dulles left his post, from mid-September to mid-October, and journeyed to Washington via London in the company of General Donovan. Their relationship, if ever close, was no longer so. Some Dulles cables contained implicit criticism of the OSS Director's policies and advanced broad recommendations that must have seemed presumptuous to Donovan. The General never approved Dulles for the position to which he aspired: head of all OSS operations in Europe. While in the United States, Dulles held extensive consultations in Washington. He spent considerable time in the OSS New York office, headed by John Hughes, which he seems to have considered his true home office and support base.

When he returned to Europe, Dulles concentrated on coordinating liaison with the intelligence units accompanying advancing Allied forces, participating in plans for the direct penetration of Germany by OSS agents, supporting the Italian resistance, and above all, designing the "German Unit" he would lead into the Reich at the end of hostilities.

In the winter of 1944–45 he received tentative, and nonproductive, feelers from certain enemy individuals offering the possibility of inducing the surrender of Wehrmacht commanders on the Western front. He also took part in the painful after-action assessment of the intelligence failure attendant of the Ardennes Offensive. The Dulles organization had not been any more successful in anticipating Hitler's last thrust than military intelligence or Ultra had. Dulles's assessments of the state of the war in late 1944 shared the overoptimism present in concurrent military appraisals that allowed the Germans to achieve surprise.

In this period, OSS reinforcements finally reached Bern. Gerhard Van Arkel of the Labor Desk largely assumed responsibility for direct penetration of Germany. Scientific intelligence operatives, including the legendary Moe Berg, came to investigate the status of the German atomic energy program. All in all, more representatives of various departments and agencies arrived than Dulles could use or appreciate. In the final months of the war, the OSS chief devoted much of his personal attention to the complex negotiations that would lead to the German surrender in Italy. As a result, he transmitted fewer reports on other matters.

OSS Bern did intensify coverage of the Japanese target, however. Throughout the war, substantial information on the Pacific theater had been obtained, including Wood messages from the German military attaché in Tokyo. Now the remaining Japanese in Europe came under closer scrutiny, and Chinese and Thai assets in Switzerland were put to account. Dulles also received indirect Japanese peace-feelers involving Per Jacobsson of the Bank of International Settlements in Basel. Contacts and exchanges continued into August and might have borne fruit if the atomic attack on Japan had not intervened.

Endgame: Operation Sunrise and the National Redoubt

The best-known success of Allen Dulles in World War II was his negotiation of the surrender of the German army in Italy (Operation Sunrise). Those involved included Dulles's assistant Gero Von Gaevernitz, Swiss intelligence officers, Swiss and Italian intermediaries, Field Marshal Sir Harold Alexander's Headquarters at Caserta, future NATO commander General Lyman Lemnitzer, a Czech radio operator secreted in German headquarters, and the most unlikely of participants in a conspiracy to surrender, SS General Karl Wolff. The documents detail this story of high adventure, as accurately recounted by Dulles in *The Secret Surrender* (1966). Examination of the full record, including the view from Washington and Caserta as well as from Bern, reveals that Sunrise was executed in accordance with high policy and was not an enterprise out of control. The White House and Joint Chiefs of Staff were kept informed at every step of the way.

The importance of this accomplishment is diminished by the late date of the surrender: less than a week before the end of the war. Still, Dulles's ongoing efforts reduced the intensity of the conflict in Italy before the actual end of hostilities and certainly saved thousands of lives. Only the disarray of the German officers in Italy and hesitancy in Washington and London precluded a more timely capitulation that could have changed the face of postwar Europe. Stalin reacted with heat to Bern's parlaying with the Germans, causing President Roosevelt great concern in the last days of his life. The Russians had every reason to believe that Dulles intended the surrender to retard their advance and speed that of the western allies, as well as to save lives. It is unlikely that the episode had a measurable effect on the decline of the Grand Alliance, since the basic conflicting interests of the parties, caused by the inherently aggressive and anti-West nature of Soviet communism, loom so much larger.

From 1944 on, Dulles reported German contingency plans, and some apparent preparations, for making a last stand in an Alpine redoubt. The German army in Italy, unless Dulles could arrange its surrender, would presumably be the backbone of this final defense. He relayed a steady stream of information that supported the redoubt possibility, and although he hedged and qualified, and noted the lack of material preparations, Washington and General Dwight D. Eisenhower's headquarters had reason to believe that the OSS chief in Bern expected the Nazi redoubt to materialize. Dulles was not alone. Allied military intelligence, the press, and the public also anticipated a Wagnerian cataclysm in an Alpine stronghold. In fact, the Alpine redoubt was part fantasy born of the unreality of Hitler's last days, and part an outright German deception operation. There was no national redoubt. To the extent that Dulles misread the situation, he contributed to an outcome he wanted least: the Western armies were distracted from full-speed advance to the east.

From War to Peace

When the war ended in Europe, Dulles traveled briefly to Italy for consultations with his Sunrise colleagues and to write up the operation. He then directed OSS Bern's conversion to programs appropriate for chaotic and devastated postwar Europe, particularly Germany. This involved identification and protection of anti-Nazis for intelligence purposes and to assist in occupation and reconstruction. In consultation with Donovan and others in London and Paris, he helped put into operation the OSS German mission that he would soon head. He was tireless in support of Germans and others who had worked for him, sometimes sparring with occupation officialdom concerned with various aspects of denazification, including the State Department's Safehaven operatives, who sought to prevent Germans from secreting assets and war booty in foreign areas such as Switzerland.

Dulles left Bern for Germany in early July 1945, amid extravagant praise from the OSS brass in Washington and other dignitaries. The departing chief received a round of parties, and wrote countless gracious thank-you notes. He left no source or contact unattended in view of possible future reactivation. His three months in occupied Germany are beyond the scope of this volume, and available documentation is meager. He divided his time between Berlin and Wiesbaden, establishing an American intelligence organization within the occupation regime, identifying German intelligence assets and individuals with good records for positions of responsibility, and assisting in gathering evidence for the war crimes trials.

Shortly after President Harry Truman abolished OSS on September 20, 1945, dividing its functions between the State and War Departments, Dulles returned to the United States. He participated in the establishment of the Strategic Services Unit, the operational successor of OSS, before leaving government service at the end of the year. He cited a long-held determination to return to the practice of law, but was also unhappy with the uncertain status of American intelligence and wanted to address the problem from the outside while the dust settled. He was never far from the subject during a 1946–50 interval with Sullivan & Cromwell. Dulles participated in the legislative and bureaucratic turmoil that resulted in the establishment of the Central Intelligence Agency under the National Security Act of 1947. He published *Germany's Underground* in 1947, an accurate account of the opposition to Hitler that helped establish the moral basis for the integration of the nation into the democratic community of the West. He was a principal author of a 1948 Presidential study recommending reform of the CIA, and he participated in numerous activities designed to help Western Europe resist Stalinism. In 1950, five years after leaving Bern, he became Deputy Director for Plans of the CIA. Following a period as Deputy Director in 1951 and 1952, he was appointed Director of Central Intelligence in the Eisenhower administration and served in that capacity until 1961.

Observations

OSS Bern and the Policy Process

How accurate was the intelligence Dulles provided, and how was it used? Beyond doubt, the Breakers and Kappa material was of first-rate importance, and in terms of volume of production Bern led all other OSS posts. Still, one is hard-pressed to identify a single example of a Dulles report in and of itself having direct impact on a top-level policy decision. Almost invariably, information from Bern was only one source among many, and integration of intelligence was badly deficient in Washington. In London, Bern reports were often checked against other sources, including the more important Ultra intercepts, and probably had utility on the strictly military level: the selection of bombing targets and drop zones for partisan support. But London did not receive all Bern cables. The Cicero case and the location of German V-1 and V-2 sites and production centers are examples of a clear Bern contribution. Dulles's procurement of detailed and accurate information on the German opposition to Hitler, both before and after July 20, 1944, was an intelligence coup of the first order and established his credibility, but it had little effect on policy.

Mountains of Dulles-originated reports reached the White House. General Donovan was slow to include items from Bern in his transmissions to the President, but in the last year of the war, having realized that the material redounded to the credit of the OSS, he made Dulles cables and phone statements the most voluminous category of OSS document forwarded to the Chief Executive. In addition, General John Magruder, OSS Deputy Director for Intelligence (responsible for both Secret Intelligence and Research and Analysis), opened a special channel to the Map Room for important OSS cables from abroad. The Bern take predominated in this material. The OSS also sent the "Boston Series" based on the information provided by George Wood/Fritz Kolbe.

In the Franklin D. Roosevelt Library, there is almost no indication of any reaction by the President or his top advisers to the hundreds of Dulles-originated papers. This is attributable in part to Roosevelt's habitual lack of annotation except to refer a document to an aide for comment, but the President did sometimes react to early Donovan memos or to those of John Franklin Carter, his personal intelligence agent/detective. The Dulles material in the Map Room files may never have crossed the President's desk. In a sense, President Roosevelt was his own intelligence officer, for no all-encompassing integrated report was prepared for him. The closest approximation was military information provided by the Joint Chiefs of Staff and Admiral William Leahy, Chief of Staff to the Commander in Chief of the Army and the Navy. The OSS provided the Joint Chiefs with many Dulles reports, but in view of the JCS's general skepticism regarding Donovan's organization, it is doubtful that views and facts from Bern appeared in the military flow of information to the President to any significant extent.

The importance of Dulles's reports lies largely in their quantity and wide distribution. If they did not figure significantly in top policy formulation, they did reach a large and prominent audience within the OSS, at the State Department, and in the military. Many of the reports were less true intelligence than the opinions of one articulate and well-placed individual on foreign policy issues, including the future of Germany, the fate of Eastern Europe, and the Soviet challenge. They certainly did have some impact on the scores of influential people in the various Dulles networks, and on the individuals who would be present at the creation of the postwar national security structure.

In his role as self-appointed psychological grand strategist for the West, Dulles had little influence on the White House or on the shape of postwar Europe. The doctrine of unconditional surrender remained unencumbered by inducements to potential resistance elements. The Allied high command was unmoved by his recommendations aimed at the hearts and minds, of Germans and East Europeans, and in any event it was military presence on the ground, rather than the state of hearts and minds that determined postwar spheres of control. Nonetheless, Dulles was perceptive in his recognition that the most effective form of psychological warfare is that which is thoroughly integrated with policy and action, and that every policy and action has its psychological dimension.

Dulles, Bern, and the History of U.S. Intelligence

The experience of the Bern OSS mission in World War II should be viewed as part of the evolution of U.S. intelligence, and also as a unique situation, never again to be approximated. The American intelligence tradition before 1939 is much maligned, and with reason. Yet in the haphazard, decentralized practices that never exceeded what an isolationist nation wanted or needed lay the basis for an effective institution. Often overlooked in this connection is the State Department heritage in American intelligence, of which Allen Dulles is a part. He learned his craft not from William Donovan, the British, or the U.S. military, but from diplomatic service in Vienna and Bern during World War I. Before a permanent national intelligence service had been established, the line between political reporting and espionage was drawn even less clearly than today. His use of sources in Switzerland in World War II was in part an extension of Foreign Service techniques already being employed when he arrived.

The Office of Strategic Services has received mixed reviews over the years. Some of its daring penetration and paramilitary operations, and its research and analysis function, are highly regarded. But its espionage activities, morale operations, security, nonmilitary political-action endeavors, and liaison with other U.S. government agencies often are accorded modest marks. The overall effectiveness of William J. Donovan and his organization was disparaged at the time and by many observers since the war, but much of this criticism is unfair, given that the OSS was created virtually overnight in wartime conditions. And the OSS is often compared with present-day national intelligence organizations rather than with its contemporaries. The Abwehr was thoroughly penetrated by the Allies. Soviet intelligence shares the blame for the unparalleled disaster of June 1941. The British have rightly received great credit for their part in Ultra and for gaining control of German agents in England. But one should not overlook the loss of agents at Venlo, the German control of Allied agents in Holland (operation North Pole), the Cicero fiasco in Turkey, and the presence of Philby and other pro-Soviet traitors in the British intelligence services. In this context, the Dulles operation in Bern, despite security lapses and instances of faulty analysis of information as discussed above, stands out as a highlight of the OSS experience and compares most favorably with other wartime intelligence entities worldwide.

OSS Bern's position as a watershed is apparent. Old-fashioned human intelligence predominated. Agents actually used recognition codes such as "Je préfère les Camels aux Gauloise." We encounter Jackpot, Climax, Little Wally, and Commandant Georges. But this was against the background of totalitarianism, genocide, and weapons of mass destruction. Subtleties of State Department cover, unvouchered funds, and scientific intelligence make their appearance. To an extent, the wartime intelligence structure survived the end of hostilities, with some of the same posts, agents, and areas of coverage remaining in place. Only the targets were different. President Truman abolished the OSS in September 1945, but the requirements it addressed continued to exist, and soon the centralized peacetime service to which they pointed became permanent.

In one area especially, Bern operations signaled transition to the modern era. Financial resources became a dominant weapon of American intelligence that neither friend nor foe could match. Aside from Order of Battle reports, the single largest category of OSS Bern's telegraphic traffic concerned funding—payments not just for agents but also for paramilitary resistance groups, political parties, labor organizations, and relief activities. As an international businessman, Dulles knew how to use financial institutions in Switzerland to obtain funds from Washington and New York for disbursement locally and behind enemy lines. He provided the means for labor unions and ethnic groups in the United States to render financial assistance to their compatriots in occupied Europe, many of whom refused to accept funds directly from intelligence organizations. This sphere of activity was a clear harbinger of postwar CIA operations.

The record of Allen Dulles at Bern is instructive for what it indicates about the man, his priorities, and his methods. Some critics of his service as Director of Central Intelligence find him lax. He was liked because he did not run a tight ship, it is said. He is deemed careless about details and security, a risk-taker confident of invulnerability to the point of recklessness. He is viewed as preoccupied with spectacular espionage coups and covert operations to the detriment of primary intelligence functions—the systematic collection, evaluation, and distribution of information. He allegedly believed that the key to understanding and influencing other nations was knowing a few influential individuals, and overlooking the increasingly complex nature of modern society. Dulles's record at Bern provides evidence of the seeds of at least some of these tendencies. He is also revealed as a Foreign Service Officer at heart, concerned more with great foreign policy issues than with the details of intelligence.

The reverse side of these alleged deficiencies constitutes elements of Dulles's strength. He had a command presence, a daring, and a breadth of vision that allowed him to succeed at Bern. He recognized that intelligence is properly part of the larger realm of foreign policy / national security policy. He saw the essential relationship between psychological warfare and the more traditional components of intelligence. His reliance on personal contacts was made possible by his great personal charm with both men and women and by his ability to establish lasting friendships. His vast network of associations and admirers was the result of his loyalty and sensitivity toward subordinates and colleagues, as well as cultivation of the well-placed and the powerful. He had the foresight to recognize the dangers of Stalinism and the need to revive Germany as part of the democratic West, despite the profound and enduring responsibility of that nation and its people for the crimes of Nazism. In assisting those who resisted Hitler, he dealt with the full range of European elements that opposed totalitarianism—landowners, peasants, generals, separatists, the clergy, bourgeois politicians, labor leaders, socialists, and intellectuals. His Bern legacy contributed to the survival of democracy in Western Europe after the war and to the ultimate triumph of freedom in the East, finally apparent in the late 1980s.

Dulles's performance was precedent-establishing in some respects, and never to be repeated in others. His broad view of his responsibilities resulted in a precursor to the CIA on a miniature scale. The Bern mission engaged in intelligence-gathering, covert action, psychological operations, and counterintelligence, all brought together in the U.S. intelligence service that emerged in the late 1940s. However, Dulles at Bern exceeded the bounds of both traditional and modern intelligence practice by intruding into the area of policy formulation. He was not just a semi-autonomous intelligence proconsul within the OSS, but a would-be grand strategist for the West. Seldom again would an American station chief range so far and wide—not even a Director of Central Intelligence, nor even Dulles himself in the 1950s. But for the historian, appreciation of the documents in this volume need not be confined to their place in a continuum. They stand by themselves as representative of a fascinating historical situation worth studying for its very uniqueness.

CHAPTER

1

An Island in Occupied Europe

November 1942–August 1943

Document 1-1

Telegram 5098, November 10, 1942

[Allen Dulles reached Switzerland on November 8, 1942, only hours before the Germans sealed the French border. He established himself at Herrengasse 23 in Bern and took charge of the minimal OSS operations that had begun earlier in the year. Although nominally a Special Assistant to the American Minister, Leland Harrison, he let his primary function be known, thus accelerating the establishment of contacts. In addition to having the OSS code number 110, Dulles was designated "Mr. Burns" in Bern for most of 1943. Due to inadequate OSS communications resources, this telegram, and many others, particularly early in the war, were transmitted to the State Department via Legation channels. "Victor" indicated that State should transmit the message to OSS headquarters in Washington.]

From Burns to Victor. Arrived Bern today, Geneva yesterday. As I crossed the French-Spanish border, news of the attack on North Africa was received, and when I talked with many people at the border and at Perpignan Narbonne, they all expressed satisfaction and relief indicating that nine-tenths of the people of France were for the United States. When I arrived at the French-Swiss frontier at Annemasse, German plainclothesmen assisted the passport inspection. I was advised that French frontier authorities had received orders that no Americans could leave France. However, after some argument on my part, Vichy was telephoned and word came through to let me pass. When my passport was returned to me, a French official stated that as I could see, their resistance is only symbolical.

The Vichy French press does not quote any of the President's messages and talks about aggression against our [invasion of] North Africa playing up British as opposed to American participation in the operations. The French people are hanging on the radio as this is the only way they can get any news, and one Frenchman asked me to arrange for the President's message to be repeated from England so that they could hear it. It is advisable, however, to repeat important messages from England over medium wave.

Document 1-2

Telegram 60-65, November 21, 1942

[From the beginning of his Bern service, Dulles considered psychological warfare a top priority. He adopted a broad definition of the term that embraced activities ranging from the planting of deadly false rumors to enhancement of the free flow of accurate, open information in Europe. 105 is David Bruce, OSS representative in London; 109 is William J. Donovan, Director of the Office of Strategic Services.]

This is for 105 and 109. Your message and the definition of my duties are appreciated. I would be very happy to have Ed here, since I believe that the development of the psychological warfare program from here will grow increasingly important. It is questionable how far this is possible by export printed material if the rigid frontier control is maintained on all sides as it is now, but I will report further after studying this problem. For the present, all the usual means of getting people here now seem to be foreclosed. We are making every effort to get the Swiss to try opening an airline to Lisbon but it is doubtful whether Swiss consider themselves strong enough to overrule the German opposition which is almost certain. It must be expected that Germany will do all that is possible to try to counteract our action to get the facts before their peoples including taking measures to restrict all of our lines of communication with our bases in Britain and the United States since the winter months which are to come are critical for the German and Italian morale, particularly the latter. The German press has had practically no war news it could print during the last few weeks and they are frantic for something to "Amuser leur public" as a keen Swiss observer remarked. Even though the Swiss press is excluded from Germany except for a chosen few, the Germans definitely fear Switzerland as a free news center. A Swiss official who has just returned from Berlin says he expects further drives to try to shackle the freedom of the Swiss press. It has been openly stated by the German press that within the European Fortress all British and American representatives will be treated as "Centers of espionage, blackmail, and subversive activities within countries concerned." To make this an effective center of psychological warfare our ingenuity will be challenged by all this, and in view of the unlikelihood of early reinforcements from the outside, I believe we should count on working with the tools which are now available. I am working particularly closely with Meyer [Mayer] of OWI and Asst. M. A. Free who are also working on certain phases of these problems and am receiving fullest cooperation from Drum, the Minister, Military Attaché and other services. Re the development of other phases of my work, I will cable my suggestions soon.

Document 1-3

Telegram 6-10, November 24, 1942 (extract)

[The OSS mission in Bern served as a crucial conduit for communication between the French resistance and supporters in Britain and the United States. A primary channel that operated for most of the war was commmunication between "328" in Switzerland and "Eva" in the United States. Innumerable messages were passed, and funds were disbursed to Maquis, underground labor elements within France, and for the relief of French refugees in Switzerland via the 328 network.]

Today I had a long conversation with 328. This conversation confirmed his usefulness for contact with French syndicalist and labor organizations provided that his contacts can be maintained despite the present border patrol. He stresses the fact that the French Labor organizations are reluctant to receive funds except from other labor organizations. Suggest that you consider the possibility that contributions be made by American Labor organizations. Provided that complete discretion as regards method of transmission can be observed, we could pass on these funds through 328. I believe that this would have a helpful psychological effect. Meanwhile we will help to modest extent which they are willing to receive from us. . . .

Document 1-4

Telegram 5688, December 6, 1942

[At an early date, Dulles provided the OSS leadership with specific psychological warfare suggestions with respect to Italy and Germany.]

For 109 and 105. The following are suggestions for the development of the Psychological Warfare Program. Any predictions herein as to future developments are based upon the assumptions that the enemy will be expelled from North Africa and that the Russian pressure on the Eastern Front will be maintained.

(1) *As to Italy.* Outside of military circles popular feeling is ready for capitulation.

Whether it comes and how effectively it will spread depends upon whether the Reich intends to defend the whole peninsula and Sicily, instead of withdrawing to a shorter line stretching from Genoa across to the Adriatic, and to a lesser extent upon developments in the Italian Army. German troop movements to Southern Italy, together with obvious reasons of prestige would indicate an intent on the part of Germany to defend the whole of the peninsula rather than to fall back upon the strategically more justified shorter line across the top of the boot.

(2) *As to Germany.* Neither the present economic circumstances, nor the morale of the people are such as to cause a rapid collapse. Short of the severest military reverses on the Eastern Front, the country is good for a year or 18 months or more. If Hitler who has shown himself temperamentally incapable of such tactics could decide upon a shorter Eastern Front and defense tactics elsewhere, the issue would be postponed even longer. Hitler's claims of infallibility and invincibility have been shaken by his failure before Stalingrad, the inability of his submarines to block our African landings, as well as by the breakdown of his policy in France culminating in the recent events in Toulon. The cumulative effect of these failures, despite their clever covering up by Goebbels, cannot be entirely hidden from the German people and should be driven home by our radio propaganda. However, little credence can as yet be placed upon resultant rumors concerning a movement in ex-officer circles to prepare to take over the government.

(3) *As to the Balkans.* There is an increasing confusion throughout this region where the Germans can least easily maintain their control due to the difficulties of transportation and terrain. If Turkey could be prevailed upon to join the Allied effort at the opportune moment, moving from Thrace, the first evidences of a German breakdown might well come from there.

Based on the above, my suggestions for psychological warfare are the following:

(a) To the Italians it should be pointed out that now that their dream of Mediterranean Empire has evaporated, they are only fighting for Germany as the Allies do not intend to take away continental Italian territory or to impose crushing terms upon them. It might soon be of assistance to form an Italian National Committee outside of the country and in this connection Sforza is the most respected Anti-Fascist abroad though he is not widely known among the people in Italy. While desirable to foment unrest in Italy so as to increase the German burden, we should not take over the policing and provisioning of Italy too soon. As Germany gradually fails to satisfy Italy's needs, with air attacks and blockade in addition, the Germans will be more and more hated in Italy. We would then be in the position of having Germany forced to abandon Italy rather than having ourselves to drive her out against a united German and Italian military opposition. Such an abandonment would result in a lesser military effort on our part and the military and economic responsibilities entailed by an occupation of Italy would be more easily met in the future than now. Of course the occupation of Corsica and Sardinia beforehand would have a deep effect in Italy and France.

A further wedge between Italy and Germany could be driven by showing that

Hitler's now discredited collaboration policy with France was in disregard of vital Italian interests, and prevented the adequate protection of French North Africa, as was so repeatedly pointed out by Mussolini. This latter point comes to me from especially well-informed quarters.

Whatever our final policy towards Germany, we should today try to convince the German people that there is hope for them in defeat, that the innocent will be protected, while the punishment of the guilty will be through legal process. The Germans have been thoroughly indoctrinated with skepticism about our assurances and made leery of reviving anything resembling the 14-point policy. The time will nevertheless come when our assurances may well be the only hope of the Anti-Nazis and such assurances may help drive a wedge between the party and the people. At this time we should do our utmost to undermine the belief of the rank and file of the German Army in ultimate victory so as to encourage desertions. The recent German statements about the treatment of their prisoners by the British and Russians and the counter-measures thereupon taken in Germany were solely to provoke reprisals so as to show the German troops that death was preferable to capture and torture by the Russians or British.

With regard to the Balkans, an effective measure of psychological warfare would be to unite the forces of resistance there, both for concluding the war and for forming a coalition strong enough to resist inevitable Russian demands in that area. Effective uniting of Anti-Nazi forces in this region can only be made if the people believe this will later make effective their existence free from Russian interference. Turkey might become the military spearhead for forming this Balkan block.

The chief ground for the hesitation of the Anti-Nazi and Anti-Fascist elements in both Occupied and Unoccupied countries about giving the United Nations their undivided support is caused by their fear of communism. It is felt that America may be too distant and the British too feeble to restrain the Soviets from exploiting the social chaos after the war in Europe and from imposing their brand of domination on Europe. The people see little to be gained from a change from Nazi to Communist domination. Any evidence we can give of an understanding with Russia to prevent this, and any statement that it is the determination of the USA, as well as of the United Nations to see that an orderly and free development of Europe takes place would strengthen us enormously in waging psychological warfare.

Document 1-5

Telegram 5792, December 10, 1942

[Dulles, the psychological warrior, sought to exploit Axis vulnerabilities whenever they appeared.]

From Burns for Victor. The Italian press is now openly commenting on the bank run which resulted from the heavy bombings and dislocation of the population, and

I believe that we should do our utmost to encourage further withdrawals of funds from Italian banks by instilling distrust of the banking system in the Italian people and pointing out to them the desirability of converting their money into tangible assets.

This should be done by radio propaganda and other means. The people will probably give little response to the present appeal of the Italian press for a wider use of checks.

Document 1-6

Telegram 5861, December 14, 1942

[Bern reports the disintegration of morale in Fascist Italy.]

From Burns for Victor. The following information has been received from source at Lugano 244 and covers information for period December 6–12 concerning Italy:

Everywhere, the morale is very bad, and notices appear on the wall reading "Fascists beware" (Fascisti prenotatevi). Fascists only appear in either companies or whole squads. Exorbitant prices are asked for everything. Because of fear of demoralizing infiltration, very few Italian soldiers are to be seen and soldiers at the front complain of getting no news from home; and letters are confiscated by censors because they are so full of criticisms and accusations. It is reported that mutinies increase from day to day. Bombing raids are extremely effective because the workers, despite the threat of dire consequences, leave the factories. News from America is believed in large part by most Italians because a great number of them still hear indirectly from their relations in the United States. It is understood by Italians that Mussolini is unable to make peace.

Italy is full of German troops, and the total estimated strength is between 150 and 200 thousand. These figures are maximum and minimum figures to be doubled shortly. The German troops assemble at Rome which is the distribution center and they come from all directions without leaders of units. Most of them are seventeen to eighteen years old; and few of them are more than twenty years old. It is estimated that one regiment a day is assembled at Rome and shipped immediately to the south.

Naples: Everyone criticizes Mussolini. There is unbelievable confusion. It is important to note that the people understand that bombing raids are necessary.

Rome: Government offices are all going to Frosinone, Avezzano, Chaeti, Aguila, and Rieti; and hotels are being requisitioned for war purposes. Although Mussolini's villa is guarded in order to make people believe that he is still living there, he no longer lives there. The Ministry of War is in the Hotel Excelsior.

Pistoia: main connection between Bologna and Florence . . . railroad bridges.

Novi Ligure: two important railroad bridges.

Verona: should be bombed immediately since it is an extremely important railroad center with many bridges, and nearly all private homes have been requisitioned by the military authorities.

Madena: At the end of January a special school for flame throwing units will graduate 780 candidates as Lieutenants.

Document 1-7

Telegram 5913, December 16, 1942

[In Switzerland there were dozens of official and unofficial figures from the Axis satellite nations of central and southeastern Europe who were willing to provide information to Western intelligence.]

From Burns for Victor. Contact established with No. 10 [*sic*]. Your 97 who reports that the Hungarians are trying to withdraw their troops from Russia since they believe that if and when Germany caves in a Hungarian army will be the only central European force available to maintain order and to enforce respect for Hungarian claims to approximately pre-1914 boundaries.

Soldiers who fought in the Spanish Civil War are being sought for among the garrisons in Italy.

If German defeat or signs of German disintegration make possible the taking over of Hungarian affairs, a group is being organized comprised of: Bethlen, Gray, Moritz, Esterhazysi, Baranyi, prominent Hungarians.

Document 1-8

Telegram 6103, December 24, 1942

[Dulles directed this message on psychological warfare and general policy toward France to James Grafton Rogers, Director of the OSS Planning Group.]

From Burns for Victor for Rogers. The following is an outline of what our present objectives should be with regard to psychological warfare in metropolitan France:

We should build organizations around someone who, when the collapse comes, can take over civilian administration.

Underground resistance groups should be strengthened such as labor and church organizations, liberation groups, combat groups and Franc-Tireurs groups. All possible encouragement and morale building material should be given the French. All possible interference with German civilian and military authority, as well as sabotage, should be organized through the groups previously mentioned and by any other means possible.

If possible, see that among these who are forced to go to Germany all these elements . . . assist in the disorganization of German industry and obstruct the further drawing of French manpower for German military or industrial production. The following measures should be taken in order to accomplish the foregoing . . . suggestions and Mayer of the Office of War Information is doing what he can to put into effect the measures mentioned, and is working with me closely. The flow of pamphlet material should be increased, if possible, by air and . . . underground from here. Underground movements should be assisted and contacts should be kept through Switzerland and London, etc., but we should be particularly careful to have regard for their security since these movements are often inclined to err on the side of indiscretion, and the utmost precaution must be observed on our part not to add to the danger of the underground movement, particularly since the German Gestapo is appearing in France.

The active participation of the French in the war should be emphasized and it would be most effective if Giraud could broadcast to France. . . . Also it would be extremely useful as a morale builder if the President could make further occasional broadcasts in French when the case justifies.

It should be emphasized that in the reconstruction of Europe, France . . . will play a real part. If it is possible not to disclose information of assistance to the enemy, encouragement and appreciation of work and risks of the underground might be given in radio pamphlets. Assistance in the despatching to Spain, Switzerland of those risking their lives for the cause, who can no longer work in France, would be of great assistance since it would serve as real encouragement, even though the number of persons actually saved would be relatively small. By this means, specialists useful in Africa or elsewhere might be assisted to leave France.

The statements of the President and Hull on the Darlan situation have been most helpful, and although I recognize that military considerations of the North African campaign render an early solution of the controversy between Giraud and de Gaulle difficult, the fact remains that Gaullism and the Cross Lorraine have been effective symbols for underground resistance, and . . . leadership is furnished, we cannot destroy these symbols without lessening effective resistance.

The most effective anti-Nazi movement in France today . . . is the Communist organization.

Even if it is possible only by propaganda leaflets and radio messages to develop the relationship between free workers in America, England, etc., and workers' organizations in France, this relationship should be developed.

I am studying the special features and the problem of Alsace-Lorraine which may require a particular type of organization.

Document 1-9

Telegram 17180 from London, December 27, 1942

[A substantial portion of the Dulles Swiss network was comprised of French persons of various political persuasions. His use of and support for French elements involved a delicate balancing act with the Swiss authorities and among the French themselves.]

1. Here follows summary of a cable which was received from 110. This is forwarded to you at his request:

A. There are increasing numbers of Alsatian refugees and militant De Gaullists arriving in Switzerland. They are in urgent need of financial assistance. The ideal solution would be to have Free French funds in London or Washington released.

B. The message above comes from French individuals in Switzerland and was forwarded by 110 to De Gaulle through us. 110 gives strong endorsement and declares that many people who would be useful to our cause will be sent to Swiss concentration camps unless they are given aid.

2. This message has been delivered to De Gaulle, and his response is awaited.

Document 1-10

Telegram 127-28, January 6, 1943

[OSS Bern sought to become involved in support for military operations of the French resistance at an early date. Geographical and logistical circumstances were daunting. Also, coordination had to be arranged with "Zulu," the British.]

Messages are being dispatched by representatives of French resistance groups in the Lyons area stressing their great need for automatic arms, radio and materials for STG work. They believe that the Nazis have discovered and are now guarding the landing fields in the area which they formerly used for delivery and escape purposes. I assume that the matters referred to above can be worked out only through London, but our friends might help designate safer places for deliveries in the future. There have been inquiries from many demobilized French officers in France requesting indications of how and where they could serve usefully. We feel under present conditions that they had best stay where they are, and await the time for action, but if you and Zulu determine a different policy, please inform me.

Document 1-11

Telegram 278, January 13, 1943

[Dulles here reports on Rumanian and German developments. 476 is Gero von Gaevernitz, a German-American businessman living in Switzerland who served as Dulles's top assistant throughout the war.]

Burns for Victor. Yesterday I had a conversation with an important Rumanian industrialist who is close to the Antonescu group. Dark picture given by latter regarding Rumanian situation. He believed that Antonescu was now convinced that it is impossible for the Germans to defeat Russia and that he is endeavoring to extricate himself. The informant who departed from Rumania in the middle of December is under the impression that German Quisling is responsible for Iron Guard action and reported Rumanian riots. In the meantime Antonescu is endeavoring to find some method whereby he can bring back some remnants of the Rumanian army for use against the potential threat from the Hungarians. It was reported by another source that 13 Rumanian divisions on the Russian front were decimated or surrounded and that Antonescu is now endeavoring to reorganize 12 divisions for home defense purposes against possible threat from Hungarian-Russian-Turkish sources.

Public opinion in Axis countries is profoundly affected by the Russian offensive, one result being that nationals of Axis and Axis controlled countries are endeavoring to develop contact with us. In Zurich on Sunday I saw a German acquaintance of 476 and 474 who is a friend of Neimuller and who is believed to be working closely with Schacht. This individual emphasized importance of being given encouragement that if Nazi leaders eliminated by resistance group negotiations for durable peace could be made with United Nations. As he pictured it, alternative was revolution chaos since, rather than surrender to Western Powers, Hitler would turn to Bolshevism. He also stated that his friends saw no reason to jeopardize lives unless there was some hope that the movement would meet with success. I personally am doubtful whether movement is seriously organized as yet.

Document 1-12

Telegram 314, January 14, 1943

[Dulles had been in Bern for only two months when he began reporting in some detail on the German resistance, a subject second to no other for him for the duration of the war. It is important to note that OSS Bern received information from leftist elements as well as from military figures and other conservatives. Source 474 is Dr. W. A. Visser 't Hooft, Secretary of the World Council of Churches in Geneva.]

For Victor from Burns. The following telegram, which gives the views of a German who is a member of the opposition group, regarding whose identity a separate report is being made, is a summary of a report written by 474.

It appears that the fact that their approaches are meeting with no encouragement or understanding is a source of deep disappointment to the opposition. The answer is always given that Germany must suffer defeat of her armed forces regardless of what new regime may be created. The view is taken that the opposition is taking tremendous risks to continue its activity, and that it will cease, by reason of the failure of the western powers to understand the oppressed peoples living in occupied countries and the Germans themselves, unless conversations are continued. There is consequently a tendency on the part of the opposition to believe that the Anglo-Saxon countries are merely theorizing and are filled with pharisaic condemnation and bourgeois prejudice. The orientation toward the east is brought about by a belief that fraternization is not possible between the present Governments, but is possible between the German and Russian peoples. Both peoples have experienced great suffering and have broken with the bourgeois way of living; both are slowly returning to the Christian traditions in a spiritual but not necessarily ecclesiastical way, and both are looking for a radical solution of their social problems. Russian soldiers are not hated by Germans, on the contrary they are respected.

According to the opposition, there is no belief in a decisive development in a military sense but only in a social one. Even after the German Army is thrown back by the Russians, when the latter's campaign comes to a halt, a revolutionary situation may spring up on both sides. Another important element in this respect is the fraternization between workers imported from abroad and German workers. The generals are ceasing to be a political factor, and the bourgeois and intellectual opposition is becoming less important there as a result of the fact that Hitler finds himself forced to play up to the laboring classes and to give them increasingly important positions. The conclusion of the memorandum is as follows: "Following Hitler's fall, a completely new Europe will be based on the brotherliness and experience of the oppressed common people."

I am transmitting the foregoing report solely because it may be of interest in connection with the program of psychological warfare and not because I am of the opinion that there is any serious organization of the opposition group in Germany or that, short of a complete military victory for the United Nations, they should expect or be led to expect any encouragement from us or any dealing with us.

Document 1-13

Telegram 18155 from London, January 18, 1943

[At the request of Dulles, London relayed this Bern cable on French refugees in Switzerland to Washington.]

. . . There is a difference of opinion among French émigrés because of Giraud–de Gaulle situation. Until this situation is cleared up, I prefer not to become involved in financial matters. Nonetheless, certain ex-French officials who might be of use to us may soon be in acute circumstances. Hoping for the establishment here before long of some French authority to handle the financial question, I am giving some help in isolated instances for services rendered.

Document 1-14

Telegram 528, January 23, 1943

[Dulles continues to offer suggestions for psychological warfare themes in light of the improving military situation.]

From Burns for Victor. It is my belief that the military situation which has developed as a result of the Russian and African successes justifies a review of psychological program of warfare so far as Germany is concerned. The issues of the present are whether and to what extent the Nazis and Hitler can conduct a war of defense, and what means would be best to counteract propaganda of Goebbels which is to the effect that, if defeated, Germans face absolute destruction which propaganda, if successful, will tend to unite the people for a war of defense.

It is personally believed by me that while the present Government remains in power, Germany can wage a war of defense, but if the Nazi regime is overthrown, it is doubtful whether resistance will be possible for any length of time. Although I am of the belief that Hitler has been a military asset for us for the past year, I also believe that he has committed sufficient military errors to help us in realizing victory, and in order to speed the break-up, everything should now be done by us to force a wedge between the Nazis and bring about a balance of the people of Germany. It is beginning to be appreciated by many of the latter that it is impossible to accomplish final victory, and in order to explain their support of the Hitler regime they are hastening to seek moral alibis.

That it is impracticable to develop a detailed post-war program at this stage for Germany is recognized, but without taking on any commitments, certain points can be emphasized which, despite the fact that forewarning has been given Germans against the repetition of our 14 point policy of 1918, may be driven home.

It is my belief that the following should be emphasized:

1. Germany's future and that of the German people depends upon the Germans. The powers are theirs to prove that a restored German Democracy is deservant of an honorable place in the international family of nations; that on equal terms with others they would enjoy access to raw materials and, under their own chosen heads, they would enjoy freedom of democratic development. It should also be emphasized that what we desire is positive safeguards against aggression of the future. Although I recognize that it is essential that disarmament be effectively carried out, do not place stress upon it in propaganda since this furnishes food for the machine of Goebbels. Threats about the destruction and the partitioning of Germany should also be avoided.

2. With a view to breaking down the strength of the Nazi party which consists of several millions, I would suggest that emphasis be placed on our recognition that, in itself, mere membership in the party is not evidence of guilt as there were many persons who were compelled to join the party; that judgment will be made not merely by party label but by the past and future acts of persons.

3. It is also suggested that machinery be worked out whereby persons who desire to establish evidence of their non-adherence to Nazism may do so with the assurance that due consideration will be given of that nature.

4. There is much speculation here as to whether Hitler dare to make an address to the public on January 30th, which will be the 10th anniversary of his assumption of power. There is also much speculation as to what will be said by him. It is my

belief that it is desirable to start calling attention by means of our radio and possibly by the press conferences of the President and the Secretary [of State] that this anniversary is significant. Details might be given of what Hitler has done in 10 years for the German people, particularly in so far as his accomplishments during the past year are concerned when he was acting in response to the "consciousness of his inner calling" (please refer to the December 22, and 23, 1941 press) and dismissing Generals of experience and took full responsibility for military developments as well as political.

It is of importance to realize within the past few weeks the people of Germany are beginning for the first time to acquire some slight understanding of what is occurring on the fronts of Russia and Africa because, after silence or complete fabrication for months, German communiqués are now compelled to make certain disclosures which are startling. With respect to this matter, I also suggest that German people be reminded of the speech which Hitler made last spring when he gave an indication as to how closely the armies of Germany were faced with catastrophe on the Russian front during the last winter, and suggest in a gentle way that this time the catastrophe is actually present and that it is aggravated by African second catastrophe.

5. Suggest that emphasis also be placed on the dollar's and pound's dramatic rise on the markets of neutral countries with the contemporary catastrophic fall of the German mark, and set forth that while vast fortunes are salted away in neutral countries by such Nazi leaders as Goering, Goebbels et cetera indefinite continuation of the war means the wiping out of insurance policies, savings and the total devaluation of the German mark and other holdings of the workers of Germany, whereas were the war to end it might mean that some these savings would be rescued.

In summary, I am of the impression that this is the moment for a drive of vigor to effect a separation of the Nazis and Hitler from the balance of the German people, and hold out at the same time hope to the German people that surrender on their part does not mean that destruction will befall the individual and the state.

I have discussed the foregoing with Mayer and he requests that the Office of War Information be furnished with a copy of this.

Document 1-15

Telegram 30-32, January 24, 1943

[Dulles and General Donovan continued to correspond on the functions of OSS Bern, especially respecting the penetration of Germany and psychological warfare.]

The following is for Donovan and is in reference to your 139.

Persons are going in the direction you indicate at frequent intervals at the present time. Included in this personnel are persons opposed political regimes who are only available for limited services, as well as some acting directly for us. We are developing all such opportunities as rapidly as it is possible to do so. In addition, through the contact mentioned in our 75, December 1, in the last sentence, we have good facilities available. At the present time, I am working on material which OWI's Mayer and I think is best suited to meet the political situation of nearby countries, and I am also preparing a program to see that printed matter is correctly dispatched and located. In reference to AL [Alsace-Lorraine], I have two aggressive natives in this location, developing all contacts possible and working with us full time. In order to be most effective, it is important for me to obtain a further idea on precise objective you now think most attainable and important, in order that definite jobs can be assigned for each trip, and so that psychological warfare efforts can be coordinated.

Document 1-16

Telegram 723, January 31, 1943

[Following the Allied invasion of North Africa, President Roosevelt and Prime Minister Churchill met at Casablanca, Morocco, from January 12 to 23, 1943. They agreed on the invasion of Sicily and effected the temporary reconciliation of French generals de Gaulle and Giraud. Most significant, Roosevelt enunciated the doctrine of "unconditional surrender" for the Axis powers, which received the endorsement of Churchill. The interpretation of this principle and its implications for psychological warfare held Dulles's attention for the duration of the war. "Burns" is Dulles.]

From Burns for Victor. I refer to yours of January 29 numbered 147 and 148. Of the Casablanca meeting, there were two things which caught particular attention:

First, the daringly conceived selection of a place which is nearly under the guns of the Germans and in an area which is generally depicted by the German press as being in a condition of chaos;

Second, the success in keeping carefully guarded the secret of the prolonged meeting.

The absence of a representative from Russia, and the fact that it was purely an Anglo-Saxon meeting in spite of the kind words of the communiqué addressed to China and Russia also committed [*sic*] here and in the countries of the Axis powers. The Swiss were not surprised at the slogan—unconditional surrender—nor did it cause any particular comment locally. Russian successes impressed the people here more than did the conferences.

I have learned from persons close to German circles that the slogan was a disappointment to Germans who steadfastly believed that negotiations might be possible or who were of the hopes that we would play along with the idea of making use eventually of the Germans to prevent Bolshevism from spreading. Although Goebbels may find temporary help in the slogan, it is believed that in the long run, it can be safely stressed as much as you desire since, as psychological warfare, it is absolutely sound. As the realization of defeat continues to become more and more general in the enemy countries, their conviction that a prolonged struggle will not result in a negotiated armistice in the long run will break down determined resistance. It is believed important, on the other hand, that it be made clear that when we insist on unconditional surrender, that it does not carry the implication that innocent German people will be subjected in the future to humiliating treatment or that it necessarily connotes intention to break up their country. Moreover, as cabled previously, it is believed undesirable to stress disarmament in propaganda of ours while recognizing its absolute necessity, since emphasis of this kind has a tendency to solidify the Army. . . .

Document 1-17

Telegram 729, February 1, 1943

[In the following message, Dulles presents detailed suggestions on policy toward Italy as the Mussolini regime continued to disintegrate.]

From Burns to Victor. Based on the best information available from Italian sources, the following is my analysis of the situation as regards the further development of the psychological warfare program as regards Italy:

An internal revolution, which is based on democratic or liberal elements seems [omission] occupation by Germans and the Fascists' present control of the Army and Navy or by individuals who do not have the personal courage to undertake big risks. Although there is no serious danger at the present time, the possibility of a communist revolution is not excluded.

Three courses of action seem to be possible:

First—When the African campaign has been concluded and preferably choosing the time when illness eliminates Mussolini from political activity, there might be made an arrangement with the group Badoglio, Ciano, Grandi, Caballero, Umberto. Of this group, some are reported to be venal and all are probably susceptible to promises of protection in the future and the hope of holding power. It is reported that they are now persuaded that the defeat of Italy is inevitable and they are faced with the loss of power and holdings to say nothing of liberty. It is possible that such a group could deliver a part of the Navy and the Army at least, their chances of success being dependent upon (1) ability to discard Mussolini, assuming the man is still living; (2) the extent to which the Germans would resist; (3) and complete victory in the Allied African campaign and control of the air. The group mentioned above would have no lasting popular support in view of the anti-Fascist sentiment which is increasing, and their only utility of any realness would be the possible ability to hold the Navy and Army in line for a temporary period. The disadvantages of a program of this kind would be the tie-up with an unpopular and discredited group, and unless there followed an early Allied occupation, coup d'état on their part might easily result in a revolution which would take a turn to communism. Unless we have early means of furnishing coal to Italy and supplying her with some assistance of an economic nature, which would tie up tonnage in large amounts, this program would be risky. Success is also unlikely unless Germany decides to abandon at least the southern part of Italy. This would also leave us burdened with the problem of getting rid of our Italian Darlans before there is a possibility of any real reconstruction. While it is not believed that this possibility should be dismissed completely, it is believed that the advantages are outweighed by the disadvantages.

The second alternative would involve the early creation of an Italian national committee under some such leader as Sforza outside of Italy, preferably in Tripoli, around which such liberal and Democratic Italian forces as are now or may be outside the country could gather. The influence and extent of such forces are problematical.

Another alternative would be to leave Italy to cook in her own gravy with idea that this would have the tendency to force Germany to expend economic and military resources in Italy in order to prevent it from being used as base against the Balkan regions. A series of revolutions might result from this, and possibly even a communist period, if German occupation is withdrawn without affecting American occupation.

The two alternatives set forth above are not mutually exclusive. The choice from among such alternatives is dependent upon military considerations with which the problem of the restoration of order in Eastern and Central Europe after the collapse or withdrawal of the Germans must be weighed.

Document 1-18

Telegram 41-43, February 3, 1943

[Dulles had a lifelong interest in psychology, which is not surprising in view of his belief in the importance of ideas and perceptions in affairs of state. He was acquainted with well-known Swiss psychologist Carl Jung. Number 105 is David K. E. Bruce, who for most of the war headed the OSS London office.]

To 105 from Burns. I have been in touch with the prominent psychologist, Professor C. G. Jung. His opinions on the reactions of German leaders, especially Hitler in view of his psychopathic characteristics should not be disregarded. It is Jung's belief that Hitler will [not] take recourse in any desperate measures up to the end, but he does not exclude the possibility of suicide in a desperate moment. Basing his statement on dependable information, Jung says that Hitler is living at East Prussia headquarters in underground quarters, and when even the highest officers wish to approach him, they must be disarmed and X-rayed before they are allowed to see him. When his staff eats with him, the Fuehrer does all the talking, the staff being forbidden to speak. The mental strain resulting from this association has broken several officers, according to Jung. Jung also thinks that the leaders of the Army are too disorganized and weakened to act against the Fuehrer. You can inform Paul M. that I am certain that Mrs. Frobe Kapteyn and Jung are OK. . . .

Document 1-19

Telegram 827, February 4, 1943

[In this message, Dulles offers an approach for dealing with would-be conspirators against Hitler.]

From Burns for Victor. Referring further to my no. 528 concerning psychological warfare against Germany, the following is suggested:

In answer to direct or indirect suggestions from German sources that there was an endeavor by groups to eliminate Hitler, the most effective reply that I have found is that so far as I was aware, Hitler was proving to be a great asset to us, and that there was not anything we could think of which would be more contributive to our military success than his keeping supreme command of the German armed forces. A line of this nature, enhanced by emphasis upon military errors made on prestige grounds following after Stalingrad and possible disaster in the Caucasus, seems to be very effective. I am still of the opinion that if Hitler were to disappear, the end of Germany would begin, and for that reason his disappearance is favored by us. However, the most effective way of speeding this is to create in Germany the impression that we desire that he remain.

Concerning the present German effort at levee en masse, I would suggest the Rathenau letter, dated October 9, 1918, to German Minister of War, Scheuch, regarding this subject might be used effectively.

Document 1-20

Telegram 44-45, February 5, 1943

[OSS Bern reported frequently on the development of secret weapons by the Nazis. Although usually carefully qualified, some of the information is identifiable even by the nonexpert as crackpot science and technology. Reports on the production of the V-1 and V-2 missiles were unquestionably helpful to the Allied cause, however. Reports sent by Dulles contributed to successful bombing strikes on the Nazi Peenemunde rocket research center, and softened the blow of surprise when rockets began to fall on Britain in 1944. Source number 490 was Walter Bovari, a German businessman who provided information on the Nazi rocket program on several occasions.]

From German sources he considers reliable, 490 reports that the Germans are producing a secret weapon whose exact nature was not disclosed to him with the exception that [it] is a flying contraption perhaps in the form of an aerial torpedo. He believes that one of his factories in Germany is making one small part of the machine. It is believed that the tests have not been completed to the satisfaction of the Germans. . . .

Document 1-21

Telegram 898, February 9, 1943

[Information in this report on conditions in France came through source 481, Louis Cruvilier, a French émigré in Switzerland; and source 477, Royall Tyler, an American League of Nations official whom Dulles had known for many years.]

From Burns for Victor. The following is a summary of reports received from French underground sources by no. 481.

1. Monseigneur Fillon, the Archbishop of Bourges, died of pneumonia which he contracted as a result of ill treatment at the hands of the Germans.

2. Violent demonstrations as a protest against the departure of laborers to Germany resulted in damage to the station at Mont Lucon, Allier. German soldiers and French gendarmes restored order, and the city was penalized by imposition of a fine of 5,000,000 francs, curfew at 8 o'clock, and a meatless period of 40 days.

3. The Gestapo seized at Lyon an organization known as "Lamitie Chretienne" which was devoted to aiding refugees. However, compromising documents were destroyed. They arrested Chaillet, who was of this organization, but intervention on the part of Cardinal Gerlier resulted in his release.

4. Franc-tireurs reported to have agreed upon united plan of action toward liberation and combat.

5. Because of the African policy both the British and the Americans are losing sympathy in France. De Gaulle is criticized as a tool of the British and Giraud is being more and more criticized as a tool of the Americans. Increasing strength is evident in the Communist movement.

6. There is a general wish for more aeroplane tracts particularly as deal with liberation and spiritual resistance, especially at Chalon, Lyons, Marseilles, Annecy and Givers.

7. It is reported from 477 that Paul Morandas is being sent to Sofia as French Minister by Laval. Former designation of Paillard, who for many years was counselor of French Embassy at Moscow, has been cancelled. Contact with Paillard, who is now in Geneva, has been established by 110. . . .

Document 1-22

Telegram 933, February 10, 1943

[Dulles commented frequently on Soviet policy and intentions, or relayed reports that impressed him. Often, the analysis was notable for its accuracy and prescience.]

Burns to Victor. In the following there is given a brief summary of a secret discussion between a trusted intermediary and an individual who is said to be representative of the Soviet viewpoint at this place.

The principal reason why the Russians abstained from taking part in the conferences held at Casablanca was that they believed that the purpose of the conference was to ratify the Anglo-American North African policy of which the Soviet does not approve because they understand it to favor the reactionary forces and likely to give to France a regime which is favorable to the Comite des Forges.

The view of Moscow that Russia alone has human material forces sufficiently adequate to conquer the Axis Powers finds confirmation in recent Russian successes. Although a second front is desired by Stalin, he is opposed to Turkish Anglo-American action in the Balkan countries. The Soviets count on Yugoslav irregulars and the Bulgarian army, and they are preparing a Bulgarian military coup to vest Slavophile generals with power at the very moment when Odessa is approached by the Red Army. Russian agents are endeavoring in Yugoslavia to sidetrack Mihailovich. Moscow is displeased with his monarchial Fascist tendencies. With regard to the balance of Europe, Moscow is building on Poland in the East and France in the West, both of which are militarily and ideologically united to Russia and which serve as a balance against the return of Prussianism in Europe. A socialist republic would be made of Poland with amputation of territory in the East but an increase of territory in the West by Silesia and East Prussia. For the Slavs of the Balkans and Central Europe, it would become a center of attraction. It is calculated by Russia that when hostilities in Europe cease, England and the United States will still be at war with Japan, and Russia, as an attitude in the Orient, can be a bargaining point in accomplishing objectives in Europe. . . .

Document 1-23

Telegram 934, February 10, 1943

[In February 1943, Fascist Grand Council members suspected of opposing Italy's continuation of the war were expelled from their posts. Dulles urged exploitation of this discord.]

From Burns for Victor. Please refer to my no. 720 [729] of February first. Discussion with individuals who are well informed on the situation in Italy indicate that the purpose of the changes in the Italian ministries was to remove from positions of responsibility those leaders whose loyalty to the Axis powers was open to question, and who might be susceptible to various forms of Allied pressure. For the most part their leaders have been succeeded by functionaries of the party who can be trusted. It is reported by a Jesuit source that some of the men who were dismissed, also the Papal envoy to Quirinal, had been putting Mussolini under pressure to ask of America conditions which would provide for Italy's exit from the war. Moreover, there is a rumor that the dismissal of Cavallero was due to the belief that an endeavor was being made by him to ascertain from the British and American forces in Africa the nature of the military terms which they would impose in the event of a radical change in the policy of the Italians.

With respect to psychological warfare I believe that we should place stress upon the following:

1. The dismissal of the ministerial leaders constitutes the first serious rend within the party ranks of the Fascists.

2. That the dismissals were the result of dictation on the part of the Germans, and that they represent German determination to make Italy proper the next field of battle. . . .

Document 1-24

Telegram 967, February 11, 1943

[The doctrine of "unconditional surrender" received public attention in Germany.]

From Burns for Victor. Reference is made to your no. 147. There is now being permitted to seep into the German press information concerning the slogan "unconditional surrender." The information is based partly on stories emanating from foreign correspondents in Lisbon and Italy.

The February seventh *Frankfurter Zeitung* contains an interesting article by its correspondent at Lisbon which assimilates the slogan to "Uncle Sam" and the "United States." After relating the story of "unconditional surrender Grant," the article concludes with a summary of what unconditional surrender provided for the states of the South. The article ends with the following: "The unconditional surrender of the Axis Powers would leave the entire nations in the same condition of devastation as were the southern states of America which had failed to recover after three generations and which the northern moneyed interests still exploit in many respects."

Document 1-25

Telegram 57-59, February 13, 1943

[In the following message, Dulles reflects on the possibility of a new purge in the Reich.]

From Burns. Hitler will probably return the High Command to the generals according to a reliable source. Apparently he himself realizes the extent that his prestige has been affected by last year's military operations, both among officers and throughout the country. A different source states that Hitler is gravitating further leftwards and that there is serious danger of a new and extensive purge. Many thousands of names have been included on a prepared list of "unreliables." (We might publicize as a step in Psychological Warfare, the likelihood of a new and extensive purge in Germany pointing out that it is about the right time for Hitler to take some dramatic action to draw attention away from his military reverses and that a purge is his probable next step.) From a German source I am led to believe that the Russians are training selected German prisoners for later internal action in Germany and that they are making strong efforts to treat German prisoners well.

Document 1-26

Telegram 1050, February 15, 1943

[In the following message, Dulles suggests a propaganda advantage to be gained from the anticipated relinquishment by Hitler of the German military high command.]

From Burns for Victor. With reference to reports concerning Hitler's possible surrender of high command, I would suggest as a measure of psychological warfare that this issue be brought into the open by us. That Hitler retain command as leading to increased tension with the military and further military errors would probably be in our interest. It is therefore suggested that we predict that he [will be] forced the surrender of the command.

Should the command be surrendered we then should say that this is a definite indication that Germany was obliged to conduct warfare of a defensive nature as the Hitler leadership was based on the theory of constant attack on the part of the Germans. Moreover, it really indicates that since the conduct of military affairs [is] now the task of supreme importance, he is not the Fuehrer any longer. Use could then be made of the phrase employed by Goebbels in his speech of January thirtieth and of like statements by Goering "Because we have the Fuehrer, we believe in victory." What will happen, however, if the soldiers do not have a Fuehrer any longer?

Document 1-27

Telegram 1051, February 15, 1943

[International business, labor, humanitarian, and religious relationships persisted during total war to a remarkable degree. Germany benefited from continuing commerce with neutral nations, and travelers returning to Switzerland provided an important source of intelligence for OSS Bern.]

From Burns for Victor. A brief summary of the views of a widely travelled Swiss businessman who returned a short time ago from trips to Cologne, Dusseldorf, Berlin, Brussels and Hamburg are given in the following:

He experienced during the period of his travels four air raids, one of which was at Cologne, two at Berlin, and one at Dusseldorf, the latter of which was especially severe. The slogan—unconditional surrender—had the effect of making the people believe that they must give their support to the Government since it was right in declaring that the war was one of survival. The unconditional surrender slogan recalled to them the surrender of the last war, Versailles diktat, inflation, the blockade.

Conditions were not bad locally, and the populace was being fed on the year's propaganda with respect to the stab in the back in 1918. They are determined absolutely not to let the soldiers on the front down, therefore, it is the belief of the informant that the home front will continue to hold until there is a collapse of the military front. In various cities, persons express the theory that the eyes of the English might soon open to the folly of continued fighting since the Empire has dissolved, with the United States having acquired Canada, New Zealand and Australia and now Africa, and after Singapore the rule of the white man in the East is finished. Therefore, why shouldn't England drop the Americans and accept peace. (This is from 110. As it is found to be considerably widespread, this theory has apparently been quietly revived in the propaganda by the Germans. A recent Goebbels article also hinted at this.)

It is also reported by the informant that in air raids, the behavior of the Germans is now similar to that of the British; that is, businesslike and unemotional. In Brussels, a Belgian pilot who was flying an RAF airplane came low over the city and shot up a skyscraper of ten stories in which was housed the headquarters of the Gestapo. This was done as an act of vengeance and it resulted in the killing of five Gestapo men. . . .

Document 1-28

Telegram 75-77, February 23, 1943

[Throughout the war, the German-Soviet relationship stood in the first rank of Dulles's concerns, especially with regard to Soviet efforts to appeal to Germans in a manner that would affect the postwar configuration of central Europe.]

It is considered possible in responsible German circles that the high German officers captured at Stalingrad may be in the mood to lead a German Revolutionary Army against the present German regime in collaboration with the Russians. Reliably informed that the bitterest possible exchanges over the radio between trapped generals and the GHQ took place. Apparently, we do not know the full Stalingrad story. In any case, the mass surrender of generals has made German officials somewhat suspicious. According to this same extremely reliable source, Rommel is in disgrace with both the Officers' Corps and Hitler. The reputation that Rommel enjoys with the United States is evidently not understood by the German military people, for they consider him as only good for offensive knockout tactics and also as one of their worst generals. Rommel's advance past Halfaya Pass was opposite to specific instructions and directly responsible for subsequent defeat, for it created an impossible German service supplies situation. This again from the same source. I believe the above is accurate, and if so, it is unlikely that he will be given command in Tunis operations.

Document 1-29

Telegram 183-85, February 25, 1943

[The Allies received numerous peace feelers from Italian sources in early 1943, as Fascists and anti-Fascists alike sought to distance themselves from the Mussolini regime at its eleventh hour. Certain contacts were made with OSS in Switzerland. In the following message, Dan is Cortese, the Italian consul at Geneva; Mary is the Marquese Marieni; and Jerry is the Duke of Aosta, a member of the royal family who held various positions in the Mussolini government over the years, including Viceroy of Abyssinia.]

This message from 110. Dan and Mary notified me through trusted Geneva cut-out of a purported offer from Jerry to send a close adviser or his wife here for discussions with us concerning the terms and timing on which an internal revolt could be effected which would put all the armed forces of the country in question at our disposal. Some understanding about general peace terms or at least a knowledge that honorable negotiations will be possible are considered necessary for success. Although he does not aspire to leadership later, Jerry does claim the ability needed to swing the deal. Zulu has been in touch with Dan, but we understand he decided to drop the matter. The move described above is from all appearances a new effort by Jerry, resulting in here detailed instructions to Dan and Mary to deal with us. Thus far I have declined Dan's request for a meeting, and assume that Casablanca decisions make the above uninteresting. It is difficult to appraise Jerry's standpoint, but most of the reports on him are not favorable. It is probable that he has some influence in certain military quarters, and anyone in this family who showed real courage might have considerable effect. Their final ability to show this courage is personally doubted by me.

Document 1-30

Telegram 188-89, February 27, 1943

[OSS Bern reported on German weapons development on an almost daily basis, on systems ranging from rockets to robot tanks. Source 490 is Walter Bovari, a German industrialist.]

490 received confidential information from important German industrialists to the effect that Hitler's secret weapon which is hoped to turn back the Russians this year is a manless tank. It is built very low to the ground, is about one yard long, and is filled with explosives. Remote control directs it against enemy tanks where it explodes on contact. The remote control is thought to operate by radio or by cable which unwinds from the tank, or by both. Mass production has been held up by the mechanism's extreme intricacy. Think that this story deserves more consideration than most of its type in view of its source and the circumstances under which 490 got it.

Document 1-31

Telegram 1381, February 27, 1943

[Axis satellite diplomats and private citizens in exile kept OSS Bern informed on internal conditions in their home countries. Here Dulles reports on an episode concerning Bulgarian restiveness under Nazi control. Ben is Buroff, a former Bulgarian foreign minister; Nabor ("neighbor") signifies Germany; Jones is King Boris, who also had the OSS designation 503; Tom and Mary are Bulgarian officials Todoroff and Matzankieff; 492 is René Charron, one of Dulles's French contacts in Switzerland.]

From Burns for Victor. Kindly refer to my February 48-52 M. Ben has forwarded the following message by emissary:

His coming to Switzerland as he intended has so far been opposed by Nabor. The fact that he is not otherwise disturbed is due to Jones who prevented all measures against him as a man to protect for the future. According to the emissary, Ben is convinced that it is possible that he leave his country within the near future in order to make necessary contacts to forward the political developments which are contemplated by him. He agrees with Jones on these political developments, but the means of action, although becoming more definite every day, are still in a fragile stage. Assistance is sought by him on one concrete point; i.e., bitter attacks on the radio by Tom and Mary against Jones to stop immediately. As against that, that is no reason to stop emphasizing with even more vigor the disastrous consequences of the policy which the present management follows. Without an army Ben cannot act. The latter is behind Jones unanimously. Everything is possible with army but the orders of Jones would be followed by it, consequently that a stop be put to the discrediting of Jones is important [*sic*]. It is felt by Ben that this request is reasonable in as much as such attacks have been completely stopped by M. radio. It was through 492 that the foregoing was received. As to authenticity I am fully satisfied.

Document 1-32

Telegram 1425, March 2, 1943 (extract)

[Number 476 is Gero von Gaevernitz, Dulles's closest assistant. Hjalmar Schacht, a leading German financier, former President of the Reichsbank and minister of economics, helped to engineer Germany's rearmament. Allen Dulles was well acquainted with him in the 1920s and 1930s. Number 491 is Kiosseivanov, the Bulgarian Minister in Bern; 284 is Max Shoop, a vital OSS agent who ran networks into France from Geneva and cooperated with the resistance.]

From Burns for Victor. The following is reported by 476 as from a trustworthy source. Schacht is no longer a member of the German Government as he was recently excluded from the German cabinet. Hitler personally ordered the exclusion about three weeks ago. This was the result of a pessimistic memorandum which Schacht submitted to Hitler, Goering and others on the political and military situation of Germany. Following his dismissal, Schacht was kept under surveillance by the Gestapo and he retired to his place out in the country. This place is about fifty miles distant from Berlin.

It is understood by 477 that 491 will probably be summoned to his home in order that a new cabinet be formed by him.

According to information which came into direct possession of 284, there has now become effective under a General appointed by de Gaulle a consolidation of French resistance groups. (Is it possible to obtain information on this), and the new consolidated group has made with Communist organization an alliance to cooperate on plans of resistance. Through 43 there has also been obtained from 284 information to the effect that there are not in France any German armoured divisions, and that regiments and divisions have been stripped, but in order to fool the Allies, some of many have been retained. In France there remains the equivalent of nineteen divisions of Germans (110 furnished this; a different source which is considered good indicates that 22 is the total).

It is also reported by 403 that according to a source (German official in Berlin), concentration of the production of submarines is now greater than on planes and tanks. . . .

Document 1-33

Telegram 1432, March 2, 1943 (extracts)

[This message was based on reports from high authorities in the Hungarian government. On March 3, Dulles cabled General Donovan that his contacts had requested nonbinding informal talks in Switzerland. Dulles noted the attractiveness of the offer with regard to thwarting the Nazis, and also other considerations that had to be taken into account, including general policy toward Eastern Europe and relations with the Soviet Union. He asked that Donovan consult the Secretary of State and provide guidance.]

Pam is the source whence the following came:

There has been straddling by Hungary. She has not been able to act otherwise because of the situation in which she is placed by her geographical position. However, Hungary was not pro-German and the fact that she never adopted Nazi ideology is proof of this. Some measures had to be adopted by Hungary in order to play up to Germany. The character of these, however, was not severe. As on Finland, the pressure on Hungary was great. In spite of the swiftness [strictness?] of its internal policy, political parties were active and Parliament was functioning. Trade unions were carrying on with finances furnished by the socialists. It was felt by Pam that in a nazified Europe this was a real accomplishment.

Two issues on which Hungary had been criticized, and with some justice, were matters which Pam wished to discuss very frankly. The first of these was the way in which the Jewish problem was being handled, and the other was the affair at Ujvidek (Novysad). This is where the killing of Yugoslavs took place. It is true that some measures had been adopted by Hungary under which the percentage of Jews in professional activities had been restricted, but against that there had been admitted into Hungary from Croatia, Slovakia, and Poland seventy thousand Jewish refugees. Some were free and some were in camps but they were being taken care of. . . .

With respect to the external situation, Hungary was not free to choose between Germany on the one hand and Great Britain and the United States on the other. The only choice it had was as [*sic*] between Russia and Germany. What Hungary would like to see is a . . . line from the Baltic south by which Europe would have protection from the Russians. Petty quarrels among the nations of the Danube was not a concern of Hungary. Rather, the future of western Europe was its concern. Was the position of the Allies such that they could do anything about this matter? American or British troops would never be fought by the Hungarians, but they must fight if the Rumanians, Russians, or Yugoslav partisans should come. The Fascists and Nazis have been beaten, but they are apprehensive about Russia. . . .

In concluding Pam adverted to Budapest's bombing. Nothing really important had been militarily accomplished by this, and he hoped that in the interest of future action a repetition would not occur. Pam stated that in the event the Allies made their way into the Balkans, the movement of troops should be made by the railroad through Zagreb rather than Budapest. He also said that the sympathies of the Hungarian population was cause. Therefore why should we turn them against ourselves by bombings and throw them in with the Bolsheviks. Message concludes here.

Document 1-34

Telegram 1496, March 4, 1943

[The menace of gas warfare as waged in World War I was a major concern of Allied intelligence. OSS Bern reported regularly on German preparations and intentions in this field. Sources 478 and 485 are the German exiles Josef Wirth and Baron Michael Goden, respectively; 497 is a Polish source.]

From Burns for Victor. 485 and 478 furnished the following. They claim that it is from a German source who is reliable. However, it is with some reserve that I repeat it.

As to whether their German sources are particularly up to date, I am not yet convinced.

There have been completed by the German Luftwaffe, offensive preparations for warfare by gas. There are now available in quantities, large calibre gas bombs. Yperite is the category in which the gas is reported to be primarily. Great increases have been made in the defensive preparations of the Luftschutz. There have been constructed in German cities new air raid shelters which are equipped with so-called "gas locks." Entry and egress is possible without permitting gas to penetrate. There has been a substantial speed up in the manufacture and distribution of gas masks for the use of the civilian population. A new type of mask has been provided for children. It covers the body from the hips on up. 110 furnishes the following: According to reports in the German press, distribution has been made of masks in certain localities. Ingen and Constance which are near the Swiss border are, strangely enough, included in these localities. Reports furnished by 497 are to the effect that the Germans are manufacturing en masse "formique acide." It is considered by source that this may constitute the base for a gas, the effect of which is a film that blinds. It was also reported that work in connection with gas warfare was carried on by Luneburgheide plant. London has received a copy of this.

Document 1-35

Telegram 1527, March 5, 1943

[German Foreign Minister Joachim von Ribbentrop, an architect of the Axis Pact, visited Mussolini to bolster his sagging regime. The following report of their meeting, if valid, indicates an irresolute attitude on both sides. Hitler's meeting with Il Duce in Salzburg on April 7 apparently did restore the latter's confidence temporarily.]

From Burns for Victor. A source which in the past has proved to be reliable has furnished the following regarding the meeting of Ribbentrop and Mussolini in Rome.

The meeting was asked for by Mussolini and he stated that it was not possible for Italy to carry on indefinitely, and consequently he asked for a free hand in order to try out the possibilities of peace. The position taken by Ribbentrop was that Europe could be held by Germany for an indefinite period. However, it was recognized by him that they had lost their chances of a decisive victory. Ribbentrop agreed that Mussolini should endeavor to make contact with the Anglo-Saxons and that so far as the immediate future was concerned the matter should be left in the hands of the latter. The basis for a peace offensive was also discussed by Ribbentrop and Mussolini, and it was agreed that an endeavor should be made to clarify the "misunderstanding" that it was their desire to bring other European nations under their domination. They also agreed that they should emphasize that in accordance with the nationality principles of the Nazis and Fascists, complete liberty should be assured to all the nations of Europe. It was agreed by them that if it should be possible to convince the Anglo-Saxons of the real danger of Bolshevism, it might be possible to make an agreement with them.

Document 1-36

Telegram 1529, March 6, 1943

[This message contains Dulles's views on what measures could be taken to hasten the detachment of the Axis satellites of southeastern Europe from the principal enemy nations.]

From Burns for Victor. I would suggest as a further measure of psychological warfare that there be reviewed by us our relations with unwilling satellites of the Axis in southeastern Europe, particularly such countries as Rumania, Hungary, Bulgaria, and also Croatia to some extent. It is recommended that we make a distinction in our policy between Japan, Germany, and Italy, which are the main Axis powers and which were the deliberate seekers of war in order to acquire territorial aggrandizement, and the satellite nationals which were obliged to cooperate with Germany as a result of occupation. The principle of unconditional surrender should be applicable to the former. As regards the latter it is suggested that we hold out the possibility of negotiation, provided we are convinced that their policy is basically anti-Axis in character and that they are willing to restrict military and economic aid to the Axis within the limits of possibility.

Although not yet able to defy the Axis powers, these countries are in a position to put sprags in the wheel of various kinds of economic and military cooperation. The disgust of the satellites with the economic robbing of their countries through the pretence of buying under agreements of clearance has already been mentioned by me. A beginning should now be made by us to find for some of their products other markets against payment, which would be blocked and which would become available only when hostilities cease, for economic rehabilitation after the war.

In this part of Europe unrest is spreading, and the Axis is experiencing difficulty in finding in these countries men upon whom they may depend unqualifiedly. For various measures of political and economic warfare, it is a fertile field.

Document 1-37

Telegram 1534, March 6, 1943

[Dulles here provides a general assessment of the various elements of the French resistance.]

From Burns for Victor. Importance of further developing program in France to build up forces of resistance is indicated in reports from that country. Several lines of contact into France have been accomplished and it is possible to develop more. Two fields of work offer themselves. (1) The old groups of resistance, Liberation Combat Franc-Tireur and so forth with whom there appears to have joined the Communists who probably are the best single group of resistance in France. It is to de Gaulle and London that these groups look chiefly, and presumably anything that is done here should be coordinated with Zulu and London. It is our belief, however, that this work can be usefully supplemented by us as, according to our information, there has been bad disruption in London contacts.

A second group, which has heretofore been neglected rather badly is centralized around former army officers and army personnel as well as other elements who are not pleased to be working with communistic elements. It is to us and Giraud that these elements look chiefly. Heretofore not much has been done to bring them into an organized body but it is our belief that work of a useful purpose could be carried out from here. However, the financial outlay might be substantial.

Reliable information has reached me to the effect that there have taken to hiding, especially in the Savoie mountains, between 5,000 and 10,000 former officers and men of the French Army. When the present severe control at the Italian frontier relaxes or as weak points in their organization are discovered, these ex-officers and men may be accessible from Switzerland. Contact has been established with this group.

This problem, I trust, will be given consideration both in London and in Washington, and I trust that instructions will be transmitted. The Military Attaché was in full agreement with what has been prepared in the foregoing. London is receiving a copy of this.

Document 1-38

Telegram 1544, March 6, 1943

[Alsace-Lorraine constituted a weak link in the frontier of Nazi-controlled territory, providing important sources for Allied intelligence and serving as a conduit for the penetration of both Germany and France. The Germans took severe steps to control the situation.]

From Burns for Victor. A good Alsatian source furnished the following.

Forty-five thousand people in Alsace-Lorraine are faced with a new threat of deportation. Evacuation of a zone 6 kilometers deep along the frontier between Delle and Bale is under consideration by the military authorities in order to prevent the escape of French prisoners and Alsatians. Between the eleventh and thirteenth of February a large number of Alsatians attempted to escape to Switzerland. Of the seventeen who were caught all except one were either hanged or shot. Balschwiller, a village near Altkirch, was surrounded and there were arrested and deported the relatives of 31 persons who escaped from this village. There are also being arrested young men who do not sign up for service in the military forces.

Document 1-39

Telegram 107-8, March 8, 1943

[Some émigrés and refugees seeking to leave Switzerland made the hazardous journey across southern France to neutral Spain and Portugal, there to embark for Allied-controlled territory.]

Before they travel west, people of different Allied nationalities get in touch with us in Switzerland. In some particular chosen cases we may extend some help. Please make up an arrangement by which they can promptly deliver their information on the Spanish side of the frontier and let us know to whom these people should report. The arrangement should include identifying passwords for our people there and for us, and we will add our own numbers for identification. . . .

Document 1-40

Telegram 1597, March 10, 1943

[OSS Bern's coverage of the Holocaust was inexplicably meager, but Dulles did transmit some reports that contributed to Washington's knowledge. Source 474 is W. A. Visser 't Hooft, Secretary of the World Council of Churches in Geneva.]

From Burns for Victor. From a Berlin source which he considers responsible, following was obtained by 474.

Fifteen thousand Jews in which were included Jews with Aryan wives and Jewesses with Aryan husbands were arrested in homes and factories between January twenty-sixth and March second. For this purpose all closed lorries in Berlin were requisitioned. They were brought to four centers including Bohemian Church and two of the main Gestapo prisons. There have died several hundred children who were separated from parents and left without food. In Berlin the shooting of several hundred adults took place. Officers who are high in the SS and who took the initiative in this action are reported to have made the decision that before the middle of March Berlin should be liberated of all Jews. Friends are sheltering about eighteen thousand Jews. That the above methods will be extended within the near future to other regions in Germany is definitely expected. The new policy is to kill the Jews on the spot rather than deporting them to Poland for killing there.

Document 1-41

Telegram 1593, March 12, 1943

[Dulles maintained close relations with the Italian literary figure Ignazio Silone, an anti-Fascist exile in Switzerland who maintained extensive contacts in northern Italy and abroad. He was given the designations "Len" and 475.]

From Burns for Victor. Len has furnished the following: Tremendous capital is being made by Fascist propaganda of the slogan "unconditional surrender." It is being used to paint a somber picture of the result of Italian defeat; that is, extreme poverty, servitude, territorial mutilation. Many liberal elements are discouraged by the formula. These elements see in it a death blow to the hopes of effecting improvement in the separate peace position of the Italians. According to a rumor that has spread, Yugoslavia expects Greece, Dodecanes Trieste, and to Senuzzi the British have promised Cyrenaica. An endeavor is made by Fascist propaganda to picture the United Nations as a matrimonial set-up between Sovietism and Americanism. It is Len's belief that the propaganda of the Fascists should be refuted in the following manner.

1. Refusal of all compromise with Mussolini is what is meant by unconditional surrender. The Italian policy of the United Nations is based on a distinction which they make between the Italian people and the Fascist Government. The United Nations do not apply unconditional surrender to the Italian people. The people will be treated in accordance with the dignity of the Atlantic Charter and the principles of liberty.

2. The concrete conditions which will be accorded Italy by the victorious United Nations depend directly on the measure in which the Italian people themselves help toward the victory of the democracies and in which [garbled] selves from the Fascist regime.

3. The imposition of Soviet or American systems on the Italians is not intended. It is exclusively on the free will of the Italian people that the future political regime of Italy depends. From the earliest days Italian history has contained traditions of

freedom which are adequate to inspire the Italians in the choice of a political regime when Fascist dictatorship collapses.

In conclusion, Len states that in order to give weight to these declarations it is indispensible that competent and authoritative persons make them public, and it is suggested that therefore the best moment would be at the commencement of agitation which is being prepared for the end of March by the Italian Socialist Party.

Document 1-42

Telegram 212-14, March 15, 1943

[Dulles often reported on wartime diplomacy in its global dimension, including the role of Japan. Number 511 stands for Swiss intelligence. Number 472 stands for the remnants of prewar French intelligence that continued to cooperate with the OSS and British intelligence in Switzerland; "472" was an important coordinator of order of battle information for OSS Bern.]

The following is from #110. This information was received from a source associated with our number 511 who is the local counterpart of number 472. Japan has agreed to offer Russia security in the Orient by ceding the Kuriles and Southern Sakhalin together with the neutralization of Manchuria. This will be Japan's contribution to an attempted Axis understanding with Russia. On this basis, Japan would act as intermediary between Russia and Germany. Withdrawal on the Eastern Front to defensive lines would be Germany's part of the agreement. It was further reported by this source that there was a change eight days ago in German-Italian strategy in Tunis. Their present policy is to strengthen and further reinforce Tunis, making every effort to hold it. Previous to this their strategy was to fight only a delaying action and even some slight withdrawal of forces. Recent visits of Goering and Ribbentrop to Italy were responsible for this change in policy. It is believed that Goering is now leaving Italy for France. . . .

Document 1-43

Telegram 515, March 21, 1943

[Dulles and OSS Bern became increasingly involved in direct support for the French resistance. Brigidier General Barnwell Legge was U.S. Military Attaché in Switzerland; source 284 is Max Shoop, an American previously employed by the Paris office of Sullivan & Cromwell, Dulles's New York law firm. Shoop ran networks in France out of Geneva for most of the war and was a primary figure in the preparation of order of battle intelligence; 405 is Philippe Monod, a French resistance representative resident in Geneva who had worked for Shoop at Sullivan & Cromwell before the war; and Henri Frenay was commander of the resistance group "Combat."]

In consultation with General Legge, I and 284 have just completed a series of conferences with 405 who came from Geneva to Bern as representative of FFCM (Forces Française Combattante de La Metropoles). This organization represents united direction Combat, Liberation, Franc-tireur. 405 particularly came from Fresnay [Frenay] of Combat but also in behalf of FFCM. It was emphasized by 405 that the central organizing committee with ex-officio representatives of de Gaulle and representatives of each group is actively directing the resistance movement's activities. The only substantial organizations outside of the amalgamation are the Communist movement and Radio Patrie. Some local liaison exists with them. Whereas FFCM operates principally in the former Free Zone, they are rapidly developing close relationship with similar organizations in the occupied Zone, particularly Organization Nationale de Resistance counterpart of Combat and counterparts of Franc-tireur otherwise known as Resistance and Liberation, also with Organization Civile et Militaire, which is numerically most important in Occupied Zone. Cairo liaison is also maintained through de Gaulle personal representatives in the Occupied Zone. Moving the headquarters to Paris is under consideration. Previous to this the chief support for FFCM came through the French National Committee in London, and some ten million francs of financing which averaged some 12 million francs monthly [?] was also received from that same city. We were advised by 405 that recently a currency shipment of about 9 million francs fell into Vichy hands.

Program and plans of FFCM follow. 1. Secret representations in Lausanne to be established as contact points for the French headquarters England and USA. At present FFCM contacts London by radio, but recently due to local conditions this has not been entirely satisfactory. . . . A summary of financial needs is as follows. (1) Sufficient Swiss funds to cover local representation. This item we have already agreed to meet. (2) To develop the organization as above 25 million francs monthly. (3) An additional amount to cover specific maintenance for guerrillas, sabotage, etc. (4) a reserve capital to take care of releve personnel. 3. There is an immediate need of materials, arms, explosives and a reserve stock of rations for guerrilla organizations. . . . 4. Assistance is desired to form a representation of FFCM in North Africa and maintain liaison permanently by air and radio. Separately comments are being submitted.

Document 1-44

Telegram 516, March 21, 1943

[Dulles raises the matter of support of the French resistance with General Donovan. Number 284 is Max Shoop; 511 is Swiss intelligence.]

For Donovan from 110 repeated London for Bruce. Companion cable gives picture concerning the position and program needs of certain resistance groups in France. Consider the source trustworthy since he has been personally known to 284 and me for over 10 years. We consider it important to plan how we may supplement from here work done from London and elsewhere to help organize these groups, particularly with the view of setting precise but limited objectives in Sergeant Fields [certain fields?] guerrilla warfare and to build up programs of general resistance. Besides the groups mentioned in the separate cable there are others such as Savoie mountain refugees, other resistance groups of Releves and possibly certain elements of the demobilized armies, Communists etc. not integrated with FFCM choice groups to support and method and extent of support requires carefully coordinated plans. We feel that FFCM view long history and existing organizations despite recent disruptive attacks deserves substantial material and financial support and that it is desirable to encourage the establishment by FFCM of liaison here for the purpose of facilitating of communication intelligence itself. We realize that if other aids are given such aids must come chiefly by air. For reasons explain separately 511 proving cooperative and this greatly facilitates the maintenance of communications across the border with groups. Have discussed the entire matter with Zulu counterpart who cable separately. General Legge concurs in the foregoing.

Document 1-45

Telegram 126-30, March 23, 1943

[This report on German strategic thinking came from Swiss intelligence via number 513, a Polish source. Charles Rochat was Secretary General of the Vichy French Foreign Ministry.]

The information contained in the following message comes from the same source as my #212 to #214 [March 15, above] and given to 513. By about the middle of April, Germany plans to have completed a substantial reinforcement program along the western front. For the present they feel they can depend on Anglo-Saxon hesitation and on the fact that, before we strike, we apparently wish to settle political difficulties with Russia and persuade the Soviet to take a definite stand regarding Japan. It is reported by the source that although German forces in France today do not exceed two hundred thousand, the period of greatest weakness in the German defenses along the French coast is already passing. He adds also that there is no important new concentration of effective German combat troops in the vicinity of the Franco-Spanish border. However, with the hope of bringing about a reduction of our strength at the Tunisian front, the Germans have sent some training forces there to strengthen false rumors of concentration. Though not yet fully tested, this source is serious.

It would seem that Germany is commencing a new war of nerves against this country. Detailed invasion plans are being planted, perhaps for the purpose of bolstering economic negotiations which may be pending. Despite the fact that immediate danger is discounted, all possibilities should be considered and plans laid accordingly.

A trusted source provides the following. At the request of the Japanese Embassy there, the Vichy government has asked the press to cease personal attacks on Stalin. However, continued attack on Bolshevism is permissible. To the astonishment of an important diplomat with whom he was conversing at Vichy, Rochat said Stalin would play an important part in the future and praised him as a great personality.

Document 1-46

Telegram 1926, March 26, 1943

[This report from 472, remnants of prewar French intelligence in Switzerland, links erratic Italian diplomacy with the danger of a separate Soviet peace with the Axis. References are to Crown Prince Umberto of Savoy and Prince Konoye of Japan, the former Prime Minister.]

472 has furnished the following, but it is transmitted with reserve for checking by you against sources of your own. Mussolini presided over a secret conference which was held on March eighth at Rome. Umberto was among those who were present. Four members were appointed to a Commission which is to proceed to Nuremberg to participate in a conference of Germans and Italians. Following the conference it is proposed that after receiving its instructions from Hitler a mixed Italian German commission would go to Japan where Prince Konoye would receive them with a view to an attempt at conversations with Russia through an intermediary provided by the Japanese.

Document 1-47

Telegram 2181, April 7, 1943

[Dulles's contacts included European aristocrats whose connections enabled them to cross international borders even in wartime. Prince Maximilian Höhenlohe von Lagensberg, a Sudeten German residing in Spain and traveling on a Liechtenstein passport, had access to Nazi leaders including Heinrich Himmler, as well as to Allied intelligence officials and diplomats.]

Max Hohenlohe, who is a Liechtenstein national, was recently seen by me. Partly because of the large holdings his wife has in Mexico and also because he hopes to render aid in eventually reconciling the Western Powers and Germany, he wishes to maintain contact. His desire is not entirely disassociated with the interest he has in preserving large holdings in the Sudeten. Contact has been made by Hohenlohe with leading personalities in Germany, Bohemia and France, where he had just made visits. Resistance of German power [German power of resistance] has been portrayed by him as largely unimpaired. Nevertheless, he is apprehensive lest certain elements will turn to the Russians in order to obtain the best terms possible. . . . Although there are in Germany strong elements who prefer to deal with the powers of the West, there are also elements which are equally powerful who are prepared to cast their lot with Russia on the theory that a Communist Germany eventually could reestablish itself as a great power by aligning itself temporarily with Russia, whereas were Germany to be defeated and be subjected to occupation by the powers of the West, it would, for generations to come, be reduced to a power of secondary position.

The strengthening of the anti-Communist elements is advocated by Hohenlohe, and this is possible only if some hope is extended to these elements. He believes that Himmler's organization is the best element available for the maintenance of internal order and to oppose communism because Himmler's prestige has been increased as a result of the recent successful counter attack of the Germans against Kharkov which is popularly attributed to SS troops.

Hohenlohe will leave within a short time for Spain. In that country he is known to the American Ambassador. His acquaintance with Samuel Hoare is also intimate.

Document 1-48

Telegram 32-35, April 9, 1943

[In this report on the status of Bulgaria and Nazi-Bulgarian relations, 492 is René Charron, a Dulles assistant. Number 491 is Kiosseivanov, former Prime Minister and now Bulgarian Minister in Switzerland. He was assigned the OSS code name "Kiss."]

At my suggestion 492 talked with 491 in an attempt to ascertain the details of Hitler's interview with King Boris of Bulgaria. Although 491 had no direct information, he believed personally that the visit was made at the initiative of Boris to: (1) Insure the delivery of military supplies to Bulgaria. (2) In order to find out Germany's attitude regarding the somewhat menacing position of Turkey. 491 believes that, although Bulgaria would defend herself against attack from Turkey alone, she is taking no aggressive action in any direction. She would, however, if the Allies entered the country, probably take the same position with regard to Germany, by permitting the passage of troops. King Boris knows that he does not have the sympathy of either Hitler or Ribbentrop, and his position is one of great indecision. 491 believes that it would be wise for us to strengthen Boris' stand and to encourage his project of forming a National Coalition Cabinet, since, he says, the present cabinet is a band of imbeciles and traitors. He is of the opinion that the presentation by BBC of Bulgarian expatriates is doing real harm, and he is confirmed that it would be wise to cease personal attacks on the King. (The SISI understand that these attacks have recently been resumed.) 491 is convinced that at the present time the Army is behind the King. Although Kiss is confident of another German offensive against Russia, he believes that the Nazi policy is to try to keep Turkey neutral, and discounts the danger of German attack. Now that the popular belief in an ultimate Nazi victory has lessened, Russia is strengthening her position in Bulgaria, and Soviet propaganda there is now strong.

Document 1-49

Telegram 173-74, April 10, 1943

[Source 512, who relayed this unsubstantiated report of German plans for an air attack on London, is Hans Bernd Gisevius, German consul in Zurich and Abwehr agent; Nabors signifies Germans.]

Test flights of approximately 40 large flying boats, whose construction the Nabors have practically completed at Rotterdam, will get under way shortly under heavy fighter protection. In making this report, 512 said that the Nabors proposed to load these flying boats with explosives and to sacrifice them in a crash suicide attack on London; the pilots will parachute to earth. While I hesitate to report rumors of this nature, I can see no particular reason for the informant planting such a story. He is in a strategic position, but he frankly says that even though his information is from an excellent source, it is not absolutely conclusive. I am informing Zulu here. It is my belief that you can judge better than I whether or not a rumor such as this is a fairy story.

Document 1-50

Telegram 60-66, April 14, 1943

[Dulles and OSS Bern devoted great effort to networks in northern Italy, both to obtain intelligence on enemy forces and to encourage the resistance. Bern served as a principal conduit for funds and messages between Italian opposition elements and leaders in exile as well as Italian-American individuals and organizations. In Switzerland, Dulles maintained close contact with number 475, Ignazio Silone of the Socialist Party, who was in touch with the resistance in his homeland. Among the prominent exiles in regular contact with 475 through Dulles was Count Carlo Sforza, a leader of the anti-Fascist, antimonarchist movement who was given the identification number 510.]

Received information from a representative of Partito d'Azione and 475 who were just here. This information shows that it is desirable for us to increase our support for the growing anti-Fascist elements. Included in these anti-Fascist groups are the Labor Party, the Socialist Party, Partito d'Azione, (and liberal democratic groups such as Giustizia Liberta). Further, all these groups are reported to be working in cooperation with each other. In order to keep in contact with us, the central committee formed by these groups looks forward to sending their representative here before long. The man they have chosen is Benedetto Croce. He is the spiritual father of the liberal movement that has such men in it as Bonomi and others. The central committee proposes to start strikes all over Italy within twenty-four hours after the Allied forces make a landing in Sardinia or Sicily. 475 and the representative mentioned above both urge that we use Sforza. He could help us strengthen and unify the Liberal Democratic elements. . . .

It is strongly urged by Representative of the Partito d'Azione that Sforza be used to give their movement standing and prestige. It is suggested that, in time with the Socialists' program of May 1st, the Montevideo declaration should be emphasized by radio, and tied in with action of the Italian democratic and liberal elements.

Please cable us any advice you may have on this subject, since these anti-Fascist elements are very strongly desirous of establishing contact here. As can be expected, they hope we will [not] be enticed into dealing with Grandi, Badoglio and others who have compromised with Fascism. They believe that this would lead to a bloody revolution as it would preclude the possibility of restoring to Italy a true democracy. . . .

Document 1-51

Telegram 260-64, April 15, 1943

[OSS Bern reported frequently on the unsettled conditions in Italy and Hungary. Nicholas Kallay was President of the Hungarian Council. 477 is Royall Tyler.]

The former Hungarian Minister to London, Barcza, is our 519. Prior to the break, he served in London, and it is claimed that his relations with the British officials had been excellent. Even during the blackest days, according to 477, the subject was consistently and firmly committed to our side, but at present, has no entree to the inner circle at Budapest. . . . It is probable that Kallay is winking at his mission here. There is no indication that he has any contact with Zulu at present. Number 520 was given to MA. . . .

We are informed by Barry that the Nabors request for 3 divisions for use in Yugoslavia and also for replacement troops for use in Russia, where the Hungarians still have some 250,000 men, was refused by Kallay. In Barry's opinion Mussolini is tied hand and foot to the Nazis and is without an avenue of escape. Furthermore, there is no leader on the horizon because the King has lost all prestige, Grandi was deliberately compromised by a recent decoration, Badoglio is too old, Piedmont is zero and Aosta, while somewhat better, spoiled his chances over Croatia.

In his long talk with the Pope, 519 found that the expectation of a wholesale bombing of big cities and an Allied attack has badly frightened his Holiness. It is the one hope of the Pope that generals commanding various garrisons will seize control and swing over to the Allies. Apparently, he believes that there are generals who are ready for such a move.

Document 1-52

Telegram 2360, April 16, 1943

[Dulles reports that the noose was tightening around Mussolini.]

The following is from Burns for Victor. A local source who is considered highly reliable has informed me that the Swiss authorities have been approached by Mussolini with a view to finding out whether they would grant him admission into their country in case of eventualities, as he has fears for his personal safety in the event internal revolution or invasion by the Allies should take place.

It was also reported by this source that consideration of the matter at this time was refused by the Swiss.

It may be recalled that a number of years ago when Mussolini was a youthful agitator, he was compelled to leave Switzerland under orders of expulsion, and that later when he came to Switzerland as a Prime Minister, the decree of expulsion had to be speedily revoked.

Since this information is known to only two or three individuals and as the disclosure thereof might betray source, it is requested that the information be given careful protection.

Document 1-53

Telegram 2483, April 21, 1943

[This message concerns the Hitler-Mussolini meeting at Salzburg April 7.]

Burns transmits the following strictly confidential report for Victor,

(a) Mussolini was in a very discouraged mood when he returned because of the rough going he encountered.

(b) Three demands were made by Mussolini. The first was a demand that, for the defense of Italy, twenty net divisions of German forces be provided. The second demand was that secret negotiations for peace with Russia be initiated. The third was that the people of occupied Europe be given better treatment. On all the foregoing points, Hitler was noncommittal.

(c) The defense of Tunisia was criticized by Mussolini. He also criticized the failure to provide an adequate supply of gasoline which is now a more critical point than is the shortage of troops. Mussolini also remonstrated against the attitude of Ribbentrop during the latter's visit to Rome.

Document 1-54

Telegram 2635, April 28, 1943

[Dulles reports on French Premier Pierre Laval's difficulties with his German masters.]

A good French source who is considered reliable had reported that Laval was expecting to celebrate April eighteenth as his assumption to power. He proposed to do this by mutual pronouncements regarding collaboration on the German Vichy side. In Paris he expected to meet Hitler or at least Goering. For the occasion a special train had been ordered, and he also had a speech all prepared. Laval completely disappointed [by] the Germans. They apparently were discouraged as regards any demonstration of formal collaboration. According to our best information, Germany felt that a collaboration pronouncement is inappropriate in as much as it was expecting to deport another two hundred and fifty thousand workers.

Document 1-55

Telegram 27-30, May 4, 1943

[Dulles offers suggestions on countering Nazi propaganda aimed at splitting the western allies and the Soviet Union. Number 491 is Kiosseivanov, the Bulgarian Minister in Switzerland.]

A good source reports that the German manuever resulting in the Russo-Polish tangle is the first move in a general program designed to split the Allies. Goebbels and Ribbentrop have been specifically entrusted with the execution of this program to see what they can do toward this end. Our informant believes that the second effort will be an attempt to upset Russo-American relations by a German discovery of alleged documents covering Communistic plots in the United States. My evidence on this subject is rather meager; I have no information on the method or time when this might be carried out. However, a statement that we know of these plans, in order to take the wind out of their sails, might be worth considering. 491 received this suggestion from a prominent Bulgarian: a secret ultimatum resulted in the Germans being given the right to pass through Bulgaria. This establishes a precedent which might be equally applicable to an Allied force if it later presented a similar ultimatum since "this would conform with the people's wishes," as our informant said. In regard to the following refer to my 1381 dated February 27, which was sent through the Secretary of State. The same informant says that Matzenkieff and Todoroff are discredited in B. He complains about their London broadcasts and says their declarations have no influence.

Document 1-56

Telegram 32-33, May 5, 1943

[OSS Bern maintained particular interest in resistance elements in the French Alps, close to the Swiss frontier. Number 520 is General Legge, the U.S. Military Attaché.]

In regard to the Haute Savoie situation, which is developing, we are keeping in close contact with it and are working in close collaboration with 520. We have given financial support totaling 2 millions. This seemed necessary to maintain morale and help build the organization. According to latest indications, there is still a good nucleus and military training is progressing. The numbers, however, are considerably reduced. . . . Parachutage has brought some encouragement this month. This is extremely important and Zulu SOE is cabling the details directly to London.

Document 1-57

Telegram 45-50, May 7, 1943

[Dulles continued to press for a more active role in supporting resistance movements, and a stronger U.S. voice in U.S.-U.K. control of special operations. Number 284 is Max Shoop; 516 is General Davet of the French resistance delegation in Switzerland; 517 is Henri Frenay, an important French resistance figure.]

Regarding your cables 18, 34, and 35, I am in close contact with Zulu, the representative of SOE. In reference to French resistance groups, I think Zulu looks upon them chiefly as adjuncts to GT and as related operations. He is reluctant to give up a monopoly that he has enjoyed up to this point. The former wish a larger role, and want to work with us also. Further, they ask for our help, advice, and financing. The contact should be with London in Zulu's opinion. From 110 and 284.

There is a bi-weekly courier system here that is operated by FFCM. We have just received their plans through this system. These cover the following points: (1) Sabotage services and railway information. (2) Including Savoie, the organization of the Maquis situation. (3) The organization of deported workers for sabotage and propaganda work in Germany, as well as work with anti-Nazi factions. Also, an expansion of the existing use of ex-prisoners. The expansion of SI work through Cheminois and other places is contemplated in these reports.

We think it is important to make a decision as to the part that we should play at this end in order to build up the resistance movements; help guide their activist operations, under the direction of Washington and London; and aid in financing these movements. This is for London and you to make the final decision on, as it is clearly seen that the primary operational headquarters must be located in North Africa or London or both. Assuming that the support of the resistance groups becomes a clearly defined joint Anglo-American operation, not completely British, we are convinced that it is possible for us to contribute valuable supplementary services although we do not have any preconceived ideas regarding our role.

After 516 arrives tomorrow, we will have further details. We recognize the fact that you may want to postpone your decisions pending closure Tunis, and an agreement between Generals de Gaulle and Giraud. In addition, if 517 makes a trip to North Africa this may have an important bearing.

There is no friction whatsoever at this end with Zulu. Due to their long experience in this field, particularly in the field of parachute work and radio, and relations with London Committee and the Radio Patrie, we are able to recognize their special position. However, as Zulu's approach to the French situation is somewhat different from ours, we recommend our independent scrutiny. Harmonious, useful work is assured once a clear understanding is reached with them concerning the American role in general and the part assigned to us here.

Document 1-58

Telegram 56-62, May 8, 1943

[With the Axis on the brink of final expulsion from North Africa, Dulles proposes that new psychological warfare blows be delivered to Italy. Leland is Leland Harrison, U.S. Minister in Switzerland; Adolph is A. A. Berle, Assistant Secretary of State.]

I wish to submit the following plan for your consideration as a measure of Psychological Warfare. I suggest that once the operations are completed in Tunis, a message from Roosevelt, concurrent with messages from Stalin, and Churchill be addressed to Italy. The messages should reassert the principle that the war is directed against the Fascist dictators and the Fascist allies of the Nazis rather than against the Italian people. The projected message should specifically make the point clear that the present offers the Italians their last chance to choose their own destiny, that it is their great chance to declare where they stand and to indicate a definite decision not to link the fate of Italy with that of Germany irrevocably with all the consequences which this would of necessity entail. It should be pointed out on the other hand that if Italians themselves should overthrow the Fascist dictatorship and drive out the Nazi intruders, then the freely elected representatives of Italian democracy could take part in the final peace negotiations together with the representatives of other free democracies, for the purpose of restoring liberty and equality of opportunity to the people of Europe now under the Nazi yoke. The explanation would be given that under such conditions, the United Nations would have no intention of depriving Italy of any preponderantly Italian territories, or of denying Italy the chance to share in a colonial regime to be established consistent with the principles of the Atlantic Charter.

It would be essential to the success of such a plan that countless copies of any such declaration be scattered over Italy by plane and that the declaration be repeated continuously over all radio programs for a considerable length of time in order to have any assurance that it would reach any sizeable portion of the people.

Although I am not able to predict that this would result in the upset of the Nazi-Fascist control, it might at least cause a sufficiently widespread disturbance to work as a continuing undermining factor for the Italian regime and the German forces of occupation, and it would also strengthen the somewhat leaderless movements of opposition to the existing government. If the Italian people reject this plan as is probable, the resulting situation would furnish a basis for future effective propaganda in order to supplement the military operations.

When this whole matter was discussed with Leland, he suggested that Adolph be given a copy.

Document 1-59

Telegram 8-9 to London, May 17, 1943

[Dulles again advocates direct aid for the Maquis of southeastern France. Number 520 is General Legge, the U.S. Military Attaché in Switzerland.]

Recently, 645 sent new parachutage directives for the Haute Savoie situation. These directives were based on the request which 520 received directly from the leader there. Zulu SOE here given our number 645. Morale there will be seriously affected if real encouragement is not given now.

Document 1-60

Telegram 3025, May 17, 1943

[Part of the intelligence picture transmitted from Bern consisted of accounts of the human suffering in occupied Europe.]

1. Radio Paris broke off relay Good (from La Pinone) Friday service when priest began prayer for Jews.
2. Germans report that some military chaplains were among victims Katyn.
3. Monsignor Stepinac Zagreb Archbishop protested to Croatian Government

against persecutions Jews Serbians and Tzigaanes. Strongly criticized racial discrimination murder innocent victims and atrocities. Archbishop sheltered 250 Slovene priests expelled from Germany, set up relief organization for 6,000 orphans.

4. Monsignor Criger of the Dalmation Erwert and several other church dignitaries recently died from starvation in Dachau concentration camp.

5. According to German order Belgian scouts organizations no longer permitted to wear uniforms and students of theology first year called for six months compulsory service.

6. Franciscan brotherhood in Germany numbers 2942 among whom 1433 are priests. 1095 serve in the army including 290 priests. 115 dead include 13 priests.

7. French Catholic Youth Association protested against French workers for compulsory labor Germany expressing regret for acceptance of such measures by French authorities.

8. Monsignor Besson Swiss bishop attended inauguration exhibition relief work of war prisoners organizations.

Persons referred to as "invalids" are transferred each month for "liquidation" to an unknown place. Clerics were no longer included in batches in recent months. Prisoners are still used in experiments for submarine fleet or Luftwaffe. Death results in ninety-five per cent of cases of prisoners. Among the victims are a few clerics, all of whom are Polish.

According to an Austrian writer who recently was released from Dachau after four and one-half years of confinement in the camp, there were still confined four hundred Germans, three thousand priests, two thousand Poles, six hundred Czechs, Belgians, and Dutch. Scourging is used as punishment for minor breach of regulations. Heavy toil is imposed on all of them. One hundred and fifty Polish priests "died" from starvation in 1942. Morale of starving Polish priests is very low, while that of the German priests is still high. . . .

Document 1-61

Telegram 103-8, May 18, 1943

[This message is indicative of the complex web of relationships that existed among U.S. and British agencies, and the array of French resistance organizations. Number 328 is an OSS Bern contact with the French opposition; 645 is McCaffrey, head of British SOE in Switzerland; 517 is Frenay; 520 is General Legge; 405 is Philippe Monod; and 516 is General Davet.]

On May 15 we received a copy of the report 328 sent to London through 645, who delivered it to us. This report indicated that our dealings with 517 group gave rise to rumors that we were intriguing against de Gaulle and trying to buy the resistance movements. The facts of the matter are that the MUR elements which we have supported are of Gaullist tendencies. We do not discuss their political views as our sole objective is to support resistance and build SI channels. Through 520 we have given a total of 2,000,000 francs in financial support to Haute Savoie and we have given 2,000,000 francs and 80,000 Swiss francs through 516 and 405 to MUR. We have no other commitments other than minor local expenses 516 which, from an SI angle, are justifiable.

Recognize London has a more complete picture of the whole situation, and activities here must be determined by the major military objectives as outlined in Washington, London, and North Africa. It is not for us here to determine the merits of the controversy between 517 group and the French committee in London. If you should decide that the former group no longer merits our support, you can depend on us for complete cooperation. While awaiting complete instructions, we propose to employ 405 and 516 for SI work since they would be valuable for work in this area. Prior to my leaving America I felt and still feel that militant resistance groups in the French metropolitan areas, exclusive of ex-army circles, were predominantly of de Gaullist sympathy. Nevertheless think it worth considering whether the French National Committee's attitude toward our direct contacts with 517 group and MUR is not due in part to the committee's desire to get complete political control over resistance movements before negotiations between Giraud and de Gaulle. Some colour is added to this by a report from yesterday's London press regarding a message from "The Council Resistance Metropolitan France" which insisted on the subordination of Giraud to de Gaulle. We are trying to get information on the council mentioned above. We had never heard of it before. We are assuming no commitments and, pending further instructions, we shall keep lines open as advised in your cables #58 and 59.

Document 1-62

Telegram 3079, May 19, 1943

[Dulles provides an overall assessment of the status of the war.]

The following is from Burns for Victor. Based on the best evidence available at this place, the following reviews the existing situation.

It will not be possible for Germany to carry through a knockout offensive in the USSR. The danger of attack against Turkey, Spain or Switzerland is discounted. The possibility of a move against Turkey exists, but this will occur only if Germany is convinced of certain attack by Turkey. It is probable that there will be offensives by the Germans on the Russian front. Unless, however, unexpected weakness among the Russians develops, these offensives will be limited to strategic objectives. They may cover withdrawal to Odessa-Riga Line which is possible before winter arrives. It is expected that the Germans will push ahead in the USSR as far as possible, following which they will withdraw to winter lines. In order to leave widest possible area of complete devastation in front of the new defense lines, they will destroy everything.

It is still a hope of Germany to tire us out and effect a compromise peace, or to conclude peace with the Anglo-Saxons and continue their move against Russia or to reverse this situation by concluding peace with Russia and moving against the Anglo-Saxons. With scant hope for an outright military victory against the existing coalition, the efforts of the Germans are directed to capitalizing through diplomacy on strong positions of defense. According to reports, some military circles among Germans are in favor of withdrawing to inner lines, i.e. Odessa Riga in USSR, the Danube in the Balkan countries and possible abandonment of Norway and southern Italy. The idea is that this would permit prolonged defense through the conservation of resources and effectives plus the concentration of flak and aircraft, thus rendering doubly difficult attacks by bomber planes. Some color is lent to this view by reported establishment of Balkan headquarters pecf [?] in South Hungary plus German preparations in the north of Italy.

It is my personal belief that such drastic measures (except possible abandonment of southern Italy and limited withdrawal in Russia) are unlikely in the near future. Such measure, if adopted at all, will be too late to prolong war effectively. Undoubtedly it is the fear of the Germans that an early attack will take place in France and, as reported previously, a large number of divisional headquarters and over four hundred thousand men have been concentrated in that country. However, probably less than half of this number are as yet trained thoroughly enough for first line combat duty. Elsewhere, other than on the Russian front, there are no threatening concentrations, although forces have been strengthened in the eastern Mediterranean area and in the Balkans.

It is indicated by several sources that it is the present German order to accord priority to submarines, tanks, and airplanes which is the reversal of the priority which prevailed during Germany's offensive period. Germany evidently considers the submarine plus her weapons of diplomacy as her present greatest hope.

How long the war will last is a question of pressure and only in terms of pressure rather than time is the end predictable.

The production of tanks and airplanes in Germany, her manpower (particularly as regards non-commissioned officers and qualified junior officers) and transportation facilities are no longer adequate to meet two front war against our heavy air superiority over a protracted period of time. Although there is no evidence of internal collapse among the Germans, it is my belief, assuming the pressure is kept up by the Russians, that Germany will capitulate well within a year after an effective second front has been established.

Document 1-63

Telegram 3080, May 20, 1943

[This report on German policy toward its satellite Croatia came from 472, remnants of prewar French intelligence in Switzerland. Ante Pavelich was dictator of Croatia and leader of the Croatian Ustachi movement.]

472 reports that Himmler during his visit to Zagreb proceeded to thoroughgoing house cleaning of Croatian administration which threatens to go as high as Pavelich whom the Germans would not hesitate to replace by a German Commissar if situation should become critical. Purpose of Germans to sidetrack all Croatian elements friendly to Italy as well as all lukewarm supporters. Germans fear many Darlans among Croats and many who would follow directives from Rome in event difficulties between Rome and Berlin.

Document 1-64

Telegram 3101, May 20, 1943

[OSS Bern reported regularly on bombing targets and results. Dulles often passed on information relating to psychological aspects of air raids. Source 470 was involved in French prisoner-of-war relief.]

Burns reports the following for Victor. Following is reported by 470 as coming from German sources which are considered good.

1. Should be possible to bomb Berlin for several days running, greatest effect would be obtained. In Berlin the morale is generally worse than at other places. Whereas there were over 1,000 fires in the last big raid that was made, the Fire Department is capable of handling only some two hundred and fifty. Great loss of efficiency would result if such bombing were to force the removal of Government offices to temporary quarters at some other place.
2. The dropping of food cards was the most effective recent propaganda, hence increase of this kind might compel the Germans to change their system of ration cards for food.
3. In Germany regional feelings has commenced to develop, and the beginnings of an anti-Prussian attitude is observed.
4. Troops have better spirit than civilians. Among the latter there are signs of apathy with personal safety and that of family being direct primary concern.
5. Because of the greatly increased losses of convoys in the English Channel, there has been a substantial reduction in this traffic.
6. Many former workers of the Krupp Works have been distributed to other factories as a result of the damage to that concern. They have been detailed to factories in Innsbruck and at nearby Woergh, those in the Munstereal Valley near Colmar, and to Skoda.

Document 1-65

Telegram 15-17, June 1, 1943

[OSS Bern frequently transmitted messages from the French resistance to compatriots in London and Algiers. In this cable, 516 is General Davet; 517 is Henri Frenay;

and 642 is Pierre Guillain de Benouville, the resistance leader also known as Lahire. General Emmanuel D'Astier de la Vigerie was another resistance leader.]

Will you please give this French message to General d'Astier: This will be at the request of 516. "After consultation with the leaders responsible for our Maquis groups and after having studied their reports, I beg to call your attention to the extreme urgency of satisfying their immediate needs in money, arms, and equipment to avoid scattering the teams whose maintenance is bound up with the very existence of resistance. It would have serious effects in the future and would discredit resistance movements in the eyes of the French people if the Maquis groups were to disappear for lack of support after initial encouragement from the Allies themselves. I beg, furthermore, to urge you to expedite the trip to London of 517 and his associate, 642.". . .

Document 1-66

Telegram 212-16, June 1, 1943

[This message concerns OSS Bern psychological operations. Dulles and his OWI colleague Gerald Mayer devoted a great deal of effort to transmitting information and propaganda to the neighboring occupied countries, but they did not adhere strictly to the instructions received from Motto (OSS Morale Operations in London) or other external guidelines.]

Cipher work takes up the full time of more than half of our Bern staff, and we are kept busy with maintenance of contacts in all parts of Switzerland. However, we will do all that is possible under these difficult conditions towards carrying out the Motto program which has hitherto been neglected because of the pressure of work. We do not like to undertake a project of such importance when we lack the means to handle it efficiently. Eventually, escaped aviation personnel may permit us to organize our cipher work properly, but until then we see no solution to the personnel problem.

About every 10 days we have been sending to France a printed news journal for the information of resistance centers, underground newspapers, etc. and have just begun a similar paper for Italy. The French journal has been edited in close collaboration with Mayer of OWI. Use can be made of the Italian journal for some of the Motto material, but it is difficult to spread information widely in Italy without the facilities of underground organizations as for instance the Socialists. Our contacts in the Italian underground would probably react unfavorably on our capitalizing on the ignorance and superstition of their fellow Italians, and I think it improbable that they would cooperate on the program suggested in your 97. As a matter of fact, I am a little skeptical that such a program would be effective in Northern Italy and doubt if we would be able to send material to Southern Italy.

We shall try to compile a leaflet to send south representing the idea set forth in your #97 and we shall keep you informed of the results. Some time may be required for this. We do not need any funds for this test. According to all reports, there is an almost unanimous Italian dislike of the Germans and the latter can be counted on to strengthen this feeling very rapidly without the application of artificial stimulus.

Document 1-67

Telegram 235, June 4, 1943

[Dulles frequently offered suggestions for accelerating the deterioration of day-to-day life in Germany.]

In order to further disrupt general travel conditions, as soon as system becomes well established, recommend consideration of donating additional tickets by air.

Document 1-68

Telegram 254-58, June 7, 1943

[This message demonstrates Dulles's willingness to venture beyond the realm of intelligence and to deal with multiple French factions.]

This information from 110 is secret. The following message from the Marshal was received through Menetrel at Vichy by a person whom we have carefully checked and believe trustworthy: The Marshal is prepared to receive the recommendations of the Americans if there is anything that can be done to assist our country. We are told by our informant M. stated that Marshal's last radio speech was completely drab and was delivered without prior German censorship. It is felt by M. that he could speak again but convey real message. We appreciate that M's reputation is questionable in view of his vanity and use of his position with the Marshal to build up his own prestige. However, a careful check on his recent activities indicates that he is strongly anti-Laval and probably anti-German as they attempted to eliminate him not long ago. In addition, he would probably like to do something to save his skin. It is felt generally by the people here that if the Marshal disassociated himself openly from Laval and his ill effect on morale and administrative machinery and from German collaboration, France would still be considerable [*sic*]. This consensus is based on careful soundings and exists despite the tremendous loss of prestige which the Marshal has suffered since November. It is clear to see that the only thing he could do would be to announce his complete retirement with an appropriate message to the French people.

Kindly give instructions if it is desired to try out anything as a message can be returned through the same channel. Perhaps a word could be sent to the Marshal from Admiral Leahy. The old man's particular mood at the moment the message arrived would very possibly determine the success of such a maneuver. It might also depend on who influences him between the time he makes a decision and the time it is carried out. If the idea meets with approval, we have other possible channels at our disposal should the Menetrel channel be considered unsatisfactory.

Document 1-69

Telegram 3651, June 10, 1943

[This message contains an additional appreciation of Italian morale.]

Burns transmits the following for Victor. A size-up of the situation with regard to Italian morale is given in the following.

That the war has been lost is the present fundamental belief of the greater part of the Italian people. Having a dislike for the Germans, they desire to find a way whereby they can get out. They feel, however, that before they can get out with self-respect, something must be done by them to reestablish their honor. Moreover, it is their desire to surrender to patently overwhelming forces following "valiant" resistance against the inevitable. The reason they feel this way is that they are conscious that they are held in scorn by the Anglo-Saxon world (whose friendship and respect they fundamentally desire) on account of the stabbing of France in the back and their Government's record in its war with the Greeks. By saying that it is the private war of Mussolini, they try to disassociate themselves from the situation. Italy is rendered a psychopathic case by this complex of emotions.

What has been set forth in the foregoing is not applicable to the large body of Fascist officials and their hangers-on. So compromised are they that they will continue to cling to Mussolini and to German alliance in order to enjoy as long as possible the power which they understand will be lost with the defeat of Germany. For them it is too late to expect any forgiveness from the Allied countries.

With respect to the Navy and the Army, it is said that there are substantial elements which would willingly follow strong anti-Fascist leader should a leader of that kind come forward, especially if the Crown should give him some support. That any such leader should come forward or that the Crown's support would be given is unlikely, especially before any actual invasion occurs. Nevertheless, it is my belief that such evolution should be worked for on the chance that it might take place.

In the initial stages of any attempt at invasion, rather sharp opposition by Italian forces should be expected, but once there has been a "vindication" of Italian honor, such opposition might collapse so suddenly that we will be surprised. As to the time when such collapse would be likely to take place would depend upon the extent of military stiffening by the German forces. According to our source of information, Germany had no intention a month ago to send any substantial forces to help in the defense of Sicily, Sardinia or southern Italy. A change of attitude, however, and substantial strengthening of German forces has been indicated in recent reports.

In the south the Anti–Anglo-Saxon feeling apparently was somewhat stiffened as a result of certain air raids on such places as Grosetto. Used widely as propaganda was the "deliberate" shooting down of women and children by machine guns.

The use of French troops in the initial attack on Italian soil is considered unwise by all sources.

It is claimed by the Socialists, Partito d'Azione and the Communists that they have organizations which are trying to prepare anti-Fascist movement to be timed with any military action taken by us. London is receiving a copy of this message.

Document 1-70

Telegram 3545, June 12, 1943

[This message on Germany was based on information provided by Hans Bernd Gisevius, an Abwehr officer stationed in Zurich. Gisevius was a member of the clandestine German resistance to Hitler and one of Dulles's most important sources.]

Burns transmits the following for Victor of OSS.

1. Because unlike Tunis which was expected, the greatest blow to Germany is the unexpected and tremendous reduction of sinkings by U-Boats.

2. Because of the shortage of scrap iron, Germany has decided to take all machinery not of vital need to military production from France. This will be carried out directly by the SS as Laval has refused to cooperate in carrying out this measure.

3. As a result of bombardments, output of iron and coal in the Ruhr is down twenty to thirty per cent.

4. There will be required in the near future another shortening of the meat ration.

5. As he believes that they are continuing to trick him, Hitler has become infuriated with the Hungarians. Their failure to carry out anti-Jewish measures have also angered him. What action to be taken is a matter which is receiving his careful consideration. Military occupation by us makes him hesitate, and he fears that he cannot move more effectively unless it is possible for him to win over the Regent (Horthy) as Imredy is considered by him to be too weak to succeed by himself even if provided with German support without the actual backing of military force. That he can win over the Regent and force Kallay out and then proceed against the "Hungarian traitors" is still a hope entertained by Hitler. (As there are rumors of a possible putsch in Hungary, I believe that the Hungarian situation warrants close following. However, according to the best information available, the Regent will remain firm and, unless Germany uses actual military force, nothing is likely to happen.)

6. No general staff planning goes on today. Any gathering together of important

German leaders is not permitted by Hitler, and various sectors are being handled as if they were separate operations. Reports by commanders of sectors are being made to Hitler and his personal organization consisting of Jodlett [Jodl] and Keitel who are described as thoroughly incompetent by my informant. Hitler still gives orders. For example, the Tunis campaign was run directly by Hitler, Zeitzler having had nothing to do with it. While some coordinating is done on the Eastern Front by Zeitzler, who is second rate, even this is lacking in plans of a unified nature. Moreover, plans involving air, land and sea operations are not coordinated. For example, the failure to evacuate Stalingrad was due partly to the acceptance by Hitler of Goering's statement that the Stalingrad army could be provisioned until spring by means of air traffic. Just as the operations at Tunis did not result from the combined judgment of the highest air, sea and land authorities, the competent military heads of the air force were not consulted concerning the provisioning by air of the Stalingrad army. According to the informant, the best German generals today are Von Kluge and Manstein, but it is his belief that none of the German Generals are equipped with political courage to compel a change in the situation described in the foregoing. Also, as already indicated, the Generals are kept apart by Hitler so as to prevent any engendering of courage by counsel among themselves.

It is my belief that the analysis given in the foregoing is worthy of careful consideration by you. It is a summary of my latest information concerning German affairs and it came from the source referred to in my telegram of May twenty-seventh, numbered 3229. London is receiving a copy of this.

Document 1-71

Telegram 305-14, June 16, 1943

[Dulles continued to report on the unstable Italian political situation and to expand his contacts. Source 660 is Adriano Olivetti of the typewriter manufacturing company. Among persons mentioned, Marshal Pietro Badoglio headed the first post-Mussolini government in September 1943. In turn, he was succeeded by the government of Ivanoe Bonomi (1944–45). Number 510 is Count Carlo Sforza; 645 is John McCaffrey, the British SOE representative in Switzerland.]

660 has come here to put himself at our disposal for any effective Anti-Fascist operations either within his country or our side. He has recently conferred with leaders of the Partito d'Azione, Communist, and certain other parties and, in addition, with the following people on the following dates. On the 7th of June he talked with the Princess of Piedmont, who was reticent, and did not expect any action by the Crown in light of the extent of Nazi control. Naturally enough, the Princess supported Piedmont's general policy and attitude. On the 9th of the month, he conferred with Caviglia who is likewise certain that the Crown will do nothing. He is

in favor of a government which will eventually be under the control of Bonomi. Says the Italian populace does not deserve to be subjected to heavy bombardments and suggests that some use should be found for Marshal Messeas, a man of great merit. (According to 660, he is too old to be of any use and regards Bonomi too weak and compromised to be effective.) On the 10th 660 conferred with Badoglio and found him alert and confirmed Anti-Fascist, who denies any personal political ambitions. In principle, he seems disposed to act, but he is doubtful about the timing of the move. He believes that it would not succeed, unless carefully coordinated with Allied forces' action. In accordance with 660's beliefs, he thought it probably necessary to dispose of the King and Piedmont, but believed it probably desirable to keep latter's son with Regency. (660 said that Badoglio is Anti-Fascist and at present time has largest following in Italy. He is potentially most helpful because of his position with the Army.) 660 talked with General Raffael Cadorno, son of a General of the First World War, several weeks ago. Cadorno, also, is a confirmed Anti-Fascist and has contact with opposition parties, among which are the Communists. He is Commander of Division Ariete at Ferrara, which is rumored to be partially armored.

Here is the general conclusion at which 660 has arrived: 2 months ago no military personnel would execute any action without order from the King. At the present time, however, he believes it is possible that something might be done with certain Army-Navy elements at the right time, but should not request them to act against the Crown. 660 has contacts in the Navy as well as in the Army, which he says are more Anti-Fascist than the Army.

Because 660 clearly understands the great difficulty of fomenting action within Italy, he has proposed a plan whereby an Italian regime should be established outside of Italy. It would be made up partly of refugees such as 510, but would be supplemented by important Anti-Fascists who could be withdrawn from Italy for this purpose. This group would join the United Nations against the Axis. In the meantime an Anti-Fascist regime presided over by Badoglio would be established in Italy which would temporarily take a stand of neutrality. This would be done, because 660 is certain that it would not be possible to lead the Italians from one war directly into another. He thinks, however, that after a short period of time, the neutral government within Italy could be linked with the belligerent committee outside the country, thereby leading Italy into the battle as a member of the United Nations.

Should this plan arouse any interest, 660 is ready to cooperate in any way toward making it a reality, including attempt intricate, definite program with Badoglio and other resistance groups, such as Communists, Partito d'Azione, and several others.

The above report consists of the results of several talks with 660. He has also conferred with 645, who is wiring London separately. 660 has impressed both of us, not only with his knowledge of conditions but also with his sincerity. We think that he may prove useful person in creating Anti-Fascist action, whatever you may decide as the possible usefulness of the plan stated above. . . .

Document 1-72

Telegram 317-18, June 17, 1943

[In this message, Dulles comments on press conference remarks by President Roosevelt in advance of the invasion of Sicily, which began on July 10.]

The statement made by the President drawing a distinction between the Italian people and the Fascist regime had great effect. We are doing all that we can to send southward. Have the opinion that this should be reiterated continually over the radio and printed in leaflets to be distributed by airplane. Our advisers on Italy including persons recently returned from there are of one mind that this is the proper course to follow. . . .

Document 1-73

Telegram 331-32, June 23, 1943

[This message concerns plots against Hitler. Numbers 485 and 478 are sources Michael Godin and Josef Wirth.]

Through 485 and 478 I have received reports which indicate that an alleged plot against Hitler was uncovered with German Generals as the plotters, and some seven arrests were made and several executions. Among the names we received were those of a General Von Arnimard, Von Witzleben, and either the Field Marshal or his brother. From a different source we have received indications that agents provocateurs are active in this field and that they had attempted to collect evidence against Halder. I am anticipating more details on this in the near future.

Document 1-74

Telegram 333-34, June 23, 1943

[This message contains a suggestion for psychological warfare.]

From reliable sources we have received reports which show that the bombing and destruction of the Moehne and Eder dams created near panic among the populations located in the neighborhood of similar dams and as a propaganda weapon, suggest that we broadcast repeated radio warnings that we propose to destroy all such German dams in due course. Also suggest that we warn all civilians living in the danger areas to leave immediately and possibly indicating the geographical possible danger limits without too much modesty. This should add further to existing dislocation caused by the transfer of populations from previously bombed areas.

Document 1-75

Telegram 338-42, June 24, 1943

[Reports from OSS Bern helped to fill out an overall picture of German rocket bomb and missile production that enabled Allied air forces to pinpoint and strike key targets, including the Peenemünde development center. This message is based on information received from Hans Bernd Gisevius.]

I have received further details regarding the rocket weapon mentioned in my #186. This additional information is from a well placed but non-technical source.

The rocket is approximately 60 cm in diameter and 3 meters in length. It is said to weigh 2,000 kilos. The driving turbine and propelling material etc. occupy four fifths of the volume, and about one fifth is devoted to the projectile. I understand that the explosions which drive the turbine are produced by a saltpeter solution (possibly meaning Nitrate) and gas-oil under a pressure of 50 atmospheres. The assembly plant and the testing grounds are in Pomerania at Tpeonemuende between Greifswald and Swinemuende. The tube is manufactured by the Deutscher Oehrenwerke Muehlhe im Ruhr and certain other parts are reported to be made by Witkowitz. Experimental tests are made in the general direction of Gdynia and the range is stated to be over 200 kilometers with a deviation of less than a half of one percent. Manufacture is now at a point where quantity production is expected for use in September, October. Our informant understands that a much larger model is in the experimental stage.

In a recent report the source of my #186 says that he contacted a person who was actually present at the tests and this person gives the same general characteristics regarding the weapon itself and the testing place, but he has nothing further to offer in the way of important technical data. Sulukas also received practically the same information from my first mentioned source above. Particularly in view of the fact that information regarding secret reprisal weapons is being allowed to leak out to strengthen German morale, neither of us are convinced as to how much of the above is a plant either innocent or otherwise. Nevertheless I feel it is my duty to report with reserve on this matter since I possess no technical knowledge of my own to form an independent opinion. I certainly feel that there is some evidence here which would indicate that the Germans are trying to develop such a rocket weapon. The first mentioned source above has also reported that long range cannon barrels, 60 cm calibre and 140 (received OMEFORTY) meters long, are being manufactured at the same Muehlheim factory.

Document 1-76

Telegram 349-50, June 25, 1943

[This message concerns German hostage-taking.]

Existing evidence seems to indicate that the Germans are developing along political lines their policy of taking hostages from occupied nations. They are trying apparently to locate relatives of outstanding and influential people, with the idea that they might then be persuaded to use their influence toward negotiations for peace. As evidence of this policy our informant refers to the arrest of General Giraud's daughter, General de Gaulle's brother, and also apparently some elderly woman who is related to Prime Minister Churchill. She was taken hostage on the Riviera. Suggest that you consider radio publicity since there is enough evidence of this policy to justify such action.

Document 1-77

Telegram 38-42, June 28, 1943

[This message discusses communications with the French resistance. Number 284 is Max Shoop; 405 is Philippe Monod; 516 is General Davet; 517 is Henri Frenay.]

Even though resistance movements may find it advisable to occasionally send secret envoys without any Swiss contacts, our experience from 284 and 110 indicates that 405 and 516 can be useful here. Our friends could be used safely as a supplementary channel both for maintaining communications between resistance movements and London Algiers and for financing the movements. They are proving to be extremely useful for SI. The frontier is becoming more difficult, but, nevertheless, their courier service with headquarters is working satisfactorily. There is some doubt as to whether 405 and 516 will stay unless their relationship is recognized as confidential official representative of MUR, or, preferably, the new Central Committee which, we understand, has merged with MUR; and unless their work is to include more than simply SI liaison work though we hope that 405 could in any event remain here for this work. We assume that you are conferring with 517 and Zulu about this whole matter. Apparently many of the clauses of your 5-9 are still inoperative, as we have no word of any action to give it effect. Kindly tell us in as much detail as security permits about plans and decisions with regard to the new United Movement; also about MUR's relation to it and the means of financing it.

Do the draft instructions in Washington with regard to 179 stand? Have given 400,000 French francs to 328 for supplementary Maquis work through his sources. Will report on these later. I have just sent through 516 and envoy of commanding officer there one half million French francs for Haute Savoie.

Document 1-78

Telegram 3894, June 30, 1943

[The subject of this cable is psychological warfare.]

. . . The statement made by Funk in which attention was called to a tendency to hoard German banknotes seems to me to be very significant for psychological warfare. It also seems to me that, in order to encourage this tendency, definite leaflet and radio program might be built around the above. Material giving details of the catastrophic decline in the mark as compared with the rise in the pound sterling and the dollar has been transmitted northward by us.

A growing anti-Prussian feeling, especially in Wurttemburg, Bavaria, Austria, etc., is indicated in evidence received by us from various sources which are considered reliable. It is my belief that this should be carefully exploited by placing emphasis on the influence of Berlin bureaucracy, the tendency to sacrifice front troops coming from areas which are not Prussian, and the general disastrous effect resulting from the destruction of German states and the Prussianization of the whole of Germany.

Document 1-79

Telegram 48-52 to London, July 3, 1943

[This message is illustrative of the complex relationships existing within the French resistance, and the Allied elements that dealt with it, of which OSS Bern was one. Number 667 was also known as Jean-Jacques; Michel Brault, a leading maquis commander, was also known as Jerome and 296. Tommy is Frederic Brown, an Allied agent in contact with the resistance; 235 is W. Arthur Roseborough, Chief of Secret Intelligence in Algiers; Max is Jean Moulin, de Gaulle's representative in France.]

The following is from 667: On June 25, arrived in Suisse after successful landing on the 19th and just released internment. Will commence work in the near future; everything is in order. Before coming here, spent one week in Haute Savoie and Savoie. 110 has summarized 667 impressions as follows: 1) They lack coordination, especially certain officers of active army who had relations with Vichy. 2) There is also a lack of equipment, arms, money, material, shoes and clothing; equipment which accompanied me is being delivered in Maquis. 3) Various leaders of the regions from Haute Savoie to Alpes Maritimes will distribute the four million FF brought by Tommy; these leaders plan to meet in a short while. 4) Groups require instructors who at least have a fundamental knowledge of handling arms, etc. Strongly advise large groups be divided into smaller units of 5 to 10; (From 110, we have already made this recommendation). 5) It is desirable that someone be sent from Andre Philips' group who is able to eliminate . . . persons who do not have their comrades' confidence, and who can bring about a union; suggest Maitre de Chezelles. (From 110, Brault has already been designated for this assignment by MUR and they are attempting to establish a contact between Tommy and him. 235 is well acquainted with Brault.) 6) Danger of additional arrests is indicated in the reported loss of Max. 7) Resistance should operate on cell method and, for the time being, all general meetings even among section groups should be forbidden. Please send 235 in Algiers a repeat of this message.

Document 1-80

Telegram 396-400, July 7, 1943

[This message concerns German intentions in Italy as received from sources in that country. Number 669 ("E.P.") is an American with contacts in Italy. Dan is Magistrati (number 812), Italian Minister in Bern and a cousin of Count Ciano.]

. . . From 110. Through a reliable source, . . . 669 . . . Dan has given us the following information: Dan has just received the following confidential report from Jerry's Aide de Camp. The Italian Royal Family secured the German Defense Plans for Italy. The King then spread them out in a Family Council. The Germans have not planned to hold Sardinia, Sicily, or Calabria on the toe of Italy for any length of time against an Allied invasion. They would, however, try to hold the Naples region and are resolved to hold Tuscany and the Po Valley at all costs. They are making tremendous defensive preparations in these regions. The Germans are also planning to suppress the Italian people and will ruthlessly smash any revolt without hesitation. Large stocks of flame throwers, tanks, and other weapons are on hand with which to carry this out. Italy has been divided into Defense Squares. The Germans would not tolerate any resistance, and they would employ every terror technique with the necessary weapons against the Italians, the same as if they were fighting the enemy. The failure of the Italians to react to President Roosevelt's address was due to their inability to resist and the thoroughness of German preparations. Dan felt that the Royal Family was powerless and that should the Allies launch a successful invasion they would probably accompany most of the Italian and German Armies toward the North. Zulu and we are quite certain that Dan has been Anti-Fascist for quite a while, and consequently it is not likely that this is an intended plant. When Dan attempted to get in touch with me several months ago, I thought it more discreet to deal with him through a middle man, in light of his esteemed local status.

Document 1-81

Telegram 401-3, July 7, 1943

[This message raises policy questions with regard to dealing with Italian Fascists.]

. . . The following is in reference to your 247. According to Zulu cables received here, and from press reports emanating from London, from recent BBC radios it seems apparent that BBC policy and policy followed by OWI are not in agreement concerning publicity opposing Fascism. Until such time as we plan to deal with

Fascists or Neo-Fascists, difficult to reconcile with unconditional surrender, we are probably being unrealistic in assuming that we can divorce Italy from Germany without internal revolution dependent upon aid of Anti-Fascist elements. It would be helpful to learn if our overall policy is as indicated your 247; since cooperating closely with Zulu, we were doing all we could to establish resistance to Fascism in the hope that there will be some nucleus of internal opposition to work with our military forces, if a military invasion takes place. Are we following the right policy?

Document 1-82

Telegram 4017, July 8, 1943 (extracts)

[Hungary was one of the key battlegrounds of the diplomatic war behind the military struggle. Reluctant allies of Germany, the Hungarians sought to preserve a measure of national autonomy by dealing with representatives of the Western allies. Dulles had numerous Hungarian contacts. Number 477 is Royall Tyler, one of Dulles's top assistants, sometimes known as "Anderson"; 646 and 655 are the Hungarian leaders Baranyai and Kallay; 519 is Barcza, former Hungarian Minister in London.]

On July fourth 477 and 110 had a conversation with 646, a memorandum of which is set forth below. 646 just arrived in Switzerland following conferences which he had with 655 and other persons of prominence in his own country. 110 has confidence in his integrity and sincerity.

In order that developments in Hungary may be understood, Regent Horthy's visit of several months ago must be reverted to. A vigorous attack was made on the Regent by Hitler on grounds given in the following:

(a) Dismissal should be made of Kallay as he is an Anglo-Saxonphile. Kallay's friendly relations with 519 were referred to. Hitler also complained of the luring of Szentgyoergyi by the British SI at Ankara to perform sabotage services against Germany (Szentgyoergi is a professor who was awarded the Nobel Prize). (b) Horthy was reproached by Hitler for the way in which the Jewish question in Hungary was handled and because of his failure to follow Germany and other countries in Europe with respect to this matter. His demand was that Jews be completely eliminated from economic life, and that they be delivered to Germany at a monthly rate of approximately one hundred thousand. (c) The failure of Hungary to provide sufficient help economically. The meeting between Hitler and Horthy ended in great unpleasantness and the latter requested that the claims of the Germans be submitted in written form to which he would reply. This was done and Hungary refused to comply with the demands. . . .

There was then described by 646 the organization of a group in the Hungarian capital whose meeting place was well known, and a formal organization in which was included persons of outstanding position who are agreed on anti-Nazi orientation of the foreign policy of Hungary. About 150 members make up the group. . . .

Six forty six stated that he was fully authorized to discuss any question, and that he had brought with him a memorandum which Bethlen drafted and which received approval by 646 and 655. As transcribed by 477, the memorandum reads: (1) 646 is convinced that the Government of Hungary would not participate in any campaign which might eventually be initiated in the Balkans and that no Hungarian troops would be sent beyond the Danube and Drave if Hungary knew: that there would not be sent against Hungary any Yugoslav and/or Rumanian troops; that Hungary would not be subjected to actual warfare.

The passage of troops through Hungarian territory can not of course, be prevented by Hungary. . . .

2. 646 is also satisfied that the Government of Hungary is prepared to wind up the commitments made by it and to refrain from entering into new commitments so that without repudiating any treaty obligations, she would attain a de facto state of neutrality provided (1) Hungary was not delivered to Russia by the Allies but afforded protection from Russia not only at the present time but at the peace conference as well; (2) provided neighboring countries were given no promises at Hungary's expense (as occurred in World War No. 1) and that there not be given any such promises from now on. . . .

646 said that although a German armed putsch against Hungary was not expected by the Hungarians, the possibility of such a putsch was not entirely excluded. . . .

Document 1-83

Telegram 4018, July 8, 1943

[This report on the situation in Italy was submitted on the eve of Anglo-American landings in Sicily, July 10.]

The following is for Victor of the OSS. . . .

Small resistance to landings on the Italian mainland or Italy's islands can no longer be expected as the Italians have recovered somewhat from the shock they received as a result of Tunis.

The German policy toward Italy has changed. When the Hitler-Mussolini meeting took place, Hitler was afraid to detail troops to Italy because he was uncertain that the Italians would fight, and German forces are now being substantially strengthened by him. According to what informant has heard, there are only five divisions of German troops on the Italian mainland, but aircraft, DCA and other services have been strengthened very substantially. Informant states that the King and persons high in military affairs refuse to separate from the Axis and it is his belief that nothing can be expected from the King for the reason that he is impressed by occupation by Germany and by idea that separation from the Axis would be tantamount to betrayal. Informant has no great confidence that Crown Princess can accomplish anything, though she is most useful.

In order to enable them to complete their preparations, the German military authorities are hoping that no attack will take place during the next four weeks.

Although ill, Mussolini is not incapacitated from doing work. An air attack on Rome is expected by the populace. Informant is of the belief that the effect of such bombing would be great. In the north the popular feeling is more defeatist than it is in the south. That a landing on the mainland could be prevented is the general feeling in Rome, but skepticism exists as to whether Sardinia and Sicily can be held against attack by the Allies. It is the belief of the informant that were these islands to be lost, a new political situation might be created with possible revolution on the part of leftists (that is, Socialist Communist). This is greatly feared in Vatican circles which are working on the King, but without success. The impression made by air bombardment has been deep, and should such bombardment be carried on over a substantial period, the way for internal revolution might likewise be prepared.

Document 1-84

Telegram 428-31, July 12, 1943

[This message illustrates the diversity of Dulles's contacts. Number 475 is the playwright Ignazio Silone, a leader of the Italian Socialist Party resident in Switzerland; 493 is Frederick R. Loofbourow, U.S. commercial attaché stationed in Zurich, who worked closely with the OSS (before and after the war employed by Standard Oil). 506 is Egidio Reale, who served as Italian Minister in Bern after the war.]

For the time being 475 has been allowed residence nearer by and contact is facilitated. He has given the following information to 493: Making plans for early contact with 506 and others in order to investigate possibilities of unified action with Partito D'Azione and Communists with idea of planning a revolt. Three possibilities are being considered: 1) Uprising of workers in Milan, Turin and Genoa; attempting to learn how much the military friends could accomplish. It is felt that this is an area where opposition is strongest, especially Communists and Socialists. 2) Combining forces in Trieste section with partisans in a revolt strategically aimed against Axis rail connection through Brenner. 3) With the help of the Italians around Pescara, the invasion of Abruzzi by Yugoslav partisans. States that the insurgents could hold out in the Pescara region for some time; the large stone bridge halfway between Pescara and Rome could be blown up causing the single rail line to Rome to be cut. Since there are no Italian troops stationed in this section at the present time, he believes that arms could be dropped safely and substantial numbers of insurgents established there. Says that propaganda from America is improving. Should reply to statement by Mussolini that there is no way out; by emphasis, that good way out is getting rid of Germans. Recommends that people of Italy be reminded of Mussolini's remark saying that he would have announced a great Italian victory if he had been in power at the time of Caporetto and that this is just what he is doing at the present time.

Document 1-85

Telegram 4158, Section Two, July 14, 1943

[Dulles's discussion of Central European boundary questions recalls 1919, when he was an influential adviser on the U.S. delegation at the Paris Peace Conference and responsible for the same matters. Number 646 is Baranyai, an important Hungarian contact.]

It is appreciated by me that it is not our desire to bind ourselves as proposed in regard to future Frontier commitments, especially, for example, if the eastern neighbor of Hungary should move more rapidly in our direction than does Hungary. I also appreciate that it is certainly well that this possibility be held over the heads of 646 and his associates. Were not some general statements made, however, against secret territorial commitments pending conclusion of hostilities which 646 might be given? It is appreciated that there is on the part of these people a tantalizing tendency to consider that they deserve special treatment because their table manners happen to be better than their neighbors, to say nothing of their irritating insistence on some deserved heritage from their history of one thousand years. It is my belief that these ideas should be knocked out of their heads if possible, and that they be brought down to cold realities of the military necessities of the situation.

These conversations should be viewed from this point of view. Since Hungary has an influential group of individuals who are close to the Government, as is evidenced by Bethlen's club, who later might conceivably be brought to the point compelling the Government to take some action of military importance against the Axis, it does not differ from Italy. In any case, even if they do not have the courage to openly oppose the Axis, the Hungarians are past masters in quiet obstructionism and in tactics of passive resistance which might be converted to our military advantage. This phase of the situation is being reported on separately, and it would be appreciated if at your earliest convenience you would furnish something for our general guidance. Of the foregoing the minister has been fully advised.

Document 1-86

Telegram 35-37, July 15, 1943

[OSS Bern depended heavily on French refugees of various political persuasions for contact with the homeland and other tasks. Pierre De Leusse was former French Consul at Lugano who had worked with Dulles before being named representative in Switzerland of General de Gaulle's French National Committee in London; René Massigli was Commissioner for Foreign Affairs under de Gaulle. 235 is Roseborough.]

De Leusse has informed Massigli of the situation of the French Refugees in the Concentration Camps here. At the present time, these refugees, unlike the Belgians, Poles, Dutch, and so forth, who receive aid from their own government, are practically left to the charity of the Swiss. If financial aid were assured, about 3,500 persons involved (100 of whom are escaped military prisoners) would legally be entitled to freedom. Many more of these prisoners, who represent anti-Vichy elements, would probably be given their liberty if they had means of support. Request early consideration of De Leusse's appeal. Please retransmit this message to 235. Confidential. Suggest that a small contribution be made under appropriate cover, inasmuch as certain of these refugees whom we select might eventually prove useful to us. Therefore feel that this action is justified.

Document 1-87

Telegram 3-5 to Algiers, July 19, 1943

[OSS Bern served as one of several channels of communications between the French underground resistance and its supporters abroad. Number 667 is a source also known as Jean-Jacques; Tommy is Frederic Brown.]

The quoted message comes from an associate of Tommy in Maquis and was forwarded to 667. "The following comes from Tommy who, in the future, will be designated as Foi: Caisse, together with a certain number of codes, has been taken. Lili and 1 operator have been arrested and post has been taken. Some of our people have been wounded or taken. At the end of next week or the beginning of the following week you will receive your radio with accompanying instructions. Do you have an operator? We will send you a French-speaking operator if one would be suitable. Please inform us by the next courier. Our service is being completely reorganized, Algiers liaison continues with one post. Foi is taking an active part in organizing an Italian service and he requests that you take speedy action at your end. We require 5,000,000 francs until the arrival of the next plane. Its arrival will be somewhat delayed because the Gestapo have taken the plane's landing field. All your friends send their best wishes."

Document 1-88

Telegram 449-56, July 19, 1943

[This message concerns Dulles's relations with the State Department and the British, and the definition of the limits of his functions. Jackpot is Whitney Shepardson, chief of SI; 140 is Dulles's old colleague Hugh Wilson of the OSS Planning Board; and Carib is F. L. Mayer. Numbers 645 and 621 are the heads of British SOE and

SIS in Switzerland, respectively. 510 is Count Sforza; 639 and 664 are Italian resistance leaders; 646 is Baranyai.]

For Jackpot, 140, Carib. This is in answer to your #288: We are thoroughly aware of your problems. These cannot be separated from the situation itself and cannot be overcome by the mechanical arrangement you recommended. In the second paragraph of your #174 you summarized the scope of our operations. We have always taken it for granted that there is just as much military significance in building up movements of resistance as in obtaining and transmitting intelligence. The handling of resistance movements should not be by way of diplomatic channels. If we abandon this important field, the effect will be to leave Zulu in sole charge in place of the partnership arrangement which now exists. Precisely the same difficulties mentioned in your cable are encountered by 645 and 621. Their work parallels mine and they file all messages independently. When, as happens time and again, their work runs over into political fields, their chiefs simply relay on to the Foreign Office. Thereupon the decision as to what is to be done is made in London rather than in Bern.

Contacts which have political implications were the inevitable outcome of support of movements of resistance and or our intelligence work, but we have tried to make these secondary to military objectives. 510 messages and contacts with Partito d'Azione, for example, were made only with an eye to keeping in touch with the underground movements in Italy for the purpose of furnishing assistance of a military nature. These contacts have been the source of valuable intelligence. Working in conjunction with 645, we hope to get 639 and 664 over to London in the near future. The latter will probably be sent to Sicily, in which spot he has utility of a military nature. I am completely in accord with your refusal to transmit 510 message because of its contents.

Leland's transmission of our messages in his cipher is not a perfunctory matter. I consult him freely. We are not able to decide the method of handling what is transmitted, but feel you and Secretary of State are better qualified to do so. If the matter has political implications we will try to send it through Legation code. We assume you will go to the State Department for their advice on such of our messages as go beyond what you are able to decide, for the purpose of finding out (1) what action to take (2) whether or not to abandon the contact, or (3) whether to let the Legation handle the matter directly. Although errors of judgment are always possible, I believe there is no need for the Secretary of State to be concerned lest I involve them. Some decent ralisation (sic) is made possible by the close collaboration which exists here, and this is absolutely necessary for the accomplishment of results in view of the small staff and large amount of work to be done.

If you are at all apprehensive because of my four cables sent recently about 646, kindly remember that this is a special situation and that Leland is being consulted closely, after you have first been referred to. The procedure followed here appeared warranted in view of the fact that so much of military significance could be accomplished with unwilling Axis satellites. I hope you will soon send instructions on this matter.

We are grateful for your expressions about the work done here, and are completely averse to embarrassing you in your relations with the Secretary of State. We do not lose sight of the fact that our function is military rather than political and our sole goal is to make use of our opportunities to the best advantage of the war effort.

Document 1-89

Telegram 460-64, July 20, 1943 (extract)

[This message from Italian Socialist Party leader Ignazio Silone to Assistant Secretary of State Berle was transmitted by OSS Bern as Allied forces advanced in Sicily.]

475 sends the following message to Adolph Berle, State Department. "The Allied invasion of Italian territory is at the present time progressing swiftly. I put my confidence in the wisdom of men like you that a working agreement may be established with the forces of the Italian people which are still undefiled by Fascism. I indeed appreciate your statements to this effect and also your thoughts on peace as expressed at Delaware, Ohio. The Italian workers are preparing to make a decisive and forceful contribution in the fight against Fascism. Therefore, I ask you that the representatives of anti-Fascist workers be permitted to take over Fascist corporations and that the publication of socialist newspapers be authorized in Italian territory occupied by the Allies." . . .

Document 1-90

Telegram 4323, Section Two, July 21, 1943 (extract)

[This extract is taken from a message that deals with German dispositions in various parts of Europe eleven days after the invasion of Sicily.]

. . . The cessation of all work by the Todt organization on the fortifications of the Atlantic coast from the mouth of the Seine to the Bay of Biscay has been ordered by OKW. From the coast, Todt organizations are being withdrawn and set to work in the interior. It is probable that they are being put to work in constructing fortifications on internal defense lines. OKW's decision to do this partly due to the recognition of the fact that they were not able to give adequate protection to important bases for submarines on the Atlantic coast with the result that some of the importance of the coast itself is lost. (110 is the source whence this comes.) The foregoing is reported with reserve as independent confirmation has not been made, nevertheless there are indications that the Germans intend flexible defense in depth rather than to make an attempt to meet coastal invasion and as a consequence some significance has been lost by coastal fortifications. . . .

Document 1-91

Telegram 4357, July 22, 1943

[In the final days of the Mussolini regime, the Allies received various Italian peace feelers, provoked in part by the first Allied bombing of Rome on July 17. In this message, transmitted by Minister Harrison through State Department channels, Dan is Magistrati, the Italian Minister in Bern. Giuseppe Bastianini, Mussolini's Under Secretary for Foreign Affairs, was involved in a number of clandestine negotiations during this period. Number 669 is an American source in Switzerland.]

After having been in Rome during the bombardment, Dan returned to his post on July 21. He called on 669 when he arrived and inquired whether it would be possible for 669 to put before the authorities of the United States the following urgent question which Bastianini put to him personally: If Mussolini got the Germans out of Italy would we negotiate with him? Bastianini was seen by Dan some hours before Bastianini left with Mussolini for his conference with Hitler.

According to what Dan said, there was no personal wish on his own part to back up the proposal mentioned in the foregoing. Dan was unable to see how it was feasible, but in as much as he had been asked to pass it on he was undertaking to do so. Dan indicated that an answer would be appreciated by him. According to Dan, Bastianini was told by him that he did not think there was any chance whatever of receiving a favorable reply, and he asked Bastianini what they were prepared to offer in order to make the proposal worthwhile to us. In response Bastianini said that they would be willing to promise the withdrawal of the Germans. It was agreed by Bastianini that direct use of his name should be made as the source from which the inquiry came. The means of giving a direct answer to him was arranged by him with Dan.

The following are the comments of Dan: The Axis has until recently counted on the establishment of peace between itself and Russia, and the previous lack of interest on the part of Bastianini in contacts which Dan endeavored to establish with Americans is accounted for by that fact. It is Dan's belief that the last hope of peace with Russia has been abandoned by the Axis, and that a radical change in their attitude was the result. In order to devote greater strength to the Russian war, Hitler's present effort was to circumscribe commitments in Western and Central Europe. According to information which Dan said he had, the Germans were fortifying themselves on the Maginot Line and it was his belief that the Germans might be glad to alter their plans to defend Northern Italy and, if a face saving device could be found by them in having Italy revert to a position of neutrality, to withdraw from the Italian peninsula entirely.

Bastianini was asked by Dan what kind of offer the Italians would make to the Germans in order to get them out, and Bastianini replied that if it was evacuated by the Germans, the Allies would likewise retire from it, and a state of non-belligerency would then be reverted to by Italy.

With respect to this, Dan remarked that even if it should be possible for Mussolini to make himself a signatory to such a peace, it would not be possible for him to last since whoever signed a peace of this kind was doomed to vanish. Both the King and the Crown Prince were said by him to be too deeply compromised to remain, and the Monarchy's prestige had suffered so greatly that the only salvation in this direction would be in the establishment of a regency for the son of Umberto with Umberto's wife as regent who, according to Dan, was greatly respected and the only man in Italy today.

A plea for the saving of the civilization of Italy from destruction, slaughter etc. was then made by Dan. In picturing the situation in Rome his comment was that it was appalling. There is general disorganization. Since nothing or practically nothing had been brought into the city recently, a great shortage of food existed. Defense by anti-aircraft during bombardment was pathetic. The planes which did the bombing could not be reached by anti-aircraft. The Italian army is so armed that it is pitiful. Old French tanks which were relics of the 1940 French campaign and which were given to the Italians by the Germans were used by Italian troops in Sicily. The Axis considered the situation in Sicily as hopeless, and as soon as the fall of Messina took place, it would be possible for the Allies to take Calabria at no cost at all. The taking of Rome and the country south of the Apennines could likewise be taken for a song.

In his journey to Milan from Rome, Dan was required to travel standing up in a third class compartment for thirteen hours because of the fact that it was overcrowded with dirty, depressed and badly uniformed soldiers whose rifles were noticeable only because of their age. Dan said in conclusion that if Italian civilization is to be saved, it might be necessary for the country to pass under foreign control for a long time.

Obviously what has been set forth in the foregoing is nothing but a desperate effort to keep us from using Italy as a spring-board for our further operations against the Germans, and it was surmised by Dan that the means and methods to accomplish this were discussed when the meeting took place.

Dulles submitted the foregoing to me. That the message has no interest whatsoever for either of us is assured by both of us. Identification of 669 and Dan can be furnished by the Office of Strategic Services.

Document 1-92

Telegram 4417, July 24, 1943

[This report was transmitted on the same day as the ousting of Mussolini by the Fascist Grand Council. Source 313 was located in Switzerland, with contacts in

Italy; 227 is Charles B. Dyar of OSS in Switzerland. The message of Roosevelt and Churchill to the People of Italy, July 16, referred to below, concludes as follows: "The time has now come for you, the Italian people, to consult your own self-respect and your own interests and your own desire for a restoration of national dignity, security, and peace. The time has come for you to decide whether Italians shall die for Mussolini and Hitler—or live for Italy, and for civilization" (*FRUS 1943,* vol. 2, pp. 330–31).]

The following was received through 313 from 227, and it is for Victor of the OSS. London is receiving a copy of it.

Having abandoned hope for Sicily, military circles in Rome now expect landings on the mainland. The points that they consider most threatened are Brindisi, Ostia and the region of Leece, and Reggio. In view of the atrocious conditions and communications in Calabria and southern Italy where the preparations for defense are only in the study stage, the greatest confusion exists in this area. In this area the population is anti-German and even anti–northern Italy and, of course, very primitive. An attempt is being made to put Calabrians in this area to replace the northern soldiers.

In Italy there is a great shortage of DCA. On the ground that DCA is vitally needed to meet attacks by Russians and Anglo-Americans, the Germans refuse to make further shipments to Italy. A number of batteries have been removed from Venice, Milan, Turin, Genoa and Trieste. Recently the work at the Fiat plant dropped almost 85%, and from this plant certain machinery was taken to Germany. The manufacture of replacement parts is what the Fiat plant has practically been reduced to.

The appeal of Roosevelt and Churchill was somewhat too high-toned for the natives of Calabria. It is therefore suggested that a practical appeal be made to them telling them that if they cease resisting the Allied forces there will be salami, bread, cigarettes, green stuffs, and peace.

Cities in northern Italy received the news of the raid on Rome with silent joy. This is particularly true as regards Turin which is the most anti-Fascist city in Italy. That the Fascist officials and the refugees in Rome were finally getting their medicine delighted the people of Turin.

Document 1-93

Telegram 4446, July 25, 1943

[On July 25, King Victor Emmanuel announced that the Mussolini regime had been replaced by a government headed by Field Marshal Pietro Badoglio. This report concerning Italian developments and German dispositions was received from source 650, known as Dumont, Doru, and M.D. It is representative of information received by the OSS from French services in Bern and Geneva.]

. . . Along with several members of their staffs, General von Stulpnagel and General von Rundstedt have proceeded via Mondane to Italy. On Sunday Prince Umberto suddenly left southern Italy for Rome where he immediately met the King for conference. Orders to proceed northward have been given German troops in southern Italy. Germans have been reproached by Italians for abandoning them and outbreaks between soldiers of both countries have occurred. There are two German divisions at Tuscany and 65,000 German troops in Milan-Turin-Genoa. This constitutes the total number of Germans in north and central Italy. For the defense of the eastern Adriatic coast, frantic preparations are being made. There are being consolidated with the German forces the eight or ten Italian divisions which are in this area. The High Command of the Germans has let it become known that Italian troops outside of Italy will be held as hostages if Italy capitulates. According to reports, OKW intends to abandon southern Greece as indefensible on account of the activities of the partisans, the lack of serviceable roads, and the difficulty of provisioning. The defense of the Balkans has been organized on a line of defense beginning with Trieste south of Epirus. It then passes inland between the Pindus mountains and the valley of Mount Olympus and reaches the coast near the city of Salonika, Greece. Thessaly and Peloponnesus are organizing a delaying resistance only. In order to meet any attack which may come both from Crete and from the interior of the Balkans, aviation is being organized. A direct attack against Crete is not expected by OKW, but rather against the Balkans from Italy and the Near East. Crete is expected to be by-passed.

A depot of four thousand light trucks is located on both sides of the highway in the forest of Marlay which is west of Paris. Since July fourth the depot has been continuously on the alert.

Document 1-94

Telegram 490-91, July 26, 1943

[This report transmitted in the aftermath of the fall of Mussolini refers to Hitler's meeting with Il Duce at the town of Feltre north of Venice on July 19. The message said to contain Mussolini's last gasp is Telegram 4357, July 22, printed here as Doc. 1-91. Number 313 is a source in Switzerland with contacts in Italy.]

A report from 313 states that military traffic over the Brenner Pass was heightened considerably after the meeting between Mussolini and Hitler. The return route via Gotthard was used by the empties. We are maintaining the closest contact with all the Italian lines but the frontier passage is becoming extremely difficult. Marshal Badoglio is a step in the right direction as a transitional leader, however, something reaching the proportions of a revolution, or at the minimum, semi-chaotic conditions are probable if Badoglio is not supported by the Army. There is a possibility that an attempt will be made by the Nazis to occupy Northern Italy including Tuscany. The message referred to in our #474 appears to be Mussolini's last gasp. An identical communication was made to Zulu by Dan 2 days after it was made to 669.

In reference to our 305. A report from 313 states that military traffic over the Brenner Pass was heightened.

Document 1-95

Telegram 12-13 to Algiers, July 27, 1943

[OSS Bern relayed various reports of the Italian reaction to Mussolini's removal. This information came from source 667, also known as Jean-Jacques.]

. . . According to a report from the conductor of the Rome-Bern sleeper, Sunday, there was much rejoicing in Rome; the supply of wine was exhausted. He states that, since the Germans still retain too much power, opinion is publicly expressed that peace is hardly possible yet. Nevertheless, as soon as they are able, the Italians will ask for peace; furthermore, the Italian forces would not resist Allied invasion seriously, and they rejoice at the news of Allied victories. However, the Germans still prefer to fight in Italy.

Document 1-96

Telegram 492-94, July 27, 1943

[The Dulles network reported that German allies other than Italy were also restive. Number 636 is Constantin Vulcan, Rumanian Cultural Attaché in Bern.]

Prior to news about Mussolini, 636 on July 25, had a telephone message from Bucharest to the effect that things were getting pretty hot and that there was considerable unrest in Bucharest. He expressed grave concern about the future developments in his country and made inquiry, which was plainly on personal basis, how R. could arrange with Anglo-Saxons an unconditional surrender. Even if it meant a complete Nazi occupation, he intimated that it might be wise to liquidate the present Government. He further stated that his minister had been recalled as a result of the intervention of Hitler himself. Hitler took it amiss that the recalled Minister had sent messages in code to the Vatican in an effort, so it seemed, to arrange the grouping of the Balkan powers. Copies of the code messages were shown by Hitler to Anty (sic). 636 believes this to be poetic justice because the minister is primarily a pro-Nazi, so the withdrawal shall be no loss.

Document 1-97

Telegram 497-500, July 27, 1943

[This message contains information concerning the fall of Mussolini. Number 472 is pro-Allied French intelligence in Switzerland.]

The following information comes from excellent German-Italian sources and is concerned with the constitution events in Italy. At a recent conference, Mussolini requested Hitler to grant substantially increased military aid to defend all of Italy. Hitler refused and suggested that the Italians withdraw their army and supplement German forces in a defense of northern Italy, possible along a line embracing Ancona and Livorno. Mussolini then returned to Rome with the proposal. The Army leaders' view of the attitude which the Italian troops in Sicily would take toward the Hitler plan was indicative of its impracticability and precipitated a conflict between Il Duce and the military. The result was the forcible removal of Mussolini and the assumption of power by the Army.

At the present time, the undeniably pertinent questions are: (1) can and will the Nazis defend above the Northern defense line, and (2) what will happen to the Italian troops in the Balkans. The consensus regarding (1) is that unless substantial reinforcements are supplied and the industrial centers of Lombardy, which are hotbeds of anti-Nazi and Anti-Fascist sentiment, are occupied, Germany cannot hold this line. (2) is still a riddle, but it is generally thought here that these forces have no longer an actual combat value. According to 472, the German SS Division, Prinz Eugen has already experienced difficulties with the Italian occupational troops in Albania.

Document 1-98

Telegram 510-13, July 27, 1943

[Dulles's network to the south drew him into the vortex of Italian politics. This message from Socialist Party member Silone (475) in Switzerland to colleagues in the United States required delicate handling.]

475 sends the following message for Luzzato and Monty. "The party denounces the duplicity of the King. He did nothing to preserve constitutional rights on October 28, 1922. He did nothing to avert war on June 10, 1940. Badoglio was called to power on the eve of the outbreak of popular riots in which military groups would have taken part as well. Badoglio's role is to sacrifice Mussolini, to save the throne and Fascism and lastly to prolong the war. There is nothing but rapid failure in sight for this manoeuver. The Italian people want an end to war, they want an end to dictatorship. We arm the workers with this watchword 'Gird your forces to impose peace and the Republic!' " I forward 475's messages to you for your information. Of course, it is up to you to determine whether to transmit them. I have also received the following statements from 475 which I send purely as an indication of his opinions and perhaps those of the Italian Socialists. I say perhaps because he is in a semi-isolated position here. "The appeal which was published in the Stampa Turin and which bore the signature of 5 opposition parties, of which the Socialist party was one, was effected at the instigation of a few elements of the Partito d'Azione. The other parties did not consent to it. We do not command the people to be silent

and calm but on the contrary we urge them to fight uncompromisingly against the Fascist Monarchy and War."

Document 1-99

Telegram 4491, July 27, 1943

[This message relays information on the composition of the Badoglio cabinet. Numbers 506 and 639 are representatives in Switzerland of the Italian center-left Partito d'Azione. Carmine Senise was the politically nimble police chief in Rome under Mussolini and successor governments.]

For Victor of the OSS. The cabinet of Badoglio contains no personalities of importance. As a matter of fact both 639 and 506 are quite unfamiliar with most names. The nomination of Guariglia who is known as a technical diplomat has no significance politically. The remainder are largely old regime functionaries. Our friends considered with some amusement the designation of Guido Rouo. He was described by them as an agreeable nullity but as a man who in his former position of Director of Foreign Press made friends through money. . . .

That Badoglio obviously has not been able to bring any outstanding personages together for his transition cabinet is believed by our friends, and they are inclined to consider that it will not exist for more than a few days or, at the most, a few weeks.

Document 1-100

Telegram 4513, July 28, 1943

[This report on Hitler and his generals came from source 485, Baron Michael Goden.]

This is for Victor of the Office of Strategic Services. The following has been reported by 485, and he claims that one of the Generals who was present is the source from which it came:

Following the return of Hitler from Verona, some fifty generals of importance were summoned to Berlin to report to him. Hitler informed these generals that in his opinion the situation on the east front was quite satisfactory, and that the psychological effect which his eastern offensive had on the German people was favorable. That the situation in Italy was not rosy was admitted by him. He had come to a decision, however, to form Lombard State, and to incorporate this in a greater Germanic Reich in which would also be included South Tyrol and Venice.

Hitler made a brusque departure after making this brief statement, leaving the Generals standing about like so many grade school boys who had failed to meet their tests. According to 485's informant, Scery has resigned from his generalship.

Scery is a German general. As to how long it will be possible to keep the situation in hand, not one of the generals had the slightest idea. Nor were any one of them able to picture what would come after total defeat which is seen on the horizon by each of them. The unanimous feeling among leading German generals is that, disregarding all requirements that other fronts will demand including the possibility that a western front will be established, they must at all cost hold the east front.

110 adds the following: Good radio propaganda might be made out of Hitler's alleged Lombardy plans.

Document 1-101

Telegram 4544, July 28, 1943

[This message contains information on the Nazi-Soviet struggle and on the fall of Mussolini. The souce was Hans Bernd Gisevius, German Consul at Zurich and Abwehr agent, OSS number 512.]

For Victor of the OSS. On the eastern front the situation of the German army is far more serious than neutral or even Russian sources indicate. That the German military power in the east is unable to achieve decisive military success is definitely proved by the failure of the recent offensive which was started at the instigation of Hitler against the advice of his generals. All Russia's available resources are not yet involved in her counter-offensive, and it is doubtful whether general retreat can be avoided by the Germans.

The most serious element of the situation is the ever increasing activity on the part of Russian partisans. Large scale military operations are now carried out by the partisans. Sometimes it is many hundred kilometers behind the German lines that they operate their own air fields and AA batteries. The rate at which supply trains are being destroyed are reaching proportions that are colossal. Many German soldiers refuse the privilege of going on leave from the eastern front because of the dangers involved. Partisans of Ukrania are concentrated on the eastern front, and preparations to invade the latter territory are being made by the Polish General Government.

Friends of the source of this information view the developments in Italy as a military putsch, and the idea that Mussolini resigned is doubted by them. While some such development was expected by them, it came about one month sooner than was anticipated by them. Hitler reproved Mussolini at the recent conference because he failed to participate sufficiently in the war effort, also because of the absence of complete mobilization in Italy, etc. In return Mussolini asked Hitler to provide large additional military help which Hitler refused. . . .

Document 1-102

Telegram 515-16, July 29, 1943

[This message concerns the situation in Italy.]

Should a defense of the Apennines be contemplated by the Nazis, there is a splendid chance to start a disturbance behind them which they would have trouble putting down. No more trainloads of food have headed for Germany from Italy via Gothard since July 26th, according to 313. On traffic the other way, there has been no material change. We have reports that Southern Italy is being vacated by Nazi troops. All Italian cities have been the scenes of demonstrations for peace. There are rumors that Scorza is a suicide and that Farinacci was placed under arrest at Cremona. It is generally believed that Marshal Badoglio's government will experience extreme difficulties in meeting critical situation. There are general anti-Fascist demonstrations in Milan, according to reports from there . . . .

Document 1-103

Telegram 534-36, August 2, 1943

[This message transmits the views of source 515, Max Höhenlohe, on conditions in Germany.]

515 has just returned here from the North and is deeply impressed by the change in morale which bombings and the events in Italy have wrought. I have seen 515, and he is convinced, from conversations with high quarters, that Germany will, in a final desperate effort, try to come to terms with the USSR and will give the latter virtually anything asked. He believes that, if this fails, it is possible that there will be a crash as sudden as Italy's. Nerves are at a breaking point. Hitler's prestige with the people has disappeared. "He has not protected our women and children from bombing raids." The fact that foreign diplomats in the German capital have been advised to address Hitler, not as Reichskanzler, but as Fuehrer, is thought to be a possible move to permit someone else to be appointed chancellor. Events in Italy came as a total surprise to Berlin; 2 days before Mussolini disappeared, their Rome Embassy reported that all was well. 515 gives confirmation of the recent meeting of the Field Marshals with Hitler to discuss Italy. However, there were no details available when he left. There are no politically strong Generals in view, but Falkenhausen and Rundstedt are both known to be anti-Nazis. Goering is in eclipse and rumor in Berlin has it that he made an attempt to get to Sweden. Bormann and Himmler are in controversy.

Document 1-104

Telegram 4639, August 2, 1943

[This report from source 650, part of Dulles's French network in Switzerland, deals with discord in Germany's satellite empire.]

. . . An ultimatum was sent by Germany on July 27 asking Hungary whether she was remaining with the Axis powers and whether she would take the place of Italy so as to defend the principles of new Europe against its foes. Germany also demanded that thirty divisions of troops be placed at her disposal immediately. Hungary would suffer the consequences in case of refusal. According to a later report from the same source, Hungary agreed to stay with the Axis and indicated that she was willing to place thirteen divisions at the disposal of Germany, armament to be provided by the latter. For the purpose of drawing up a military agreement with the Hungarians, a German military mission is proceeding to Budapest. (This is from 110. Unless it is solely intended as a stall or unless the present government in Hungary falls, I question whether the attitude of Hungary is reflected in the foregoing, as authoritative information has just reached me direct from Budapest that prior to the departure of Mussolini, Germany made a specific request for troops for Albania upon Hungary. (and was refused)? [*sic*] The situation in Hungary is very tense, according to another source.)

650 also furnished the following: Military leaders in Russia, the Balkans and occupied countries have been called to confer with Hitler in order to discuss the consequences of Italian defection and the following situation. Although Germany needs thirty-five divisions of troops in the Balkans, she has only fifteen there. Plus eight divisions to replace the Italians in France and ten divisions to constitute a strategic reserve for the Vienna area, Germany needs an additional fifty thousand DCA and fifteen divisions in order to assure occupation of Bulgaria, Rumania and Hungary. It was temporarily decided to fill these needs partially by the withdrawal of twenty divisions from Russia and by withdrawing substantial forces from Norway and Finland. The twenty divisions from Russia would require retirement to the defensive line at Dneiper.

Document 1-105

Telegram 530-33, August 3, 1943

[This message reports on the devastation caused by bombing in the Reich and suggests methods for further sapping German morale. It also presents a badly over-optimistic assessment of the chances for the early collapse of Germany. Source 496, "Warren," is Maurice Villars, General Director of the Electro-Bank in Zurich; 227 is Charles Dyar of OSS Bern.]

The following report was given to 496 by a refugee who departed from Hamburg on the 27th of July; Munitions factory at Wilhelmsburg, as well as oil depots in vicinity have been destroyed; flaming oil and explosions have caused great damage. It is estimated that there are 20,000 to 30,000 casualties; 100,000 people are now homeless. The railroad to Berlin has been knocked out of service. At the present time, the only avenue of escape for refugees is toward Lubeck. All reports point to the overwhelming effectiveness of these non-stop raids on Hamburg.

The following is from 227 and 110. If and when conditions permit, a similar non-stop raid on Berlin would have a tremendous effect on the already weakened German morale if this raid could possibly be timed with Italy's withdrawal from the war.

Working under the assumption of: 1) The surrender of Italy; 2) Repetition of raids such as those on Hamburg; 3) Some foothold in the Balkan countries; 4) Continued victories by the Russians; we should be prepared for anything that might happen in Germany. It is futile to attempt to foretell the precise timing since it might occur at any time; however, if we keep applying pressure, it most likely will happen before the end of the year. There is a possibility that it might occur before point 3 or if landing in France replaces point 3 since Germany probably must now take a chance and allow a semi-protected situation to exist in France.

Document 1-106

Telegram 544-48, August 3, 1943

[In this message, Dulles requests permission to promote certain French resistance operations and to enhance contacts with dissidents in Hungary. Number 477, Royall Tyler, spent much of the interwar period in Budapest for the League of Nations and as a financial adviser to the Hungarian Government; 646 is Baranyai, also known as "Barry."]

Your #342 is appreciated here. We are aware, however, of how hard it is to arrive at an adequate principled accord with the Secretary of State while it might still be of use in this crucial period. It is for that reason that we propose trying to get the War Department to clear a number of definite projects, such as that of gathering forces of resistance in France for the job of severing communications between France and Italy. In this connection, consult my #17-21 to Algiers. At present we are going over with MUR a plan by which Mt. Cenis would be cut off with the aid of MUS. Do you approve of this?

The following is with reference to Hungary. After additional talks with 110 and 477, 646 went back to his capital. My messages having aroused no comment from you, we gave him nothing much except some frank words about the complacent attitude of his nation. He seemed satisfied, however, and now proposes:

1. To try to manage to have a Minister appointed there who for purposes of contact, has the unqualified confidence of his faction.

2. To give consideration to a proposal which was very tentatively put forward by us, i.e., that radio operators and equipment might be despatched by us for them to use in hidden locations. These operators could send information direct for advice our military authorities via code messages. If this proposal interests you, he has hopes

of despatching a technician here to talk over the details. If you are not, we believe that Zulu ought to be given the opportunity to pursue the matter. It involves no political significance of any sort.

3. To support the withdrawal at once of all their military forces from the USSR.
4. To inaugurate agitation favoring severance of relations with the Axis.
5. To attempt to set up contact with Mihailovich. He wanted to know whether we could be of assistance in this scheme. Kindly send us instructions. Also kindly send us the previous questionnaire about Hungary, covering both economic and military angles.

Document 1-107

Telegram 125-26 to London, August 4, 1943

[By virtue of its strategic position, Allied intelligence in Switzerland was often involved in espionage and counterespionage operations based in other areas. In this case, Dulles assisted a French agent in getting to London via Spain. Number 520 is General Legge, the U.S. Military Attaché in Bern.]

Roger Hullen, a French aviator, should be permitted to proceed; he was recently sent to Barcelona to report to American Consul for the purpose of securing transportation to London as a double agent. In order to reveal other French aviators sent to London for espionage, an agent of 520 is using Hullen as a plant on Germans. Refer to our message to Washington, #487. About July 22, he left Paris in German black Cadillac, #160 Z.S. which was driven directly to Barcelona. When he arrives in London, he will communicate with de Gaulle Deuxieme Bureau. Kindly handle with Barcelona and, upon his arrival there, should appreciate your notifying us.

Document 1-108

Telegram 541-43, August 4, 1943

[This message concerns Dulles's official expenses as OSS mission chief. References are to Spencer Phenix of the OSS New York office, which Dulles headed before going to Switzerland, and to 227, Charles Dyar, who managed OSS finances at Bern.]

At the end of 9 months there is almost nothing left of the 40,000 Swiss francs which were deposited in the Union Banques Suisses at Geneva and the Credit Suisse at Bern, or of the remainder of the funds which Phenix advanced for the trip. These funds were employed for rent, travel, entertainment, living expenses and other incidentals, as well as in connection with outfitting an apartment which did duty as an extra office. When I have completed my term of service, you will receive some refund. About $1000 a month is needed to cover the expenses listed above and to keep up the establishment on the same basis as it is at present. Please let me know if you think this too much; if you do I will take care of the difference out of my own pocket. Travel and entertainment are integral parts of the job, and the cost of living is high. It seems to me that we arranged that although I would not receive a salary, you would take care of all out of pocket expenses, of which I am keeping adequate records. Kindly let me know whether you will send money directly via banking media or whether I should have the above accounts reimbursed by 227.

Document 1-109

Telegram 552-53, August 4, 1943

[Dulles continued to relay fragmentary reports and opinions on the situation in Italy. Number 475 is Ignazio Silone.]

A July 29th private report of an important neutral diplomat in Rome expressed conviction that the Italian monarchy is through. He further stated that Rome quarters do not yet know what Germany intends to do about occupying all or part of Northern Italy. In a conversation today with 475 and other competent sources, the unanimous opinion was that unless the Badoglio government brought peace immediately, on any terms, the government would be promptly discredited. Further, they agreed that the Badoglio government should be liquidated in favor of one with no previous Fascist connections, and no Fascist attributes, if we desired to support the Italian people.

Document 1-110

Telegram 4721, August 4, 1943 (extract)

[This message consists of reports received from 513, a Polish source in Switzerland, from various German-controlled areas. The extract printed deals with Italy, where labor unrest erupted in major cities on August 3. Cardinal Ildefonso Schuster, Archbishop of Milan, was regarded as friendly toward Mussolini.]

. . . Instructions regarding the occupation of the Italian zone have been received by Rundstedt, and for this purpose several divisions, including SS divisions in the area of Marseilles-Avignon-Valence-Lyon, have been assembled. No direct dealings have been had with Italian headquarters at Grenoble by OKW since July twenty-sixth.

The reports regarding popular loyalty to Badoglio, the Crown and the Vatican et cetera which were spread abroad were almost entirely propaganda which Ciano had prepared beforehand. The demonstrations of the workers in Genoa, Turin, Milan and Rome were directed against Badoglio and the King as well as the military authorities, and they were outspokenly anti-militaristic, socialist, and communist to a certain extent. A demonstration against Cardinal Schuster was included in the demonstrations held at Milan on July twenty-sixth. That these demonstrations were in his favor as was set forth in reports sent abroad is entirely false, since he is particularly unpopular on account of his relations with the Fascists. . . .

Document 1-111

Telegram 142, August 7, 1943

[On August 1 almost 200 U.S. B-24 bombers from bases in Libya devastated the oil facilities at Ploesti, Rumania. A quarter of the planes were lost, but the Axis supply of oil was reduced significantly for months. Number 493 is Loofbourow.]

This is from 110 and 493 for Victor. The following information was furnished by a Rumanian [who was in] Bucharest on the first of August and passed by Ploesti on the fourth of August. The train on which he traveled was the first to pass through the wrecked area.

The entire fire of the seven pieces of flak installed at Ploesti was drawn by a few raiders which passed over at a high altitude. The main force then swung around a small hill of three hundred meters to the northeast. As they swept in they skimmed the tops of trees on the main thoroughfare of the town, waved to the populace on the avenue, and dropped their bombs squarely on the refinery of the Credit Ulminier which is adjacent to the railway station of Ploesti. They demolished seven refineries and damaged another one, and the explosion blew tank cars on to the roof of the station. Not until Wednesday were trains able to get through the station and even then the heat from the fires could still be felt. Those of the coils that were still erect were white from the fire.

Credit Ulminier, Unirea, Steana Romana, which on Wednesday was still smoking, and Astra Romana (Shell) were among the refineries which were destroyed.

On Tuesday night people in Bucharest could still see the fires burning.

All of the bombs which were aimed at Ginrgin fell into the river. This is the locality where the pipe lines meet the Danube.

Approximately sixty airmen were made prisoners of war.

The raid had an excellent psychological effect for the following reasons:

(1) Sunday was the day on which the raid was made in order that the workmen would not be hit.

(2) Waving by the pilots.

(3) Completeness of the job.

(4) The equipment of the above sixty prisoners was very impressive as it consisted of a slide rule which contained a hack saw for each man; supplies of Balkan money of all sorts; a sufficient supply of Camel cigarettes; letters which stated that the airmen were Americans and not Russians—these were written in Rumanian, and silk scarfs which, when held up to the light, showed a map of the Balkans.

(5) The bombing was limited to targets of a military nature.

Document 1-112

Telegram 583-87, August 10, 1943

[This message describes negotiations between the Badoglio government and opposition parties. Number 639 is a representative of the Partito d'Azione, also known as "Carr Phillips"; 645 is John McCaffrey, head of British SOE in Switzerland.]

639 had just reached here, having traveled from Rome direct. What follows is a digest of his report to 110 and 645, which is being cabled to the War Office in London by the latter.

Representatives of 5 opposition parties were received by Badoglio on the 3rd of this month. He was handed a joint statement expressing insistence that an immediate armistice be sought through every possible effort, and declaring that whatever the consequences might be, they would be willingly accepted by the people of Italy. Badoglio hinted that he was in touch with the United Nations, and gave as explanation of his procrastination the statement that the country could be taken over by the Germans, and that in order to allay their suspicions he was obliged to act most discreetly. He made the claim that because of the unexpectedness of the coup, he had not been prepared for dealing with the critical situation.

On the 8th of this month, 639 saw Mario Badoglio, who is a longstanding friend of his. He pointed out to him the decided opinions of the parties in opposition, and showed how far his father was putting himself in a compromising position. Mario admitted no concrete contacts with us, and no answer from us. (It is uncertain what he had in mind making the latter statement.) He inquired of 639 whether he could make such contacts. 639 answered in the affirmative. He stressed his disagreement with the policy of Badoglio, and said that he and the Partito d'Azione were extremely anxious to know whether action ought to be delayed by themselves and the other opposing parties. As 639 is staying on here, prior to his return south, any message could be forwarded directly. 639 believes that a stiff message could be sent, since both ourselves and the opposition parties might use it as a means of putting before Badoglio and Victor Emmanuel the choice of doing something promptly or of personally accepting the responsibility of having to explain to the nation the consequences of additional delay. More information will follow.

Document 1-113

Telegram 4877, August 11, 1943 (extract)

[This message is based on reports on conditions in Germany and German-occupied areas, from 513, a Polish source. Beginning in late July, the city of Hamburg was subjected to a week-long Allied aerial bombardment.]

. . . Approximately one hundred and fifty thousand people left Hamburg in mass evacuation. In this city three hundred and fifty thousand persons were rendered homeless, some seventy-five thousand homes having been destroyed. The destruction of Hamburg was particularly severe to the marine industry of Germany, the marine construction works of Cuxhaven, Emden and Wilhelmshaven having been moved to Hamburg in order to receive the protection afforded by the concentration of night fighters and flak at Hamburg. Night fighters and flak were not available in sufficient quantities to provide protection for all these cities. The backbone of German U-boat production and German shipping was also broken by the demolition of Hamburg. . . .

Document 1-114

Telegram 4883, August 11, 1943 (extracts)

[This message contains a further report from source 639 of the Italian opposition on conferences held with the Badoglio government in Rome on August 8. Reference is made to an August 6 meeting between foreign ministers Joachim von Ribbentrop and Raffaele Guariglia that failed to slow the movement of Italy away from Germany.]

It is stressed by supporters of Badoglio that they are at the mercy of the Germans because of the lack of military equipment for Italy and also because of the reinforcements that the Germans have placed at strategic positions, particularly as regards aviation. . . .

Recently when Guariglia and Ribbentrop met at Tarvisio, the latter began by being abusive and concretely stated that the Germans had no intention to leave Italy and that there must be a fulfillment of the promises given them by Mussolini. . . .

That Italy is not in a situation to do much without our support was also one of 639's conclusions, and it was not possible for him to see how the occupation of the Genoa-Rimini line by the Germans could be prevented by the Italians, if the Germans should definitely decide on such occupation. . . .

We were rather indiscriminate in our last raid on the city of Naples, according to what 639 says, and he thought that it might be better if during the next few days we endeavored to limit our bombing activities to objectives of a military character outside the population zones, since raids against cities in the north might cause upheavals of disorder against Badoglio and premature intervention on the part of the Germans. 639 is entirely opposed to Badoglio but it is his belief that this ought to be organized and timed with the action we take.

Coquarone, the Minister to the Royal House, was the moving figure behind Mussolini's overthrow. It was he who carried on the negotiations between the right wing Fascists and the King, and made the arrangements for the convening of the Grand Council in order to provide the King the constitutional basis on which the elimination of Mussolini was brought about. Until then the King was worried about his constitutional duties. The whereabouts of Mussolini is not known as yet. After his last meeting with the King on the Sunday when he was dismissed, he apparently suffered a complete physical collapse. Before that he had met with failure in an endeavor to arrange for the arrest of the men who had been against him when the Grand Council was held. . . .

Document 1-115

Telegram 610-12, August 16, 1943

[OSS Bern continued to provide a channel of communications between the resistance within France and its supporters in the United States. Number 328 is a French member of the Dulles network based in Geneva; Eva is a contact in the United States serving as liaison with French individuals there.]

328 sends the following message to Eva: "Received 50,000 for the Socialists, the CGT and the Christian Unionists. Many thanks. The reorganization of Socialist Party in France is making rapid headway. Newspapers like the *Populaire* are being widely circulated throughout France. Comrades are thankful for the financial assistance, which ought to be continued. The growth of de Gaulle's prestige in the last few months has been extraordinary. He is backed by a strong popular current in favor of a democratic France with pronounced socialist tendencies. The French resistance movements find it impossible to comprehend America's attitude toward the National Committee of Liberation, which has a dangerous tendency to strengthen pro-Russian sentiment among the French. The resistance movements believe that it will be necessary to change the nature of the Committee of Liberation ultimately as it is not sufficiently representative of the heart of France. However, this does not occasion any immediate concern. . . .

Document 1-116

Telegram 5003, August 16, 1943

[This message contains information on a number of subjects during the volatile period between the fall of Mussolini and the Italian surrender on September 8. Numbers 667 and 313 are agents in Switzerland with sources in German-occupied areas; 506 is Egidio Reale, a member of the Partito d'Azione; 510 is Count Sforza. General Andrei A. Vlasov was the commander of captured or defecting Red Army troops fighting on the side of the Germans.]

This is for Victor of the OSS. German aviation staff headquarters in northern Italy has been installed at Cicenza, according to reports received from 667 and 313.

It is estimated by Italian sources from whom 313 obtains his information that there are in the area of Vicenza, Trento, Bolzano, Verona and Merano nine divisions of German troops. It is confirmed by both sources that north of Brenner a substantial concentration awaits transportation, depending on what developments take place. Trees are used to camouflage the new runway at Staube.

Information that Mussolini is on the island of Ponza between Rome [garble] has reached 506. It has also been reported that there are in the area of Savona approximately two divisions of German soldiers, and this report has been confirmed by two other sources. Removal of all refugees from the Lipari Islands has been effected.

An excellent Paris source reported to 110 that Schiff Giorgini prepared the Nitti letter supporting Badoglio Government. Giorgini, who was formerly an associate of 510, is an anti-Fascist refugee in France, and he was subsequently summoned to Rome with the apparent intention to detail him to proceed to Portugal with a view to having him make contact with 510 to ascertain if it would be possible for him to accomplish the same result with 510.

The presence of General Vlasov in France was confirmed by another source, who also confirmed that German troops in the Bayonne Toulouse region were being reinforced by troops of White Russian soldiers.

In reference to previous telegrams concerning the rocket guns of the Germans, it has been reported by three independent sources that the rocket gun has not proved to be a success because the volume of explosive that is propelled to its mark is not great enough and because of the inaccuracy of its aim. One of the sources who reported this is a well placed neutral.

Document 1-117

Telegram 616-18, August 17, 1943

[OSS Bern reported on Japan and East Asia throughout the war, intensifying coverage in 1945. The source of this report, Dr. Hack, was a former Krupp representative in Japan, resident in Switzerland.]

Living here is Dr. Friedrich Hack, a German opposed to the Nazis, who acts as confidential adviser to the Japanese. Dooman perhaps will remember him. We refer to him as 673. It is our belief that although he is prejudiced in favor of the Japanese on matters which affect them, he may be of use in providing information about the Reich which can be obtained via Japanese channels. Hack is on close terms with Nomura who left Berlin a short while ago to return to Japan where he became a member of the Supreme Japanese War Council. The Nazi military situation is believed hopeless by the Japs, according to Hack; Japs tried to effect a Russo-German agreement, but met with failure; the Japs are therefore turning their energies toward bettering their relations with the Soviets, and for this end are furnishing them with tin, rubber and other strategic materials. The Japs have as their ultimate goal the achievement of an entente embracing Nanking-controlled China, the Soviet Union and themselves. German generals, according to Dr. Hack, recently approached Oshima, Japanese Ambassador to the Reich, and asked him to place before Der Fuehrer certain opinions which they themselves did not have the audacity to present.

Document 1-118

Telegram 5014, August 17, 1943 (extracts)

[This report of dissension within the German submarine fleet is not consistent with other information available at the time or with studies prepared after the war. Number 472 is pro-Allied French military intelligence in Switzerland; 650 was a French source.]

. . . According to reports from 472, the German authorities themselves have been obliged since May 1943 to assign personnel to man submarines because of inadequacy of volunteers for such service.

Pending a further check, 650 transmits the following with reserve:

The Naval High Command has been advised by certain submarine commanders at Kiel that they are not willing to proceed to sea with their present crews and units. This is in consequence of orders from Admiral Friedeburgs to the effect that there should be used on submarines on the same basis as German sailors, natives of Holland, Belgium, etc. . . .

Lack of crews held up fifty-five submarines which were ready to proceed to sea. . . .

In Germany the general belief is that when tonnage figures of sinkings are announced, the commanders making such announcements invent sinkings with a design to protecting themselves against retaliation.

Document 1-119

Telegram 621-22, August 19, 1943

[This cable is illustrative of OSS Bern's role as a channel of communication between the French resistance, exiles in Switzerland, and supporters in Allied territory.]

Kindly transmit to Eva the message which follows, from 328: From now on, I will number messages to Kingdom. Remittance from Katia Adler is acknowledged with thanks by Eksel. Anschi is in good health, and received remittance. The following have been deported: Brechenmacher, Eugen Eppstein and his wife, Riess and Walter Bergner. In comparative safety are Seehof, Orozlan, Zienau, Hardekopf, Kloth, Cohenreuss, Hirschberg and Schwalbach. Good work is being accomplished by Robert

Le Fonctionaire. He sends regards to Bure and Vignaud. I will send news on the activities of Vignaud's Syndicalist friends, who in turn would like news from him.

Document 1-120

Telegram 623-27, August 19, 1943

[From August 14 to 24, President Roosevelt and Prime Minister Churchill held the Quadrant Conference at Quebec. They scheduled a cross-channel invasion of France for May 1944 and decided on landings near Naples and in southern France. Meanwhile, Dulles submitted a major statement of his views on psychological warfare aspects of the war.]

Thus far in this war, our political warfare has lagged behind our military warfare. To vitalize our psychological warfare, can we not do something during or after the Quebec Conference in the way of appealing to the masses in the Axis countries? I am aware of the fact that the terms of unconditional surrender must not and will not be altered, but Axis propagandists have distorted this into synonymity with the oppression of the common man and the enslavement of peoples in the capitulated countries, etc. Could not Allied leaders emphasize that while surrender is admissive of complete military defeat, it actually will inaugurate a new life for the oppressed in Axis and Axis-controlled countries; that it means the end of the war, the end of bombing raids, the end of the Gestapo; the resumption of labor's right to organize for its own protection; of the people's right to choose their own government, to exercise the right of free speech, to have old age pensions, social security, currency stabilization (in the sense of putting a firm foundation beneath world values and thereby protecting workers' savings). These are the things that the enslaved peoples of Europe are interested in today—not future nation boundaries. If we take concerted measures in both the psychological and military fields of warfare, we can crack Germany and end the war this year. This is not more wishful thinking; it is the opinion of tough military critics here and the consensus of calm persons who have watched and are watching the situation in Germany, and in the Satellite and occupied countries. Germany is a fighter who has been knocked down a couple of times. She can go for several more rounds if we let her get her breath. If we hit her with the hardest military and political punch we have, we can bring about the collapse.

Document 1-121

Telegram 628, August 20, 1943

[Dulles repeated whatever news of possible military significance he could obtain from within German military circles.]

Source of the following will be identified later. It is rated good. Warnings of a possible attack on the coast of Norway by British and American forces have been received by authorities in Berlin. The general region of Trondheim is mentioned. It is believed that Scotland and Iceland will be used as bases from which the attack will be launched.

Document 122

Telegram 629-30, August 20, 1943

[Dulles received peace feelers in the days before the Italian surrender, as reported in this message. Dan is Magistrati, the Italian minister in Bern.]

A reliable cutout (not 669, who is sick) has transmitted to me a report from Dan which states that Italy, according to Foreign Minister Guariglia, remains prepared to cease resistance on condition that we can guarantee plane protection against the Nazis, and are willing to open the airports, and so forth. It would seem that Dan is anxious to be in touch with me directly. It is very possible that Guariglia and Rosso are making use of him here. Until I receive instructions, I am continuing to handle Dan with care, as an intelligence source only, and by means of cutouts.

Document 1-123

Telegram 164-66 to London, August 21, 1943

[This message discusses the appearance of "George Wood," possibly the most important agent-in-place of World War II. His real name was Fritz Kolbe, and he was a mid-level official in the German Foreign Ministry. He approached OSS Bern in August 1943, having first been turned away by British intelligence. Wood, an anti-Nazi, brought with him copies of recent German documents and offered to serve the allies by returning to his post in Berlin. During the course of the war, he provided Dulles with more than 2,000 document texts and summaries. Number 521 signifies British intelligence in Switzerland; number 105 is David Bruce, head of the OSS office in London.]

Please consult our #628 sent to Washington. You will receive a message from Zulu Office sent by 521 containing information about Wood who is now given our number 674. This matter is highly secret. We want Wood's assistance, and although we inaugurated this contact which may have vast consequences on subject discussed by 521 since certain matters were of immediate concern to his people, we are making the necessary checks to verify Wood's bonafides. For 105: please take care of the matter with Zulu under your personal supervision. For Jackpot: please do likewise at your end. Every existing security safeguard must be observed and employed in spite of the fact that this may prevent desired action on certain revelations on the quantity of Wood material which is already available and which will be forwarded as security regulations permit. This material is based on Wood's statements except where labeled Wood, then it is documentary as indicated to 521. Mayer of OWI deserves a good word; and intermediary of 674 approached him first, but since the matter wholly pertains to us, he is not sending a report to his office.

Document 1-124

Telegram 5150, August 22, 1943 (extracts)

[This message contains information from source 8219—not further identified—on German dispositions, especially in Italy. It also cites rumors of General Ludwig Beck as a focal point for opposition to Hitler.]

. . . Notification has been given to the Italian Government by the Germans of the latter's intention to occupy the Pisa-Ancona defense line as this is considered as absolutely essential in holding the railway line running between the following points: Spezia-Parma-Bologna-Rimini. The Germans requested Badoglio to deliver his reply to them by the eighteenth of August. (110 says that the above is reported with reserve as strategic disposition of troops does not yet indicate that the Germans intend to hold the line as far south as the points mentioned. The possibility exists, however, that they have sounded out the Italian Government's reactions to such occupation.) . . .

It is rumored that army circles in Germany are discussing the possibility of constituting a military government, and that General Beck is generally considered to be the only person who possesses the necessary stature. (According to 110 General Beck's name is mentioned in various quarters as being a possible German Badoglio.). . .

Document 1-125

Telegram 5163, August 23, 1943 (extracts)

[This message transmits information from source 639, a leader of the Partito d'Azione also known as "Carr Phillips" regarding the negotiating position of the Badoglio regime. Italian talks with the Allies in Portugal and elsewhere resulted in the Italian armistice and surrender in early September.]

639 who has been in Rome since August 17 returned to Bern late in the evening of August 21. He reported that his trip was a nightmare, having been compelled to travel on foot some 15 kilometers to Milan in order to make connections. His survey set forth the following:

The situation has made a prisoner of Badoglio, but this is not entirely contrary to his wishes. By giving some posts to the opposition and by convincing them that Fascism has been undone, Badoglio has hypnotized a part of the opposition. . . .

Delay is operating in his favor and that the war will swerve around Italy are the things upon which Badoglio is playing his card. Also the threat of the Germans to use gas etc., and the impression that the Germans are trying to make by saying that the offensive in Russia is approaching the end, and that conferences with the Russians are taking place. . . .

It is claimed by Badoglio that all the endeavors toward making contact with the Anglo-Saxons have been futile. . . . Marchese d'Ajeta and a General have been sent to Lisbon, and Berio of the Foreign Office to Tangiers. The latter is an old member of Ciano's gang. Grandi has been sent to Madrid. There have also been some talks with Osborne in the Vatican. All the activities are a smoke screen for the delaying action, and in the meantime there is taking place the regrouping of the old forces which functioned under Fascism. Of the big Fascist profiteers, not one has suffered any molestation.

In spite of what has been set forth in the foregoing, it is believed by 639 and his friends that if Badoglio is sure that we mean business, we can, with bold action, win him over. . . .

It is the belief of our friends that concerted action on our part with some help from the Government to prevent the use of strategic railways, gasoline stores, etc., plus the same kind of action by parties of the oppositionists, could make untenable the position of Germany in Italy except regards the immediate vicinity of Brenner. . . .

Through 639, Partito d'Azione recommends that there be sent through Osborne at the Vatican to Badoglio a stiff message to the effect that our patience is exhausted with the Government's policy of vacillation and delay, and that if the Government has anything to say, it be said at once through 639's contact in Switzerland. . . . the next step would be for us to inform 639 that Badoglio should detail, . . . a secret military delegation to military headquarters in North Africa or in Sicily to make arrangements, . . . for measures of concerted action by the Italian Government and by our forces in order to free Italy from German forces. Our own terms would then be prescribed . . . . the Badoglio Government would coincidentally create some kind of incident with the Germans, and this would be taken by the opposition parties as a signal for general uprising against the Germans. . . .

. . . If Badoglio should become absolutely convinced that his country will become an immediate theater for military operations and that this can not be escaped as a result of an Allied landing in France or by some accident in Russia, then his Government will go along with the United States. 639 feels that it is the fundamental desire of Badoglio to find his way out on our side if mere delay will not enable him to win.

From the viewpoint of ability and integrity I have confidence in 639 and it is my belief that he is sincerely anti-Fascist. 645 joined in the conversations which I had with 639, and a corresponding report is being sent by him to the War Office in

England. The foregoing is reported as information and with no comments from me. . . .

Document 1-126

Telegram 651-53, August 25, 1943

[Upon establishing contact with OSS Bern, Fritz Kolbe, also known as George Wood and 674, immediately began to provide information on possible Nazi penetration of Allied communications, as indicated by this message.]

The source of the following information is 674. Please inquire discreetly whether Parker of OWI sent a cable on approximately August 7 from Cairo presumably to Washington in Secretary of State code. The context of the message is substantially as follows, making allowances for double translation. "Expecting the arrival next week of 2 English generals from London in connection with future developments in the Aegean and Italy, therefore, I am not flying to Washington immediately. Radio report of Allied General Staffs from USSR states that last month Russia suffered tremendous losses in both men and equipment. They did not achieve a corresponding result for their losses. It is presumed that the Nazis will change their lines further, but as yet there are no visible indications of a general withdrawal under pressure." If such a message was transmitted, either the Germans have an inside agent or they know the code used. The latter has been alleged. Since any evidence that we have this clue would have tragic results, it is essential that this matter be handled with the utmost discretion and without any direct contact with OWI. For 105 in London: This is in connection with the general investigation we, Zulu, are making of 764 [674]. Please advise us of results. This information is to be regarded as secret.

Document 1-127

Telegram 5223, August 25, 1943

[This message provides additional information on Italian peace feelers through Magistrati, the Italian Minister in Bern ("Dan").]

Consul Squire informed Minister Harrison on November 12, 1942 of Dan's earlier attempts to attract our notice. At that time it was learned through reliable channels that Dan had stated that he wished to work with the British and ourselves. He stated that his relations with Il Duce had always been friendly but that Ciano had opposed Dan's suggested selection as Minister to Switzerland last year to succeed Tamaro.

After this contact we have received by round-about means from Dan, reports regarding the conditions in Italy. These reports were not very useful because of their lack of objectivity and the frequent interpolation of propaganda. Our subject has stated, with probable accuracy, that he is anti-Fascist. Dan's monarchist leaning probably explains the effect by Badoglio and his people to use Dan as the intermediary for presentations to us.

Both intermediaries X and Y are from neutral countries and are well reputed members of the diplomatic corps with whom I am personally acquainted. I am convinced that their motives in this connection are of the best and spring from their personal compassion for the Italian people and for Italy. . . .

Document 1-128

Telegram 654-57, August 26, 1943

[This message contains an initial installment of information provided by "George Wood" (674) from German Foreign Ministry documents. The flow would continue until April 1945.]

The following data is supplied by 674. Goebbels' appeal for civilians to evacuate Berlin precipitated such a serious reaction that the original plan to transfer the Ministries from Berlin has been postponed for the time being. . . .

As a result of the Ruhr bombings and the consequent dislocation of factories, the production of the Suhler Waffen Werke whose normal output is 500,000,000 rounds of ammunition per month, dropped to 430,000,000 during June. An important objective is the Telefunken plant at Lichterfelds near Berlin. It produces radio locators, and plane detecting devices. Important armament factories which are in the woods and are well camouflaged are located at Mus[c]hlhausen, Thuringia.

German and Japanese submarines have a rendezvous east of Cape of Good Hope in line with Port Elizabeth. The German Consulate at Lourenco Marques gives important information concerning the movements of Allied ships. This is communicated via Lisbon. The Consulate also infiltrates spies into South Africa who are drawn from the Malan group of Boer diehards. Werz, a member of the Consular Staff, is probably the leader of this work. He was born in Switzerland.

2,000,000 gold marks of bribe money was shipped a short while ago to the German Chargé d'Affaires Meynen in Buenos Aires for Ramirez.

Spain is carrying on negotiations with the Germans for armament. Because the Germans are vitally in need of tungsten, they will probably have to accept the rather harsh terms which Spain proposes. Eiselohr is in charge of these negotiations for Germany.

Document 1-129

Telegram 658-60, August 26, 1943

[This message is representative of a constant stream of rumors regarding German separate peace negotiations that came to the attention of OSS Bern. Numbers 646 and 655 are Baranyai and Kallay, respectively; 513 is a Polish source; 511 is Swiss intelligence; 651 is Roger Auboin, a past or present official of the Bank of International Settlements.]

For Jackpot and 105. 447, source of 646, reports the following: According to reports received by 655, German-Soviet discussion are being held in order to ascertain the possibilities of Germany's agreeing to abandon Bulgaria, Rumania, and "Russian" territories. Have received information from my 513 stating that he has reports which are, in essence, the same as above. Furthermore, 513 asserts that secret Anglo-Saxon military conversations are being held with OWI [OKW?]. I said to him that it was my opinion that this report was pure, unadulterated bunk. Although we recognize this as probably only a war of nerves, nevertheless, felt it was my duty to report his stubborn views since the reports of 513 are distributed throughout 511 and possibly elsewhere from there. . . .

Document 1-130

Telegram 5240, August 26, 1943

[This cable comments on the appointment of Reichsfuehrer Heinrich Himmler as Minister of the Interior on August 24.]

. . . It should not necessarily be assumed that the control of the Nazi Party will be strengthened as a result of Himmler's appointment as would have been the case had they chosen Bormann, who is Himmler's rival. It has been indicated for a long time by my best German sources that military and conservative circles, who realize that little can be accomplished by them with the help of SS machinery, might use Himmler as a bridge. The appointment of Himmler is no doubt related to the necessity for stern measures to control the home front in the face of general bad news as well as bombings. Himmler's appointment might be compared, without too much optimism, to the choice of Scorza by Mussolini some time back.

Mussolini is now on the island of Maddalena, according to latest reports. Maddelena is between Corsica and Sardinia.

Document 1-131

Telegram 5269, August 26, 1943

[Dulles reports further on contacts with the Badoglio regime through Anglo-American intelligence in Switzerland.]

. . . Early today 639 departed for the Italian Capital carrying the response which has been received by 645 from London replying to his companion message referred to in the ultimate paragraph of my telegram number 5163. [See above.] Zulu informed 639 in effect that:

Our military operations for Italy will not be hindered by any additional impeding efforts of Badoglio. He will be given a statement of our terms when he asks for it. The acceptance of those terms is the only means of persuading our military authorities to delay their timetable as it is now outlined.

Authority to transmit this information to Badoglio was given to 639; in addition, the latter was authorized to tell him that his failure to request our terms or his refusal immediately to request them, will cause opposition to the present regime in Italy to act instantly. (This from 110. Previously Zulu's counsel to 639 was that for the nonce those opposed to the present regime should restrain radical moves.) In addition, 639 was told that the moderate element should perfect their scheme: (a) to precipitate action by Badoglio and then to set up a government based on the principle of representation and (b) to prosecute all manner of sabotage and hindrance possible against the Germans in case they occupy Italy. With regard to the claim of Badoglio of his inability to set up adequate liaison with the Anglo-Saxons, Zulu indicated that no adequate response would be forthcoming via any intermediary without duly authorized agents requesting a statement of terms from us.

For the information of Victor from 110:

Lacking specific directions, I abstained from participation in communication being carried back by 639.

It is my judgment from this vantage point and with my knowledge of the connection of 639 to the present status of events, the communication transmitted would appear to be both rational and in conformity to good business practice.

The above has not been duplicated to Algiers nor to London.

Document 1-132

Telegram 666-68 to London, August 28, 1943 (extract)

[In this message, Dulles comments further on his relations with the French resistance and French intelligence. Number 105 is David Bruce, head of the OSS London Office.]

For 105. Through MUR, we are receiving a large quantity of GI [SI?] reports. As yet, however, no separate financing is needed; if any outlay is required we have sufficient means to take care of it. . . . MUR's understandable feeling that SI given us should also be at the disposal of the Fighting French Intelligence in Algiers and London constitutes the only problem. They might show even greater activity in this field, if this could be managed. Would it be feasible, or wise, from your end to pass on to the Fighting French such SI data as we send to Washington and London marked "Source MUR"? . . .

Document 1-133

Telegram 5313, August 28, 1943 (extract)

[The cable of which this extract is a portion was a two-part, six-page message discussing German dispositions. At least half of the information transmitted by OSS Bern during the course of the war concerned enemy order of battle, troop movements, and armaments.]

In the direction of the Soviet, as well as toward France, there have been large movements of military personnel and equipment from the heart of the Reich. Moving by train, by motor lorry and marching six, or perhaps seven, divisions of troops from the southern part of the Reich traveled in the direction of Nancy from Kehl during the week ending August 22. Equipment for the generation by chemical means of dense mist was carried in two of the ten freight trains sent to Nancy loaded with equipment. Most of the soldiers were youthful. Bound for the Soviet there proceeded from the area around Dresden and Leipzig during the ten days just preceding August 20, eight or ten divisions of soldiers who had scarcely completed their training period. . . .

Document 1-134

Telegram 5317, August 28, 1943 (extracts)

[This message contains miscellaneous reports on the situation in Germany, as provided by 513, a Polish source.]

(1) Hamburg stood at the head of the list of metropolitan areas to suffer bomb injury. More than 150,000 buildings were either wrecked or made useless; Cologne with 112,000 comes next; the city of Essen lost 70,000 while Duisburg [Düsseldorf?] . . . had 56,000 houses wrecked, and 24,000 in Wuppertal. . . .

(4) Doenitz, Ribbentrop and Goering were sustained by the leading generals in their opposition to the scheme of Hitler for using harsh measures in Italy. This occurred during conferences at the Reich general headquarters. . . .

(7) The Reich continues its scheme of giving the homeland and production centers priority in fighter aircraft defense, nevertheless the problem of the heads of the air force has been made more difficult as a result of the day bombing expedition by US air forces over Austria, because of the fact that there is a deficiency of fighter planes to cover all needs.

(8) Since the latter part of June patriots in presently occupied former Russian territory have been active in sabotage efforts so that the whole railway system in the vicinity of Kiev is no longer safe. These Russian patriots have pursued their work especially in the section north and west of Kiev. . . .

Document 1-135

Telegram 5341, August 29, 1943

[Through influential contacts in Bulgaria, OSS Bern obtained important intelligence and sought to influence the internal political situation of the country in favor of the allies. Bulgaria had joined the Axis under pressure on March 1, 1941, and declared war on the United States on December 12 following Pearl Harbor. Kiss is Gheorghi Kiosseivanov, the Bulgarian Minister in Bern, number 491. King Boris of Bulgaria died under suspicious circumstances on August 28, 1943, just after having met with Hitler.]

The following report, which is from 110, is for Victor of the Office of Strategic Services:

Following a visit to Sofia, Kiss recently returned to Stockholm. Maneuvers by him were so made that he would be summoned by Boris and this enabled him to report direct to Boris instead of to Filoff. He presented the message given in our no. 214 at the first interview. Apparently Boris was very much impressed with the message. He retained a copy saying that he desired to give study to each word in the message. At that time Boris was calm and his health was good, and he stated that at all costs his one objective was to keep his country from participating more actively in the war. The impression that Kiss gained, however, was that Boris, dominated by fear, was aware that the Germans disliked him and that they would go to the extent of even bringing about his death. During the second interview, Kiss informed Boris that at this stage he was not prepared to lead a national union Government to which Boris replied that it was his intention to form a transition Government so that some of the pressing problems might be liquidated and so as to prepare the way for a national Government, the head of which he wanted Kiss to be. According to Kiss, an incident occurred after this meeting which discouraged Boris. There came from Turkey a Bulgarian, name not revealed by Boris, who brought with him a message from Earle which was to the effect that the situation as concerned Bulgaria was desperate and that Bulgaria would be fortunate if she could escape partition; also that there was a great divergence of views between the British and the Americans as regarded the position. This message had the effect of a cold douche as concerned Anglo-Saxon relations, particularly in view of the Soviet Minister's activity. The Soviet Minister was causing to be spread reports to the following effect:

(1) That no Anglo-Saxon landing in the Balkan countries would take place so long as he was in Sofia.

(2) That when the war was won by it, Russia would insist on a common frontier, giving North Dobrudja to Bulgaria, and that it will also support a large Bulgaria.

It is said by Kiss that in view of the alleged message from Earle, Bulgarians, including even those who are anti-Communist and anti-German, have come to the conclusion that their only hope rests with Russia and that while this may mean temporary communist rule in their country, it will be of help to them in having their national aspirations fulfilled.

In the meantime, a card is being played by Filoff, circles in the Government and others on the possibility that Russia and Germany will conclude a separate peace. There is a lot of talk about the Free German Committee in Moscow, and the idea of separate peace is encouraged by this talk. Kiss says that according to what he has heard, Marshal Bock is the representative of this committee in Germany. (110 says that this is very doubtful but interesting in that it serves to indicate the nature of rumors that are current in Bulgaria.)

According to Kiss, propaganda broadcast by the London BBC for Bulgaria has had the effect of creating hopelessness among Bulgarians so far as the Anglo-Saxons are concerned, and this feeling of hopelessness has thrown the Bulgarians into the camp of either the Germans or the Russians. At the present time they take the view that going into the Russian or German camps, plus separate peace which would bring about the joining of these camps, are the only choices open to them.

According to Kiss, there are not many German troops seen in Bulgaria, but he has been told that there is a rather large concentration of troops near the old frontier between Turkey and Greece. It is the hope of the Bulgarians that an attack will be launched in the upper part of the Adriatic by the Anglo-Saxons, as Bulgaria would be kept south of the battlefield in such an event. Relations between Bulgaria and Turkey are not unsatisfactory. Those American flyers who were compelled to make forced landings in Bulgaria when they were returning from the bombing of Ploesti are quoted as having said that strict orders to refrain from bombing Bulgaria had been given them.

According to Kiss, a considerable stir was created by his visit, and it is popularly believed that plans for a national union Government were made. Fully aware of this reaction, the German Gestapo and Filoff regard Kiss as an Anglo-Saxon tool.

No report of the conference between Boris and Hitler has reached Kiss direct, but it is his assumption that an ultimatum with regard to Bulgaria's participation in the war was given by Hitler and that this culminated in the death of the king, either directly or indirectly. Following our no. 669 the text of this message has been repeated to Algiers for SNAFU. London has also received a copy of it.

Document 1-136

Telegram 676, August 31, 1943

[In Telegram 497-98, August 28, General Donovan (109) informed Dulles, Eddy in Algiers, and Bruce in London that Count Sforza, an important anti-Fascist exile, was worried about lack of communication with the Partito d'Azione, feared that the internal Italian situation might deteriorate into a clash between communism and neo-Fascism, and thought that the Allies should give full support to moderate democratic elements. His reply indicates that Dulles considered the Donovan cable to be criticism of his handling of relations with Italian sources.]

From 110 to 109. Since I have kept direct and constant contact with the leaders of this party and have deluged you with cables on the subject, the first point of your #497 is inconceivable. The Partito d'Azione leaders feel that 510 has failed to keep adequately in touch with them. However, this may be attributed to communication difficulties. With reference to the preceding information, consult my 4883 of August 11, 5163 of August 23, and 578, 583, 638, and 661. The first-mentioned cables contain principally information obtained through 639 and the policy of the Partito d'Azione which he represents. Further, consult my #4584 dated the 30th of July and #5196 dated the 24th of August, containing memoranda which the opposition parties submitted to the Badoglio government; these were received through representatives of the Partito d'Azione. At present 639 is in Rome on behalf of Partito and I expect a report from him in the near future. Point 2: Up to this time the Communists have been stalling and have not yet put their cards on the table. It is possible that a conflict as indicated might materialize. Point 3: We are not able to see what our policy might be relating to opposition. My 5269, dated August 26, gives an idea of Zulu's policy. With reference to this see your #247 which seems at this time to be both out of date and inadequate.

Allen Dulles, Chief of the OSS mission in Switzerland (Source: CIA)

General William J. Donovan, Director of the Office of Strategic Services (Source: U.S. Army Military History Institute)

General John Magruder, OSS Deputy Director for Intelligence, gave Dulles's reports highest priority distribution in Washington (Source: RG 226, Entry 133, National Archives and Records Administration)

Whitney H. Shepardson, Chief of the OSS Secret Intelligence Branch in Washington and an old friend and supporter of Dulles (Source: RG 226, Entry 133, National Archives and Records Administration)

Ambassador Hugh R. Wilson, member of the OSS Planning Group and a Dulles friend and associate since 1919 (Source: RG 226, Entry 133, National Archives and Records Administration)

Colonel G. Edward Buxton, Assistant Director of OSS, Donovan's right-hand man for administration, and frequently Acting Director (Source: RG 226, Entry 133, National Archives and Records Administration)

Brigadier General Barnwell R. Legge, U.S. Military Attaché in Switzerland (left), and Lieutenant Colonel Alfred R. W. De Jonge, a member of his staff (Courtesy, D. R. Rexford, Wilmington, Delaware)

Leland Harrison, U.S. Minister in Bern who worked closely with Dulles (Source: Library of Congress)

Eduard Schulte, a German industrialist in Swiss exile and an important OSS source (Courtesy, Ruprecht F. Schulte)

SS General Karl Wolff, who was instrumental in the surrender of German forces in Italy (Operation Sunrise) (Courtesy, Papers of Allen Dulles, Mudd Manuscript Library, Department of Rare Books and Special Collections, Princeton University Libraries)

U.S. General Lyman L. Lemnitzer (seated), British General Terence S. Airey (right), and Major Max Waibel of Swiss intelligence, all key figures in Operation Sunrise (Courtesy, Papers of Allen Dulles, Mudd Manuscript Library, Department of Rare Books and Special Collections, Princeton University Libraries)

Allen Dulles and his top aide, Gero Gaevernitz (Courtesy, Papers of Allen Dulles, Mudd Manuscript Library, Department of Rare Books and Special Collections, Princeton University Libraries)

CHAPTER

2

The Invasion of Italy, Resistance Movements, and Balkan Intrigues

September 1943–January 1944

Document 2-1

Telegram 682-83, September 1, 1943

[Dulles and Mayer of the OWI waged psychological warfare on a large scale even though they were dependent entirely on local resources and functioned under the scrutiny of Swiss authorities. They managed to produce millions of items on clandestine printing equipment for distribution in enemy territory.]

Please inform OWI of the following, explaining to them that it seemed best, for apparent reasons, to send the information through this channel. Mayer, of the OWI, and I have been working together in preparing for the publishing of an underground edition of the *Frankfurter Zeitung*. This will be issued monthly, and will probably commence in September, with the disappearance of the famous old newspaper. It is to be printed on Bible paper, and will appear in four pages, with identical makeup, in reduced format. We will endeavor to discover some method of getting copies to Washington. . . .

Document 2-2

Telegram 182-84 to London, September 2, 1943

[This message relays an appeal from French resistance representatives in Switzerland regarding repression in Italian-occupied areas of France. Number 516 is General Davet.]

The following is for BCRA through 516 from Comite Directeur MUR: "Italian occupying authorities have redoubled repressive measures; refractaires put to death, hostages taken into custody. Request that the Allied radios give French and Italian notices stating that, after the armistice, the defeated army will be punished implacably for the crimes they committed. Personally know those who are guilty. Wish to bring attention to the chief offender, General Vercellino who is in command of 4th Italian Army. Under the impression that results can be secured with strong and repeated admonitions."

The following information is from Faure for BCRA, "Stress urgent need for parachutages. Maintain the August plan for September. Because of the lack of arms, the morale of H.S. threatens to crack. In view of lack of armament, the August losses amounted to 80 prisoners, 20 wounded, 10 killed and all this with hardly any loss to the Italians. Because of failure to supply arms, cannot completely organize as units."

Document 2-3

Telegram 5453, September 3, 1943

[This message reports the establishment of a new Hungarian contact. Number 477 is Royall Tyler, Dulles's foremost expert on Hungarian affairs.]

Bakach-Bassenyey has been ordered to Bern from Vichy as Hungarian Minister, probably to act as intermediary with United Nations, since he is reputedly against the Nazi. . . .

The above-mentioned diplomat conversed a short time ago with informant 477 and expressed the hope on the part of Kallay that Budapest could be spared, since there was but little industrial production there for the Germans. Bakach-Bessenyey also stated that during a call at German headquarters a short time ago, the Hungarian Minister of War asked that the 80,000 or more Hungarian forces who were in support on the eastern front be brought home. This was turned down, so Kallay did likewise with a German order that Hungarian forces be prepared to occupy the Balkans. Bakach-Bessenyey was also requested by Kallay to sound out our side with regard to Hungarian preemption of an area in Croatia extending to Fiume. He did not wish to act in this connection without the concurrence of the Government of Yugoslavia and asked that we sound the latter in this connection. The repatriation of their troops in Russia and collaboration with the Allies when they invade the Balkans was given as the ends to be achieved by Hungary. Allied approval to joint action by Rumania, Bulgaria and Hungary to maintain discipline in the Balkans whenever the grip of the Reich is withdrawn, was a third scheme of Kallay's which was broached by Bakach-Bessenyey. The latter had seen the Regent and while the latter execrated Hitler, he felt that desertion by Hungary of the German-Italian-Japanese combination at this time, when it is on the wane would earn naught but the contempt of the British and Americans. Hungarian leaders adhere to this attitude rather generally and the information should be passed on to OSS according to informant 110.

Kallay's naivete was greeted in a humorous vein and he was given no assurance that his ideas would be transmitted, according to informant 477. For your confidential information it is suggested that Bakach-Bessenyey may well become a valuable informant but, at the same time, there is the danger that he may use us for political expedients in Hungary after he has presented his letter of credence here. For that reason I have advised informant 477 to be very careful in all transactions that follow and to keep the Minister informed in detail.

Document 2-4

Telegram 693-97, September 7, 1943

[OSS Bern continued to play a significant role in support of the French resistance, as the information provided in this message indicates. Number 284 is Max Shoop, formerly of Sullivan & Cromwell's Paris office, Dulles's top assistant in Geneva. Shoop managed networks extending into occupied France.]

From 110 and 284. In reply to your #516. A.S. is a skeleton officer organization which has been in existence for a long time, according to the data which we have. It is ready to gather action forces together rapidly in the Southern Zone. There is nothing about the Northern Zone in our recent information. MUR, in general command of Maquis groups, has officers of A.A. associated with him. The former had planned originally guerrilla and SO work, but we did not develop these plans because we were advised to play down guerrilla work in our original instructions from London, and we did not have authorization, not to speak of lacking material and funds. Until these groups have been given a chance to prove their effectiveness, we would hesitate to forecast their value. The arms and supplies needs of the Maquis groups, as well as their numbers (which have probably decreased by now), have been indicated in several of our cables. . . .

A detailed report on the present status and the possibilities of operations in the area to the East of the Rhone will be prepared at a meeting I am arranging with the A.S. Head of the Savoie Regions. Another purpose of this meeting will be to get further details as requested by London on the Mt. Cenis project. Due to the importance of the element of time in this matter, you may want to give us specified and limited objectives for the Savoie Area, if practicable, while awaiting our report. We will then be able to discuss possibilities with the following considerations in view:

1. What can be done without having to wait for more supplies.
2. What can be done under the assumption that deliveries of certain specified materials can be made. . . .

Document 2-5

Telegram 5548, September 8, 1943

[In this report on the unstable Italian situation, 664 is a major opposition figure also known as "Green"; 660 is Adriano Olivetti. On this date, the Italian armistice, signed September 3, was announced. On September 9, Allied forces invaded Italy at Salerno.]

From source number 110. After conversations with persons connected with the Badoglio regime, it appears that the marshal has made progress toward arranging a truce according to (Carr Phillips) our informant number 639 who recently came from Rome and will return thither soon. The people around the top feel that only to the point of terminating hostilities and not beyond, will Badoglio receive the aid of groups opposed to the regime. The same restriction applies to the Partito d'Azione according to the same informant, who goes on to say that it is possible that the Germans may try to make a grab for power and even go to the extreme of attempting to abduct his majesty. He adds that the Reich forces near Rome have been augmented and that, while opposition to Badoglio is increasing, that against the King is even more pronounced. While 639's data on military subjects is very incomplete, he is convinced that Reich forces are not sufficient and would have to retreat even north of the Apennines before they would be able to make a real stand. He said that there were two divisions of Elite Guard panzer troops and three other similar divisions of the regular army as well as some other forces. . . .

In spite of the woeful dearth of material, Badoglio is making every effort to equip the Italian troops under General Carboni in the vicinity of Rome, in order to frustrate any attempt at a coup d'état on the part of the Germans. A yearning for peace is most prevalent among those German soldiers whose morale has been sapped by long association with the Italians. From the control center in Rome, both our informant 664 and also Lussu are very busy on behalf of the Partito d'Azione. Return to

Rome before long is the plan of 639. Doubtless on account of recklessness in his efforts to establish a liaison with the Americans and British, informant number 660 has been arrested by Badoglio.

Document 2-6

Telegram 5565, September 8, 1943 (extract)

[The spectrum of Dulles's reports included highly unlikely rumors, such as this indication of possible German air attacks on the United States.]

. . . It is said that Gotham, and other points on our Atlantic seaboard, will be subjected to bombing by planes that are now being installed in several U-boats. According to number 110, this oft recurring rumor is passed on again because of the serious view taken of it by the person contributing the information. . . .

Document 2-7

Telegram 703-5, September 9, 1943

[This information on German troop movements and rocket development came from Eduard Schulte, a German industrialist.]

A report from 643 states that *Das Reich* and *Adolf Hitler* panzer divisions are in the area of North Italy, most likely in the vicinity of Villach. These divisions were recently transferred from the front at Kharkov. According to this source which, although non-technical, is exceptionally well-informed, there are 15 German divisions in Italy. Source stressed the point that rocket bomb should be taken very seriously. It is his conviction that, at the present time, the weapon is sufficiently perfect to allow the effective bombing of cities; further, that the margin of error has been cut to 1000 yards. A delay of 1 to 2 months in assemblage work was caused as a result of the bombardment of Peenemuende; however, there is still much there to be destroyed. It appears that some assembly plants on the island are located underground; however, there are important surface objectives which have not yet been demolished.

Document 2-8

Telegram 710, September 10, 1943

[Responding to the Italian surrender and the Anglo-American invasion of Italy, the Germans seized Rome on September 10 and moved swiftly to disarm Italian forces in Italy, France, and the Balkans.]

According to report from an individual who arrived from Lyon this morning, the regular railway transportation in that section is almost motionless. It is difficult to ascertain the actual direction of troop movements because the military trains are scurrying in all directions. Door to the Swiss French border is closed; Germans have taken over.

Document 2-9

Telegram 711-12, September 10, 1943

[Dulles comments further on the situation in the aftermath of the Italian surrender and the German seizure of power in Italy.]

At the present time serious intelligence work is blocked by the crowd of rumors. We are making every attempt to obtain information on Italy, but crossing of the frontier has been suspended and new measures of control are in effect on both sides of the border. Therefore we are in effect isolated for the time being here in Switzerland. 284 and other agents are covering developments on the Savoie frontier, and we have two men working independently in the Chiasso and Lugano region. We must expect that Hitler will carry out any steps of revenge or destruction which he can effect against Italy. Except in areas which our forces are occupying and policing we must anticipate general chaotic conditions in Italy in the immediate future.

Document 2-10

Telegram 713-17, September 11, 1943

[In this message Dulles presents his views on psychological warfare activities in response to a communication from the OSS Morale Operations Branch.]

The objectives mentioned in your #552 have our complete approval. The only difficulty lies in their execution. It must be remembered that this is a neutral nation, and the greatest care is demanded in operations. We would only risk suppression by the police if we were to set up a separate office. For the past 6 months the person numbered 677, whom our Drum #113 mentioned, has been working full time for us, and, since it is not wise to transmit reports by cable, we have been doing a great deal more along the lines indicated than you know. Separate networks are operating in all 4 points of the compass, and there is an even flow of data in all directions. Will investigate any chances of enlarging the work. Up to this point, I have shared budget with Mayer (678), and can meet all reasonable expenses out of funds now at hand. You are assured of our greatest interest, but to be frank, I have not completely agreed with your views on the practicability of a rumor campaign of the sort previously presented, using this place as a base. Rumors must be spread from mouth to mouth, and there are simply no agents willing to risk their necks in this game. There is a great number of rumors as good as yours already current in the surrounding countries; and also, your rumors are often greatly exceeded by the realities. For instance, the sound wave bomb is mere child's play as a horror weapon when compared with the devastating effect of the phosphor-bombs. Germany is now ripe for material of a more constructively destructive and serious type than your rumors. They are getting some medicine from us, and we will enlarge the doses with the encouragement which your cable has given. Have you any program to give us misleading military material to plant?

Document 2-11

Telegram 718-21, September 11, 1943

[This message provides additional information on French resistance capabilities. Number 516 is General Davet, French resistance representative in Switzerland.]

The following reply to your #516 is sent by 516 after having conferred with the local Maquis agent here:

A.S. has available at once an aggregate of 10,000 trained troops, 3,000 of whom are armed, for Hautes Alpes, Haute Savoie, Savoie, Isere and Drome. These troops are made up [of] 7 groups, Maquis and A.S. men subject to call. There are another 7,000 men who must obtain munitions and arms, presumably by parachute, if they are to be used as guerrillas or for other military action. . . . Dynamite is available for small sabotage jobs, but bigger jobs demand high explosives and light arms.

We have 516's assurance that, if this material is obtained, and instructions are issued, those forces will be able to: 1. Destroy railway lines at many and well separated points, and so halt traffic. 2. Either as part of military operations or as preliminary guerrilla work, attack local garrisons at many different localities. 3. Provided they can depend on the prompt arrival of around 2,000 of our troops by parachute or plane, hold this region for a time. 4. Sabotage essential services as indicated such as power plants, viaducts, et cetera.

We are waiting for your directions on these matters.

Document 2-12

Telegram 5674, September 12, 1943

[This cable deals with the Rumanian political situation and relations with the Germans. Number 636 is Constantin Vulcan, Rumanian Cultural Attaché in Bern.]

. . . After extensive conversations on the 4–6 of September with Michael Antonescu, informant number 636 returned from Bucharest yesterday. The purpose of his visit was to convince Antonescu of the serious need of a break with the Germany-Italy-Japan combination by Roumania immediately. Antonescu, who is not yet 40, was found by his intimate friend (our number 636) looking elderly and weary, said he was amenable to relinquishing control at any time but that the Marshal was tenaciously sticking to the agreed upon direction and gave him, Antonescu, considerable trouble. The Marshal stands by his deal with Hitler because he claims to know the British as a result of his tour of duty in England as Military Attaché, and feels that the British respect loyalty and as a result would understand his adherence to his pact.

All exertions were under way to evacuate Roumanian forces from Soviet territory, the move having been started on the fourth of September by the four divisions in the Kuban valley. Antonescu dropped the suggestion that a general retreat was under way leaving Roumanian forces only in Transnistria. He made a suggestion that exchanges were now under way toward the end of bringing about peace between the Reich and the Soviet, an end which Antonescu greatly feared. He further stated that for four months or more, between the Fuehrer and himself, contact was strained. Antonescu stated that he lived in fear of his life every day, a statement attested by the fact that his will lay on his desk. This fear grows partly out of his denunciation by Sima.

A million youthful recruits will have completed their training by November, but they possess only light equipment and additional material was refused at this time by the Reich. He pointed out that in the event of a break with Germany these troops would be lost to Roumania and would be used by Germany instead. Another argument against a rupture at this time was the fact that the Germans would commandeer Roumania's 450 tons of gold as well as her bumper crop of seven million tons of grain, including 3 million tons of wheat. Efforts are under way by the Roumanian government to break up this crop into small family holdings, including a special winter grubstake of about 22 pounds of white flour per person. Reich DCA troops and coast defense units of other kinds are at Constanza but, according to Antonescu, all the rest of the Black Sea shore from Odessa to Varna was defended exclusively by Roumanian forces. There might be a total of 40,000 Reich forces in Roumania according to his analysis. In the event of an invasion by the Allies, Antonescu was ready to look to the best interests of Roumania and resign, he said. The Minister of Foreign Affairs of Turkey advised him to retain control, said he, and continued that he had maintained an entente cordiale with the government of Turkey and had kept the latter supplied with information in detail regarding the disposition of Reich troops in the Balkans.

Conversations had been held with Maniu, Bratianu and others opposed to the regime toward the end of working out plans for an interim government under a military man, after the pattern in Italy. Plans were under way, meanwhile, to transport the outstanding opposition people over into Turkey or to Switzerland in case of eventualities. The Roumanian troops hold a sharp resentment against the Germans because of the manner of the latter's retreat from the Soviet, according to the view that informant 636 encountered.

Document 2-13

Telegram 726-29, September 13, 1943

[Following the Italian armistice, Dulles sought to mobilize sources in Switzerland to enhance intelligence-gathering and special operations behind German lines in northern Italy. Dan is Magistrati, the Italian Minister in Bern.]

In our #4357 of July 22, our #629, and our #671, we have spoken of Dan. With recent developments in mind, and certain of his sincere anti-Fascist beliefs, we decided to confer with him personally. Some of our existing lines of information have been cut by recent happenings. We can expect little at present through the services of either 475 or 638. After the armistice was announced, 639 departed for the south and we have not heard from him since. It therefore appeared necessary to discuss frankly with Dan concerning the possibility of employing the aid of Italian diplomatic and consular and SI channels in Switzerland, in an effort to build up SI and SO behind the Germans in North Italy. Although this is out of Dan's sphere he consented to look into the picture and put me in contact with the most satisfactory Italians here for the development of this program.

We received a sad description of the officials of the Italian diplomatic consular office from 671, who asserts that there is no actual intelligence service here except . . . CE. We have reports which indicate that the Minister is not dependable, despite your #221. We feel, however, that we should not turn down even last minute converts if they can be employed to advantage.

In connection with SO, what is the situation with Zulu? Since the occupation, 671 has had no official or other contact with Rome. As to SI, we assume that you approve underground SI work . . . even with Italian officials. . . .

Document 2-14

Telegram 734-35, September 14, 1943

[This report of Himmler's plans for a social revolution came to Dulles from source 487, Hans Opracht, a Swiss socialist.]

487 requested to see me yesterday to give me this report. It was given him by a lifelong friend who has just come from Baden. This man is an honest and well-intentioned person, who has a reasonably good knowledge of current developments in Germany. He is, however, made especially receptive to any alleged Communist danger by his background, both political and religious. A report from reliable quar-

ters in Berlin had reached him to the effect that Himmler is preparing a radical social revolution. Himmler, it is said, is convinced that defeat is unavoidable. He hopes to pull off a revolution and thus win Moscow's sympathy. This revolution is scheduled to take place between 3 and 8 weeks from now. We are transmitting this report with reserve.

Document 2-15-16

Telegram 5752, September 15, 1943 (extract)

[OSS Bern continued to transmit reports on German development of secret weapons.]

. . . In addition to the two secret weapons already mentioned, this informant spoke of still another, but had no knowledge as to where it was being built or even of any great detail about the construction of this weapon—a plane powered on the rocket technique and which was said to have unusual speed in climbing.

Our source 110 commented that this informant's estimate of the damage from air raids at Peenemunde far exceeded estimates from other quarters, the former claiming that damage above ground amounted to 80 or 90 per cent. No harm was suffered by the electric generating plant which is a sub-terranean one. While some persons said that General Jeschonneck took his own life because of chagrin over the raid at Peenemünde, our informant said the General was a casualty of the raid itself. . . .

Document 2-17

Telegram 5781, September 16, 1943

[This report on the tenuous state of affairs in Hungary was provided to Dulles by source 519, George Barcza, former Hungarian Minister in London.]

. . . On the tenth of September, in the capital of Hungary, the regent presided over a conference consisting of the present and former prime ministers, the present and former ministers of foreign affairs (with the exception of Bardossy and Ihredy) and the Minister of Home Affairs. At this meeting it was decided to send a delegation to the Fuehrer's headquarters, composed of outstanding army and civilian leaders. Kersztes, Fischer and others supported this idea, which was first broached by Bethlen in a manner to attract favorable attention. The projected delegation was to expound the following points:

All Hungarian troops being used to garrison Soviet territory to be sent home right away. (While instructions to these troops to come home had already been issued secretly and without consulting the Germans, the move was to come out into the open in case the Germans should refuse to accede to a formal request toward that end, as was anticipated. The gravity of this move was quite apparent to those at the council.)

The protection of the homeland was to be the sole consideration of the Hungarian government from now on, and none of their soldiers were to go beyond their own borders but were to remain at home as a defense against guerrilla bands. While orders would be issued to Hungarian troops not to fight any British or American forces, the attempt of the Germans to requisition these soldiers for use in the Balkans were turned down completely.

Routes skirting the capital, viz., from Pecs to Szombathely by way of Barcs and from Szolnok to Losoncz via Hatvan, were to be prescribed for the movement of German military personnel and equipment.

On the ninth of September Reich Military leaders in Hungary demanded that the Minister of War make certain moves with regard to Italy, viz., arrest of all nationals of that country in Hungary on military missions and so forth; give all planes that belong to them to the Reich; stop shipments of oil; cut off similar shipments from Rumania.

Hungary did not cooperate in any of these measures but Rumania did divert to Reich army units in the Balkans her oil that was meant for Italy. The Italian Minister to Hungary is received as coming from the Italian crown and the Minister from Hungary to Italy was directed to act as though he were accredited to the crown.

Document 2-18

Telegram 5829, September 18, 1943

[OSS Bern continued to report the views of the left-center opposition to the Badoglio government in Italy. Number 510 is Sforza; 645 is John McCaffrey, head of British SOE in Switzerland. References are made to Randolfo Pacciardi, exiled Republican Party leader; the anti-Fascist historian Gaetano Salvemini, an exile in the United States since 1925; and General Vittorio Ruggiero of the Italian Army.]

. . . Informant 510 is able to inform you about the life history of informants 683 and 682 who have recently come upon the scene and who held a conference in Lugano on September 17 with informant 638. One of these, R, was liberated not long since after 13 years imprisonment on the Island of Ventotene and is a member of the Partito d'Azione. The other, T, is a member of the same group and is a competent Milanese attorney. Both of these men begged me as well as number 645 for aid and comfort for those groups in Italy which were opposed to the old regime and which would not countenance a single Fascist survival. According to the view which these men hold, the upheaval of the 25th of July was not for the purpose of saving Italy but rather to salvage the crown. None the less, they offered no opposition to the scheme because it offered a means of getting rid of the Germans. They wish to avoid any act that would hinder the return of peace, but feel that the crown is utterly in bad repute and they have no wish to cooperate with it. Those elements in Italy which have been opposed to the Mussolini regime have found their hopes blighted to some degree and they seek verification that to achieve and maintain freedom for free men is the purpose of all this fighting. They maintain that Badoglio is not in a position to voice the thoughts of free Italy and they regret that our side had not allowed Sforza, or another representative of their same opinion who was outside Italy, to speak without restraint. With regard to Badoglio, they say that he will be unable to integrate Italian opposition, that he cannot even exercise command over the army. Only a person who has the best interests of Italy at heart and is a firm believer in freedom, can organize and start Italian resistance. Among the persons they list in the latter category are Pacciardi, Sforza and Salvemini, who can work with others of similarly unsullied history. The first of those three, they hoped, might lead in organizing an Italian army. Most of the Italian generals procured their positions through Fascist political means and are therefore not to be depended upon in the least. These men regret that when our side asked for cooperation from within Italy, the plea was made not on behalf of the people of Italy, but on behalf of the crown. The group of which we speak hopes that Italian leadership will go to someone with an unsullied record who has given no hostage to fortune, though they appreciate that military considerations come first.

To both of the informants who have just entered the scene, we stressed the fact that at this time military considerations take precedence over political ones and that the wholehearted cooperation of the elements in Italy of which they speak can render great assistance to the Allied armies through guerrilla tactics, intelligence work and sabotage, and thus aid in clearing northern Italy of all Reich troops.

These new informants, who very recently left northern Italy, give a very depressing picture of conditions in that section. There is a stupendous amount of looting of everything worthwhile, in which the Mussolini crowd are aided by the Germans. Everybody who felt released from restraint by the events of the 25th of July, and has expressed his opposition to the Fascist regime since, is now being picked up and either shipped off to some unknown point by the Fascisti, turned over to the Germans or merely given a beating. Men of an age that would make them available for military service are being put into concentration centers and will be shipped to the Reich, it is thought. Every sort of vehicle has been requisitioned, and that includes bicycles. General Ruggero went back on his word and told the Germans and surrendered to the latter all the arms, ammunition and so forth which he had agreed to give to Milanese opponents of Fascism to the number of 6 thousand, who had planned to make a street to street defense of the city against the Germans.

Document 2-19

Telegram 763-67, September 21, 1943

[OSS Bern reported whatever evidence it could identify concerning German resistance elements. In this cable, Dulles cites the danger of Germany seeking an accommodation with the Soviet Union, a persistent theme in his reporting throughout the war.]

. . . As yet there is no coordinated opposition other than the following nuclei with whom we are developing every possible contact: (1) Certain Protestant and Catholic church circles. (2) Labor elements which are both unorganized and isolated. (3) Communists. (4) Special departments of the government. (5) Various Army circles. The work of these groups is hidden and all of them lack coordination. If a change were to come it would most likely come from the top much as it did in Italy although at the present everyone here agrees that an attempt to organize would only bring about ruthless suppression.

Two conflicting plans are favored by the opposing groups but when a crisis is reached and some feel this is not too distant, the attitude of the military leaders will probably influence the decision. One of these plans is the Western solution which entails opening the door to the Anglo-Saxon occupation forces; the other plan [is] the Eastern solution, that is, by approach to Russia. At present, the military attitude is not clarified, but the Gestapo tends to favor the Eastern solution. . . .

Document 2-20

Telegram 5876, September 21, 1943

[OSS Bern's leading Hungarian contact was Baron Bakach-Bessenyey, Budapest's Minister in Bern. He provided a running account of the agony of Prime Minister Nicholas Kallay's government as it sought to escape both short-term German enslavement and long-term Allied retribution. Number 477 is Royall Tyler; 495 is Gregoire Gafencu, former Rumanian Foreign Minister.]

. . . Bern's number 684 has been given to Bakach-Bessenyey who has told number 477 that he has learned from Kallay, that the scheme of occupying some parts of Yugoslavia had been given up entirely and that, regardless of the course of events, no military forces would be sent into the Balkans. The course of events has rendered any collaboration with Bulgaria out of the question. The possibility of getting into difficulties with the Soviet caused Kallay to stall, though Antonescu is making offers. The complete domination of Italy by the Germans is held to be a harbinger of what the Hungarians could expect if they were to withdraw at this time from their connection with the Germans. While Kallay suggested that he is willing to take chances, he feels that his judgment would be better guided if he were assured that the Allies understood the serious position that Hungary is in and the obstacles that confront her. Through the medium of Bakach-Bessenyey, Kallay has requested that we repose confidence in him to the best advantage and to get out of his present bad position as soon as possible. Since Hungary lacks transport facilities, Kallay's efforts to repatriate all their forces on the Soviet front must have the consent of the Germans. The Hungarian Minister of Foreign Affairs and the Chief of Staff plan to visit the German headquarters just as soon as they can get an appointment, for the purpose of demanding the return to Hungary of all her soldiers for home defense. Attention is called to a telegram of the 16th of September, number 5781, in this connection.

Hungary would sacrifice all possible means of assisting the Allies at the right time, according to Kallay, if they were precipitate in their action now and gave the Germans a basis for taking complete control of Hungary before the latter could offer any resistance, and then proceed to commandeer everything of value in the country, ship all the Jews out of the country, conscript workers and so forth.

There is an interesting parallel between the attitude of Rumania (Antonescu) and that of Kallay with regard to precipitate action inviting occupation by the Germans, an event which they are willing to risk in a move to upset the government, according to their information to number 495, if our side thinks it opportune and essential. With the data about subversive movements in the region referred to contained in a telegram sent over a short time ago, in mind, it poses the question whether it is advantageous to overturn the present regimes in Rumania and Hungary now and thus bring about a possible comparatively cheap occupation by the Germans or whether we should postpone action until [garble]. . . . According to information received from 495 from elements opposed to the present regime in Rumania, they are greatly impressed by events in Italy and by the questions posed above and by the similarity of the positions of Hungary and Rumania. They are not of a mind, if left to their own devices, to essay a revolution at this time and thus bring about closer military cooperation through a government favorable to the Allies, which both Hungary and Rumania would be willing to set up as hostage to fortune. However, there is another consideration involved in immediate and joint action by the two countries, viz., such a move might hurry along the day of German collapse by messing up their transportation facilities and cut off their oil supplies.

Document 2-21

Telegram 777-79, September 22, 1943

[This cable contains information on German submarine operations as obtained from number 472, prewar French intelligence elements in Switzerland.]

The following material on submarines comes from 472. It has been alleged that Doenitz indicated in a recent report that there have been revolutionary tendencies noticed among naval personnel. Unsatisfactory protection of submarines, especially artillery DCA personnel, has caused much discontent. During surface attacks these artillery DCA men have no protection and suffer severe casualties. Attacks by single submarines was substituted for hunting in packs at the end of July. The detection hull is being given insulation covering of buna so as to allow the U-boats to escape the enemy. Units which are actually in the Atlantic are being tested. (A similar report comes from 496.) Results of tests of a new type of silent motor proved satisfactory. After the raids on Hamburg, production of U-boats was transferred, principally to Kiel. The age limit for submarine crews has been changed to 46; it was formerly 30.

Document 2-22

Telegram 783-84, September 24, 1943

[This cable regarding potential resistance forces in northern Italy was part of the ongoing OSS Bern effort to provide information helpful to special operations behind German lines.]

According to message dated September 12th from a dependable contact in Turin to 110, there are concentrations of Alpini troops at Torrepellice, Dronero, and Boves. They need radio sets, arms, and ammunition. Officers have ducked out, and therefore, they are also in need of leaders. Morale is good. Our informant is from Camp 49 Fontanellato which is located in the vicinity of Parma. He says that Larry Allen, American Associated Press correspondent, was sent from there to Chieti Camp where there is a concentration of American prisoners. This message was brought to us by an escaped British Officer.

Document 2-23

Telegram 5971, September 24, 1943

[In this cable, Dulles provides an extended exposition of his fear that effective Soviet psychological warfare might result in a Communist Germany after the war.]

. . . General von Daniels and General von Seydlitz are considered to be officers of high military accomplishments as well as of unquestioned personal honesty, so that great importance is attributed by well-informed circles in Germany to the group of German army officers in the Soviet capital. It is said, in secret, that they tried at the point of their pistols, to coerce von Paulus into abandoning Stalingrad contrary to the orders of the Fuehrer and before the last opportunity to do so had passed. This experience at Stalingrad crystallized their latent anti-Nazi feelings. General Hube is the purveyor of this story. He was wounded at Stalingrad and is one of a small minority of ranking Reich army officers to be sent back for that reason and is now fighting in the vicinity of Naples. The person telling the story feels that it is indicative of the earnestness of this committee of officers, who were held in esteem by their colleagues on the Russian front, that Stalin should have given his approval to their efforts.

It is suggested as within the realm of possibility that these officers may establish communication, if they have not done so already, with German officers now leading troops against the Russians. There is the suggestion that would furnish a way out for the German military and that is that they might even be won over to the idea of reversing the direction of their armies, returning to the Reich and, with the aid of Soviet forces, to overthrow the Fuehrer and his party. This idea is forwarded by the embassy with reservations.

Soviet propaganda may be able to make excellent capital out of the activities of the Committee of German officers in Moscow because of the growth of radical thought and lowered standard of living within the Reich as a result of bombing and the fact that workers have been brought in from foreign countries to the number of a million or so and also because of the fact that about a million people have been forced to leave their homes. It is felt that the morale of the home front is such that it may be susceptible to such ideas.

With regard to the activities of the Communist Party within the Reich, a dependable informant, who is close to labor and religious groups, contributes three items which are as follows:

The man who was once leader of the Communist Party bloc in the German Reichstag, Torgler, is now in the capital of Bohemia, where he is active in an element that is said to have been instituted by Heydrich but which is now thought to be cooperating with Daluege and Himmler. In other words, odd to relate, it would appear that the Gestapo has placed an anchor to windward, by setting up its own Communist group with a carefully selected personnel picked by the Gestapo itself.

The thought is gaining ground among leading army people that Germany's hope rests with collaboration with the Soviet. While they have been in a dilemma as between Russia and Britain and the United States, they have finally concluded that the latter two countries are determined that the German army clique as well as the Nazi Party should be completely annihilated.

Because of the presence of large numbers of Soviet prisoners and laborers and the spread of the philosophy of control by the lower classes, there has been a noticeable change in the attitude of labor groups within the Reich.

From number one ten comes the editorial comment that the material given above, in summary, is worthy of mature thought. The fact is that Soviet propaganda has been busy and successful in the field of politics, while the English and ourselves have been adhering to the demand for unconditional surrender. The devastating effect of the Russian advance and the result of bombing together with the Russian activity in the political field have brought about an alteration, psychologically, within the Reich so that the appeal of democratic thought to all of Central Europe may be weakened.

Document 2-24

Telegram 5974, September 25, 1943

[OSS Bern continued to report on Rumanian developments. Number 686 is Raoul Bossy, former Rumanian Minister in Berlin; 495 is Gafencu. Reference is made to opposition leaders Iulio Maniu and Constantin Bratianu. OSS Acting Director Buxton sent a paraphrase of this message to the Secretary of State on September 30.]

. . . Number 686, whose praises are sung loudly by number 499 [495?], reached Bern a short time ago from Bucharest and says that he had agreed to take over a new place in the government only after an understanding with Maniu and other outstanding figures among the opposition, and after persistent urging by the king of Rumania. The latter, he says, is, to all intents and purposes, a captive and his opinion is never sought. Number 686 consulted with all the leading figures in the opposition, including both the Messrs. Bratianu and Mihalache, who represented Maniu during the latter's illness. He has verified the statement made in my telegram number 5876 [Doc. 2-20] with regard to the willingness of those opposed to the present regime to overthrow the government of Antonescu and thereby take a chance on complete domination of Rumania by German troops, if the British and Americans are convinced that this is an opportune moment for them to act. In fact, completely integrated arrangements for planned action are already made. Maniu and all the people who think as he does appreciate that our side will look at the affair solely from the standpoint of Allied Military expediency, but they are willing to jeopardize themselves if we are convinced that this is the moment to move.

The data from number 495 as well as that contained herein, are definitely meant seriously but I can give no assurance as to what will actually be done if our side acts at this moment. Nevertheless, in consideration of number 600 from that end, it is my suggestion that you give thought to transmitting to Maniu and those who are with him, some helpful comment, which could go through number 686 and number 495, if plans are worked out for making the movements of our army fit in with internal action within Rumania. Naturally, one must not overlook the importance of action in this sphere to the Soviet and see to it that movement is in harmony with any moves of theirs.

Document 2-25

Telegram 5985, September 25, 1943 (extracts)

[This five-page message on German battle order and troop movements in Italy was one of thousands of similar cables sent by OSS Bern during the war. Such reports on military subjects represented a substantial portion of the mission's overall contribution.]

. . . During the four days ending the 20th, additional Reich troops arrived in Italy, the latest increment being about one and one half divisions, described in different quarters as armored, light or substitute, which reinforcement raised the total of troops in the country to 27 or 28 divisions.

Of these troops, six divisions are fighting in the Salerno region and two in the vicinity of Foggia, making a total of eight divisions to the southward of a line between Anzio and Pescara. . . .

The 200,000 Reich soldiers which were held as a strategic reserve in Carinthia before the capitulation of Italy have now departed, some having gone to Italy and the balance to the Balkans.

The Nazis are very unhappy about the presence of Mussolini in the Reich because he is such a perfect example of what a dictator looks like after he has been deposed.

Document 2-26

Telegram 794-97, September 28, 1943

[After the Italian surrender, OSS Bern continued to provide a channel of communications for left-center opposition elements in Switzerland. Number 510 is Sforza; 638 and 506 are representatives of the Partito d'Azione.]

To 510 from 638, 506 and their friends. "The program of the Partito d'Azione has not been altered. This group will not share governmental responsibility with the Badoglio regime, but it does not want to cause trouble for the latter. This stand is not only a result of idealistic antagonism, but also is designed to keep the main force opposition from allying themselves with extremist or Communist factions. The program outlined in cables from 510 and in our preceding declarations is the only solution to which the majority of the people, the active factions in particular, would agree. It is absolutely imperative that an official decree be issued which states that anyone, whether private citizen or military official, who works with the Nazis will be considered a traitor and will be punished accordingly, and that anyone who commits an act of cruelty will be looked upon as a criminal and will be prosecuted as such."

638, 506, their colleagues, and others recommend that financial aid be solicited from Italian organizations in America in order to raise enough money to provide for political refugees here, no matter what party they belong to as long as they are opposed to Fascism. If money were provided so that a number of these refugees could be released from camps, it would aid our work in general. Some of these people might be able to help us in our activities. The above is from 110. . . .

Document 2-27

Telegram 58-61 to Algiers, September 29, 1943

[Dulles maintained great interest in furthering special operations in enemy-controlled territory and sought guidance for coordination of activities in association with the British and the SO Branch of the OSS. Colonel William A. Eddy was OSS representative in Algiers.]

For 109, McKay, and Eddy. Since there is no Consulate in Lugano to use as a cover, I am having some difficulty working on your #43. Am using everyone possible on this project but lack sufficient American personnel who can speak Italian. My opinion that there is good chance for SO to work south from points along (local) Italian border and also opportunity for SI to get information regarding groupings of Italian soldiers, points for parachutage equipment, and data on centers of local Italian resistance. Because of delays and disappointments in satisfactory working out French Maquis situation, please decide as soon as possible exactly what kind of service you expect from this end and how you desire our SO activities coordinated with ZULU's. My work well synchronized with ZULU SOE who has built up workable organization to the South during the past 2 years. It is essential that we know who will be responsible for action here, and who, on your end, will issue instructions and effect coordination. Will compare notes with ZULU, but keep up altogether separate SI organization, as formerly. Since our basis of action is too restricted to allow efficient division of territory, SO handled from here should go through one channel. Does the fact that Italy has now been invaded alter the situation resulting from our agreement with ZULU, of June 1942, in view of which we have not specialized in SO work?

Document 2-28

Telegram 799-801, September 30, 1943

[Dulles devoted great effort to the transmittal of unclassified material including press reports with a view toward providing a database for both intelligence and psychological warfare. Number 678 is Gerald Mayer, OWI representative in Bern. The "Hugbear" channel was named after John C. Hughes and Frederick Dolbeare of the OSS New York Office.]

. . . I have made plans with 678 to transmit through him to their New York branch as Press Wireless, certain non-classified information which we receive via our channels, but which perhaps would be interesting to both OWI and you. Such data will not be in cipher, but will be sent direct to New York in plain text and will not be subject to State Department delays. The cables will be addressed Miller, Barnard Hugbear, followed by serial number. Hugbear is our code word in honor of our personnel in New York. Kindly inform us, after this system has been tested for a short time, how the arrangement turns out. Please make this facility known to OWI. . . .

Document 2-29

Telegram 805-6, October 1, 1943

[This cable contains information on Italian matters.]

1. The following is a message from 506 and 475: "We believe that it is urgently required that Pacciardi go back to Italy to help in organizing armed opposition behind the enemy's battlelines."

2. It has been reported that Prince Louis de Bourbon-Parma, the Princess and their two children were taken prisoner by the Gestapo near Cannes around the 13th of last month. The princess is the youngest daughter of King Victor Emmanuel of Italy. It is assumed that they were sent to Germany as hostages.

Document 2-30

Telegram 809-10, October 1, 1943

[This report concerns Hitler's command arrangements. Number 643 is Eduard Schulte.]

Lately from the north, very competent and well informed, 643 said in a conversation that East Front developments are no longer receiving Hitler's personal interest. General Staff, Manstein, von Kluge, etc. are being left with this, while Hitler takes a direct personal interest in Balkan and Italian campaigns. Though, our informant states, Rommel is not personally in agreement with Hitler's program for defending outposts in Italy and Balkans, Hitler's orders are still decisive here. Hitler's insistence that everything should be held if possible is not in accord with Rommel's belief in the strategy of withdrawing to lines which are more defensible.

Document 2-31

Telegram 6137, October 1, 1943

[This cable provides additional information on the possibility of German accommodation with the Soviets. Number 227 is Charles B. Dyar of OSS Bern; number 313 is a source who reported from time to time on communist and Soviet matters.]

The following information comes from number 227 and is intended for the OSS. It is a resume of a conversation held a few days ago between number 313 and a well informed figure from Russia whose integrity 313 greatly respects.

The Japanese, the Prussian army clique and the big Reich manufacturers are the leading figures in urging a negotiated peace with the Soviet. Nippon's interest is to avoid attack from the rear in view of her present struggle with Britain and the United States, which is for her very life. It is said that the Japanese desire at least a friendly neutrality or, better yet, an actual alliance with Russia. For these reasons, the pressure by the Japanese in offering their services as peacemaker becomes greater in direct proportion to growth of the difficulties confronting the Reich.

The contention is made that Reich manufacturers are in a cul-de-sac with the only outlet a negotiated peace with the Soviet and, after that, a similar move with Britain and the United States.

Ranking Reich army officers consider that a deal with the Soviet would maintain their social status and assure their futures.

It is only to procure an advantage in manoeuvering that has caused the Soviet to refrain from denying the gossip with regard to negotiations for peace between Germany and Russia. In fact, the officials at the Kremlin even foster such gossip as a good foundation for the projected conference between Great Britain, the United States and the Soviet. The Russians retain their old fear of fascist inclinations in Britain and America. The Soviet will not be contented with the downfall of the Fuehrer and the Nazi Party but will demand a governmental set-up within the Reich which will not only give other assurances, but will give the Soviet a complete feeling of freedom from any German incursion for many years to come. Failing in that, another conflict is sure to follow. Since this is the Soviet's first goal, her primary step will be to set up a Free German Committee in the Soviet capital.

In spite of all the stories going around, such negotiation with the Reich is preposterous and would receive serious consideration in time to come only in the event that the Soviet were so worn down that such negotiation were more in her favor than would be the continuation of the conflict. The upshot of it all, therefore, in the opinion of 313's source of information, is that such talk of a negotiated peace is a useful tool in the hands of the Russians, but has no real basis.

This dissertation on German-Russian relations is said to represent the point of view of 313's source rather than that of Americans here, but does seem to be a sensible exposition. One possible eventuality is omitted, and that is the possibility of capitulation to the Russians by communist elements within the Reich.

Document 2-32

Telegram 811-20, October 2, 1943

[This message discusses possibilities for a more active Allied role in influencing events in Hungary. It is interesting to note that Dulles concerned himself with operational details. Number 477 is Royall Tyler, Dulles's top assistant on Hungarian matters; 684 is Bakach-Bessenyey, the Hungarian Minister in Bern.]

I have gone over your cable #637 and earlier cables with 477. Our mutual opinions are set forth below:

1. After 110 and 477 recommended informally that we should have a reliable person in Berne to whom we could deal on problems such as those mentioned in your cables, 684 was sent here. 477 has now conferred with 684 several times and has received assurances that his first mission in Berne is to keep contact with us.

2. 684 is suggesting that it be arranged in native country to accept and hide people whom we might dispatch with material. This could be accomplished through

a pretended forced landing in connection with a raid on some objectives such as Savedrave Bridges, if not too costly, or else by parachute landing. I am requesting 684 to get the location of a landing field for the former or exact coordinates for the latter, and to give us detailed information about the reception committee and similar matters. We do not prophesy their reply but we regard this as an extremely good chance.

3. The people for such an undertaking must be selected carefully and at the beginning there should not be too many. Perhaps 3 or 4 people in addition to the normal operational personnel of the airplane in the case of a pretended forced landing, so that the operating personnel could be officially made prisoners to quiet possible German suspicion or investigation. It would be better if we did select Aryans for this Mission and not former citizens of any surrounding nation. It would be fine if a Hungarian-speaking person were available, otherwise some of the people should speak German. There is no objection to using as second man or leader a straight American but, if we can get one, he should know something of the Danube countries.

4. We assume that plans for the pick-up could be arranged by radio from landing party directly to our GHQU in Italy.

5. We take it for granted that the mission would not itself carry on subversive activities against the existing government; however, we will make it understood that the arrangements concerning the sending or the reception group do not bind us in this or in other respects. Although our reports here show that such an attempt now would be premature, there may be a time when it will be useful to replace the present government. Even the Socialists, with whom we maintain independent contact, are inclined to back the existing government as long as it employs the policy of combatting demands of the Nazis. The Socialists take this position to preclude a possible coup d'etat by the small Imredy-Progerman group which might make the most of the situation if the Leftist factions began active opposition.

6. With regard to political connections, we have fine contacts with 646 and others not in the government, who are ready to take control at the proper moment.

7. Based on 655's specific question, 684 has asked 477 whether, following our occupation, their Minister might remain at Quirinal without chancing his internment. 477 did not commit himself and made it clear that it was impossible to give any assurances. From the practical viewpoint, we suggest that it be handled discreetly if the Hungarian Government continues its recognition of the King's Government.

8. 684 reports the German GHQU and Hitler conferred recently with the Chief of Staff. As a result of the conference, the Germans completely refuse to allow Hungarian troops to be sent home from the Eastern front in the fear that this will give the Rumanians a precedent. The Germans did agree to an additional withdrawal to the west, to the region between the former Polish border and Lemberg. From the practical viewpoint, troops could go home on foot from there if an emergency arose.

9. We see no benefit at this point of involving Balassy and Pelenyi in the above plans although we believe that our friends inside the country trust them.

Document 2-33

Telegram 840, October 8, 1943

[The material provided by Fritz Kolbe in Berlin, number 674, included items of immediate military or naval interest.]

The information below comes from 674. From Lisbon, German authorities received secret word that submarines would find it propitious to assail an Allied convoy the 7th of this month in the vicinity of the Azores.

Document 2-34

Telegram 843-44, October 9, 1943

[The information received from Fritz Kolbe ("George Wood," 674) caused great controversy in Washington and London because its authenticity was doubted. It was also feared that should the Germans become aware of the Wood leak, they would conduct a thorough security investigation that might place Ultra in jeopardy. The Allies were doubly concerned because the channels of communication Dulles used to transmit the voluminous Wood traffic were considered less than totally secure. The diplomatic cipher from the Legation in Bern, often used by the OSS, was especially suspect. Dulles's efforts to respond to cipher security concerns are evident in this convoluted message. The following code words were identified in a subsequent message: Alpha, German two-way secret Foreign Office cables; Beta, the security of Minister Harrison's channel; Gamma, Wood's cross examination; Delta, the particular value and authoritative quality of the Wood material; Epsilon, the paraphrasing of the cable prior to transmission; and Zeta, this extremely important and valuable line. Number 105 is Bruce; 109 is Donovan; and Jackpot is Shepardson. Sulu is Zulu, the British; 521 is British SIS (MI-6) in Switzerland.]

For 105, 109, Jackpot. I have recently secured about 200 mimeographed pages of Alpha which deals with a wide range of economic, diplomatic, and military subjects. They take in a 6 weeks period and cover through the 3rd of this month. Source: 674. Especially since we are no longer sure of Beta, it will take weeks to handle . . . situation. However, we will endeavor to do our utmost and, as Alpha is of vital concern to Sulu, we will divide with 521 because of the emergency. 105 will relay this to you. I am fully convinced of Delta, after a careful study of yesterday's Gamma and (garble). This opinion is based on all internal evidence, 105 and London reaction. The whole formation and set-up of Alpha, as was given by 521 in his cable of around the 22nd of August, is necessary for proper handling. Therefore, unfortunately, a great deal of valuable material is unavoidably lost in Epsilon. Yet, there is no sure alternative. I will continue to refer to Alpha as 674 as I have in the past. In order to preserve Beta, complete discretion must be used in dealing with Alpha.

Document 2-35

Telegram 850-51, October 11, 1943

[This report on Italian matters was received from Fritz Kolbe / George Wood, who was assigned two numbers: 674 and 805.]

805 reports that the headquarters of Il Duce and the official establishment of his government are being transferred to Belluno. Mussolini attacked the German scorched earth policy in a recent discussion with Rahn. The former said that this policy would make the Italian people so angry that it would result in preventing any effective cooperation in fighting alongside the Nazis. 674 is the source of the following information: Schloss Hirschberg, located in upper Bavaria between Weilholm and Murnau, is a meeting place for important Fascist Italian refugees. Ciano and his wife were both at Schloss Hirschberg a short time ago. Minister Dornberg is providing liaison between the Nazis and the Fascist Italians.

Document 2-36

Telegram 852-53, October 11, 1943

[This message is based on German Foreign Ministry correspondence intercepted by agent Fritz Kolbe (source 674 and 805). It concerns counterintelligence and German relations with Turkey. Nabors signifies Germans; Vinta is the code name for Foreign Minister Ribbentrop; Milit is von Papen, German Ambassador in Turkey; Nicod is the Italian Consul.]

Nabors received from Nicod, at Magro, information allowing them to proceed with the Allied shipping observation. This observation was formerly a common job. 674 says that Doctor Wertz at Magro has a weakness for women and that he could be of great assistance if approached in this manner. The source of the following information is 805: A fortnight ago Vinta sent Milit a strong message informing him that under the circumstances there is no chance of realizing his efforts toward persuading the Italians to hand the Dodecanese Islands over to Turkey voluntarily. He was instructed not to pursue this project any further. In addition Vinta dispatched a secret message to Milit a few days later. This latter message was evidently an answer to an inquiry from Milit and was to the effect that the reported negotiations between the Russians and the Nazis are completely false, and that this is obviously a British propaganda move designed to influence Turkey to agree to English wishes.

Document 2-37

Telegram 869-71, October 14, 1943

[In this message, Dulles discusses U.S. relations with the French resistance. Regis is Reginald Foster; Jackpot is Shepardson, Chief of SI; Trump, also known as Carte, is the French resistance figure André Girard, who was in the United States in October 1943; Sulu is Zulu—British.]

From 110 to Regis and Jackpot. With reference to your 688. We have not gotten in touch with Trump's organization since this was a Sulu matter. A tactfully conducted investigation shows that there is some doubt as to whether his organization is still operating effectively. Since we have a paucity of evidence, however, we cannot form a conclusive opinion in this matter. I do not give much weight to Trump's allegation that resistance groups are anti-American. We are now having a conference with their authorized agents and they are very congenial. As far as our work here is involved, they are cooperating with us. Without a doubt there is a feeling that our Secretary of State is hostile to General de Gaulle. This has had certain bad effects, since the militant resistance organizations work under the banner of de Gaulle and his followers, who are a symbol of the spirit that resisted the Nazis from the most somber days of 1940. This symbol has more power and is more extensive than the influence of the man who, regardless of his virtues, has acted cantankerously, as I am well aware. I certainly would regret any endeavor to establish an anti-Gaullist resistance organization. Although the military and bourgeois factions are not particularly pro-Gaulle, in character, I am completely of the opinion that we should collaborate with them as well as with the militant resistance movements.

Document 2-38

Telegram 880-87, October 16, 1943

[This message contains additional information based on German diplomatic communications, apparently from Portugal, intercepted by agent Fritz Kolbe in Berlin. Grand is the German Foreign Ministry; Porto signifies a German embassy or legation; Bonty means Lisbon; Henry is the Brazilian Foreign Minister; Fonda signifies the Germans; Gerbo means Hungary; Sarto is Portuguese Premier Salazar. The nature of this material could have contributed to the unfounded thesis that Kolbe/Wood was a plant. The material presented here may have been interpreted to be designed to undermine Allied solidarity and trust in the security of several U.S. and British agencies.]

. . . 2. In the month of September the following reports to Grand from Porto, Bonty.

a. According to a secret report Henry says that there is depression in United States circles over the prospects of the Moscow conference. This is occasioned by the doubtful attitude of Stalin, his demands that cannot be realized and his failure to deal clearly with his Allies. Stalin's latest demands were for a share in the administration of the occupied Italian territory and for recognition by the South American States. Negotiations between Rio de Janeiro and Washington for recognition have not met with success.

b. Quoting from alleged American and British diplomatic sources, he reports the growing fear in both these countries of the negotiations between Russia and Germany. He claims that London and Washington evaluate the danger of the Bolshevisation of Europe to be so serious that the lull in the air raids on German cities is occasioned by the wish not to weaken Germany in view of the coming Russian offensive, and that no additional concessions will be made to Russia.

c. The statement that heavy attacks are being readied against the German GHQU are attributed by a confidential source to the chief of the American FBI in Bonty. GHQU plans were delivered by a high-ranking Italian officer, who is well acquainted with them, to the Allies. The FBI Chief indicated that the Italians gave the Allies good advice concerning the Nazi military situation.

d. In relationship to the Timor and Azores problem, he reports confidential data allegedly stemming from sources in the American Legation pertaining to their attitude on these two points. He finished by saying that very serious consequences for the Nazis, in their acquisition of raw materials, including wolfram, will result if the Americans are successful in obtaining a base on the Azores, or possibly on the mainland.

e. An alleged statement made by a British General Staff officer is reported to account for the halt of air raids on Germany as being occasioned by the quick advance of the Russians and an attempt to equalize Russian and Nazi losses. A decisive change in the policy of England and the United States towards Russia is made possible by the rise of anti-Russian sentiment in the United States and the resignation of Undersecretary of State Welles.

f. Fonda realizes that American and British Legation members meet at the home of Baron Radvanski with the personnel of Gerbo Porto, and especially with press and commercial attachés. Whether policy negotiations of a serious nature are worked out there, is not known yet.

g. Reports attributed to the Chief of the American FBI state that landings are to be effected by the British in northern France and by the Americans, in southern France; both are to take place in September. The same source originated reports that landings are to take place at Trieste.

h. The latter part of August. Reports on the crisis in the Timor situation. Recommends that Japan be informed that the Nazis view a war between Portugal and Japan as an extremely unwelcome development, and that Germany is therefore anxious that a peaceful solution be worked out.

i. Gives substance of a lengthy conference with Sarto. Sarto expressed his bitterness at the fact that the British show no comprehension of the Bolshevist menace. Sarto is quoted as being hopeful of staying on a neutral basis with Germany. Although the British have caused difficulties in economic affairs, they are satisfied with Portugal's policy of neutrality. The British are making no demands, such as approval of the landing of troops, or such as the ceding of air bases, which would be likely to cause war with Germany. Sarto is quoted as saying that Monteiro owes his whole career to Sarto himself, and that although his weaknesses were apparent, he would take no action which would be contrary to the interests of his country. This was in connection with the rumor that Monteiro was seeking the position of Minister President. Sarto also stated that he was amazed at the strength which the Nazis have evidenced, and at their ability to withstand bombing raids. . . .

Document 2-39

Telegram 6600, October 21, 1943

[OSS Bern remained in touch with the Rumanian opposition.]

. . . Another message has just been received by Y from Maniu which contains confirmation that the opposition is willing to make an endeavor to effect a change in the government, creating a temporary government consisting of military and of individuals who have the opposition's confidence and indicating that his majesty is inclined to cooperate along these lines. It was felt by the spokesman of the opposition, however, that in as much as the allies are too far distant to give assistance, a change at this particular time might carry more risks than benefits to the cause of the allies. However, the opposition has indicated again that they are willing to act if a change of that kind fitted into the plan of the allies and if they wished such a change.

Document 2-40

Telegram 245 to London, October 22, 1943

[OSS Bern frequently became involved in the rescue of Allied flyers downed in enemy territory. U.S. B-17s suffered especially heavy losses in bombing the German ball-bearing manufacturing installation at Schweinfurt, October 14–15. Number 520 is Brigadier General Legge, U.S. Military Attaché at Bern.]

12 of our pilots coming back from the Schweinfurt raid were forced down in the vicinity of Nancy. This information was reported to 520 by means of Polish contacts.

Would it be possible for you to have the right organization contact them? 520 is trying to get in touch with them by means of local sources, and would like to know if there is a specific addressee in that region for this very purpose?

Document 2-41

Telegram 76-77 to Algiers, October 25, 1943

[This cable consists of a message from Italian Socialist leader Silone in Switzerland to Count Sforza, prominent Italian anti-Fascist in exile.]

To 510 from 475. Allow us to congratulate you on what you have said recently. Maintain contact with us. We have dealings with three resistance groups in north, whose complete destruction is being arranged by the Fascist militia to take place at the end of this month. Our strength is sapped by the lassitude and complete personal deterioration of the troops who remain with Badoglio. It is of the utmost importance that they receive vigorous propaganda against the Nazis, which shall be sincere and stirring and will arouse the people. It is equally pressing that they be sent more aggressive instructions. Is there any chance of forming a nucleus of leading Socialists (if any of them have managed to get away from Rome to the south) in the liberated region? I urge that they work on an agreement with Partito d'Azione. Will you kindly assure them that our efforts go on in the north in connection with their [garble] Milanese companions.

Document 2-42

Telegram 919-21, October 25, 1943
(extract)

[The Dulles network continued to further the activities of center-left Italian opposition elements by providing a channel of communications. Number 475 is Ignazio Silone; Monty is presumably Vanni Montana, Italian Socialist and aide to Luigi Antonini, prominent Italian-American labor leader in New York. Italian Socialists in Italy and neighboring countries received funds from American labor because they refused to be funded by Allied intelligence.]

From 475 to Monty. There was not enough time to send a message for Columbus Day, but I hope to get one off very soon, since in the name of socialism I want to express the gratitude we feel toward the Labor Council for the help it guarantees us. If money is to be collected to help rehabilitate the Italian Labor Movement, great care should be taken as to who handles the money and by what method the money is managed. I make the suggestion that the composition of the committee be given to the newspapers for publication. Tell them that the committee will be made up of myself, Modigliani and American-Italian Labor Council members. The Swiss have received our proposed plan for international worker relief for after the war. . . .

Document 2-43

Telegram 924-25, October 25, 1943

[Dulles transmitted erroneous as well as valid information. He had a good record, however, in identifying dubious reports for what they were. Number 477 is Royall Tyler.]

1. 477 has received the following report from French sources. The Wehrmacht plans to withdraw from the southern and central regions of France. They will include the Atlantic and Channel coast to estuary of the Seine in their evacuation and will establish a line extending to the southeast along the Seine and across to the Vosges. According to this plan Paris will be held as hostage inside the line. The same sources report that there are more and more indications of the likelihood that the Wehrmacht may execute said plan before the Allies land.

2. Believe you should have this information because 477's contacts are extremely good; however, I am forwarding it to you with great hesitancy due to the fact that there is no substantiating evidence.

Document 2-44

Telegram 78-79 to Algiers, October 26, 1943

[OSS Bern took great interest in refugee relief as well as in the French resistance. This message relates to the thousands of French citizens who fled to Switzerland to escape the Nazi/Vichy regime in their homeland. William Eddy was OSS representative in Algiers.]

From 110 to Eddy. . . . Forward to Massigli, or in his absence Jean Monnet, the following personal message: lacking receipt of funds from the Committee for carrying on modest aid for French refugees here, the relief committee will be sure to dissolve almost immediately. This will seriously effect the prestige of the French cause here. Numerous cables from the Legation have dealt with this subject. More than a month ago, the message reached us that the committee was remitting 100,000 francs for this purpose to de Leusse. In confidence, and for your information alone, the liaison established with French refugees through the existing committee is of great assistance in our work with the French. We hate to see this useful connection cut off.

Document 2-45

Telegram 927-29, October 26, 1943

[This cable reports further on the situation in Hungary. Number 684 is Bakach-Bessenyey, the Hungarian Minister in Bern.]

We have received word from 684 in connection with your suggestion. He indicates that in principle this proposal meets with their approval, but they want to hold off for the time being until alterations in the General Staff, now pending, are effected. They offer by way of explanation the statement that the General Staff was loaded with pro-Germans before '36. In view of the delays which this would entail, the reply does not fully satisfy either 477 or myself, and we are having additional consultation to push the matter ahead. 684 states that Kallay's entourage has received reports that American contact in Lisbon and British contact in Turkey advise them to remain quiet and to take no action. These conflicting advices have confused Kallay's group, and as a consequence there is opposition to running the moderate risk which our suggestion would entail. The Italian Legation staff in Budapest is divided in its allegiances, 5 being for Mussolini and 13 for King Victor. The Nazis are pressing for internment of the latter group, but their request has been denied up to the present time. 684 reports that although the Minister is still accredited to the King, the Quirinal legation has withdrawn from Rome. The Nazis have threatened Hungary in case all Hungarian officials withdraw from occupied Italy. Therefore, although the whole staff except the counselor has gone back to Hungary, Pap remained in Venice. Pap has been directed to make no contact with the Mussolini government.

Document 2-46

Telegram 83-84 to Algiers, October 27, 1943

[Dulles was a persistent advocate of special operations in support of resistance movements. In this message he again prods OSS Algiers to take action.]

It would be desirable for us to start some parachuting in the near future, judging from our reports, as token encouragement to resistance groups. It goes without saying that you require information as to the leaders, the needs, and the exact locations and numbers involved. Groups whose whereabouts enable them to be most effective in guerrilla activities or sabotage should be the ones chosen. Procurement of this type of information concerning groups in the vicinity of our frontier will be undertaken by several envoys whom we have sent out for this purpose, collaborating closely with Zulu. As soon as we obtain exact data for your purposes, we shall cable you. It is our opinion that best arrangement then would be to forward WT sets to approved units. You can handle from your end just as soon as WT communication is set up between units and south. Whatever information we can obtain will supplement above.

Document 2-47

Telegram 930-31, October 27, 1943

[OSS Bern performed a secondary role in Yugoslav affairs, which were managed from London and Italy and received heavy personal attention from General Donovan (number 109). Dulles did report occasionally on the subject and also interacted with Yugoslav refugees in Switzerland, as indicated in this message. Number 663 is a source on Yugoslav matters also known as Beki.]

With the help of 663, a method of keeping in touch with the following Yugoslav officer refugees here has been set up. We have been informed that these men assisted in the coup on March 27, 1941, and are certain they met our 109: Capt. Kalafatovitch Ratko, Major Alexitch Radaie, Capt. Milosavlievitch Petar and Capt. Alexitich Panta. Believe that they all are acquainted with Yugoslav MA in Washington. If we are able to get them out of camp, they are willing to do work for us in Italy. Please confer with MA and if he confirms, make all arrangements to have Yugoslav legation here attempt to expedite their release, thereby placing them at our disposal for duty in Italy. Because of the involved Serb-Croat situation here at the legation, it would be wise to make no reference to the fact that this recommendation originated with us, nor should any reference be made of 663.

Document 2-48

Telegram 946-47, October 29, 1943

[This message concerns Eduard Schulte (number 643), a German industrialist, who provided OSS Bern with vital information on the Nazi extermination of the Jews, the V-1 program, and other subjects. His contribution is examined in detail by Laqueur and Breitman in *Breaking the Silence* (1986). Number 487 is Hans Opracht.]

We referred to a memorandum, prepared by our 643 and a few of his local friends, 675 and 676 among them, which contains a plan for economic reconstruction in the postwar period. Although aware that this is out of my line, 643 is believed to be a very valuable contact not only by myself but also by 487 who first established contact with him. He is a prominent business man who, we feel, can be depended upon to cooperate with us after G's [Germany's] collapse. Consult your 105, Moffet. Further development of this contact would be advanced if attention were given his document by parties concerned with problems of this nature, the Lehman outfit for example, and some comment sent back here to me which I could relay informally to 643 the next time he comes. Caution must be used in guarding the source. Please notify me when the document reaches you and what steps are taken in reference to it.

Document 2-49

Telegram 6761, October 29, 1943

[This composite collection of reports on Germany contains an early indication of Nazi plans to develop a final defense area and to continue underground operations in the event of defeat. It also includes an erroneous report on the projected disbanding of General Vlasov's anti-Soviet Russian army, which continued to exist until the end of the war.]

. . . According to informant number 1023, the Reich has lost 1200 technicians and 50 U-boats as a result of the aerial bombing of U-boat bases along the shore of the Atlantic and the North Sea during the months of August, September and October.

From other sources come information that the number of desertions into Switzerland from the Reich army has increased greatly. . . . Beginning last month, defense construction has been under way in valleys of the Austrian Tyrol, to the southward of a line between Imst and Bludenz. This work is being carried on by the Todt organization. Training schools for prospective Nazi leaders (Vogelsand being the outstanding one) were the recipients of directions not long since, to cover the contingencies of the loss of this war by the Reich, the disappearance of Hitler or like events. In such cases they were to inter all papers and then continue to maintain the grapevine liaison among party groups toward the end of keeping party principles alive with the view of bringing Nazi rule back again some day. The matter is not being propagandized but, for the second time, a mass draft is under way in the Reich. This move particularly applies to workers in manufacturing plants. The age limit for reserves from the army living abroad has been raised to 50 years and in some cases men even 55 years old are being recalled to active duty. There is a report that General Asov [Vlasov] is under arrest and that the so-called "army of liberation" in the Soviet, which had enlisted Soviet prisoners of war in the Reich, is to be disbanded.

Document 2-50

Telegram 962-63, November 1, 1943

[Communications security was an ongoing problem for OSS Bern. Number 670 is Eduard Waetjen.]

Convinced the Germans have adopted a definite plan by which they are trying to discredit our codes here, so that people will be frightened from getting in touch with us. Not long ago a friend of 670 was arrested after visiting in Switzerland, and a rumor started to the effect that because a cable from the Legation had been deciphered in which his opinions were expressed he was arrested. Have not been able to locate a cable by any American service about him, but he used little discretion in conversations with the chief of an important news agency in Zurich and others. We treated this man with some caution as we knew that he was in contact with Himmler.

Document 2-51

Telegram 965, November 2, 1943

[This message discusses German intelligence and, in particular Walter Schellenberg, head of the SD intelligence service. Number 511 is Swiss intelligence.]

Gamma and Mueller are in charge of Beta Gestapo. Kriminal Polizie [*sic*] Verwaltung is called Kripo. Main responsibility for foreign CE and SI belongs to Schellenberg who is under Alpha. Our information, received from inside channels, is to the effect that Schellenberg intends to try to get in touch with 110 either directly or through indirect means. He often goes to Switzerland and believe he is in touch with 511 chief which bothers us some. You are aware that Abwehr organization under CE is completely separate and primarily concerned with military intelligence; it is frequently in conflict with Schellenberg's outfit.

Document 2-52

Radiotelephone Transmission No. 30, November 2, 1943 (extract)

[In the fall of 1943, Dulles established a regular radiotelephone hookup from his residence to OSS. Several times a week for the duration of the European war, "Bertram L. Johnston" placed an evening call to "Charles Baker Jennings" in Washington. Security constraints limited what Dulles could cover, but he provided a much-valued, up-to-date account of European perceptions and gave his own analysis of events. He also used the evening transmissions, called "flashes," to supplement sensitive information sent by cable. Dulles gained a considerable audience, and by mid-1944 OSS was sending Flash material to the White House on a regular basis.

Secretary of State Hull, British Foreign Secretary Eden, and Soviet Foreign Minister Molotov met, at Moscow, October 19–30, 1943. Basic secret decisions were made including affirmation of the principle of unconditional surrender for the Axis powers, agreement on a May 1944 date for the Anglo-American invasion of France, and establishment of a European Advisory Committee to plan for the postwar settlement. Public pronouncements calling for establishment of an international security organization, an independent Austria, and the punishment of war criminals were made.]

. . .

Moscow Conference

1. The result of the Moscow Conference will probably be received less enthusiastically in this part of the world than in America, because it fails to give any answer to the question of the fate of small states, and in particular the future of the Balkan states, Poland, Finland et cetera. On the whole, however, the public statement gives more in the way of precision than was generally expected; and it is, of course, universally interpreted here as a death-knell to German hopes of separating the Allies prior to German defeat.

2. The German official DNB press reaction is that the communiqué is a mass of words, in which the idea of the League of Nations of unholy memory plays a role; that Stalin succeeded in eliminating consideration of all questions which interest him; and agreement was only reached on the common enmity against the national state of Europe. As regards the Austrian proposals, the DNB suggests that this is only a device to make some reference to the problem of small states without treading on Stalin's toes. That's the end of the German press comment.

3. There are two or three points in the Moscow communiqué which furnish starting points for affirmative activity on our part. First Austria: The precise declaration on Austrian independence should give a basis for building up the increasing separatist tendency there. The first and most important thing is to see that this decision regarding Austria becomes known as widely as possible there. Then we must find ways and means of following it up. In its strategic position in the rear of German communication lines to Italy, any disturbance in Austria will have direct and immediate military significance. Second: The declaration on war criminals should furnish a basis for further steps to undermine the Gestapo. Membership in the Gestapo, if retained to the end of the war, might well be deemed prima facie evidence of participation in the crimes for which the Gestapo organization as a whole is responsible. Those who continue to support the organization by continuing to work for it might well be deemed to be disqualified for any governmental position in the future German state, even though the participation in actual Gestapo work may have been a minor one. If we can break the morale in the lower ranks of the Gestapo, it will begin to crumble. Those at the top of the Gestapo know that there is no salvation for them. We must persuade those at the bottom that the days during which they can rescue themselves are numbered.

Document 2-53

Telegram 967-70, November 3, 1943 (extract)

[Dulles's sources kept him informed about Italian resistance developments.]

I conferred in Lugano on Sunday with 683 and 638. They told me that a Committee of National Liberation was recently established in Rome as a unified action body made up of 5 anti-Fascist parties. This committee has organized regional committees at Genoa, Milan, Venice and Turin, as well as a special committee with headquarters at Milan, known as the Special Committee of National Liberation for Northern Italy. . . .

Document 2-54

Telegram 971-74, November 3, 1943

[Dulles began to offer suggestions for the treatment of postwar Germany at an early stage, as indicated by this cable.]

From 110 to Carib and 154. We will supplement the material below after further study of your interesting suggestions. The following had been drafted before we received your message #764.

There is no way of foretelling the date when Germany will collapse, but when the crackup does come it will be with a suddenness which may catch us unprepared unless painstaking plans are laid now. I have given below a partial list of the subjects which I feel we should be studying in addition to fundamental problems of military occupation and the financial and economic measures that breakdown and possible revolution in Germany will make essential;

1. German personnel whom we could trust to aid in putting an interim economic and financial regime into force and in helping military occupation forces. We have contacts with trusted people within Germany, who hold certain key positions. In addition, there are several scores of refugees here who might be of some assistance, though I do not think we should place too much hope in refugees. We are working on lists of both types of people and are also keeping well-abreast of the activities of secret resistance factions. I believe it unwise, however, for reasons of security, to cable much information about the latter elements.

2. Course of action for rapid seizure of records and documents:

a. To aid in providing evidence for determining guilty persons.

b. For purposes of acquiring any useful data regarding the Far East for use versus Japan.

c. To reveal any military inventions which are in process of development.

d. To obtain data which will aid occupation forces in associated Axis nations and in Germany itself.

e. To uncover all data concerning German SI services all over the world; Nazi SI work in the Far East and South America would be included in this search, as well as Europe itself.

3. Organization for salvaging elements of the German War Machine which might be employed to advantage in the Far East. Defeated and possibly revolutionary German forces may sabotage the fleet and considerable other war material to prevent us

from having it. We may, by careful planning, be able to so arrange things as to aid in saving the greater part of the German fleet, especially subs, if we so wish. . . .

Document 2-55

Telegram 985-88, November 4, 1943

[In this message Dulles continues to prod higher authorities to take a more activist role in support of the Italian resistance, even at the risk of friction with the British.]

As a result of recent re-examination of our Italian activity through Lugano, we are convinced that it is imperative to make a decision soon in regard to coordination here of our activist work in northern Italy with that carried on by Zulu, including backing given to National Liberation Committee and isolated resistance units, SO work and the like. Think that Zulu rather leans toward the opinion that they should take over the bulk of this work by virtue of their present organization in Northern Italy and perhaps also because of 1942 agreement re London's 17. Sincerely hope invasion rendered said agreement null and void. Up to now I have not adopted Zulu's opinion as to what their share in the work should be and will wait until I receive directions from you since I feel that the steps which we take to back resistance in Northern Italy may be important politically and do not want to give impression that we are giving up this activity or turning it over to anyone else. However, closest coordination is necessary because of the small base from which we carry on operations. In addition I realize that we are sadly lacking in qualified personnel to get complete and tangible results and we are badly handicapped by the lack of consulate at Lugano. However, Zulu is not in much better shape than we are though they do have a consulate at Lugano. . . . Believe following action wise in regard to giving support to resistance groups; we should give North Africa exact details regarding needs, locations and numbers so that if they think it advisable, a TSF operator can be sent and thenceforth direct communication maintained with GHQ. On the other hand I am now examining certain SO objectives in this locality that might be dealt with from here, though to do so, supplies from GHQ would be necessary. Then too, the Milan National Liberation Committee is arranging to send delegates soon to contact Zulu and ourselves. Am sorry that up to now have been able to supply so little information concerning resistance groups but generally the couriers that we have sent out have not come back and the Italians here are inclined to avoid taking risks due to the widespread disinterestedness and exhaustion from war. Please send us instructions as soon as possible.

Document 2-56

Telegram 994-95, November 4, 1943

[Dulles continued to monitor the situation in Rumania; one of his top sources was number 636, Constantin Vulcan, the Rumanian cultural attaché in Bern.]

. . . Yesterday number 636 was very persistent in his request for advice to give Rumania. I think 636 acts with his chief's knowledge. He again set forth their willingness to take action provided we could give them any assurance that Rumania would not be handed over to Russia completely. Up to this time I have been careful not to give any advice whatsoever except to say that my personal belief is that United Nations would be more favorably disposed toward them if they had entirely severed connections with the Axis before its ultimate collapse than if they remained with the Axis to the last. Can we give them anything more definite to go on? Am not certain that they are intrepid enough to take any action at present, but circumstances are driving them to it.

Document 2-57

Telegram 1012-16, November 8, 1943 (extract)

[OSS Bern gradually expanded its ties with the left-center Italian opposition. Attom is Ferrucio Parri, a future Premier of Italy.]

In the following message the Milan Liberation Committee will be designated as Motta and one of its important representatives as Attom. I have met Attom of Motta; the former was accompanied by Leo who went to Rome from Algiers not long ago. Am of the opinion that both the Zulu signal corps and our own are familiar with Leo. Zulu and I are convinced that Motta is a serious organization and I am arranging for current contact with it. In view of the danger and difficulty of getting money out of Italy, Motta may require some financial backing here. If additional analysis of their program and requirements reveal that it is justified, SOE, Zulu and I might combine in making an advance to them. Report by Attom places 20,000 to 30,000 scantily armed men as the total number of dependable fighting men that the resistance movement in northern Italy has available to it. Even though there are numbers of Alpini in hiding in the mountains the 4th Army is no longer in existence as a unit. Most of the generals of this unit are of no use with the single exception of Operti. In order to present [prevent] reprisals against the civilian population, which would hinder the work of the organization, the current plan for resistance is confined to organization and not to making direct attacks on the Nazis. . . .

Document 2-58

Telegram 1018-20, November 8, 1943

[On November 1, 1943, the OSS Secret Intelligence Branch transmitted an extensive list of questions concerning conditions in Germany, the Nazi Party, and possible opposition elements. Dulles responded over a period of weeks. Carib is F. L. Mayer; 154 is Whitney Shepardson, Chief of SI.]

This background of facts about Germany should precede answers to your #784 from Carib and 154: organized opposition does not exist in Germany. Gestapo terror effectively prevents their organization. Oppositional groups exist and some of them are known to each other, and are linked together by members who belong to more than one group. The former leaders of German parties who are still in the country are not very important. Many are too old, and a great number of others have died. Still others are in concentration camps or under surveillance of Gestapo. Possibly the young men, who have belonged to secret opposition groups for a long time, and who are unknown to the outside world, will step forward. Both Catholic and Protestant clergymen oppose the Nazis, but are at present unable to act. After the Nazis have been liquidated, the clergy should play an important part. Security makes concealment of names of opposition leaders advisable. Of the 75 percent or more Germans opposed to the Nazi regime, there are only 2 groups who could possibly initiate practical action. These are the labor and military groups. As an example of this point of view, the generals could remove Hitler and the Nazi regime by using the armed men at their disposal. Labor can start sabotage in industrial plants, transportation lines etc. to obstruct the war effort. Hence, propaganda should be directed together with other attempts towards teaching sabotage to workmen and encouraging action by hesitating generals. Code word, Bakus, will be used to refer to our cable and flash answers.

Document 2-59

Telegram 105 to Algiers, November 9, 1943

[OSS Bern often transmitted scraps of information that contributed to the accumulated knowledge of conditions and practices in enemy territory necessary for the successful conduct of espionage and special operations.]

In answer to your #78 about identity cards we report the following: an identity card is the only document required according to a woman who has just reached here after travelling in the Milan, Turin, Genoa and Varese regions. She was also asked to show food card whose number is checked with that of the identity card. Investigation precise method endorsement of numbers on food cards. Military documents are also necessary for men of military age.

Document 2-60

Telegram 1023-28, November 9, 1943

[This report on the situation in Germany was received from number 515, Count Max Egon Hohenlohe von Lagensberg.]

The following are the opinions of our 515, which he gained on a journey to Vienna, Prague and Berlin from which he has just come back. In the course of this journey, he held a lengthy discussion with Herr Himmler and other leading personages. Public morale is stiffer to some extent than it was immediately after the collapse of Il Duce. Other than battling it through, the population does not see any way out. This belief has been caused by Nazi propaganda founded on the unconditional surrender policy and by the publicity about the desperate circumstances of Italy.

On the other side, however, important personages are extremely pessimistic and 515 believes that at any moment dramatic changes might occur. Herr Himmler denies that he would take any action to unseat Hitler, and he realizes that he could never become Chancellor. Nevertheless, Himmler and others foresee the eventuality of Hitler's disappearance although there is a wide tendency to avoid transferring from Hitler the responsibility for the inevitable collapse. There are 3 bases of power at present, according to 515's analysis:

1. Himmler and the SS organization.
2. The Nazi Party organization, Adolf Hitler, Bormann and the Gauleiters.
3. The German Army.

The source is of the opinion that Himmler possesses the best organization, considering the power of the police and the SS. In addition, he has intimate connections with the Air Force and the Navy. Himmler's own thought is to remove power from the Nazi Party and focus it in the Ministries. He is reviving Herr Goering to offset the growing strength of Speer in the economic matters. Nevertheless, Speer is non-political.

Some of the leaders of the Nazi Party and most of the Army leaders feel that their sole hope is ultimate agreement with the Soviet Union and they generally understand that the biggest hindrance in the way of doing this is Adolf Hitler. At present, Hitler and his clique do not favor rapprochement with the Soviet Union. They would rather deal with the Western nations. (This report is prior to the Moscow agreement. The main interest of the source is that the German situation be settled in an orderly manner, to safeguard his property interests. The person most able to do this, he feels, is Himmler. His impression that Himmler is antagonistic to an orientation toward the Soviet Union should be viewed with some caution. The above parenthetical remarks are by 110.)

Neubacher may take the place of von Ribbentrop, who is through. Himmler is withdrawing his people from the Foreign Office. Manstein is in semi-disgrace and no longer on the Soviet front. Wolff has been dispatched to Italy by Himmler, to be his representative there.

Mussolini is creating difficulty and wishes to retire from his current position. The Nazis are sorry that they aided him in establishing a new Fascist Party, for they would rather have an outright German occupation of Italy and no Italian political involvements. The source understands that it has been decided to carry on a semi-guerrilla war in Italy, retreating northward. It is probable that there will be a substantial evacuation of forces from North Italy. Von Rommel [*sic*] is also in partial eclipse. There is a rumor that Jodl has been selected as OKH representative for strategy on Italy.

There are opposing views about the secret rocket weapon. Opinions differ whether it should be employed now, because of the serious doubts as to its effectiveness and a dread of the effect on morale should it turn out to be worthless. There is wide apprehension whether they will be able to maintain the Soviet front this winter, and there is extreme indecisiveness in top circles concerning future policy. There are no Nazi Party leaders or Army generals who have the ability or the wish or the political courage to begin action, even though the opinion is general that the Fuehrer may not last much longer.

Document 2-61

Radiotelephone Transmission No. 34, November 9, 1943

[In this evening "flash" message, Dulles set forth information on conditions in Germany. He addressed particular questions presented by the OSS SI Branch in telegram 784-88, November 1.]

. . .

Germany

What follows is number one in the Bakus series. I shall number the paragraphs for reference. More will follow on succeeding days.

1. The following are the leading party men, given in order of their importance: Hitler, Himmler, Bormann, Goebbels, Goering, Ley, Ribbentrop, Rosenberg. Besides there are two expert executives of outstanding importance, closely affiliated with the Nazi Party. Saukel, charged with the mobilization of labor in Germany and German-controlled territory. He is considered very able, much abler than Ley, head of the German state-controlled labor union. Then Speer, Minister for War Production. The latter's position is steadily gaining in importance, and important economic structures, which up to now had been under the control of the Ministry of Economics, have been transferred to Speer's Ministry. In this connection it should be mentioned that Fischer, the administrator for the German oil industry and one of the leading men in the I. G. Farben concern, who so far has been under the authority of the Reichswirtschaftsministerium, will probably be placed under the authority of Speer. Thereby the entire German oil industry, including that of German-controlled Europe, would be placed under Speer's command. In the economic field Speer has surpassed Ley and Funk.

2. The relations between the above men are difficult to analyze and they undergo changes from time to time. However, it may be said that there is a certain antagonism between Himmler and Bormann; also between Himmler and Ribbentrop.

Except for Hitler, the relationship of most of the above men to the military is cool. German military leaders bow to Hitler, but to hardly anyone else in the party. The gauleiters are the men who are most important in the party hierarchy, because they are directly under Hitler, and in Hitler's absence under Bormann. They are responsible to no one except to Hitler and Bormann. Hitler passes his orders to the gauleiters through Bormann. They are the administrators of the German Gau—administrative districts which in the majority of cases follow the frontiers of the former German states and Prussian provinces. The gauleiters are dictators in their respective districts, and are more powerful than the former kings of Bavaria, Saxony, etc. Some of the better-known gauleiters are: Goebbels, gauleiter of the city of Berlin; Terboven, the gauleiter for the Rhineland, and at the same time administrator for Norway—a ruthless and bloodthirsty fellow; Koch, gauleiter for East Prussia, at the same time administrator for the Ukraine; Mutsthman, gauleiter for Saxony; Hantke, gauleiter for Silesia—able, said to be the son of a locomotive engineer, and former assistant of Goebbels; Sprenger, gauleiter of Hessen, including Frankfurt; Wagner, gauleiter for Baden and Alsace; Gieszler, acting gauleiter in Bavaria; Baldur von Schirach, gauleiter for Austria; Kaufmann, gauleiter for Hamburg and at the same time commissioner for the merchant marine.

3. Other important men of the regime are Frank, the governor of Poland; Frank (a man by the same name), secretary of state in the protectorate of Bohemia and Moravia. Frick, former Minister of the Interior, is today of no importance; his position as Reich Protector of Bohemia and Moravia is more or less nominal. For many years he has been an opponent of Gestapo methods, but he has been unable to make his opposition at all effective.

4. The principal political changes in the administration of Germany in recent times has been the appointment of Himmler as Minister of the Interior. His disappointment at the terror in Germany has greatly increased. The Volksgerichtsof (People's Court) is working overtime passing death sentences for offenses which up to now had been considered as minor ones. For instance, anyone expressing the view that the war might be lost is liable to be punished by death. The change in the situation is characterized by the following fact: formerly it was preferable for anyone accused of so-called political crimes to be brought before the jurisdiction of the court, rather than to fall into the hands of the Gestapo. Now the reverse is true: it is preferable to fall into the hands of the Gestapo rather than into those of the People's Court, which in most instances passes death sentences. Needless to say, however, the Gestapo has not become any milder in its practices.

5. The former political leaders of Germany play a role of limited importance, and as to the future not too much should be expected from them. Some of them are in concentration camps with their health broken; some, although technically free, are under the surveillance of the Gestapo; some are compromised by having accepted pensions from the Nazi government. Many of them are dead and some are too old to be of any consequence.

Document 2-62

Telegram 1054-55, November 12, 1943

[This message contains a bombing report from the French Alps and a proposal for a follow-up special operation.]

Concerning the Modane raid, an SNCF employee reports that the car bars [barns?] and the station were destroyed by fire. Whether there will be an interruption of traffic is yet unknown. The informant reports that there are 15 double pylons between the tunnel and Modane station and that if these were destroyed, traffic would be halted for quite some time. The informant is in contact with people at Modane who are prepared, if we are able to deliver equipment to them, to execute this project.

Please inform us if you have any interest now in an SO operation here. If we are able to supply the landing grounds, is there any chance that equipment can be dropped by parachute?

Document 2-63

Radiotelephone Transmission No. 37, November 13, 1943 (extract)

[Dulles commented frequently on Nazi propaganda and the broad geopolitical aspects of the war.]

Germany

1. German propaganda is stressing more and more that three essentially non-European powers, namely the United States, Great Britain and Russia, are proposing to settle the fate of Europe, and that they will settle this in a way to make Central and Western Europe into a vassal state whose economic life and future will be controlled solely in the interests of non-European powers. This propaganda is having some effect, taken in conjunction with the ceaseless German propaganda that the only interest of the United States is business and that representatives of big business are following in the wake of the armies to insure that we get all the economic plums which the newly-occupied territories can offer. . . .

Document 2-64

Telegram 115-21 to Algiers, November 15, 1943

[As this message indicates, Dulles's heavy reliance on French intelligence sources within Switzerland (472) created political difficulties. Number 520 is General Legge, U.S. Military Attaché; 511 is Swiss intelligence.]

. . . The following is confidential: Both 520 and myself believe that the organization under Pourchot is a source of information of the greatest value. 110 assumed the financing of the Deuxieme Bureau a little while after it was suppressed by the Vichy Government. It is mainly because agents use Consulate and Embassy covers that the bureau is still able to function under present peculiar conditions. The Consulate and Embassy staffs are largely anti-Vichy and are working whole-heartedly for the cause, although they are technically still under Vichy. Their services have been much more worthwhile than their rumor-mongering critics in the French Colony of Lausanne, Geneva and so forth.

Several senior consul officials and the principal members of the Embassy staff (with the exception of the Ambassador who has never interfered with Pourchot's activities) made it clear several months ago to Algiers that it was their wish to place themselves at the disposal of Algiers and were asked for the time being that they stay at their posts. An understandable request has now been made by Algiers that anti-Vichy personnel discontinue their connections with the Embassy and Consul. I doubt whether it is fitting to press them (except perhaps in the case of 472 people) to place their futures in danger by keeping their current affiliations even though in view of the circumstances these people are of greater value in their current posts than they would be if they left them to join the refugee colony here. However, a distinct loss to Allied work here will be suffered by wholesale withdrawal of current consular and Embassy employees and even if Pourchot should agree to stay, 472's services in particular will be jeopardized. It is axiomatic that any employees placed by Lavalle [Laval] and sent here can be expected to cooperate with the Gestapo. It will be hard for Pourchot and his staff to work under the same roof with them with any degree of safety. On the other hand Pourchot's withdrawal will place his ability to keep on working in even graver danger. This is due to the fact that the Swiss may be forced to assign Pourchot a residence outside of Bern and forbid the continuance of his current activities.

Pourchot has been of the greatest value as a contact with various branches of 511 services, in addition to his Battle Order information. We were just working on the development of a new German service through 511 and Pourchot. Naturally, Rivet would have access to all of Pourchot's material.

I recommend that you discreetly talk over the foregoing with Rivet and Massigli, to whom Pourchot is sending a wire through us, and determine whether they have any suggestions to offer. Massigli is a personal friend of mine and understands the problems of the Swiss situation completely, so you may point out to him that 520 and myself have read his cable exchanges via the Legation in strict confidence and understand Algiers' desire that the Consular and Embassy people here end the ambiguity of their position. Certainly neither Pourchot nor the others should be requested to keep their Consular-Embassy affiliations unless expressly asked to do so by Algiers and with sufficient assurance that their fellow countrymen will eventually be clarified on the nature of the sacrifices that they are making. If, as an alternative, it is suggested by Algiers that Pourchot's work should be continued under the cover of the delegation which Algiers is thinking of setting up here, I would add that in view of the delegation's delicate position as well as the precedents set by Swiss policy of neutrality, that I doubt if this type of work should be undertaken by the delegation until its situation is solidly assured. In addition . . . delegation will not have consular cover, and in all probability only attenuated diplomatic cover. I have discussed the above message with 520 and the Minister in its entirety.

Document 2-65

Telegram 1085-87, November 17, 1943 (extract)

[This message concerns the funding of European labor elements via OSS Bern.]

. . . The fact that no word from Eva has reached 328 for some time is causing him concern. 328 was also given to understand that funds for French socialists would be forthcoming at the present time; he has, however, received none. We find that 328, who is at present engaged in active work with us in setting up lines to Germany, is a completely top-notch individual, and is invaluable for the maintenance of our contacts with syndicalist and socialist organizations in Germany, France, and Italy. He is hesitant to let us provide him with financial assistance; therefore it is of great importance that we make it easier for him to secure funds from American labor circles. I am, however, giving him an advance in French francs to the amount of about 8,000 Swiss francs, since the situation in French socialist work is at a critical stage. Kindly investigate the possibilities of aid from your end, and advise us of the prospects. . . .

Document 2-66

Telegram 1093-95, November 18, 1943

[A November 2 cable from the OSS in Washington suggested that Bern contacts encourage Poles and Czechs in German units in France to escape to Spain. OSS Bern suggested the alternative that they be organized where they were for future use. Number 284 is Max Shoop; 498, source "Simpson," apparently was a Czech resident in Switzerland.]

Looking at this procedure from here, we do not think that it is a very wise idea. Only a limited number of people would probably be able to escape to Spain in the winter, and for reasons of security access to this route of escape should be given to specialists only. Any attempts to escape in large numbers would probably destroy the route. When the hour for action arrives, we think that the Poles and Czechs in France will be of more use in France than in North Africa. 284 has talked over this problem with 498, and the idea developed from their talks of trying to work out some joint action on the part of the Poles and Czechs with the objective of secretly naming, for each unit which is made up of a good sized contingent of each nationality, a single leader who could assume command in the event of a revolt. At many points in France there is a like situation to the one you describe as existing at St. Etienne. We might be able give some help from this end if the above proposal is agreeable to both London and Washington. . . .

Document 2-67

Telegram 1096-98, November 19, 1943

[This message responds to criticism of the quality of intelligence data provided by Bern and casts light on the composition of the Dulles network.]

The strength of Algiers' reaction, as expressed in their #86 to SI data is appreciated. I would be grateful for any recommendations to better the service. The principal obstacle is the lack of trained people able to take care of the quantity of material obtained. The largest part of French Battle Order Intelligence reaches us from 8 different networks, to-wit, 472 relying on 511 CER service via 616, and 4 established by 284. In addition, there are numerous individual sources. Generally speaking, we are not in touch with the individual agents in the network, since the labor of dozens of individual agents is represented in the information which comes across the border in bulk. Although I am confident of reliability of individual networks, I cannot maintain control over the sources used by individual agents. Hence it is possible that "plants" may take place.

Since we do not think it advisable to freeze our ideas, reports which are at variance with previous items have been consciously included.

I have no liking for performing a somewhat haphazard job in this field which I realize the situation to be at present. Would you rather have us continue current arrangement of submitting bulk transmittal and having you make your own appraisal or should we, by sending less material, endeavor to make a careful cross check ourselves. In the interim, attempting to reorganize this work within the limits our small staff allows.

Your #844 and similar reports prove of great value because they aid us in the prompt elimination of a useless agent. Furthermore, in order to discard unsuitable agents in various services, it might be to our advantage if you, Algiers or London, upon occasion, could advise us of possible plants or points of error.

Document 2-68

Telegram 1128-30, November 23, 1943
(extract)

[While users were critical of Bern's order of battle information at this point in the war, Dulles did receive moral support from Washington on his overall performance.

On September 22, Colonel Buxton and General Magruder, the number two and three ranking OSS officials, cabled: "We are pleased to say well done and extend the highest appreciation for the excellence of your advice and high calibre of your reports." On November 19 the SI Branch extended congratulations and thanks on the occasion of Dulles's first anniversary in Bern.]

. . . Many thanks for your #617 and #863. The credit for the work belongs to the entire group here, which is small but hard-working. Will you please let us know the results of the Thanksgiving Day football games?

Document 2-69

Telegram 1140-45, November 24, 1943
(extracts)

[Having again consulted with Bakach-Bessenyey (684), the Hungarian minister in Bern, Dulles assesses the reasons Budapest was reluctant to break with the Germans.]

The following is a report on an additional and full review with 684 of the Hungarian situation. 684's principals do not like parachutage but they are willing to accept and work with our agent. 684 wishes to know whether our agent could be gotten across the border. He proposes Croatia and he is requesting his people to give the precise particulars. . . .

The indecisiveness and slowness of his people have clearly disappointed 684. He has gone so far as to intimate that he will finally resign unless they take more realistic action. He conveyed the impression that Kallay has suggested that unless we furnish some proof of our power to defend Hungary against Germany, or give some other encouragement, they ought to sit tight and develop Hungarian armaments. . . .

For broad background information, Hungary feels that her status under the Treaty of Trianon is the worst fate which can befall her. It is not likely that the Hungarians will take a line of action which carries immediate risks with it, for the following reasons: we do not offer any signs of betterment, the Soviet Union is almost sure to support Yugoslav aspirations, the Hungarians feel that the Soviet Union may wish to repay Rumania for ceding Bessarabia and similar territory by backing Rumania's claim on Transylvania, and, lastly, the Hungarian population is easy-going and not given to heroism. It is their hope that at the time of collapse, should they be able to keep local order and keep their army whole, that they can find some solution.

Document 2-70

Telegram 1151-53, November 26, 1943

[This message transmits a report on conditions in Germany received from Carl Burckhardt ("B"), member of the International Red Cross and former High Commissioner of Danzig.]

The following is reported by B who has recently returned from a short visit to Germany. He was there on business for his organization. B states that there is no evidence that Himmler proposes to move against Hitler, although Himmler's power is increasing. If H is persuaded at last that there is no hope of making a deal with the Anglo-Saxons he may flop over, although at the present time he does not favor the Russian solution. A reversal of Alliances is still hoped for by the Nazis.

Germany's prospects leave B pessimistic. B can not see a personality or authority coming to the fore that would be able to surrender in time and still keep internal order. B is of the opinion that the odds are heavily in favor of Communism arising in Germany. The leaders of Germany are aware that she is defeated but others are still in hope that Hitler can work a miracle like an agreement with Russia or some such stunt. The only force which keeps the people together is Hitler and if he should vanish, rapid degeneration would follow, accompanied by war among would-be successors, all of which would be followed by Bolshevism. All the Nazis that B saw ladled out the identical sop about Germany only fighting to save the world from Bolshevism. For aiding Russia, both Great Britain and the United States are traitors to civilization. B affirms that in view of the vast capacity that the Nazis have for self delusion and overlooking the facts, that they forget that 3 years ago they were ready to share the world with the Bolos as their partners and really seem to believe the statements made above.

Document 2-71

Telegram 1157-58, November 27, 1943

[The relationship of Admiral Wilhelm Canaris, Chief of the Abwehr, German military intelligence, to the Allies may never be understood with precision. It is known that he maintained indirect contact with British intelligence, permitted his organization to become a center of resistance elements, and paid for his dubious loyalty to Hitler with his life. Dulles assigned him source number 659, but the extent of Canaris's actual and intentional assistance is obscured in a thicket of intermediaries, including Abwehr agents and Swiss intelligence, and oblique connections. On November 12, 1943, Dulles reported that Canaris might soon be visiting Switzerland.]

The following data is secret: it is thought by the German SI that the United States received notice from the Soviet Union that the latter does not require additional tanks from the United States. 659 gave the impression to his friends here, in the course of the visit reported in my #1053, that there was no sign of Allied troop concentrations for important action on the continent in the near future. He also gave the impression that the Nazis were amazed that the Allies had not attacked the Balkan states, because of the impossible situation of Nazi lines of communications in that region. . . .

Document 2-72

Telegram 1159-61, November 27, 1943

[This message contains suggested themes for psychological warfare against Germany. Number 678 is Gerald Mayer of OWI.]

A large part of the bombed-out refugees from Berlin . . . are being evacuated to Bavaria. Considering the increasing anti-Prussian sentiment in Bavaria, I recommend that this situation be utilized by dropping leaflets and by clever radio propaganda in order to aggravate the anti-Prussian feeling. Together with Bavarians, 678 and I are preparing the wording of such leaflets. . . . The following has to do especially with reports of the Berlin raids: one of the gravest aspects may be that Speer's ministry was damaged and that their files on construction activities and war production were seemingly destroyed. The most important ministry at this time with reference to war and other economic topics is Speer's. Considering the huge quantity of foreigners in the Todt organization, I recommend as an additional propaganda weapon that workers be told by radio propaganda that they should take advantage of the chance to get out of the organization, since all files have been destroyed. . . .

Document 2-73

Telegram 1162-68, November 29, 1943
(extract)

[Dulles and OSS Washington began planning for the postwar occupation of Germany and other liberated territory at an early stage. This cable discusses the teams that would be dispatched immediately upon the end of the war. Dulles did indeed head such a "German Mission" after VE-Day, although he did not assume his new responsibilities until July 1945. Numbers 493, 244, 476, 477, and 110 are, respectively, Loofbourow, Stalder, Gaevernitz, Tyler, and Dulles.]

Concerning the collapse of Germany, at whatever date it may occur, there will be a concomitant if not a prior collapse in the satellite and Nazi occupied countries. Presumably, arrangements are being formulated to prepare for military administration and occupation. A parallel arrangement pertaining to civilian representation should be prepared to coordinate affairs, which are not of a military nature, in each one of the different ex-enemy centers and in the capitals of the liberated areas of the Allied countries. This problem was not adequately thought out after the collapse in 1918. I know this from my own experience; our representatives arrived at their posts late and poorly equipped technically to cope with the difficult conditions as they then existed. Upon the collapse of Nazi Germany the difficulties will be vastly larger.

If this is in line with your plans, we could get a small group in readiness here which might include 493, 244, 476, 477 and 110 to go on at a moment's notice to a point chosen in Germany, in order to keep you informed of developments. This point may or may not be Berlin. We have contact with a German group which, from the information we now have, seems to be the most probable to seize the power, at least temporarily, when Germany collapses. The exception will be if there is a Communist government. We have additional sources there which can be rapidly developed and, in the meantime, I am of the opinion that a workmanlike job can be done until, in the light of developments, the form of our more permanent civilian representation is determined. The shipment of this group should not be put off until safe conditions prevail and quite ready to take the chances involved. . . .

Document 2-74

Telegram 7520, November 30, 1943
(extracts)

[This message concerns Yugoslavia. General Milan Nedic was the chief of the puppet Serbian government; 681 is M. Z. D. Dragoutinovitch of the Yugoslav Legation in Bern; Ante Pavelich was the head of the Croatian puppet government; Draja Mihailovich was leader of the pro-monarchist Serbian resistance.]

. . . The latest conference between Neditch and Hitler has been reported to me by informant No. 681 as follows:

Two requests were made by Neditch, the first being that the Serbian Army be enlarged to 120,000 soldiers. The other request was that the right of Serbia to that portion of the old area which is now under occupation by Bulgarian soldiers to Montenegro, South Dalmatia with Eastern Bosnia and Cattaro be recognized.

In principle these requests were complied with except that it was only promised that the Eastern Bosnia frontier would be rectified. Surmia was also demanded by Neditch but this was refused. Neditch also requested diplomatic representation in other countries, but this was also rejected by Hitler. According to reports the latter showed much sympathy for Neditch. He is also reported to have told Neditch that Pavelich was useless and that he (Neditch) was the only constructive individual in this region. . . .

According to information given to 819, the allegation that negotiations are going on between Mihailovitch and the Germans is not true. The objective of Mihailovitch is to keep his forces intact for the future and with this in mind it is possible that there exists a silent agreement between Mihailovich's people and the Nazis to keep from clashing with one another. It is the belief of 819 that Maeditch [Neditch] is probably in accord with the general policy; that is, that he probably favors the playing of a waiting game policy. . . .

Document 2-75

Telegram 1183-85, December 1, 1943 (extract)

[In this message, Dulles provides additional information on Mihailovich and on his own opinion. Number 476 is Gaevernitz; 521 is British intelligence in Switzerland.]

. . . 3. The following, from 476, comes from a person close to the Nazi SI: Whenever it was a case of fighting the "Communists" in Serbia, Mihailovitch has been in collaboration with the Nazis. Mihailovitch's relations with the Nazis is becoming more intimate as his relations with the British cool off. Some of the funds which the British paid to M. passed through the Nazis hands and part was pocketed by the German agents. The following is from 110: There are extremely conflicting reports concerning Mihailovitch. Informed by 521 that his people have sent him word indicating that London has evidence of collaboration between the Nazis and M. In my opinion, I lean toward the belief that both M. and possibly Neditch will be with us when the time comes, even though the foregoing information is qualifiedly true. Today the Croatian Partisans are a more important anti-Nazi element than M. For my own guidance, I would like to have your opinions on the information contained in this message.

Document 2-76

Telegram 7535, December 1, 1943

[OSS Bern here supplies additional information on the position of neutral Turkey.]

. . . On November 27, 1943, Bergery, the French Ambassador to Turkey, who was on his way to Vichy, passed through Geneva, Switzerland, and in a conversation with acquaintances there he is said to have made the following statements.

Unless the Allied Nations are able to place 70 divisions of troops on Turkish soil, Turkey will not go into the war. The British Secretary of State for Foreign Affairs was unable to convince the Premier of Turkey.

Military authorities of Turkey state that Russia has 400 divisions of troops at the present time and that the Germans have only 275 Divisions which can be brought against them. These authorities further say that a third of these divisions consist of less than 7,000 men each, and that a great number of them are in a bad state of fatigue.

The view taken by the Turks is that should Turkey enter the war, it invites occupation of her territory by either the Germans or the Russians. The aviation craft of

Turkey could hold out only about seven days, and within thirty days their aviators would not be able to fight at all because their stock of spare parts would be exhausted by then. There is a feeling among the Turks that just as the Fifth Column assisted Germany in Poland and France, so would a similar set-up made up of hundreds of thousands of men which the Russians have disposed of, help Russia when she invades countries occupied by the Germans.

Bergery also said that Turkish military circles expect the war to end this coming June, but that these same circles are also of the opinion that the Allies and the Russians will be at war with each other by October, 1944.

The above is interesting principally because it may be an indication of the sort of thing that Bergery is reporting to his people as well as to Nazi friends in this country. There is a possibility that it is a reflection of what Bergery has been told by the Turks.

Document 2-77

Telegram 1187-88, December 2, 1943

[Dulles knew Noel Field, number 394, former League of Nations official and relief worker, from the interwar period when both were involved in disarmament matters for the State Department. There is convincing evidence that Field was a Soviet agent in the 1930s. In 1949 he disappeared behind the Iron Curtain, only to be imprisoned in Hungary and identified in Stalin's East European purges as a spy for Allen Dulles. This background begs many questions about Field's service to OSS Bern during the war, which available documents do little to answer. They do establish that Field worked intimately with Dulles on relief and refugee matters. Robert Dexter was the Lisbon director of the Unitarian Service Committee.]

The following is from 394, and is for Dexter. Kindly be advised, and notify Lisbon, of the following: "According to the Swiss Legation in Vichy, French authorities holding singercox (sic) funds for USC and ready to turn over to an appointed representative of France for relief purposes. Dr. Zimmer is doing first rate work and is in contact with both foreign and French groups. However, he is short of money. Subject to conditions set up by you or me, e.g., for relief for refugees lately freed from the Castres prison, or for medical assistance for Maquis, kindly authorize payment of the money under discussion to Dr. Zimmer. Kindly direct him to utilize me as alternate intermediary, as he seems to find it difficult to keep in touch with you."

The following is from 110. Consult Joy's message for 394 which was sent through Lisbon and which concerned relief. Are you able to furnish us with any background for 394's guidance? Because of the necessity for prior organization, it is improbable that a large amount can be wisely spent before the 1st of next year. Neither blocked francs nor dollars can be used. Moreover, the entire matter necessitates careful handling with Swiss authorities.

Document 2-78

Radiotelephone Transmission No. 43, December 3, 1943

[In this transmission, Dulles summarizes his views on the French political situation. He was assisted in this statement by OSS staff member Royall Tyler and had the views of his numerous French associates in Switzerland on which to draw.]

. . . Any broad generalizations with regard to France would be erroneous, except for the generalization that they are practically unanimous in their hatred of the Germans and in their contempt for Italy. There are many currents of political thinking, depending on the social strata and ideology of the individual. These currents are more and more coming to the surface as the French recover from the stupor of their defeat.

3. The number of persons who are pro-German in France today is negligible. They are chiefly those who have sold themselves to the Germans and who would be irretrievably compromised when the Allied victory comes. These few will inevitably fade from the scene. In addition there are some persons, chiefly in the higher economic strata, and including some regular army officers, who are not pro-German but who would prefer some compromise solution which would not entail a Russian victory. Their attitude is motivated by fear of socialistic legislation, or even of a communist movement which would deprive them of their privileges or social prerogatives.

4. Among the great bulk of the people who are frantically anti-German, and desire an Allied victory, there are many divergent currents. Among the young and the militant Gaullism dominates. It is not personal allegiance to the General, but rather allegiance to the ideal of resistance to Germany which General de Gaulle incarnates for these Frenchmen. Many of them realize de Gaulle's personal shortcomings, but they do homage to the fact that he has never wavered and has never compromised. They also feel that with all his blunders he has fought to defend French interests and French prestige.

5. Communism is gaining strength. The communist methods and cell organization, which are necessarily incident to any effective underground movement, have given the communists an important place in the resistance. Further, the communists who billeted [benefited?] from their long-time clandestine organization are probably better organized and better armed than the other groups.

6. Of course Russian prestige is immense throughout the continent of Europe, because of her victories over Germany; and many who are not communists themselves feel that a close collaboration with Russia, for the next few decades at least, would be the safest insurance for France.

7. Here I wish to interpolate that there are many, particularly in bourgeois, labor union and parliamentary circles, who, while favoring collaboration with Russia, still view with alarm the importance assumed in Algiers by the French communist depu-

ties who were imprisoned in 1939 for trying to sabotage the war against Germany. While the French are ready to collaborate with Russian communism, they do not trust French communism. They feel that Russia has worked through the bloody stages of its communism and has given up all revolutionary ideas. Therefore Soviet Russia is a state with which one can well cooperate. On the other hand they believe that if the French communists came into power in France, France would then have to go through the same bloody revolution as Russia. These persons feel that the French communists belong to the old Trotsky, rather than to the Stalin school of thought.

8. To the right of the communists and the groups of militant resistance there is the large body of the French peasant, bourgeois, and small business and professional class. Of course certain of these are directly in the resistance movement, but, for technical as well as often for family or professional and business reasons, most of them are not participating actively in the resistance groups. They represent the persons who are likely to mold public opinion in the future France. While they are probably Gaullist in the sense of supporting the ideals of Gaullism, they are not particularly happy at developments in Algiers, partly because of the apparent communist influence there, to which I have referred, and partly for other reasons which I will note. They would like to see Algiers devote itself more to military, and less to political matters. They regret the apparent strife between Algiers on the one hand and Americans and British on the other. Many of them suspect de Gaulle of overweening personal political ambition of the Boulanger variety. They do not like the somewhat mystical hero-worship of the man de Gaulle by his young adherents. The French people have an inborn skepticism of their political leaders. Among these people are a vast number of government functionaries in various state administrations, prefects, and all the people attached to prefectures, railway employees, and the like. These people have had no chance to join Algiers. To keep the machinery of administration going, they have had to stay at their posts. They resent the fact that Algiers ascribes all virtues to itself, and forgets the day-by-day, unremunerative, thankless task which those at home are doing in order to feed, clothe and keep the life of the country going under the almost impossibly difficult conditions existing in France today.

9. These people do not want any military or political dictatorship, and despite all the weaknesses of the Third Republic, they wish to see a parliamentary regime restored. They are entirely conscious that there was something gravely wrong with this regime as it existed in the last years before the war. They do not quite know what it was, but they are seriously disquieted to see many of the men who were closely associated with the regime in the pre-war years now coming back into power in Algiers.

10. To conclude: In France today the apprehension of a fratricidal civil war and terror is only second to their fear and hatred of the Germans as an underlying motivating force. Yet they also fear the danger of a military dictatorship. What they would probably like most of all would be a short occupation, chiefly by Americans,

until they had time, undisturbed by personal vendettas and civil strife, to get on their feet and organize their own political life, their own police and army, and put their own new chosen leaders in the saddle. They do not want a French colonial army under either Giraud or de Gaulle to play this role. . . .

Document 2-79

Telegram 1212-15, December 4, 1943 (extract)

[This message records a conversation between the Hungarian minister, Bakach-Bessenyey (684) and Royall Tyler (477) on December 3.]

. . . 684 remarked that while he understood thoroughly that no assurances for post-war could be given to a country which had declared war on us, when it was our policy to give no such assurance even to allies, his people nevertheless complained that no positive encouragement was given to them. The extremely difficult position of his government should at all times be kept in mind. If German occupation should result from the course adopted by his government, a great number of those in the ruling circles would most likely be annihilated. In spite of this, 684 knows that unless some major act of violence occurs before the end of the war to show that Hungary is an unwilling partner of Germany, it would be a disaster. His only hope is that occupation by the Nazis may be limited to the briefest possible period.

684 stated that Goebbels would find an invaluable confirmation for his most effective piece of propaganda in the speech by Marshal Smuts recorded in the Swiss papers on the 3rd of December. This propaganda charges that victory by the Allies would result in turning Europe over to Russia, with the exception of the small maritime nations which would come under British domination.

Document 2-80

Telegram 7607, December 4, 1943

[The Allied air offensive intensified in late 1943. On November 18, British bombers carried out the heaviest air raid against Berlin to that point in the war. Number 513, a Polish source, provided an account of bombing results. This message was transmitted by State Department channels and circulated to the office of James Clement Dunn, Adviser on Political Relations.]

The bombing by air of the Reich capital has proven that the essential line of supply and transportation to the north Soviet front is susceptible of being put out of commission for 120 to 148 hours and that the repetition of such bombings at 5 or 6 day intervals can disrupt such service permanently.

The Germans are now increasing the speed of goods movement on inland waterways, particularly that between Stettin and Berlin. Along this waterway are two points that would be vulnerable bomb targets; viz: a trifle over six miles to the eastward of Eberswalde the Liepe locks and also right at the latter town, where a concrete aqueduct conveys the canal over the railway which runs from Stettin to Berlin. Whenever there is an air raid alert, an artificial fog is sent up to screen the ship raising device and Liepe locks. . . .

Exclusive of prisoners of war and soldiers, some 7,100 persons were killed in the big air raids, and 10,000 homes and 100 factories producing war material were demolished. The plans for passive defense in the Reich capital failed to function entirely and chaos was general. . . .

Document 2-81

Telegram 1220-25, December 6, 1943

[This message describes a conversation between Bulgarian Minister Kiosseivanov (491), and René Charron, number 492.]

Our 491 Kiss informed 492 as follows Dec. 3: The Council of Regency and the Bulgarian government are completely German controlled. A little known archeologist who strayed into politics, Filoff is dazzled by his own rise and piles on evidence of his adoration of the Germans who raised him to position. Cyril has no prestige or authority, is a colorless personality, and unable to pursue a national policy. An SS gangster, the German Minister, alone has authority in a government composed of puppets; he knows of all government decisions before they are put into effect.

According to Kiss, a coup d'état is the country's only possible salvation. He thinks a brave group called Zveno is contemplating this move. In the group are some army men, Damian Veltcheff, and Kimon Gueorguieff. The latter two had coup d'état experience in 1934; it was during this unsuccessful coup that Kiss saved Veltcheff's life. Gueorguieff possesses great prestige.

Veltcheff was once head of the military school at Sofia, has kept faithful friends in the Army and seeks vengeance against the dynasty. In addition, these men have contacts with communism. Kiss maintains these men have the means to upset the government and put in its place a government of national union.

Kiss is ready to cooperate in case this movement exists as he feels it does. He is staying with his job here just to have access to the means of communication and information related to this. He is, however, afraid that if the movement began, it would run away with itself and drag Bulgaria directly into communism. Kiss is of the opinion that in case revolution comes before Russian occupation, he can hope that in the light of the Moscow agreements occupation would be not wholly Russian in nature, but inter-Allied. If, however, the Russians occupy Bulgaria as a result of military operations and prior to the overthrow of the current government, he believes country is ready for it and communism will be the result. With Veltcheff and Gueorguieff and their group, Kiss wants to work for the first-mentioned objective. He does not have authentic information about the plans of this group, however, and dares not communicate via his courier on the matter. Realizing it would reach us, he suggested the following to 492: that without alluding to this discussion or Kiss, we should find out from Momtchiloff in London if the latter knows or thinks that Zveno have any plan of action of the sort discussed above. Kiss would be agreeable to contacting Momtchiloff and trying to correlate their respective actions if he receives a favorable reply to the above. He thinks he may have a way of getting in touch with K and G and making arrangements for him to dispatch his confidant to Bern.

For 105 and Jackpot from 110: In reference to following up above in London, kindly arrange this between yourselves. We will wait for instructions before acting further. Cannon at State is well acquainted with Kiss, and we think the latter's position in Bulgaria is such that this cooperation in the plan would play an important part in its possible success.

Document 2-82

Radiotelephone Transmission No. 44, December 6, 1943

[In this message, Dulles reports the reaction in Switzerland to the assertion by Prime Minister Smuts of South Africa that Russia would dominate Europe after the war.]

General

1. The speech of Marshal Smuts is continuing to cause a real sensation here, not only among the Swiss, but among arrivals here from neighboring countries. No speech which has been delivered in the past year has caused as much comment. In the camp of the enemy it is, of course, acclaimed as evidence of their thesis that the Anglo-Saxons are ready to deliver all of Europe to the Russians. It has made more difficult the task of our friends here who have been maintaining that an Allied victory did not mean a Russianized Europe.

2. It is possibly difficult for you in Washington to realize the extent of the real apprehension of Russia in this part of the world. They view Russia as the same country which invaded Finland and the Baltic States, and made the pact with Germany dividing Poland and Rumania. They view developments in the Balkans and in France as evidence that Russian domination may extend far beyond the limits of the 1941 boundaries. I have had many talks recently with persons from Hungary and Rumania, where fear of Russia is the dominant preoccupation. Now these people see in Smuts' speech the confirmation of their fears.

3. I give the above merely so that you may get an idea of opinion in this part of the world—not as sharing these fears and apprehensions. However, in judging psychological factors as affecting the reactions of peoples and governments, we must necessarily reckon with these feelings in judging the European situation.

4. The Smuts speech is accepted generally as being an authoritative statement of British policy. It is assumed here that it could not have been made during the critical days of the conferences among the heads of State unless it had also been approved by the British government. Whether it was approved on our side of the Atlantic is a question that is generally being asked, and to which no answer can be given. In a few quarters I have heard it suggested that the speech never was intended to see the light of day, but leaked out in garbled form which forced its premature publication.

5. Any clues that you can give us would be most helpful, as this is a speech which will not be soon forgotten. Unfortunately we do not yet have the full text of the speech and it is always possible that certain phrases were taken out of their context and given undue importance. . . .

Document 2-83

Telegram 1244-45, December 8, 1943

[OSS Bern reported frequently on the threat of German chemical and biological warfare.]

Formerly employed in bacteriology research in connection with its warfare manifestations, Prof. of Biology Hellmuth Simons, a German Jewish refugee, who worked at I. G. Farben, now works at the Zurich Polytechnic Institute. He feels that bacteriological warfare using toxin "bacillus botulinus" will be the German secret weapon. According to Simons the toxins can be readily produced in quantity in such plants as the following: I. G. Farben at Hoechst, the research laboratory in Berlin of Heereswaffen Amtharden Bergstrasse, or the Behring works at Marsburg. Prof. Simons says he has worked at the British Museum Library and at Cambridge's Minteno Institute, where Wickham-Steed and Prof. Keilim were both very familiar with him.

Prof. Simons appears to have reached his conclusions through deductive evidence rather than from exact new evidence from Germany. Please inform us if this matter is sufficiently interesting to you to merit my following up the preliminary memorandum he has given me.

Document 2-84

Telegram 1246-47, December 8, 1943

[This message contains a report on Austrian resistance elements.]

Through sources that are usually reliable, we have been informed that an anti-Nazi organization with about 5,000 members, mostly communists and leftist socialists, exists in Vienna. We have been in touch with envoys professing to represent this organization. They want to establish contact in order to suggest industrial and military targets, secure instructions as to sabotage and pass on to us secret intelligence. Previously their organization communicated only with Moscow over Prague. They now want a radio transmitter and an operator, and they will notify us when they finish with reception preparations now being made. According to them, 2 Swedish communists with a radio transmitter parachuted into Austria recently from a plane which might have been Russian, in order to cooperate with their organization. Do you know about this?

Informants state that the organization in question goes by the unusual name of Jonny. We are probing deeper into the matter.

Document 2-85

Telegram 7708, December 8, 1943 (extracts)

[This telegram on Hungary, sent through State Department channels, was circulated to the Office of the Under Secretary and to the Division of European Affairs. Numbers 477, 646, and 655 are Tyler, Baranyai, and Kallay, respectively.]

477 had talk with 822 just arrived here whom he knows intimately. 822 says Hungarian Government stalling deliveries Germany up to point of actual rupture. . . .

822 has not visited Germany except transit for last four years but sees many German businessmen. Believes German Generals incapable seizing power against Party. In absence of great increase Allied effort believes war will last another year at least. . . .

822 says when 646 returned to Budapest last August he mobilized his political friends to induce Government to disassociate Hungary from Germany even at risk German occupation. 655 willing in principle but apprehensive open break would mean occupation Hungary not only by Germans but also by Rumanian and Slovak troops, drafting and mobilizing Hungarian labor for German purposes and slaughter of anti-Axis Hungarian leaders. 822 says Hungary between devil and deep sea as Russian occupation would drive many Hungarians including himself to kill their families and themselves. Developments in Italy since armistice discouraging to Hungarians as showing lack coordination between Allied diplomatic and military effort and that Marshal Smuts' speech makes prospect appear doubly menacing. Relations between Hungarian Government and Germany so bad that if Hungarian Socialist Deputy were taken into cabinet Germans would make use pretext to occupy Hungary. . . .

Document 2-86

Telegram 1248-50, December 9, 1943

[This message contains another psychological warfare suggestion.]

A highly competent observer of the German situation recommends the following as psychological warfare procedure: German people should be told this kind of thing by Allied propaganda: "We know that millions of you are on our side. You do not know how to show it, but we are watching you, both we ourselves and our friends within the Reich see what you are doing. We will notice if you give a piece of bread to a foreign worker. We will be told of your help to our prisoners in one way or another no matter how small it is. Your help to patriots who are trying to free Germany of Nazis will be remembered, and you will be rewarded when the Nazi machine is destroyed. If you are afraid that the Gestapo is reporting on your activities, you are perhaps right in your fear, but do not forget that your friends are also observing and reporting what you do. Yes, you are watched, but you are no longer watched by the Nazis only; now you are also observed by secret, friendly organization, which will credit you with every good deed you undertake, and every step you make to help get rid of the Nazi Hun. . . .

Document 2-87

Telegram 1257-61, December 9, 1943 (extract)

[OSS Bern continues to report on the German rocket development program. Number 321 is Evert Smits; 493 is Frederick Loofbourow of OSS.]

The following is from source Sanders, our 321, by way of 493.

1. Rocket projectiles.

They weigh 40 tons and have a speed of 800 kilometers per hour for 25 minutes and a range of 333 kilometers. This is told to us by an electrical expert who was employed to measure their speed and course. They are launched by catapults and each one contains 6 mechanical and 22 electrical ignitions for explosive charge. Accuracy within 2 seconds is called for in specifications. It is said that a rocket projectile fired from Peenemunde landed in Sweden, and that trees within a thousand meter radius were destroyed. They are still being assembled at Peenemünde, and this expert says that only the drafting room there was destroyed. Both the Air Force and the Army are working on projectiles, but it was impossible to meet Hitler's deadline of November 30. The general in charge of the matter does not want to begin using the projectile until he has 1,000 catapults ready. Professor Braun is the scientist behind it. According to the expert, the final difficulty lies in finding the right moment for ignition—whatever that means.

Document 2-88

Telegram 1266-67, December 10, 1943

[Information on German submarine warfare received priority attention. Number 496 is Maurice Villars, a Zurich banker.]

Construction of a quantity of new type subs in Germany is reported by a competent source through 496 to be under way. According to this informant, a larger number of these newly designed submarines are being constructed than exist at present of the old type. The new subs reach high speeds on and under water and are designed so that they do not have to come to the surface as the current model finds it necessary to do. The old type will be utilized just for coastal service in the future. Tests of one sub of this new type were successful and orders have been given for quantity construction. A large number will be ready by spring. The opinion of the source is that it will be essential for the Allies to revamp their system of convoy protection in order to deal with this new factor in the situation. The following is from 110: Although I acknowledge the vagueness of the above, the source is such that consideration is, I think, justified.

Document 2-89

Telegram 1272-73, December 11, 1943

[OSS Bern operated under the constant scrutiny of Swiss authorities and occasionally encountered difficulties.]

To Jackpot and 109. We think you should be informed that local officials are making a detailed investigation of our alleged network here, apparently at German insistence. Several relatively insignificant arrests have been made down the line and 809, 328, 244, and 667 have been questioned. To date our work has not suffered especially with the exception of the part described in my #855. In the latter case, we are trying to overcome the handicap of lacking consular cover.

Although we are not expecting serious trouble, in case there should be protest via diplomatic channels, we thought it would be advisable to prepare you. It is essential that all precautions be redoubled and it might be advisable to obtain an official cover for 284. As yet, I do not believe anything serious has come to light, but some contacts are burned. We depend upon you to assist us in maintaining our cipher communications' security.

Document 2-90

Telegram 1274-75, December 11, 1943

[Commercial travelers between Germany and Switzerland often provided information either to the Axis or to the Allies, and sometimes to both.]

In order to secure a visa, German businessmen who come here are frequently required to do some SI work for Abwehr or the Gestapo and they are provided with a group of questions concerning which information is wanted. The following is an example: (1) What method is employed by the American Legation in Bern to transmit its information to America? Have the Swiss made an airplane available to them for this purpose? (2) Are there any signs of deals among the Japs, Russians, and Chinese for establishment of a political bloc? (3) Are the Japanese being provided with American made airplane motors by Russia in payment for supplies of tin and rubber? (4) What was the reason for Halifax departing from the United States at the precise time Prime Minister Churchill arrived there? (5) Is the Swiss press receiving monetary assistance from Americans?

Document 2-91

Telegram 7789, December 11, 1943 (extracts)

[This cable containing information on German matters from source 513 was sent via State Department channels and reached the office of the Adviser on Political Relations, Mr. Dunn.]

Resumption of Ambassador post by Abetz in Paris indicates attempt to follow new policy regarding France following advice of Goering and Foreign Office. Himmler and Goebbels said to be opposed as indicating sign of weakness. Ribbentrop believes France is good field for German European bloc building policy as French even including Gaullists are enraged at being excluded from both war and postwar decisions. . . .

4. Germans again considering reprisal plan of locating prisoners, civil internees and hostages in cities where bombing is likely. . . .

Document 2-92

Telegram 1305-6, December 13, 1943

[This message contains additional information on Yugoslavia. It is significant that several Dulles sources reported that General Mihailovich had reached an understanding with the Germans.]

Our source 819 says that lately a non-aggression pact has been made between Mihailovich and the Wehrmacht, though the former is not pro-German. Mihailovitch would, according to our informant, join up with the devil to vanquish the Croats. As a result of his troops' consistently joining the Partisans, Pavelitch has been almost liquidated by Hitler, who has refused to have Croat forces abroad brought back and has recently turned down a request for arms from Pavelitch's Minister of War.

According to our informant, Machek's position in the estimation of the people is still stronger than Tito's, though the latter's is powerful. Machek will possibly be the important personality if he manages to stay alive, as he better represents the

Croat people. Negotiations are proceeding between the Partisans and Machek. In order that M may be watched more closely, the Gestapo contemplates removing him to Zagreb.

Document 2-93

Telegram 1309-11, December 14, 1943

[This message concerns plans to send Sparrow mission to Hungary. Number 684 is Bakach-Bessenyey; 477 is Tyler; Aramis is General Ujszaszy, a top Hungarian intelligence officer.]

The secret directions described below were received by 684, and we feel that they can be regarded as authentic. It is up to us to decide upon either Lyon or Paris as the place in which his people will receive our SI man; they have made arrangements to do so at either of the places which we designate. "Semper" is to be the password and "idem" the reply. In order to make necessary preparations they want to be advised 2 weeks in advance as to time and place of arrival. Aramis will meet the SI man. The person chosen for this assignment should have, for the success of the mission, a captain's rank, at least, and should have the type of personality to work with senior officers. He ought to be able to speak German if unable to speak the local language. . . .

I am entirely aware of the responsibility this plan entails; however, 477 and I have now done all we can to make arrangements for the reception, and we both believe that it is wise to go ahead with the final plans without delay, providing suitable personnel is available and if it is technically practicable to put the men across the frontier at either of the places mentioned above. Since this matter has to be handled with 684 Headquarters through a courier please send instructions at the soonest possible time.

Document 2-94

Radiotelephone Transmission No. 49, December 14, 1943 (extract)

[In this evening telephone message, Dulles sets forth a pessimistic view of the battle for European hearts and minds that he believed was taking place between the West and the Soviet Union.]

. . . I think it is fair to say that there has been a very decided change in the psychological outlook of this part of Europe in the last five months, since the fall of Mussolini. While military considerations undoubtedly have prevented more aggressive action on the part of the Western powers, a great psychological moment was lost when we were unable to exploit more fully the fall of Mussolini. Ever since that date, as a result of a combination of circumstances, the impression has been steadily growing that the future of Europe will be decided by the Russians. These circumstances are: first, the events in Italy which I have mentioned above; second, the apparent lack of understanding between the Algiers Committee and the Anglo-Saxons, and its apparent orientation towards the communists; third, the disillusionment in France since winter has come without any signs of an early invasion, which has resulted in a growing radical tendency there; fourth, the events in Yugoslavia, where Mihailovich, the original choice of the Anglo-Saxons, is apparently petering out as an anti-German force, while Tito, with Russian backing, is capturing the imagination of the people; fifth, the quarrels between the refugee governments in London and Cairo and their people at home; sixth, the Polish-Soviet break, which the Anglo-Saxons have so far failed to heal; seventh, the fact that the air warfare of the Western powers inevitably tends to create social conditions which make the people turn to Russia rather than to the West; eighth, the Russian-Benes treaty which in certain quarters here is taken to mean that there is no longer a completely clean slate in which to form the new Europe, and that Russia, in effect, has created her first post-war alliance in the heart of Europe; finally comes the candid speech of Smuts—a man whose reputation for honesty and forthrightness is high—who draws from these premises the conclusion which, as I have said above, is fast gaining ground in this part of the world. There is another consideration which is most important: in the social conditions prevailing in a large part of occupied Europe and even in Germany itself, the Russians are catching the imagination of the masses, and we have so far failed to do so. For some reason or other, we are viewed as reactionary and desirous of reestablishing the old pre-war order of privilege. This is a difficult and rather intangible idea to get over to you, but I am certain that it has for us a dangerous reality in the minds of millions of people. In the foregoing I have merely tried to interpret as objectively as I can the large mass of reports and of conversations of people from neighboring countries and of keen observers here. If it seems distorted to you, you must realize that here we have a very distorted world.

Document 2-95

Radiotelephone Transmission No. 51, December 16, 1943

[The Dulles network in Germany was able to provide on-site reports of bombing damage, as in this case the effect of air raids on central Berlin.]

Germany

Here is a summary of some late reports on the bombing damage done to Berlin.

The Wilhelmstrasse government quarter is not fully destroyed, but practically every house has some damage in this particular area. In the Foreign Office, the

Propaganda Ministry and in the special office of Ribbentrop, work is being carried on only in the cellar and on the first floor. The British Embassy has been burnt down. The Air Ministry and the Gestapo Headquarters in Prinz Albrecht Strasse had some hits, but on the whole remained intact. Unter den Linden suffered heavily. The French Embassy and the building of the Speer Ministry in the Pariser Platz have both been made entirely unusable by fire and water. . . . The administration building of I. G. Farben has been heavily damaged. The Russian Embassy, the Ministry of Culture, the Hotel Bristol, the Hotel Kaiserhof and Hotel Viktoria have all been very heavily damaged. . . . The palace of Kaiser Wilhelm I, the Prussian State Library, the University, the State Opera House have also been heavily damaged and most of them were entirely burnt out. . . .

The old Reichstag Building also received incendiary bombs, this time not placed there by Goering; but the building still stands.

. . . In the workers' quarters there is also great damage and entire housing quarters were destroyed. According to the best reports we have, the number killed is placed at around 35,000 in all these various Berlin raids. The number of homeless is many hundred thousand. It is difficult to describe the reaction of the population: the people are so busy trying to take care of themselves that they have not had time to draw many conclusions. The Nazi leaders are busy spreading among the population such phrases as "English cannibals" and "British air pirates," but my informant does not think that this propaganda has had any very great effect. He says that people are even heard to say that it would have been better if they had never started the war. The list of factories hit is a long one, and that will be sent separately. . . .

Document 2-96

Telegram 1347-50, December 17, 1943

[Dulles here presents his considered estimate of the Hungarian situation, in response to a request from OSS headquarters.]

1. Under existing conditions, I have serious doubts regarding the chances of separating Hungary from the Axis. Were we to penetrate the Balkans in strength, the picture might be otherwise.

2. There is greater fear of the Russians than of the Germans among the Hungarian governmental strata at the present time. It is the belief of these people that Hungary will suffer through Russia's intent to compensate Rumania for the probable loss of Bessarabia and perhaps Dobrudja. Hungarians believe that Russia's hostility toward their country is even greater than the Soviet's enmity towards Rumania.

3. Since fence-sitting is an art highly developed by the Hungarians, I do not think that they will line up with us openly unless we give them assurances of [*sic*] regarding the Soviet, or unless we succeed with a penetration of the Balkans. The former is presumably not to be considered.

4. Hungarian policy has been influenced by the general impression in Europe that the Russians will be allowed pretty much of a free hand in Europe by the Anglo-Saxons. This was pointed out in my flash of the 14th of this month.

5. Although the Hungarians consider that they are in a desperate situation, they hope that their small army will be in a tolerable state when Germany collapses, and they will possibly be able to retain at least a moderate amount of territory if the Russians are tired at that time as the Hungarians hope they will be.

6. In the opinion of the Hungarians, as has been pointed out before, the only thing that can hit them which would be worse than the Trianon Treaty would be a Russian occupation and they are not certain that the Anglo-Saxons will protect them from the latter eventuality or allow them anything better than the aforementioned treaty.

7. There are numerous Hungarians in the neutral countries who wish to gain favor for themselves by passing along pleasant but, in my opinion, unrealistic views of the Hungarian policy and attitude.

8. I am of the opinion, however, that Hungary would like to have an anchor to the windward with us and therefore it is not impossible to make use of them in certain ways. For an example of this, refer to my #1309. Moreover, even at the present time, they will exhibit independence of the Reich up to a point. They will not, however, take such steps as might make Nazi occupation a probability. I am informed by 964 that it is out of the question to obtain directly from the authorities the battle order for which you asked in your #838. 964 is entirely pro-Ally, but he takes a realistic view. The authorities are afraid that the Russians would have access to the battle order were it in our possession.

Document 2-97

Radiotelephone Transmission No. 53, December 18, 1943 (extract)

[Roosevelt, Churchill and Stalin met at Teheran, November 28–December 1, 1943, solidifying the Grand Alliance. The second front was discussed at length, and Stalin put forth claims to Polish territory. Few major decisions were made.]

Germany

1. Reports from Germany indicate that in government circles they are endeavoring to persuade themselves that the Teheran Conference was not a success. Apparently there is a confidential German report circulating that Roosevelt and Stalin had a very serious difference of opinion with regard to the Far Eastern situation, and this report alleges that Roosevelt for the first time discovered certain secret arrangements between the Russians and the Japanese, possibly with regard to mutual supply of war materials, which led to friction between the two men. The German report

stresses that whereas the Moscow declaration indicated certain concrete points of agreement, there were practically nothing but generalities in the Teheran declaration. This, the Germans conclude, indicates that there was no agreement on concrete matters, and that in effect the Teheran Conference represents a worsening of relations between the Western Allies and Russia. I give the above merely as indicating what I believe is being passed around in German official quarters. . . .

Document 2-98

Telegram 1280, December 20, 1943

[The security of communications was an ongoing concern.]

To Sherman, Carib, and Jackpot. We will be grateful for a reply to our #946. The following information is secret. OVSJBI contacts with 497, perhaps with 110 also, have been found out and he arrived Top barely before Jerry. It does not appear impossible that the BKRZLC communication system from this end may be prejudiced. This arrival may possess significance of great importance. For the present, however, it has to be maintained secret.

Document 2-99

Telegram 311-15 to London, December 22, 1943 (extracts)

[This telegram transmits a summary of a report received from CER, the Paris executive committee of the French resistance, suggesting bombing methods and targets and relating them to sabotage operations.]

From 284 and 110. . . .

1. Stressed in this report is the distinction between SO and air objectives and between Zero hour and immediate action.

2. In reference to the railroads the report recommends that the attacks, whether they are by SO or from the air, should be made on open ways devoid of detours. Bombs should be directed 100 meters apart for several kilometers. As a general rule yards and stations do not make good objectives because within a few hours transit is restored. In general, it is useless to gun trains and engines from the air, as this results in the unnecessary death of SNCF personnel who are loyal to the cause of the Allies. With the exception of important depots of engines and cars, similar to Longeau where large yards and 1200 cars were destroyed by attack from the air, the best results on rails and traffic can be achieved by SO on TCO movements and trains selected at the last minute. . . .

5. When zero hour finally arrives, if the CER service FER is furnished with material it will be organized to disrupt traffic, as per instructions, in nearly all of France for a period lasting 15 days. This is in accordance with plans that already have been set. CER is awaiting information regarding the areas that SO wants, both at zero hour and at the present time. . . .

Document 2-100

Telegram 1443-47, December 27, 1943 (extract)

[This report concerns relations of Bulgaria with Germany and Turkey. It is based on information from 513, a Polish source.]

About the 5th of this month, the Germans demanded that Bulgaria order a general mobilization, and become incorporated into the Nazi Luftwaffe organization. These demands were presented through General Meister and General Warlimont, and were conditioned by the degree to which the Turks might make concessions to the Allies. If the Allies invade Turkey's territory or territorial waters, the arrangements are to take effect at once. . . . The Bulgarians accepted the Nazi demands, but only with conditions which the Nazis found unsatisfactory. These conditions included the withdrawal of Nazi soldiers from Bulgaria, and the calling in to Bulgarian territory of all Bulgar troops. It would appear that both of these steps were urged upon the Bulgarians by strong representations from the Turks. Von Papen was ordered to make energetic counter-representations to Ankara when this information reached Germany. . . .

Document 2-101

Telegram 1466-76, December 29, 1943

[In December 1943, Fritz Kolbe ("George Wood"), an official in the German Foreign Ministry who offered to work for Allied intelligence in August 1943, brought a large batch of documents to Bern. Many of them deal with the question of Turkish neutrality. In this telegram, Yellow stands for Turkey, Grand for the German Foreign Ministry, Milit for the German Ambassador in Turkey (von Papen), and Penni for the Turkish Foreign Minister. Cicero was the code name for Nazi spy Elysea Bazna, valet to British Ambassador Knatchbull-Hugessen in Turkey. Information provided by Kolbe and forwarded by Dulles contributed to the detection of this agent.]

KAPPA. Yellow. Cables to Grand from Milit are given below in reworded versions:

December 12, #1804: Penni was informed by Milit that the granting of air bases to the Anglo-Americans would be the equivalent of declaring war. Milit further stated that Hitler was unwilling to sacrifice European interests and therefore refused to join four-fold alliance embracing the Soviet Union. Penni declared that no serious debate took place in Parliament; that the Teheran Conference did not make decisions on the second front, but instead took up the question of the most effective means of involving Yellow in the war; that in order to keep the Soviets in the war, Churchill and Eden had abandoned Eastern Europe; and that his own ideas on the Soviet's imperialist aims in Greece, Yugoslavia and the Mediterranean in the period after the war had been bolstered. In addition, Penni stated that he did not give straightforward answers to the Anglo-Saxons, and that he invariably offered new reasons for keeping out of the war. He substantiated the statement about the Teheran Conference made by Cicero. In continuation, he declared that there was no reason to anticipate a surprise landing by Anglo-Saxons in Yellow. Should the latter land, they would find no munitions or gasoline available; Yellow retains complete control of air defense.

14th of December, #1811: Following reported by Cicero: (1) By the middle of February, air bases in Yellow will be ready. (2) Capture of Rome about the middle of January is expected by Anglo-Saxons. 3 groups of medium bombers will then be based in Cyrenaica to halt traffic on the Aegean. (3) Yellow must reach a decision by the 15th of February on receiving 20 Allied air squadrons. (4) Other plans will be made in the event of refusal. In the event of acceptance, a program called "Accolade" will go into effect, directed against Rhodes and Crete, with the 10th Indian Division supporting the 4th English Division in this plan. (6) (sic). For operations against the Crimea, 6 to 8 submarines are to go through the Dardanelles to the Black Sea. (7) The "Anvil" (sic) program, directed against Salonica, is to follow the "Accolade" program. Cicero's report ends with this.

If the tentative answer to the Anglo-Saxons made yesterday by Yellow is as negative as Penni states it to be, it is questionable, Milit adds, whether equipment for Istanbul and Smyrna air defenses will be delivered by the British. These deliveries were supposed to arrive on the 15th of February. As the necessary number of transports is not available, Milit also is doubtful that "Accolade" will take place before this date. Observance of the most strict confidence is requested by Penni.

18th of December, #1842: Milit was called for a talk by Penni, who declared: Yellow's entrance into the war was settled upon at Teheran, even if, in order to bring it about, it might be necessary to apply force. The full arming of the Yellow Army and Air Force must take place first, however. The British will take care of this within a few months' time. In order to gain time, Penni declared that he deliberately estimated transport requirements above the figure which the English could possibly manage. To satisfy Yellow's needs, he thinks 6 months would be necessary.

Penni looks to 2 possibilities: (1) Occupation by force. Yellow's defenses are prepared, and anti-aircraft are ready to fight in this event; or (2) Yellow will be made ready for war by British propaganda.

It was demonstrated by Penni that the cause of the Anglo-Saxons would be aided if the Bulgarians and Germans took counter-measures during this tense period.

Decision was firmly reached by Penni and Harem to play for time and to keep Yellow out of the conflict. In Penni's opinion, a gain of 5 or 6 months time will result in stabilization of the Eastern front and a decision in the West as a result of successful Nazi defense against invasion from Britain. Question posed by Milit argued: Why did you not call 70,000 to arms if this is your policy? . . .

Following is Milit's summary of this conversation: (1) The situation is of extreme gravity. (2) He urges that Germany prepare with the greatest possible secrecy so as not to augment sentiment for war. (3) Yellow must be clearly informed by Bulgaria that the latter will fight should Yellow enter the war.

December 22, #1863: It is anticipated that there will be an increase in ship movements to Mersin and Alexandretta. . . .

December 24, #1875: Milit was advised by Penni that a near break resulted from a violent discussion he had with the British Ambassador.

In order to force Yellow to enter the war, the British Ambassador had tried to present a collective demarche on the part of the Allies. Penni declined to accept this document, upon which the Ambassador gave notice of the arrival in the near future of the Allied Land, Air and Sea Commanders-in-Chief. Permission for them to enter would be refused, Penni claims to have said. The British later inquired whether their chief adjoints might come to confer. Penni again gave a negative answer, with the result that another crisis took place. The arrival of several officers of the General Staff was later announced by the British Ambassador. This met with acceptance, and Penni stated further that his conscience is now clear.

The Russians have not taken part in these discussions at the Yellow Foreign Office during the last week.

Since it tends to drive a wedge between the Russians and the English, Penni feels that the continuing flow of arms shipments to Yellow is a favorable sign.

This is the conclusion of this set of Milit cables.

The personal evaluation given by Woods is: that Yellow is playing both ends against the middle, or that air defenses of Yellow are too weak, or that Milit is permitting Penni to deceive him. The latter possibility might be caused by Milit's anxiety to have rose-colored picture to present for protection of his own position. It is not impossible that Milit would fade out of the picture altogether should he lose his job.

Document 2-102

Telegram 1477-79, December 29, 1943

[While the second large batch of Wood Traffic documents was being processed and transmitted by OSS Bern, doubt remained in Washington and London concerning the authenticity of the material. Wood was too good to be true; was he a Nazi plant? In this telegram, Dulles stakes his reputation on the validity of his source.]

More than 200 notes are included in the most recent catch. (Refer to our #868.) They are to Vinta and Grand from different Waldos and Portos. Certain traffic from

Vinta is also included. In addition, an oral analysis, provided by Wood, of considerable further correspondence which he obtained from original documents. As an indication of documentary source, I will place a D after our indicator, so that you may be able to recognize such messages. . . .

I now firmly believe in the good faith of Woods, and I am ready to stake my reputation on the fact that these documents are genuine. I base my conclusion on internal evidence and on the nature of the documents themselves. We are keeping close watch on cipher security in re-wording.

Document 2-103

Telegram 1484, December 29, 1943

[In this document from George Wood, Tosar is Sofia; Trude is Hungarian Lieutenant Colonel Hatz, a key figure in the abortive OSS Sparrow mission, an attempted penetration of Hungary; Ragon is Istanbul. The naval officer in question is probably Admiral George Earle, President Roosevelt's personal observer in Turkey, who was recalled for a series of indiscretions.]

KAPPA. Orange. From Tosar, Trude has given the Germans very full particulars of his connections in Ragon with our personnel, among whom a Navy officer is included, seemingly. It seems from the document that perhaps Trude is pulling our leg and, in addition, Zulu's. If you wish, I will send a more complete report. I urge caution.

Document 2-104

Telegram 1486-93, December 30, 1943 (extracts)

[This message consists of miscellaneous reports submitted orally by George Wood.]

KAPPA. . . .

1. About a month and a half ago production on a new fighter plane, having a top speed of almost 1000 kilometers, was begun. Reports on this plane by Gallant, leading test pilot in the Reich, were enthusiastic. Junkers at Dessau, which has not been bombed as yet, produces parts for this plane. Assembly of the planes takes place at the Messerschmitt factory in Augsburg and at Oschersleben in Harz. The new high speed of this plane was obtained through an increase in motor power, thereby greatly cutting down the time that the plane can remain in the air, due to gasoline consumption. This plane has no changes in armament. . . .

7. Hitler, Himmler, Goering, and all of the other bigwigs are at the General Headquarters in East Prussia. Part of the Nazi F. O. has been transferred to Krummhueblim Reisengebirg.

8. The entire Nazi idea of the British and American battle order for invasion

troops has been viewed by Wood. This battle order states that there are 50 to 60 divisions stationed in the south of England and prepared to leave. The Nazis think that they know exactly where each division is located. . . .

11. The following was contained in a message to Dublin from Grand, dated the 16th of this month; Grand proposes that, to avoid being interned, Nazi airmen landing in Ireland should claim that they are on a practice flight. Munitions and bombs are to be dropped overboard prior to landing. On the basis of such actions by Nazi fliers, the German Government is to request that De Valera release all Nazi airmen who land in Ireland from now on. Then perhaps a civilian airplane could fly to Ireland for the purpose of picking up these fliers, thereby affording Grand a chance to send a new German official to Dublin.

12. The following information, dated the 16th of this month, was sent from the Legation in Dublin to Grand; this message was not received by Grand until December 21st: 600 airfields in England are in readiness for use in a large Allied offensive, which is on the point of starting.

13. A secret radio transmitter is located in the Nazi Legation in Dublin, and the Irish are aware of its existence. Regular cables from Dublin are sent, with considerable delay, by way of Bern; the Nazis are keeping the secret transmitter for emergency use only. The Irish are putting pressure on the Nazis to give up this transmitter, but the Germans are stalling.

14. On the 22nd of this month the Fuhrer decided to ignore the 2nd note from Sweden in regard to Oslo students. He ordered Grand to draw up a "Swedish Calendar of Crime." The task was assigned to Leitner, and he is said to have stated that he could not locate any Swedish crimes. (Note from 110: with reference to our #113; desire to revise my appraisal of Leitner on the basis of additional information. He is not a Nazi, although he is cautious.)

15. East Jutland is most appropriate for the landing of agents from Sweden; it is not well defended.

16. Grand received a letter from OKM, dated the 15th of this month, in which the latter asks Grand to put pressure on the Japanese to give up Portuguese Timor. OKM feels that the United States may use the Japanese occupation of Timor as a pretext to establish air bases on the Iberian Peninsula or occupy the Cape Verdes Islands. German sea warfare would be gravely hampered if the United States took either of these steps.

Document 2-105

Telegram 1496-97, December 30, 1943

[This message is another instance of OSS Bern's reporting of the Nazi effort to exterminate the Jews. "Kappa" signifies material received from Fritz Kolbe, assistant to Ritter in the German Foreign Ministry; "D" indicates that the text is the translation of an actual German document rather than a summary by Kolbe; Green stands for Italy. This document appears to be a message from German Ambassador Rudolph Rahn in Rome to the German Foreign Ministry. General Kesselring was commander of German forces in Italy.]

KAPPA. D. GREEN. Oberstrurmbannfuehrer Kappler has been instructed from Berlin to seize the eight thousand Jews living in Rome and to take them to Northern Italy where they are to be liquidated. The city commandant of Rome, General Stahel, informs me that he will permit this action only if it is consistent with the policies of the Reich Foreign Minister. I am personally of the opinion that it would be better business to use Jews, as in Tunis, for work on fortifications and I shall present this view, together with Kappler, to Field Marshall General Kesselring. Please advise.

Document 2-106

Telegram 1498-99, December 31, 1943

[This message indicates that the Germans were resorting to extreme measures to preserve their position in Italy. "Kappa" stands for material from Fritz Kolbe, "D" for actual document text, Green for Italy, and Grand for the German Government in Berlin. Field Marshal Wilhelm Keitel was Chief of Staff of the High Command of German Armed Forces. He was executed as a war criminal in 1946.]

KAPPA. In conjunction with my #1496–1497. The following is additional D Green communication, despatched by Keitel from general headquarters to Grand and all Military Naval Services involved, on the 12th of September: The following treatment shall be applied at the command of Hitler, to all Italian troops who permit their arms to come into the possession of rebels or who in any manner unite with rebels for mutual ends; if captured, 1) Officers are to be shot at once; 2) Soldiers and non-commissioned officers, avoiding as much as possible any passage through Germany, are to be dispatched at once to the East and put under Military Command for labor.

Document 2-107

Telegram 1500-1502 (part 1), December 31, 1943

[This message based on George Wood material provides additional information on the status of Turkey. Harem is Sukru Saracoglu, the Turkish Prime Minister.]

KAPPA. Following message concerns Yellow.

1. 1769, to Grand from Milit on December 6. Harem stated he was pleased at

the assured manner with which military developments were being met by Hitler. I stressed our preparedness for any eventual attack and the decision Hitler made to send additional forces to every Balkan position. Identical resolution in Sofia. Harem is resolved to stay out of war since even winning the war would mean that Yellow would be under Russian control. He stated assurance that president would bring good results from Cairo. He stated his indignation with regard to Smuts' proposed plans for after the war. He recommended, since the French were indignant and realized now what to expect from England, that we had another chance for building a strong foundation for a European settlement by reaching a fair peace with French.

2. 1768 to Grand from Milit on December 5; neutral diplomats were informed by Penni that rather than bring Yellow into the war, he would give up alliance and the Spanish minister was informed by Harem that alteration of neutrality policy was opposed by all party leaders.

3. 1668 to Grand from Chargé Jenke while Milit was away on November 15; sent to Milit and foreign minister: This relates the reply Yellow gave to English demands concerning her entering the war and various other matters of very little practical interest now except the remark that Rumania and Yellow are arranging for moving gold from former to latter.

Document 2-108

Telegram 1503-5 (part 2), January 1, 1944

[This message based on George Wood material contains more information on Turkish neutrality, and also on Cicero, the Nazi spy. This document contains British secrets intercepted by the Nazis and in turn intercepted by an OSS agent, Wood. It is noteworthy that Dulles took it upon himself to give British intelligence in Switzerland (521) evidence of the leak in the British Embassy in Turkey.]

KAPPA. D. Yellow. 4. The following is contained in message #1642 to Grand from Milit, on November 10: The material given here was learned from an extremely dependable source which must not be jeopardized. In Cairo, Eden made a demand for airfields. Harem refused on the ground that this would mean war with Germany. Eden answered this by saying that Germany would simply make a protest, as in the instance of Portugal, and that deliveries by the United States would halt should Yellow persist in refusing. The political leaders and the ministers were informed by me that to yield even one airfield would mean war. I will wire if greater pressure by Berlin is required. For the present, I feel it would be wisest not to reveal any anxiety and to go on assuming that Yellow will continue as a neutral.

5. The following is from 110. 521 has been given #1576, dated November 3rd, #1600, dated November 5th, and #1603, dated November 4th, for transmission. These are all to Grand from Milit. They deal with documents on which Milit clearly placed great value and which, seemingly, were taken from the Zulu Embassy

through a source designated as Cicero. This source has been referred to earlier. Among the wires was a list of questions which the Zulu Ambassador took to Cairo for his own guidance for consultation with Eden. Also included was a Foreign Office memorandum of October 7th, with the title, seemingly, "A Long-Range View of Turkish-British Policy." Via a special SD person, these and additional documents were dispatched to Berlin. Among the additional documents dispatched, there was a memorandum which, it seems, dealt with steps which the English were taking in Yellow in preparation for war, and which was referred to in the list of questions.

Document 2-109

Telegram 1534-38, January 2, 1944

[This message, based on German documents intercepted by George Wood, raises grave questions about Colonel Hatz, an OSS Hungarian contact. "Black" signifies documents dealing with the Balkans; Beckerle is a German representative in Bulgaria.]

KAPPA. The following is documented information on Black:

. . . 24. This message is #2029 to Grand from Beckerle, dated December 14. Have been unable to unearth any evidence of any connivance between Tito and Hungarian Border Troops, although this situation does exist according to the Chief of Military Intelligence. The Hungarian, Lieutenant Colonel Hatz, has been chosen as MA in Turkey. It is reported confidentially that he is in touch with Americans. The Zulu Embassy in Ankara made him an offer. The Americans there also made him a proposition. However, Hatz declined at once to act in a manner unbecoming an officer. When the Americans said they sympathized with Hungary, Hatz replied that the U.S. lost Hungarian sympathy when she began to collaborate with the Soviet. The Americans' answer to this was that Russian domination of Europe was even more offensive to them than German domination, and that the real solution lies in a federation of Europe founded on democratic principles. The Americans also indicated desire to keep in touch with Hatz. The latter says that he reported this to Szombatelyi (sic), Kallay and the chief of Hungarian SI. They came to the conclusion that Hatz should retain his connections with the Americans so that he can secure information for the Germans. Hatz is reliable and pro-German. However, he is short of funds and has numerous affairs with women. There is also an unconfirmed report to the effect that he is in touch with Jews who are paid by the Hungarian intelligence and that he shares in the profits which they make from smuggling currency.

25. This is message #2050, dated December 17, to Grand from Beckerle. Conferred further with Hatz. Canaris was advised in the meantime. According to Hatz, the Americans and British got in touch with him through a Hungarian agent, Andreas Gyorgy (sic); he could not recall the names of the Americans and British,

though he did recollect that 1 American was called Kellog or something close to that. 2 Americans, 1 from Navy (reported not to be Earle) and close to President Roosevelt, got in touch with him later on. After the second talk between Hatz and the Hungarian Chief of Staff and Kallay, they instructed him to continue in touch with Americans in Istanbul. The Americans desire to be in touch with a Hungarian officer in preference to a diplomat made an impression upon Dremieh Kallay (sic). If anything crooked were planned against the Germans, Hatz promised to advise them of it.

Document 2-110

Telegram 1555-56, January 3, 1944

[Dulles addresses the question of the physical penetration of Germany in this message.]

110 to Carib with reference to your #1037. According to information reaching me, DAF was infiltrated by numerous old trade unionists. However, DAF will have to be reorganized thoroughly. I am placing 476 at work obtaining the information you wished to have. Each of us here is extremely interested in these questions.

The following paragraph is for Jackpot. We are aware of the importance of your #1051. It is practically impossible to dispatch people back and forth across the border lawfully due to visa regulations both in the north and locally. Crossing the north border illegally is most dangerous but we are doing everything possible. For this, however, we have to depend almost completely upon communist and leftist groups. Perhaps the most feasible channel at this time is to penetrate by way of France, including Alsace. We are trying to take advantage of this channel, as well as of all other which it may be possible to use.

Document 2-111

Telegram 1604-12, January 5, 1944

[A document received from Kolbe revealed a serious indiscretion by Vice President Henry Wallace, who had discussed the results of the Moscow Foreign Ministers Conference of October 1943 with his brother-in-law, Grunn. This account reached German hands and was transmitted to Berlin, apparently through Switzerland. Dulles viewed the content of the Vice President's remarks as innocuous but noted the danger posed by the possibility of similar future leaks to Kolbe/Wood and to Allied security generally. The tenor of observations reported is so at variance with the pro-Soviet outlook of Wallace that it is possible that Grunn, or someone in the transmittal pipeline, tailored the report to conform to Berlin's illusions.]

KAPPA. Lomax divided into 10 paragraphs the cable you requested in your #1061. Although aware that such a message exists, Zulu is informed about none of the details and is sending no wires on the subject. London was not sent a copy of my #1509. The cable is given below:

1. K.O. Schweiz (Note by 110: This refers to Kriegs Organization, which is comparable to our SI or MI) Jassnen reports of Grunn, which were based upon talks with VP. According to these reports, at the start of the Moscow Conference the Americans and British tried to vindicate both the past and future actions of the Allied GHQUs; however, their Russian partner exhibited practically no sympathy or appreciation of their position. On the other hand it seems that the foundations were laid for coming military cooperation. Not until a second front has been opened up, i.e., not until the Allies have carried out a successful invasion of France, will this plan for cooperation go into effect. Until then Russia retains the right to unrestricted action in military and political matters. VP stated, however, that Russian conditions for more complete military cooperation will soon be met.

2. There was no agreement on the German question. The Soviet requested that the ravaged areas of Russia be rebuilt by German labor, and with the use of German materials. On the theory that this would involve complete Soviet control over Germany, the granting of this request was refused, and the decision was put off; the question is to be referred to the European Commission for a solution.

3. The request was made by the British and American delegations that Russia agree to total German disarmament. However, no agreement was reached. Russia favored the establishment of an anti-Nazi "Kampf Gruppen." The American opinion on this proposal was that, if carried out, it would constitute the building of a Communist army controlled by Russia. This problem was also left to be decided by the European Commission.

4. Russia indicated her willingness to a plebiscite, controlled by the Allies, in the Baltic states. Aware of the farce of the 1940 plebiscite, the British and Americans were worried about the freedom of the polls.

5. VP declined to discuss the Finnish question with even his intimate friend, which signifies that Russia is adamant on this point. Special problems arise relative to this in view of the fact that the 1939 Russian aggression in Finland was emphatically denounced by public opinion in the United States.

6. Russia made 2 proposals in regard to Poland. (1) An independent Poland, governed by the exile London government, provided Britain and America agreed to the Ribbentrop line. (2) If the first proposal is not acceptable, Russia is prepared to establish a large European republic which would include all the original Polish territory and should then seek to become connected with the USSR. VP says that Russia promised not to take any steps toward fulfillment of this plan, either politically or through propaganda, as long as there is a chance of effecting an agreement with the exile London government. The Russian opinion of the exile government is that it is made up of "an entirely unrepresentative bunch of émigrés." No solution

was reached, and this problem was turned over to the European Commission, which in effect means that Russia will take steps to carry out the 2nd suggestion.

7. There was only an interchange of opinions on the question of south East Europe. Grunn was not in a position to state whether or not Russia discontinued her opposition to landings on the Dalmatian coast in return for a guarantee that Bulgaria and Rumania would not be involved in the operations. The European Commission was presented with the Balkan question also.

8. The paragraph on Austria is regarded as nothing but political strategy to attack a vulnerable point in Germany's inner front. The consensus of opinion was that Austria is the first place that disorders and revolutions might be expected to break out.

9. VP's general political comments on the Moscow Conference were the most interesting parts of Grunn's report. The American delegation set out for the Conference with little optimism. And now that it is over every one who is familiar with the results of the Conference is certain that the British and Americans alone must win World War II, possibly even against Russia, and that Russia means to dominate the whole of Europe and has already made substantial progress toward this end. The main outcome of the Moscow Conference is not apparent so much in the resolutions adopted as in the realization that the ideology of a World Revolution is still alive. Although Russia agreed to the majority of the British and American suggestions, she always succeeded in leaving herself a loophole. The assumption is that she will endeavor to put the western powers on the defensive so that after the war the various national communistic organizations in all countries will be guaranteed freedom of action. Since this is diametrically opposed to American ideals for peace the American government may be compelled to make momentous decisions very soon. The gravity of these conclusions is in no way tempered by the conciliatory atmosphere in which the conference was conducted. Secretary of State Hull was not blinded by the Russian subterfuge, however, and admitted, "that he knew less now about what was going to happen than he did before he arrived in Moscow."

10. The Grunn report is a valuable supplement to the reports from friendly diplomats which I (Lomax) sent earlier. The reason that the above report contains so much more concrete information than the data which came to Bern from the American and British governments is due to the fact that VP was talking to Grunn, his brother-in-law, in the greatest of confidence.

A final remark is inserted by Lomax to the effect that the Moscow Conference reminded him of the Molotov Berlin tactics in 1940. It was clear then as now that Russia had not abandoned her inclination toward World Revolution.

Document 2-112

Telegram 205-7 to Algiers, January 6, 1944

[Plans for the penetration of Hungary moved forward.]

SPARROW. For Pflieger and SO, Washington. . . . 684 verifies the fact that all arrangements are now completed, and they are prepared to receive either one or two of our men, with 10 to 14 days' warning, at either of the locations designated in our #1309. The passwords and all other preparations are verified. The envoy may be in uniform; but, in order to attract less notice, should also wear a trench coat. His story should be that he was with the Partisans and was constrained by circumstances to leave. He will then be taken to the General who has been specified prior to this. It is felt that it would not be a good idea for the envoy to ask for him at the outset. It is preferable that the envoy be a sturdy intelligent American specimen, rather than one possessing any foreign traits. They have no aversion to receiving two men, one to perform the headwork and the other a radioman. They concur in the opinion that carrying a transmitter over the border is not a good idea, and if local machines turn out to be insufficient they are even prepared to dispatch a transmitter by courier from here. The envoy ought to speak German, and in this case Hungarian would not be required. The following is for both Washington and Algiers: We will miss quite an unusual chance if we do not succeed in completing this project. 684 speaks with authority. In order to go ahead, we wish to hear at the earliest possible date.

Document 2-113

Telegram 1633-35, January 6, 1944

[This information provided by George Wood surely received scrutiny as a possible German plant, containing ostensible indications of bad faith among the Allies and lack of security and discretion.]

KAPPA. The following is Part III of a D message concerning Blue. To Grand from Huene, #3462, dated October 11. Count Wohl, Polish Chargé at Algiers, just back from Washington, informed a member of the American Legation that the United States War Department was aware that the best American military equipment sent to Russia was not dispatched to the Front but was deposited in the Urals for employment in the ultimate French Communistic regime or for employment against Japan.

The same, Huene to Grand, #3570, dated October 17. It was ascertained through the Zulu Embassy that an official American telephone conversation revealing the Americans about to occupy the Azores was intercepted by a Zulu. Under treaty alliance the British then forced through an immediate agreement. Extreme disappointment was felt in Washington which was shared by President Roosevelt over the Azores agreement, and the American Legation was instructed to watch British Intelligence more closely.

The same, #3902, dated November 15. I was assured by Salazar that the concessions regarding the Azores were confined to us by British of Terceira Air Field and use by the Allies of Horta, also that the rumors were false which claimed the reinforcement of Horta and Pico Island and the stationing of U.S. planes in Terceira. He informed me that British use and protection of the airfield alone were allowed, and there were no indications of any more requests by Britain.

Document 2-114

Telegram 190, section two, January 8, 1944

[The battle cruiser *Scharnhorst* left port on December 26, 1943, to attack two Anglo-American arctic convoys. Aided by Ultra intercepts, the Allies located and sank the German warship.]

. . . It is said that the reason the Scharnhorst put to sea was because the big convoy of supply vessels bound for Murmansk was thought to be transports of troops, under protective forces. As observed on Christmas Day, the out-of-the-ordinary protective measures for war vessels gave added credence to that thought. It was the opinion of the OKW that these imagined troops were being sent to occupy the fjords and islands in that section around Vanno and the North Cape which is so cut off from outside contact, and thus to sever the Reich lines of supply to the front around Petsamo and in that way give aid to an offensive in northern Finland by Soviet forces, rather than for an invasion of the northern part of Norway. Commands had been given to make use of all forces possible, and that included the Scharnhorst, in order to put a stop to such an operation. The safety of that vessel would not have been jeopardized merely for the purpose of raiding a convoy of supply ships.

Document 2-115

Telegram 1655-57, Part 2, January 8, 1944 (extract)

[Information from "George Wood" indicated that the Germans planned to augment their defenses in Scandinavia.]

KAPPA. November 1. Bearing no number. From Keitel, General Headquarters, East Prussia, via Grand to Commander of troops in Denmark and to Ritter. Fuehrer orders utmost speed in building defenses in all of the West, including Norway and Denmark, because he believes Russia will insist at Moscow on an early opening of a second front by the British and Americans. Political considerations should be subordinated to these new defense efforts. Defensive fortifications in Jutland must be built up. Workers must be contributed by Danish people who benefit by the operations of the German Wehrmacht, especially since there are 28,000 unemployed Danes. Fuehrer expects action at once, and if any difficulties arise inform me at once. . . .

Document 2-116

Telegram 1671-73, January 8, 1944

[This message contains George Wood information on France. Apple is Otto Abetz, the German ambassador; Vinta is Ribbentrop.]

KAPPA. The following is Part IV of a D message concerning Red.

3. Apple, dated December 6th. American and British influence with relation to Petain's draft law is verified by reports from Switzerland. It is said that Petain was advised by Giraud that, if the National Assembly met with the right to select a successor to Petain, Giraud would consider him as Head of State after the Allied occupation of France. Despite abandonment of the draft law for calling together the National Assembly, Petain's retinue will not desert [discuss?] a move assisting the British and Americans. It is vitally important that Menetree (sic) Jardel, General Campet and Romier be removed. Romier and Jardel might be dismissed and then arrested by Nazi agents. Petain is getting ready a draft for answer to letter from Vinta. Continued machinations must be looked for, if we are not able to pin Petain down on the subject of names of the new Minister.

4. Apple, dated December 16. With respect to members of the Deriot party joining the Cabinet, Deriot's headquarters imply that they do not wish to participate in the government unless the Cabinet is selected by Deriot himself. This is contrary to my directions. I recommend that Deriot be kept from departing from the Russian Front, but his retention there should be based solely on military reasons and any biasing of his use politically in the future should be shunned.

5. Although there is no evidence to prove the reality of such communications, we have an extensive cable relating to correspondence which is claimed to have taken place between Petain and Giraud.

Document 2-117

Telegram 190, Section One, January 9, 1944

[A coup in Bolivia on December 17, 1943, brought to power a pro-Axis government that was recognized only by Argentina. This report indicated possible extended significance.]

It is reported that the recent coup in Bolivia is a link in a program designed with a view to creating an Ibero-American confederation of Portuguese and Spanish speaking countries as well as Catholic countries in order that there will exist, in addition to the Soviet, United States and British bloc, a fourth bloc of world powers. That the United States would not interfere with a modernized version of Fascism in South America, provided such Fascism was weaned away from the Axis, is apparently believed by Franco, Salazar and Ramirez. The next objective is Peru, and army officers are waiting to establish the new order in that country. Chile and Uruguay will come next, and if Brazil does not follow, she will thus be isolated. A number of the Bolivian rebels were processed in Nazi schooling, hence the Foreign Office in Berlin is aware that the Bolivian rebels are in whole-hearted sympathy with Ramirez and Franco. It is not believed by the Foreign Office, however, that tin deliveries will be impeded by the Bolivian putsch, since it is expected that a friendly attitude will be shown toward the United States by the new Government. The purpose of showing an attitude of that kind would be to mask the real objective of the new Government to set itself up firmly in Bolivia as one of the members of the confederation mentioned in the foregoing. (The source which is cited is 513). . . .

The advances made by the Russians in the area of Kiev and Winnitza are considered a catastrophe which is due to the foolhardy counter-offensive of Manstein against Kiev in the middle of November and to the OKW's under-estimate of adverse forces. . . .

A start toward carrying out instructions to stop Zulu supplies of material from reaching Tito was commenced by Marshal von Weichs on the 24th of December. The reason this action was taken is that OKW desires to ascertain whether an attack on the Eastern Adriatic is intended by the Allies this winter for serious cooperation with Tito or whether the concentration of the Allies in Apulia and Taranto are simply intended as a diversion to tie up coast defense and combat units of the Germans. These will be withdrawn soonest if major operations in the Adriatic are not really intended by the British in the Adriatic on the assumption that the Allied attack on the western Balkans has been postponed or has not been prepared sufficiently.

Document 2-118

Telegram 1684-85, January 9, 1944

[Dulles maintained contacts with many prominent Swiss.]

To Jackpot. Have received tremendous amount of help from Emil Oprecht who is with Oprecht Verlag Top, very reputable publishing house. He wired Walter Lippmann concerning permission to publish here the latter's book on United States foreign policy; please advise Walter that if he is not already involved in other arrangements, it would be impossible to find a publisher more devoted to Allied aims than is this man. . . .

Document 2-119

Telegram 230, January 10, 1944 (extract)

[This message notes German development of artificial fog.]

. . . In preparation for coming raids by American bombers facilities for the creation of artificial fog have been greatly increased, as that device is considered, at this time, the most adequate defense against such raids, particularly those which occur in day time. Special protection of this type has been provided for power and industrial plants and locks on canals located outside of large urban communities and also for smaller establishments scattered all over Austria and south and central Germany. . . .

Document 2-120

Telegram 1692-93, January 10, 1944

[OSS Bern frequently transmitted reports on German secret weapons. Flute was a prominent Swiss scientist, Dr. Paul Scherrer.]

Number 827 has been assigned to Flute, whom we mentioned in our #1336. He says that according to an eye witness, the speed of the rocket is not so great as to prevent the eye from following its flight. The rocket left a visible wake of steam in its path. Flute believes this is the result of the condensation of the exhaust gases when they contact the carbon dioxide which vaporizes from the layer of dry ice. He also thinks that production of the most highly refined parts for radio location and radio direction of projectiles is no longer carried on in Berlin but has been moved to Forschungstelle E., Bisingen Wurttemberg. This deduction is based on a letter which he received from the latter place about the 10th of December, written by the top ranking German shortwave expert employed in this work, in which the latter referred to his transfer to the above address from Berlin. . . .

Document 2-121

Telegram 1705-8, January 12, 1944

[This message indicates Dulles's support for Sparrow mission.]

477 has been informed by our 684, BB, that he has dispatched urgent warnings to his own country that it is imperative to decline German aid against Russia and urging the most strenuous opposition to German demands for use of Hungarian railroad, on the premise that to allow this would make Russian occupation of the country inevitable. 684 further states that he has emphasized the point that Germany is in no position to devote from 10 to 15 divisions to the occupation of Hungary at this time and he insisted that Hungary does not want German troops and, what is more, should resist them if they were sent.

In an interesting report on the strategic position of the Nazis on the Eastern Front, our 485 emphasizes that Hungary could be of tremendous assistance to the Allies if she could now assume the status of a nonbelligerent and cut off German transit at the same moment that Soviet troops reach the Hungarian Carpathian frontier. In this way Hungary could help in cutting off the southern from the northern German armies; consequently the latter would be compelled to depend upon the precarious Zagreb railroad and their communication problem would be desperate.

This paragraph is addressed to 109 and Jackpot. Please consult my #207 to Algiers and those previous to it. If it is at all possible I urgently recommend that the Sparrow project be carried out. After nursing this project along for 6 months we have now reached the point where H. authorities have shown that they are willing to go ahead. 477's extraordinary personal influence is more than a little responsible for this. I am aware that Pflieger in Algiers is making every possible effort but, in my opinion, the kind of persons recommended in his #141 and #119 are not suitable for this particular work. This project ought to be regarded as a matter worthy of the attention of our highest military authorities, not to be handled as simply a routine parachute job. We have worked very hard on this matter, believing it had your deepest interest, and we would be grateful if you would reexamine the entire project and reach a decision as soon as possible as to the course of action to be taken in this matter.

Document 2-122

Telegram 349 to London, January 13, 1944

[OSS had incomplete knowledge of French agents. Number 284 is Max Shoop.]

With reference to your #438. Arrangements had been made to receive T after he left this place, in consideration of the data received by Zulu and ourselves which seemed to confirm the fact that he was a double agent. 284 has just informed me of the execution today of T and his companion.

Document 2-123

Telegram 1746-50, January 14, 1944

[This message contains information from sources in Germany on Nazi strategic thinking, and Dulles's own views. Jackpot is Whitney Shepardson, Chief of the OSS Secret Intelligence Branch and prewar associate of Dulles in New York.]

Recently OKW's von Solms was in Bern. A reliable informant told us he informed the German Legation of the following: We now look upon the west front as the principal one, and the east front as secondary this year. In order to meet invasion, substantial material and troop preparations have been made. The latter throws light upon the current eastern withdrawal. We believe it is decisively important that we defeat the Anglo-Saxons completely, and though the actual counter attack will come only after sufficient troops have landed, the Anglo-Saxons will also pay heavily for landing. They must be defeated grimly enough to shake the farthest reaches of Britain and, especially, America. We will dispose of all possible forces for this purpose. The morale effect of such a defeat will be great, particularly, in the United States, and Churchill and Roosevelt will be finished politically. This success is also needed for effect on the occupied territories. When they did not land last year, the Anglo-Saxons committed a fatal error. At that time, France and Italy were nearly open and a daring blow would have meant our ruin. There will be rapid stabilization of the eastern front once we turn back the western invasion. The Russian lines, as well as ours, are thin; the average caliber of Russian forces has dropped; the Russians are superior in material for the time being, and this gives their concentrations power to strike. By withdrawing the front, we feel we can withstand their attacks. The situation will be speedily reversed if we can dispatch to the east in summer or fall reinforcements and material from the west. If we stave off the invasion attempt, the Russians will not have the push to defeat us. We anticipate that the war will last another 3 years. This finishes the report attributed to Solms.

The following is from 110: There have been less detailed reports not unlike the above from other good German sources, (consult the end of the 1st paragraph of flash #66 concerning Hitler attitude), suggesting that Hitler's policy is to crush the attempt at invasion at the sacrifice of other fronts. It is almost impossible to ascertain how much of this planted propaganda. From my sources, I derive the following impression, however:

1. The Nazis anticipate an invasion attempt during the next few weeks or months and are making their plans on this assumption.

2. Troop concentrations in the N. France region will not necessarily reveal the spot where the Germans anticipate the principal onslaught, as a large portion of the German troops will be kept in positions to the rear until the precise point of the landing attempt or attempts is made certain.

The following is for 105 and Jackpot: Please do not give the Solms report to Zulu since they will receive it soon. It is preferable not to indicate the fact that you received it before, if you again receive it later.

Document 2-124

Telegram 1754-56, January 15, 1944

[This report is illustrative of OSS Bern's role in counterintelligence.]

Easy from 110. The information herein is from a document purporting to be the examination of Heinrich Rieder, a German deserter, by the Swiss in October 1942. Witness claimed that he entered the German SI in February of 1942 and received his SI training under Col. Gawantka in Munich. Baron von Malsan-Pronikau was head of the Political Information Section of the school. 5 of his colleagues were sent to the United States in June and evidently were among the group arrested after landing from a submarine. None of the 5 are referred to by name. Dr. Werner Pyrkosch was one of Rieder's comrades. Pyrkosch was previously director of the Hong Kong Branch of some Boston firm. In the middle of July Pyrkosch was sent to Pernambuco with his wife and was supposed to go from there to Chicago to take charge of the Chicago area. The plan was for Rieder to go to Chicago also and be head of Section 2-C-8 (Military Political Department) in the same area. An uncle of Rieder's who had a leather goods factory and knew of Rieder's activities was to meet and hide him in Chicago. (Uncle's name not given.) Rieder maintains that he declined to implicate his relatives and made his escape to Switzerland. The following is from 110: Would like to know whether the FBI can confirm any of the above since there is a chance that further information may be secured from this source.

Document 2-125

Telegram 367-69 to London, January 17, 1944

[The Dulles operation continued to play an important role in supporting the French resistance by providing a channel of communication and as an advocate with Allied authorities. Iris is the French resistance delegation in Switzerland; Barres is Benouville.]

Iris to Azur for Dastier Frenay from Barres, #54. A dramatic financial situation prevails here. Resistance was forced to halt all activity. We understand your difficulties. We realize your lack of Pound Sterling and French bank notes. The Comite Centrale has given me the mission of "informing the Allies of our difficulties. We beg them to help you at once to find a solution. We remember that if you deposit Registered Pounds with Baring Brothers, London, for the account of Lombard, Odier & Cie, or Pache, both bankers in Geneva, and if you so inform Iris who has become the general delegate for the resistance by adjunction of the delegate of the northern Zone, Suffren, then we will find in France, as equivalent a limitless number of French bank notes at an advantageous rate of exchange. The same process can be effected with dollars. This solution eliminates the risk of sending funds by parachute. Put a monk or whomever you appoint, in contact with the French payer designated by the Swiss bank. I count on a reply from you before the 25th, when I return to France. This is a desperate call. All services are in debt. Maquis about to disappear if we do not, at all events, obtain an instant advance of funds." I am repeating this message for Washington and Algiers because I have been specifically asked to do so by Barres with whom I discussed the above situation yesterday in its entirety. I am convinced that we should help to arrange for adequate financing of the resistance groups at this critical stage. Information as to your plans in reference to the above situation would be appreciated here.

Document 2-126

Telegram 1807, January 19, 1944

[This message concerns Mussolini's daughter, the widow of Count Ciano.]

We have learned from a source that has proved trustworthy in the past that Edda Ciano has just been permitted to enter Switzerland with her children. We are attempting to have this verified.

Document 2-127

Telegram 1811, January 19, 1944

[Dulles reports further on German strategic expectations and on Edda Ciano.]

I have received the following information from an extremely dependable source who is in close touch with persons who are in a position to know: The Nazis expect the Allies to attempt an invasion of western Europe any time after the end of February but not before that date.

The following is in reference to our #1807: News of Edda's arrival has now been received by our newspapermen who say, however, that they have been absolutely forbidden to send out this information.

Document 2-128

Telegram 1841-43, January 24, 1944

[Bern reports on the situation in France. Source 802 is Devignat.]

The following report is from source 802 and deals with the general French political situation. Plans for the rebuilding of the Radical Party were gravely affected by the death of Sarraut. However, attempts are being made to keep going along these lines. A manifesto is being prepared by a committee composed of 4 members, one of whom is Laurent-Eynac. This manifesto will be publicized via Geneva. Its main features are: (1) a statement of regret regarding the policy adopted by Algiers toward the Parliamentarians and of hope that this policy will be revised to allow an agreement to be reached; (2) agreement with the resistance groups and reaffirmation of the policy of resistance; (3) denouncement of the policy of collaboration and finally, (4) a statement in favor of getting rid of any Parliamentarians who have accepted positions in the Vichy Government.

Rightist elements are in the process of reorganizing. The Radicals have once more established contact with other political parties. The Socialists, whose position is to the left of the Radicals, are very divided among themselves. The Leon Blum supporters are working in opposition to the views of Paul Faure, a pacifist and supporter of the Munich Agreement. Resistance groups have made every effort to persuade the Radicals not to commit themselves to a policy which would exclude the Communists. The Radicals have contacted the Communists very discretely, and the latter seem to take a reasonable attitude. Algiers is regarded as too exclusive by the Communists, who say that they are interested only in having a hand in the government and do not desire a revolution.

Document 2-129

Telegram 1875-78, January 26, 1944

[Planning for the Sparrow mission continues.]

Consult cable #168 from Algiers. 684 came to see 477 and myself to discuss further particulars relative to the Sparrow project. After describing the crucial decision now confronting his government, he said that he had advised the Foreign Minister and 655 to decline German assistance and resist it, should this be necessary. He then proceeded to question us as to whether there was any chance of finding out whether Russia would halt its invasion forces on the Carpathian Line, provided Hungary would decline and resist German assistance and prevent Germany from availing herself of any facilities within her borders, for example, transit air bases and the like. Although fully aware that this might result in open hostilities with the Reich, 684 believed his country had now reached the point where it would be willing to assume this risk. We told him that it was unlikely that this hypothetical question would be placed before the Russians at this particular time. Next he wanted to know whether we would see that such a plan were presented provided he was authorized by his government to make a definite proposal. Our reply was that for the time being at least we thought it more advisable simply to report what he had said as a matter of military importance. He said that it was his sincere hope that some clue would be forthcoming which would help his country determine her course.

It should be pointed out that 684 is a trained, discreet man. He was extremely serious and spoke with complete awareness of the significance of his statement. Although it is entirely possible that in the end his government might be afraid to make such a desperate decision, he made it plain, that in his opinion, they would risk a break with Germany and try to defend their own frontiers provided they were granted any safeguard against an invasion by the Red Army. The discussion was on military matters exclusively and no political questions were raised. From his conversation it was quite clear that he felt Anglo-Saxon occupation would be welcomed by his government.

I thought it advisable to pass the above information on to you, and, if you deem it wise, the Joint Chiefs of Staff might also be informed. As has been stated earlier, 477, more than any other American, enjoys the confidence of the Hungarians.

Document 2-130

Telegram 403-5 to London, January 27, 1944

[This report on conditions in Germany came from George Richter (817), a German trade unionist residing in Switzerland.]

From 817 to Sandy. In reference to your #489 to Vogel. The German people have shown good self-control during the bombing raids. There is excellent organization of fire fighting equipment and food services for people who have been bombed out. However, in places where evacuees are sent there is a great deal of friction. Those who have been bombed out of their homes, realizing that their destroyed property can only be replaced by a victory of German arms, are fanatically insistent on a continuation of the war. The middle classes in particular have been roused to fury against the Allies by the air raids. Although there is no lowering in the morale of Germany's troops, there is an increase in the number of draft evaders and deserters.

The bombings are held by pious people to be a retribution for anti-Semitic pogroms. Most of the people no longer have faith in the possibility of ultimately winning the war. They have become indifferent. Except for potatoes, food supplies are holding out in the urban centers. The beer is very bad, and wines cannot be bought.

The underground connections of the Social-Democratic Party extend all over Germany, radiating from an illegal center. There is not much Communist activity in the southern part of the country. Some separatist feeling exists in Austria and southern Bavaria, where it is joined to bitter anti-Prussian sentiments. Throughout the country, inconceivable terror exists. People are often executed for repeating jokes about the Nazis. In Nazi Ordensburgen, an organization has been established to assassinate all Germans cooperating with the forces of occupation. A successful anti-Nazi revolt is out of the question. The Party can be overthrown only by the Army, but nothing can be accomplished along this line until serious defeats have been inflicted on the latter. Village folk are frightened to death of foreign workers imported into the Reich. German women are arming themselves. The Nazi opposition is drawing up a list of Party members to be executed. The youth of Germany is expected to develop a pronounced swing to the left in the future, although a definite prediction cannot be made with any certainty.

Document 2-131

Telegram 406-8 to London, January 27, 1944

[Labor leaders associated with Dulles in Switzerland frequently passed information on conditions in occupied Europe to their associates in London.]

Sandy Eclair from 328 for Oldenbroek. Although it has not yet been set up on an organized basis, work with the Rhine barge men is going forward. Information on conditions in Germany secured through personal contact. Rhine barge men are anti-Nazi and look forward to the downfall of the Hitler regime. However, they do not participate in activist work for fear of the terrible consequences. Our opportunities are also lessened by the reduced amount of traffic. They provide the following information: (1) Through sabotage efforts of French patriots, the canal bridge system in France has been disorganized, especially in the Chalons-sur-Marne and Chateau Thierry region. (2) For the first time there have been incidents of sabotage on railroads in Germany. (3) In order to cut down desertions, new Alsace recruits have been incorporated in Waffen SS scheduled for the Soviet front since the Reds are merciless in battling the Waffen SS. (4) The people of Baden and Hamburg are delighted by the bombings of Berlin because they feel the war will end just that much sooner as a result. (5) Mathis factory at Strasbourg-Neudorf ought to be attacked from the air. It is working for Junkers. (6) Tanks move about within the large Dresden factories, where a quantity of French workers are employed, in order to guard the workers and frighten them as well. (7) There are big underground factories manufacturing munitions and chemical products located in the forest between Aschaffenburg and Darlstadt.

Document 2-132

Telegram 409-10 to London, January 27, 1944

[This telegram contains a message from Ignazio Silone (475) to fellow anti-Fascists in London.]

From 475 to Lussato. Ivanoe Bonomi, who is president of the Rome Liberation Committee, and Meuccio Ruini are both supporters of "Democratie du Travail." The Republican Traditionalist Party has been organized under Lawyer Conti in Rome. A small Christian Socialist Party is quite busy in the north. In Milan, a new Communist Party under the leadership of Onorato Damon and Bruno Maffi publishes "Prometeo." Lawyer Basso heads the Maximalist Socialist organization which has also been set up in Milan. The Republican Socialist Front is the name given the united front combination of Republicans, Maximalists and Christian Socialists. This week a publication appeared in Zurich entitled "L'Avvenire dei Lavoratori." This is the organ of Italian Socialists who lean toward Federalist and Democratic principles. This group is part of the Italian Socialist Party of Proletarian Union. It opposes Nenni's proposal to unite with communists within the party.

Document 2-133

Telegram 1888-89, January 27, 1944

[In early 1944, Dulles alerted Washington to the coalescing of German opposition elements he called "Breakers." Some of the group's efforts to contact the West were made in Spain and Portugal. Number 659 is Admiral Wilhelm Canaris, Chief of the Abwehr, German military intelligence; 512 is Hans Bernd Gisevius, German consul in Zurich and Abwehr agent; Gorter is Eduard Waetjen, another Abwehr officer in the German resistance.]

The German oppositional group, called Breakers, is composed of various intellectuals from certain military and government circles. They have loose organization among themselves. Luke's surname is John and have been given to understand that he is one of 659's men for Spain and Portugal, intended especially for Anglo-Saxon contacts. Rocky is Zulu's Ambassador to [*sic*] Campbell in Lisbon. Beaulac of our Madrid office is known as Bearcat. You may be interested to know that for the most part, Breakers maintain their foreign contacts and communications through 659 organization and both our 512 and Gorter act as intermediaries here in Bern. (Note from 110: I quite understand that you may doubt the foregoing statement but I am convinced of its accuracy after examining the situation for a period of months.)

For a number of reasons, I have not talked with Zulu about the Breakers situation at this particular time, and pending further developments I recommend that you also refrain from doing so on the basis of information in my messages.

Document 2-134

Telegram 1890-93, January 27, 1944

[Dulles here provides the SI Branch with additional information on the German resistance. Gorter is Eduard Waetjen.]

To Carib and Jackpot. With reference to your #1051. We have at the present time, by means of Gorter, secured a line to Breakers which we think can be used now for staying in close touch with events. Since any slight break would be disastrous, no constructive purpose would be served by cabling particulars. The Breakers contain 3 tendencies, on the whole, i.e., evolutionary, revolutionary, and military. The 1st of these factions takes the stand that, in the face of history and the people, complete responsibility should be shouldered to the grim conclusion by the leader and his cohorts. In general, the other two groups think that drastic action should be taken to get rid of the leader, and that a new government should be organized before the fighting stops so that it could thereupon join in the negotiations. In spite of these contrary opinions, these groups keep in touch and are very eager to obtain political ammunition from our side. They consider this to be sadly wanting, and they wish it to reenforce their movement at the present time and following the collapse as well. Western orientation is preferred by the Breakers over Eastern orientation, but they fear that their nation is being directed by events toward the influence of the East. They are in favor of extensive social changes.

Are you able to check, in an extremely judicious manner, the word which we have received that an associate of Gorter, whose name is Luke, has been in contact with Bearcat and Rocky? It is very likely that this is exceedingly secret. I am informed by Gorter that he and his friends are inclined to doubt the encouragement which Luke has received from Rocky regarding the idea that negotiations would be facilitated by putting the Military in power and changing the government.

I would appreciate hearing of any indication with which you could supply me regarding what you would be interested in achieving via the Breakers, and could be pursued effectively at this time. I do not understand what our policy is and what offers, if any, we could give to any resistance movement.

Document 2-135

Telegram 415-17 to London, January 28, 1944

[This message from the French resistance to London via Bern discusses plans for sabotage and disruption of communications at the time of the Allied invasion.]

The following Zeus, given below in substance, was transmitted by Legrand, Chief of FER Service of CER to 284:

SNCF Service is ready to act when the moment comes. They strongly recommend that action at that moment be restricted to sabotage or plane attack against important military railroads and troops movements instead of against railroads and equipment in general. Since the Nazis make use of the civil reserve to meet military requirements, the latter course only creates critical internal supply problems. The SNFC Service asserts that transportation will be absolutely tied up at the zero hour. . . .

[Here follows a list of targets.]

. . . The plan for the zero hour is to trisect France into zones radiating from the point of the landing:

Zone A: 100 kilometers deep
Zone B: the adjoining 200 kilometers
Zone C: the remainder of the country

It is planned to bring about total paralysis in the first 2 zones, but in the last zone action will be taken only against military movements. The following methods will be used to disrupt movement: sabotage of telephones, demolition of water supplies for engines, destruction of exits from engine depots, severing of lines, etc.

Legrand hopes to depart for London presently.

Document 2-136

Telegram 1913-14, January 29, 1944

[This cable futher describes the German resistance group "Breakers."]

110 for Carib and Jackpot. (Falstaff.) These groups are made up of well-educated and liberal individuals, but nevertheless, they do not have rightist tendencies and are confident that in the future the Government will have to be really leftist. The Fat Boy of Germany is popularly considered the German Ciano, and as I see it, he currently commands no support in reputable opposition circles. I believe that Gorter may be considered trustworthy for existing purposes, but like the majority of such Germans, he is acting for the future welfare of his own country, and hence his opinions may not always check with ours. I am satisfied by the evidence before me that he wants to wipe out every element of the current Nazi group. Recommend that you use Breakers for my contacts except for the Fat Boy's group and Falstaff.

Document 2-137

Telegram 1920-22, January 29, 1944

[OSS assisted Italian anti-Fascists in seizing Campione. Number 809 is Donald Jones, the OSS officer in Lugano; 812 is Magistrati.]

The Italian enclave, Campione, which borders entirely on Switzerland or the waters opposite Lugano, has a population of about 600 and is anti-Fascist almost to a man. An anti-Fascist, De Baggis, took over the administration de facto January 28th. The following is confidential: from our point of view this matter has possibilities if it is dealt with carefully, as De Baggis is working in close touch with our 809. A wire to Badoglio to recommend the Legation's appointment of a commissioner is being considered by 812. We feel that a request of this kind should receive backing if the request can be effected without precipitating trouble with the Swiss.

It stands to reason Germans and Neo-Fascists will urge the Swiss to grant them permission to dispatch a detachment for taking over Campione. However, since only the King's government is recognized here, it should have the right to dispatch officials to Campione. The Swiss will find the matter very delicate and may feel they must assume the administration of Campione temporarily, as the presence of an anti-Fascist enclave reveals real possibilities. However, since there has been no public disturbance in Campione, they may keep hands off. If Campione faces an acute financial situation and 812's funds are not adequate for the job, we may feel it wise to aid Campione secretly through 812.

Document 2-138

Telegram 425-27 to London, January 31, 1944

[This message concerns the plight of the French resistance. Iris is the resistance delegation in Switzerland; Jerome is Michel Brault, a resistance commander.]

For Azur from Iris; from Jerome and Cheval to Gen. de Gaulle and Dastier (#62). "The position of the Refractaires is tragic. Almost totally without arms and suffering from lack of financial support, we are losing 100 men weekly; the Germans take no prisoners and slaughter all the wounded. In spite of our shortage of arms, we inflict twice as many casualties upon the enemy. MUR has, in the southern zone, an effective complement of 22,000 men in cadres, and in the north 14,000. Half of the men are in camps, only 10% of them armed, and the other half are scattered but can be mobilized at a moment's notice. The cadres are strong, and manned by seasoned soldiers. In spite of what seems to be indifference on the part of the Allies and Algiers, the morale remains very high. We have taken, with you, the serious responsibility of encouraging uprisings by continual propaganda without furnishing material assistance. We have assured responsible Maquis that our men are ready for any sacrifice, but we want to be sure that you clearly understand the value of contributions the Maquis can give to Allied military action through the guerrillas' dispersion throughout the whole area. The Maquis need money, munitions and arms immediately in order to carry out such action, or else the Refractaires, weary of meaningless words, will be reduced to murder and pillage, and the country will feel itself abandoned by the Allies and Algiers. This message was relayed with the approval of Cleanthe [?] and all responsible military leaders." The following is from 110: At Iris's request, this was transmitted to Algiers and Washington for their information. We sincerely hope that it will be possible to offer effective assistance.

Document 2-139

Telegram 1923-24, January 31, 1944

[In this message concerning Rumania, 495 is Gregoire Gafencu. Iuliu Maniu was a leader of the Rumanian Peasants' Party.]

I have been informed by our 495 that Maniu has requested him to serve as his agent outside of the country. 495 has contacted Zulu, as he is very eager to leave here. If no other means presents itself, he is thinking of running the danger of a secret getaway through France. 495 is a realist with regard to his country's present situation and he has been of the opinion for quite awhile that they ought to attempt to deal directly with Russia despite the risk involved. He was the last Rumanian Minister to Russia and he feels that the associations he has in that country would aid greatly in establishing direct contact at the present time. 495 realizes, however, he is gambling on a long shot.

CHAPTER

3

Prelude to D-Day; The Rise of the German Opposition

February–June 1944

Document 3-1

Telegram 1937-38, February 1, 1944

[This report of an imminent German withdrawal to a defensive line well north of Rome proved to be erroneous. Rome was not liberated until June 1944.]

472's wire #42 to Algiers on January 31st, is summarized as follows:

The Nazi Command has decided to organize their resistance on the line La Spezia–Pistoia–Rimini–Dicomano. There are four facts which indicate that there will be an early exodus south of this line: The first indication is the order issued to Nazi civilians to leave Italy not later than January 31. The second point is the fact that Italian refugees are forbidden to move south of this line. The third important sign is the cancellation of orders the Nazis had given to Italian industrial firms south of this position. All industrial machinery in these factories has been moved to Northern Italy. The fourth factor is the situation in Rome. No attempt has been made to insure provisions for the capital and the garrison has not been strengthened with any new additions.

Document 3-2

Telegram 1945-46, February 3, 1944

[Devignat, source 802, provided this report on German exploitation of French labor.]

The following report is from source 802. A short while ago, Saukel came back to France and made demands for the supply of 150,000 workmen by France to Germany in February and for a similar number of workmen in the following month. In addition, Saukel demanded appropriate legalization which would enable the speedy mobilization of all males between the ages of 18 and 60. (The reason for this is to get all men in this age group out of the way in case there is an invasion.) Saukel also demanded a law to permit a special census of all women from 18 to 25 who are not married or who are married but childless. It would then be possible to send such women to Germany or put them to work in French war industry. The Vichy regime refused Saukel's requests and negotiations are being continued by the latter. The source reports that this is an indication that Saukel has defeated Speer in the matter of additional requisition of French workmen. The informant also states that he is of the opinion that any demand which would require that French women be sent to Germany would result in the most extreme reaction in French popular feeling.

Document 3-3

Telegram 1963, February 4, 1944

[A Polish source, 513, reported on a possible German secret weapon.]

Number 513 informed me in the course of a discussion with him that he felt certain the Nazis were making ready big amounts of oil fire bombs especially for use against invasion forces. Such bombs spread oil on water which is set on fire when it touches water or some other object. Number 513 admitted that he was unable to supply with [precise details] but stated that he thought the manufacture of these bombs was centered mainly in the vicinity of Vienna.

Document 3-4

Telegram 1965-66, February 4, 1944

[Dulles continues to report on the German resistance movement "Breakers."]

To Carib and Jackpot. The names listed below may possibly be of interest with reference to my wires on the subject of Breakers:

1. The socialist leader, Leuschner, previously the Minister of Interior in Hesse.

2. General Oster who was previously 659's right-hand man. Some months back, he was taken into custody by the Gestapo but was released. However, he has been kept under watch. I am informed that Keitel has just discharged him officially.

3. The former Mayor [of] Leipzig, Goerdler. He is a capable organizer.

The Breakers are inclined to be leftish and I understand that they feel that someone like No. 1 would be a more acceptable kind of person, if it is assumed that neither the communists nor the military dominate the transition period.

Document 3-5

Telegram 1992-94, February 5, 1944

[In this cable, Dulles relays an appeal from Italian resistance leaders to Count Sforza regarding Trieste.]

The following communication was sent by Motta via Leo to our 683 and 826, and they in turn asked that it be forwarded to 510: "It is imperative that you get in touch with Allies and responsible Yugoslav leaders so that some course of action may be decided upon in regard to Trieste, whereby better Yugoslav-Italian collaboration may be effected there. We recommend that the problem be dealt with as follows and also suggest that similar action be taken in regard to Fiume: Italy should retain its sovereignty over Trieste in conformity with the principle of self-determination; the port should have a free custom zone and be made an international corpus separatum. We are organizing contacts with [forces?] fighting Germans and Yugoslav Partisans. Please answer as quickly as you can." The message is signed Adolph Tino.

In addition Motta substantiated the reported cooperation between Italians and Yugoslavs in the Trieste region and said that between the 15th and 25th of last month there were numerous incidents of sabotage and fierce encounters with the Germans northwest of Gorizia.

Concerning the message for 510, which was presented to Zulu as well, I pointed out to 826 that in my opinion it was absolutely preposterous to consider any negotiations at this time between local Italians and Yugoslavs in connection with future plans for Trieste. I also advised him that I felt quite certain that 510 would not be given the message. Nevertheless, I believed you should be advised of this. Zulu SOE are taking the same stand on this matter.

Document 3-6

Telegram 450-53, February 8, 1944

[Dulles and Max Shoop (284) continue to work intimately with the French resistance, raising problems for U.S.–U.K.–Free French relations.]

From 284 and 110. In reference to the new Maquis plan mentioned, which seems to have been agreed upon by the French, British and yourselves, we are most eager to get additional information about the matter. The part America will play in the support—is disturbing to us. You have no doubt seen the desperate wires Iris has been dispatching because he has not received financing in the past weeks.

We have no desire to cross any wires; however, we are of the opinion that we could give aid at this end since our contacts with resistance have been steadily improving. We are restricting ourselves to the following work: 4,000,000 each month for Maquis through Iris; acting as a means for sending their messages to Indigo and Asur and receiving miscellaneous operational and intelligence information such as Zeus, Ulysses, and Hercule. Up to now, there has been no basis for Zulu's fears regarding liaison with resistance. Recently the Iris delegation here was reinforced by the representative of north zone and, for the past weeks, Barres has been here trying to make arrangements for the needed financing.

Confidential. Because of the direct military significance of resistance groups in France, it is my opinion that we should think about taking active steps and make certain that sufficient financing is afforded to these groups. I realize that it is important to work in closest harmony with Zulu but am of the opinion that this should be on an equal basis, especially since our position in France is stronger than Zulu's since the Smuts incident; furthermore we can be more effective than they in certain ways.

Would like to learn whatever you can safely tell us regarding any coordinated program for resistance which you may have. Based on our current information, we are truthfully distressed at seeing the military possibilities of resistance tend to disintegrate as a result of the delays in supplying effective assistance both in materials and money; also by the absence of evidence to support the fact that the relationship between resistance groups and the United States is being developed fully. We are aware that we can not know all the political cross currents of the French situation at this end; nor do we know the complete picture. We can only furnish you with our own conclusions drawn from the reactions which resistance affiliations have displayed.

Document 3-7

Telegram 2026-30, February 11, 1944 (extracts)

[Dulles concerned himself with the activities of French Vichyites, as well as resistance figures in Switzerland.]

Although some resistance people believe that Jardin is trustworthy, I myself am of the opinion that he is attempting to play safe by performing favors from time to time for resistance. He is playing a peculiar part here, trying to get himself into the good graces of resistance circles at the same time that he is keeping up his relations with Vichy. I refused to see him; however, I am keeping check on what he is doing through 492. . . .

Jardin claimed that he had been invited by Marshal Petain to accept the position of the latter's Chef de Cabinet, but that he declined because the entourage was suspicious of him. Jardin states that Petain's entourage believes that Pierre Laval entrusted him with a special mission in Switzerland, but that this suspicion is unfounded. . . . The following is for Algiers: I would be grateful if you would make cautious inquiries with Couve de Murville, as well as other individuals, and let me know what opinion Algiers holds regarding Jardin. I request this because Jardin's maneuvres at this end may take on importance and because certain people who trust him (which does not include 492) might find their relationship with Jardin a grave matter should it turn out that Jardin is actually employed by the Nazis.

Document 3-8

Telegram 242-44 to Algiers, February 11, 1944

[The case of use of the enclave of Campione ("Quail") is a rare instance of Dulles taking a more cautious approach than SO in London and Algiers. He knew that Allied use of the territory depended on the forbearance of Swiss authorities. Number 812 is Magistrati, the Italian Minister in Bern.]

Would appreciate your cooperation in the Quail matter. In reference to the 1st point of your #191, however, current advice is adverse to droppings in the enclave or lake since such a plan would mean flying over Switzerland. This might and probably would mean being spotted, and detection of any Quail activities would doubtless force the Swiss to eat Quail, with subsequent loss of other possibilities. There is no reason why there should not be dropping on Italian soil in the vicinity of Quail for transit through the Quail area. We are attempting to secure pin pointing of the most satisfactory dropping two (sic). As a tentative or possibly a permanent refuge, we feel Quail can be utilized by a fairly small number of people. Although tremendous discretion is necessary, we plan to use Quail in penetrating Italy. At present we are working with 812 on the organization of a new Quail administration. Since the former possesses almost no money, I have financed up to 5,000 Swiss francs for this month because if such action is not taken the new and friendly Quail administration may crumble.

I am extremely doubtful about the project utilizing Swiss territory as secret headquarters for penetration east and north. The police in Switzerland are very highly organized and watchful. It would be hard to go across the borders and return. I feel that the simplest penetration of Germany is through France with connection with current facilities for transit from France to Spain or Switzerland. Nevertheless, if your people arrive either Quail or here, will do all within our power consistent with the security of our present position, which is at best hazardous, due to Swiss police measures.

Document 3-9

Radiotelephone Transmission No. 85, February 12, 1944 (extract)

[In this evening telephone call, Dulles discusses psychological warfare aspects of the administration of liberated areas.]

Italy
As an important measure of psychological warfare, we should do more to give publicity to what is happening in the liberated areas in Europe. Two things have recently brought this to my attention. One was Sforza's statement praising what the AMGOT has done in Italy. Coming from him, both as an Italian and sometimes as a critic of our policy, this is important. We should try to get over to the areas of Europe under Nazi domination, and to Germany itself, what we are doing and planning to do in the way of returning the liberated territories to the administration of their own people. Then there was recently in the *London Times* an interesting article about the reforms introduced in the educational system in Italy. The University of Messina was especially cited. Teachers and professors in Germany and Nazi-controlled countries would be tremendously interested to know about the educational regime installed after an Allied occupation, and how once more scholars are allowed freely to develop and teach their own ideas. They would also be interested to know that professors and teachers were appointed because of their intellectual attainments and not because of their political views and subservience to party doctrine. . . .

Document 3-10

Radiotelephone Transmission No. 86, February 14, 1944

[Dulles here discusses the postwar German internal political outlook.]

Germany
Certain observers of the political scene in Germany believe that there are only two political forces in Germany on which any new democratic government can be based. First the Socialists, and second the Catholic Centrum Party. This is on the assumption, of course, that after the breakdown, Communism and anarchy do not prevail in Germany. As a matter of fact, the democratic cabinets in Germany from the end of the last war to the advent of Hitler were primarily built around these two

political forces. As an outstanding example of this one can cite the government of Otto Braun in Prussia, which lasted longer than any democratic cabinet in Germany, i.e., for about twelve years. This was based on the Socialist Party.

. . . Of the democratic forces, namely the Socialists and the Catholics, the Socialists will be by far the stronger once political life is reestablished in Germany, since they should be able to rely on the masses of German labor insofar as the latter have not gone over to the Communists. Immediately upon the Nazi collapse, a considerable force of the Socialist labor union officials should again become available to help organize German labor and to win them over to a democratic form of government. The labor leaders from outside Germany with international experience and connections should also be of help. The former German labor union officials, of course, had to discontinue all political activities under the Nazi regime; but many of them remained in the factories of Germany as workers waiting for the day when they can resume their political work. Undoubtedly the Communists will try everything in their power to gain control of the German labor movement, but if the situation is properly and efficiently handled, and if the period of chaos after the German collapse is not too long, it seems likely that German labor—which has no desire to exchange Nazi dictatorship for Communist dictatorship—can be won over to support a democratic system. (To be continued: telephone circuit failed at this point)

Document 3-11

Telegram 482 to London, February 15, 1944

[Just as the British hesitated to accept the authenticity of Fritz Kolbe / George Wood as a source, they also questioned the accuracy and value of Dulles's information on the German opposition. In particular, British intelligence distrusted Hans Bernd Gisevius, number 512, wondering whether his loyalty lay with the OSS and the Allies or with his Abwehr connection and Germany.]

Obtain source of your information sent us in message #545 if you can possibly do so. The message is unclear, and the data contained in it will in all probability be second hand if it emanates from Zulu here. What do you mean by compromised and from what angle? I see 512 once in a while and I keep myself informed and up to date on his activities. It would be useful to have any facts or clues should Broadway ever be able to supply them, but I usually find that their data on subject is incomplete.

Document 3-12

Telegram 483 to London, February 15, 1944

[This cable concerns the Dulles role as a channel of communication for French resistance elements that were not controlled by General de Gaulle.]

To Tertius. I hope that your French collaborators appreciate the fact that the Indigo and Iris messages relayed by us to you usually originate in Resistance centers in France, and thus their form and substance can not be disputed by either Iris or us. I have been considerably disturbed even to have to send out certain of these dispatches, in view of their immoderate phrasing. However, I hope that you and Algiers will be able to inform the proper authorities confidentially that I am not responsible either for what these messages say or how they say it, and I have no control over the matter.

Document 3-13

Telegram 2054-56, February 15, 1944

[In early 1944, Dulles and OSS Washington intensified their efforts to identify "useful Germans," individuals who could be counted on to contribute to the development of a peace-loving, pro-West, and democratic Germany after the war.]

Please refer to your #1181 and previous cables.

The lists mentioned in paragraph 1 of the above cable are receiving my active attention. I have classified useful Germans into the following categories for convenience: also included, for reference purposes, are names of people in Switzerland who may be of future aid to us in completing our list, and some of whom might be useful after the war in Germany proper. 1. Labor leaders and Socialists: O.B. (mentioned in our #1828) assigned our number 830. W.D., V.B., and G.R. are assigned our numbers 831, 832, and 833 respectively in addition to our numbers 817, 500, and 328. 328's wife, who is very competent, came from Germany originally. She is somewhat like our Eva in N.Y., although able to make her own decisions even more effectively. Both 328 and wife intend to go to Germany and help organize German Labor along democratic lines after the war. (This couple may be extremely helpful.) We have Weigl and Linder, on the Austrian side, who have been assigned our numbers 835 and 834 in that order, as well as our 656 who might be of assistance by way of Luxembourg. 2. Scientists and Intellectuals: Beeking, Roepke, Dessauer, and Linsom. Further listings will be sent later.

Document 3-14

Telegram 2057-61, February 15, 1944

[Dulles here provides the names of additional Germans believed to be competent anti-Nazis worthy of postwar responsibilities. He also presents ideas on occupation policy.]

This is a continuation of #2054-56. 3. Lawyers and men of business: Max Doerner, our 670, who was once connected with the Dresdener Bank; Willy Dreyfus, once head of the firm of J. Dreyfus & Company; Rathenau's brother-in-law Andreae, designated as our 643. [Incorrect. See code number list at the back of this book.]

4. Officials of the government: see my #1828 for references to Dr. Wilhelm Abegg, given our number 836; also in this class is our 512.

5. Prominent Catholics: Father Augustine Galen, the bishop of Munster's brother; also our numbers 801, 821 and 478.

6. Outstanding Protestants: Besides our 665, there is Freudenberg, with whom our 474 has been associated.

Later on we will make some additions to all of the above classifications, and we will also send similar lists of publishers and journalists. We will also send material on the 4th paragraph of your #1183. If you feel that it is necessary to have more detailed accounts of any of the people named above, kindly let us know.

Although it is not easy to make generalizations on the subject of your 3rd paragraph, we feel that a number of priests are in a position to be of help to us, as are certain carefully chosen Protestant clergymen. Adherents of the Bekenntniskirche may be especially useful. So far as the greater number of school teachers is concerned, we have reservations about the possibility of their being of use. We are not sure what you mean by "academic administrators." There should be many government job-holders who will be useful after the ousting of the Nazis now in control. In all categories it will be difficult to settle upon a method of selection. Since we feel that each locality, village or town will be quite familiar with its own Nazi and anti-Nazi personalities, as a result of bitter experience, we suggest giving thought to the wisdom of establishing local committees. These should be made up of known anti-Nazis in whom confidence may be placed; their function would be to provide the authorities of occupation with their estimates of individuals suggested for administrative jobs. They would set in an advisory capacity. In any case, we feel that the powers who occupy the country ought not take in with them a set of fixed judgments based on a list which could be made up at this time by either you or ourselves.

As psychological warfare move tending to aid the preparation of occupation organization, we advise that announcements be broadcast repeatedly at some time in the future, addressed to all individuals whom the Nazis ousted because they did not hew to the line of Nazi doctrine. These individuals should be urged to keep themselves at the disposition of the new administration which the occupying powers will establish. For such classes as police, teachers, university professors and government functionaries, dismissal by the Nazis for failure to conform ought to be satisfactory proof of their usefulness to us.

I hope that thought is being given to the functions of UNRRA in the fields of education, amusement (for example, motion pictures), literature and things spiritual. It seems to me that UNRRA here will have almost the same importance as UNRRA in the sphere of material things.

Document 3-15

Telegram 2068-73, February 15, 1944

[This message presents Dulles's views on the historical configuration of German politics and its implications for postwar occupation policy.]

. . . . Without question the Communists will attempt to attain control of the German Labor Movement. However, provided the period of chaos following Germany's downfall does not last too long, and if the situation is handled capably, it is likely that German labor can be induced to back a democratic government since they have no wish to replace a Nazi dictatorship for a communist one. The only closely knit Bourgeois element which is not linked up with Nazi ideology is the Catholic Centrum element. This applies especially in western and southern Germany because the Catholic influence there was anti-dictatorship whether of the communist or Nazi variety.

There never was a Protestant political block in Germany. Protestants usually scattered their votes among parties representing the right, middle and Democrats. It is regrettable that there were numerous Protestants who gave their support to military Junker nationalism. On the other hand there is a good element represented in Bekenntnis Kirche which is prepared to support attempts by Catholics and Socialists to establish a Democratic system.

For the purpose of averting political chaos in Germany which would promote the setting up of a Communist State, as a matter of policy, we should give serious thought to whether or not, in the first stages of occupation, we should support those political groups, especially Centrum and Socialists as a foundation for the establishment of a democratic government. Such a policy would not mean the exclusion of any other constructive democratic forces which may develop. New individuals and new parties will take their place in the political scene here just as occurred in Italy.

Although we may be inclined to let political matters in Germany develop in a natural fashion, such a course might turn out to be extremely dangerous because of the absolute destruction of all political machinery at the hands of the Nazis. In spite of the fact that the old German political parties were far from perfect and the future may witness enormous changes, it is still true that the Centrum and Socialist parties alone could be speedily re-formed after the collapse and they are the only ones which may be strong enough to give direction to political life in Germany. The German people will need sound guidance politically in order to develop a democratic system after the collapse. If we neglect to help supply this, Germany may be the scene of unbridled political passions in commotion the result of which might be a new type of dictatorship which would be a serious problem for the country whose forces occupy Germany.

There is a chance that the Socialist and Catholic parties may cooperate and discover a basis for joint action. Outstanding refugees, representing Catholic and Socialist points of view, have conferred here on various occasions and although they were confronted with difficulties on education problems, they were not far apart when it came to the broad political outlook for Germany after the war.

In conclusion, I suggest that we assist in the establishment of political life in Germany beginning on the ground floor and that we achieve this by using local communities as a basis for our activities and centering our efforts around labor leaders and church leaders who have not been guilty of compromising their own beliefs.

Document 3-16

Telegram 252-53 to Algiers, February 16, 1944

[This message illustrates the clandestine intelligence aspects of OSS operations in Switzerland. Number 809 is Donald Jones, OSS representative in Lugano.]

What password will the agent use? At what point is he making his entrance into Switzerland and where is the cut-out wanted? In the event that time does not permit you to give us this data and if he is coming from the Lugano region, he should call our 809 . . . at the Hotel Splendide. This call should be made from a public telephone booth and he should employ the password "Pocatte." Additional particulars will then be arranged by 809. In the event that there is any postponement in leaving, I would prefer to work out transportation through Campione, concerning which I hope to wire the particulars shortly. I am afraid that your plan does not give enough weight to the tight police watch and very fine counter-espionage organization which exist at this end. There is a very great possibility that he will be apprehended very quickly if there is not the most cautious planning of each detail beforehand. In addition, I do not favor very much the utilization of 809 in this affair, because his situation is extremely uncertain. However, I cannot find any other way of proceeding in the light of the lack of time mentioned in your wires. Should you notify me that there has been any delay, I may revise this arrangement. Bear in mind that telephones are not secure and that Lugano is 7 hours distant; consequently, everything must be arranged through messages by courier.

Document 3-17

Telegram 2083-84, February 16, 1944

[From time to time OSS Bern reported on the views and activities of Japanese personnel in Europe. Number 513 is a Polish source.]

513 is the source of the following report. (From 110: the accuracy of this material is impossible to control; however, 513 claims he received it from a reliable source.) A conference of Jap military attachés, at which were present all the attachés in Eu-

rope who were able to get there, took place last month in Budapest. The precise attendance has not been ascertained. The general point of view was held to be that the Allies would not be successful in establishing a foothold on the Continent this year. Those who participated in the meeting are said to have reached the conclusion that the USSR could persist at the present rate for another year, and that the breaking point for the Nazis might not occur for the same length of time. According to their estimate, on the 1st of the year 12 U.S. divisions were in the region of the Mediterranean, out of a total of 26 American divisions calculated to be in the European-African Theater. They estimated also that in 1944 the U.S. could send across 4 more divisions each month.

Document 3-18

Telegram 2086-87, February 16, 1944

[In this message, Dulles discusses policy concerning defection of Nazi officials.]

The information that some of the Nazi officials serving at Ankara had frankly joined us has been remarked with interest here. In connection with the situation at this end, I have never given encouragement to movements of this sort, as they serve only to paralyze and deprive of any value particular individuals who might be potentially useful to us. If, however, such movements become more frequent, I can understand that they could have genuine psychological repercussions in Germany, and it is possible that some Nazi officials here would be tempted to follow the example. I would be grateful for any help in regard to this situation, especially if the Nazis make any inquiries along the following lines:

1. Whether or not we want them to join us now.
2. Whether we will offer them any protection, if they keep their current status in order to be of greater assistance to us.

Document 3-19

Telegram 484 to London, February 17, 1944

[The Allies were constantly concerned about the German naval threat to convoys bound for Russia. Although the battleship *Tirpitz* had been immobilized by British submarines in September 1943, it remained a perceived danger. The following report was inaccurate; the *Tirpitz* remained inoperative in Norway due to British air attacks and was finally sunk in November 1944.]

A communication in conventional language has been sent to S-G by his Naval informant, and he alleges that the message translated says: "At 4 o'clock in the morning on the 26th of this month the Prinz Eugen and the Tirpitz, accompanied by a dozen destroyers, will depart from the Norwegian Fjord, headed north-northwest."

Although I am aware of your doubts apropos of this affair, and though I share them, it seemed to me to be my duty to relay this information to you. It came into our hands with no financial obligations attached.

Document 3-20

Telegram 2089-94, February 17, 1944 (extracts)

[Allied efforts to convince Hungary to break with Germany proceeded side by side with discussions with certain Hungarian officials concerning "Sparrow" mission, the parachute-dropping of OSS agents to make contact with anti-German opposition elements. Number 684, Baron Bakach-Bessenyey, the Hungarian Minister in Bern, was the point of contact for both OSS and the U.S. Legation; Royall Tyler, number 477, was the primary adviser to both Dulles and Minister Harrison, as well as a channel to the Hungarians.]

On Wednesday, when the Sparrow matter was under discussion, 477 and I were informed by 684 that the latter now had a reply from Foreign Minister Ghyczy apropos of 684's emphatic recommendations as to the policy which Hungary should pursue. 684 had urged that Hungary's position should be that she would undertake to defend the Carpathians, unassisted, and resist pressure from Germany or German offers of support. 684 believed that in this policy lay the only hope of preventing the Soviet from treating Hungary as enemy territory. In reply, Ghyczy gave the usual reassurances that Hungary would not resist British or American forces but had no confidence in the Soviet, and that in spite of preferring to defend the Carpathians single handed, Hungary was not in a position at this time to resist Nazi forces dispatched to the Carpathians against the Reds. . . .

. . . I feel that 684 is making every effort to persuade his countrymen to take action to eliminate the very legitimate grievances which the Soviet has against Hungary; however, a solution will be extremely hard to find, even if one assumes that he is successful in convincing his people, which is doubtful, since Russian antagonism on ideological and social grounds is basic as I'm inclined to suspect a large number of Hungarians believe.

Document 3-21

Telegram 1026, February 18, 1944

[Dulles reports that the German legation is gathering information on U.S. domestic politics.]

For Victor from 110. Usually reliable source furnishes the following. Minister Bielefeld who recently attached German Legation here has been given task by Staats Sekretaer von Steengracht in Foreign Office to collect all information available here covering developments in United States of America; in particular he is to follow election developments which now specially interest Germans. Bielefeld was once in charge of economic section of German Embassy in London.

Counselor for Legation von Straempel reported as having been in United States of America until outbreak of war and since then information section of Foreign Office arrived Bern February 15 for a short visit. He has task of inserting articles in Swiss press which are directed against Roosevelt "in order to influence presidential elections in United States of America."

Informant states that German Legation here considers this project as indicative "of entire infantile character of foreign policy of Ribbentrop and Steengracht." In addition they believe it is hopeless to attempt to circulate here propaganda material that is directed against the United States of America.

This source also available Zulu and no copy of this should go to them.

Document 3-22

Telegram 498-99, 501-2 to London, February 19, 1944 (extract)

[This cable is based on material delivered to OSS Bern by Fritz Kolbe of the German Foreign Ministry. "Kappa" indicates Wood/Kolbe material; "Purple" connotes miscellaneous subject matter rather than country-specific. Reference is presumably to the Moscow Foreign Ministers Conference of October 1943.]

KAPPA. Purple. "It is the opinion of the Fuehrer that it is not impossible that the current Moscow Conference will be the scene of a renewal of strong pressure exerted upon the British and Americans for the establishing of a second front at an early date. Such pressure would be similar to those second front demands which Russia has recurrently made. The Fuehrer therefore orders an immense activation, with all possible speed, of the construction and preparation of fortifications along the entire western front, Norway and Denmark included. He demands that work to meet the military necessities of the situation be carried through, even though this may make necessary a most drastic subordination of those political considerations which have been observed up to the present time . . ."

Document 3-23

Radiotelephone Transmission No. 89, February 19, 1944 (extract)

[Dulles again recommends that the Western Allies look beyond unconditional surrender and plan for the postwar period.]

General

1. The aspect of the European war has undergone a vast change in the last few months. This has come about so suddenly that possibly we have failed fully to recognize it and to draw the consequences.

2. Under no circumstances now can Germany win even a partial victory. What is left of Germany after the bombardment, the blood-letting in Russia, and the destruction of its social fabric, could under no circumstances reorganize and rule Europe. No matter what the future course of military events might be, the most Hitler can now do is to help create chaos. The people of Europe—and tacitly most of the Germans themselves—recognize this. Hitler's dream of a New Order is as dead as the dodo. What Hitler has today is great nuisance value, and the ability to keep his war machine and SS organization functioning for some months longer. The Nazi machine has now forever lost its forward drive, its grip over the minds and souls of people; it still has a grip on their lives by the SS terror.

3. The only real question today is whether constructive regenerating forces will control and direct the fate of Europe, or whether forces of disintegration and anarchy will prevail. The answer to this question depends firstly upon the policy adopted by Russia, and secondly upon the vigor, strength and direction of the policy adopted by America and Great Britain.

4. Our policy seems to have been predicated upon the idea that a military victory plus unconditional surrender was all that was needed. This, I think, is mistaken. We in the West have as yet failed to understand the social and spiritual factors which are playing a vital part in determining the trend of events in Europe today. As a result it is Russia rather than the Western powers which is tending to dominate the scene, not only because of its military victories but on account of the growing belief in many parts of Europe, particularly where Russia is little known, that the common man will fare better in a Europe under Russian than under Western influence. The principles of the Atlantic Charter appear to be subordinated to the idea of unconditional surrender, and the latter is interpreted as meaning not only a military surrender but also the acceptance of whatever terms in the social and economic fields the Western powers choose to impose. We have not yet dictated and given to the people of Europe any clear indication as to what economic and social regime we propose to favor, or to give life and figure to a program which appeals to the common man.

5. The people of Europe have moved far to the Left. By and large, they do not want communism. But they do want a new social order, which will constitute a very definite break with the past. They feel that in our Italian and French policies the Western powers have shown a disinclination to break with the past, or to seek the aid of those forces which, I believe, will be the coming elements in the Europe of tomorrow.

6. As regards Germany, we are certainly reaching a point where daily more and more people are becoming reconciled to a Russian solution. This is where Hitler's nuisance value can still play a considerable role, as everything seems to indicate that he would sacrifice the Eastern front and turn Germany over to the Russians before he would let us and British into the European fortress. This policy seems to be

creating allies for him in this endeavor, even among people who normally would turn to the West rather than to the East.

7. I recognize that what I have said is very general, and that it is far easier to criticize than to construct. It is only an attempt to put on paper impressions received from talking with a great many honest and sincere people come into this oasis from the tragic surroundings on all sides of us. It is only intended to convey the thought that we should look to our weapons of political warfare with the same attention as we give our planes, our battleships and our armies. . . .

Document 3-24

Telegram 2137-42, February 21, 1944

[On February 21, Dulles reports receiving an eight-page handwritten memorandum from "George Wood," his agent in the German Foreign Ministry. This new information was transmitted incrementally in cables bearing the code designation "PACA." "Yellow" signifies Turkey; Milit is German Ambassador von Papen; Penni stands for Turkish Foreign Minister Menemencioglu.]

KAPPA. The following is PACA Yellow material.

1. In the opinion of the German Government, the Allies have suffered a setback in their first political offensive in Turkey, and the situation there is calm. On the 9th, Milit reported that relations between Russia and Turkey were poor. He reports that on the 3rd, the English military mission departed with no concrete achievements to show for its visit. Milit asked Penni about U.S.-British operational plans, but has not received any reply as yet. The obstacle to any Anglo-Turkish agreement lies in the question of rearmament and, in particular, air rearmament. Penni explained to Milit that the Turkish Government had refused to submit to England's demands and determined to stick to the argument that the country would have to rearm completely before coming into the war, which would take at least 5–6 months. Prior to that, he said, no air bases would be granted. . . .

7. We are informed by Wood that there is no way of finding out who Cicero is or where the information about Cicero and Teheran originated. He suggests, in connection with this, that the leak might have come from an Albanian-born private secretary of Inonu whom the President took with him to Cairo.

8. Since the 15th of December, Kujurdechki [Koymoudzinsky?] has been a member of the American Economic Mission in Istanbul. He is a friend of Elisha Friedmann. Berlin regards him as possessing great influence and importance. Filoff resides in his house.

Document 3-25

Telegram 503-4 to London, February 22, 1944

[This message concerns aid to the French resistance.]

For Tertius . . . .

1. Jerome is an old friend of 405, 110, and 284; Hinn pleased to hear that you are in touch with him.

2. I am thoroughly convinced that, unless we, as well as the British, give our complete co-operation to French resistance, the latter's potentialities of direct assistance to our armed forces will not be completely fulfilled. In this connection, our end has usually taken the lead in contact with the resistance in the light of the British attitude, well known to you, about working from here.

3. . . . If Washington agrees, and provided it can go on providing us with Swiss francs, we could supply further monetary support. Although we possess enough reserves for immediate needs, they would vanish very quickly if we began to finance resistance to any great lengths. The Macuis [Maquis?] departments are still getting the equivalent of about 80,000 Swiss francs per month from us.

Document 3-26

Telegram 2143-45, February 22, 1944

[George Wood frequently provided information on the Pacific war. "Scarlet" connotes Japan.]

KAPPA. The following is a Scarlet Paca message:

1. Grand was formally notified on the 8th of this month by Kawahara, Counsellor of the Japanese Embassy in Berlin, of a meeting between German Ambassador Ott (From 110: I do not understand this name; perhaps it is misread in the COF text) and Shice Mitsu. This meeting took place on January 24 in Tokio. The proposal was made by Shice Mitsu that a Russo-German agreement be concluded. Acting under orders from Tokio, Kawahara started discussions again with Berlin, forwarding the view that Germany's attitude toward the USSR should cease to be definitely affected by the former's claims on the Ukraine. In the light of the Italian debacle, Germany could spread out unhampered in the Mediterranean, in North Africa, and so on. Kawahara alleges that Ott's response to this was that although the Germans agree to such a plan in theory, only following an unsuccessful Anglo-American invasion would they make advances to the Soviet. In the eyes of the Japanese, it would be too late by that time. Grand has requested Ott to interpret the consultations from his point of view.

2. The Nazi Military Attaché in Tokio reports the following state of affairs in the Pacific: A British offensive on a large scale against Burma is not anticipated. Landing vessels have been remarked in Calcutta alone. Since early this month the Japanese position in New Guinea has grown extremely serious. The Japs, who are surrounded, have no opportunity to push through to Madang. Air raids have nearly demolished Rabaul. The Japanese are in hopes of holding it until June, at which time they consider that their airplane manufacture will be fairly under way. In New

Britain the Japs are reduced to receiving provisions only on black nights from small boats along the shore, as America has total air superiority there.

3. In the face of Japan's monthly output rate of 80,000 tons of new ships, an average of 140,000 tons are being sunk each month.

Document 3-27

Telegram 2160, February 22, 1944

[In trying to solve the puzzle of Hungary, Dulles and Washington had the benefit of knowing what the Germans thought was going on in that country, courtesy George Wood.]

KAPPA. This material is PACA and concerns Hazel.

1. The Hungarian Cabinet decided at meeting on the 9th of this month that they would mobilize the country when the Russian troops had penetrated to Lemberg. The Hungarian army will co-operate with the Germans in defending the Carpathian Mountains.

2. Before they were to stand trial about the middle of last month for committing atrocities against the Jugoslavs, 3 Hungarian officers escaped to Germany, and to date the Nazis have declined to give any satisfaction to Hungarians.

Document 3-28

Telegram 2173-75, February 24, 1944

[This message concerns the demise of Admiral Canaris (659) and the Abwehr. Hitler dismissed the Admiral in February 1944 and had him executed in April 1945.]

659's position and his whole outfit has been seriously jeopardized by the developments in Argentina and the V affair in Turkey. Abwehr will probably be taken over by Himmler due to the fact that Hitler is reputed to have personally intervened in the matter. It is likely that 659 and SD will be the recipients of an "extended leave." It is unlikely that 659 will offer a strong protest since he is somewhat of a Buddha. Hansen, 659's chief assistant, is mainly taking care of the matter with Keitel.

The possibility that V may make certain disclosures concerning present relations between Turkish and Nazi Intelligence is a matter of grave concern to the Nazis. This presents a possible clue to Cicero and also has bearing on point #4 in my #2139.

The question discussed in your #1247 and our #2086 is brought up again in a different light due to the possibility of a general weeding out of Abwehr men abroad and their replacement by Himmler's men. It may be wise to encourage certain Abwehr men in important jobs to decline to go back to Germany, if as appears probable, they will lose all value for our purpose. We are thinking especially of our 512 who would not go back under any circumstances. Gorter, who just got back here after much hardship caused by above shakeup, has family problems. Excellent relations exist between the Swiss police authorities and 512 and the latter is trying to influence them to stop replacement by SD of any recalled Abwehr. However, his chances of success are very slight.

Although the liquidation of 659's group is not an accomplished fact as yet and they might overcome present difficulties as they have former ones, our above mentioned contacts, who were formerly optimistic, now feel that the situation is quite devoid of promise.

Document 3-29

Telegram 2183-85, February 24, 1944

[This message addresses the possibility of Germany seeking an "eastern solution."]

. . . I concur that there is nothing to support the statement that Himmler is losing ground. It is my opinion, however, that some rivalry exists between Bormann and Himmler and that Bormann is more positively committed than Himmler to the possibilities of a Soviet orientation of Nazi policy. At the right time, however, Himmler is limber enough to shift his position. In the last few months, there has been an increase in strength of groups who would rather surrender to the Russians than the Anglo-Saxons, when the crash comes. Even though overtly, Nazi policy and propaganda is bitterly opposed to the Soviet Union, there are a number of realists within Germany who are aware that Germany must surrender, sooner or later. The Nazis are convinced that the choice will be theirs, regardless of anything we may have to say, between surrendering to Russia or to us rather than to the United Nations.

Document 3-30

Telegram 2188, February 24, 1944

[Dulles here comments on postwar zones of occupation for Germany.]

For Carib and 154. I am grateful for your #1251. I completely realize its significance and the potentialities which exist. Please refer to my flashes respecting federalism. The solution of the coming problem of Germany, in the era when the occupation shall be ended or lightened, might be facilitated by organizing the new local administrative set-up in Germany along natural regional lines. With regard to the prospective establishment of boundaries for occupation zones, you ought to keep in mind a proper arrangement of the German states, instead of allowing rivers, or latitudinal and longitudinal lines, to govern the grouping in an arbitrary fashion.

Document 3-31

Telegram 2189-93, February 24, 1944 (extract)

[This message on Austria was based on information from Josef Johan, a financier.]

The following report is from source 680 and deals with Austrian affairs:

1. During the preceding few months, there has been very little development revealed in the situation at Vienna. The food problem is growing more acute. The statement on Austria which was issued at the Moscow conference caused no strong change; however, the Austrian public are nearly all opposed to staying with Germany if it is possible for Austria to become a member of a large economic entity composed of perhaps Hungary, Croatia and Czechoslovakia. This position is even shared by the Socialists. Open resistance or even organized secret activity is nearly impossible because of Gestapo control over such tendencies. The movement favoring the Monarchy possesses some force, but it is doubtful if it has the support of most of the people.

2. The scheme of moving industries to Austria from Germany is not being put into effect any longer. Movements of this kind are now principally to Bohemia and Silesia.

3. There are extensive efforts made by men ordered up for Army service to bring on temporary defects to cause their rejection at the physical examination. This is accomplished through the use of drugs. The source of this report recommends that it is worthwhile to supply amounts of drugs suitable for this purpose. . . .

Document 3-32

Telegram 1191, February 28, 1944 (extract)

[Dulles reported frequently on declining German morale caused by defeats on the Eastern Front.]

For the purpose of making a personal inspection of existing conditions in that area, Hitler was urged by Manstein and Kuechler to make a trip to the east front. On the advice of Himmler, however, who believes that the attitude of the troops is such that they might attempt to assassinate their Fuehrer, Hitler declined to follow Manstein's and Kuechler's suggestions. Himmler is presently using his influence at headquarters, and the attempt to free ten divisions of troops from entrapment at Korsum was instituted upon his recommendation. Sensing that the attitude of the troops and the populace have reached dangerous heights, Himmler has endeavored to persuade Hitler to forbid publication of the losses which these divisions sustained. The bitterness which prevails among the staffs and formations on the east front has been increased by this loss, and the loss has also aroused the feelings of the more youthful officers who have urged for some time that Hitler's strength be tested. Manstein and the other higher ranking officers, however, still decline to let Hitler down. Rating A-3 should be given this paragraph. . . .

Document 3-33

Telegram 2226-28, February 28, 1944

[Although Dulles feared communist and Soviet ascendancy in Europe after the war, he advocated cooperation with communist elements in resistance movements. Peter is Joseph Modigliani, an elder statesman of the Italian Socialist Party residing in Switzerland and brother of the deceased painter.]

To 305 and Jackpot. In reference to your #1264-65. Serious doubts present themselves over the sagacity of our forwarding this message. Peter might construe our transmission of the message to mean that we approve its subject matter. He is already rabidly anti-communist. In my opinion, from the standpoint of the current military position in Italy, this message is not wise. Moreover, we ourselves, should not sponsor any movement which would split the current united front of the anti-Fascist[s] and which would, I fear, lessen the opposition to both the Nazis in northern Italy and to Fascism. In addition, I have gleaned from conversations, especially those with 475, that Monty's political judgments are not of serious consequence. You are not realistic in some of the opinions contained in your #1264. Finally, since Peter is loquacious, I do not consider it wise to perform the office of transmitting agency for messages of this sort due to the current delicate condition of our relations with Moscow. I would not be able to guarantee that Peter would be discreet about the channel by which he received the message. Pending your further instructions, the message will not be forwarded.

Document 3-34

Telegram 2242-43, February 29, 1944

[This message concerns relations with the French resistance and postwar implications.]

A memorandum which 642 drafted for me was the basis of my Flash dated the 26th [28?] of this month. 642 has spent several weeks here with Iris, but has now gone back to his work with the resistance. He is impulsive, youthful and his judgments are somewhat immature; however, the point of view set forth is fairly representative of the younger militant resistance elements. For this reason, I believed you would be interested in it. There is no doubt about the devotion and sincerity of these people. It is questionable, to what extent their political views will dominate in the future France, but it is a viewpoint that must not be overlooked. In my opinion a statement from the President to the French people and the French resistance at some time before the invasion would be considerably valuable psychologically and even militarily. However, if such a statement is to be entirely effective, a reference must be made to General de Gaulle, at least as the man who never doubted the final victory over Germany and the man who has persistently struggled to release France from the domination of the Nazis.

Document 3-35

Telegram 2263, March 1, 1944

[This report identified potential bombing targets.]

The following vital targets in the Berlin area have not as yet been hit.

1. The electrical plant at Klingenberg.
2. The Niederfinow dam.
3. The factories in Fferstenwalde sector.
4. The big bunker near the zoo which is headquarters of ARP and air raid defense.
5. The important military training center located at Gatow.

The foregoing information has come from an untested source.

Document 3-36

Telegram 2282-85, March 3, 1944

[In this report, Dulles relays information received from 513, a Polish source, on German thinking respecting Turkey, the Allied landing at Anzio/Nettuno on January 22, and the anticipated Allied assault on the coast of France.]

The following information was supplied by source 513:

1. Dated February 15, Turkey. AMT, AUSW and OKW are highly suspicious of Anglo-Saxon–Turkish differences. The fact that members of the special mission remained after the special commission left, and the fact that many British agents and officers in mufti are allowed to come into Turkish Military zones have both served to strengthen their suspicions. It would not surprise the Germans if Turkish air bases and seaports were suddenly made available to Anglo-Saxon forces in the Near East.

2. Dated February 18, re Italian fronts: OKW has granted Kesselring permission to use all available reserves at his command, including forces which were intended

for defenses against an eventual Allied landing north of Rome (Corsican zone). He hopes to win supremacy at Nettuno through a quick movement of light artillery units detached from infantry divisions for this purpose. The Germans have 2 air divisions, 15 army divisions and 1 Waffen SS Brigade, making a total of 17½ divisions, which represents total German strength on both the Italian battle fronts.

3. Dated February 20, re Atlantic Invasion: The Nettuno landing is regarded by OKW as simply a general rehearsal for the invasion of the Atlantic coast of France. In the opinion of German military circles, the Allies can break through any concentrated Nazi artillery defense and set up a bridgehead successfully if they have good air support and a minimum of 600 naval guns or 8 battleships of 160 guns, 50 destroyers of 240 guns and 20 cruisers with 200 guns. It is further believed that General Eisenhower will establish 3 bases of this kind on the Atlantic coast of France and bring in large armies and supplies to these 3 points in preparation for simultaneous advance to the interior later on.

4. Dated February 22, re Nazi air defenses: According to OKL calculations, it would be necessary to withdraw from 25% to 35% of present fighter planes from Germany itself in the event of an Allied invasion on the north Atlantic coast. The result would leave Allied bombers almost unmolested to raid at will and the effect on the morale of the German people would be terrible. . . .

Document 3-37

Telegram 2288-92, March 3, 1944

[Dulles asks General Donovan's support in working out the final details of Sparrow Mission, the parachuting of agents into Hungary.]

For 109 and SO. The following is vital and urgent. We have now secured 684's agreement to a plan which should allow the immediate execution of the Sparrow project under circumstances, which to my mind, curtail the risks attendant on any project of this nature. This is the result of months of work. Algiers' attitude, however, disturbs me. This attitude was expressed in Brewster's wire dated the 27th of last month which was not repeated to Washington. Brewster said that unless a more exact plan was evolved for getting in touch with General Ujszaszy than the one recommended in our Algiers #264 point 5, that the Sparrow project was a leap in the dark. In addition, Brewster insisted that it was necessary to notify the frontier guards and added that there was no justification for wasting 3 men on a blind parachutage into Jugoslavia and then their attempting to make their way to General Ujszaszy past frontier guards who do not know the plan. Nevertheless, he recommended pinpoints . . . situated in territory currently occupied by the Hungarians according to all the information which both 477 and I have available and the problem of passing frontier guards is not involved. In addition, you will observe from my Algiers #293 that the Hungarians are currently in accord with the plan to parachute men in on their side of the line. Algiers fears about eventual meeting with Ujszaszy are not understandable unless we make the assumption that the Hungarians are hoaxing us about the complete matter. This does not seem logical to me, however, since the last thing that the Hungarians want to do is to alienate or deceive us.

I am sure that our men will reach General Ujszaszy if they are safely dropped on Hungarian soil and to include subordinate guards in the secret would risk revelation of Hungarian collaboration which might destroy the Sparrow project and precipitate far reaching Nazi demands on Hungary. We were asked by Operations in their wire #227 dated the 28th of February not to repeat to Washington the details of the Sparrow project but only a general survey. I felt, however, that you should possess this information in view of the questions of principle involved in our late cables relevant to this matter.

If you send instructions to Algiers, please do not mention this wire as I am anxious to avoid trouble with them. I do want to emphasize, however, that the point has been reached in the Sparrow project where we must either tell the Hungarians that we have abandoned the project or else go ahead immediately in a business-like way. This point can only be settled between Algiers and yourself and I trust that you will be able to do this with all dispatch.

Document 3-38

Telegram 2301, March 4, 1944

[This cable concerns Gero Gaevernitz, number 476, the closest aide of Allen Dulles.]

With reference to your #1281, the proper spelling of brother-in-law's name is Gerovoh S. Gaevernitz. Von Schultze Gaevernitz, the noted German professor who died a few months ago, was his father. Refer to our #501. Considering that the contacts 476 has established for me are diverse and include especially contacts with Social Democrats and even Communists, it is evident that he does not share his brother-in-law's prejudices. 476 believes that his brother-in-law is afraid he may compromise his anti-Nazi friends in Germany by broadcasting and therefore he is unwilling to do so.

Document 3-39

Telegram 2307-11, March 5, 1944

[Dulles here reports on Nazi measures against suspected internal resistance elements and on relationships among Germany's top leaders. Number 659 is Admiral Canaris; 800 is Adam von Trott zu Solz.]

KAPPA. We have received an additional report by way of Breakers, according to which 659 has been placed "zur Disposition" and given a naval promotion pro forma. The following have lately been placed under arrest; Madame Solf, wife of the well-known German diplomat, now deceased; Kiep, who was once Consul–General in New York, probably for not keeping his mouth shut; Scherfenberg, who did liaison work with the OKW; and Helmut von Moltke, a man close to Breakers, and adviser to OKW on international law, who, prior to the war, often visited London. The probability is that Kaltenbrunner will draw on the Abwehr to create a new MI service, for the nonce maintaining as an independent organization the Foreign Service division of the Sicherheitsdienst, which is chiefly concerned with political and counterespionage matters. The Foreign Office and Himmler's service have lately been feuding as a result of certain mistakes that each has made in granting exit visas, particularly in the case of Mrs. Vermehren. The latter is in part due to the activities of our 800, whose security is thereby to some extent affected. It seems that the Foreign Office accorded the lady an exit visa for a journey to Turkey. In an attempt to break off her journey, the German military in Sofia closed the border between Turkey and Bulgaria to her. However, Madame Vermehren, unbeknown to them, secured permission through the Foreign Office to go by courier plane and thus reached her destination. As a result of this incident, the Foreign Office came in for some sharp criticism from the Schutzstaffel. Subsequently, a number of Sicherheitsdienst agents in Argentina declined to come home after the break in relations occurred, and the joke was on the Schutzstaffel, as the Foreign Office gleefully pointed out. Nevertheless, Breakers information states that a truce has been declared, and that Ribbentrop's and Himmler's mutual fear of Bormann's mounting influence has now caused an improvement in their relations. The following is Gorter's analysis of the political setup in Germany: On the one hand, though Goering and Himmler are still faithful to Hitler, each is hopefully counting on the possibility of inheriting his mantle of power. In contrast with this attitude, Goebbels and Bormann are fully aware that they are dependent solely on their relationship to Hitler for their authority and that, should the latter go, they would count for nothing as neither could possibly hope to succeed him. It is not because of any partiality to England or the U.S. that Himmler is pursuing a policy of so-called Western orientation but because of purely selfish reasons. Correctly or incorrectly, he believes that he would be completely out of the picture in a German policy that was directed toward the East, for the reason that Stalin would insist on his execution. The following summary of Himmler's personal views, though fantastic in nature, in my opinion comes from sources who are in a position to know what the subject really thinks. He is especially interested in matters relating to Japan, such as the samurai tradition, and so forth. It was on his initiative that the Japanese were declared to be Aryans. Himmler is looking forward to the possibility of leading Germany into a Japanese-German attack on Russia, which would form part of a compromise peace settlement with the Western powers, and which would have their blessing.

Document 3-40

Telegram 2318, March 6, 1944

[This message concerns efforts to recruit German sources, in this case Wolfgang Krauel, the Consul General in Geneva.]

To Carib; with reference to your #1278. The data we receive tends to confirm 140's and yours. We are almost certain that this is not a plant. However, our primary concern is to how he may be used at this time. Anti-Nazi Germans are not terribly enthusiastic about working with us since their anti-Nazi feelings are somewhat mitigated by fear that they may be assisting in the dismemberment of Germany by us and the Russians to the ultimate benefit of the latter. I am making arrangements to set up contact indirectly with K, whom we have designated as our 838, and I will send you more details later.

Document 3-41

Telegram 2321-22, March 6, 1944

[OSS Bern filed this report on German troop movements in southern France.]

The following report was made by some French railway workers who reached Geneva on the 4th of this month. Southern France is boiling with German activity. A temporary suspension of civilian freight and passenger traffic in this area has been decreed during major shifts of troops and material from northern to southern France. This information is in line with general indications of troop movements and TCO's that we have received before. Although the Germans may be carrying out a major reinforcement of southern France or Italy, there is also the possibility that they may merely be making a show of so doing. However, the reports we have been getting indicate that the Germans may be under the impression that there will not be any grave danger in the north of France and on the Channel coast for another 60 days or more, and that they intend to launch one more concentrated attack on the Anzio front in an attempt to force a withdrawal and thereby produce a psychological effect on landing operations planned for the future.

Document 3-42

Telegram 2327-28, March 7, 1944

[Dulles again urges material support for the maquis in southeastern France.]

284 [Shoop] has been informed lately to the following effect by the Chief of the Maquis in Haute Savoie: in the "Maquis des Glieres" between Thones and Petit

Bornand where especially propitious defensive prospects are afforded by a natural plateau and mountain defenses, concentration of this Maquis is taking place. Great appreciation is felt for the valuable items which were dropped there early in February. In addition to the present 800 men, the capacity of this Maquis is sufficient to hold 1600 more, who are being collected with the view of creating a fortress for the area there. I should like to point out the advantage of strengthening this as a nucleus with the possible parachuting of military troops into the area in the future. Particularly under the circumstances created by the snow at this time, defense against considerable forces could be maintained with the arms now accessible. There are sufficient quantities of milk and meat on hand there; however, larger amounts of other foods, particularly dried fruits and vegetables, are required.

I would be grateful for word from London or Algiers as to whether they have any directions to offer respecting the working out of this set-up and whether they are in touch with this Maquis.

Document 3-43

Telegram 2341, March 9, 1944

[This message reports on the Allied bombing of Castel Gandolfo, the location of the summer residence of the Pope.]

According to a trustworthy Vatican source, bombardment of Castel Gandolfo resulted in the injury of about 1,000 people and the death of about 300 more. The highness of the figures is due to the fact that the area was crammed with refugees. Our source says, however, that the village of Castel Gandolfo was packed with Nazi military equipment and soldiers, and the same bombs which caused the college to explode destroyed tanks which were parked before the palace. Again according to our source, the Vatican is looking at the bombing fairly, though it felt forced to protest against this bombardment of its territory.

Document 3-44

Telegram 2355, March 9, 1944

[OSS Bern relays a report on German use of the Maginot Line.]

28 F [284 F] has sent us a report, in response to your earlier questions about the Maginot Line, which advises that the Nazis are amassing supplies in France and moving them into the Maginot Line, where they are safeguarded in underground rooms. A check is being made regarding the kind of supplies involved; no information was provided concerning this.

Document 3-45

Telegram 2381, March 11, 1944

[This report provided by "George Wood" gives an account of a conversation between Marcel Pilet-Golaz, the Swiss Foreign Minister, and Otto Kocher, the German Minister in Switzerland.]

KAPPA. The following is TEBA material from Switzerland. On the 2nd of this month, Pilet-Golas once more spoke to Minister Kocher in connection with an Anglo-German settlement. Pilet-Golas says that England exhibited no interest in the possibility of a people's revolution in Germany. He is aware that no government of England at this time would be in a position to show any desire for negotiating a settlement, but that, if the projected invasion should not succeed, negotiations might be possible. Furthermore, according to him, Russia's refusal to fight Japan is causing more and more indignation in America and Great Britain. "Kocher is holding himself in readiness to act on orders."

Document 3-46

Telegram 2408-11, March 14, 1944

[This message concerns the Vienna network ("Cassia"), with which contact was established by Lanning McFarlard ("Packy"), OSS chief in Istanbul. "Diana" is the industrialist Franz Josef Messner. When the Germans invaded Hungary and captured the Sparrow mission in late March, they also arrested the principal members of Cassia in Vienna.]

I conferred with Diana, the leader of Cassia, several times during the weekend and have now absolutely ascertained that the envoy and group are those described in my cable #1284. I have given 840 to Diana as a designation. Several wires based on data obtained from him are being dispatched separately. Contact existing between Packy in Algiers and 840 was described in detail by the latter, and a plan was developed for establishing liaison between us, to take care of the situation if Packy's lines are interrupted, and to supplement Packy's current lines. . . . We get the impression from what 840 says that he knows of Sparrow or a similar operation, that he has expectation of receiving a transmitter and that he is going to set up contact with Sparrow representatives. This sounds as if it would be practical. However, I recommend that Sparrow envoys exercise extreme caution as far as dispensing to local military men any information regarding Diana Cassia situation is concerned [*sic*]: Army groups are seething with pro-Axis elements and greatest care is essential.

I wish to offer my congratulations to Packy for his accomplishments in developing this line; 840 impressed us very favorably. We are convinced that he is worthy of all our support and we will make arrangements to give him some modest financial assistance from here if he requests it. . . .

Document 3-47

Telegram 2435-39, March 14, 1944

[This report on aspects of German war production was received from sources in Vienna.]

The following is from source 840:

1. The high frequency laboratory at Gatow in the vicinity of Berlin, employs 600 technicians engaged in research on rocket direction. It is reported that a month ago there were 300 rockets ready for use. 2 batteries are among the more than 1000 parts of which each rocket is composed. Each missile is 15 to 17 meters long and has 8,000 to 12,000 lbs. of explosive. The problem that still confronts the technicians is a deviation of as much as 500 meters radius over 230 kilometers.

2. Although their program in May called for the production of 124 submarines a month, only 30 a month are actually turned out, The steel presses are the bottleneck. (This is from 110: I assume that this is the source of your earlier information from Istanbul giving tremendous figures for submarines. I was told by 840 that this was the program only, and that it is altogether unattainable. . . .)

. . . Starting the first of next month, . . . the Continental, located in Hanover, will produce soles of thick rubber. Because of the scarcity of leather, these will be cemented onto marching boots with thin leather soles. . . . This development was put off to this time by officers who like a brisk and noisy goose step.

Document 3-48

Telegram 2460-64, March 15, 1944

[This message describes ambiguous relations between the Swiss and German intelligence services. Brigadier General Roger Masson was head of Swiss military intelligence; General Henri Guisan was commander of the Swiss Army.]

For 109 and Jackpot, SECRET. Outside information, beyond the Wood material, points to a perilously close association between Masson, the head of Swiss G-2, and Schellenberg of the Gestapo, and forces me to reach the conclusion that the Nazis are receiving information from certain officials in the Swiss intelligence Service, which the latter obtain through their diplomatic and military channels in the United Nations Countries. I am disturbed at the convincing nature of this evidence.

I firmly believe that the controlling Swiss authorities have a basic desire for an Allied victory. There is danger, however, in the complaisance of certain of the Swiss

Military men, whose activities evoke some encouragement from those of their countrymen who hope to see a compromise peace, or who harbor an extreme fear of the Soviet.

With the above in mind I believe that we should earnestly contemplate presenting evidence (the Wood material included) in strictest secrecy to the highest Swiss Quarters, to prove to them that material is handed over to the Nazis from here, which has been obtained in confidence from the Allies. I appreciate the delicate questions which are raised by my Kappa 1509 and #1604 which provide the most shocking examples. However, no new information will reach the Swiss by this move. They will merely be informed by us of our awareness of what is occurring and will learn that we are advising the highest Swiss Quarters, where this information may be unknown.

Of course, it is absolutely necessary to protect Wood and this future source of information, which we hope will supply us with further data within a fortnight or so. It is our opinion that the disclosure could be made in such a manner as to implicate the Lomax shop, which the Swiss already know to be very leaky. General Guisan has just indicated his wish for a confidential conversation with me, and it is to him, and to him alone, that I would personally submit my evidence. I am convinced that his integrity and devotion to our ideals are unimpeachable, and that the discovery of what is occurring (presumably unbeknownst to him) might move him to act. This might result in a housecleaning here, and remove the danger of critical leaks which remain inevitable during the tenure of certain military officials in their important intelligence service posts. Refer also to my #2417-23 in regard to the above. I await your recommendations. Meanwhile I have shown this cable to Leland 520 in strictest confidence.

Document 3-49

Telegram 2465-66, March 15, 1944

[Dulles here offers another assessment of the state of German morale.]

The question you bring up might well arouse contrary opinions in fair-minded individuals approaching the situation from the identical geographic angle. The morale of the Nazi population is at present in what could be described as the "desperation psychosis" stage. Their reaction to the repeated raids is rather like that of an injured animal held at bay without any obvious means of escape. The animal is not affected by additional wounds regardless of how deep they go, but he may die of loss of blood. I have not secured adequate proof since Hamburg that the Germans' morale has been influenced to any great extent by the recent raids, but there is not an accurate instrument to measure the rise and fall of their morale. At the present time the Germans can see no way out except to continue the battle. They fail to see any prospect of hope from the East or West. I had no intention of indicating in my previous flash that the final collapse might not occur at any moment now, but I think that this will be the result not of the collapse of the morale on the inner front, but rather because of one of the following reasons:

1. Military collapse.
2. Breakdown of the economic machine, transportation of war production.
3. Coup d'état which would completely abolish Hitler and probably other Nazi authorities.

Document 3-50

Telegram 2469-72, March 16, 1944

[This message concerns developments in Yugoslavia.]

From 110. The following information is from source 819 and is derived from reports recently received from Zagreb [and] Belgrade:

1. Krnievic from London is no longer enthusiastic about rapprochement with Tito. Recurrent indications of weakness in the Tito movement are due to the unfriendly reaction of the peasants, the heavy losses that have been suffered, and the failure of Machek's Peasant Party to continue their support. They had joined the Partisans but now have been ordered to sever their connection.

2. The appropriation of the food by the Partisans has caused the peasants to regard them with fear and hatred.

3. General Glaise-Horstenau says that before there is an allied invasion of the Balkans, which he does not anticipate until the summer or even next year, the Nazis will have eliminated Mihailovic after first getting rid of Tito.

4. During the Fuehrer's recent visit, Peric, the Foreign Minister, and Mandiccro as Premier secured an agreement in principle concerning the return of the Croatian forces at present in France. All dealings with Serbia regarding territorial matters are to be held in the balance until the war is over.

5. Machek is ailing and is incommunicado in a sanitorium in Zagreb.

6. Mihailovic's political formula has changed. It is to be Yugoslavia now instead of greater Serbia. A recent mass meeting of Mihailovic's supporters was allowed by Nedich. Although the Nazis apprehended some who went to the meeting, new followers are rushing to join up while some of Mihailovic's lieutenants have arranged local deals with the Nazis. The Nazis regard Tito as enemy #1 and Mihailovic is looked upon as enemy #2. By avoiding a fight to the finish with the Nazis, Mihailovic continues his policy of protecting his followers from annihilation. Mihailovic is gaining ground.

7. Tito's chances in Croatia are not as good now as they were a few months back. Machek is the Croatians' choice and if he is still alive he will have a united country behind him when the day of liberation dawns. However, the Russians may force

Tito on the people. 819 thinks that things are going Mihailovic's way and that the national union of Serbia is taking shape around him.

The following is from 110. Because 819 sees the situation from a somewhat detached viewpoint and has excellent contacts we thought the above material might interest you. However, advise us if it is a routine duplication and lacking in interest. We are aware that you have a direct contact with the situation in Yugoslavia.

Document 3-51

Telegram 2473-76, March 16, 1944

[This cable discusses the position of Rumania, with reference to a letter from Czech President Benes to former Rumanian Foreign Minister Gafencu (495).]

Your expression of interest was gratifying to our 495. He would eagerly accept any chance to leave Switzerland and aid in the attempt to get Rumania out of the war. On the assumption that the newspaper reports of Stirbey's activities are accurate, 495 would willingly get in touch with Stirbey to help him in every way possible. (This is from 110: It is my opinion that 495 is a firm friend of ours and of Great Britain, and that his attitude toward the Soviet problem is both realistic and honest.)

The remainder of this cable is a summary of a confidential message which Benes sent to 495 last month. Perhaps it has already reached you either from the English or from Benes, himself: I reviewed the Rumanian situation with Molotov and Stalin, and informed them that in Hungarian matters Czechoslovakia stands with Yugoslavia and Rumania, and holds to the belief that Transylvania should be part of Rumania. It is my earnest hope that Rumania will be able to establish the sort of relationship with Russia which will enable us to resume our amicable relationship with the former country. Molotov informed me that it is essential for Bessarabia and the northern portion of Bukovina to continue within the Soviet Union. He is, however, in accord with the Czech viewpoint on other Rumanian issues and his country is prepared to support Rumanian-Hungarian matters, and to embrace a good neighbor policy in general toward the former country. Both Stalin and Molotov stressed the need for a more militant Rumanian opposition, so that Rumania's break with Germany would not come too late. Stalin emphasized the importance of having Transylvania remain Rumanian so as to insure Rumanian democracy; he evinced deep interest in Maniu. The attitude toward Hungary, as I observed it in USSR was exceedingly unfavorable. There is, however, general sympathy toward a democratic Rumania and an unswerving intention to respect its sovereignty. It is my belief that much can be salvaged for Rumania by an early initiation of a proper policy. The Russian attitude toward Transylvania as conveyed to the British was identical with that expressed to me. Warmest greetings.

Document 3-52

Telegram 540-41 to London, March 17, 1944

[In this message, Dulles offers a deception proposal for use in the air war against Germany.]

. . . We think that we appear too eager to get Nazi fighters into the air. It is likely that most Nazi tactical military errors are due to the Fuehrer's initiative since his orders in the military field are still absolute. If it were possible by some subtle insinuation to make the Fuehrer think that our plane casualties are great and that the continuation of those catastrophes would tend to weaken morale in the United States, he might disregard the opinions of his military experts and call out his fighters. The Fuehrer seems possessed with the theory that he can quench the American fighting spirit and also our concern with European affairs by causing us severe casualties. It is apparent that he is deliberately sending selected forces out against us. We advise that the idea be initiated secretly that we are having trouble getting replacements for bomber personnel and that our losses are greater than we announce and so forth.

Document 3-53

Telegram 2501, March 17, 1944

[In this message, OSS Bern reports a connection between anti-Nazi Germans in Switzerland and the Soviet Union.]

Have received reliable information to the effect that although originally the activities of the Freies Deutschland group here were in no way connected with Moscow, not long ago such contact was set up. Moscow has granted approval of their work and has also issued orders to prepare lists of especially treacherous local Nazis and establish cells among the anti-Germans at this end.

Document 3-54

Radiotelephone Transmission No. 106, March 17, 1944 (extract)

[The text that follows was sent to President Roosevelt by General Donovan on March 20. It was standard procedure for Donovan to transmit numerous reports to the White House under the cover of memoranda prepared for his signature. From March 1944 to the end of the war, he sent dozens of items of Bern origin, the largest single category of material sent to the President in this manner. The covering memos almost always identified Bern or Dulles as the source and seldom included comments by the OSS Director.]

Germany

1. I have here a detailed memorandum with regard to the treatment of Russians in German prison camps, which brings out some rather interesting points. At first, that is in 1941, the Russian prisoners were far more closely guarded than any others, and on the whole received far worse treatment. Most of them arrived in the prison camps in a pitiable condition. They were given completely inadequate food and practically no medical attention, and were forced to undertake heavy manual work even though in most cases they were really too weak and too undernourished for this. Also the French and British prisoners were absolutely forbidden to do anything to help the Russian prisoners, but notwithstanding this there were many cases where the British and French shared their parcels with the Russians whenever they were able to get in contact with them. The mortality among the Russian prisoners was extremely high, and there seemed no doubt that the German government in its treatment of Russian prisoners violated all international conventions and is responsible for the death of thousands of Russians. Those Russian prisoners who were eventually distributed in small groups on farms to help with the harvest and other farm work quickly gained the sympathy of the local population. People were tremendously struck with their extraordinary ability to learn German—many spoke it better after two months than other prisoners after two years. A great change has come about in the treatment of Russian prisoners dating from the initial Russian successes in December 1941. This is due in no small measure to the influence of the returning German soldiers who generally have a high admiration for their Russian opponents. My report refers to a characteristic incident which took place in the summer of 1943 at Karlsruhe, where a group of Russian and French prisoners were engaged in cleaning a street following a bombardment. A group of German soldiers from the east front, disobeying all orders, went up to the Russian prisoners, engaged them in conversation, and offered them cigarettes—and when anybody gives a cigarette away in Germany it means a good deal. In 1943 the Germans, taking into account the fact that the Russians received no packages from abroad, started to give them even larger rations of bread than the other prisoners, and generally improved the rations given the prisoners. At the same time there has been a very noted change in the attitude of the German civilian public toward the prisoners. In general, the Russian prisoners have retained their faith in Stalin and their absolute confidence in final victory. Russian prisoners never complain of the regime, and have been on the whole impervious to German propaganda. In general the Russian prisoners can read and write, and take great pride in their country. It is remarkable to note how many simple workers and peasants among the Russians know about Russian literature and take a real interest in it. One of their first requests made to the German authorities was for reading material. The Germans have also been highly impressed with the qualifications of Russian technicians among the prisoners. This above report, from

someone who knows what he is talking about, generally conforms to other information on the subject which we have received here. . . .

Document 3-55

Telegram 317 to Algiers, March 20, 1944

[In this telegram, OSS Bern relays a message from Ignazio Silone to Count Sforza.]

475 to 510. I am very grateful to you for your message of March 8. Please advise us whether Saragat is with you. We regard him as our most able representative. We are convinced that it is impossible to win the peasants to the democratic cause unless there is a strong alliance in southern Italy between the Partito d'Azione and the Socialist Party for the liquidation of the Latifundists and establishment of a republic.

Document 3-56

Telegram 319-21 to Algiers, March 20, 1944 (extract)

[Dulles continues to advocate support for the Italian resistance.]

1. In Lugano, this past weekend, I conferred with Motta representatives and other organization Maquis work to be undertaken this spring. An urgent request for funds was submitted by Motta; they want 100,000 SF immediately, this month, to carry on their work and are asking Zulu to supply an equal sum. In my opinion, it is wise to strengthen Motta in preparation for the spring offensive. Apparently they are relegating politics to a back seat; however, we should realize that Motta is not sympathetic to Badoglio's government. On the other hand, if we back only those elements behind Badoglio and the King we will not secure maximum activity in the north. Kindly advise what course to pursue.

2. In dealing with the delicate Maquis situation, a satisfactory division of responsibility has never been decided upon between our organization and Zulu. The latter is inclined to work on their own lines in absolute secrecy and can appreciate the fact that, from the point of view of security, it would be bad policy to put all our eggs in one basket. Has the field been divided in any way between Zulu and OSS? In the event this has been done, we could arrange the same division at this end, but if this is not the case, it would be well for you and Zulu at operating end to let us know exactly what is expected of each or dispatch identical instructions to Zulu, SOE and myself re lines of operation and common activity. Judging from the standpoint of both safety and efficiency, the independent services operating from the Lugano Chiaso region are far too numerous. . . .

Document 3-57

Telegram 2518-22. March 20, 1944

[In this message, Dulles expresses apprehension over the projected work of the War Refugee Board (Garbo).]

In further reference to my #2492 of March 17. We are very much concerned over conditions which may arise as a result of Garbo activity.

1. If it were publicized that I am in any way connected with refugee relief work I would be swamped with a multitude of applications, visitors, and irritations which would gravely handicap me in carrying out my other duties.

2. Quite aside from the attitude of the Swiss Government, I am not at all convinced it is wise to try to transport large number of refugees here.

3. Such action necessitates establishing underground channels and there are not many individuals employed in relief work who have the technical abilities or who are emotionally qualified to carry on this work. The Gestapo will soon uncover many of these underground channels and as a result people who are trying to get across the border will be executed as well as their friends still remaining in occupied territory. It is quite likely that a greater number of unfortunate persons will lose their lives if they employ these methods than if they continue in their present surroundings.

4. If an effort is made to establish underground channels for refugees, it will interfere with SO or SI lines set up for immediate military uses, since only a limited number of these channels can be maintained safely. This is explained by the fact that only a very small number of reliable individuals are available who can carry on refugee relief or be used for immediate military purposes and they cannot be used safely for both types of work.

5. Consult wire from Secretary of State, Dexter and Joy to Field, #107 to Consulate Geneva. The Department of State should be aware that consular codes are not safe. It is regrettable that the use of underground methods were discussed and that mention was made of our #328.

6. The Nazis unquestionably are familiar with the main outlines of the Garbo plan and they will now have a splendid chance to use this to plant more agents here and other places as well.

7. Zealous individuals who are ignorant of conditions and who do not have the necessary technical training can do the refugees the greatest amount of harm. My opinion is based on an intimate knowledge of the hardships these people have had to endure and I submit the above as much from the standpoint of their good as from concern for the work extremely important for military operations.

8. In special individual cases it will be possible to work out plans in connection with underground operations and we can be of assistance in this. In addition numerous people will get here unassisted, on their own, without the aid of new under-

ground channels or those already in existence and a great deal can be done to receive and care for them.

9. There is a tremendous need for work now neglected, among refugees already here, especially Jews and Italians, without bringing in a new avalanche of refugees.

Document 3-58

Telegram 2523, March 20, 1944

[This message illustrates the complex overlapping and interaction of Dulles's intelligence, religious/charitable, and personal interests. The Countess Wally Toscanini Castelbarco, daughter of the renowned conductor Arturo Toscanini and wife of an Italian later to serve in the government of Premier Ivanoe Bonomi, spent the war in Switzerland involved in relief work. She and Dulles developed a close personal relationship that continued after the war.]

Please deliver this quoted message to Toscanini, Riverdale, N.Y. It is from his daughter and is signed Wally. "I am very much distressed by my inability to alleviate the suffering of Italian political refugees among whom are numerous musicians, Jews and various other friends. I beseech you, Menuhin, Volodja, Heifetz and other magnanimous friends to assist me in furnishing help even if only on a small scale. I am well and send you my love." The prospect of opening up this specialized line interests me. Wally can be of assistance to establishing contact to the south and this cover which has a genuine philanthropic basis can be employed.

Document 3-59

Telegram 324-25, March 21, 1944

[On March 15, Dulles reported that Lieutenant McCollum, an American pilot downed west of Cuneo, Italy, had taken part in partisan operations before making his way to Switzerland. This message provides further information on the resistance bands.]

. . . Another 4 Americans of the same crew are supposed to come here by the same passage; however, they were scheduled to arrive some time ago. McCollum was under the impression that the most powerful partisan force in this region is the band located south Boves and Borgo. An Italian major is in command of 1000 men. This outfit has made a successful fight to prevent the Germans from entering the valleys and the enemy has taken revenge by burning large sections of Boves and Borgo. It is reported that, via parachute, the band has received food supplies, radio transmitter and arms. They are said to have communicated with Naples via the transmitter. No information has been secured concerning passwords or signals. Small Maquis bands throughout entire region foothills Cuneo plain. The population of the whole mountain is definitely anti-German and continues to be sympathetic with the Partisan cause, notwithstanding reprisals inflicted by the Germans.

Document 3-60

Telegram 2526, March 21, 1944

[On March 19, 1944, German forces occupied Hungary and replaced the Kallay government with a completely subservient regime. This meant disaster for the Sparrow Mission, which had been dropped into Hungary on March 15. The team was turned over to the Germans on March 25 and spent the remainder of the war in captivity.]

In reference to my March 20th Flash. I have no direct news about the German coup because all communication lines between Switzerland and Hungary were closed for 48 hours. Up to this time no work [word] has come out of Germany. Nothing of what is happening is known to the Hungarian Legation here. 684 has requested to see 477 and me later today. 684 will probably decline to comply with the instructions of any Quisling government in Hungary.

Document 3-61

Telegram 2541-43, March 22, 1944

[This message concerns continuing financial aid to anti-Nazi European labor through OSS Bern.]

. . . The following is from 110 and refers to your #1363: The problem of financing 328's work was the subject of discussions between 328 and myself. The two of us concur that it is impossible for him to receive appreciable sums for secret undercover work via regular channels, and transmission of such funds through the use of other names seems inadvisable since it would entail the possibility of investigation by the Swiss. If you approve, we would stand ready to advance funds in Bern for clandestine work, within the suitable limits necessitated by the status of our reserves of Swiss francs. All regular relief funds would reach 328 via regular channels. Against ultimate reimbursement to you, I have given him 5,000 francs in advance. Please advise me in this matter.

Document 3-62

Telegram 2544-47, March 22, 1944

[Gheorghi Kiosseivanov ("Kiss"), the Bulgarian Minister in Bern, was a pro-West OSS contact. In this message, Dulles advises General Donovan that Kiss plans to visit Sofia with the hope of facilitating Bulgaria's withdrawal from the war. Number 492 is René Charron, an adviser to Dulles on the Balkans.]

For 109 and Jackpot. SECRET. 492 conferred with Kiss on Wednesday the 22nd. The latter has made up his mind positively to go to Sofia at once provided such a journey is possible at the time. He wants it kept absolutely secret that he is to make the trip. It is not to be revealed even to Momtchilov since he does not want the news of his coming to reach Sofia in advance of his arrival so that rumors and possible demonstrations may be prevented. He made very vigorous protestations of his determination to make every possible effort to extricate his country from the war and to find out what the chances are of accomplishing this. In view of the impending Sobrante meeting, he would have the opportunity to see all the main political figures and he also intends to get in touch with Sveno. Kiss says that Veltcheff and Guerorguieff were not placed under arrest but are in residence Surveillee, and that Peter Todoroff is free and and maintains close contact with them. Kiss believes that Todoroff is permitted his liberty for this very reason. In addition, Kiss expects to confer with Lukas, Chief of General Staff and naturally he anticipates seeing Cyril and his sister Udoxia whom he considers a very dependable person. According to Kiss, Bojiloff who is now Prime Minister, is prepared for maneuvers. Kiss knows him very well indeed and considers him a crook. If Kiss feels it is possible to accomplish anything he will request his government to authorize him to handle all negotiations. If this occurs he intends to come back to Switzerland inside of a week or 10 days since he thinks Ankara is the wrong place to undertake negotiations, giving as his reason the presence there of various individuals whom he thinks would prove harmful to the cause and at the same time expressing the opinion that Ankara is too Levantine and Balkanic to attain the best results. He gave his listeners to understand that if events turned out as described above, he might like to contact 492's friends, namely ourselves, when he returns. The preceding account was absolutely unsolicited and 492 offered no comment of his own. The chances of getting through to Bulgaria are still doubtful; however, I shall advise you if he leaves here.

Document 3-63

Telegram 2548-49, March 22, 1944

[OSS Bern finally received information on the German occupation of Hungary, as reported by the Hungarian Minister in Bern.]

The following wire from the Foreign Office in Budapest has now been received by 684. . . .

The Nazis executed a coup de main on strategic points in Hungary on March 19 (supposedly March 18th–19th) during the absence of Regent, Gheczy, Csatay Szerbythely who had gone to Hitler's headquarters to demand that Hungarian troops be sent home from the Soviet front. Three reasons are cited for the German move: (1) They were aware that negotiations were underway between the Anglo-Saxons and the Hungarian government. (2) An Hungarian version of the Badoglio affair was undesirable. (3) The presence of almost 1,000,000 Jews in the rear of their troops was intolerable from the German standpoint.

The Government has resigned. Among those arrested by the Germans were Deputies Rassay, Peyer and Bajesyzsilinszky and the Governor of the National Bank, Leopold Baranyai.

Document 3-64

Telegram 2557-58, March 23, 1944

[In this message, Dulles reports further on Hungary. Number 678 is Gerald Mayer of OWI.]

477 and I were just given a statement by the Hungarian Minister here, our 684, which he intends to release today to the effect that, since he is not able to recognize the new Magyar government's legality, he finds it necessary to halt all affiliations with this government. 678 is cabling the text of this message.

2. 684 intends to stay on in the hope that later reports will reveal the new government was not appointed by Horthy as Chief of State, or that Horthy was forced to do so under such pressure as to nullify the action. 684 contemplates resigning at once if future events verify that Horthy did appoint the puppet government or if the Swiss recognize the new government.

The following is from 110: Among certain assets which the Hungarian Government has here are 30,000,000 francs gold. Recommend that the neutrals be cautioned against any action which would allow the Nazis to control the puppet Magyar Government and abscond with such assets for Germany's gain.

Document 3-65

Telegram 2563-67, March 23, 1944

[Dulles participated in detailed planning for the OSS role in the occupation of Germany. From an early date, he anticipated that he would assume a leading position. He foresaw a vigorous postwar OSS, active in Germany and elsewhere, and certainly did not expect that the organization would be dismembered by Presidential order within two months of the end of hostilities.]

I am working on the matters mentioned in your #1328 and would be grateful if you would advise me on the points listed below:

1. Is the aim of the operation to furnish Washington and the occupation officials with social, military, economic, political, etc. intelligence?

2. Advise me what relationship an organization of this type would have with occupational authorities, State and War Departments and so on. Under what cover, military or administrative, will it function? Will the organization be partially civilian as it is now or will it be purely military?

3. If Germany is divided, for occupation, between Russia, Britain and the United States, I take it for granted that our permanent headquarters at such time would be in the American occupied region, and that we would have branches in the Russian and British held portions of Germany. Will we consider pre-Munich Germany as a unit for this purpose, and would we have other headquarters in Bohemia, Austria and so on?

4. As soon as the breakdown occurs in Germany, it will be desirable, I think, to establish a central headquarters at a strategic point there. It might be advisable to do so even prior to the completion of occupation. Provisions should be made at that same time for direct communication with London, Washington or both via radio. The initial headquarters should probably be set up at the location of the greatest concentration of German administrative machinery. This would facilitate our securing prompt control of papers and records etc. regarding Germany and, where possible, the situation in the Far East. A suitable location for this place after the collapse cannot be predicted now, though at the moment Berlin would seem to be the location. The nucleus I described in my #1162 is available here for use in the above scheme; that is, taking it for granted that 493's and 477's respective offices authorize them for such work.

5. With the idea of developing contact with local federalist tendencies in previous German states, branch headquarters should be established in important centers; e.g., Hanover, Munich, Breslau, Frankfurt, Hamburg and Cologne.

6. It is impossible to predict what Europe will be like following German collapse. At present, all we can do safely is to collect material and personnel to be prepared for any sudden developments, to proceed immediately into regions which will appear strategic in view of developments and to have dependable means of communication available so that they can be used under the greatly confused circumstances which will probably prevail until occupation is effected.

7. We will be partly dependent upon the support of German individuals we can trust for the success of our efforts. It would seem advisable to have a cover with some economic and reconstruction background in order to make collaboration with the right kind of Germans possible. Such a background would be calculated to enlist the support of these people through their motives of self interest. I am busy working on the construction of a list containing such Germans and on plans for developing rapid contact with them.

8. When I receive your answer to this preliminary survey, I will reply further.

Document 3-66

Telegram 2569-71, March 23, 1944

[This telegram contains a message from a German socialist exile in Switzerland concerning the postwar fate of the state of Prussia, of which he had been president before 1932.]

This is a summary of a message to Weichmanns from Otto Braun, in answer to the one contained in your #1195 of February 5. "I appreciate your birthday greetings. My personal plans depend on developments. I feel that American Government officials should have their attention called to these facts: if East Prussia and other land in Eastern Germany should be transferred to Poland under the terms of the peace treaty, Germany would be deprived of agricultural territories absolutely necessary to the production of her food supply. Germany would then be forced into close collaboration with the Soviet on economic matters and this might be followed by political understanding between the two countries in which case Poland might be the victim of political pressure from both Russia and Germany and this in turn might bring on another war. Consult page 34 of my book entitled *Von Weimar Zu Hitler.* Also bring out the fact that in the interim between the 2 wars, Prussia was the most democratic and progressive of the German states and should not be confused with the old Prussia of the Hohenzollern era which was militaristic and reactionary. I trust you will find it possible to have my above mentioned book published in America. This historical evolution is explained therein. I think it would be advantageous for the socialist parties of all nations to make contacts for the preparation of an international socialist conference to [be] called as soon as the war ends with a view to influencing peace plans. Trude and mother are in good health. Have received no word from Herbert's mother. I am well. Sincere regards."

Document 3-67

Telegram 548-49 to London, March 24, 1944

[OSS Bern faced serious problems of cooperation and coordination with British intelligence in Switzerland (521) in providing nonduplicative and swift information to the Allied entities that required it.]

A certain amount of duplication in Unison material is unavoidable. This is in reference to your #592. Headquarters of 521 are located in Geneva and frequently there is a lapse of 10 days before it is possible to make a cross check. In addition Algiers likes to be given K-2 material promptly, and it is easier and quicker to transmit than to check with 521. Do you have any arrangements whereby you can transmit Unison information to Algiers? The main purpose of Unison is to avoid false confirmation of intelligence. If Broadway is in earnest about wanting to assist in preventing duplication they ought to make arrangements to move their Headquarters to Bern since 520, K-13, 472, Poles and everyone else, including ourselves, centralize their activities here. It is all right with me for the British to make use of K-2; however, this is mainly a 520 source, an integral component of the 472 system, which according to my understanding, is financed exclusively by us. Duplication may also come through Unison K-13 which may develop into a valuable service. I have just come to an understanding with Zulu; we are going to finance it on the basis of an advance of 15,000 Swiss francs per month from each of us and the output will also [be] shared by both. In my opinion the establishment of a precedent giving exclusive rights of any kind here to Zulu would be a bad policy.

Document 3-68

Telegram 2576-81, March 24, 1944

[OSS Bern was a source of scientific intelligence. This routine "secret" cable reveals a surprising knowledge of atomic energy matters ("Azusa"). "Flute," number 827, is Paul Scherrer, a prominent experimental physicist at the Federal Institute of Technology in Zurich. Later, he was point of contact for Moe Berg, an American agent who sought intelligence on the German atomic energy program.]

AZUSA. Owing to the illness of our most reliable source, we unfortunately could not meet your deadline. The following is a report secured from Flute by 493:

1. Damage as a result of the bombing has disorganized the KW Institute for Chemistry at Berlin-Dahlem. The right side of the Institute, containing high tension apparatus, was not touched, but the left side was destroyed. They have commenced reconstruction with Tag heading reorganization. Tag is a fine person and not a Nazi. Flora, an associate, is a youthful, good and honest person. Other associates are as follows: Hendrick who works on mass spectrograph, Miller, a good physicist, 33 years of age, who works on the disintegration of uranium products and does not sympathize with the Nazis, and Brelenne, whose specialty is nuclear physics. Anton has taken leave of Tag and proceeded to Reichspost which possesses an excellent apparatus for nucleus smashing, manufactured by Phillips Eindhoven. Anton's specialty is theoretical work on cosmic rays and nuclear physics.

2. A super-Nazi, Lorens of Berlin-Lichterfelds-Ost is a financial and scientific swindler. He boasts of constructing an uranium bomb but does not have adequate equipment. Lorens' associate is Breit who was previously a Communist, was apprehended in Russia, but released in 1939 after which he turned into a fervent Nazi. Breit's work is in nuclear physics.

3. Ernst, at the KW Institute for Medicine at Heidelberg and assisted by Stenson and Haas, is constructing a cyclotron which will contain 50% more iron in the

magnet than the one at Zurich which is the best one in Europe to date. Ernst is, in addition, working on the construction of the Jolliot cyclotron in Paris.

4. At Strassbourg are Lender and Ebert. Lender has extremely pro-Nazi sympathies and he is a pure theorist. Zurich University will not allow him to lecture there. Ebert of nuclear physics took leave of the KWI in Heidelberg to join Lender, and also a scientist by the name of Droste.

5. Grippe and Goethe of the Chemistry Institute in Munich work on the separation of isotopes and are not Nazi. The latter visited Zurich in 1943. However, as I understand it, no other scientists on your lists have been visited in Germany by Swiss scientists or have been to see them in Switzerland.

6. Jolliot and his wife, Eve Curie's sister, voiced their sympathy with the Nazis previous to the war and they are felt to be unreliable. Two pupils of the physicist, Christopher, namely, Rudert who is doing theoretical work on mesons and Zeit who is in nuclear physics, have, together with Ritzler, joined Jolliot in Paris. The political views of Rudert and Zeit are not known. KWI for Physics in Berlin-Dahlem has the greatest living German physicist, Christopher. He is working on cosmic rays and projectile trajectories for long range guns, disseminates Nazi propaganda. Otto, his pupil, is doing practical work on mesons. The latter is young and his political views are not known. Ludwig prepares books on electron interference. He is in bad health, aged and against the Nazis.

7. Italy's Poli, whose work has been with the theory of nuclear physics, is definitely against the Nazis. Where he is or what he is doing is not known.

8. In Switzerland: Cello works under Flute in Zurich with the largest cyclotron in Europe. He is extremely reliable. Jacobs, whose specialty is the theory of mesons, cannot be depended upon politically. Orff in nuclear forces and Baum in electron optics are both considered reliable, although the former is German. Thomas is also reliable; he experiments on neutrons but not uranium.

9. Flute is not acquainted with the individuals he leaves unmentioned. However, we are attempting via other sources to obtain information on them.

Document 3-69

Telegram 2600, March 26, 1944

[Wrenching changes in German intelligence and military organization continued. Number 512 is Gisevius.]

The following has been verified through 513: Canaris is not Chief of Abwehr and Himmler has assumed control of Abwehr organization which operates under Kaltenbrunner under Hansen's direction, the latter being General Oster's successor and former right hand man of Canaris. Military intelligence is still handled by Abwehr. Schellenberg continues as head of SD activities; his position is on a level with Hansen's and he is also under Kaltenbrunner.

512 makes the following statement in connection with changes in the German command on the Eastern Front: Kuechler will face a court martial for his failure to hold the Leningrad front. The replacement of von Kluge might be in some degree attributed to a bad automobile accident which occurred 3 months ago, and which has hospitalized him. Busch typifies the Prussian soldier. Kuechler's replacement, General Model, is an inveterate Nazi, similar in type to Rommel.

Document 3-70

Telegram 2612-17, March 28, 1944

[This revealing summary of the Dulles organization as of early 1944 should be considered with reference to the information on OSS source number and code/cover names at the back of this book.]

To Jackpot. Replying to your #1360. This answer does not fully reveal the extent of our network, due largely to the fact that the questions in your cable are not completely applicable to our complex setup. It should be remembered that for the 3 years of the war during which we did nothing, the various other Allied services picked up all the available agents in Switzerland who were suitable for assignment to the east and the north. Furthermore, since the border was shut down soon after we began our work, suitable agents for numerous assignments could not be brought in and a large enough administrative staff could not be built up.

(a) Including the branch sections at Geneva, Lugano, and Zurich, there are 5 staff officers and 12 for ciphering, translating, and secretarial work. Although 493 is mainly on another payroll, he is included as a staff officer. The individuals listed below are also assimilated, but without official cover, to the staff officers: 667, 476, 496, 677, 394, 477, 668. (b) Numerous agents and subagents come under about 14 services, i.e.: K13; K23; 245 [284]-B, D, E, F, G; 472, 513, 475, 802. (c) Apart from 513, we provided all the foregoing with funds or expenses. A number of the above services are shared with either Zulu or 520. No precise figures can be stated on the number of subagents in those services who are either directly or indirectly doing work for us; however, they number more than 100. Only a rough picture of their distribution can be given, running somewhat as follows: Italy, 20%; France, 70% (including agents working into Germany from France); and the rest to eastern Europe and Germany.

The following offices take care of the principal other paid agents: Lugano, 6; Bern, 14; Geneva, 7; and Zurich, 13. Apart from 2 for Italy and 2 for Germany, these agents are based here. The majority of them are located here but possess contacts estimated at 20% in France, 15% in the Balkans and eastern Europe, 50% in Germany, and 15% in Italy. The above agents handle about 20 subagents, most of whom are voluntary.

All individuals who are assimilated to the staff officers mentioned in (a) above, possess wide contacts, and among them are about 20 subagents of major importance, most of them voluntary rather than professional. Priceless collaborators such as 492 are not included in the above. Furthermore, I don't know if you look upon a close continuing contact like Breakers as an agent. Numerous people of like category are handled by staff officers, as well as by others, including 477, 492, and 476.

Although this is as clear a picture of the situation to date as we can let you have, it is by no means an accurate one if you desire to know how many people we can count upon after the collapse of Germany. The reason for this is that a great many would then return to the service of their own countries, especially the Italian, German, and French, and therefore their continued presence on the battle order staff must not be expected.

Document 3-71

Telegram 339-42 to Algiers, March 29, 1944

[This report describes conditions in Italy.]

From 110. Recently our 685 reached here from Italy, and he will go back there in the near future. 685 says that he had a talk with Major Ralph Harrison in the vicinity of Rome, and that the latter inquired about me. Major Harrison went on to the Apennine region, according to 685.

685 states that conditions in Rome are in a tragic state, and he forcefully protested that a lot of valueless and highly destructive bombing attacks are currently being carried out in the region of Rome, and in Terni, Viterbo, Arezzo, and so forth. He reports that all of the railroad lines to Rome are already severed and that all we are doing in effect is bombing graveyards and making it impossible to supply civilians in the urban areas with provisions, and that the best propaganda material that the Nazis now have are these air raids. The raids are seriously impairing the morale of the people and divorcing them from the Allies according to 685.

685 alleges that practically all Nazi war transportation is currently carried on at night by truck. During the day, however, the Nazis run ghost trains for the most part vacant or filled with civilians, just as bait for raiders.

He says that the current population of Rome, including refugees, is 2,750,000 and that there are virtually no reserves of food. Bombing is gradually destroying 75 trucks and certain trucks which the Vatican has loaned for the job of carrying food into the city. There is a grave danger of pestilence in Rome, which has no electricity or gas and little water. He says that after the landing at Anzio the major part of the Nazi services and troops were withdrawn from Rome. Some skeleton services remain in Rome at the Flora and Excelsior Hotels, and General Mafitzer is there as well as about 500 Nazi police. He further claims that a circular road around Rome is employed for bringing supplies to the southern and Anzio fronts instead of going through Rome itself. He gave the names of Professor Di Georgis and Zanetti as 2 alleged agents of ours who are operating in Rome, at the present time.

685 says that he saw a copy of a secret Nazi report about the drastic shortage of chrome ores, and advises that notice be paid to the alleged shipping of these ores by small craft across the Adriatic Sea from St. Giovanni di Medua.

685 is a bit scatter brained and tends to exaggerate in his presentation. Nevertheless, a picture of the expanding and dire situation of civilians in Rome is given in other reports which we have recently received.

Document 3-72

Telegram 336-37 to Algiers, March 29, 1944

[This message is representative of the numerous obscure and baffling intelligence matters faced by OSS Bern.]

Do you or Zulu have any information on the following matter? It was reported to us by source K-13 A and C: A man identifying himself as Don Silvani Alberto Lorenzo (this name, he admitted, was a pseudonym but he would not disclose his real identity) reported to be a Trieste industrialist gave K-13-C one-half of a lira note bearing the serial number 829643-543. He then requested a passport and aid from K-13-C in getting to Lisbon, and claimed that the person holding the other part of the note would help him to accomplish this. Lorenzo claims to be on a mission from General Giuseppe Locatelli who is currently Commander of the Adriatic coast (exact location unknown) and was formerly Commander of the Rovigo District. The purpose of the mission was to meet Admiral Leonardi in Lisbon with the goal of helping the forthcoming landing of the Anglo-Americans in the Balkans. Lorenzo's story is that Locatelli is willing to cooperate with TSF personnel and so forth. As yet can not find the other half of the note. K-13-C is keeping close watch on the envoy.

Document 3-73

Telegram 2627-28, March 29, 1944 (extract)

[Dulles reports further on Hungary in the aftermath of German occupation.]

Reliable information about Hungary is still shut off from us. Since the German occupation of Hungary, nobody has reached Bern. Press accounts of events should not be accepted at full value. It is likely that we lost most of our best contacts as a result of the coup. However, our activities later on should be aided by any underground opposition, if such has been organized. It is probable that the best way of effecting contact now will be through Croatia, provided we are able to accomplish air infiltration. It is regrettable that it is a simple matter for the Nazis to control the channels from Hungary to Switzerland. . . .

Document 3-74

Telegram 2630-31, March 29, 1944

["Castle" messages deal with the German threat to Switzerland. "General G." is Henri Guisan, commander of the Swiss army.]

CASTLE. To 154 and 109. In reference to your #1382. I fully understand your attitude and am governing my actions along those lines. Recently I talked to General G. and made known to him that the situation in general was causing me some concern. He said that he would begin an investigation on his own. I think that his reason for requesting a talk with me was to try to gain some indication of whether or not it is probable that France will be invaded in the near future. It is evident that he fears the threat to Switzerland present in the fact that the Nazis may wish to use Swiss railroads to transport Nazi forces into safety in the event of a retreat of the Germans from the South in case the attack is carried on simultaneously in the North and South. We have assigned General G. our 839.

Document 3-75

Telegram 2633, March 29, 1944

[Dulles relayed an additional report on organizational turmoil in Germany. Number 670 is Eduard Waetjen; 512 is Hans Bernd Gisevius.]

SAINT. The Ribbentrop Bureau has been liquidated according to 670 and 512. It was previously housed in a building on Margarethen Strasse which Rosenberg now uses. They also say that it used to be under the supervision of Stoengracht. We are trying to secure material pertaining to the lower echelon of this organization as you requested. It is alleged that Luther is now in jail and that Wusson is in Portugal. Both these individuals have been associated with the Bureau.

Document 3-76

Telegram 2634, March 29, 1944

[This message reports the impending establishment of a new German military headquarters.]

We have been advised that the civilian residents of Bratislava have been evacuated in considerable measure in order to clear the way for military headquarters there. Reports from sources indicate that a sizable Nazi headquarters is currently being established there, for the direction of operations in Southeastern Europe.

Document 3-77

Telegram 2651-53, March 30, 1944

[Dulles here discusses additional contacts with Hungary.]

From 110. In reference to your #1335. 684's Lisbon associate has advised him that Deak, subject of the above message, is very active in Lisbon and is trying to represent himself as a special envoy to conduct Hungarian affairs. He has fostered the idea that he is acting in behalf of both Eckhardt and the Secretary of State. Deak has spread the propaganda that our Hungarian connections here are known to the Nazis, that our communication channel is insecure, that he is in a position to transmit cipher communications to Eckhardt, and that it would be wise for Hungarians to communicate in this fashion. In addition, Deak has cautioned Lisbon to be wary of dealing with "lesser dignitaries." The latter, according to Deak, are subject to Czech control.

684 is greatly upset over this information and his Lisbon associate with whom he maintains close contact is also worried. Personally, I'm not in a position to evaluate the accuracy of this data. We presume that both the Secretary of State and you realize that the Hungarians do not like to operate through their excountrymen such as Deak.

Deak is well known to me. He is somewhat of a schemer but has ability and initiative. For our own information kindly let us know if Eckhardt would be an acceptable candidate for the leadership of, or membership in the Free Hungarian Movement. When I departed from Washington, I had formed the opinion that his usefulness is considered rather questionable. He is more or less in disrepute, and in consideration of the enmity felt by certain leftist Hungarians, Czech and Jewish circles, it is best not to advocate using him in such a position.

Document 3-78

Telegram 2659-67, March 31, 1944

[This telegram is a reply from Dulles to Donovan on questions of German morale.]

From 110 to 109. With reference to your #1406–1410. I am extremely concerned over the inquiries put forth in your message, and I should like to give you my present opinion before going ahead with the matter.

1. If I or any other official is involved in any way with distributing the 2nd and 3rd questions, the idea may be formed a) that we are suggesting or preparing to offer a new definition of unconditional surrender, and b) that we might be interested in negotiations with a minority group if such a group were created. Unenlightening and very likely uninteresting responses will be elicited if on the other hand, the questions are disseminated anonymously.

2. In our candid opinion here, allowance is not made in these queries for the current state of affairs in Germany or for our own policy toward the German nation to date. If my co-workers, Breakers, for instance, were presented with this questionnaire, I would be at a total loss to reply to the questions they would ask of me. Unison K-24 is a paid agent, of comparatively low class.

3. The following are the replies which I think would be given by the Germans to these inquiries. This material is not founded on idle theorizing but on innumerable reports and on extended consultation with individuals qualified to discuss such topics, who have come from Germany.

4. Regarding the 1st question: The Germans are certainly aware of an inescapable trend. Their hopes at the present time consist solely in: a) diminution of Russian interest upon attaining the 1941 boundaries, or else friction between the USSR and the western Allies; b) frustration of endeavors to land in the Balkans or in France, added to war-fatigue on the part of the western countries, the forthcoming elections in the United States, and the degree to which the United States views the war against Japan as its primary concern; c) a miracle of some sort, such as a secret weapon, although this hope is fading; d) an era of chaotic confusion throughout Europe, from which Germany would emerge in as good shape as any other country.

5. Regarding the 2nd question: The majority of Germans believe it very possible that the Allies wish to ruin the economic as well as the military strength of Germany, and thus to demolish what they feel to be a normal and successful civilian life. The expression "unconditional surrender" therefore signifies to most of them total catastrophe for the country and for the individual German, as we ourselves haven't done a thing to offer them any hope of any more optimistic meaning for this expression. It has never been indicated by us that military and party leaders are the only groups to which "unconditional surrender" refers. The Germans' pessimistic interpretation of "unconditional surrender" is supported by lack of statements from the United States, the widespread feeling that the Atlantic Charter has been discarded or at least does not hold good for Germany, and by the Prime Minister's mention of compensation to Poland by giving her German territory. It is a debatable question whether any new and to them more optimistic interpretation of "unconditional surrender" could be effectively impressed upon the German people, in the face of the propaganda system of Dr. Goebbels; however, granting the issuance of authoritative and harmonizing proclamations by Churchill, Roosevelt, and Stalin, it is probable that it could be achieved in time. Up to this point, back-handed encouragement from the Free German Committee in Moscow has been the only source of hope for

the Germans, although this committee is regarded as a trap by a large number of people.

6. Regarding the 3rd question: Unless the following chain of events occurred—the murder of Hitler and certain other Nazi potentates followed by the assumption of authority by the Military—it is believed by the majority of Germans that no minority faction could now seize authority over the existing ruler. At the present time no effective opposition group, military or civilian, exists which favors the western powers. Most anti-Nazis who desire western orientation at this time do not see any justification for risking their lives in order to promote the materialization of any plans submitted to date by the western powers insofar as concerns Germany. Other anti-Nazi elements in the Reich prefer to have the authority and responsibility maintained by the Nazi and Military cliques until the ultimate debacle, so that the whole blame for the War and for Germany's downfall will rest on the shoulders of Hitler and the Military for all time. The German Socialists, especially, do not intend to assume control as they did the last time and thus have to answer for the armistice and peace terms. The Catholics' point of view is much like this. The Communists possess no known leader. Of course, a new group probably would be created in case we chose to offer any indication that such a group would be able to engage in dealings with us; however, until the capitulation, the strength of this group would be insignificant. In the conviction that such a proposition was unwise, untimely, and opposed to our policy, I have never given any stimulation to this notion.

7. The above opinions constitute my candid beliefs, proffered after discussion with other persons here. Refer to my January 31 Flash, which I believe still holds true, with respect to the overall state of affairs in Germany. I am waiting for additional directions from you concerning the treatment of the actual questions in your message. I do not favor any sentimental approach to the German problem, but it is my conviction that the war could be brought to a quicker conclusion by the exercise of a more realistic attitude in the sphere of psychological warfare.

Document 3-79

Telegram 2674-75, March 31, 1944

[OSS Bern continued to report on the deployment of German rockets.]

The following information is from source 284-F and deals with rocket torpedo installations on the Cotentin peninsula. It is dated March 30th. Underground batteries, composed of galleries sloping at a constant angle, launch these projectiles. An electric gun system, in which the gallery plays the part of a gun tube, projects the torpedo. It is not until the projectile reaches a particular initial velocity that it is ignited. The galleries are built of cement and are completely without metal, because of the fact that the propulsion is electric and in order to eliminate magnetic interferences. By projecting the rocket torpedo together with a chariot, which drops off while the rocket is moving through space, the initial problem of separating the chariot from the projectile was solved. The newest model of rocket torpedo is equipped with a device which allows it to be guided by "telecommande" employing Hertzian waves. Only German laborers participated in the construction of the underground batteries on the Cotentin peninsula. These batteries are alleged to be bomb-proof and are successfully camouflaged. It is recommended by the source that the sole means of demolishing them would be by employing French Commandos who have a good knowledge of that area or by partisan activity.

Document 3-80

Telegram 355-56 to Algiers, April 3, 1944

[This message concerns contacts with the resistance in northern Italy. Number 809 is Donald Jones.]

809 in Lugano was contacted by couriers of the Padua unit of Motta, which claims to have branches in the Veneto region, then indicated their wish to establish direct contact with us because of the trouble encountered in obtaining useful assistance from Motta. If we are desirous of giving them assistance, they will give us complete particulars in connection with the leaders, organization, and opportunities presented in both the mountain territory to the north of Padua, and conditions on the Veneto Adriatic beaches, the places along the beaches where their supplies could be landed. Should this interest us, kindly transmit this message on the 10th to the 15th of this month at 21.30–23.30 hours over the Italian Service identified by the following phrase: "L'olefanteo arriate." As soon as this signal is received, they say they will send us a courier and the information. They claim that they could assist us in breaking the Trevisio line, if we could furnish them with the equipment. Request that you advise us if you are interested and of the steps taken in this connection.

Document 3-81

Telegram 2724-26, April 6, 1944 (extract)

[Evert Smits, a German source, provides additional information on German rocket deployment.]

From source 843. 1. The Swiss, according to advices received by our source, possess drawings of rocket projectile catapults on the invasion coast. Source recommends that possibly we can arrange an exchange with them, since the Swiss would like very much to obtain the design of German radio equipment for beaming attacking airplanes. Our source says that the British captured the latter design in 1942 in a commando raid on Boulogne, and that he has this from a German inventor. Also according to information received by our source, not one rocket projectile catapult on the invasion coast has remained unbombed. . . .

Document 3-82

Telegram 2714-16, April 6, 1944

[Dulles continues to report on the German resistance group, Breakers.]

To Carib, Jackpot and 140. The wire which goes with this one, and which comes from Breakers, is a short resume of a lengthy talk I have had with Gorter and 512, who have just come back from the north. Tucky is the general whose name is also that of Kippy's first wife; Lester is number 3 in my #1966. The Breakers message, I understand, is founded on talks between Lester and Gorter and on communication "H" from Tucky. They are eager to know if we are interested in pursuing this subject, and point out that the time in which successful action could be carried out by any such group is quickly drawing to a close. They want to make it clear that while they say they are ready to attempt a coup, they cannot guarantee success. I made few remarks beyond expressing my strong belief that we would never take any kind of action without the Soviet's knowledge. I do not feel too sanguine, especially since Tucky and Lester have both been too much acclaimed as potential heads of such a movement. We are bound to take it for granted that the Gestapo is aware of the situation and is letting matters hang fire, either because they plan not to crack down till the situation has matured further, or because they wish to have an anchor to the west. I should like, in any case, to have any directions you can supply.

The Breakers message brings up the old predicament of capitulating to the east or to the west; the Germans can never perceive the third alternative of capitulating to both at the same moment.

Document 3-83

Telegram 2709-10, April 6, 1944

[This message discusses the status of Baron Bakach-Bessenyey, Hungarian Minister in Bern.]

A confidential report which 684 received directly from Budapest via a safe channel, is the basis for the part about Hungary in my Flash of the 3rd of this month. I think that the report is genuine. 684 has wired the government in Budapest to the effect that he does not recognize it and is stopping all communication with it. The Swiss have indicated that until a letter of recall signed by Horthy is received they intend to continue to recognize 684 as Minister. In view of this 684 is going to hold fast, which appears to be the best procedure for him to follow in order to forestall the creation of a Quisling Legation in Switzerland. It is 684's opinion that at the moment Horthy is completely isolated. 684 still hopes, however, that the Regent will awake to his error in appointing a new cabinet, especially since his most intimate friends have been apprehended by the Nazis, and that he will discontinue any collaboration with the Nazis. 684 is keeping us posted on developments.

Document 3-84

Telegram 2712-13, April 6, 1944

[Dulles presents his evaluation of U.S. broadcasting in comparison with the BBC.]

From 110 to Jackpot. In reference to your #1438. . . . I am reluctant to admit that I believe that to the majority of the population in the countries to which you have reference, radio broadcasts from our side are almost identical with those of the British Broadcasting Company. Since the British Broadcasting Company broadcasts the news in well-prepared digests at convenient times, I listen to them at least once a day myself, and seldom tune in American stations. Too, it is almost always possible to hear the BBC programs. I have talked with countless individuals and have gathered the impression that the effect of American shortwave programs from the United States is slight. Programs relayed through the British Broadcasting Company are most often tuned in. Interest in Africa is increasing, but up to now there has not been much talk of Italy.

Document 3-85

Telegram 367 to Algiers, April 7, 1944

[This message describes fighting in southeastern France.]

According to a report just received, 350 Nazis were killed during their attack on the Glieres Maquis; however, heavy losses were inflicted on the 600 Maquis. The Nazis are currently engaged in a search of the outlying territory for escaped Maquis men and cleaning up the Glieres plateau. In reprisal, the Nazis have burnt some villages. Milice did not enter into the actual battle but was actively engaged in espionage operations handling prisoners and applying the methods of the Gestapo.

Document 3-86

Telegram 2718-22, April 7, 1944

[By April 1944, Dulles could report that the "Breakers" opposition group in the Reich was gaining strength and audacity. Carib is F. L. Mayer, an officer in OSS headquarters concerned with the penetration of Germany; number 140 is Hugh R. Wilson of the OSS Planning Group, former Ambassador to Germany, and a prewar associate of Dulles; Tucky is General Ludwig Beck.]

To Carib, Jackpot, and 140. This is a resume of a declaration made by Breakers: Germany's position is fast coming to a head and the conclusion of hostilities in Europe can definitely be seen. The opposition group led by Tucky and Lester say that at this critical point they are now willing and prepared to try to start action to oust the Nazis and eliminate the Fuehrer. Theirs is the only group able to profit by a personal approach to Hitler and other Nazi chiefs, and with enough arms at hand to accomplish their ends. Their group is also the only one in Germany having enough power in the army and with certain active army chiefs to make the coup feasible.

The condition on which the group is ready to act is that the Anglo-Saxon powers give assurances that, once the Nazis have been overthrown, the group may negotiate directly with the Western powers about practical action necessary. The group is especially concerned that they should not have to negotiate with Moscow, but that the dealings be carried on through London and Washington. The group cites as precedent the procedure followed, though in reverse, in the instance of the recent negotiations for peace with Finland. The Finns dealt with Moscow alone, despite their being at war with both Britain and the Soviet. The group, though grasping fully that conditions are not at all the same in the instance of Germany, bases its request on the fact that the people who are planning this coup are rather conservatively minded, although willing to cooperate with any available elements of the Left, barring the Communists. The chief reason for such a request on their part is their ardent wish to keep Central Europe from coming under the sway of the Soviet, factually and ideologically. They feel certain that in the latter case democracy and Christian culture and all their accompanying benefits would vanish in Europe, and that there would merely be a switch from the current Nazi totalitarianism to the new totalitarianism of the radical left. The group declares with great emphasis that we must not dismiss lightly the perils of such an eventuality, particularly in the light of the millions now living in Central Europe who have become completely proletarian. The group also states that if the capitulation is to be primarily made to Russia, the negotiations would be carried on not be [by] Breakers, but by another group of persons. The Wehrmacht generals now commanding in the West, particularly Rundstedt and Falkenhausen, would be ready to cease opposition and to help Allied troops land, once the Nazis had been ousted. Similarly arrangements might be worked out for the reception of Allied parachute forces in strategic spots in Germany.

Document 3-87

Telegram 2729, April 7, 1944

[Dulles advises that Gerald Mayer will be using the nightly radiotelephone channel to transmit to OWI (headed by Elmer Davis).]

For Jackpot. Use of our Flash channel for 1 night every week, perhaps Wednesday, is wanted by 678 in order to send Elmer the semiconfidential part of his weekly summary. It is necessary to lighten the burden on the code facilities of the Legation, which is the reason for this request. Subject to your approval, I shall be glad to oblige 678 in this. He should make the call on our regular system, using the same call we do but starting off with "Weekly Summary for Elmer." The advantages of this arrangement are that it would allow 678 to benefit by Flash partner's excellent facilities for reception, would mean greater economy by not having to work out a new arrangement, and furthermore, in confidence, would give you an opportunity to look over this summary, which might be of interest to you. 678 is wiring Elmer, and, for greater security, I have arranged here that you would bring this matter up to Elmer in confidence.

Document 3-88

Telegram 2732, April 8, 1944

[This message concerns Yugoslavia and Hungary.]

Do you have any data on the following matter: It is vital that we make certain what Tito's reaction will be in connection with work beginning here through 684 and others to recreate lines to Hungary. Also, if it would be a good move to encourage armed Hungarian bands to anticipate a friendly welcome by Tito if they cross over into Croatia.

Document 3-89

Telegram 2751, April 9, 1944

[Dulles discusses the Japanese intelligence target.]

110 to Jackpot. To date, it has not been possible for me to uncover Japanese data of this kind here. I think that our greatest chance of securing such information lies through persons like Wood. I feel that the Japanese forward only a small amount of interesting material here and that they have been withholding a great deal of information from their Nazi partners for some period.

Document 3-90

Telegram 568-69 to London, April 10, 1944

[Funding of the French resistance through Bern continues.]

For Tertius, concerning your #620, Washington #1437. Through Iris, we are providing the Maquis in the departments of Haute Savoie, Isere, and Savoie with a monthly sum of 80,000 Swiss francs, which at first had a value of 4,000,000 French francs but have now increased to more than 5,000,000. Neither 284 nor I see anything wrong in having this amount raised to 150,000 Swiss francs a month. However, if only those 3 departments are to benefit thereby, the current general budget for the resistance movement might become rather disproportionate and you might feel that the field of activities for which the CCR could allow an increase should be extended. Naturally, a great deal more money could be used, provided our Army authorities wanted to see these three departments develop into real centers of strength. Kindly advise us.

Iris has dispatched a communication from Marcus to Indigo concerning Indigo's scheme to build up an emergency operating reserve of Swiss francs here. 284 and I are in close collaboration with Marcus and feel that this scheme has a lot of merit, especially since there is a chance that some parts of France may, for a while, be cut off from other sources of monetary assistance at crucial moment. And furthermore, if any special parachutage of money should be lost, this reserve would come in handy.

Document 3-91

Telegram 2787-92, April 12, 1944

[In April 1944, Fritz Kolbe ("George Wood") visited Switzerland and provided Dulles with a large batch of new documents copied from originals in the German Foreign Ministry. OSS Bern processed and transmitted this material incrementally in telegrams bearing the indicator Kapril. This cable and a memorandum from Acting Director Buxton describing Dulles as a source were sent to the White House on April 15. Although some Boston Series items based on earlier Wood Documents as relayed by Bern had been sent to the White House beginning in January 1944, this cable and Buxton's highly laudatory memorandum were Dulles's real introduction to Presidential circles. From this point forward, the OSS frequently sent Bern/Dulles material to President Roosevelt under the cover of memoranda from Donovan. For the last year of the war, information from Bern was the single most voluminous category of OSS data put before the President.]

KAPPA. For 105 and Jackpot. This is a Kapril message. Sincerely regret that you are unable at this time to view Wood's material as it stands without condensation and abridgement. In some 400 pages, dealing with the internal maneuvering of German diplomatic policy for the past two months, a picture of imminent doom and final downfall is presented. Into a tormented General Headquarters and a half-dead Foreign Office stream the lamentations of a score of diplomatic posts. It is a scene wherein haggard Secret Service and diplomatic agents are doing their best to cope with the defeatism and desertion of flatly defiant satellites and allies and recalcitrant neutrals. The period of secret service and diplomacy under Canaris and the champagne salesman respectively is drawing to an end. Already Canaris has disappeared from the picture, and a conference was hurriedly convoked in Berlin at which efforts were made to mend the gaping holes left in the Abwehr. Unable now to fall back on his favorite means of avoiding disconcerting critics by retiring to his bed, Ribbentrop has beat a retreat to Fastahl and retains a number of his principal aides at Salzburg. The remainder of the Foreign Office is strung out all the way between Riesengibirge and the capital. Practically impossible working conditions exist in the latter, and bombing shelters are being permanently used for code work. Once messages have been deciphered, a frantic search begins to locate the specific service or minister to which each cable must be forwarded; and, when a reply is called for, another search is required to deliver this to the right place.

Either Bormann or Neubacher will step forward if Ribbentrop is sacked, and one of them will carry out Gestapo diplomacy. Ample evidence of what this will mean is contained in 100-odd pages of Wesenmeyer cables describing the situation in the Hungarian capital. There, however, the drama involves that old fox, Horthy, playing the role of a 1944 Petain. Wesenmeyer's cable dated the 20th of last month ends on the following querulous note: "Within the last 24 hours, I have had three long talks with von Horthy. As a result, I am becoming more and more convinced that on the one hand the regent is an unmitigated liar and on the other he is physically no longer capable of performing his duties. He is constantly repeating himself, often contradicting himself within a few sentences, and sometimes does not know how to go on. Everything he says sounds like a memorized formula, and I fear that it will be difficult to convince him, let alone win him over."

In Sofia, cagy Bulgarians are playing all sorts of tricks on Beckerle and going off to Turkey on pleasure trips, while Nazi offices are accusing each other right and left of letting traitors clear out from under their noses. In Bucharest, Antonescu's harried aides try to think up excuses for the Stirby-Chastclain incidents that will satisfy the Nazis, while the Marshal himself receives reports that looting German troops are just ahead of the Russians.

The final deathbed contortions of a petrified Nazi diplomacy are pictured in these telegrams. The reader is carried from one extreme of emotion to the other, from tears to laughter, as he examines these messages and sees the cruelty exhibited by the Germans in their final swan-song of brutality toward the peoples so irrevocably and pitifully enmeshed by the Gestapo after half a decade of futile struggles, and yet at the same time also sees the absurdity of the dilemma which now confronts this diplomacy both within and without Festung Europa.

Document 3-92

Telegram 572 to London, April 17, 1944

[This message discusses a possible Hitler-Mussolini meeting.]

We are informed that Mussolini is critically ill and because of this we doubt that Hitler and he met recently, although Mussolini had been persistently asking for such a meeting. In any event, the Germans would scarcely use a meeting such as that to talk about their withdrawal plans, if they had such plans. The probabilities are that they would first withdraw and then inform Mussolini. There is no direct proof at this end of withdrawal plans. Nearly all Italian Swiss reports emanating from Chiasso are without foundation.

Document 3-93

Telegram 2966-69, April 17, 1944

[OSS headquarters responded to Dulles's telegram 2787-92 of April 12 by asking him if he wanted to modify it in view of its importance as an appraisal of the current state of German diplomacy. Acting Director Buxton sent the substance of this follow-up cable to the White House on April 19.]

KAPPA. From 110 to 105 and Jackpot.

1. Having weighed your #1488 very carefully, I do not want to mitigate my #2787–92 as a description of the current Nazi diplomatic and political scene.

2. Even though the Kapril messages and a long oral commentary by Woods are responsible in the main for the picture presented, other reports from sources like Gorter and 512 and the general background data available in Bern are in accord with this view.

3. It was not my intention in my message to give the impression that the morale of the entire Nazi Army (with the exception of the so-called Gross Deutscher, Slav and other non-German elements whom the Nazis cannot rely on) has yet reached the point of collapse. Therefore, fierce, perhaps desperate opposition may be given to any attempt to invade. I do not believe that any able Nazi military officials are prepared as yet to throw open the western front to us. I do believe, however, that the collapse of Germany might follow a very few months afterwards, if we could get a solid toe hold in the west, opening in this way a 4th front to Italy, Russia and the Balkans.

4. Woods supplied the information that the wastage of Nazi fighter planes was nearing critical proportions as a result of our bombing attacks during the day.

5. The psychological timing of the invasion attempt may be of vital importance. The mass of the regimented German people are still war weary and apathetic and even in influential Nazi circles there is evidence of the identical type of psychological depression which existed last August and September. The Nazis may catch their second wind if the Russian front can be stabilized once more and they would then be able to make an even stronger fight against the invasion.

6. You will have had the greater part of the Kapril messages by the time you receive this wire. The precis of these messages which I wired, is not very adequate

but will provide an additional basis for arriving at an independent judgment about the inner diplomatic and political condition of Germany.

Document 3-94

Telegram 3034-36, April 18, 1944

[Rumania sought to make contact with the Allies through Bern, hoping to avoid going down to defeat with Germany.]

To 105 and Jackpot. . . . A request from Mihai Antonescu with the approval of the King and Maniu was just received by our 495 via a special courier from Bucharest. The request was to find out what the political terms of the Allied Nations would be and what practical action was to be taken. The message states that the King and Mihai Antonescu have been able to preserve 8 entire infantry divisions in the vicinity of Bucharest. Due to the ungratifying results of the Stirbey mission because of the collapse of communications and excessive notoriety, this step is being initiated through 495. In addition, 495 is afraid that Stibey committed the error of not handling the Russian side of things correctly. The special courier is remaining in order to return with any answer which may be sent to 495. The particulars of the above message have been simultaneously transmitted via the British Minister and via Benes' representative in Bern to Benes for Moscow. The following is from 110: in view of our experience in Italy it is probably impossible to await the outcome of protracted political negotiations if any use is to be made of these 8 alleged divisions. I recommend, in the event that you are interested, that it would be desirable for the Soviets, the British or ourselves to try and find out at once, what the best way to establish direct contact would be and where and with whom this meeting could be arranged.

Document 3-95

Telegram 387-88 to Algiers, April 20, 1944

[OSS Bern reported the arrival of U.S. airmen shot down over Italy.]

Recent arrivals here were Lieutenant Potter and Sergeant Johnson, 2 more members of McCollum's crew (see our #310). A partisan group of about 2,000 men were contacted in the vicinity of Fobello 0418 West Rome 4553 North. Their chief was a supposed Communist and former lawyer at Borgosesia by the name of Muscatelli. . . . There was also a man called Frank, an Australian ex-PW, who inspired the unit with fighting spirit. This man was not identified. On the 10th of last month, the band was attacked by a Nazi motor convoy and obliged to break up because of a severe lack of weapons. It is thought that later on it was reorganized with fewer people. A lot of partisan units are in this area but they do not cooperate. It was observed that this unit was giving protection to 5 German deserters, 2 of whom are in Switzerland at present.

Document 3-96

Telegram 2543, part 3, April 21, 1944

[The Nazis and the Vichy French clashed over the allocation of champagne and cognac.]

. . . The authorities of France cannot let the refusal by the Germans to raise the price of champagne for their troops stand and now the Ministry of Agriculture of France has the matter under advisement. The Germans had insisted that during this calendar year quantities of cognac delivered to the German army by the outstanding producers be increased so that Martell and Hennessey would ship a total extra amount of 79 thousand cases while the smaller producers' deliveries would be reduced. According to the French, the outstanding producers would be unable to ship more than the amount planned but that the Government of France would agree to make available 75 thousand hectolitres of cognac which would be, in part, of inferior grades, to the German Army. The situation with regard to cognac has been ordered investigated by the Germans.

Document 3-97

Telegram 2560, April 21, 1944

[Dulles advocated measures to strengthen the noncommunist German labor movement.]

The following information for the OSS from a source which will be revealed in another message has been sent also to London as number 668.

For a considerable period the obstacles cited below have hampered our efforts to set up a liaison with the underground of labor circles within the Reich:

(a) Everybody outstanding in labor circles is under special surveillance by the Gestapo.

(b) Leaders of labor within the Reich who are opposed to the Nazi regime are not able to get out to non-belligerent countries, even to Switzerland.

(c) There is no contact between leaders of labor in the Reich and reliable Germans who can go to Switzerland.

At last contact has been established with an individual thought to be in contact with dominant figures in the underground movement of Socialist labor circles and the following views of theirs are expressed:

While the two movements are entirely separate, both the Communists and the

Socialists maintain underground organizations in labor circles within the Reich, with skeleton organizations in the bigger urban communities. For the following reasons the former organization commands a broader influence, is more active and is better organized:

(a) The ideology of the Communists finds a fertile field because Germans by the millions have lost all their material possessions.

(b) A central committee of the Communists exists in the Reich to coordinate and direct their activities within the country and to maintain contact with the committee of Freiesdeutschland in the Soviet capital, from which government support is received. Soviet war prisoners and workers by the millions facilitate this contact with Russia through a Moscow-directed secret organization. The fewness of their German guards is a great aid to them.

(c) The Soviet maintains a steady flow into the Reich of constructive ideas and schemes as a program to provide for the rehabilitation of the Reich after the war. Such plans and ideas are being disseminated widely among the masses of the German people through the whispering campaign that the Communists have organized very well.

In contrast to the activities mentioned above there is complete ignorance as to the ultimate objectives and the practical ideas for the future of central Europe maintained by the Allied powers. The leaders of Socialism within the Reich say with emphasis that this uncertainty must be clarified as soon as possible in order to counteract the growing influence of Communism. This tendency toward the ultra-radical has grown stupendously and its momentum is gaining rapidly. If it is not stopped the leaders of German labor are afraid that even if the Allies achieve military victory, the peace will be quickly lost and a new dictatorship may take the place of the present one in central Europe. The adoption of a policy of a constructive nature in dealing with the masses of central Europe is urged as a means of dealing with this very dangerous development. The leaders of labor in the Reich suggest the following policy of a moderate nature for orderly reconstruction in order to attract the German laboring element:

(a) Some responsible person in the United States to make an encouraging statement which could be transmitted through the channel mentioned above in confidence to leaders of Socialism within the Reich.

(b) Some basic statement with regard to the problem of self-government for Germany in the future as well as some intimation of the extent to which the independent operation of the German's own administration will be permitted by the Allies. Self-government by local communities and regions should be stressed particularly, it is recommended.

It is suggested that the Allies issue a series of statements to the laboring classes within the Reich of an encouraging nature and which would stress the prospect of their collaboration in the reconstruction of Germany. These statements should also extend a welcome to the leaders of Socialism to join in the future government of Germany.

There should be a statement that it is not the intention of the Allies to do as the Nazis have done and set up in the Reich a puppet regime composed of German quislings who will govern the Germans and represent the interests of the Allies. Such an idea is obvious to us but the fact that these German leaders of the opposition request assurance on the point is a good example of the bewilderment in the German mind instilled by the long continued propaganda of the Nazis.

These same leaders of labor offer the suggestion that air raids be focused as nearly as they can be upon industrial and military objectives as the bombing of big urban centers is rapidly making all of central Europe entirely proletarian.

Because of the fact that I believe that these opinions are representative of those labor leaders who are opposed to the present regime in the Reich and who are basically agreeable to taking sides with us, I hope that these views will be accorded due consideration even if some of them have a naive appearance. Such an impression can be accounted for by the fact that for many years the people of the Reich have been isolated from honest news and have had, instead, vicious propaganda as a result of which even some basic truths have been distorted. Now they must relearn some fundamentals of the simplest nature.

Some statement should be made that the labor element in Germany will be encouraged and allowed to organize their own labor movement along their own lines and with no interference from the anti-labor ideas of the capitalist elements among the Allies.

There should be an active exchange of thought set up between forces of a progressive nature in the Allied nations and the socialist movement among German labor in order to counteract the close contact that prevails between the Russians and German communists.

Bombarding Germany with leaflets was ineffective during 1939 when German arms were victorious but now the people are open to such propaganda if the material used is prepared on the basis of the constantly shifting trend in the psychology of the masses of the German people. The best effect would be achieved by not dropping bombs and leaflets simultaneously and such large numbers of the latter should be dropped as to make their quick removal by the Gestapo impossible. To implement the constantly changing psychological point of view of the German people these leaflets should be compiled with assistance of the resistance movement in the Reich.

Document 3-98

Telegram 3152-53, April 25, 1944

[This message relays a rumor regarding enemy biological warfare research.]

TOLEDO. Through a trustworthy middleman we have received an additional short item from Briault indicating that the information given earlier is still in effect and that "when dogs are inoculated with serum from Leporides infected with Tularemia, a dry bacillus is produced which is extremely poisonous and contagious, and which causes terrific congestion." We are also advised that in Paris dogs are being requisitioned in large numbers, and that Tularemia is being studied by Japanese scientific groups. The same informant declares that a bombing attack should be launched against St. Gobain at Chauny where containers are produced. However, we are also advised that prior to the bombing photographs should be made of the place so that new works buildings may be identified.

Document 3-99

Telegram 3163-65, April 26, 1944 (draft)

[Dulles defends the authenticity of Fritz Kolbe as a source.]

KAPPA. Jackpot and Carib from 110. Fully appreciate force of suggestion your 1508 and have endeavored throughout to analyze Kappa material critically from this viewpoint. I appreciate danger of becoming so enamored with one's own sources that one falls into such traps. While possibility you suggest should never be excluded my present views are:

(1) As yet no evidence of plant in material itself. If plant had been intended last trip would have been logical time to try it out.

(2) Having critically examined hundreds of these Documents internal and external evidence has persuaded me of their genuineness.

(3) Local intermediary is I believe above question though of course he might be fooled also.

(4) Wood while intelligent is somewhat naive and appears to have none of the characteristics which would qualify him to pull off double-crossing game. So far under hours of questioning he has failed to give any clue which would raise question of his genuineness.

(5) Have analyzed entire scheme under which material procured and transmitted and it is logical and feasible.

(6) Wood claims to be, and I believe is, working with anti-Nazi group which includes Alpha Beta Gamma.

All of foregoing while persuasive is not conclusive and agree with you on importance of continuing critical examination. So far only disturbing element has been some evidence of recklessness on Wood's part but this is quite usual in conspirators.

Document 3-100

Telegram 3167-69, April 26, 1944 (draft)

[Fritz Kolbe provides material on German activity in Ireland.]

KAPPA. Your 1506. Evidence is unclear but cables indicate see also our 2643 that if German Legation lost any possibility of using its own radio it would be thrown back on some form of telegraphic channels which Blarney might be able to keep open for them. Reference to Senderweg apparently relates solely to method of acknowledgement by Grand of Hempels cables. It appears in several of his messages. Very possibly this was done by radio from Berlin. Full text of significant section Hempels 610 Dec. 22 see our 2779 reads: I told Walshe that possession of transmitter, view present situation in which British with Irish agreement control entire post and telegraph connections, was naturally matter of great importance. Loss of transmitter meant complete dependence on our enemies. If I indicated willingness to surrender transmitter that would mean great concession to De Valera's appeal on behalf of Irish neutrality. I would make this concession on condition that Irish would do everything possible to insure continued functioning of telegraph communication. I also raised question of resumption of direct wireless communication with Berlin. If Irish did not have any transmitter they could use those which they had just seized. W. first tried to avoid issue but then said this was not presently possible. However Irish Govt. would naturally do everything possible "um fortbestand Nachrichtenverbindung sicherzustellen."

Document 3-101

Telegram 405 to Algiers, April 27, 1944

[Bern reports setbacks suffered by the Italian resistance.]

Motta has just received information to the effect that their organizations in the Genoa and Torino regions have been practically obliterated. Attempts are now being made to form them once more.

Document 3-102

Telegram 586-87 to London, April 28, 1944

[This message concerns Ignazio Silone and the Italian Socialist Party.]

Report made by 475 that Nenni is in Rome and that Silvio Trentino is no longer living. In addition, 475 states: at the moment one of the headquarters for the Socialist Party is located in Naples; Oreste Longobardi is its leader. A second headquarters is situated in Rome led by Professor Colorni and Pietro Nenni. A 3rd headquarters in North Italy is currently scattered and no names can be furnished. Some members of this 3rd headquarters are at present refugees in Switzerland. In the Party they think of Nenni as head of the Pro-Soviet trend and as advocating a merger with the communists. The opposing trend is fairly powerful but it is not possible to predict at the present time which trend will finally win.

The following is for Washington: 475 is wiring Harper Bros. in New York that he is readying a story as the foundation for a movie depicting the brotherhood existing between Americans and Italians as shown by the experiences of escaped Britishers and Americans who were both helped and hidden by northern Italian peasants. Because of the psychological value of such a movie as well as my wish to help 475, would appreciate it if Harpers could be discreetly contacted, on basis of 475's direct wire, in an effort to discover, if the material can be delivered to them, whether they would be interested.

Document 3-103

Telegram 3228-29, April 28, 1944

[Dulles addresses Nazi use of the press in neutral nations.]

From 110. The following concerning the Swiss Telegraph Agency is submitted with reservations. A source close to the Nazi Legation in Bern says that the Nazis are utilizing the Swiss Telegraph Agency's British and American facilities as an information service, and are generously underwriting its communications expenditures. It seems that the Swiss Telegraph Agency's correspondents, Keller in London and Joseph Mannheim and John Schwab in New York, do not realize that many of the questions they are asked are of German origin. The same source also reports a Nazi program to start a magazine in Stockholm. It is to be under the supervision of Kircher, of the *Frankfurter Zeitung* and Matuschka, of the *Berliner Illustrierte*. The latter will be stationed in Stockholm and the former in Bern, since, if they can secure sanction, they hope to distribute the magazine in Switzerland. It is to be called "Globus," and will be illustrated. Zulu, who obtained it from the same source, also has the above.

Document 3-104

Telegram 3238-39, April 29, 1944

[Dulles urges that the Allies foment prisoner escape and sabotage operations in Germany.]

It is indicated by people who are acquainted with workers' and prisoners' camps in the Reich that control precautions have been weakened a good deal, with the purpose of drafting men for combat duty. Guard duty thus falls to young men who have been wounded and to old men, whose morale is dubious and who are not well armed. This state of affairs raises the prospect of arranging large scale sabotage and escape activities in connection with invasion, by means of selected organizers who would be parachuted in with arms and equipment.

The Nazis would engage in harsh reprisals, obviously, against any people whom they succeeded recapturing. However, a few such outbreaks by prisoners and workers would have a grave psychological result in Germany. It would also tend to tie down large Nazi forces for keeping order internally and it might be possible to engage in various sabotage activities.

To be candid, we do not possess sufficient data at this end regarding the exact places where it would be possible to carry out such activities. However, we will try to formulate a more detailed program if you are interested in this suggestion.

Document 3-105

Telegram 590-96 to London, May 1, 1944 (extracts)

[As an official under Ritter in the German Foreign Ministry ("Auswartiges Amt," or AA), Fritz Kolbe was able to provide detailed information on Foreign Minister Joachim von Ribbentrop and the organization he directed.]

KAPPA. . . .

2. In general, Ribbentrop's relations with departments outside of his own are poor and his position has grown weaker since Germany has been forced to pursue a defensive foreign policy. Ribbentrop has disagreed sharply with Funk concerning leadership in foreign trade negotiations and with Saukel regarding the question of foreign workers. He also quarrelled with Goebbels when Goebbels attempted to open a branch propaganda office in Paris. He continually disagrees with Keitel on the question of exempting FO people from military service. . . .

4. Staats Sekretaer von Steengracht is in charge of administering AA with Graf Mirbach as his assistant. The latter took over the position after Minister Bielefeld, who is at present in Bern, had vacated it. The administrators of the 4 principal departments under von Steengracht are listed below with the departments they head:

A. Political Department: Henke with Minister von Ermannsdorf as his assistant.

B. Political-Military: Ritter. He is responsible for liaison with every military department. Minister Frohwein and Minister Leitner assist him.

C. Law Department: Though Ambassador Gaus is in charge, he is usually at Fuschl, so Minister Albrecht is really doing the bulk of the Berlin work.

D. Economic Department: Ministerial Director Wiehl with Schnurrf as his assistant. Negotiations where foreign trade is concerned in charge of Clodius. . . .

5. SD is the term generally applied to the foreign service of the Gestapo with which Abwehr is mostly joined at present and RSHA is the headquarters of SD.

6. Ribbentrop's customary residence since he left the Fuehrer Hauptquartier

about 3-4 months back, is Schlossfuschl in the vicinity of Salzburg. There he resides, accompanied by a modest personnel staff, including an adjutant but no private secretary. . . .

Document 3-106

Telegram 3256-59, May 1, 1944

[Information provided by Fritz Kolbe included estimates and views of the Japanese on the situation in Europe. Some of this material reached the German Foreign Ministry via normal exchange of information between the enemy allies; other items had been obtained by the Germans through surreptitious means, including espionage in Tokyo and Berlin.]

. . . KAPPA. The aggressiveness and fighting power of the Soviet troops is still highly rated by the Japanese. They are currently mobilizing 16-year-olds. The opinion of the Japanese General Staff is that the principal goal of the Soviets is to push southward with its most powerful forces from the region of Zhitomir. According to the Japanese Military Attaché's report on Europe, the Germans, by making relatively scant use of earth fortifications and accepting longer front lines, sometimes heighten the difference in forces.

2. The Japanese Staff questions whether a chance will be taken on a large-scale landing by the Anglo-Saxons. An attack on Spain, the stirring up of rebellions in France, a landing northwest of Rome, and so forth, may occur prior to such a major undertaking, if it is attempted, however. If a landing is tried, it will be a concentric invasion of the channel coast probably east and west of Toulon and north and south of Bourdeaux. Considering the political pressure on Finland, small-scale landings on the northern Norwegian coast are also within the realm of possibility. Since it is counter to Russia's desire for the Anglo-Saxons to progress in the Balkans, it is not as probable that Albania will be invaded.

3. Nazi war industries so far have not been critically hurt by bombings, and the production of new arms appears to be advancing well.

4. At most, 40 reserve divisions of Nazi troops are now being created, according to estimates by the Japanese Staff.

Document 3-107

Telegram 589 to London, May 2, 1944

[This message reports bombing results in France.]

Below are results of bombing reported by source 284-D CCR the 28th of April:

1. There were 2 trains packed with men on leave, 2 trains carrying munitions

and several trains carrying supplies, all at the freight yards of Veyres in the vicinity of Lagny sur Mer on Est railroad line when the April 4th-5th air raid blew up the munition trains, killing approximately 1,800 Germans. All the above trains were bound for Germany. . . .

Document 3-108

Telegram 3261-68, May 2, 1944 (extracts)

[Messages from the German Ambassador in Rumania to Berlin, copied by George Wood / Fritz Kolbe and provided to OSS Bern, indicated that the Nazis were having difficulty maintaining control of that wavering satellite nation.]

. . . 2. Message #1067, dated March 22: Information on the departure of Stirbey and Boxshall, his daughter, was secured through an agent. I issued order to retain Boxshall in Svilengrad because of the suspicious nature of the situation. Mihai Antonescu expressed disapproval of this action, insisting S. was a Rumanian. Declared that the Rumanian Minister in Ankara had invited Boxshall and Stirbey, since he was a relative of the latter and a friend of the former; pointed out that the trip was made for this reason and had no connection with political situation.

A diplomatic pass was issued to Stirbey who is very pro-English and one of Maniu's backers. He has numerous English friends in Turkey. Mihai knows about Stirbey's journey and is without a doubt acquainted with the secret reason for undertaking the trip. Through the Rumanian Foreign Ministry, agents have found out that Crezianu stated that Stirbey went to Cairo and that Stirbey's English friends in Turkey were behind this because he had highly valuable information and went on Mihai's behalf carrying valuable papers with him.

3. Message #1275, Grand from Killinger, dated April 3: I received the following written statement from Marshal in reply to a statement that General Hansen and I made to the effect that his complaints were greatly overstated. . . . (D) A German column, with 160 horses, billeted in the Commune of Dulsesti, robbed the Mayor's home, . . killed his swine and made off with meat, stole forage from the people of the town. . . . (E) . . . German soldiers pay no attention to the military traffic regulations of Rumania and try to intimidate Rumanian traffic officers with pistols, break into homes and rob them, bother women on the streets, rape them and carry them off in German automobiles, go about thoroughly intoxicated, drive through towns at outrageous speeds causing 4 fatal accidents . . . .(G) . . . Tartar soldiers, wearing the German uniform, broke into a cooperative grain storage . . . killing swine and making off with cattle.

A portion of your instructions contained in #521 dated April 1 (Note from 110: To advise Marshal that Rumanian homeland is being protected from Bolsheviks by German troops) has ceased to apply since the Reds have made their way into Moldavia as well as Bessarabia, and doubtless Marshal will bring this to my attention. Please advise whether I am to change your instructions to fit the new conditions.

Document 3-109

Telegram 3274-76, May 2, 1944

[This telegram contains a report of a Nazi secret weapon against bomber aircraft.]

The following report is dated the 19th of April and was received from source 284-F:

1. This deals with a secret weapon used for defense against heavy bombing planes. According to a report, the Nazis have produced a device which will freeze the atmosphere to the temperature of 250 degrees below zero by the use of one tube which is connected to the underside of each wing of a fighter plane. The plane is then supposed to fly over the bombing planes on which the device is to be used, ascertain the altitude of the bombers and release the mechanism, which then will cause ice to form immediately on all planes within the refrigerated area. It is reported to suffer the following defects: the period of refrigeration is brief, being merely a few minutes; the zone which is refrigerated is small. The mechanism is still experimental; however, the Nazis regard the results as definitive and have hopes of commencing manufacture in considerable quantity shortly. . . .

Document 3-110

Telegram 3278, May 2, 1944

[This report indicates declining German morale in Italy.]

The following is from source 331 through 227: it is reported that the representative of the Vatican who went last week to Austria by train through the Brenner Pass from Italy informed an intimate friend that ranking German officers in his compartment spoke openly of the mess the German forces find themselves in Italy. Further, that they intimated a slow retreat was scheduled.

Document 3-111

Telegram 3297-98, May 3, 1944

[Donald Jones, OSS officer in Lugano (809), provided additional evidence that the Germans planned to withdraw from Italy.]

The German Military Commander at Milan was reported by source 809 as having recently made the statements below to his ranking officers.

Serious events will take place within the next few days. We have received directions from Berlin on the subject of Allied invasion and these will be announced publicly when the time arrives. As you may at any moment be ordered to depart for any destination, even Germany, be constantly on the qui vive. In order that not even 5 minutes need be wasted in the event of departure, a parcel holding your personal effects must always be on your bed. Go about armed in groups and make use of arms against anyone even Italian or German soldiers. Bear in mind that our lives are dependent upon our actions. Our fellows in anti-aircraft artillery and infantry who are at present stationed in the country will come back to the city. Italians will take their places in the country. The faithful Waffen SS, the Storm Troops and the SS will be the last units to depart.

Document 3-112

Telegram 3282-91, May 4, 1944 (extracts)

[This message was based on various German cables copied by Fritz Kolbe and delivered to OSS Bern. Subjects include papal displeasure with Allied bombing in Italy, and Russian terms for Rumania reported from Turkey. The latter messages appear to indicate defective U.S. communications security at Istanbul or Cairo.]

KAPPA. KAPRIL.

1. #180, To Grand from Weissaecker, Vatican: My authority for stating, in my March 14th message #166, that the Pope denounced Allied air attacks on Rome in an unusually sharp way has as its basis a reference in the Pontiff's speech which evoked applause from the crowd before St. Peter's. An indication of the meaning which the Pontiff placed upon his words was revealed by an inquiry of the Cardinal Secretary of State, when he asked whether the Pope's statement was sufficiently clear. The Pontiff's speech provoked bitter comment from the British Minister to one of his associates. Notes from the Vatican are sent to the Anglo-Americans almost every day about the bombing of the Holy City. The purport of the protests is as follows: There is no justification for the bombing of Rome by the Americans and British, nor for their excuses on the basis of military objectives. Did these bombardments or those at the Monte Cassino Monastery and Castel-Gandolfo reach even a single Nazi soldier? The demolition of the Monastery on Monte Cassino resulted in no military advantage for the Allies. The Cardinal will bolster representations verbally to the British Minister. He went on to say that an appropriate declaration from the Nazis would give added weight to the argument sent to Washington and London. . . .

5. #162, dated March 17th, To Grand for Under Secretary Hencke from Twar-

dowski (sic) Istanbul states: According to claims made by American sources, Stirbey was given the following conditions by the Russians in Cairo:

Frontiers to be those of 1940 with the addition of the mouth of the Danube.

All Rumanian ports on the Black Sea to be under the control of the USSR.

Rumania to get back Transylvania.

Abdication of the King.

Government officials to be delivered to the International Tribunal for War Crimes, and Marshal to be handed over to the Russian War Tribunal. . . .

The Communist Party is to be organized and supported. . . .

It is said that the Americans are furious at these conditions; however all of this should be reported with reserve.

6. #451 dated March 22, to Grande from Von Papen: A telegram from the American Legation in Cairo to (From 110: next group garbled) Soviet Russian stipulations for the Rumanian armistice follow:

1. Government of Rumania to be a democratic republic.
2. King Michael to take title of Prince of Transylvania following his abdication.
3. Soviet flotilla to be placed at mouth of Danube which is to be placed under Russian control.
4. For two years the Danubian ports of Galati and Braila are to be placed under Russian control.
5. Constanza to be a free port.
6. The Russians are to nationalize the oilfields and supervise the process.
7. The new government of Rumania will be "advised" to give authorization for the Communist Party again.

Document 3-113

Telegram 3301-9, May 4, 1944 (extracts)

[The documents provided OSS Bern by "George Wood" when he visited Switzerland included material on the war in East Asia, such as this report from the German Ambassador in Thailand.]

KAPPA. KAPRIL Thailand. #103 dated the 23rd of March, received 30th of March, very secret, to Grand from Wendler.

[The Prime Minister] was not afraid at the present of an attack from Burma by the British. The British are obviously determined to limit themselves in greater part to defending India. However, he voiced concern over the United States increasing naval superiority over the Japanese. . . .

. . . The Prime Minister went into the matter of neutrality as the better way, in great detail, stressing the informality of the discussion. . . . Thailand was not ready for war, either physically or morally, to say nothing of total war. I replied that . . . Thailand's position is such that she could not stay neutral forever during a war in the Far East and today it was not possible for them to go back to any variety of neutrality. I referred to the campaign against European neutrals made by the Anglo-Saxons and also that no sympathy could be had by even those neutral countries who wanted to remain idle bystanders in the historical war against Bolshevism. The Prime Minister answered that the fate of Thailand hinged on Germany's defeat of Bolshevism since, if Germany did not win, Thailand would be overrun.

The Prime Minister then called to notice rumors that the European war might be over the end of May and the reports of a separate peace between Germany and England or the Soviet Union. He went on to say that because of racial affinity the most natural move would be for England and Germany to come to terms. If the choice rested with the Siamese as to who they would like to see win, Japan, Germany or England, they would choose Germany.

Section 2.

Rounding out the foregoing interview, the following is founded on numerous talks with the Japanese Commander and Ambassador and other observations:

1. A profound impression was made on the Prime Minister by the air raids on Bangkok. He is afraid of further heavy damage to Thailand and fears for his own life.

2. The Prime Minister . . . the notion of neutrality perpetually reoccurs in his conversations.

3. Since the middle of 1943 attempts to get in touch with the opposing side have been observed. . . .

4. The wish to get out of the war was stimulated by the bombings of Bangkok and other cities. Both the people and Government are weary of the war.

5. By nature the Siamese are lazy and easy going and consider the war as an evil which the Japanese visited upon them. . . .

Document 3-114

Telegram 3320, May 4, 1944

[OSS Bern now learned that Sparrow Mission contacts in Hungary had been shot.]

SPARROW. It has been indicated in a report received subsequent to the one contained in the above message that the lady mentioned in that message was Aramis' mistress and she, too, was shot. The rumor presently circulating in inner circles in Budapest states that these 3 executions were the result of meetings held in her home in Budapest with English parachutists who reached there a few days earlier.

Document 3-115

Telegram 3321, May 4, 1944

[Dulles reported further on the absorption of the Abwehr by the SD.]

We learn from a reliable source that the rank and file of the Sicherheitsdienst have now been transferred to the same barracks which quarter the Abwehr near Berlin. This is one more step in the direction of combining the Abwehr and the Sicherheitsdienst, which in all likelihood will result in the eventual disappearance of the higher echelons of the former including Hansen and everyone.

Document 3-116

Telegram 3327-33, May 5, 1944 (extract)

[This German message, as provided to Dulles by Fritz Kolbe, contains indications of a Soviet perception of secret Anglo-German negotiations.]

1. Shanghai. (In all probability during journey of sender.) #260 to Grand from Stahmer dated the 31st of March.

The following was received from Russian circles by KO: repeated reports of British-German negotiations in an Iberian seaport have been completely confirmed by the Russian Intelligence Service. Because of this, Russian leaders are extremely angry and have abandoned all faith in the chances of honest cooperation with the Anglo-Saxons. It is thought that the attitude of the British is caused by dread of the diffusion of Bolshevism all over Europe and the tendency to save other Slavic countries from the influence of Russia and to forestall Russian domination of the Balkans, for which Germany is only possible support since Russia has all the other controlling positions. The Russians feel that their position is sufficiently powerful to counter any action taken against them. To counteract the Anglo-Nazi developments the betterment of Turkish-Soviet relations is being forwarded. Compromise with Japan consolidated policy in Asia. The march of the Japanese into India is being observed with interest. KO has already reported that the Russian military organization has been strengthened on the Indian border.

2. Shanghai. #237 to Grand from Stoller dated March 28th: Information from KO: The Russians have finally decided, because of the peace offers to Finland, to carry on European policy from now on without taking the Allies into consideration, since Russia is persuaded that the refusal of the Finns was due to Allied intrigue to forestall Russian penetration in Scandinavia and without this the Russian Army would now be located along the Norwegian-Swedish boundary. . . .

Document 3-117

Telegram 3343-44, May 5, 1944

[This message concerns the role of international business in wartime and its interaction with intelligence.]

It seems Axe was never able to obtain a German visa to proceed to Switzerland. He was apprehended by the Gestapo and taken off the 19th of March. One of our close contacts for Austrian affairs who is in addition adviser in legal matters for Axe and the Swiss bankers who are looking after Axe's interest, may have the chance to name a high class Swiss to the company board, and also furnish us a line which will be of some use. An appointee of this sort would of course do what he could in the company for American interests. If it would bring about black listing, the Swiss nominee will not act. Under tight existing rules, black listing would automatically result, that is, unless confidential arrangements were made with MEW and OEW exemption from it. We will probably be able to work this out locally, but we did not want to go ahead without letting you know. The matter can be confidentially mentioned to the Americans referred to in your #166 if you wish. It must be remembered, however, that my interest is not protecting private American investments but establishing a communication line.

Document 3-118

Telegram 3345, May 5, 1944

[OSS Bern reports on Berlin's lack of trust in the German diplomatic corps.]

Ribbentrop lately issued secret directions that members of families of German diplomats who were recalled to the homeland were not to be allowed to stay in Switzerland any longer. These people must go back to Germany with the head of the family. Consul Craf [Graf], who was attached to the Consulate General, Zurich, was recalled to the Reich and it was in connection with this that the above data was secured.

Document 3-119

Telegram 3377-79, May 8, 1944

[Dulles discusses the status of Franz Josef Messner (840).]

KAPPA. To Jackpot, with reference to your #1582. Concerning 840, I am inclined to concur in Packy's opinion. 840 is tied with a chain which includes K-6 and K-5 as well as various other people who have been acquainted with him for an extensive period and whose honesty, I feel, cannot be doubted. He gives a very fine personal impression. It is not probable that he would operate in behalf of Nabors for money, in view of his standing in the community. The possibility that he may be a Nazi by ideology or temperament is one which I discount. 840's arrest does not seem to be a trick. Because even people in high places obtain and transmit a large amount of bunk with good faith, I doubt if a conclusion founded exclusively on a comparative analysis of reports is definitive.

I favor weighing sources critically and analyzing them with great care but I feel that eventually you should understand that reasoning persons now are aware that Germany is destined to lose the war. Consequently, only those people who have been utterly compromised or [garble] are likely to be engaged in operating double-cross schemes for them. I feel that genuine opportunities may be lost to us if we are unduly suspicious. As an instance of this, I have the feeling from my dealings with Zulu that their services, because of the leg-pulling they suffered in gloomy times of 1940-1941, are unaware on occasion of the degree to which the situation has been reversed, even in the field of intelligence. Several of my finest sources would have been lost to me had I pursued their course.

Document 3-120

Telegram 609-10 to London, May 10, 1944

[This message concerns important Croatian personalities.]

We have had some assistance here on certain matters pertaining to Croatia from Ivan Pavelic, whose brother is acting as secretary to the Ban of Croatia in New York. He says that General Vladimir Velebit, who is at present in London for Tito, was once a law associate of his in Zagreb. Pavelic wants Velebit to be notified that his parents and sister in Belgrade are in good health but that this brother-in-law is not well. If Velebit likes, Pavelic would be able to send the former's parents both news and money. You might find this message a useful means of getting in touch with Velebit and perhaps it would help us to build up Pavelic's relations with Croatia, if Velebit decides to communicate with him. We could also make use of Velebit's check on Pavelic.

Document 3-121

Telegram 611-16 to London, May 11, 1944

[Dulles discussed D-Day preparations with a Maquis commander.]

Tertius. A very short time ago I consulted with Bertrand here in Bern. He and David are in charge of military resistance in the 10 departments named below: Ain, Ardeche, Drome, Haute Savoie, Jura, Loire, Isere, Rhone, Saone-et-Loire, and Savoie.

Major Constant at Algiers and Delphin of BCRA know Bertrand as Perimetre. I was very highly impressed with him and have made arrangements through 492 to maintain uninterrupted contact with him. The information he wanted to pass on can be condensed as follows: (1) In the 10 departments there are about 20,000 available men; 6,000 of these are mobilized and in the Maquis. Besides these, the

Communists have between 6,000 and 8,000 in these departments under FTP leadership. However, there is no close relationship with FTP. (2) Supplies of arms are being received satisfactorily via parachute and forces will be fairly well armed in about a month; however, the supplies listed here are urgently needed: . . Clothing . . . Belts . . . Shoes . . . Radios . . . More money. . . . Cadres are also urgently needed. . . . Complete plans for H Day for cutting road and railroad communications have reached him from Allied GHQ and he is ready to put them into operation. . . . This is confidential. Bertrand stressed the fact that the resistance forces are very anxious for America to have a more direct role in assistance because they have a great deal of confidence in the United States. He indicated that in his opinion the morale and eagerness of his men would be increased tremendously if they were given some evidence of American aid and, later on, some personnel from the United States. Finally, Bertrand wanted to know why General Eisenhower did not assume direct command of the French resistance. Bertrand did not get in touch with Zulu here but he consulted with Iris. . . . I would be glad to know what you and Algiers think of Bertrand. Also please let me know whether you think his demands are reasonable and whether any action can be taken to comply with them. My own personal opinion is that it is very important that U.S. assistance to military resistance in France be activated so that they will feel that the Americans are supporting them just as the British are.

Document 3-122

Telegram 3401, May 11, 1944

[Dulles learned from Roger Auboin (651) of the Bank of International Settlements that the Germans planned to seize French gold.]

I have been informed by 651 that he is the recipient of secret information from Paris pointing out the danger of an attempt to seize both the French Treasury and Bank of France's gold and foreign exchange at this end. It is my understanding that financial matters for the CFLN are handled by Vaidie advising Mendes France directly.

David in my London #611-16 is Didier and Bertrand is Major Descour.

Document 3-123

Telegram 3423-31, May 13, 1944

[In this message to General Donovan (109) and others, Dulles reports that the Breakers group actually was willing to help western forces enter the Reich, provided German forces were allowed to maintain the Russian front. Gorter is Eduard Waetjen; Tucky is General Beck; Ladder is General Halder; Zeta is General Zeitzler; Theta is General Heusinger; Eta is General Olbricht; 512 is Gisevius.]

To Carib, Jackpot and 109. See our #2718. An important oral message was delivered to Gorter and 512 from Breakers not long ago. The text of the message as I received it, was that the opposition group which includes Tucky, Rundstedt and Falkenhausen (discussed in my #2718), plus Ladder, Zeta, Theta and Eta were ready to help our armed units get into Germany under the condition that we agree to allow them to hold the Eastern front.

The aforementioned military authorities have worked out the following technical details of the plan: (1) 3 allied Parachute Divisions to land in the Berlin region with the assistance of the local Army commanders. (2) Amphibian landing operations of major proportions either at or near Bremen and Hamburg along the German coast. (3) The isolation in Obersalzburg of Hitler and high Nazi officials by trustworthy German units posted in the Munich region. (4) Although the preliminary plans for landings on the French coastline will be difficult to formulate, since they can not count on Rommel for any cooperation, the above plan will normally [be] followed by such landings.

This same opposition group is reported to feel that the War has been lost, and that the last hope of preventing the spread of Communism in Germany is the occupation of as large a section of Europe as possible by the Americans and the British, and that helping our armed forces enter Germany before the fall of the East front is the only possible means of accomplishing this.

The courier was received by 512 who sent him back North, saying he believed that it would be of no use even to discuss the plan, because of the proposed proviso on the matter of our offering assistance in regard to holding the Eastern Front. He did this without first consulting me, solely on the basis of his understanding that we would give no consideration to plans which would result in dishonorable dealing with Russia or in a breach of faith. Later 512 was sent a short wire stating that "for the time being" he should do nothing more.

In spite of this, however, both Gorter and 512 think that this is still an open subject. They appreciate the theory that having our forces get into Germany while the Russian front is still held by the Wehrmacht is not realistic, and they think that the core of Breakers plan is only that we should attempt to beat the Russians in getting our own forces firmly entrenched in Germany.

I told him I believed that the Americans would probably think that the plan for parachuting troops into Germany was a Nazi ruse and that they would assuredly be surprised to find Zeta's name among the list of those assisting Breakers. In regard to the 1st objection, they said that since they were not Army men they would not offer their opinions, but in the event that some plan could be arranged, we would have sufficient opportunity to demand all the requisite precautions by contacting the Military authorities directly beforehand. In reference to Zeta, they replied that he had been persuaded by Theta and Eta. They added that his military pre-occupation was in connection with the Eastern front exclusively, and that thinking of his own future, he would agree to cooperate in any program which would bring about a systematic military liquidation of the Eastern front, in order to prevent his having to accept the blame for the disaster which is feared.

Gorter and 512 presented the argument that it is completely a military matter if some of the Nazi generals want to aid our invasion of the continent and to try themselves to take over the Nazi regime. It should be considered on that basis alone, provided that all conditions are eliminated, so far as the Eastern front is concerned.

I did no more than listen to their argument, but did once more stress the fact that we would abide by our agreements with Russia both literally and in the spirit.

The foregoing leads me to the opinion that there are actually some Nazi generals who want to liquidate their responsibility to history by collaborating on the construction of a firm Anglo-American bulwark against a Russian-controlled Europe. Furthermore, I am certain that Gorter and 512 are in touch with such a group. I am rather doubtful as to whether or not this group would actually have the courage to act effectively when the time comes, although we might be able to use their activities to weaken the military morale of the top echelon.

I can investigate any aspect of this matter, if you are interested. I think that we should not rule out the idea at this particular point, that there are Nazi Army leaders who, confronted with the situation as it stands now, have resorted to the plan of collaborating with us to bring about an Allied occupation of Europe instead of a Russian occupation. Since this group can safely contact Switzerland and since their contacts here are more secure than anywhere else, I have received assurances that this group has not presented similar ideas in other places.

Document 3-124

Telegram 3443–46, May 13, 1944

[The volume and nature of order of battle intelligence from France that was transmitted by OSS Bern did not change dramatically in the weeks preceding the Normandy invasion. It continued at a steady level of more than one report a day. This message is representative of the information provided by the Dulles network.]

The following is a Battle Order on France, which was furnished by source 472-K-1:

1. Dated the 6th of this month: Concentrated in the Paris Zoo, there are approximately 500 vehicles of all types. Between Marseille and Nice there are 10 armored trains. . . .

2. An alleged 3 divisions of Marine infantry from Germany have reinforced the garrisons at Chaumont, Besancon, Auxerre, Dijon, and Langres. At Mulhouse, heavy units of motorized artillery have been concentrated in preparation for pro-

ceeding to Hamburg at an early date. A division in the Miramas area is getting ready to move out. Two divisions in the Rennes section have been exchanged against 2 others in the Galasis area. Between Bordeaux and Toulouse, there is a Schutzstaffel division of Poles, Mongols, and Austrians. The foregoing is dated the 5th of this month.

3. There are approximately 500 French and 150 American care [POWs?] in the 323rd HKP at the Caserne de la Garde Mobile in the town of Hericourt. The flyers stationed at Vesoul and Belfort are a part of the 303rd Luftwaffe Regiment. The 271st Division, containing the 788th and 789th Regiments, is stationed between Lunel and Sete. The above is dated the 1st of this month.

4. Dated the 1st of this month: The following are the locations of the main staff headquarters in Rennes: In a series of buildings between the Boulevard Sevigne, the Rue Ernest Renan, the Rue Pointeau, and the Rue Waldock, there is a Panzer Division with all services. The Feld Kommandatur is in the Faculté des Lettres. Luftwaffe elements are at the Ecole Primaire on the Rue Danton. Panzer elements and the office of the General Lieutenant are in the Caserne MacMahon on the Boulevard Verdun. At the Hippothome des Gayeulles (sic), there is a park of motorized units. The Gestapo is housed in the Maison des Etudiants on the Avenue Ferry. Telephone and radio central is in the Lycee des Garçons on the Avenue Jean Tanvier. Luftwaffe officers of higher rank are quartered in a chateau 100 meters east of the Asile d'Alienes.

5. One hundred and two troop and supply trains passed through Lyon from Russia between April 27 and May 1, bound for Valence and Avignon.

6. At Belfort, a great many young Schutzstaffel troops belonging to the *Adolf Hitler* and *Das Reich* Divisions were seen.

Document 3-125

Telegram 3464, May 14, 1944

[Additional Documentation received from "George Wood" in May 1944 was transmitted to Washington in the Kamay series. This message concerns the aftermath of the Sparrow and Redbird projects, and the enigmatic Colonel Hatz, who apparently worked for both sides.]

KAPPA. This is a Kamay message. Following is information received from the legation at Sofia and is dated the 19th of April: When Colonel Hatz applied for a visa for a journey to Vienna, he stated that one of his colleagues had been contacted by a group of Americans who asked that a transmitter be delivered for them to a specified individual in Vienna. Hatz proposes in this way to uncover Austrian Resistance movement. (Wood has supplied the following data which came to his attention from other sources: Hatz was apprehended by the Nazis in Hungary early this month.)

Document 3-126

Telegram 3460-63, May 15, 1944

[This message based on George Wood materials provided information on an apparent Turkish desire for German assistance in resisting Allied pressure to enter the war, and on German knowledge of British intelligence operations in Greece.]

1. Cable from German Embassy in Turkey dated the 7th of this month said, "Moyzysch was notified thus by a bekannter Vertrauensmann May 5th: The Stadt Praesident would like the German Government to know that he wishes von Papen's prompt return. At the month's end, it is expected that Allied pressure will be renewed and this the Turks wish to circumvent. Von Papen is an opponent of the Allies, for whom there is no substitute, in the delicately balanced Turkish policy based on the single aim of avoiding entry into the war.

Because this information was so important, I requested confirmation of it from Moyzysch through Nacip Erkel, the head of Turkish Secret Service. May 6th I received full confirmation with the added information that no official action could be taken for understandable reasons and this means of getting the information across was thus employed.

He added, too, that the Turkish action relating to the chrome issue was basically different from that of the Spanish Government since England and Turkey were allies. Consequently, they, as contrasted with other neutrals, must make special concessions. In his speech the special stress of Numan was meant to give expression to his Zwangslage. The Turkish Government hoped that this Zwangslage would be understood by the German Government. Signed Walter."

2. The 3rd and 5th of May, the Legation at Athens reported concerning English espionage ramifications which go as far as the ante chamber of the Minister of the Interior. The Minister President seems to be connected, but Minister Derfilis and Minister Tavoularis are especially involved. Present intention when Neubacher goes back to Athens is to remove these 2 ministers from their positions. It will then be possible to arrest them without bringing on unwelcome publicity. In due time, there will be 100% replacement of the cabinet.

Document 3-127

Telegram 3484-91, May 15, 1944 (extracts)

[Dulles reported on political developments within the French resistance on the eve of the Normandy invasion, and served as an additional channel between the resistance and the Allies.]

1. A message of importance from 802 describes the late developments in reorganization in France of the Comite National made up of elective officials who include

all the French political parties (unless the Communists are exceptions, which is possible). Lorraine, identified elsewhere, is the guiding force in the organization, along with members of the Radical Socialist Party. . . . 802 claims that some 300 leading people of the foregoing sort have become associated with the Committee and that local organizations are being established in the East, North, and Paris regions, while some are already in existence in the Southwest, Normandy and Brittany. The Comite wishes to have liaison with the Allies and to dispatch a representative to insure such liaison. 802 inquires whether London and Washington will agree to this. If so, how and where could the liaison take place where security could be properly assured?

2. The Comite wishes to know if the Allied Governments concur with the following formula of the Committee for Readministration of Liberated Territories: "It would be guaranteed by the French Civil Administration under the Allied High Command while military operations are in progress. Since no administrative function could be carried on without the consent of the elected officials, those of the latter who would be given a local mandate by the National Committee would necessarily have to be consulted about the appointment of officials. The latter would be regarded as having been mobilized and their appointment would be merely temporary.". . .

4. In addition, the Comite sends the declaration it adopted the 7th of this month. . . . "The affirmation is made by the Comite that there can be no lawful authority except that based on respect for the Constitution. . . . General de Gaulle has, since Armistice, stood for France's profound sentiments of resistance to Germany. Now, when de Gaulle is at head of our forces abroad and preparing for combat on French soil side by side with our Allies, the Comite indicates its confidence in him and promises full collaboration. . . . On the eve of momentous happenings, all French are reminded by the Comite that only in discipline, united action and respect for Republican legality can they be guided to deliverance and be returned to the freedom and order which France now more than ever hopes for after so many mistakes."

Document 3-128

Telegram 456 to Algiers, May 16, 1944

[Dulles confirmed the arrest of Franz Josef Messner (840) in Vienna.]

KAPPA. KAMAY. For Jackpot. A substantial amount of data from separate sources convinces us that there can be no doubt as to the arrest of 840. We believe that further contact with this group would be dangerous, prior to additional clarification as to what is happening, particularly in view of the fact that 840's assistant in Cassia work was also apprehended, indicating the possibility that her arrest was caused by this connection. We are afraid that lives may be placed in jeopardy by lack of coordinated action in handling the 840 matter. . . .

Document 3-129

Telegram 630-31 to London, May 16, 1944 (extracts)

[OSS Bern reported on the disintegration of the German Navy.]

1. The information which follows is a resume of the wires which K-1 sent to Algiers. The information in the 2nd paragraph originates with 511 and was received through deserters from the German Navy. 511 has stated that as a result of the attempt to incorporate the navy men into the army, a great number of naval deserters are now reaching here.

2. The following naval ships are docked in German ports: the Tirpitz is immobilized at Altenfiord; a damaged light cruiser is at Bergen; there are approximately 12 submarines at Danzig; the Admirals Cheer [?], Prinz Eugen, 2 training ships and 3 light cruisers are in the port at Gdynia. . . . Substantiation of the report of the loss of the Hipper in Norwegian waters has been received. At Danzig, Koenigsberg, and Kiel obsolete and damaged Nazi naval units are being disarmed and their cannon employed in the defense of the coastline. . . .

Document 3-130

Telegram 3518-19, May 18, 1944

[Baron Bakach-Bessenyey (684) provided Dulles with information on the state of affairs in Hungary.]

The following information comes from 684, who has just met the individual with whom Regent has spoken. Regent indicated that he was furious with the Nazis, but reports with naivete that civil war would be brought about by his resignation and that the army would become completely uncontrolled. It seems plain that Admiral Horthy is pursuing Petain's course, and I feel that we ought to make every effort to oust him, so that his control over the army will be broken.

I approve, consequently, the MO plan described in your #1584–5, and I advise that we endeavor to make the Nazis think that Admiral Horthy is actually following Darlan's example and that we would like to have him stay in power, so that we can use him and the army to open the way to Hungary.

In addition to the above information, 684 states, although it is not definitely substantiated, that Bethlen is being held as a prisoner in Germany. Consult #658, from London.

Horthy has signed 684's letter of recall, and they have been received by the Swiss authorities, by whom it is probable that they will be accepted, although this is not definite.

Document 3-131

Telegram 3565-66, May 23, 1944

[Gisevius and Waetjen supplied new information on the demise of the Abwehr.]

Sources 512 and 670 provide the following information: top officials of the combined Sicherheitsdienst and Abwehr organizations recently held an important meeting in Salzburg for the purpose of completing the merger of the two organizations into a unified intelligence service. Himmler presided over the session; both Schellenberg and Hansen were in attendance. The latter has been acting head of the Abwehr since Canaris was ousted. Confidential: according to the sources, Hansen will soon be ousted also, and a high Nazi official will take his place. At the last moment, a statement which was to be delivered by Hansen, as representative of the conservative army groups, was cut out, and Schellenberg gave a long speech.

Document 3-132

Telegram 665 to London, May 24, 1944

[Dulles again proposes material aid to the French resistance. Number 284 is Max Shoop.]

With a view toward speeding up the services and preparing for growing frontier obstacles and for a possible effort to close up the frontier when the invasion comes, we would like to give radio transmitters to our various intelligence services in France. Safe facilities for reception and transmitter contact in Geneva have been arranged by 284. Provided we give dropping grounds and other details, would you or Algiers in theory be able to parachute the transmitters?

Document 3-133

Telegram 3589-90, May 25, 1944

[This report reveals that certain German financial interests still believed they would have a voice in postwar reconstruction, as if there were to be no occupation regime. Number 644 is Thomas H. McKittrick, an American, the President of the Bank of International Settlements in Basel.]

Not long ago our 644 had 2 lengthy conversations with Puhl of the Reichsbank. The latter was extremely depressed, not so much by the idea of Nazi defeat, but by the situation which Germany will have to contend with later. The Reichsbank has been engaged in work on plans for the reconstruction, and evidently they are unable to see where an effective beginning can be made. Puhl can not understand how Germany will succeed in procuring the necessary importations for construction work: it will be necessary to import large quantities of goods in every field especially to meet damage caused by the raids; the possibility for export is restricted, if not negligible. The Reichsbank is still located in Berlin and special vital services of the finance ministry are still there, although the administrative branches of the ministry have been transferred to an unidentified place.

Document 3-134

Telegram 3595-97, May 25, 1944

[Dulles reports on a meeting with Constantin Vulcan, Rumanian Cultural Attaché in Bern.]

This morning, 636 handed me 3 documents which Bucharest had sent to the Rumanian legation. In the first report, it is stated that the Rumanian Government has papers proving that the Soviets have committed atrocities in Russian-occupied Rumanian territory (that is, apart from Bucovina and Bessarabia). Although no particular instances are mentioned, there is a list of the types of atrocities committed. The next report presents an outline of the statements made to the German and Rumanian newspapers by Mihai Antonescu on the 18th of this month. The statements are in general meant for German consumption, but they stress the alleged fact that Rumania is carrying on a defensive struggle for existence. He declares that the people of Rumania have never waged war against England or America, and that in return the Allies are now viciously bombing hospitals, universities, churches, and so on. He says also that the country is standing by its loyal feelings for friends of yesterday. The third report says that the hitherto favorable Rumanian feeling toward the Allies is fast waning because of the air raids by American planes. The report emphasizes the fact that the raid on the capital destroyed civilian targets and that, although the first bombing of Ploesti was carried out with great care and precision, during the past 60 days the raids "have been made with utter disregard and scorn for the most basic rules of protection for the civilian population." I finally had to expel 636 forcibly because he became so violent. This was an unusual display on his part for hitherto he has always shown pro-U.S. feelings. Before he left, he gave voice to his extreme disappointment at the terms which the Soviets had presented. I got the general idea that the Rumanian Legation here does not think the chances of reaching an agreement with the Soviets are very favorable.

Document 3-135

Telegram 3650, May 31, 1944

[This message assesses conditions in Germany and the public state of mind.]

Current conditions in Germany were reported to us by envoys dispatched by 328-K-15, whose contacts were for the most part with leftist groups and Nazi labor. A resume follows of the information which was derived therefrom:

1. Those who continue to believe that the Nazis will be victorious comprise only a small minority of the population.

2. Substantial quantities of people are convinced that if the invasion effort is met effectively, a compromise peace will be made possible. The hope for an immediate invasion comes from this notion, since most of the Germans believe that it will be increasingly difficult to counteract the invasion the longer it is put off.

3. No hope is felt by the people of Germany. They despair of their fate in the event of defeat, and they have a skeptical attitude toward everything. All of the Germans are burdened by an emotion of common guilt. Goebbels' underground propaganda, with the following approach, promotes this feeling: "The people of all the countries which we have occupied will avenge themselves upon us for our many detestable actions and we may anticipate no mercy from the Allies. As we have annihilated Russians, Poles and Jews, etc., destruction will likewise be brought upon the people of Germany. Our only chance lies in fighting in an effort to achieve the impossible." This mental state produces a blind alley, which is encountered by activists who are against the regime, on occasions when they attempt to enlarge the scope of their activities.

4. The fact that Allied propaganda has done nothing to destroy this vicious circle is lamented by German friends of the Allies, who bemoan the fact that the Allies have neglected to declare distinctly that the German people will be liberated by the defeat of Hitler. They are aware that such liberation carries with it the absolute obligation to make good the destruction which the Nazis have wreaked upon the European continent. To ensure the thorough destruction of the forces which fostered the coming of Nazism, i.e. the Military, the Junkers and Capitalism, they want strict Allied control. The only way to create effective points of resistance and to escape from the blind alley described above is to employ propaganda of this nature.

5. The masses of the German people, including the working classes, are terrorized by the fear of Communism and the prospect of a Russian regime. Occupation by the British and Americans is preferred by the workers.

6. In spite of the enormous corruption permeating the Gestapo machine, it remains intact.

7. Efforts against the regime are still being made, despite the Gestapo and the dismal future:

a) Such an effort was made in the fall of 1943 in certain military groups under von Hammerstein, working with certain liberal bourgeois groups. The latter also tried to set up connections with workers. The affair was brought to the attention of the Gestapo, and a number of arrests followed. Von Hammerstein's death occurred, and was attributed to an operation which the Gestapo organized.

b) An attempt was made recently to establish an association throughout Germany with the title of "European Union." Communist factions were the source of inspiration for this movement. The Gestapo stepped in and condemned 8 members of the Union to death. One of them was Hawermann, the prominent chemist.

c) In some factories the workers tacitly recognized one of their group to be a confidence man who will be responsible for action at a given moment. This leader in the Boclurner-Verein was arrested recently with 20 other workers by the Gestapo.

d) German resistance is scattered: it has no central organization. Persons belonging to opposition groups are acquainted with each other only locally. It would be possible to establish a convergence of important resistance groups to combat the regime, if a more propitious atmosphere for underground work were established.

Document 3-136

Telegram 3674-83, June 2, 1944

[Dulles again reports on French resistance elements based on the prewar political parties. Number 492 is Charron; 802 is Devignat.]

Lorraine Part I. In order to give 477, 492 and me additional information on the program of the group described in my #3484 and #3495, our 802 came here secretly in that group's behalf. 802's explanation included the group's desire to cooperate with the British and Americans for France's liberation. 802 stressed the fact that the Comite National, which is headed by 14 deputies and senators, is supported by about 300 parliamentarians and is in close touch with the Conseils Generaux and Municipaux in considerable areas of France, including the larger part of political factions who wish to cooperate with the Western democracies. In addition, CN is in touch with churches, local and state administrations and teaching bodies.

2. As demonstrated in my #3484, the platform of the Comité National is to safeguard the democratic constitutional framework, to throw out the Nazis, to resist arbitrary government be it from the left or the right and to fight the hazard of civil war. . . .

4. The CN acknowledges de Gaulle to be the chief of the Army and stands ready to put all its influence in his hands to liberate France. However, CN thinks of itself as the constitutional representative of France, until such a time as elections may be held. . . .

5. The Comite National criticizes the Algiers Committee severely and the pretensions of men such as Dastier, Le Troceur and the like who say they speak for metropolitan France. . . .

6. The Comite National is alarmed over the magnitude of the control which the communists have secured in the resistance movement. . . .

9. CN is currently looking for effective liaison with the Allies in London to advance military cooperation with de Gaulle and to put all of the metropolitan groups behind the invading armies. . . .

Document 3-137

Telegram 3702-7, June 3, 1944

[Dulles presents his analysis of the Lorraine group.]

This is part 4 of Lorraine cables and contains my remarks on the previous 3 parts.

1. 802 is an individual of great personal integrity and capability and I think that his opinions are representative of a very widely-held viewpoint in France.

2. The work I have been doing and will go on doing has been predominantly with the resistance groups and the Military groups connected with them. All my contacts are with such groups. I have held to the opinion right along that Gaullism represents the outstanding aggressive element in France at the present time and that, if we are faced with a choice between supporting Gaullism and other groups at the beginning of a military operation, we will have to support the de Gaullists. This fact is fully appreciated by the Lorraine group and they are evidently desirous of bridging the gap between the de Gaullists and the middle-road, Parliamentary, church, middle-class group. You should observe that they maintain that many of their members are Parliamentarians who voted against awarding full powers to Petain, and that others among their members are Parliamentarians who rejected later collaboration, although they had previously voted for Petain full powers.

3. I will agree that the Algiers Committee per se does not have the complete support of the French people; it is considerably less strong than de Gaulle. I think that it would be unwise to allow the idea to arise that we are cool towards de Gaulle, or at odds with him.

4. Because of their 1940 abdication, and the loss of standing which has fallen on a number of the members, the constitutional argument of the Parliamentarians (that of still holding the legal right to represent France) does not impress me. I think, however, that a considerable number of these non-collaborationist Parliamentarians wield a great deal of authority locally and that if a gap between the moderates and the de Gaullists could possibly be bridged, the solidarity and effectiveness of French assistance would be greatly increased. If, however, as I said before, we are ever forced to choose between the de Gaullists and the Parliamentarians, we will have to support the de Gaullists. The Moderates could naturally use as their spokesmen and leaders, those men who voted against full powers; this would in no way be prevented by the vigorous part Lorraine has had in the movement.

5. I wish that you would explain the connection between Beta and the "Secret

Army," as well as that between Beta and the Military group which is working with the Resistance Movement, since this bewilders me.

6. There is some foundation of truth in the criticism of the resistance movement, although it is exaggerated. The estimate of the Communist and extreme left-wing resistance factions is probably correct, although I am not sure that they offer the degree of danger that is feared by the moderates.

7. In all my relations with 802 I avoided making any commitments or offering any encouragement and only listened to his story and tried to clarify the opinion which he and his friends represent. His most intimate friend at Algiers is Queuille, although he also said that Giaccobi, Jacquinot, and Mendes France of the Algiers Committee are moderates who have the confidence of his friends.

Document 3-138

Telegram 688-89 to London, June 5, 1944

[Dulles corresponds with General Donovan and David Bruce concerning order of battle reporting.]

110 to 109 and 105. I am fully aware that first importance should be given all French order of battle information. I think that it is better to go on following the current procedure of sending this material, i.e. sending summary of the full reports gathered from individual sources instead of trying to select certain items as mentioned in your #686. Do you and Washington agree that all the French battle order cables should be directed to London for action with information copies for Algiers and Washington rather than sending action copies to Washington and information copies to London and Algiers? The breakdown of travel in certain sections of France threatens to hold up the arrival of material and it has been necessary to set up bicycle couriers, since we can no longer rely on railroads and the Nazis have redoubled their supervision of travelers. In addition, we are trying to set up radio communications between several SI field units and Bern.

Document 3-139

Radiotelephone Transmission No. 151, June 5, 1944 (extract)

[On the evening that Allied forces entered Rome, Dulles reports the reaction in Switzerland and his thoughts on the new situation in Italy.]

Italy

The occupation of Rome overshadows all other events here. The question which particularly interests us here is the effect it will have on the situation in Northern Italy, and how this great military and psychological victory can be best exploited to render more and more untenable the German positions in the Po valley. The strengthening of the Italian government, the inclusion of new and democratic elements, if possible the inclusion of persons who have taken an active part in the underground resistance in the North, would be a constructive move. Hidden in Rome during the German occupation were a considerable number of persons who were in intimate touch with the Committee of National Liberation in Milan. These people should be able now to make their influence felt. Further, as soon as our position is consolidated, it should be possible to extend more direct aid to the Partisans in the North. The Germans have found it necessary to keep some six divisions in the north of Italy. Now they will badly need those divisions to help build a new line, possibly from Germany [?] to Spezia or south of there. If, however, the Partisan activity in the North is kept alive, the Germans will not be able to group these divisions South, since what they have in the North now is a very minimum force to hold down a population which is becoming more and more restless, and a Partisan movement which is slowly getting better organized. The Neo-Fascists see the handwriting on the wall, and only those brigands who are completely compromised will have any further enthusiasm to support the German cause. The new Italian government is strengthened by elements which come directly from the resistance and do a good deal toward strengthening the resistance to the Germans and the Fascists in the North. It might be well for the Italian government, when installed in Rome, to issue a proclamation in general terms the type of aid and support that thereafter will be given to the Partisans, specifying that all those who, after a given date, of their own free will give any aid and comfort to the enemy, that is, to the Germans or to the Neo-Fascists, will be considered as traitors. The information should be given to those that are forced to enroll in Neo-Fascist military formations as to how they can best sabotage the German war effort and encouragement should be given to them to desert at the earliest opportunity. As the Germans retreat north, they will come nearer and nearer to the area of active Partisan activity, and if we can effectively increase that activity, their rear-line communications can be rendered most precarious. . . .

Document 3-140

Telegram 3722-26, June 6, 1944

[On D-Day, OSS Bern sent this report on the status of German transportation and communications in France.]

The opinions of 802 with respect to various transportation matters are set forth below:

1. Communications with Germany by the Cologne-Jeumont-Paris route have been made uncertain by the air raids. No serious effect on communications along the lines to the south of Ardennes has been suffered as yet. To do this, it would be necessary to cripple Sarrebruck and Metz (Sablons). Communication by way of

Strasbourg also has not been gravely hindered to date. It would be advisable to go on with the methodical raids on the line from Dunkirk to Basel. Raids on Epinal would not be as effective as at Charlesville-Mons.

2. Communications in northern France are nearing the point of utter paralysis, while the Paris area has suffered extensive injury. It would be worthwhile to destroy the Grande Ceinture at several places.

3. There has been no important effect on communications in the Loire area and toward the west.

4. The lines between Marseille and Paris have suffered injury; however, traffic has not been halted to date.

5. The Todt organization, with special trucks, is used by the Nazis for repairing railroad lines. They also impress French workers in the locality for such repairs.

6. It is revealed by a significant reduction in the numbers of TCO's that the Nazis are employing mainly the highways for moving troops. These road movements are disguised by them in every possible manner.

7. To halt traffic from Germany to France, it is urgent that, at the final moment, the bridges on north south rivers be demolished by specialized paratroopers.

8. To combat the risk of a general strike, the Nazis have dispatched from 7,000 to 11,000 of their own cheminots to France. These workers are old, demoralized to some extent and, from contact with their French colleagues, it appears that they do not wish to place themselves in jeopardy. It is recommended that when the Nazi cheminots are sent into the northwest area, the locomotives should be machine-gunned.

With reference to general military problems, 802 gives the following information:

(a) To mislead our intelligence operations, the Nazis are setting up in France "ghost" divisions with false headquarters and false insignia.

(b) The general opinion is that the Nazis are constructing fortifications nervously and, to some degree, arbitrarily.

(c) From the mouth of the Eschult (sic) River to the mouth of the Seine River, Nazi measures against a landing are especially powerful. Between these rivers, at a distance of about 30 kilometers from the coast, there are practically solid lines of fortified places or fortifications. Not only are there fortifications running parallel to the coast, but there are 3 defense lines running north and south along the Seine River toward Basel, along the Somme-Aisne Rivers and along the Maginot.

(d) Toward the interior, from the Cherbourg peninsula, there are powerful concentrations of soldiers. In Brittany, the troop concentrations are not as strong. In general, there are weak defenses along the Atlantic coast from Brittany south.

Document 3-141

Radiotelephone Transmission, No. 152, June 6, 1944 (extract)

[In his evening telephone call, Dulles discussed first German reactions to the invasion of Normandy that began that morning.]

The Invasion

The invasion, of course, overshadows all other news. As yet it is too early to have an accurate picture of the reaction in France or in Germany. I have here some hastily penciled notes which I have just made on the basis of the evening edition of the *Neue Zuercher Zeitung,* which comes out in Zurich about nine o'clock here. According to the Berlin correspondent . . . , the German people only learned of the invasion in the afternoon, which tends to indicate that the authorities were caught a little by surprise, and waited to give the news until they had prepared their line of propaganda. According to the *Neue Zuercher Zeitung,* the German people were apathetic. The general theme of the newspapers, however, was that the Allied landing was "on orders from Moscow." *Der Angriff* has a full across-the-page headline stating that on orders of Moscow the invasion had begun, and another evening headlined news British and Americans land "on orders of Moscow." The general line of German propaganda also apparently is that this is a desperate attempt of the Anglo-Americans to obtain some real success, that they were not fighting in their own interest, but in the interest of Bolshevism.

With the change which this great event will bring, it will be very useful to have a review from your end as to the subjects which you would particularly like to have covered in these flashes. As soon as information is available, I will, of course, give all important news we can get from this vantage point behind the German lines. Undoubtedly, every effort will be made by the Germans to tighten the control of access to Switzerland, but this will require troops, and these they can spare with difficulty. The general impression here is that with the main attack apparently coming from the North, Switzerland itself is not in any immediate danger from the Germans. . . .

Document 3-142

Telegram 3747-48, June 7, 1944

[This message indicates that Berlin questioned the loyalty of its diplomats abroad.]

A visit to Switzerland has just been made by Schroeder, who is head of the personnel department of the Foreign Office at Berlin. The purpose of his trip was to check all employees and officials to avoid repetition here of the Vermehren affair. A considerable number of people about whom there are doubts will be called back to Germany.

Another recent visitor here was Ambassador Pruefer, who was previously in Brazil and Argentina. He came to establish contact with South Americans. In addition, Reinbeck, who was previously the Minister to Guatemala and is the Chief of the American section of the Foreign Office, was here. The purpose of his trip here was to reorganize the reporting on America when Prince Urach comes here as Press Attaché. The Nazis have tried to induce ex-Consul General Krauel and ex-Ambassador Stohrer to go back to Germany. However, these men are declining to do so, using the manufactured alibi of sickness. Berlin was seemingly especially disappointed by Krauel's failure to comply, since they invited him to accept an important job in the Foreign Office. Zulu has not been given a copy of the above information, since they will obtain it indirectly via the same source. It is preferable that they remain ignorant of the fact that we obtained it, for local reasons.

Document 3-143

Telegram 3749, June 7, 1944

[The author of *All Quiet on the Western Front* had the opportunity to aid the Allies.]

At Porto Ronco, in the vicinity of Locarno, there is a conveniently situated house which belongs to Erich Maria Remarque, the novelist. We are informed that he is in the United States at present. Can you make arrangements with him for this house to be placed at the disposal of someone named by us for the period of the war?

Document 3-144

Telegram 3750-51, June 7, 1944

[OSS Bern continued to cooperate with French labor elements.]

From 328 to Eva.

1. "Regular contact with Poimbouef and Dominique is wanted by the Christian Syndicalists. I can serve as the go-between. Am dispatching a lengthy Christian Syndicalist report by way of Eclair for Dominique.

"2. At the moment, we are paying special attention to our work on Germany. Have re-established relations with some of our friends in Germany. Kindly let us know if certain sums from Kingdom funds are earmarked for our political activities. I have in mind promises made by Dominique with reference to European resistance."

The following is from 110: 328 has good possible worth for northward penetration. I would be happy to have some word from Eva on the matter, in order to stimulate this. 328's contact with his American friends seems to have been discontinued of late. Would be very happy to have this renewed in a small way, with special stress placed on German matters.

Document 3-145

Telegram 3758-59, June 9, 1944

[This message concerns U.S.-U.K. joint sources.]

K-25 attempted to sell his services to Zulu as well as to ourselves. Zulu has been handling him. Personally, I am not certain of his reliability as he has shown himself to be unreliable on certain technical matters. His bomb damage data always appeared to be interesting. However, we must bear in mind the fact that the Nazis want to plant information with us which reports complete demolishment of factories in a great number of cases where there was only part damage or where the machinery was unharmed for the most part and shipped to some other point. Both Zulu and ourselves have reserves about K-24, although I believe Zulu is inclined to have a little more confidence than we have.

Document 3-146

Telegram 3787-91, June 10, 1944

[The Breakers group provided more information on the military situation as viewed from Berlin.]

BREAKERS. The report presented below was supplied by a courier from Breakers. This courier departed from Germany just prior to our landing in France:

1. Italy. It is felt that Germany suffered a major military disaster when the Allies broke through south of Rome. Marshal Kesselring was amazed by the strength of the Allied blows, as he had believed he could maintain his stand south of Rome for an extensive period. It is now believed that the Germans will not make any stand before reaching the Apennines, to the north of Florence. Moreover, it is questionable if the Nazis will be able to maintain a stand even there, because of their big losses in material.

2. France. From a viewpoint of Nazi defense in France the situation is held to be far from rosy. The prevailing opinion in Military circles is that the battle for France will be lost if the Allies are successful in creating a number of strong bridgeheads.

3. Soviet Union. In the near future a large scale offensive is expected. However, the Nazi General Staff does not believe the Eastern front to be as grave a problem as that in France and Italy. They are aware of the fact that the Nazis will have to retreat even further, but the opinion is generally held that a defense line can be set up and held at some point between the Baltic and Carpathians. Generally speaking the Nazi High Command considers the Nazi retreat from the Soviet Union's great distances as a successful military performance; however, if Adolf Hitler had not continuously disrupted the Army's plans the retreat would have been even more of a success. Hitler and Hitler alone bears the responsibility for the great mistake of attempting to defend the Crimea. It is felt that Soviet infantry is not as good as the Nazi, although Soviet artillery is thought to be better.

4. The principal motive of the conservative Army group is to prevent the Soviet Union from entering Central Europe. In the event that the Allied invasion of France goes well, there are some German generals who want the Allies to reach Berlin

ahead of the Soviet armies. One of the people whose assistance Breakers hope to secure is Gen. Blumentritt, who is said to be opposed to the Nazis. He is a member of von Rundstedt's staff. (By 110: In considering the foregoing, it is necessary to bear in mind the inclination of Breakers to stress the opinions of the conservative Army element, as opposed to the Nazi viewpoint. It is likely that the above report is based to some extent on wishful thinking. However, according to every report, it appears that the Nazis regard the situation caused by the successful French landings as grave and critical. It is possible that nearly anything could occur in Germany if we obtain a good grip and develop a front which will pin down a considerable number of Nazi divisions. In view of the slow destruction of their industrial output and our superiority in planes, the Nazis simply do not possess sufficient material, transportation facilities and manpower to distribute all around.)

Document 3-147

Radiotelephone Transmission No. 155, June 10, 1944 (extracts)

[OSS Headquarters in Washington forwarded this message to President Roosevelt on July 5, perhaps in part due to its discussion of the Himmler postage stamp.]

Germany

The tones of the press reports from Berlin on the invasion have changed. They have taken on an air of great seriousness, almost of pessimism. Here are some of the high points as reported in the Swiss press from Berlin: "The military situation in Normandie demands from Germany the greatest efforts and the greatest determination." The report continues that the Allied position in Normandy is reported to have remarkably improved. Repeatedly it is emphasized in the Berlin reports, possibly to explain to the German people the delay in bringing up more German troops to meet the invasion, that the Germans must expect landings in the various other parts of the coast. . . .

A new fact which will tend more and more to decrease German production is the effect which the victories in Italy, Russia, and France are having on the will to work of the foreign workers in Germany. Reports indicate that, in the early days, the foreign workers, and particularly the Russians, used to turn out a good day's work; now, since the impression of German defeat is becoming more general, the situation has been radically changing. It is not so much a question of systematic sabotage—although there is plenty of this—but an almost more important factor is the passive resistance, delays, and general negligence. It is one thing to work for a victorious master; it is a very different thing to work for a tottering slave-driver. Of course, the fact that the Germans have had to take away the best guards and supervisors of the foreign workers into military service, and in many cases have replaced them by old, tired, and even war-sick veterans, means that the foreign worker is not supervised as he was, and can with impunity lie down on his job.

Some months ago, I reported briefly about a mysterious Himmler stamp, which had turned up here in Switzerland. Since then, I have had someone investigate some stamp dealers the situation [*sic*] with regard to this stamp, and the mystery seems to deepen. The *Stamp Collector's Journal,* published here in December 1943, had a brief article with regard to the stamp, with a facsimile and a full description, and the editors of the journal, who apparently accepted the stamp as genuine, asked for further information from any of their correspondents. The next number of the paper, printed early in 1944, had a further article about the stamp, and stated that apparently it was not an official issue of the German post-office, and that there was some sort of mystery involved. The paper also quoted from a letter which the magazine had received from the German post-office, which briefly and curtly said that the notice their previous number regarding a Himmler stamp did not correspond to the facts. As far as I can find out, pressure was brought to bear on the editors of the stamp journal by the German authorities to play the matter down, and they have since become very uncommunicative about it. Meanwhile, one Himmler stamp has turned up here in the hands of stamp dealers, and is for sale. Though it appears to be genuine, no stamp dealer will give any guarantee as the German post-office has repudiated it. It does not appear that this is merely a stamp dealer's trick, as otherwise there would probably be more spurious examples on the market. It may have been a trick pulled by some of Himmler's enemies to make trouble for him, or it may be that some enthusiast in the Ministry of the Interior thought it might be nice to honor Himmler in this way, possibly in connection with some charitable drive. In any event, the mystery of the stamp has not been cleared up.

France

The report I gave last night about the situation in the Belgrade area appears to be duplicated in some other regions in the general Savoie region. The French Partisans in the Grenoble area are reported to have revolted in force. Despite the counsel given them from London, it is practically impossible to temper the impatience that the men of the maquis [*sic*], and despite the danger of severe reprisal, these outbreaks may nevertheless tend to serve notice on the Germans as to what would happen if they withdrew their troops in order to reinforce the present front in the North. If we assume that the Germans had some forty to fifty divisions in France at the date of the invasion, a very considerable number of these would be absolutely essential to keep down the country, and can never safely be sent to the front, or, if they are sent to the front, all German lines of communication will be threatened, and control over the civil population will be lost. It will be a nice calculation for the German High Command to try to decide exactly how many men can be spared for front-line duty in the North, and what is the minimum required to prevent open rebellion behind the lines.

Document 3-148

Telegram 3793-94, June 12, 1944

[This message concerns U.S.-U.K. coordination of intelligence from Italy.]

. . . Both Zulu and I realize that duplication of reports does occur; the main sources of this is K-13 namely SIM and K-23 namely Milan Headquarters of CNL. The set up with regard to these two sources is as follows: the information reaches both Lugano and Bern at approximately the same time. However, Bern cables usually go out about a day before the Zulu messages since Zulu cables are made up and transmitted from Geneva. In view of the fact that we are able to hold only bi-weekly discussions in Bern, we cannot check each cable before it is transmitted. If we waited until after we had a meeting before we sent the material out, a serious delay would ensue. The only way to avoid this duplication, if it is important that it be eliminated, is for you to make arrangements with London for either Zulu or us, exclusively, to relay the information from one or both sources. As it now stands, Zulu transmits to London only and London in turn relays to the south. I, on the other hand, send to Algiers direct and the information transmitted concerns this theater particularly. The sending and preparing of these cables is at present, to a great extent, a mechanical proposition. Since Zulu has an expert on naval matters here, I arranged for them to take care of certain recent cases of naval material from K-23 and K-13.

Document 3-149

Telegram 3800-3806, June 12, 1944

[In this report to General Donovan, Dulles cited German and Austrian contacts who could have a role after the war.]

From 110 to Carib, 109, and 105.

1. There is an idea prevalent locally that my work includes a review of problems concerned with postwar Central European settlements. Although I never indicated that this was a fact, I did not think it was a good idea to deny this rumor because it was valuable as a cover and uncovered several SI channels which would not have been available to me if contacted from a direct SI approach.

2. The above situation has resulted in my receiving several recommendations and memoranda from German circles. These may be worthwhile from the point of view of the occupation forces. These have been summarized in part by Flash but the greater part are too involved for such treatment.

3. I concur that it is not probable that Nazi refugees will take a leading part in the new Germany and they ought not to be "supported" by us. However, some of

our German contacts locally have kept up close personal association with friends in Germany and others of them have arrived from the Fatherland just lately and under conditions which set them apart from the majority of Nazi refugee[s] in England or America. I am not familiar with the Nazi refugee problem in Sweden and other places, but Switzerland, with its literature and newspapers printed for the most part in German and with the majority of its nationals speaking that language, is in a better position to maintain contact with Germany than other countries are, regardless of the fact that the German-speaking Swiss are fundamentally opposed to the 3rd Reich philosophy.

4. The problem comes up whether contacts such as those noted below can be employed to advantage in evolving plans for the occupation and if so, just what use to make of them. We are aware that this lies a little beyond our actual province but we cannot escape the fact that our organization in Bern has established these contacts and in the interest of security it would not be a simple matter to hand them over to other people.

5. Noted below are individuals whom I believe possess real worth and who are engaged in questions concerning postwar occupation of Germany. It is my belief that all these people can be relied upon as true anti-Nazis:

A. A memorandum concerning industrial and business reorganization of Germany is being prepared by our 643. Gorter, and Rathenau's brother-in-law, Andrea, would be of assistance in this same work.

B. 665 is a prominent person in the Protestant field and 801 is a front-rank Catholic layman. We are cooperating in an active manner with both these individuals in matters pertaining to the church. In the Protestant field, Professor Schmid at Basle would also be of help.

C. Wirts, an authority on questions relative to the youth movement and Roepke, a prominent author in Geneva, are both available to work on the problem of education.

D. Our 500 and our 328 (his wife is of German origin and remarkably competent) are both available for the labor relations field.

E. Our 817, 830, 836 and 512 have had varied training in police affairs and the administrative field. In addition, 478 can be used in this connection and also in work concerning the church.

F. Also, a separate group is engaged in work on the Austrian situation. Members of this group include 837, Klein, who is concerned with labor-socialist matters, 834 and attorney Grimm, the latter in Zurich.

G. There is, in addition, a group devoting their attention to the Bavarian question, comprising among others 817, 845 and 801.

6. The individuals mentioned above represent abilities that ought not to be disregarded in establishing experience and background data for the Herculean job of occupying and reeducating Germany. During the past 1½ years we have earned the

confidence of these persons and we would be grateful for your advice concerning ways in which we may effectively employ these contacts.

Document 3-150

Telegram 3818-22, June 14, 1944

[Swiss contact with Allied intelligence intensified as the war progressed. Number 839 is General Henri Guisan, commander in chief of the Swiss armed forces.]

1. 839 stated in a private talk which I had with him yesterday that he felt a renewed sense of unrest regarding the local situation, in view of the developments in Italy and the presence of a substantial number of Nazi reserve troops on his northern border. He said that their SI services had located 35 Nazi divisions in the general vicinity of Alsace, Vorarlberg, Wuerttemberg, Bavaria, Black Forest and Baden; they estimated that the total Nazi strategic reserve amounted to 60 divisions.

2. He was aware that the greater part of the 35 divisions were in all probability either recuperating or training and that a majority of them were only two regiments strong. He stated, nevertheless, that they had identified among this group two air divisions and several veteran field divisions. Therefore, in the light of this, he was exercising every possible precaution and was calling up additional troops.

3. 839 mentioned that the Brenner Pass was becoming increasingly precarious and that, in all probability, Mont Cenis would be out of order for 3 months and this made the local situation more difficult. He said that if the Italian approaches to Simplon and Gotthard were destroyed, Nazi pressure would be rendered less effective.

4. A report concerning Nazi preparations for bacteriological warfare was being carefully checked by 839's SI services. According to rumor, scientific experiments were conducted in laboratories at Lyon, the product was produced and then forwarded to Leipzig.

5. The above approximation and location of Nazi reserves is neither understood nor credited by 520 or us. Even though it is possible that, in the general region surrounding the Swiss border mentioned, there may be several hundred thousand convalescents or trainees, no other source has supplied us with information indicating that there were any such number of organized divisions stationed there. We do not think that there is any actual cause for worry over the local situation. We, however, do have reports which state that more and more Nazi deserters are coming over; this of course, would require larger patrols along the Swiss border.

6. Rumor received from another source, states that, in view of the developments in Italy and France, the Swiss are weighing the possibility of preparing some defense at the frontiers, instead of immediately withdrawing to reduit in the event of attack, and as a result, are planning that the forces outside of reduit are to be increased.

Document 3-151

Telegram 724-25 to London, June 15, 1944

[Dulles became involved in acrimony between the French resistance and the Anglo-American allies.]

A cable for CFLN, has been submitted by Iris for transmission to Indigo (copy to Azur): it says that a request has been made by the Departmental Liberation Committees of 10 departments, asking that the CFLN be informed of the emotional reaction resulting from the passage in Churchill's speech withholding recognition from the CFLN, and of the serious repercussions occasioned by bombing of civilians, such as that in Lyon. The message ends with a plea to the Allied powers to understand that in denying recognition to CFLN they are delivering a dangerous weapon to the enemy, since such a refusal is construed as an indication that the French resistance is not trusted.

From 110. I informed Iris that our facilities were not available for political denunciations, that they were designed for work of an activist character against the common foe, and that I could not transmit messages such as the foregoing, which was purely political in character. The above message appears to have been prepared in France before our invasion of Normandy. Do you agree with the foregoing?

Document 3-152

Telegram 3825-29, June 15, 1944

[This report discusses differences within the French resistance.]

Lorraine. Following information is dated the 7th of this month and was furnished by 802:

1. The Lorraine group is thoroughly against having any business with Rigaud or Lemaigre-Dubreuil. The group has not been in contact with either of the latter and does not intend to establish such contact.

2. According to Lorraine, Fabry, former Minister of War, went to Madrid with the sanction of the Nazis. Fabry asserts that he talked with Middleton, Stevens and the American Ambassador and it is said he was asked to go on to Washington but that he refused this offer. (Following comment is from 110: There is a possibility that the reference to the Washington bid and the above mentioned conferences may be in error in which case it would be of assistance if we could be so informed.) When he returned to France, Fabry made known his opposition to de Gaulle and the fact that he was in favor of Petain. He intimated that he had attempted to establish contacts with the United States in the Marshal's name.

3. Lorraine knew in advance of Fabry's journey and had warned the latter that

neither Lorraine nor his associates would treat with Fabry or with any Parliamentarian who were supporting Petain. Fossati, who went with Fabry, pointed out to Lorraine that Stevens had referred to the latter as the individual with whom the United States had established contact. Lorraine said he had no contacts outside the country. (Following is from 110: It is most unwise that our contact should be revealed in such quarters if this has actually happened.)

4. It is the opinion of the Lorraine group that certain Parliamentarians who have lost caste because of their support of the pro-Vichy viewpoint will now make an attempt to regain favor by setting up contacts with the Lorraine group and try to put the latter in an unfavorable light in other countries. The incidents involving Fabry and Lemaigre-Dubreuil indicate how bad this situation is. The Lorraine group refuses to admit any and all individuals who have yielded to Vichy dictates or activities.

5. Fabry is a member of that group of Parliamentarians who, using a study bureau with offices on Avenue Victor Emmanuel II as a cover, have joined together various journalistic and literary elements of the Parliamentary faction. Boucher is the President; he was Deputy des Vosges and a former Cagoulard, Benoist-Mechain and Montigny are included among the associates. Although it is not probable, the group asserts they have organized about 40 Parliamentarians. In any case, the Nazis direct this group and employ it in attaining their political objectives.

Document 3-153

Telegram 734-35 to London, June 16, 1944

[This message is another example of OSS Bern's contribution to the Allied counterintelligence effort.]

An employee of the Nazi SI, Gabriel Sagrera or Saguera, who resides in Paris at the Hotel Central, 58 Rue Labruyere, will soon depart for Spain. He will be accompanied by Maria Reuck who has secured a passport under the name of Patricia Barillet. Miss Reuck, although German, has a French mother, Madame Barillet, who resides in Paris at 3BIS Rue Rotrou, Asnieres. She intends to get in touch with Ushor at the British Embassy and to donate her services to the Red Cross. Among Miss Reuck's papers is a letter for an alleged fiancé, an American whose parents live at 1862 Beacon Street, Brookline, Massachusetts. Their name is Randall.

Document 3-154

Telegram 736-37 to London, June 16, 1944

[As the Red Army approached Bulgaria, OSS Bern's channel via the Minister in Switzerland was threatened.]

I have been informed by 492 that the new Bulgarian cabinet includes people who are unfriendly to Kiss and that, at this time, Kiss contact and homeward channels of communication will more than likely be restricted. Should you contact Zulu, it may be desirable for you to inform them about this matter. In the very near future, we hope to have a reliable courier departing. There was a letter for General Mihov, Sofia, included in the message MOM sent for Kiss via Zulu. Suggest you ask MOM if we should employ channels other than Kiss to forward this letter.

Document 3-155

Telegram 738-44 to London, June 17, 1944 (extracts)

[Twelve days after the Normandy invasion Dulles submitted this area-by-area report on the status of the French resistance ("Fres").]

An agent who left France the 14th of this month makes the following report on the French internal situation.

A. Jura: Fres hold the open country well. (From now on will employ the word Fres to mean Maquis, French resistance and the like.) Bourg is encircled. General Touchon [Fouchon?] who was the former military governor of Lyon, disciplined the Fres and controls them militarily. . . . The population is being terrorized by the Milice. Most of the civil officials and general Sauvaceon [Sauvageon?] have been apprehended. Chalon/Saone: the Nazis are not able to suppress sabotage and are in a state of great worry. . . .

B. In the central sector the Fres is well organized. The Fres hold Brive and Tulles and are working jointly with General Jieunesse, who is prefect. . . . The Nazis are determined, no matter what the cost, to cut down the Fres in the central region. . . .

E. Paris area; comparatively quiet. Because of the transport situation, provisioning is critical, spelling famine to the poorer class of people. . . .

F. Region of Lyon: situation quiet. The Nazis are trying not to incite the population. There is a military guard at the prefecture since they fear a "coup de main" by Fres and the Nazis have made ready for a siege. . . .

Document 3-156

Telegram 3854-55, June 19, 1944

[This message illustrates Dulles's use of religious groups for contacts and information. Individuals under reference include John Foster Dulles, Norman Armour, and Hamilton Fish Armstrong, editor of *Foreign Affairs*. Number 800 is the German resistance figure Adam von Trott zu Solz.]

A Swiss citizen by the name of Philippe Mottu, who has been engaged in work on postwar questions for the Political Department, has just departed for the United States. He is going on a private mission; however, the Political Department is aware of his trip and has given its consent. He is to make a study of work in progress in America on the problems of postwar settlement. Mottu, who is a Buchmanite, will go the Buchman meeting at Chicago. It is thought that Mottu's opinions are satisfactory, but it is likely that he follows the general (and what I feel is the somewhat unrealistic) trend of this faction. I gave him introductory letters to my brother and to Hamilton Armstrong. I recommended to Armstrong that he might arrange for Mottu to contact Norman, Isaiah and yourself. I think he will be able to supply you with some valuable background information concerning the German resistance organization, especially about our #800 and his associates.

Document 3-157

Telegram 3866-68, June 20, 1944 (extracts)

[This report on analysis of a downed German bomber indicates that Dulles had indirect access to certain Swiss intelligence and underlines the ambiguity of the relationship between the OSS mission and British intelligence with regard to exchange of information.]

Some weeks back, a Dornier 217 came down by mistake in Switzerland. It was equipped with the night-fighting mechanism which is described below and which the Nazis are vigorously trying to protect: there are 16 dipole antennae on the nose of the airplane. These receive and send on a wavelength of 60 centimeters. As a result of their number, they produce an extremely narrow beam which makes it possible for the pilot to locate on an oscillograph any hostile bombing planes which are flying on the direct course of his plane. . . .

A different source, which has not been tested, calls this device the "Fernsch [Kernsch?] beaming apparatus."

With the exception of the information in the preceding paragraph, the above data was secured through 493 from Flute our 827 K-16. Through 484, the same information may possibly be given to Zulu at a later date.

Document 3-158

Telegram 3878-79, June 21, 1944

[Dulles maintained close contact with General Guisan, Swiss army commander (number 839), and with Swiss intelligence (number 511). The Swiss also exchanged information with German intelligence. Therefore, reports obtained locally were both vitally important and subject to critical examination by OSS Bern and General Legge, the American Military Attaché (number 520).]

The report supplied by 839 concerning sizable Nazi concentrations in the general region of the northeastern border of Switzerland has not been verified by information which we and 520 are receiving. The Nazi divisions in that sector seem to be mainly ersatz divisions which are being established and they have comparatively little strength. In addition, various sections of 511 do not believe that reports of such Nazi concentrations are correct.

We are of the opinion that the chief of 511 and various of his principal assistants are being misled by the Nazi SD. We are aware they are in contact with the latter. We feel that it is possible this fact accounts for somewhat amazing data reported in our #647–658 to London, to which you stated your reaction in your #689–90. In spite of the fact that this report reached 520 from K-3, K-3 had been away for a number of weeks on another assignment. He did not analyze or prepare the report. It is quite possible that the SD planted this report on our local friends.

Document 3-159

Telegram 602-3 to Algiers, June 25, 1944

[OSS Bern frequently relayed reports on the situation in northern Italy to Algiers and served as a channel of communication for the resistance.]

On the 17th of this month, Chris courier brought the following:

1. The Committee for National Liberation at Turin asks that fields which have been rejected for dropping purposes be signalled. This will enable them to take away the persons who have been watching such fields, obviating the great danger in maintaining guards for a lengthy period.

2. It is thought that 2 ex-Fascist leaders in Turin named Salvatore Cipullo and Paolo Zerbino were in Rome when the Allies took the city. These 2 men were to blame for the execution of the Military Committee of the Committee of National Liberation of Turin, which requests that they be arrested and tried as war criminals.

3. In northern Italy, leaflet propaganda should be stressed, especially for Fascist troops and Maquis organizations. The former are ready to desert the Fascist army but they are unable to listen to much radio propaganda.

4. They ask for 3-pointed nails (for the purpose of puncturing tires) and for additional medical supplies.

5. The Val d'Aosta section of the Committee for National Liberation is not very cooperative. They do not like the supervisory officials Turin dispatched to them and they have had some differences with the Committee for National Liberation.

6. The Partisan groups in the Val d'Aosta sector were attacked on the 28th of last month by Fascist soldiery and German customs guards. This was not a clean-up

campaign, although they destroyed numerous homes. Other than increasing the number of Maquis, this action had no effective consequences.

Document 3-160

Telegram 3908-15, June 26, 1944 (extracts)

[OSS Bern continued to report on conditions in France and on disarray among elements of the resistance.]

The following information on France is dated at Paris the 17th of this month, and was furnished by source 802. . . .

3. After the invasion, 17 officials of the SNCF, including President Fournier, were placed under arrest. . . . The Gestapo had made the arrests without asking the advice of either the technical authorities or the Oberkommando der Wehrmacht. Laval had a talk with Abetz, who went to Rundstedt, after which the release of all arrested persons was ordered. The Gestapo had planned these arrests a long time before, as part of a general scheme to seize hostages.

4. It is very difficult to get any positive information on what has happened, due to the fact that the Germans are in control of telephone and telegraph communications, and that railroad communications with the west, southwest, and north have been stopped. . . .

5. In general, little attention was paid to the orders for restraint issued by London. The fear has been expressed by leaders of the French resistance that premature uprisings and resultant countermeasures by the Germans would nullify attempts to act methodically in harmony with the invading forces.

6. Less violent groups of the resistance are trying to keep discipline. . . . The Communists are everywhere starting uprisings in order to keep up their prestige and strengthen their political position. If the resistance elements avoid following their example and jumping the gun, the whole region between the sea and the Loire is ripe for general action. . . .

7. There has been an improvement in relations between the resistance and the Lorraine group. At present, the new leader of the Socialist Party is trying to establish contact with Lorraine. Although there has not been any interruption in the talks with Parodi, the latter is becoming more and more dictatorial and hard to handle. Results can already be observed from the delay in recognizing the Provisional Government. The Lorraine group is getting an increasing number of requests to arbitrate between the different groups, but has been refusing as it does not want to become involved. . . .

9. . . . Lorraine understands that London and Washington may think that, because of their lengthy enforced silence, there are no more supporters of the Third Republic in France. This is far from the facts, and Lorraine still hopes that the Allies will receive its representatives and listen to their opinions on the country's true position.

(From 110: the Lorraine group has not yet proved its effectiveness. I report the information in paragraphs 7–9 in its original form, not because I am in favor of the political opinions given, but because I believe 802 to be a well-informed and honest reporter.)

Document 3-161

Telegram 770-72 to London, June 27, 1944

[On June 13, 1944, Germany began launching V-1 "Vengeance Weapons" against London. These rocket bombs killed thousands during the course of the war and had a devasting effect on civilian morale. The V-1 was the long-promised German secret weapon.]

Although the reports are not all in, Swiss correspondents in Berlin have gained the general impression that the low morale in Germany had gone up quite a lot as a result of the initial German propaganda reports about the secret weapon. Over a period of some months the latter had been given an extremely powerful build-up. A large part of the population feels that only a miracle can save the country, and the propaganda led some of them to believe that at last the miracle might have happened. No permanent effect will be produced by this shot of adrenalin. As a matter of fact, if this secret weapon does not lead to any positive results, such as delaying the 3-front offensive, or decreasing the air raids, it is likely that German morale will fall to a new low. It is evident that the Nazi chiefs are afraid of having gone too far, as the newspapers have tended lately to advise the people against too cheerful an outlook so far as regards immediate concrete results from the use of the secret weapon.

328's German friends report that the appearance of the new weapon has caused a few people to think that there is now a chance for Germany. This may mirror the view held in labor and leftist circles. Most people, however, are still holding to the belief that in a few months the Allies will have developed countermeasures which will bring about an even greater deterioration in the situation. Many say they would rather have had the invasion keep on according to schedule, as in that case the war might come to a close sooner, but that the secret weapon will only lengthen it. In view of the foregoing reasons, 328 reports, there is no indication of much jubilation in those circles. Undoubtedly, one of the reasons for the paling of the first flush of enthusiasm is the fear of countermeasures by the Allies.

Document 3-162

Telegram 3918-20, June 28, 1944

[With V-1 attacks against England already in process, Dulles sources reported on Germany's development of an even more potent weapon: the V-2, a true guided missile.]

The report which follows is a brief summary of the information given to us by 3 separate sources including Breakers: V-2, a large rocket, is the 2nd secret weapon of the Nazis. It is charged with a new and more potent explosive which very likely is liquid air and it is fired into the stratosphere from underground chambers in practically a vertical direction. During the tests made with unfilled rockets, a high degree of accuracy was shown, although charged rockets at a high altitude almost always went to pieces. According to one of our sources, this rocket is being manufactured at Freifssberg in the vicinity of Stettin (this may be Greiffenberg or Greifenberg). A 2nd source indicates that it is being produced in lower Silesia at Marklissa and will be used on London very soon, according to Nazi plans. One source describes it as weighing between 12 and 14 tons with a maximum range of 400 kilometers and a speed of 1000 kilometers per hour.

As nearly as we can determine from these reports, the torpedo receives its first impetus in the same way that rockets are propelled and when it reaches the stratosphere, it travels on its way by virtue of its imparted momentum. It proceeds at very great altitudes until its momentum is lost, and then it falls to earth. In the past, we had many reports of the explosion of such rockets while being tested, since the problem of stratosphere operation has evidently not been solved by the Nazi experts. Realize that this information is extremely indefinite, but it may offer you some leads.

We have more information from a Nazi deserter indicating that recent raids on Kluftern in the vicinity of Friedrichshafen have evidently had little effect, since production is still going forward on a secret weapon there.

CHAPTER

4

The Failed July 20 Plot Against Hitler; The Liberation of Western Europe

July–December 1944

Document 4-1

Telegram 775-77 to London, July 1, 1944 (extract)

[Dulles continued to supply a channel of communication for his socialist/labor French contacts in Geneva to correspond with their compatriots in London.]

From 328. Action: Eclair, London. (By 110: The following is transmitted to Washington for information only.)

1. I do not possess any intimate friends in the areas which have been freed or in the adjacent regions. My contacts in France are very uncertain at this time. I am trying to set up contact once more with Tarbes, Marseille, Paris, Montaubon, Lyon, Aix-en-Provence, Toulouse and Chambery. I am sending our friends the directions set forth below: They should report to the local Allied Headquarters as soon as

their area is liberated. They should ask to speak with the Civil Affairs officer. After introducing themselves by supplying their real names and surnames, they are to state that they come from Antoine. . . .

2. It would be possible for us to utilize comrades at once as liaison agents. Our friends are prepared to accept them. Their stay at this end creates no problem. We are able to dispatch them to their native country without excessive danger. . . .

Document 4-2

Telegram 3966-68, July 4, 1944 (extracts)

[This message was transmitted to President Roosevelt by General Donovan on July 10. It is based on information received from "George Wood" in June and therefore bears the designation "Kajun."]

KAPPA. KAJUN. . . .

2. The following is dated the 24th of last month: the Nazi Legation in Brussels expects landings in the near future in the vicinity of Ostend, Antwerp, Rotterdam and/or the mouth of the Somme River. Woods believes that landings close to channel would be assisted by the disastrous food situation in Belgium and the north of France. They have reduced the Belgian bread ration to 250 grams; greater reduction is imminent. Seven hundred railroad cars are required every day for normal Belgian food supplies and only 163 are available at the moment. The transportation system will become more critical in the next few months. . . .

5. A Nazi agent reports from England the 10th of last month, that a British bombing of Dresden, possibly with new weapons, is planned as a reprisal for the shooting by the SD of 54 British officers. Eden interpellation was the first knowledge the Nazi Foreign Office had of the shooting.

Document 4-3

Telegram 3988-90, July 5, 1944

[General Donovan forwarded this message to President Roosevelt on July 10. It concerns German submarine warfare in the Western Hemisphere.]

KAPPA. We have just obtained from Wood more material which is dated the 3rd of this month. We will send it to you under the indicator PBKLY and we will label documentary information as we did before.

In a message dated June 22nd, the Seekriegsleitung (hereafter referred to as SKL) reminded the Foreign Office that after the middle of July, 1943, it had been agreed with the Foreign Office that submarines were not to operate off the coast of South

America below the latitude of 28 degrees South. SKL advised that it was considering ending this limitation and requested the concurrence of the Foreign Office in this decision. The reason given by SKL for this proposal is that the rupture of diplomatic relations with Argentina terminates the necessity, in SKL's opinion, of maintaining the restriction. The proposal would not involve the limitation against sinking or seizing Chilean or Argentine vessels. SKL wishes to be free to operate in this region since they will not have to contend with any organized protection system, especially none like the powerful enemy air patrol operating off the coast of Brazil. This fact offers a prospect of success in this region. According to SKL's plan, just one or 2 U-boats would be used at the beginning. In the event that it should appear possible to obtain greater successes, more submarines would be used.

In its answer, the Foreign Office inquired of SKL concerning the amount of tonnage which it could be fairly assumed would be sunk. If the tonnage were to amount to merely some tens of thousands of tons, it would not justify running the chance of Argentina declaring war; however, it would be worth the risk if the tonnage they expected to sink were to amount to hundreds of thousands of tons. By July 3rd, SKL's answer to this inquiry had not yet reached the Foreign Office.

Document 4-4

Telegram 3991-97, July 6, 1944 (extract)

[This message concerning the German V-weapon program was transmitted to the White House by General Donovan on July 10. "George Wood" provided specific information on the location of certain production facilities.]

KAPPA. This is a PBKLY message.

1. With reference to the rocket bombs, extremely secret information from Paris (Koerperbau) reveals that the "gerade laufapparatur" is produced in Gdynia, at the Ascania works; both the V-1 and V-2 models are made in Hersograd (sic), which is located in Niederdonau, in the vicinity of St. Valentin; the "Dobsen" [? illegible] are built at the Krupp works in Wuppertal; additional parts which are not named are manufactured by the Siemensplania factories at Wurtenberglesh (sic), situated 50 kilometers north of Augsburg. (By 110: Wood is not sure regarding the final identification above.)

2. Approximately 10% of the V-1 model rocket bombs will have short-wave transmitters installed in them. The purpose of this will be to direct the path and aim of the rocket bomb. The problem which arises with respect to this, however, is whether waves transmitted from England will be able to interfere with the apparatus.

3. To the best of Wood's information, Berlin has not been able to obtain any first-hand information regarding the consequences of the bombing of southern England. . . .

Document 4-5

Telegram 4001-3, July 6, 1944

[In the weeks following the landings in Normandy, OSS Bern reported intensified disarray in the German hierarchy. This message was sent to President Roosevelt by General Donovan on July 10.]

Through a Norwegian source in France, previously shown to be fairly dependable, we have obtained the information reported below:

There was a critical situation last week in the OKW High Command for France. Hitler ordered both Rommel and von Rundstedt to appear before him, as the result of the latter's threat to give up his position because of his quarrels with Rommel. From the start of the landings in Normandy, Rommel had insisted upon bringing up the full German reserves; on the other hand, von Rundstedt retained sizeable concentrations of troops in the Black Forest and to the north and east of Paris because he feared huge paratroop landings by the Allies to the east, possibly even in the Vosges region and along the Rhine River. It is reported that the Fuehrer himself had given his approval in advance to von Rundstedt's plan. Von Rundstedt was bitterly angry against Rommel for arguing against this plan directly with Hitler. It is stated that the Fuehrer settled the feud and Rommel will not make his reports hereafter to Hitler directly, but will send them through von Rundstedt. It is felt that this reconciliation will have brief existence.

The source advises that from every corner of Europe, forces are reaching France to take part in the Normandy struggle. One division has come from Hungary, one from Rumania, one from Norway, and two have arrived from East Prussia. The Nazis are faced with important difficulties because of transportation troubles and now by the lack of gasoline. Large numbers of Nazi troops were forced to halt south of Paris en route to the front as a result of the fact that supplies and heavy equipment did not reach them from the warehouses in Germany. According to the report, the Germans are according priority to the Normandy front over to the Russian front until the close of July. The Nazis are aware that the Soviet armies are likely to have reached the Vistula River by then; however, at that time Hitler will take up a stand. Families of officers residing to the east of Koenigsberg in East Prussia are moving to Austria, according to information reaching these officers.

Document 4-6

Radiotelephone Transmission No. 171, July 6, 1944

[General Donovan sent this message to President Roosevelt on July 8, 1944, with the following suggestion: "It occurred to me that it is the kind of story which you may consider represents a common ground on which de Gaulle and yourself may meet in a public condemnation of these atrocities and in a promise to end them." From this point until the series terminated in April 1945, the Dulles radiotelephone "flashes" were sent by Donovan to Roosevelt with increasing frequency.]

France

Here is a report regarding the situation in certain parts of the interior of France which has just been received and deals with the events of a few days ago. The person making the report was in the Limoges area. Here is the report: The trip from Paris to Limoges cannot be made by road. There is a prohibition against travel on the part of the Germans. There is grave danger of being machine-gunned on the road. The maquis have requisitioned all vehicles in the regions which they control. By railway, with several detours, it was possible to make the trip in two days. In Limoges the situation is dramatic. The city is in a virtual state of siege. The center of the city is entirely cut off by barricades and block-houses held by the gardes mobiles and the milice. The prefect and all the administrative authorities have been deprived of their powers. The person in command is a lieutenant of Darnand named Vaugelas, former aviator known for his oppressive measures against the Haute Savoie maquis. He has installed himself as dictator, mobilized some civilians, forced the young men to enroll in the milice, and requisitioned all existing stocks. He arrests anybody he pleases without any judicial procedure. From time to time, in armored trucks, he leads expeditions into the surrounding country. Thus he went to Gueret at the head of his men to arrest the Secretary General of the prefecture and certain number of notables there, and brought them back to prison at Limoges. The Germans, who number about 2,000 at Limoges, are installed in the casernes. They patrol the streets and control the city, where the Gestapo is creating a reign of terror. In the country, the maquis is in control, but it is divided between the FTP, of Communist tendencies, and the FFI, military elements of the secret army, and special groups which obey only their local chiefs. After the invasion, these various elements all wished to make known their presence by various acts of sabotage and even terrorism. They proceeded to enroll a large number of people, and, by their disorganized action, brought down terrible reprisals by the Germans. These reprisals have bathed the whole region in blood. Everywhere there are large numbers of civilians who have been executed by the Germans. After the maquis was driven out of the city, the two most serious developments in this region [were] those which occurred at Tulle and at Oradour. At Tulle, the maquis, after having taken the city, wished to take a small garrison of about a hundred Germans. The inexperience of the men of the maquis cost them heavy losses. When they were finally able to reduce the garrison, they massacred their prisoners. They also executed a certain number of persons they suspected of being collaborationists. The Germans, accompanied by soldiers, arrived the following evening and decided to raze the city. On the intervention of the Prefect, and considering that a certain number of German wounded had been saved from massacre and cared for by the inhabitants, they decided to execute only a part of the population. After two days of terror, they ended by hanging from the balconies of the principal street of Tulle 150 hostages taken haphazard throughout the city. Adding to this the number of persons killed at the time of the action and during the razing of the city by the Germans, seven to eight hundred persons were victims of this adventure. The savagery of the Germans at Oradour is inexplicable. An SS detachment arrived at ten in the morning of the tenth of June. It was market day, and many people from Limoges had gone there to get supplies. There were also a great number of children sent there for their vacation—a total of about twelve hundred persons. On the pretext of searching for clandestine munitions depots, the SS commander had all the men shut up in two or three barns, and all the women and children in the church. The abandoned village was then pillaged. At two o'clock, the houses were set on fire, then the barns. The Germans machine-gunned all who attempted to escape. At five o'clock, the church was set on fire. Here again machine guns were used. One woman only managed to escape. The German general commanding at Limoges acknowledged before the prefect that this act dishonored his country. He permitted the bishop and the prefect to visit the ruins and authorized a funeral service at the cathedral. In the face of these barbarous acts, the whole region trembles. The peasants hide in the woods, and scouts signal the arrival of any German vehicles. The country has at one and the same time the violence of the enemy, of the maquis, and of the milice. There is no longer any legal authority. The Prefect is powerless. A wild anger pervades the terrorized people. The fate of Limoges and that of all the cities in the center of France, is very much the same. At the mercy of this terror—almost impossible to describe. The only comfort in this frightful situation is to be found in the intense patriotism of these people, in their hope for prompt deliverance, and in the reaction which is developing against all violence. It is true that all hope for the constitution of the regular army and the reconstitution of a legitimate authority (sic), but it is high time that these hopes and aspirations are supported by concrete and serious action.

Document 4-7

Telegram 4019-25, July 7, 1944 (extracts)

[General Donovan transmitted the full text of this telegram to President Roosevelt on July 10. Among the documents obtained for OSS Bern by agent "George Wood" in Berlin, it concerned German efforts to prevent the defection of its Bulgarian satellite.]

KAPPA. This is a PBKLY message from a documentary source. The following is the substance of a secret message sent to the Minister of the German Legation in Bulgaria by von Ribbentrop. The message is dated July 2 and states that it is for the Minister himself, with reference to his #537 dated June 30th.

Please deliver at once the following message from me to the Bulgarian Foreign Minister. It should be transmitted orally:

1. In the military and political matter of removing various military installations from the coast of the Black Sea, which is of such great importance to us, it is extremely unfortunate that Draganoff reached an agreement with the Russian chargé d'affaires to make such removals without notifying us in advance and without obtaining our concurrence beforehand. Consequently our own situation is affected adversely.

2. Any impression of giving in to Soviet demands should have been avoided, even if we can, from the military aspect, remove or disguise such installations along the coast.

3. We feel that the note of May 18th which the Russian Legation submitted is obviously an ultimatum in its nature. As a result, to have yielded to the Soviet Union in part on the matter of the military installations will not prevent them from urging the establishment of Russian consulates in the harbor cities of Bulgaria. In addition, it is probable that the Soviet Union will make larger demands. This will cause them to apply ceaseless pressure on Bulgaria.

. . . Consequently, in preparing the reply to the Russian note of May 18th, it is necessary to give full study to all military and political factors affecting both Bulgaria and Germany. As has already been agreed, we therefore request that you consult with us on the reply to this note, following the completion of the military study. This closes the directions for your discussion with the Bulgarian Foreign Minister.

Please advise the appropriate German military command in confidence of the foregoing directions and inform them they should protect their interests in the matter of the military installations along the coast. . . .

Document 4-8

Telegram 4029-32, July 7, 1944

[General Donovan forwarded this telegram to President Roosevelt on July 10. It consists of a message sent by the German Ambassador in Turkey to the Foreign Ministry in Berlin, where it was intercepted by George Wood.]

KAPPA. PBKLY series. Doc. This concludes the PBKLY series. The following is a cable to Ribbentrop from von Papen, sent about the middle of June. (Although the number and date have been cut, the latter can be determined from the information given at the end of the cable.)

1. Yesterday the first reception for heads of missions was held, and Saracoglu had a talk with the Bulgarian Minister. I consider the talk they had an extraordinary one. Bulgarian Minister asked if a fundamental change in policy should be read into Numan's departure. The Turkish premier's remark that Turkey would not use her rights against the Allies might be interpreted to mean that henceforth she would yield to Allied demands for conceding bases. This received a categorical denial from Saracoglu. Should Turkey enter the war, Bulgaria would automatically be the first

to feel the effect. However, he fails to see why there should be any change in relations between the two countries, which he stated were altogether amicable. He did not consider the mobilization of the Bulgarian army as a move against the interests of Turkey, but rather as a perfectly natural step. He had received advice that the new government in Bulgaria was firmly maintaining order and was trying to stop [illegible] any break with the USSR if possible. Saracoglu recommended that this policy be continued. Turkey would be confronted with a difficult situation if Soviet armies were to begin operating in Bulgaria. Nor should the Soviets forget that at their lowest point, when the Nazis were in the Caucasus, Bulgaria held firm against German pressure to enter the war. To the Premier's amazement, Balaba replied that this statement was incorrect and that the Reich had never put pressure on Bulgaria to enter the war against the USSR. The talk appeared to have satisfied Balaba, who left with the belief that the prime minister's assurances were sincere, certainly for as long as there was no change in the situation on the Rumanian front.

2. The Turkish President went to Thrace on a trip of inspection.

3. Yesterday, for the first time, radio programs were exchanged between the United States and Turkey. Introductory speeches were delivered by Salim Sarper, Ambassador Steinhardt, and his wife.

Document 4-9

Telegram 4033-36, July 8, 1944

[On July 7, Dulles received what appeared to be an attempt by Marshal Pétain to contact President Roosevelt. General Donovan transmitted this message to the President on July 10.]

110 to Jackpot and 109. On the evening of July 7, a special courier arrived at the French Embassy from Vichy bearing with him an unsigned paper dated the 22nd of last month. Menetrel is supposed to have handed this himself to the courier, saying that it was from Marshal Petain personally and was to be handed over to me in the hope that Roosevelt would get it. 472 gave it to me, at which I said nothing and did not undertake to forward it.

The document is 3 pages long and seems, in my opinion, to be authentic. It takes up the question of French administrative problems under the occupation, saying that British and American troops are landing on French soil in order to free it from the Nazi invaders. It declares that the French people are willing to suffer without protest, the destruction that will inevitably accompany their liberation and are aware that the Allies will have to establish all sorts of strong military services. However, they do not see the necessity for any replacement of the legitimate French civil administration by a U.S.-British administration or by one which they appoint. It implies that a civil war might result from trying to force this on the country and that even Communism might be the eventual outcome. The document insists that Petain still bears a regular mandate of authority from the National Assembly and as such is the sole legitimate symbol of French sovereignty, regardless of whether the complete exercise of this authority is prevented by circumstances. In consideration of the foregoing, the document goes on to say that the following principle should be observed: The Allies should keep in office all regularly appointed officials, with the exception of those who have excited public opinion by their attitude. In addition, whichever officials are substituted for them "will act only in the capacity of deputies and their appointment will be solely on a temporary basis, so long as it is not ratified by the head of the State, Marshal Petain."

Unless you wish me to, I do not intend to forward the complete text. I understand that this is a delicate business and if you so wish I can send the document back to the Embassy by way of 472. The latter has been immensely valuable, and the only contact I have had and will have with him is in the interests of obtaining intelligence.

Document 4-10

Telegram 4045-46, July 10, 1944

[Dulles's informants included Evert Smits, number 843, also known as "Source Sanders." Smits was apparently a publicity manager for Germany's Fokker manufacturing concern. He was able to provide political, economic, military, and industrial intelligence from various parts of the shrinking Nazi empire.]

1. According to information received by 843, construction will shortly be completed on the new 150-ton submersibles being built in Hamburg. As a safety measure against beaming, they have double shells.
2. A big munitions plant, including fuses, has been made out of the old Trumpf chocolate factory north of Berlin and south of Buch. The red buildings are not camouflaged; the chimneys are tall. The sulphur used in manufacturing is making the employees sick.
3. Since D-Day, German troops in the Netherlands have been visibly reduced.
4. A rumor has it that Goebbels is criticizing Ribbentrop and wishes to put the current minister to the Vatican in his place. Another rumor says that Goering has had to relinquish the fighter output program to a man from Speerorg.
5. After a Messerschmitt 110 night fighter crashed in the Netherlands, 843 friends made off with its radio device for beaming hostile aircraft in order to determine their size and distance. He hopes he will be able to smuggle it here. It does not seem to be linked up with any gun. It resembles a small steamer trunk in size and shape.

Document 4-11

Radiotelephone Transmission No. 173, July 10, 1944 (extract)

[Dulles devoted many of his evening phone calls to in-depth analysis of the situation in Germany. General Donovan transmitted this Flash extract to President Roosevelt on July 12 and invited his attention to Paragraph 2.]

Germany

A neutral observer gives his impressions of Germany as follows: A revolution is not to be expected; the people are too apathetic and too closely supervised by the police. A collapse can only come as the Allied troops arrive. Further, no Badoglio development is likely there. The opposition movements are not in any position to take such a step. Germany is destined to continue until the end and until the complete defeat. This is true even though there are divergencies within the ranks of the Party. At the present time, Goering is under suspicion. The foreign workers are almost as much a cause of internal alarm as the Allied or Russian armies. In certain agricultural areas of Prussia, for example, there are only women, children, and aged, and hundreds of Polish and Russian workers. Even though the latter are not armed, they could easily overcome the handful of guards. The same source reports that the German High Command is now reconciled to giving up a great deal of territory in the East and to seeing the Russians at the frontiers of the Reich. The Germans think that, at that time, they would have many who would support their efforts to find peace, for example, the Pope, and various neutral countries. In any event, the present watchword is, withdraw at the East and hold firm at the West.

Here is an amusing story which I pass on, rather as gossip, because it will not admit of confirmation. The various Nazi chiefs will not seek death in case of defeat, and will not surrender. They will go to various countries: the Argentine, Japan, Ireland. Hitler, so the report runs, has chosen Ireland, as he is convinced that the Irish would not turn him over to the English. Goering will go to Sweden. At the critical moment, it is said that the Wehrmacht would gladly facilitate the departure of Hitler to avoid having the problem of delivering him to the Allies, and thus leave to the Allies the difficult and delicate task of obtaining his extradition. In connection with this somewhat extravagant story, it is interesting to conjecture whether the astounding inactivity of the German submarines could possibly be tied in with a German program for a massive delivery of submarines to Japan, possibly tied in with a flight there of leading Nazi personalities. Japan will probably not be anxious to receive the Nazis, unless they got good value with them; but if Germany could deliver with a few Nazis a hundred submarines, plus crew and technicians, the Japs might take the high Nazis thrown into the bargain. There is, as yet, no evidence whatever to back up this hypothesis, and I merely throw it out as something that might be worth watching. I do not know technically how many of the German submarines could be re-equipped to make this long journey, or how they could be refueled en route.

I call your attention to Goebbels' speech given, I believe, yesterday, in which he dramatically admitted that the German people were in danger, and again played the tune that it was a question of complete destruction or fighting on with every ounce of strength to ultimate victory. He also stresses here the theme, which we expect to have repeated from now on, that Bolshevism is on the threshold of Europe.

Those acquainted with German military affairs say that the loss of General Dietl is a very serious one for the German Army. Dietl was the outstanding German expert in mountain warfare, and might have played a considerable role in the end phases of the war in defending the inner German line, such as the Alps and the Carpathians. The other German general particularly competent to command alpine troops is General Schoerner, who is presently operating in the Carpathians. While Dietl was extremely popular among the rank and file of his troops and could command their full cooperation, Schoerner, on the other hand, is quite unpopular with his men. . . .

Document 4-12

Telegram 4067-68, July 11, 1944

[Dulles consistently urged financial and military support for the resistance in northern Italy. Motta is the Committee of National Liberation in Milan; Attom is Ferrucio Parri, one of its leaders.]

To 109 and OPS. In a group of messages . . . I have told of the pressing request of Attom for a substantial amount of money to back Motta from this point on the basis of 25,000,000 Lira every month from us, and the same amount from Zulu. I feel that we should give financial support to Motta and I can add that there is justification for this as proved by the intelligence reports I have been given here. I do not believe, however, that I should start on such a far-reaching plan without orders from you since I do not know about other possible programs to provide money for Italian resistance by parachute groups from the south, or by some other means. Current talk of a possible Nazi retreat has brought about a sharp rise here in the exchange rate of the Lira which has mounted from 55 to 115 Swiss Centimes per 100 Lira. Please instruct us on this as soon as you can.

Document 4-13

Telegram 804-7 to London, July 12, 1944

[The OSS Bern sources included number 667, "Jean Jacques," who began reporting in 1943. This contact appears to have been associated with labor elements in Geneva that ran networks into both France and Germany.]

1. Reports state that there was ruthless suppression of the strikes in the Heinkel factories, but that strikers in the Osthofen factory in the vicinity of Worms remained out for 3 days. There is still a tense feeling among the workers.

2. Hitler youth receive their glider training at the Emmendingen Field in the

vicinity of Freiburg. The field is utilized exclusively for this purpose. Following their training at the field the students are dispatched to Focke-Wulf factories to finish their training.

3. The shipment of army supplies is being held up by a bottleneck at Rastatt on the Rhine Canal.

4. Small speed boats and barges are being built at the Durmens naval plant in the vicinity of Pforzheim. Vital marshalling yards are located there and in nearby Muehlacker.

5. Saboteurs cut the Pirmasens-Kaiserslautern line.

6. Air raid of the synthetic gasoline plant in Homburg highly effective. They are building smaller decentralized plants in the outlying regions of Homburg.

7. The following description given of Nazi worker sentiment in the Rhineland: the opinion is universally held that collapse will come momentarily and they anticipate an armistice before the harvest. The peasants are tired of feeding the victims of bombings and there is great dissension both in rural districts and in factories. The Nazi leaders enjoy safe places behind the lines while the Reich's best men are exposed to sudden death in the occupied countries. Anti-Hitler sentiment is mounting. (Following from 110: the foregoing is a little too optimistic.)

The following is from 328: labor syndicalist groups are convinced that the Nazis will not surrender but would rather "plunge the entire population into the abyss," and that the Nazis if necessary would not hesitate to utilize gas against their own people. People arriving from Germany still report "mass shootings." (The following is from 110: in the form in which it was presented I am inclined to doubt the Winkler report described in Washington #1769. I do not have any confirmation of the material.)

Document 4-14

Telegram 4085, July 12, 1944

[In this message Dulles gives clear forewarning of the events of July 20. He indicates that Gisevius had returned to Germany to join the plot, that Goerdeler was in hiding, and that von Trott du Solz was involved.]

BREAKERS. To Carib and Jackpot. There is a possibility that a dramatic event may take place up north, if Breakers courier is to be trusted. We expect a complete account this evening. However, it is not only possible but probable that any news will be suppressed by violence if necessary. Henceforth 512 will be known as Culber. He has gone north for discussions with Tucky and others. This goes along with your #1782 but we believe 800 connection was also with Zulu. G, mentioned in the last sentence of my #4080 is in hiding. The Chief of Police in Berlin, Helldorf, will henceforth be designated as Bobcat, and Risler will be the new name for General Fromm.

Document 4-15

Telegram 4110-14, July 13, 1944

[Dulles provided additional information on the German opposition one week before the July 20 attempt on Hitler's life.]

BREAKERS. With reference to our #4085 [July 12, above]. A courier from Breakers, who came here a short time ago, advises that the Soviet victories have given new vigor to the Breakers movement. The success of the Allied landing in Normandy and the local developments reported below have also contributed to the impetus of this movement:

1. Breakers have gained a new member in Risler. He holds a responsible command over the reserve from the Berlin region.

2. The headquarters of the Oberkommando der Wehrmacht have been shifted to Sossen (in the vicinity of Berlin) from East Prussia. As a consequence, it is in the vicinity of Berlin that Eta, Zeta and additional generals who are supposedly in the opposition are chiefly concentrated at this time.*

*Refer also to the declaration by Prime Minister Churchill yesterday, in which he stated that it would be better if the people of Germany were themselves to oust the Nazi regime. With respect to this, please consult the flash which I am transmitting this evening [No. 175, below]. I am not making any forecasts regarding the prospects of success for the Breakers program, as reported. Without any doubt, the Gestapo is keeping its eye on developments and it is possible that the Gestapo may get rid of the leaders. Moreover, it is quite probable that the military men, whose action is indispensable to the achievement of these ends, will lack the "intestinal fortitude" to act, just as they have earlier. Furthermore, I am not unaware of the strength of the idea that Germany's defeat must be connected with the criminal program of the Fuehrer and the Nazi clique. Nevertheless, the moral consequence of a display of bravery in taking steps toward setting their own affairs to rights would be valuable to Germany's subsequent status in the Europe that will exist after the war. In the face of all this, however, I am of the opinion that we are warranted in issuing now a general declaration regarding Germany along the lines stated in my flash and in the preceding portions of this message.

Document 4-16

Radiotelephone Transmission No. 175, July 13, 1944

[On the evening of July 13, Dulles transmitted a detailed assessment of the situation in Germany and announced that the end was in sight. He urged that the United States issue a statement declaring that "unconditional surrender" applied to the Nazis and the German war machine, but not to the German people if they took it upon themselves to overthrow their criminal government. General Donovan transmitted this message to President Roosevelt on July 15.]

Germany

The end for Germany is in sight. How long it will be before the collapse comes is now not only a question of the success on the various battlefields, but it also depends upon the extent of the German people's willingness to continue to wage a hopeless struggle. A great percentage—how high, it is impossible to state—of the German people are now persuaded that it is a hopeless battle. Many, however, who have this realization, fight on or work on because they see no alternative, no hope, no future. Goebbels' propaganda to the effect that the Allies, if victorious, intend to annihilate the German people for generations, to reduce them to slavery, has been effective. This propaganda is believed in wide circles in Germany. Goebbels has taken and twisted the slogan unconditional surrender and made the people feel that the slogan means unconditional annihilation. More than ten years of Nazi propaganda and more than four years of war, plus the bombardments, have reduced the German people to a state of fatalistic lethargy in the field of intellectual matters. Most of them no longer think or reason, but merely react. The youth, with no knowledge of anything but Nazism, is still fanatical, and furnishes the cannon-fodder. The workers perform mechanically because they must eat and because of the Gestapo terror. In this situation, we cannot expect very much of a reaction from the German people, but still there are some people in Germany who might conceivably act if we could get over the idea that, by so doing, they could in some way help to improve the future lot of the German people and help a reformed Germany to take an honorable place in the Europe of tomorrow. Under the conditions existing in Germany today, any form of opposition to the Nazi regime involves the gravest risk of immediate execution. Persons are not likely to take this risk unless they feel that, by their action, and very probably by their sacrifice, they are doing something to aid their country's future and to lighten the lot of their fellow citizens. These people ask themselves why they should risk their lives, if the ultimate result, as far as Germany is concerned, is exactly the same as if they remained passive and allow the inevitable collapse to come in due course and time. While the story of Italy over the past year is hardly a brilliant one, nevertheless, now, most Italians realize that, despite their suffering, they will be better off for the future because they have contributed in some measure themselves to rid their country of Fascism. Those who are now fighting with our troops, or in the Italian mountains, will furnish the nucleus around which a new and more virile Italy can be built. These Italians have had this chance only because, with our aid, they staged a kind of revolution. I do not believe that we should make any political or territorial promises of any nature to the Germans. Unconditional surrender must remain the principle for the German military machine and its Nazi rulers. However, this does not mean that we could not and should not help the German people to force this unconditional surrender by explaining to them what we mean, and by holding out some hope that the fate of the individual

German, after such surrender, and his future will be tolerable; that a reformed, demilitarized Germany has a necessary and vital place in the life of Europe.

Many Germans are beginning to realize that there is no hope of any consideration from the Allies as long as Hitler and his gang are in power. They do not know, however, whether there is any hope for them if the Nazis are removed and the military machine is smashed. Of course, one difficulty lies in the fact that there is no hope of a revolution in Germany without the aid of the military, and therefore any statement which couples the destruction of Nazism with the destruction of the military tends to throw the army into the hands of the Nazis. The time is fast running out when any action within Germany would be of great value to us, as military victory may be around the corner. It may be some months off. Those opposed to the Nazis realize this and recognize that the next few weeks may be their last chance to show that they are willing to take some risks in making the first move to clean their own house. We must judge, on our side, whether the encouragement of any effort towards a revolution in Germany will, at this juncture, help to save thousands of lives of Allied soldiers fighting on the various fronts.

Prime Minister Churchill, in a statement attributed to him in the paper today, in the House of Commons, emphasized the desirability that the German people themselves should take steps to overthrow the Nazi government. I believe that it would be helpful if a similar and somewhat expanded statement could be authoritatively made on our side at this time. Possibly coupled with this statement, some indication could be given that the individual German citizen, who had not been a party to the Nazi crime, need have nothing to fear and something to hope from an Allied victory. The German people might be challenged to show the falsity of Goebbels boast that there is not a single man in Germany who is not back of the Nazi leaders. We might well say that we have never and do not now believe Goebbels, and do not believe that the whole German people has sunk to his level. We could tell the German people that their fate lies in their own hands, and those who say that the United Nations mean to exterminate them or reduce them to slavery are merely deceiving them in order to perpetuate themselves in power; that now is the last clear opportunity for the German people to show that they will not continue blindly to follow Hitler to the inevitable catastrophe.

I do not predict that this line will produce a revolution in Germany, but if there is any slight chance of it, and if we wish to help to bring it about, a statement of this nature would certainly be timely. I admit that I have at times wavered between the idea that we should leave Hitler and his gang at the helm until the ship sinks, and the idea of a constructive form of psychological warfare to wean the people from Hitler and bring about an internal revolution. Today, with the Russians at the door of East Prussia, with the invasion a success, and Italy practically lost to the Germans, Hitler stands before history as a beaten leader, and encouragement to internal revolt may be given without much risk that the Hitler legend could rise again on the myth of a stab in the back.

Document 4–17

Telegram 818-21 to London, July 15, 1944

[As the events in Germany approached a decisive point, the political infighting regarding the future of France continued. By providing a channel of communications, Dulles furthered the interests of that narrow base of former parliamentarians who had not been compromised by association with the Vichy government and who sought to avoid the arbitrary imposition on France of a government headed by Allied military authorities, General de Gaulle, or the Communists.]

A friend of former Prime Minister Herriot, Andre Enfiere, has come here. He uses the fictitious name of Lamballe. Through 477 and 284, he has asked that the following message be given to Louis Marin. I am submitting it for your information and so you can decide if it would be proper to deliver the message. Please let me know what you do.

"I have reached Switzerland secretly to carry out a project for Herriot and his friends. At the time I departed, Herriot was in good health, both mental and physical. . . . In behalf of Herriot, I request you to make arrangements for me to travel by plane from France. Georges Bidault, who is the Chairman of the Comité National Resistance and a friend of mine, very much wishes me to make this journey. Kindly make it clear that regardless whether Herriot is alive or dead, I carry with me the backing of his supporters for the reinstitution of a democratic and parliamentary republic. This still constitutes a powerful force among the people of France and we desire to inform supporters of a republic of our opinions regarding the formation of a government, control of the press and election procedures. . . ."

Lamballe indicated verbally that he was a supporter of General de Gaulle to the extent it was necessary to recognize him as the person who upheld the honor of France. However, he states that he and his associates desire to make certain that General de Gaulle really plans to submit himself to the decision of the nation. Consequently, they desire to have genuine republicans surrounding de Gaulle.

The following is for Washington: Lamballe was the source of the material dealing with Herriot contained in my flash of July 14th. Kindly send London a duplicate, making reference to this wire. 802 was the source of the remainder of the material in the above mentioned flash.

Document 4–18

Telegram 4111-12, July 15, 1944

[On the basis of sources within Germany, Dulles now reports that the conspirators had the cooperation of the Berlin police chief, Count Helldorf (Bearcat/Bobcat). He also reiterates his suggestion for a Presidential statement to encourage the resistance.]

BREAKERS. The Breakers group is receiving the cooperation of the Bearcat group, which is composed of a considerable number of anti-Hitler elements working separately from the Gestapo. The next few weeks are believed by Breakers to represent the final opportunity to start action to prove the desire of the German people themselves to overthrow Hitler and his organization and to set up a respectable government. The Soviet threat of invasion of German soil in the eastern sector gives the impetus to this movement. The Breakers group wishes to keep as much as possible of the Reich from falling into the hands of the Russians. Consequently Breakers' plan of action would call for an ordered retreat from the West, and the dispatch of all the crack divisions to defend the Eastern front. Luben [Luber/Gisevius] has made a trip to the North to take part in the discussions there and hopes that he will be able to convince the generals to wage a final struggle against Nazism.

The following is from 110. A presidential announcement to counter Goebbels' line about the Allies' plans for complete annihilation of the German people would encourage the anti-Nazi groups. Attlee's statement, made recently during a debate in the House of Commons, seems to have made a great impression on German groups.

Document 4-19

Telegram 4148, July 15, 1944

[Dulles reports that the Nazis were taking steps to counteract the bane of all totalitarian regimes: contamination of personnel by exposure to the external environment.]

We have been informed by a reliable source that at Baden-Baden there are no elements of the Foreign Office, but that it has been turned into a reception camp for foreign service personnel who are coming back. Its purpose is to "readapt" them to the German ways after returning from foreign posts. I suppose that this is to give the Gestapo a chance to decide whether or not they are correctly permeated with the Nazi ideology; it is a kind of intellectual delousing station.

Document 4-20

Telegram 4154, July 15, 1944

[Dulles continued to promote the fortunes of progressive Italian elements. In this instance he forwarded a message from Edigio Reale, a leader of the Partito d'Azione, to a prominent liberal Italian-American publisher.]

Would you please give 506's message which follows to Max Ascoli if it is possible: "Hope you are alleviating our family dissents, as I am troubled by them; having Pacciardi and others like him in our country is extremely useful; I am grateful to you and Dr. Johnson for the information regarding the old appointment in the new school. Italian and German editions of book on Italy were recently published, and the essay on Sforza is being published; think over the possibilities of dissemination among Italian circles or otherwise. I am in contact with our friends in Italy. Substantial help is needed here by thousands of Italian refugees."

Document 4-21

Telegram 774-76 to Algiers, July 18, 1944

[Always desirous of promoting an active and independent American role in supporting resistance movements, Dulles hectors OSS Algiers about alleged acceptance of a subordinate position with regard to the British in supplying aid to the Italian resistance.]

After I had dispatched my cable #767–69, your cable #512 was delivered to me. It would take me a long time to determine whether a definite field had been activated, nor can I determine which one of a great number of agents operating in Italy has signalled the field direct. You have asked me to do the impossible. The only information I can pass on to you is whether the same pinpoints have been cabled by Zulu SOE here. Kindly inform me if you want me to stop forwarding pinpoints claimed by Zulu. Such a position however, would restrict our actions a great deal, since the making of broad claims is in keeping with their general policy. I am of the opinion that Como is not in touch with the British and he has informed me that no fields were given to the British by him.

I believe your wire indicates that you have not taken into consideration the actual conditions of the situation in northern Italy. The fact is that every conceivable avenue is utilized by the partisan bands in order to signal their fields to us or to Zulu. The action to be taken can be determined at your end only by Zulu and yourself. It is my private belief that confusion will continue until you and Zulu decide upon separate fields of operation.

I am very much perturbed about the situation. This matter seems to have been taken over more and more by Zulu in spite of the fact that the Italians greatly desire help from us. Yesterday I received some disheartening information concerning actual droppings on fields which we signalled. Please bear in mind that until orders are given to Zulu SOE concerning our working together with reference to the material each of us should drop, proper coordination at this end is extremely hard to attain. It also seems possible that fields which they have not as yet been able to put into operation are being retained by Zulu.

Document 4-22

Radiotelephone Transmission No. 178, July 18, 1944

[On the eve of the July 20 attempt on Hitler's life, Dulles commented on the German position on the Eastern front and on an incident that illustrates Germany's precarious situation in Italy. General Donovan transmitted this message to President Roosevelt on July 21.]

Germany

A military critic, viewing the German situation in the East, remarks that, while it is very serious, it is not absolutely hopeless if dealt with in a purely military way and without regard to questions of prestige. A capable German military command might be able to pull the chestnuts out of the fire for a time; but if the decisions are left to Hitler, this critic views the situation as practically hopeless for the Germans and believes that the next two weeks will go far towards telling the story. If Hitler insists on maintaining forces in Finland, holding his army in the Baltic, this critic feels that there is no prospect of building up an effective German defense in the East, and, judging by Hitler's past experience, he assumes that Hitler will refuse to withdraw from any of the exposed positions to which his prestige has committed him, and that sound military practice will not prevail.

Here is a report as to possible developments in Germany, which is still in the field of speculation, but, I felt, worth passing on.

As soon as the enemy army reaches the German frontier, the German government will proclaim "a people's war for the defense of the Fatherland." The SA, which has been somewhat reactivated lately, will be entrusted with this people's war—Volkkrieg. German factory workers will be given arms to defend their factories, but at first arms will be distributed only to factories which are near the front line. In this way, the armed workers would constitute a second armed [force?] on the home front, next to the SS, which has had the monopoly of armed power at home up to the present time. My informant explains this somewhat strange prediction by stating that the purpose of this is to help counterbalance the armed force of the Wehrmacht once it has retreated and taken up a position on German soil. Apparently the SS realize that the Wehrmacht, under these conditions, might try to suppress the SS, and that the position of the latter would be stronger if there were, in addition to the Wehrmacht and the SS, a third armed power in the interior; in this way, the SS might be able to turn the workers against the Wehrmacht and play the role of a controlling force between the two. However, it is reported that this plot of the SS is already known to the workers and that something in the nature of a working arrangement between the Wehrmacht and the factory workers may be in preparation, and that numerous contacts have been made between groups of the Wehrmacht and [illegible] with reserve, as I doubt whether the SS would dare to arm workers to any extent at the present time. Further, there are not a very large number of male German workers of military age to arm.

Italy

On June 25 a bomb was thrown into a bar frequented by German soldiers in the city of Genoa. No one knows who threw the bomb, but one German soldier was killed outright, and five died of their wounds. The German soldiers, who were in relatively small numbers in Genoa, and who had feared a Partisan raid on the city, lost their heads and started shooting at random. A group of Polish soldiers with the German forces, thinking that the Germans were firing at them, fired back, and a panic spread through the city which reached such proportions that the general impression of a serious raid on the town was created. This first-hand report is indicative of the state of mind of the German troops in Genoa.

A report received from North Italy states that the Fascist Party is to disappear largely from public view, but that its members will continue to work as underground units in small squads of action, grouping trusted members of the Party organization. Substantial sums of money have already been distributed to finance these groups.

Document 4-23

Telegram 847-48 to London, July 21, 1944

[On July 20, 1944, Hitler survived an assassination attempt when a bomb exploded in his headquarters in East Prussia. The coup planned by certain German officers to accompany Hitler's death was quickly crushed by the Gestapo and other elements loyal to the Führer. Accurate accounts of what transpired did not reach Bern immediately. The following cryptic message was among the first from Germany.]

From 110. Today a reliable member of the Norwegian legation who is closely associated with us, received a strange phone call from a man using the password Leo Kreuz. The legation member has a German contact who uses the pseudonym Leo Kreuz. The following phrases were then dictated. The person spoke high German. "To the 3 nobles: the roads cross, Abraham likes to sing, Friedrich will come, not all men are married. To the 3 princes: silence is golden, the front remains the front, the colonel passes judgement, there is wine on the Rhine." He then made the request that this be broadcast with the following introduction on the afternoon of 23 July. "Ferdinand sends the following greeting to you." To our friend's query the following reply was given, "The entire world should be informed that everything continues. The proper men are still in their proper positions." The connection was then broken. We are sending this on to you to determine if it coincides with information possessed by Zulu or you. It is meaningless to our friend and to us.

Document 4-24

Radiotelephone Transmission No. 180, July 21, 1944

[This evening transmission was the first report by Dulles on the July 20th attempt on Hitler's life. General Donovan sent a copy to President Roosevelt on July 22.]

Germany

No very clear picture of the situation in Germany can yet be pieced together from the information reaching here. There is no information as yet from arrivals from

Germany, and the radio material is available to you as quickly as it is to us. The developments did not come as a great surprise, except to the extent that there were reasons to doubt whether any high officers of the German Army, who had remained in positions of power after successive purges, would have the courage to act. As reported to you, many high German officers realized, however, that the time was growing short within which the anti-Nazi forces in Germany could act to rid the country of Hitler and the Gestapo, if this was to be accomplished prior to Germany's collapse. These officers considered that Hitler's military conduct of the war was a catastrophe, and that the only hope of saving anything from the wreckage was to remove Hitler. These persons hoped that they could make some sort of a deal with the West, along the lines of the Italian pattern, and thus be in a better position at least to restrict the extent of Russian occupation of German territory. The evidence seems to indicate that possibly the Putsch was staged prematurely, probably because the action of the Gestapo forced the hand of those who were plotting to remove Hitler. Rundstedt's removal and then, more important still, the recent removal of von Falkenhausen in Belgium, indicate that the Gestapo was fearful of a military coup. Certain other persons who were probably to participate in the plot were also forced to run to cover before it took place. I do not believe the report circulating here that the story of the attempt on Hitler's life was fabricated or exaggerated in order to justify a thorough-going purge of the Army. If Hitler desired to make a purge, he would not wait for any such excuse. His statement, and those of Goering and Doenitz are hard to explain on any such theory. These statements would have too disturbing an effect on German morale to have been planted merely for the purpose of facilitating the arrest of certain generals. Further, we have had ample advance warning that a plot was in the wind to discredit rumors that it was merely a Gestapo concoction. In fact, I believe that what has just taken place in Germany represents the one and only major attempt during the past eleven years to overthrow the Hitler government. No Putsch in Germany is possible without strong military backing. The Gestapo are numerous, determined, and ruthless. The SS military formations in Germany could probably be counted on fully by Himmler. To meet these forces, the German generals opposing Hitler would need initially to secure the backing of several OKH divisions strategically located. Only if they could succeed in winning [illegible] and holding for a time certain strategic points could the revolt have any chance of success. As yet, we have no evidence that they have succeeded in this. If they had, it would have seemed likely that certain powerful radio stations would be in the hands of the revolters, and we would be getting news of developments. Apparently, certain Nazi stations are off the air. Whether this means they are being fought over, or whether there are other explanations, we do not know. Whatever may be the result of the putsch, the moral effect on Germany and on the Army will be very serious. I do not believe that the Army will for long accept and fight effectively under SS leadership. Of course, certain Nazi-minded generals, such as Rommel and Guderian, may be able to hold their troops for a time. I doubt whether von Kluge is an out-and-out Nazi, despite his apparent pledge of loyalty today. He certainly was not such some years ago. While it is too early to indulge in predictions, I think it is safe to say that even if, as seems to be the case, revolt is being or has been suppressed in a Gestapo purge of leading generals, the Army's morale will receive a severe shock from which, in its critical situation, it will be difficult for it to recover. There is no doubt that there is a real crisis in the High Command, with men like Zeitzler and Keitel both apparently involved, and this can hardly be hidden from the men at the front. Further, Army circles have always had great respect for Beck, and if he has been executed, as reported, this will be a great shock to the rank and file of the OKW officers. It is particularly significant that Hitler apparently found no outstanding general to address to the Army the same type of appeal which Goering made to the air force and Doenitz made to the navy, and that he was not able even to give the name of the general from the East Front who he stated in his last night's speech was to be second to Guderian, who replaces the diplomatically ill Zeitzler. Outside of the opposition group which was responsible for this Putsch, I do not believe that any other group exists in Germany which would have any chance of staging active armed opposition. If this attempt has failed, the Germans will probably have to wait for the complete military collapse of Germany to rid themselves of the Nazis, and the next group to attempt this might be the Communists, probably aided by disorganized returning German army and foreign workers and prisoners, if there is any lapse of time between the military collapse and the Allied occupation. Certainly what Hitler refers to as the Heimatheer is the only military organization now stationed in Germany which is powerful enough to stage an action against the SS forces, and if Himmler's command of the Heimatheer becomes effective, any possibility of revolt will be largely removed.

Document 4-25

Telegram 4199-4202, July 22, 1944

[In this report on the July 20 Hitler assassination attempt, Theta stands for General Heusinger, HM for Helmut von Moltke, and 670 for Eduard Waetjen.]

BREAKERS. Apparently Breakers are breaking. In all probability the movement is the one explained in my #4110 and earlier Breakers communications. It was planned that certain men in the inner circles, such as Theta, our 3432, would be at the meeting when the bomb went off because the only chance for planting the bomb was in conjunction with a conference attended by many of the chief military leaders. One of the members of the group was Stauffenberg who served as liaison between the older officers on active duty at General Headquarters and the younger group, formerly headed by HM, see our 2307. Stauffenberg, in addition, acted as councilor to Lester and C, referred to in my #4085, who in the future shall be designated as Leper. Luber was involved in all these proceedings and we have established close contact locally with our 670 who at the present time is the contact man here.

The outcome of the revolt at present rests with the Reserve Army "Heimatheer" and their willingness to follow Himmler as their chief or whether they will stick to their old commanders some of whom, as pointed out in my #4110, appear to be involved in the plot. Naturally, the blood purge will be unmerciful.

One of the disheartening facts seems to be that Breakers do not have adequate radio facilities at their command. However, it has come to our attention that a report from Reuters states that a message dispatched by the rebels from Frankfurt-am-Main this morning was interrupted.

However, a thorough perusal of the Goering-Hitler statements would apparently infer that the rebellion was not put down at once. If the opposition find it possible to maintain their stand in any region of Germany, we may possibly consider action along lines as indicated below: (1) Some word from the President. In this connection refer to my 4110–14 and my flash dated the 13th of this month. (2) Air raids on the Nazi stronghold in the region of Berchtesgaden. Although the immediate military effectiveness of such action would be unimportant, it is possible that the psychological reaction would be great. Naturally, any break in the communication channels between the region of Berchtesgaden and the rest of the country would be especially valuable. (3) Providing the rebellion gains any momentum, some announcement to the effect that any German town which sides with the opposition would not be attacked whereas Gestapo centers and Nazi strongholds would be bombed unsparingly. (4) Large-scale dissemination of pamphlets from the air.

Document 4-26

Telegram 4204, July 22, 1944

[Dulles assesses the events of July 20 based on the reaction of German diplomats in Bern.]

Up to 1 p.m. today the Nazi Legation had not had any news from the Foreign Office, not even the customary "sprach regelung." This is the Nazi term for instructions on how to lie. There are positive signs that if a revolt did get under way, several Nazi officials at this end would abandon the sinking ship.

Document 4-27

Radiotelephone Transmission No. 181, July 22, 1944

[In his evening telephone call, Dulles reports that the coup in Germany had failed and offered some initial suggestions for psychological warfare exploitation of the incident. General Donovan forwarded this message to President Roosevelt on July 24.]

Germany

Until some trustworthy persons arrive from Germany, we will not know the full story of what took place, but it seems clear now that any prospects of an armed military revolt growing out of the Putsch against Hitler have been crushed. I am inclined to believe that the Gestapo probably had a good deal of prior information about some of the persons involved, and were ready to strike and to strike hard. Himmler was probably glad to have an opportunity to do this before the retreating German armies were themselves on German soil, as it is far easier to deal with the Heimatheer than it would be to deal with the troops fresh from the defeats in the East, West, and South. But, in any event, a good deal of benefit to the Allied cause can result, as this attempt at revolt should help to undermine the will of the German Army to keep up the struggle. Obviously, an attempt is being made in Germany to play down the importance of those who were alleged to be in the plot, and therefore our tactics should be just the opposite. The personality of Beck gives us a good opportunity. He was a man of the highest military attainment, who enjoyed great respect from his colleagues, and who at the same time from pre-war days refused to play along with Hitler's wild program of military conquest. Zeitzler, too, is a figure who can be used, as no one believes the story of his illness. Keitel's position is still obscure, but I am inclined to doubt the story that he was implicated in the plot. Apparently Manstein, too, had nothing to do with it, as, according to excellent reports, he is undergoing a serious eye operation at Breslau. This attempt to overthrow Hitler was largely engineered by men who desired a western orientation of German policy, even though apparently they received no encouragement from the West, and acted on their own initiative entirely. The next attempt to overthrow the Hitler regime from the inside is likely to come from an eastern oriented group, possibly after a part of East Prussia is occupied and a German government à la Seydlitz is installed there. It is probable that the failure of Beck and his friends will still further increase the influence of Russia in Germany and somewhat decrease the influence of the West. Russia has throughout played a more realistic policy in dealing with the internal German situation than has either the United States or England, and it is possible that, from now on, the Seydlitz Committee will increase in importance and have a larger scope of action. This is a development we should not underestimate, particularly now that the western-oriented dissident group in Germany, in and outside of the army, has received a serious, if not a fatal setback.

I have a report here that, since about July 1, petrol has been so short in the Koblenz area that shipments transporting workingmen to distant factories have been largely cancelled, and the men concerned have often had to stay at home. This is believed to be the case in other nearby areas.

Austria
Here is a memorandum from some well-informed Austrians here, which answers certain questions which you have put. Eighty to eighty-five per cent of the Austrians are in favor of an independent, democratic Austria. Germany and the Germans are now very unpopular. There are daily causes of friction. The Moscow declaration is generally known, but comes in for some criticism because of its passage with regard to Austria's share of responsibility for the war. A new cause of grievance of the Austrians against the Germans results from the German occupation of South Tyrol, and there is a strong feeling that the South Tyrol should be joined to a Free Austria, as its population is still two-thirds German speaking and closely tied in sentimentally with the North Tyrol. The relations between the foreign workers and the Austrians are good, and foreign workers are receiving secret support in various acts of industrial sabotage, particularly faked illnesses, strikes, placing of time-bombs after bombardments, and various acts of railway sabotage. The oil production of Zittersdorf is again increasing and is now over one million tons a year. Since the heavy damage to the Austrian refineries, the oil is being taken for the most part to the Protectorate by pipe-line.

Document 4-28

Telegram 851-55 to London, July 23, 1944

[Dulles presents an interim after-action report on the failed July 20 attack on Hitler in a message to David Bruce, head of the OSS office in London. Clearly, Bruce and OSS London had not received the full benefit of Dulles's advance information on the impending coup.]

BREAKERS. From 110. Action: 105, London, with reference to your #809. Information: Jackpot, Washington.

1. The Breakers series of cables contains the background of the attempted assassination of Hitler. Some of these wires were sent to Washington only, but I take it for granted that Washington informed you of them. In addition, I am treating various aspects of this affair in my daily phone reports from Bern, which I recommend that Washington repeat to you as far as they believe you will be interested in them. In the future, every wire dealing with this matter will be duplicated to you.

2. The heart of the scheme was either to isolate or do away with the Fuehrer and his staff and gain control over the Heimatheer through Eta and Riesler. The latter were participating in the plot, with the support of Theta and Zeta at General Headquarters. Various key people in the former 659 group were giving their assistance. In case their attempt proved successful, Leper and Tucky were to take over control. (By 110: Leper is the same as Lester.) The Berlin situation was to be held by Bearcat. It is my opinion—but I am unable to prove it—that the Gestapo had been tipped

off in advance from the inside and acted with too much speed for the plotters when the attempt to kill Hitler with the bomb proved unsuccessful. Perhaps the courage of a number of plotters failed them at that time. (By 110 for 105: If you do not have all the foregoing code names, kindly arrange to secure them from Washington.)

3. There is no reliable information here regarding any developments in the situation. I think that the majority of the newspaper accounts originating here and at Stockholm are simply rumors. Since the people in the plot seemingly failed to control a radio station at any time, I am inclined to believe that the affair never reached the proportions of a grave military revolution. However, I think that the general position adopted by our radio and newspapers is right, for psychological factors, in emphasizing the affair. This is especially true with respect to stressing the eminence of the army leaders who were killed or removed, by the admissions of official Nazi sources.

4. It is likely that Luber was deeply involved in the plot. We will be able to learn what happened if Luber should be lucky enough to make his escape. I am in continuous contact with his associate, 670, but the latter does not possess any inside information. This is also the case with respect to the Nazi Legation here, even including General Horn, who has just come here to serve as Military Attaché.

5. I am very eager to find out if Zulu had any advance notice of the plot, perhaps via 800. I refer to this in connection with the official German claims that a foreign country had played a role in the matter. This raises the possibility, if Zulu is not made the object of attacks on this ground, that they may try to involve me because of my dealings with 670 and Luber. However, unless the persons seized make revelations or some other people prepared memoranda, no evidence should be in existence against me.

With reference to #1861 from Washington, please refer to our #4085. 512 is Luber.

Document 4-29

Telegram 859 to London, July 24, 1944

[Even at the height of excitement over the events of July 20, the regular flow of intelligence information from Bern on subjects such as bombing targets continued.]

The following information has been received from a person who reached here from Koblenz. We were favorably impressed with this individual. However, he is an untested source. He informs us that the anti-aircraft guns at the important munition factory of Concordia-Huette, a part of the Krupp works, are not manned on Sunday during the hours between 1600 and 1900 German time since the employees of the plant who operate these guns are off duty at that time. It is his suggestion that the plant be bombed then. The plant is located on the right bank of the Rhine River 7 kilometers north of Koblenz near Bendorf.

Document 4-30

Telegram 860-61 to London, July 24, 1944

[This message discusses the question of sharing Breakers cables and information with the British.]

BREAKERS. For Jackpot and 105 in reference to your #817-19.

1. Provided Washington approves, I have no reason to oppose your handling of Breakers as suggested.

2. I originally preferred not to have this information go to Zulu, because of his attitude as described in our #181 and #545. Realize that Broadway (see your #198) rather changed their position but 512 endeavored to establish contact with Zulu through us as soon as the Breakers movement started to grow. London rejected this when 521 offered it to them, although I made it obvious that I was eager to have their assistance in deciding upon such a tenuous case.

3. I would be grateful for any particulars on the developments resulting from relationship with 670. This may have been through our 476 who had a contact like this before we entered the war.

4. Schacht's arrest as reported appears to be quite possible, since he and Luber were great friends. On the other hand, Neurath was not at all popular with Breakers, so that if he really was arrested, it was not because he was concerned directly but because of the general purge.

Document 4-31

Telegram 4214-19, July 24, 1944 (extracts)

[This message indicates that Dulles had access to certain diplomatic correspondence of Germany's Hungarian satellite government.]

I have secured duplicates of certain Hungarian diplomatic communications which apparently were disseminated by the Foreign Office for their legations. This information was supplied by 684 who still maintains a line into his old shop. This source should be thoroughly safeguarded. . . . Dated the 24th of last month, from the Consul General at Belgrad to the Foreign Office: Mihailovich's forces are still working in conjunction with Nedich and the Nazis against the partisans but are careful to avoid open collaboration which might compromise their position with the English. Negotiations are underway between Nedich and Mihailovich. The latter is being represented by Pavle Djursic, head of the Montenegrin nationalists, who is endeavoring to obtain a united Serbian front against Tito in Montenegro. Mihailovich is seeking revenge against his personal adversaries within the Nedich group. . . . Dated the 22nd of last month, from the Consul at Prague to the Foreign Office: the secret ambitions of the Czechs have been answered by the landings in Normandy and they anticipate vital developments as a result. Despite this feeling, the Czechs continue to bow to the Nazis and maintain their efforts to enlarge Germany's war potential. Regardless of propaganda spread by the English or the statements of Czech émigrés, the population on the home front are unwilling to take any chances unless the war situation improves to the extent that such dangers are minimized. . . . Dated the 27th of last month, from the Legation in Venice to the Foreign Office: the Nazis look upon the Italian theater as of secondary importance and Florence will not be defended. However, they do intend to hold the Rimini-Spezia line. . . .

Document 4-32

Radiotelephone Transmission No. 182, July 24, 1944

[This message provides new information on the July 20 attempt on Hitler's life, and Dulles's recommendations for psychological warfare based on opportunities presented by that occurrence. General Donovan forwarded it to President Roosevelt on July 24.]

Germany

The Berlin correspondent of the *Neue Zuercher Zeitung* today gives the first detailed report on last week's attempted anti-Nazi revolt. Obviously, the report had to be carefully worded on account of German regulations. It contains some interesting hints with regard to the internal situation in Germany. The report states that photographs appearing in the German press of Hitler bidding farewell to Mussolini, after his visit to headquarters, may indicate that Hitler's right hand has been wounded, since he is giving Mussolini the left hand. Likewise, only the left side of Hitler's face is shown, giving rise to the supposition that possibly the right side of the face is wounded. According to the same report, even the name of General Beck as a participant in the plot has been altogether withheld from the German public and has only been given to the foreign press; nor have the Germans been informed as to the names of any other prominent men involved. (End of the comment from the *Neue Zuercher.*)

It appears that only when Hitler felt that he had coped with the immediate crisis, was Goebbels allowed to start in with his official propaganda, which is doing its utmost to play down the importance and scope of the attempted action by emphasizing again and again that only a very small group of retired reactionary officers were responsible for the plot. It seems possible that Goebbels was not in accord with the somewhat hysterical and blundering handling of the propaganda phase of the matter by Hitler, Goering, and Doenitz in their original speeches. Actually, every indication points to the fact that a considerable number of outstanding German military and civilian leaders were behind the attempted revolution. The knowledge of this fact can have a far-reaching effect on German morale at home and at the front, and may well hasten the end of the war. Never during the course of this war has the Allied propaganda had such an opportunity to strike at the heart of the Nazi war effort. In answer to the lies of the official German propaganda, it should be emphasized to the German people 1) that the attempted revolution was the first major attempt to overthrow the Hitler regime since its inception; 2) that a large number of leading generals and members of the General Staff, as well as many younger officers, were apparently back of the attempted plot; 3) that it is more than likely that the Chief of Staff of the German Army, Zeitzler, and others of this rank were involved because they were of the opinion that it was useless to continue the war and to sacrifice more German youth for a hopeless cause; 4) that a group of prominent civilian leaders were ready to take over the government after the military government had cleaned out the Nazis; 5) that the new government had intended to bring peace to the German people as quickly as possible; 6) that now the time had come for every German to do his share to overthrow the Nazis, to end the war, and to save for Germany whatever can be saved.

A special broadcast might well be addressed to German soldiers and workers giving directions how each one of them could contribute to bring about peace by disobeying orders, staying away from work, returning home to their families, etc. So far, Russian propaganda has been particularly astute in making use of this opportunity. In this connection, the recent appeals of the committee, Freies Deutschland, to the German people, especially to the German soldiers and workers are outstanding examples. Up to now, we have had nothing effective to offer. If this situation continues, the result may be that the Germans in their plight will turn increasingly to Russia, or to the committee Freies Deutschland, for leadership. This development is accentuated by the fact that Russian troops will probably be the first to reach German territory, thus opening up the possibility of establishing the first center for anti-Nazi activities upon German soil, possibly under the auspices of the Freies Deutschland Committee.

I have just heard tonight from a good source that Berger, Hitler's co-worker, who was the only one who was immediately killed at the time of the attack on Hitler, was Hitler's double. Possibly Stauffenberg, who probably did not know Hitler well, made a mistake.

General Guderian has not always been in Hitler's favor. In December, 1941, he was ordered to make a tank attack at Tula, near Moscow. He argued against it on account of the cold. The Fuehrer ordered him to proceed. He did, and in a few days, reported back to Hitler that all his tanks were frozen and what should he do next. Hitler did not show any sense of humor, and Guderian was out of a job for more than a year.

Here is what purports to be a statement from an anti-Nazi Prussian official, which just came to me: wounded soldiers on leave from the front state that morale in the East is about ready for collapse. The fighting morale has been so weakened that bloody altercations have taken place at different sectors of the front. For this reason, special commandos, called UK (Unterdrueckungs Kommando) have been formed. These flying police forces are ordered into action whenever the Nazi faithful troops are endangered by the depressed soldiers. The depressed troops are then transferred to new Wehrmacht units. The report continues that the higher Nazi bosses are already moving with their families to sparsely populated districts along the Austrian frontier. The opposition believes that many Nazis flee to Spain when worse comes to worst. Diplomatic baggage is being sent to Spain every day. So far, diplomats are taking large packing cases, and countless valuables have already been shipped from the Reich to that country. In South Germany, the population has been ordered not to have any conversations with soldiers on leave from the front, as their pessimistic stories are not to be believed. The Gestapo say that they tell things from sheer nervousness which are detrimental to the unity of the people.

Document 4-33

Telegram 4222-24, July 25, 1944

[Dulles reports that the Gestapo is now aware that members of the Abwehr had been involved in the plot of July 20.]

BREAKERS. 1. Following is with reference to the last sentence of London-Washington #855, the first sentence of your #1857 and the last sentence of your #1861. I prefer to postpone giving additional particulars. (For reasons of security I am giving certain numbered persons new names. Although I am aware that this creates confusion, the situation is such that I wish to exercise the utmost discretion.) Subject has passed every test and I am confident of his reliability.

2. The Gestapo is now certain that 659 organization members were employed in the Breakers matter and this will speed liquidation and assimilation with SD. We have received trustworthy information to the effect that not long ago Schellenberg furnished the Chief of Swiss SI, Masson, with the names of the entire membership of 659 in Switzerland with the idea of having them expelled. However, we think it unlikely the Swiss will take any action despite the fact that Masson plays ball with Schellenberg.

3. It is our understanding that Lunter was seized before the coup. This man worked in close conjunction with Leper and was aware of the Breakers plans. Waner, another member of the Breakers group who was associated with the 659 organization, received advance information of his impending arrest and disappeared from the scene.

4. On looking back over certain of my notes, I realize that before the putsch my Breakers associates had advised me concerning Stauffenberg as I indicated in my #4199 but at that time we did not realize the part he would play.

Document 4-34

Telegram 4229-32, July 25, 1944

[After the Normandy invasion, the leaders of Vichy France fell into a state of desperation. Further, the grip of Nazi Germany on this most subservient of satellites began to weaken.]

The following intelligence was brought by Paul Morand, the newly arrived Vichy ambassador. It was relayed on to us by source 472-K-1.

1. Bonnard, Deat and Bichelonne together composed a letter to Hitler stating that French collaboration on the current basis was finished, and that the only line possible to France would be a declaration of war on the British and Americans. This letter was written without the knowledge of either Petain or Laval. Laval heard of the letter through the Nazis, and summoned a council of the ministers. Deat refused to attend the meeting, at which Laval fiercely attacked both Bonnard and Bichelonne. (The following from 110: I voiced my amazement at Bichelonne's stand, to which 472 replied that he had learned that over the past 2 or 3 months Bichelonne has virtually gone wild, perhaps because he is numbered among the first 10 for execution by the patriots.)

2. Recently, Petain summoned all the neutral and Vatican diplomats and told them that if news should reach them that he was gone from Vichy, they could assume he had not left of his own volition and that he was being held prisoner. Renthefincke attempted to get an audience with Petain, when he heard of the foregoing, to lodge a protest. Petain denied him an audience stating that he, Petain, was not at Renthefincke's disposition, but rather the latter was at his disposal.

3. Reynaud, Blum and Mandel were returned to France by the Nazis. Laval was informed that they were being handed over to his custody for execution should Algiers kill any more collaborationists. It is reported that Laval told Renthefincke, who delivered this message, that he would ignore his visit. Laval further stated that if he had any message for Algiers he should deliver it through Spanish diplomatic channels. To all appearances Laval would not accept the custody of the 3 men and the Nazis took them away. During one of their transfers in France, the Milice attacked Mandel's car and he was killed. Nothing is known of the whereabouts of Blum and Reynaud.

Document 4-35

Telegram 866-67 to London, July 26, 1944

[This message contains Dulles's recommendation that the Russians not be supplied with a full account of the Breakers movement and his relationship to it. Following the events of July 20, however, OSS London was brought into the circle of knowledge on Breakers, and soon thereafter British intelligence in London. An MI-5 officer, Kim Philby, the Soviet agent, received access to the Breakers cables and presumably was able to pass on some of what he learned to Moscow.]

Breakers. I would like to point out to you that the Breakers connection was established in order to secure intelligence and for more than a year this contact has proven itself to be a real value to us. At all times they were entirely on their own and at no time did they receive any encouragement or political communications. I believe that by now communicating with R[ussia], it would needlessly single this connection out from other contacts of a like nature which are employed for intelligence purposes, and in addition would give too much importance to a connection which at this time may be broken. However, the decision naturally, rests entirely with you and Washington. It is my opinion that certain of the Breakers personnel are still in hiding, and to give out names at this time to R may very well place in jeopardy those people who may still be in vulnerable positions.

The Berchtesgaden thought was mentioned in the event the movement might get started. At this time it is very likely that the idea is academic. I do not now fear the development which I mentioned in my cable #851-5, paragraph 5, in view of the passage of time and the Nazi tendency to minimize the event.

Document 4-36

Telegram 4233-36, July 26, 1944 (extract)

[This message contains a report of German plans for strategic withdrawals in Italy and southern France.]

The following is a portion of a wire sent by 472 K-1 and K-2 to Algiers on the 24th of this month. (The 1st to 4th items, inclusive, were obtained from a Swiss source.)

July 7th. (1). A Reich defense conference held on July 7th came to the conclusion that the Nazi forces should be regrouped and that the front should be shortened in part. This should be done, first, in Italy. The army there should retreat to the Alps; however, the Allied forces should be held off for the greatest period possible. Second, arrangements should be made at once to withdraw from southern France. It is stated that the Fuehrer opposed this program for some time but ultimately was forced to consent. . . .

Document 4-37

Telegram 4247, July 26, 1944

[When General Donovan expressed interest in an intensification of support for the resistance in northern Italy, Dulles expressed hearty agreement. Number 809 is Donald Jones, OSS representative in Lugano.]

To 109. In reference to your 1862. I am in agreement with you that this is the time to strike hard in this region. As often as I can, I get over to the Lugano area since the center for such action is there. 809 is now doing very good work in that region. Your above mentioned cable came at a very opportune time and I am very grateful for it. Certain key personnel of CNL are coming south [north?] soon and your message will be very encouraging to them.

Document 4-38

Telegram 4270-72, July 28, 1944

[In the aftermath of the July 20 putsch attempt, Dulles remained concerned about the possibility of separate peace on the Eastern Front through the auspices of captured German generals who had been co-opted by the Soviet Union.]

Cutout secured the following information from a member of the Freies Deutschland group here who may reflect the opinions of the Moscow Committee. I do not feel that too much reliance should be put on this report as it may be not as much fact as speculation, but it may prove of value in showing the trend in the local Freies Deutschland. The leader of the real German military opposition to Hitler is in the Pskov region on the Russian front, and one of the leaders is General Busch. (Note: this was composed before rumors of latter's "suicide.") The Generals in the east are only holding off until there is another Stalingrad so that Hitler's military weakness will be proved beyond doubt. Nine months ago the eastern opposition generals and those in the west who were behind the uprising on the 20th of this month ceased all efforts for negotiation. The leaders in the east are following the Tauroggen policy and they will try to bring about a peace with the USSR after German defeat is a certainty, with the possibility that an armistice will be signed at Tauroggen. The junior officers are picking out those known to be anti-Nazis who favor socialistic ideals and the eastern generals are organizing "Vertrauensraete" among the troops. The principal reason for this is to insure against anarchy when the collapse occurs.

Document 4-39

Telegram 844-50 to Algiers, July 29, 1944 (extract)

[Although repeatedly frustrated by British obstructionism and American hesitancy, Dulles was tireless in his efforts to activate U.S. special operations in support of Italian partisans. Gadfly is B. Homer Hall, formerly of the OSS Swiss Desk in SI in Washington, and then head of the same function in Algiers and later Caserta.]

From 110. To Gadfly, Caserta, or to whom it may concern.

1. We have not received any word from you for almost a fortnight as to whether

any of Chris, Como or other drops can be activated, and a crisis is approaching in the matter of the aid we may be able to furnish Italian Partisan movements. . . .

3. We have built up through the Chris service, a constant, and to date, safe, communication with the Val d'Aosta area, in direct contact with the Partisans in this region. Urge that you dispatch at once to Dondena field an operator and a transmitter. . . .

4. I am aware that Dondena field was signalled to Brindisi, but have been told that over the past 10 months Zulu has made only 1 little parachutage and this was over 4 weeks ago. According to a reliable source this area has 3,000 armed men and 6,000 unarmed reservists, and that this has been especially developed via our Chris service. There is no reason why this whole region should be monopolized in theory, but not activated, by Zulu. . . .

6. Statement was made by the CNL representatives in a written document given to the chief of the Chris service that Franchi, alias Sonia, a British agent, told them that all parachutage must be asked for through his organization. If not, these requests would not be activated. This has set up the idea in Turin region that Zulu has a monopoly. Kindly let us know if this is the case and we will not raise any false hope that there will be U.S. assistance.

7. Carrying out the aforementioned program will be taken as a test of whether or not we will be able to conduct operations in this region. This is vital if we are to build up our operations at this end and keep the Chris organization intact.

8. If possible, urge additional support for the Val d'Aosta groups, parachutage at Nivolet field, Valsavaranche. . . .

9. Would very much like to receive prompt opinion as to whether foregoing action can be taken and advise me what the approximate date would be. In addition to sending via BBC, I would probably be able to send signal by messenger. I believe the operation to be of real importance.

Document 4-40

Telegram 892-93 to London, July 30, 1944

[This message provides explicit evidence of difficulties between Dulles and certain British representatives in Switzerland.]

For 105 and Tertius. In reference to Tertius' #840. I have made a thorough investigation and think you can disregard Zulu's information about Niveau. Am not able to discover locally any valid basis for censure, and experience will iron out any defects which exist. In my opinion he made an understandable mistake by getting in touch with Zulu at this end and perhaps is disposed to overlook the obstacles and dangers which a more experienced man would discern. These are mistakes, however, which time will cure. The foregoing is strongly seconded by 520 who saw Niveau.

The following is strictly confidential: Am sorry to state that the Bern Zulu-SOE Chief's general attitude is to try to monopolize relations with resistance, and in the absence of confirmation, criticisms from this source about U.S. contacts with both Italy and France, should be overlooked.

Document 4-41

Telegram 4300-4303, July 30, 1944

[On July 29, Dulles reported receiving a letter written by former Hungarian Prime Minister Kallay, then in hiding but unable to leave the country. It presented a picture of terror and near chaos with 50 percent of the "upper classes" in jail and revolution brewing. Kallay emphasized the threat of the Soviet Union and communism to Hungary, favored continuation of the Horthy government for the time being, and raised the possibility of the eventual restoration of the Hapsburg Monarchy and confederation in central Europe.]

To Jackpot and 105. Our cable #4286-93 is a short resume of a 6,000 word letter 655 succeeded in smuggling out to 684, who in turn handed it over to 477. This communication was meant for certain dissident ministers, especially Wodianer, Ambro and 684. The author of this letter asserts that he is still Premier and that his ministers abroad remain as Hungary's representatives and ought to demand recognition, work in [illegible], and take care of their funds. He offers the suggestion that Apor is situated in the best spot for action and it is more desirable that he conduct the central negotiation. The writer is aware that Ullein-Revicsky will follow his own dictates. He advises that perhaps the Ministers could publicly denounce the government's betrayal and show that the root of the trouble is the terror of Bolshevism. He says all the guilt ought to be placed on the Nazis. Horthy ought to remain but merely to salvage what is possible to rescue as he comprehends the situation but refuses to assault Germany from behind. In addition, the author of this communication cautions the Ministers against permitting Benes to have everything as he wants it, that it is possible to accomplish worthwhile measures, and that they ought not to allow themselves to serve merely as a hindrance as Benes has. The writer counsels against partisan operations and works of sabotage until the country has been awakened to the true situation and then, he says, all will work out for the best. According to this person, the population of Hungary is still deluding itself that the Nazis will be victorious in spite of the situation at present. This he attributes to Imredy's attitude and the propaganda disseminated by the British.

At the end of his letter, the writer stated that he was forced to write it in 2 hours and he requested 684 to edit it prior to forwarding it and to see that the communication was safeguarded in order to prevent any embarrassment to his hosts, as he had assured them his letter would not give rise to any political issues.

Following is from 110 for 105 and Jackpot: the letter leaves the impression that the writer is a desperate and worried individual and that he wrote the letter very quickly, as it is poorly composed and contains much repetition. Probably it is desirable that this information not be disseminated to Zulu, and we suggest much discretion in its handling in order to safeguard the source.

Document 4-42

Telegram 4305-7, August 1, 1944

[This message from Dulles to Donovan concerns the security of Breakers material, and particularly with the question of making it available to the Russians.]

110 to 109. 105 only, London. . . . The above messages would seem to indicate that this business has been fully and competently settled. I am in complete accord with the plan and policy that you outline, and also agree that we shall be forced to allow the Germans to fight it out within the country with no help from us.

I am, however, sorry to say that I have neither seen nor heard anything which might indicate that Russia will follow the same procedure, and I believe that the second item in my flash of the 29th of last month and my #4270 point the course which future developments will take.

In the meantime, we should at least keep away from any action which might unduly jeopardize any who might still take part in anti-Nazi action of Western oriented tendency, even if we do not identify ourselves with them in any way.

I was for this reason stunned by the broadcast over the BBC on the night of the 29th, in which they abused Bearcat and pictured him as a vicious anti-Semite, and identified him as being among the undisclosed leaders in the plot against Hitler. I am not in a position to apologize for Bearcat, and it may turn out later on that we shall want to investigate his history, but it still seems poor propaganda to give the participants in the plot a bad name and very unwise to reveal names until they are broadcast by German sources. I also think that unless Bearcat has already been taken, he may be sheltering those who got away. I am certain that Luber felt that the help Bearcat furnished was one of the essential parts of the Breakers action. I would like to know where the BBC got this information and what reason they could have had for using it in the way they did.

Document 4-43

Telegram 4314-18, August 2, 1944 (extract)

[Dulles moved forward quickly on augmented funding for the Italian resistance, pursuant to Donovan's approval.]

To 109. My CNL Italian friends were greatly encouraged by your authorization, but the transportation of large sums of money from here is a hard task for the time being, by reason of local market conditions, with the partial drying up of buying possibilities, and also because of unexpected complications in crossing the border.

Today Zulu and I had a talk with the financial representative of CNL. This representative thinks that he can get substantial amounts of lire from commercial houses and large banks in North Italy, on the condition that a guarantee is given that when North Italy is liberated the lire will be repaid. . . .

Document 4-44

Telegram 4348-49, August 4, 1944

[OSS Bern received new reports of Bulgaria's drift away from Nazi Germany.]

Reports outlining the policy of the Bulgarian Government are being sent to Kiss for the first time since Minister here. These reports gave evidence that the Bulgarian Government felt that they could continue their relations with Turkey even though Turkey severed relations with Germany.

Their policy is to do as much as they can to fulfill Russia's demands and yet to maintain their relations with Germany. Bulgaria has been granted certain concessions by Germany such as the withdrawal of the Nazi naval units from Bourgas and Varna. These forces are now being concentrated in Constanta. Kiss feels that he may soon be asked to contact the Anglo-Saxons by his government.

Document 4-45

Telegram 4332-44, August 5, 1944 (extracts)

[Dulles continued to cooperate with the Lorraine organization in its struggle to prevent either General de Gaulle or the communists from arbitrarily displacing the vestiges of the Third Republic in France.]

LORRAINE. 802 and the Lorraine organization have sent 850 here from Paris to give us a report on the situation within France. He has just arrived and we are making arrangements with him to obtain current information from the numerous sources he is able to tap, as well as those which are available to 802. Their attitude, as reported by 850, is condensed into the summary which appears below: Varying anti-Nazi and anti-Vichy French viewpoints are represented in the Lorraine organization. . . . It is claimed that the Lorraine group's executive committee (designated hereafter as Acropole) represents not just members of the Chamber of Deputies and the Senate, but also represents the local urban and departmental elected chambers. These latter bodies have generally retained the trust of the population. . . .

Our friends stress their sympathy with the U.S. policy of refusing to grant recognition to any regime which has not been selected by the people of France. Nevertheless, they believe that, if all previously elected officials are dropped and others arbitrarily chosen, which is what General de Gaulle's delegates in France claim will take place, then it will be impossible for the French people to freely give expression to their will, since men so appointed would have control over the election results. . . .

850 feels certain the excessive criticism of the Third Republic by the Reds is, in effect, directed toward the destruction of all potential opponents. . . .

850 is in intimate contact with Alpha (see our #3696), with General de Gaulle's delegate in the occupied areas of France, and with the Committee of National Resistance which includes a representative of the Lorraine executive committee. He has talked over these matters with them in all frankness. Nevertheless, he is certain that the Reds exert a preponderant influence in the Committee of National Resistance and furthermore that even Alpha has been shuttled into a position from which he is unable to acquaint General de Gaulle with the real situation. Thus the latter in all likelihood knows nothing of the degree in which popular representation has been superseded by the Reds, taking their orders from an unidentified source.

The French nation, however, is not Communistically inclined, as the Reds well know. Therefore they are out to grab the controls at the very beginning and have received a strong boost from their success with the Committee of National Resistance. . . .

Document 4-46

Telegram 4361, August 5, 1944

[OSS Bern reports on the aftershocks of July 20 in Germany.]

BREAKERS. It would seem that the net is being pulled tighter around the Breakers group, in view of the information that the Nazis have posted a reward for Arthur Nebe following a like report on Goerdeler. We know a good deal about Nebe. He is an old Gestapo officer and Luber had been in touch with him for more than 10 years. Nebe was a clever but rather routine official to whom the methods of the Gestapo had sometimes been shocking. This accusation that he was involved in the Hitler plot would seem to prove that some elements of the Gestapo had a hand in the scheme.

Document 4-47

Telegram 896-99 to Algiers, August 7, 1944 (extracts)

[This message concerns penetration of Austria and the Austrian resistance.]

REDBIRD. From 110 to Chapin and Joyce, Bari. 1. We are sorry that especially since the downfall of Redbird our lines to Austria have been so unsatisfactory. We have fine passage here over the border to Vorarlberg but this latter region is hopelessly distant from the active center of Austria and only a scant number of persons use this route. In view of this, we feel that your plans for penetration are right. . . .

4. We have found through our dealings in Austria that, with the exception of Redbird, the possible opposition forces are too weak-kneed to take chances on contact with foreign elements and would rather sweat it out than hazard their lives to expedite an end which they feel at present is merely a matter of time. Furthermore, the Moscow Declaration failed to bring forth any hosannas since there has been nothing else forthcoming of a more concrete nature regarding Austria's future. In addition there exists an attitude among some of the left wing crowd and among some of the Socialists to countenance a merger with a big Socialist or leftish Germany rather than to remain an isolated independent government. These are all contributing factors which sap the vitality of any activist Austrian movement and this is so in spite of the fact that the country has an inbred hatred of the Nazis and of Prussia.

5. We shall cooperate in all possible ways and we shall attempt to establish possible channels especially since at this time you will possess facilities, previously lacking to us, by which you can develop these potential lines to your advantage. . . .

Document 4-48

Telegram 4382-83, August 7, 1944

[In this cable to General Donovan, Dulles discusses the clandestine purchase of arms in Switzerland for resistance forces.]

110 for 109. Our problem is not quite covered by your cable #1915. Every once in a while, I buy Black material which may be obtained in this manner, and no authorization from anyone is needed. But such sources are restricted and on the whole leave much to be desired. We now have the chance to obtain a number of modern arms by completely legitimate means, ostensibly for storing here but actually we intend to use them chiefly in French and Italian maquis, especially to arm escapees and internees who have come back, which we are shipping to Valdaosta and Valdossola. There is nothing illegal about their coming back, and giving them arms is practicable. 520 can legitimately and openly buy a number of arms, after which, with his assistance, I can get them out. [We need] to have the authorization of the War Department for the buying operation. Once this is obtained, we will be able to obtain a good quantity of arms. Furthermore, in order to supplement the plan in your cable #1899, arms would be kept in reserve.

Document 4-49

Telegram 935-37 to London, August 8, 1944

[Dulles once more addresses matters of psychological warfare against Germany.]

BREAKERS.

1. Would appreciate your telling General McClure and PWD that I shall be delighted to give any assistance I can. I recommend that the rift between the Schutzstaffel and the Army be widened as an effective propaganda line. Himmler and the Gestapo took advantage of the Putsch to finish off the job, begun years before, of destroying the power of the Reichswehr and making the Schutzstaffel supreme. This began prior to the war, when the Gestapo framed Generals Fritsch and Blomberg and later on managed to dispose of every military chief who did not think along the prescribed lines. If I were to make a prediction, I would say that the next Chief of Staff will in all likelihood be SS General (so-called) Sepp Dietrich. The latest signs of this trend are the decree against the Army salute and Himmler's appointment of the domestic army. One objective of the Schutzstaffel is to get the Army entirely under its thumb when the latter comes home, so that in the final death throes the SS will have an army which, if need be, it will be able to turn against the German population itself. Reports which we have received here show that the rift between the Schutzstaffel and the Army is getting to be more and more threatening and that we should be able to help demoralize the German resistance by emphasizing this rift. We refer you to our Washington flash last night.

2. We have evidence that the Nazis are also locking up generals suspected of favoring the eastern and Seydlitz policy, though the Putsch was conceived by generals favoring peace in the west.

3. If possible, would you let me have the source of the UEC (sic) report about the reward posted for Arthur Nebe, in which connection see my cable #4361. Perhaps this is a clue to what happened to some of the people in Breakers.

Document 4-50

Telegram 4394-95, August 9, 1944

[Dulles reports that the German army attempted to seize power in Paris at the time of the July 20 coup attempt.]

Report received by 472-K-1 from a French source he considers excellent states that the German Army took measures toward assuming power in Paris simultaneous with the attempt by the Wehrmacht against Hitler, and the proposed assumption of power in the German capital. Informant said he observed events which took place at a Gestapo headquarters on the Avenue Du Bois and claims that about 30 soldiers seized Gestapo members to take them to Fresnes. Gestapo Chief Knochen and his aide were seized on the Rue des Saussaies. They were attacked, bound and taken to Fresnes. An SS division on its way to Normandy was sent instead to Paris to reestablish order. General von Stuelpnagel attempted suicide; the bullet cut the optic nerve and blinded him but failed to kill him.

Document 4-51

Telegram 4396-4400, August 9, 1944

[With the liberation of France and Italy well under way, General Donovan intensified OSS concentration on the penetration of the German homeland. Dulles responded by setting forth his estimate of opportunities as viewed from Bern.]

110 to 109.

1. Your cable #1899-1905 was much appreciated, and its great significance is well understood here. We shall strive to do twice as well in the future, for we are not content with the work we have done to date in this field, both in Austria and in Germany.

2. We wish to put a number of problems before you, not with any intention of letting them hold us up but only because we would like to know whether you can give us some assistance on them.

A. Personnel. The few people we have here are driven to and beyond the limit of their capacities and we shall be laboring under a heavy handicap until we are able to get some more into the country legally to occupy posts at Schaffhausen and Bale. Should the Italian or French borders remain closed for some time yet, do you suppose you could drop them by parachute, after which we could get them over to Campione, whence they might be able to make legal application for a visa and thus enter the country legitimately. Anyone who has not entered the country legally, that is, with a Swiss visa, is not given diplomatic protection or allowed to travel freely.

B. It is far from easy to beat the border between Switzerland and Germany and Austria. Although the Swiss are not particularly concerned about what goes on across the French and Italian borders, so long as these are carried out with a certain amount of discretion, they are extremely energetic in seeing that nothing like this takes place on the German border. You must keep in mind the fact that the Swiss have mobilized a good part of their army and that one of the few things for this to do is to keep watch over the border, which they do with great effectiveness. Another problem is the topographic one, as the Rhine forms the border with Germany except at Schaffhausen and Bale, while a close watch is kept over the Voralberg window, which leads to comparatively unproductive territory anyway. All in all, therefore, we have a very grave problem in maintaining secret liaison with Germany and effecting secret passage. The Swiss are anxious to avoid border incidents with the Reich and will go to any lengths to prevent them.

C. Switzerland is most incorruptible neutral nation in existence, and we must exercise the greatest tact in getting anything done here. The Swiss counter-espionage is extremely wide awake and any mistake we made would eliminate the section of our organization which was involved—a serious matter with the absurdly small staff we possess.

D. The Anglo-U.S. plans for Germany, or rather the lack of them, do not give rise to any powerful feeling on the part of the population to lend us assistance in our activities. The people of the Reich wish passively that the war would come to an end but much stronger than this is the individual will to protect themselves and sail before the wind. Because of this, not many have any desire to incur last minute risks by giving us assistance. There was a possibility that Breakers would pay dividends, but this is probably no longer the case. The most efficiently organized body for work is now the Communist group. We might be able to do some work among the syndicalists and labor unions, and I am handling this matter independently, as well as the problem of foreign workers and prison camps.

3. I consider that Slovenia and northern Italy are now the most likely areas for the penetration of Austria, while Alsace and eastern France, together with the Low Countries, afford the best entries to Germany. (More to come.)

Document 4-52

Telegram 4401-6, August 9, 1944

[This message is the second part of Dulles's exposition on possibilities for the penetration of Germany, prepared in response to General Donovan. "Gerplan" connotes messages dealing with Donovan's plans for Germany.]

GERPLAN. This is a continuation of our #4396-4400 (IN-16744). The rather hasty East-North movement of the Nazi units in Italy and France ought to add to the opportunities of setting up secret bases there. In the meantime, we would set up additional bases from here, in Alsace especially. . . .

4. We are driving SI to its limit. On the whole, even if the agents dispatched to Austria and Germany are thoroughly trained, unless they have available contacts established in strategic locations or have technical information at their disposal in the field of their specialty, they are of small use. At the present time we are eliminating generalities and most of the information collected by run-of-the-mill agents. We are trying to establish a German SI by direct means as well as by means of experienced Alsatian and French workers.

5. SO matters: (a). Because of the scarcity of men and equipment and the extreme trouble in transporting men back and forth, it is very hard to conduct raids from here. In addition there is an urgent need for Nazi documents. Checking the Rheinfelden project now at the instigation of Algiers in their #532-4. Would it be possible for you to furnish explosives and some operating personnel by parachute provided

we could plan the project and secure some personnel? (b). In reference to London #829: Some of 328's associates in the Syndicalist field are available in London ready to be dropped and then sent on to associates already in Germany through Bern. This is a constructive plan and we are trying to work on it with 328. (c). 500 and his associates ought to develop some contacts and we are endeavoring to get them started.

6. The Laborer and Prisoner situation: Optimistic outlook here. A separate report will be submitted by 284 in Geneva who is in contact with a resistance member for their work with PW. Whenever this develops, however, the Russians will gain the most.

7. I have already made up a complete list of possible German resistance leaders in Germany and here. The Communist group will probably take the next step, as a result of the failure of Breakers, although the Socialist groups and non-communist leaders may take some kind of action. However, you must appreciate the complete lack of coordinated resistance activity.

8. In reference to your mention of Zulu. Unfortunately, even collaboration has become extremely difficult as a result of the seemingly jealous attitude exhibited by Zulu-SOE and their efforts to monopolize the show. They have gone in for a lot of undercutting in French and Italian spheres. This is not true of SI activities or of our relations with 521 or PWE.

9. Should groups be sent into the Reich, we recommend that every one of them be given definite SO objectives, or, if they stay, prepared liaison to receive, hide, and assist them. You should not put your faith in any general public desire to help, except perhaps in some sections of Austria.

10. We are not too sure of what you mean by "stay-behind" agents. Could you elucidate?

11. We are now attempting to activate 2 special Maquis schemes in Italy, one in Valdaosta and the other in Valdosolia. The former is designed especially to help complete block between France and Italy. This is a field in which we can really do something. I know that Algiers is doing the best they can. However, after a flood of cables from us and some signs of interest, we are unable to obtain any action, such as transmitters, munitions, liaison agents, parachuting, and so on. Would like your assistance.

Document 4-53

Telegram 4111-15, August 9, 1944

[Dulles solicits Donovan's support for particular special operations.]

GERPLAN. From 110 to 109. With reference to my #4396-4400 and subsequent messages, we advise that all wires relating to your general plan be labelled with the code designation Gerplan in order to facilitate the handling of these communications.

284 reports as follows concerning his discussions with Grainville, who represents the French resistance "Movement National des Prisonniers de Guerre Deportes," commonly known as MNPGD. This man was in Geneva not long ago. Beginning last winter, we have been trying to influence MNPGD along the following lines: A. Preparation for direct action by workers and prisoners as soon as the time is ripe. B. Establishment of a system of secret intelligence through the workers. Although their funds are insufficient, MNPGD has already made contact with groups in 45 out of 60 Nazi prisoner camp areas and also has around 30 inspectors going in and out of France. Among these are some individuals who travel under official Vichy protection. Approximately 15 assistants are assigned to each regional leader, and these agents operate under cover of proved liaison men between the Nazi control staffs and the prisoners. Not long ago, MNPGD dispatched representatives under this same cover to circulate among the French workers in the Reich. It is thought that this organization is sufficiently well organized to stimulate current sabotage and to unite the eventual French resistance in the Reich. They are ready to increase their activities to bring about these measures if they receive monetary backing equal in round numbers to 10,000,000 French francs each month. These funds are to be used for travelling expenses, reserve funds for men in camps and for bribery.

The scheme would include dropping food, arms, and other supplies by parachute at previously designated camps on D-Day. In addition, it is hoped that arrangements can be made for this group to continue to operate in the Reich even if France is made inaccessible by the battle lines.

The local agent for MNPGD has advised us that we cannot look for assistance from subversive elements in Germany with the exception of the Communists, and this element will only help to the extent of current sabotage and the creation of disorder on D-Day. In a nut shell, our informant means to imply that no true German maquis will oppose the Nazi forces. (Note from 110: We do not agree entirely with this presentation as we feel that among the non-communist labor factions we may be able to rally a little support and it is possible also that some factions of the Wehrmacht may rebel against the Gestapo.)

We feel that this movement may be developed more practically through France than directly from Bern. Following is from 110: Because the matter is imperative and since there is not time to wait for an answer from you because of the early departure of the courier, I propose to advance a sum equal to 2–3 million French francs, a portion of which will be in Nazi currency, to expedite the work mentioned in the above paragraphs. I should be grateful for your orders concerning additional financing and also your views on the material discussed in this cable.

Document 4-54

Telegram 909-10 to Algiers for Caserta, August 10, 1944

[Dulles advises OSS Caserta of a possibility for the penetration of Austria.]

Joyce and Chapin from 110. . . . There have been wide repercussions as a result of the recent events in Germany, especially because of the execution of high Wehrmacht officers. This may lead to the opening up of new Austrian lines; if so, we will pass them on to you at once. We understand that Count Thurn who has a large estate in Carinthia is a possible center of anti-Nazi activity. Count Thurn had Heimwehr connections and his wife is Stahremberg's sister. I expect to send a courier to him shortly to secure full information and to obtain an exact location for a drop or for reception possibilities. Do you have any information on Thurn? It is a contact of a rightist nature so should be handled carefully. His estate might prove to be of use as an operational base, but it would probably be wiser not to plan a Labor Desk operation from there. When referring to Count Thurn, use the name Turtle; when referring to Carinthia, use the term Kansas.

Document 4-55

Telegram 943-45 to London, August 10, 1944

[In planning special operations in the French Alps with his French syndicalist source in Geneva, 328, Dulles again encounters the need to avoid friction and overlap with the British.]

328 is back, and I have gone over your cable with him in detail. We are ready to cooperate in receiving, hiding here, and arranging northward passage of the individuals pointed out in your cable. In my opinion, it would be better to drop them in the Haute Savoie region, perhaps to Niveau, who would be able to get them through to us. Notice must be sent to us well in advance so that we can prepare to receive them. 328 will soon be replying to your other questions. This is in strict confidence. You are aware of the fact that 328 is working both for Zulu and for us but keeping his two jobs separate. There are a number of parachute grounds in the Savoie region which he has staked out for his work with Zulu and which are so being used. Of course, he has no desire to have his work with us clash with that. Please let us know if your program should be carried out as an independent U.S. project or in cooperation with Zulu and also how 328 and ourselves should take care of the problem in connection with Zulu over here. I hear that 328 has been in touch with Eclair through our channels as well as those of Zulu. Would like to know whether Eclair is now doing work only for us or whether he is doing Zulu work as well.

Document 4-56

Telegram 950-51 to London, August 10, 1944

[Dulles was involved in several infiltration plans simultaneously in August 1944, including a plan for the penetration of Alsace.]

A plan designed to infiltrate Alsace at the earliest possible date has been developed by a group of about 20–30 Alsatians, the majority of whom have had past army training and some of whom are officers. The plan calls for a northward movement to a prepared spot in an area 35 kilometers due east of Besancon with assured liaison here. I am thoroughly acquainted with the leader of this group and he has requested that we assist them. He advises me that we have a liaison officer located at Mont Deliad. Is this true? Do you want us to encourage this kind of activity or should it be handled exclusively by General Koenig's group? Has General Koenig any liaison officer here besides Commandant Georges with whom matters of this sort could be talked over?

Document 4-57

Telegram 912 to Algiers, August 11, 1944

[During the course of the war, scores of Allied bombers made emergency landings in Switzerland. This raised delicate questions respecting Swiss neutrality and was a propaganda issue as well.]

To Colonel Glavin. No case of any nature has come to the attention of myself or 520 giving the least credence to the report that American airmen are attempting to evade any more combat by landing here. I believe this is nothing but ill-willed propaganda inspired by Nazis, since I learned in a confidential talk with Gen. Guisan a short time after many U.S. planes landed here, that under his orders each case was thoroughly investigated and it was determined that none of the planes could possibly have returned to its home field. A complete report has been forwarded to Arnold by 520. Naturally, the information from Gen. Guisan should not be disseminated.

Document 4-58

Telegram 4443-46, August 11, 1944

[During the summer of 1944, Dulles's sources in Germany provided additional information on the July 20 putsch and its aftermath.]

BREAKERS. We have received the following information from our courier who has just returned from Berlin. While he was there, he saw our 512 who is presently in hiding. He reports that a grave break occurred among the conspirators at the very last minute before the putsch. 512, Goerdeler, Beck and some of the others involved, were in favor of the western solution, while many of the Breakers generals, Stauffenberg included, desired to conclude a peace with the Russians. (The attitude of these generals evidently had undergone a recent change, as Breakers, before the end, never informed me of this.)

The conspiracy was known by both Rommel and Kluge, however, the former maintained that only if Goebbels, Himmler and Hitler were done away with, would he collaborate. At present, Rommel is in the Reich and is seriously sick. At the time of the conspiracy, Kluge stated that on the western front, he would be able to hold out for only 21 days; Rommel maintained that the time was even less than that. 512 sent us a suggestion that in the west, Kluge held the keys to the entire situation in his hands and that if we could pick a suitable German officer from those we have captured, who could be dispatched to Kluge, we might now find him disposed to cooperate with us in the hope that this move would permit the Western powers to occupy portions of the Reich sooner.

The following are additional names of those taken into custody and of those who were killed: All of Stauffenberg's children, his wife, his brother and wife were killed. Oster was killed. The following were imprisoned: Schacht, Neurath, Pupits, the former Prussian Minister of Finance, Helldorf, and our 800. All of these taken prisoner are shackled.

This portion from 110. While we cannot positively substantiate the names hereinabove mentioned, it is our opinion that they come from a source sufficiently reliable to justify your broadcasting the information concerning the killing of the Stauffenberg family over the radio. We have been informed that General Stauffenberg came from loyal Catholic stock and that he had a big family. The incarceration of Schacht and Neurath and the killing of Oster might be mentioned, however, do not mention 800 in these broadcasts.

Our messenger came out of the German capital with news that all that is necessary now is for us to shake hard and the entire structure will collapse. All information advises that the Army is outraged and shocked and that a real reason exists for the driving of a deep wedge between the SS and the Army.

Document 4-59

Telegram 4438-39, August 12, 1944

[Gregoire Gafencu (number 495) had served as Rumanian Foreign Minister (1938–40) and Minister Plenipotentiary in Moscow (1940–41). He was an important source on Rumania for OSS Bern.]

It is felt by our 495 that, because of his Russian contacts, he could aid in the Rumanian crisis at this time. He is very desirous of learning if means of leaving Switzerland can be furnished him. He indicated a desire to have his wife accompany him and is not adverse to risking an airplane pickup. I told him it would be unlikely that he could take his wife under any circumstances. He feels that Stirbey may not have been suited to job of negotiating Russian phase of matter and says that Maniu, who appears discouraged at Stirbey's lack of success, also desires that he go.

Document 4-60

Telegram 4471-73, August 12, 1944

[As the outcome of the war became apparent, widespread speculation arose regarding a Nazi last stand in the Alpine regions and creation of irregular units of fanatics that would continue the fight after formal German surrender. OSS Washington requested Dulles's views on this speculation.]

To 154. In reference to your #1939. The problem mentioned in the above communication has 2 aspects. (1) The possible establishment of a Nazi reduit as was taken up in my flash dated the 10th of this month. (2) Underground union of rabid Nazi factions within territory held by the Allies. Concerning the first aspect, 511 has a rather grave approach to the situation, due to the fact that any such reduit could be flanked by the Swiss and therefore they are paying close heed to this matter. He seems to feel that there is some leaning towards a concentration of materials in this region. Switzerland has accorded the reduit boundaries which are slightly more extensive than those indicated in my flash and they have suggested that a portion of northern Italy might be included providing an outlet to the ocean in the region Trieste-Venice. It is not beyond the realm of probability that some such project is being devised but the evidence is not conclusive at the present time. The Nazi theory is that by stationing 1,000,000 troops on the Vorarlberg, Austrian and Bavarian Alps, together with sufficient material, they could resist for a period extending from 6 to 12 months.

The 2nd scheme, i.e., going underground within Allied controlled territory is mentioned in many reports which have been received but all of these lack conviction. These accounts are usually based on Ordensburg Hitler educational institutions where rabid young Nazis are trained. These would supply the core for underground movements in the future. As we receive trustworthy data we shall add to the above information. . . .

Document 4-61

Telegram 966-68 to London, August 15, 1944

[Dulles and OSS London exchanged information with respect to the failed coup of July 20. On August 12, London sent a British report emanating from Stockholm to the effect that Breakers figures including Waetjen (670) and von Trott (800) had at one time been part of a left-leaning German opposition group that sought to establish a socialist government. Dulles's comments follow.]

BREAKERS. I found your #867-70 highly interesting but not a sufficiently full picture of the matter as I understand it. 670 is not qualified to be a leader and never acted as such. He is a useful envoy although greatly inhibited. He may be led to more determined action, however, because of his current indignation over his friends' execution. The unnamed official of the 659 organization you refer to is probably 512. He was the courageous man of action, and always dominated 670 here. 512 worked directly with the generals, Tucky in particular, and also with the Leper group, as Breakers always told me that without Wehrmacht leadership, action was impossible. Only when Oster and 659 were eliminated did Hansen become prominent. 800 is very highly regarded but von Cramm is not taken very seriously.

In reference to paragraph 6, refer to your #397 and my 241. I surmised that at that time Zulu perhaps did not want to take us into their confidence. This may account for their refusal, last October, to communicate this message to us.

Document 4-62

Telegram 4478-79, August 15, 1944

[The OSS continued its role as a channel of communication between the Italian opposition and Italian-Americans in the United States.]

Request has been made by Targetti, Boeri, Gasparotto, Migliano, Mazzonimo, Facchinetti and Jacini, all ex-Italian deputies, that the following message (which has been translated and reworded) be given to Mayor La Guardia for them. I hope you will be able to deliver this message as I know most of these men and think them to be all right. Let me know what action is taken.

"Your friends, recalling your work in Italy, which they always supported, express, as true interpreters of the unanimous thought of the Italian people, their deep gratitude to you for your noble affirmations of encouraging solidarity, and hope that your great people will approve your generous appeal."

Document 4-63

Telegram 4489-92, August 15, 1944 (extract)

[Dulles here transmits a list of Fascist "spies" as provided by the Como organization of Italian partisans. It is surprising that he seems to have accepted this information at face value. Como was later revealed to be a questionable source.]

From 110. A roster has been drawn up by Como's men, listing around 40 active Fascist spies in northern Italy. This roster details the offenses of each man. We have selected the following 10 as the most dangerous. Como urges that BBC broadcast this list in Italian, to act as a warning to people who might be fooled by them. We do not know whether this practice is a good one or whether it is consistent with your policy. Kindly let us know what action you take, and if you want the balance of the names. . . .

Document 4-64

Telegram 4498-4500, August 16, 1944

[In *Breaking the Silence*, Laqueur and Breitman describe the important role played by German industrialist Eduard Schulte (number 643) in alerting the Allies to Nazi extermination of the Jews. Arriving in Switzerland in 1943, Schulte was also a source of information on conditions inside the Reich and provided advice on postwar occupation and reconstruction.]

I have been constantly in touch with 643 since he fled . . . here last December. (Refer to our #1280.) 643 has been engaged in drawing up plans for postwar Germany of an economic-industrial nature. I believe that he is anti-Nazi and entirely trustworthy. He is one of the few technically able and up-to-date persons who could be of service to our army of occupation following the collapse of Germany. In addition, I trust his judgment on anti-Nazi groups who might be relied upon to work with us. 643 is entirely realistic about the Reich and is aware of the need for both a complete clean sweep and a long occupation. In large part he is responsible for the idea contained in my flash dated the 14th of this month about an advisory German committee to help on personnel. 643's background can be given to you by Sherman.

Even though I am aware that this matter is a bit out of our field, I would like to be advised whether we can give some encouragement to men like 643 and whether any directives could be given by the men working on occupation plans, naturally without making any commitments. There will not be many Germans of this kind that we will be able to locate and I believe that those persons responsible for planning the U.S. zone of occupation might find it advantageous at this time to line up a carefully chosen group of people available at this end, so that if we need them we will have first crack at their services.

I have also been advised confidentially, that there are a few Swiss police who speak German and have been trained, during the war, in anti-Nazi work. These police would welcome work after the war with the occupation forces. They would be most useful because of their language qualifications. Are our people interested in the foregoing?

Document 4-65

Telegram 4511-14, August 17, 1944

[This message from an important labor operative in Geneva was directed to French individuals in the United States.]

From 110 to Wolf. In reference to your #1932. Following information is for Eva from 328: The funds intended for the Socialist Party were forwarded regularly to the region center in Lyon, when Juste Evrard was at its head, and to party headquarters in Paris. The party's organizational activity and their clandestine publications have been greatly furthered due to this financial assistance. The party's present Secretary, Daniel Meyer [Mayer], wishes to extend his grateful appreciation to the trade unionists in the United States for their considerable contributions. Liaison with Paris has been seriously jeopardized since last June. The latest information concerning the party goes back to the last part of July. At that time, all was in order at headquarters. The Socialist Party has fine opportunities for recruiting and building up progressive democratic factions and those Catholics with leftist tendencies. All assistance possible should be forthcoming for this work. The party has taken a definite stand with respect to communists.

The funds intended for the Christian Syndicalists were forwarded regularly to Brodier. We have received acknowledgement from him of the last remittance of 400,000 francs which was sent the beginning of last month. The syndicalists were able to establish their liaisons with these contributions. A lengthy courier was dispatched 3 months ago from Van Hove and Brodier through Eclair. However there has been no acknowledgement of this communication. Van Hove is negotiating a wide-spread dissemination of Temoignages Chretiens.

The funds intended for the CGT were forwarded to Lacoste. They were appropriated in part for use locally in the dissemination and publishing of informations sociales, to finance visits to Switzerland of syndicalist associates engaged in my activist work and to organize liaisons with Toulouse and Paris. At the start, this financial assistance was of primary importance to the militant syndicalists who reorganized the CGT.

The funds intended for activity in the Reich made it possible to establish contacts, to send associates into the country and to make some arrangements locally for effective operations in the fatherland when the time is ripe.

Vital negotiations are under way with European resistance elements in order to promote sympathy for a European federation. We are in close touch with associates in the Reich, France, Italy, and Holland. Propaganda is appearing in French entitled L'Europe Federaciste and is being disseminated in Italian under the title L'Unita Europea. Several other documents are being brought out which are intended for European resistance factions. It is necessary that effective assistance be extended to this activity.

Trust we will see you in the near future.

Document 4-66

Telegram 4532-34, August 18, 1944

[In this cable, Dulles offers additional information on the east versus west factionalism in the Breakers movement.]

BREAKERS. To Jackpot, wishing him a pleasant journey. In reference to your #1955. I interpret the situation in the following way: some little time prior to the putsch, some type of union existed between the eastern and western oriented factions. Both groups had identical immediate goals, the destruction of the Hitler gang. I believe that 512 was not aware of this move until he arrived at headquarters. The foregoing is only a guess but I call to your attention the opening paragraph of Breakers #3423-31, describing the reaction 512 received when he returned the messenger with the information that there was no possibility at all of making a deal with the west on the basis of allowing the Nazis to maintain the Eastern Front. In addition, refer to the answer which 512 received. It is entirely probable that Breakers decided at that point to collaborate with the east oriented faction. Even though the identities of several generals involved were furnished to me in advance, the fact that participants who were just as prominent (possibly those who were eastern oriented) were not mentioned makes me think that 512 had no knowledge of this development before he returned.

This appears to be the most probable answer to your query rather than any change in the policy or mentality of Becky-Leper and their group.

Document 4-67

Telegram 4535-36, August 19, 1944

[On August 19, OSS Bern received new information from "George Wood," its agent in the German Foreign Ministry. Subjects covered included the Far East, France, Turkey, and Yugoslavia.]

KAPPA. This morning we received a letter from Wood containing information dated the 16th of this month from his home town. The attack on Hitler does not seem to have made any change in his position. However, he has not much to say with regard to it, merely that, in spite of July 20, he is still working with the Volksmilice project. (Together with a number of friends, he was trying to organize the members of a Volksmilice to assist Allied parachute troops, landing troops, and so on.) Wood himself might very well not have any inside information on the affair, for it seems that not much was allowed to be made public inside the Reich after the first publicity and information about the trial. For instance, a well-informed Spanish courier, just back from Berlin, declared that there was far more knowledge in Switzerland about the affair than there was in the German capital.

We are starting in to process this Wood data right away. The code word Kagust will be used in sending it to you.

Document 4-68

Telegram 4551-54, August 18, 1944 (extracts)

[This message contains information on the Pacific war and other matters as obtained by George Wood from German communications.]

KAPPA. This is a Kagust message. Following is information received in a message to [from?] the German MA from Tokyo, dated August 10th. Because islands such as Truk, Rabaul, Wake, West Guinea, and Bougainville, which were by-passed by the Americans, are situated in the outer ring, they have no value for general defense, as they lack offensive means. However, the islands of Yap, Bonin and Palau are located internally, and landings on Yap and Palau are anticipated. The Japanese Admiralty expects the next American offensive action to take place at the Philippines, and not at Okinawa. . . . The Admiralty also feels that there will be air raids on the Japanese mainland from the Marianas before the end of this month. Defeatist attitude is prevalent among the Japanese. The people are more and more expressing their opinion that Germany's example was followed. . . .

4. To the Foreign Office from Bern Legation, dated August 12th. In reference to a request from Minister Stucki, Vichy, regarding the use of a radio transmitter, Pilet-Golaz stated that he was aware that the German Legation in Bern has been using a transmitter to send telegrams. As a matter of fact, the Legation began using the transmitter about 3 weeks ago. Transmission has now been disconnected, but they are still receiving.

5. By order of OKW, key positions are now being built in Italy north of the existing front lines. Gauleiter Ruiner and Hofer who were respectively in Trieste and Posen, have been put in charge of this work by Hitler. Mussolini's statement that both were looked upon as advocates of Germanization of Italy was disregarded. This was a hard blow to Mussolini, according to Ambassador Rahn.

Document 4-69

Telegram 4537-42, August 19, 1944 (extracts)

[This German message obtained by George Wood deals with the death throes of the Vichy regime and Nazi efforts to control it to the last.]

KAPPA. This is a Kagust message. Documentary. Message to Grand from Abets dated the 14th of this month. The following is the French inner political situation:

1. Petain is striving to reach Paris, providing we approve and guarantee him freedom both on the journey and for his stay in that city. Petain wants to dispose of the current government and work with those political and military people approved by America. He wishes to summon a National Assembly and then, supported by a vote of confidence from them, to wait in Paris for the arrival of the Anglo-Americans.

2. With respect to Laval, he is trying, apart from Petain, to effect the summoning of the National Assembly and has set up contact with Herriot and other influential Parliamentarians for this purpose. By this means, Laval hopes to forestall Gaullist and Communist coup d'états prior to and during the Anglo-American advance. Although Laval claims not to have received any assurances from the Americans for his

personal safety, and in truth anticipates imprisonment or assassination, and even though he was advised by the parliamentarians he contacted that he personally could hold no place in the future government, Laval believes it to be his duty to the nation to stay in Paris. . . .

4. Lately the resistance movement has been strongly reinforced in departments which are not occupied in strength. The resistance movement has taken the stand that they will not abide Laval, Petain or any new Vichy Government of the National Assembly. We are in danger of having Petain either assassinated or removed from our power by the Anglo-Americans and forced to issue a decree for total mobilization against us, since a landing in the south of France can be expected in the near future and the Maquis draw ever closer to Vichy.

5. The summoning of the National Assembly is to the Reich's advantage in this instance. However, it is of secondary importance whether it is really allowed to meet. Aside from the propaganda value this will afford us against dissidents, communists and Roosevelt, the summoning of the National Assembly provides us with the only chance to get Petain out of Vichy of his own volition, and in this way to keep the legality of the French Government on our side, should the Anglo-Americans further occupy France. . . . To this [some] city in the east of France we would move the Bank of France, the State intelligence and radio services, the 1st French Regiment, Milice, and the official journal. In this way we would join all the attributes of the legal French Government, and keep them under our own control.

Document 4-70

Telegram 4568-72, August 19, 1944 (extracts)

[This German report intercepted by George Wood in Berlin and forwarded to Washington by Dulles contains assertions that could have contributed to the growing Allied perception that General Mihailovich was cooperating with the Nazis in Yugoslavia.]

KAPPA. This is a Kagust message. To Grand from Neubacher, Athens, dated the 8th of this month, subject Draha Mihailovic:

(A) 1. We have information from DM's camp that Neditch's political influence has waned to such an extent that DM is practically in full control of the political situation in the region of Serbia. . . . (2) Concurrently there is an increasing animosity towards the British in DM's camp because the Chetniks feel the British have betrayed them by arming the Partisans and giving their support to the latter. . . .

(B) Attempts to contact the authorities in occupation are supported by the viewpoint that the latter might be forced to evacuate Serbia in the near future because of the war situation. This would be the signal for a show-down engagement between the Communists and the Nationalists. Therefore DM's idea is most likely to cooperate with the Nazi Army, during the short time left in which he thinks those forces will be present, in efforts to lessen the effectiveness of the Tito partisans. He then feels that he will be right on the spot and will be able to take over the Germans' positions without a struggle when the Nazis flee. In addition, using their common fight against Communism as a tool, DM would secure as many weapons as possible from the Nazis. All this would be preparation for his ultimate encounter with the Tito partisans in Bulgaria and Croatia.

(C) Situations as described above make DM more willing to bargain. He appears to be desirous of conferring with me. . . .

Document 4-71

Radiotelephone Transmission No. 198, August 19, 1944

[In this evening telephone call, Dulles provides some insights on the state of mind in Germany and reminded Washington to use the liberation of Paris for psychological warfare purposes. The Allies entered Paris on August 25.]

Germany

In civilian circles in Berlin, the recent putsch apparently made far less impression than we had expected and believed. Here are the reactions of a man just arrived here from Germany, whom I shall describe separately. The generals behaved as usual with little energy or foresight. They all sat around in a room and waited to be captured. They weren't very effective conspirators. The people and even the Army were not quite unprepared [prepared] for any coup; they did not know what was going on or being attempted, and did not react. The failure of anything so badly organized was a foregone conclusion. The Germans generally are too tired to do any thinking about such matters. They know the war is going badly, they believe that if they lose it they will be overrun by the Russians, and that in that event everything will be lost. Living and working conditions are so desperately bad that all one does is one's daily task, and then tries to get some sleep. There is no leisure or desire to think or even worry about political developments. There is only the daily routine and the struggle to find food and shelter and get to one's work. In supplement to the above, we must remember that executions are no new thing in the Third Reich, and that removal of Army officers has been the rule rather than the exception. But in military circles the "hanging" of the generals was the crucial mistake which Himmler made. The Prussian military spirit could as a matter of discipline, accept almost anything else, but hanging meant a deliberate humiliation of the Army by the Gestapo. This man had not heard anything about any of arrests among civilians in government offices in Berlin.

That is all I have tonight, really. These days of military developments at the front overshadow everything else. Again, I emphasize, don't neglect the psychological factor involved in the taking of Paris when it falls. This will clearly show the German people that the myth of the European Fortress is absolutely destroyed.

Document 4-72

Telegram 4573-79, August 20, 1944 (extracts)

[As Soviet troops approached the borders of Bulgaria, Germany sought to coerce and cajole its wavering satellite into resisting. This message from the German Ambassador, obtained by George Wood / Fritz Kolbe in Berlin, describes an eleventh-hour meeting with the Bulgarian leaders. On August 29, Russian forces entered the country, ignoring its protestations of neutrality. The following day, German troops withdrew. The Soviet Union declared war on Bulgaria on September 5, provoking an immediate surrender.]

KAPPA. Kagust. Doc. The following is to Grand from Beckerle, dated the 14th of this month. In accordance with your orders, I went to Chamkoria to meet Bogdan Filoff. I delivered to the 3 regents the representations you summarized for me. They were greatly affected, and tears came to Filoff's eyes while Kyrill kept tapping his fingers on the table. Most of the talking was done by the former, who has more leadership and political insight than the others. He took the line that we had drawn the wrong conclusions and were not being fair. The foundation stone of his country's foreign policy, he declared, was still her alliance and amity with the Reich. His government believed that the course most favorable to us was to avoid, for as long as we could, making the Balkans a battlefield. We should, therefore, evaluate everything from this angle and have faith in their allegiance. Since the future of Bulgaria depends entirely on the victory of the Reich, all must be directed toward guaranteeing this victory. The only way to make the Bulgarian people ready for war would be to prove that their government had done all it could to avoid an armed clash with the Soviets. . . .

There ensued a lengthy discussion regarding the general attitude befitting Bulgaria as a little nation and the fact that she should not talk above her station and irritate people. However, they were our allies and would stand or fall as we did. There should be no question of a change in Bulgaria's policy. At that point, Kyrill broke in, declaring with heat that he vigorously protested the implication that his government had altered its policy and that I was completely incorrect in making any such accusation.

My opinion is that the regents, especially Filoff, are sincere in wanting to preserve the alliance with Germany. Filoff exerts a preponderant influence in the regency, but they are swayed by their fear of domestic difficulties arising from dealing with the USSR and from a declaration of war. . . .

Document 4-73

Telegram 4602-5, August 22, 1944

[With the Red Army a short distance from Warsaw, the Polish Home Army rose against the Germans on August 1, 1944. The Soviet offensive then paused, and over the next two months the Nazis virtually exterminated the Polish fighters in the city. "George Wood" in Berlin obtained this German propaganda statement targeting

Polish forces in the Allied ranks. Ironically, the Nazi information, discounted by Wood himself, bore more than passing resemblance to the truth.]

KAPPA. This is a Kagust message. End of Kagust series. The following was contained in a message from headquarters in East Prussia to the German Embassy, Fasano, dated August 10th. The Foreign Minister has asked that it be distributed through all means at our disposal, in particular to the Polish forces in the Near East and Italy. This is a quote from DNB Berlin, dated August 9th. "The following was an intercept of a broadcast by Polish Partisans from behind the Russian lines at Kovel to a Polish station located in Bari, on August 9th: 'The Russians have taken away our arms. This is the finish of the Polish Army, Long Live Poland.' Kovel asked Bari to pass this on to all the Polish stations. A great deal of dismay was caused among the Poles by this broadcast, as they were relying upon erroneous advice and the whispered propaganda of the Americans and the English, and had been led on by Bolshevik promises. The Poles had instigated armed uprisings and sabotage, and had sacrificed themselves before German guns, so that they might, they thought, be of assistance to the British and Americans in bringing about Polish liberation. Instead they actually led their country into slavery. While at the suggestion of the Americans and the British, the exiled Mikolajczyk travels to Moscow to talk over terms of a compromise with the Russians, with whom a compromise is impossible, Stalin again informs his British and American Allies of things that have already taken place, such as the disarming and imprisonment of Polish units behind the Soviet lines. It has been found out that Polish officers have been taken away from their troops and sent to Kiev where they will receive the same treatment as befell their compatriots at Katyn. All elements that were non-Bolshevist have been separated from the troops. In this manner all possibility of the Pole insurgents receiving assistance from the Anglo Saxons or the Russians has been ruthlessly eliminated. Their position is without hope. Their sacrifice of life has been useless, and Stalin continues to kill their countrymen. Stalin's plan to destroy the Polish people, and to force Bolshevism on Poland, is very evident. Any partisan who is captured by the Russians will never again look upon his native land." This concludes the report from DNB. Signed by Timmler. (From 110: This appears to be the converse of MO material; From Wood: The foregoing falsified account is self-explanatory.)

Document 4-74

Telegram 4608-9, August 22, 1944

[The collapse of the Vichy regime brought difficulties for OSS Bern because important intelligence operations were conducted by persons associated with or having contacts in the Vichy French Embassy.]

Paul Morand, who is the Vichy French Ambassador in Bern has informed 472-K-1, of his intention to resign if he finds out that Petain is held captive, or if the mission of the Swiss Minister to Vichy is brought to a close. Jardin also intends to resign, but for the present he will remain to take care of the Embassy affairs. The latter action has been taken in accord with 472, as a formal closing of the consulates and the Embassy would be a hindrance to his operations. The foregoing is confidential. In the meantime, the matter of Algiers representation here has been left in a state of utter confusion. Information stating that our 516 had been appointed by Algiers, with the approval of the Swiss, recently went through our Indigo Iris service. It has since been reported that Algiers has altered that decision. The following is for Algiers: can you quietly inquire into this matter, and determine the true state of affairs. It is said that Laval has taken refuge at the chateau of Louis Veillard at Morvillars, which is located 12 km. from Belfort on the road Boncourt-Delle-Belfort, and is 10 km. from the Swiss border. The press reports this, and 472 believes it to be confirmed.

Document 4-75

Telegram 4610-11, August 22, 1944

[This message reports on conversations between General Legge, the U.S. Military Attaché in Bern (number 520), and Colonel Rakolczai, the Hungarian Military Attaché (number 844), concerning possible operations in Hungary. Perhaps mindful of the failure of Sparrow project, Dulles assumed a cautious attitude.]

520 has held several meetings with 844 and has later discussed his conversations with me. He has reported to War Department that from 844 he has the information that Voros, Chief of Staff, is ready to order a revolt of the army if a parachute force of sufficient size can be dropped. 844 has suggested that a liaison officer should be dropped to arrange all the details with Voros.

From 110: I personally feel that the Hungarians would be glad to be through with the war if they could extricate themselves without losing their own skins. I am rather dubious as to their courage at the last minute, especially if they are faced by the Gestapo, the SS and other repressive forces. We must also take it for granted that the Germans are watching these very possibilities and will have placed the Army in a situation where the possibilities of revolt are at a minimum. From our reports it would seem that the majority of the Hungarian fighting units are at or near the Carpathian front. Some such program might well be considered if feasible from a political standpoint at the time when Bulgaria withdraws from the war and the Southeastern front folds up completely.

Document 4-76

Telegram 4616-18, August 22, 1944

[Competition between OSS Bern and British SOE in Switzerland with regard to assistance to the Italian resistance became increasingly bitter, as indicated in this message.]

The head of Zulu SOE in Bern (645) has just given me a copy of a letter he sent the local military representative from Milan Committee of National Liberation. He requested that the representative send the letter on to the CNL in Milan stating that, to end baseless stories that we were doing more than the British (which did not come from either American or British sources) he would list the tonnage parachuted (From 110: probably North Italy) during recent months: May: English, 95 tons, Americans 50; June: English 180, Americans 123; July: English 201 tons, Americans 97; First week in August: English 47, Americans, 20. (From 110: this is contrary to the spirit of our united effort, but I would like to know if the statistics are even approximately correct.)

To Algiers: Re #501. You might use the above statistics for strengthening your demand for more equitable allocation of tonnage.

I asked the military representative of the Committee, through 809, why we had failed to receive any information from Motta lately regarding activist work. The answer came back that a British mission with Motta passed all the information through their channels. Is this so? Should I continue to finance Motta (refer my #4612-3) or should the British handle this too? I have no moral commitments beyond September. I feel once liaison is established between groups in North and South Italy we in Bern should have nothing further to do with the work.

Document 4-77

Telegram 1018-20 to London, August 23, 1944

[With Allied forces about to reach the Swiss border, Dulles communicated with Donovan about augmenting the Bern staff, establishing a base in French territory adjacent to Switzerland, and arranging a personal meeting.]

I was very glad to receive your #894 from London and #596-99 from Algiers.

1. It would be no trouble to pass men here from the Haute Savoie region. However, in order to work as regular staff members they must have Swiss visas when they arrive here. We will expedite this matter here if you will let us know the names of personnel and the jobs they are to have, as Vice-Consul, code clerk, clerk, etc. However, applications for visas should be made at the point of departure. We would receive people here merely to pass them secretly to the Italian Maquis, of course, but this was probably not your intention.

2. I also recommend that you give your attention to the desirability of setting up a small working office, on the Swiss border but actually in France, where certain activities could be prepared without the necessity of considering problems of neutrality. For instance, during the last war there was a British center at Pontarlier and a French center at Bellegarde, which were supplementary headquarters for Swiss activities.

3. I think it would be useful if I could report personally, whenever air transport from anywhere in this vicinity becomes possible. If hydroplane transportation is

possible, the French waters of Lake Geneva should be safe now, with Evian or Thonan as embarkation area.

Document 4-78

Telegram 1047-48 to London, August 25, 1944

[Dulles corresponded further with Donovan regarding planning for conditions created by the evolving military situation. Jigsaw is Lieutenant (J.G.) Robert Wauchope, an OSS officer who coordinated special operations in Italy.]

From 110 to Jigsaw and 109. Presumably the arrival of U.S. troops at the Swiss border indicates practical control of the Alpine region from the Mediterranean to Lake Geneva and raises the issue of coordination of our military action with that of Partisan groups across the border in Italy. We have set up many contacts with these Partisans and also gathered together a sizeable amount of documentation. At the moment a messenger from the Turin CNL is here and is trying to determine whether it will be possible to make arrangements for any contact between him and our forces during the weekend. Please advise whether we have anybody with our forces in this region or someone whom it would be possible to dispatch to coordinate on the spot possible military activity to the east via the mountain passes in support of Partisan operations in that region. In addition, please advise what are the prospects of sending arms, through our forces in the Savoie region and southward, to the Italian partisan groups, especially in the vicinity of Torino and north of there.

Document 4-79

Telegram 4673, August 25, 1944

[News from the depleted German resistance movement continued to filter into Switzerland. Number 670 is Eduard Waetjen; Tucky is General Beck; Leper is Carl Goerdeler; 800 is Adam von Trott zu Solz.]

BREAKERS. Not long ago, a Breakers courier contacted 670 and said that the movement was still going on, although naturally slowed down by executions and arrests in addition to the fact that evidently the Gestapo have found a lengthy list of the names of those individuals scheduled to assume the top posts in the new Tucky Leper regime. He verifies the arrest of 800. It is thought that he is in serious danger of being liquidated; however, probably will be held for Leper's trial.

Document 4-80

Telegram 1069-70, August 27, 1944

[Control of French-Italian border areas was a particularly difficult issue in the latter stages of the war and led to profound discord among the Allies. Dulles sought to alleviate the problem by encouraging liaison between French and Italian resistance groups operating in the region.]

We have reached an agreement here with Iris, after due consultation, and 3 Motta representatives, Jacini, Silvio (CLN, Turin) and Morone (who organized our Chris service) have gone to Haute Savoie to get in touch with the French Maquis authorities. The plan is to coordinate French-Italian activities along the French-Italian-Swiss frontier. Though the mission is the result of initiative on the part of the French and Italians, I can recommend the Italians highly. You should advise our military authorities nearest the particular area involved so that if the project is feasible, they, too, should get in contact with the group.

Document 4-81

Telegram 4697-98, August 31, 1944

[Although military and political events of fundamental importance were occurring daily, Dulles continued to take interest in international intellectual and cultural matters. Professor William Rappard was one of many European friends and contacts that Dulles assisted in liaison with American institutions.]

From 110 to 140 and Carib. I have received a cabled communication from Joseph Willits of the Rockefeller Foundation, asking that I cable a confidential account of the Rappard Institute at Geneva. I would be grateful if you would convey the following to him: the future use of Geneva as a hub for international work, will have the greatest influence upon the future of the Rappard Institute. You are better able than I to judge these possibilities. It is my opinion that the Institute has performed beneficial work in the past, and that Rappard is steeped in the principals for which the United Nations are fighting. He has attempted to gather about himself an earnest group of students and teachers, and has met with some success in this effort. I believe the success of the work depends to a great extent upon his remaining as the head and guiding power, and on the considerations aforementioned. . . .

Document 4-82

Telegram 1100-1101, September 2, 1944

[As the Allies gained the upper hand in Europe, OSS Bern devoted increasing attention to the Japanese intelligence target and to what the enemy allies reported about one another. Dr. Friedrich Hack, former Krupp representative in Japan (number 673), was the source of the information in this message. Bern also notes that Admiral Canaris, former head of the Abwehr (number 659), had been arrested.]

Following information has come from 673 who has based his report on data secured during a discussion with Sakai who is thought to be one of Japan's foremost intelligence officers in Europe and who is assigned to the Embassy in the German capital: the Germans realize now that it was a tactical mistake to hang the Wehrmacht generals as it had a bad effect on their standing with the satellite states and with their ally Japan. Nazi ideology was not the selling point when these countries allied themselves with the Reich but they did have faith and confidence in the Wehrmacht. The elements in these countries who championed collaboration with the Wehrmacht are at the present time sorely disillusioned and they have lost influence because of the humiliating treatment the Nazi Party has accorded the Wehrmacht. It is apparent that Sakai thinks the abrupt reversal of sympathies in Bulgaria and Rumania was brought to a climax by the fact that the Wehrmacht has sunk so low. Presumably this same feeling is prevalent in Japan where the Wehrmacht was also held in high esteem. General Fromm is being held in custody but he has not as yet been executed. Our 659 has been apprehended.

Document 4-83

Telegram 4699, September 3, 1944

[Dulles reports that the blood purge in Germany is continuing.]

According to 670, as an aftermath of the July putsch von Haeften of the Nazi Foreign Office was brought to trial and hanged. This trial was conducted in secret. Both 670 and his associates confirm reports we have had from other sources, that the Nazis are aware of the unfavorable reaction of the people to a public trial of the main participants in the putsch. It is expected that all these trials from now on will be conducted secretly. The hanged von Haeften was the brother of Ober Lt. von Haeften who was officially reported shot on the 20th of July.

Document 4-84

Telegram 1135 to London, September 5, 1944

[Dulles asks to be a recipient of the harvest of German documents captured in France.]

I suppose that during the occupation of France and the consequent capture of German and Gestapo headquarters we have acquired a great many documents, such as German passports. Has anything been done to coordinate this work and place these documents where they may be used for future penetration of Germany? If this has been done, kindly see that we get some at this end.

Document 4-85

Radiotelephone Transmission No. 206, September 5, 1944

[This message discusses conditions in France, Austria, and Germany at the moment when Allied forces reached the French-Swiss border.]

France

Several short visits to France across the frontier from Geneva are hardly adequate to permit a judgment as to French conditions, but there are one or two points which occurred to me from what I have observed. The town which we visited is typical of many French rural towns where the forces of the resistance have been particularly strong, and have contributed substantially to clearing out the Germans. These forces, which have contributed to the liberation of France, now feel, and quite naturally, that they should control its destinies. In this town there is a strong organization of the FFI and a parallel and almost equally strong organization of the FTP. Each has a large headquarters, its own personnel and followers. Probably in this area, the Haute Savoie, the FFI is somewhat stronger numerically and is tactically in military control of the situation. This situation in Haute Savoie is quite typical of that in many other parts of France. However, the prolonged existence of such semi-military, semi-political organizations possesses [poses] a real problem for the future development of France. To an outsider, it would seem that the only solution was a prompt mobilization in France which would incorporate the greater part of these elements into a regular disciplined army and remove the potential threat which such organizations present upon the political angle. However, it would probably be difficult for the French to feed, clothe, and arm so many soldiers under present conditions, and thus the task of mobilization would not be an easy one. Also, de Gaulle and the present French government may well consider that their strength depends upon the loyalty and devotion of forces such as the FFI, the FTP and the old resistance movements, and they may be loath to break them down into a non-political military organization.

Austria

A report from one of the leading Austrians here in Switzerland indicates that the Austrians feel that they are neglected and forgotten, that, with the great world-shaking events of the past few weeks, the Austrian problem has somewhat merged into the German problem and nothing more is apparently said of Austria. This man feels that, to give life to the Austrian movement, we should now do something concrete such as forming a separate Austrian corps and giving as much publicity as possible to this move. He feels that we should create the impression that we are not putting the Austrians into the German caldron, but are holding out some hope to them. I agree that it might be wise to do something to give life and vigor to the idea of an independent Austria, and possibly my friend's suggestion may be worth considering.

Germany
According to a report in the Swiss press, the assistant German press chief, Hellmuth Sundermann, in a recent article, calls upon the Germans to be ready for the people's war within the German boundaries. . . . "No German cow is to feed the enemy, no German mouth is to give him any information, no German hand is to provide help for him. He should find every bridge destroyed and every road blocked. He will encounter nothing but death, destruction and hatred; he will meet death on every inch of German soil which belongs to us and which he wishes to rob us of."

I just cite this as the kind of twaddle they are handing out to try to get the last ounce of resistance out of a people whose resistance is rapidly breaking down.

Document 4-86

Editorial Note

[On September 6, Allen Dulles seized the opportunity of the newly opened border to leave Switzerland for a month of consultations in France, Britain, and the United States. After a brief stay with French resistance elements in an area between Geneva and Lyons, he linked up with General Donovan, who had spent considerable time in France since D-Day. They flew from a small airstrip to London and are reported to have been in the Savoy Bar on September 8 when the first V-2 missiles hit that city. During this period the two OSS leaders discussed the possibility that Dulles might replace David Bruce, OSS chief in London, and become head of all European operations. Donovan decided against this realignment and prevailed on Bruce to remain for a time. Subsequently, he was replaced by Russell Forgan, thus denying Dulles the opportunity to become OSS European chief.

Donovan and Dulles then flew across the Atlantic (Dulles and his partner apparently got the better of the OSS director in bridge games during the crossing). They arrived in Washington on September 15. Dulles remained in the United States until October 7 but spent much of his time in New York and saw little of his superior. His activities centered on the OSS New York office headed by his old friend John Hughes. On his return trip, Dulles visited London and Paris, reaching Switzerland on October 21.

In his absence, Gero Gaevernitz acted in Dulles's stead in running OSS Bern. Charles Dyar and Royall Tyler also transmitted a number of cables. Telegraphic traffic was somewhat reduced in Dulles's absence, but familiar subjects, including Breakers, were reported on. A new shipment of material from George Wood arrived in early October. There seems to have been an unusually high degree of friction with Swiss authorities during this period. One notable OSS Bern success in the absence of its chief was the relaying of information that permitted decisive air strikes in support of partisans fighting near Campione. Gaevernitz sent a number of messages to Dulles to keep him abreast of developments. The evening telephone call routine was maintained, but subject matter was limited to press coverage.]

Document 4-87

Memorandum from Allen W. Dulles to William J. Donovan
New York, October 7, 1944

[During his stay in the United States, Dulles wrote two important statements of his views on the future of Europe and the German situation. Presented in terms of postwar East-West relations, this overview foresaw the Cold War.]

To: General William J. Donovan
From: Allen W. Dulles
I enclose copies of two notes, one on the general European situation as I see it and one on the German situation. The latter you have already seen in earlier draft. I have prepared these memoranda more or less to clarify my own thinking. I am sending one copy to you and have left one copy here in the New York office.

[Attachment 1:]

7 October 1944

NOTES ON THE SITUATION IN EUROPE

1. Russia now believes that she is entitled to a dominating position in Eastern and Southeastern Europe. By the term is meant Poland, eastern Germany, Austria, Hungary, Czechoslovakia, and the Balkans with the possible exception of Greece. Russia does not intend to impose a strictly Communist regime on this entire area but there will probably be a very general liquidation, expulsion or subordination of the bourgeoise elements. Leftist regimes will be installed and pledged to cooperate primarily with Moscow.

2. This development will change the face of Europe and will limit the area in which Western culture and Western democracy will have the chance of surviving for the immediate future. The Russians *know* that we will not try to prevent Russian domination by force and hence we should not bluff about it. For the moment, the most that we can do is to act as a restraining influence by insisting on keeping our observers in this area and thus keep ourselves informed as to what is going on. Russian activities may be tempered somewhat by the desire to maintain working relations with the United States and England and hence they will try not to go beyond the point which would mean a serious disturbance in these relations. Russia certainly does not wish a clash in Europe with the United States or England at the present time. She feels quite confident that she can accomplish her primary objectives without any risk of this. She will be somewhat sensitive, but not overly so, about public opinion in the United States and in the British Empire and this may prevent her from going beyond certain limits. If she can move quietly without our knowing much about what is going on she will be able to go much farther than if

she is apprehensive that we are currently and accurately advised of what she is doing. Russia realizes that democracies like the United States and Great Britain can do little unless their governments are backed by public opinion. She will, therefore, try not to stir up public opinion here or in England against her.

3. In this situation it is of great importance that we be quite realistic as to what we can and will do and give our attention primarily to the areas where there is a real prospect that the principles of western civilization can be maintained and developed. These areas are primarily France, the Low Countries, Switzerland, Italy, Scandinavia and possibly Greece. Also there will be the two zones of occupation in Germany where, under the influence of British and American occupying forces, we may be able slowly to reconstruct a social system integrated with the West. Hence, we should concentrate on these areas as some of them are not too sure, in the hope that the influence that we can there set in motion will eventually spread and that an example can be set which will slowly enlarge the area of Europe committed to the principles of a democratic Western civilization in which a peaceful Europe may be reconstructed. We shall concentrate on these areas rather than embark on adventures in other areas where our intentions will not be backed up with an adequate force in the face of a predominant Russian position.

4. The situation in France presents a real opportunity. We should not be frightened by the leftist tendencies of the Resistance. We should give them economic and other backing and help them rebuild France. In particular, we should strengthen rather than weaken the hands of de Gaulle's government and persuade it that their interest lies in looking to the West rather than to the East.

5. The Italian problem in particular will require careful handling. There is a strong Communist movement in Italy, but the great majority of Italians prefer the Western to the Eastern form of civilization and will be with us if we handle them properly. The fate of Italy lies largely with the Italians of the north who are still under German occupation and the crucial time will come when North Italy is free. It is important that this area be freed by American and British forces rather than by Russian troops advancing through Yugoslavia. In the latter case the tendency of North Italy to go Communist would be very strong.

6. Austria and Czechoslovakia lie on the border line between West and East. Czechoslovakia will lean primarily on Russia for the immediate future but due to Benes' foresight as to the Russian position, Czechoslovakia will probably enjoy a greater degree of independence than its neighbors to the north, south and east.

Russia will make every effort to occupy Vienna before the Anglo-Saxons. Vienna today is of more significance to Russia than even Berlin. The areas of occupation of Germany are already agreed and Russia's position in Berlin is assured. If, however, Russia is in Vienna before the Anglo-Saxons it will help to consolidate her predominant position in the entire Central European area and will give her added influence in northern Italy. Even though an eventual joint occupation of Austria may already have been accepted, a few weeks of exclusive Russian occupation of Austria prior to the arrival of American or British troops will largely determine the future character of that occupation and will insure that friends of Russia are installed in important administrative positions. In view of Austria's key situation both in relation to Italy and to our zone of occupation in south Germany it now deserves our special attention and should be the subject of most careful and realistic planning.

7. This outline is intended to give an objective analysis of the force factors in this general area of Europe as they stand today. It is not intended to convey the idea that Europe, upon Germany's collapse, will be divided into two mutually hostile zones, the one under Anglo-Saxon and the other under Russian control, which will be pitted against each other. Rather, the conclusion to be drawn from this is that there may be two areas where different types of political and social orders will predominate, the one turned toward Russia and the Russian social structure, the other drawing its inspiration from Western culture and democratic institutions. How far the one system or the other will spread its influence will depend upon the inherent force and vitality which lie respectively in the Russian or the Western systems. Either may be able to extend its influence by peaceful means.

[Attachment 2:]

7 October 1944

NOTES ON THE GERMAN SITUATION

This memorandum represents the conclusions reached from approximately two years' study of the German situation from Switzerland and contact with persons of various nationalities intimately familiar with Germany's conditions, including a large number of Germans, both those who are still resident in Germany and those who have been refugees in Switzerland for varying periods of time. Obviously, this heterogenous group of people have not always been in agreement, and this memorandum represents my own conclusions based on all the evidence available to me.

1. We have two problems to meet—punishment and settlement. These two must be kept distinct. There must be punishment, but if the settlement is itself a punishment it will not be lasting.

2. No overall settlement of the German problem can properly be reached in the early days following the German collapse and it would be a grave mistake to prejudice the future by hasty partial solutions. Germany must be administered by a United Nations military administration for a considerable period, and the final settlement should only be reached after a period of such administration. It is recognized however, that it may be necessary to deal with the eastern frontiers of Germany at a relatively early date as the dispositions reached with regard to the administration of East Prussia and Upper Silesia will affect, and possibly determine, the ultimate solution.

3. When the military collapse comes in Germany there will probably be no German government with which to negotiate an armistice and it would be a mistake to attempt to create one ad hoc. There is today in Germany no constitutional machinery which would install any government in Germany having a legal basis, and any group of men who might attempt to succeed Hitler and call themselves a gov-

ernment would have no authority to speak for or bind the German people. We should not encourage a deal with any such group. If we could find, and this is problematical, a group of anti-Nazi leaders who might call themselves a government, they might well be viewed in the country as usurpers or quislings and, if, individually, they had any merit or utility for the future, they would tend to disqualify themselves by assuming responsibility for the German surrender.

The Russians will probably wish to serve up to us a readymade German government out of the Seidlitz Committee and it is partly for this reason that it seems wise that we start out with no central government in Germany. It might be difficult to reject a "made in Russia" government and then present a government with an Anglo-Saxon trademark.

4. When the collapse comes and the individual Generals in the field have laid down their arms and Germany is occupied, the United Nations' authority should unilaterally announce the terms and conditions which should be effective for occupied German territory for the immediate future until other disposition is taken. Such measures, in addition to the necessary military conditions, would include the automatic dismissal and presumably the detention for trial of all persons in leading positions who have served the Nazis. In order to maintain in operation the essential government services such as railways, food distribution, public utilities, banking, and the like, the permanent officials in the various Ministries who are the least contaminated as Nazis should be temporarily maintained as technical functionaries until time permits the weeding-out process and the installation of persons who are trustworthy.

5. To guide the occupational authorities, one or more small confidential groups might be set up composed of trusted anti-Nazis, competent in various fields of government activity, or leaders in the churches who could confidentially advise the occupation authorities as to the trustworthiness and integrity of the officials to be selected or to be continued in various administrative offices. If great care is exercised, absolutely trustworthy persons for such purposes can be found.

6. The rebuilding of political life in Germany prior to the constitution of any central government must begin in the local communities and then in the German states. For example, to take Bavaria as an instance, we should first select trustworthy Burgermasters for the various Bavarian cities, then we should choose small city and communal councils, then we should allow these bodies to select a central council for the state, thus building up local State government before any attempt is made toward the organization of a central government for the territory that may remain German.

7. As regards the issue as to whether Germany should be partitioned or not, no decision should be reached at the present time. Personally, I am inclined to believe that an enforced partition of Germany would be an error. If the natural tendency of certain areas of Germany is to break away and if, for example, the Rhineland should prefer to join up with France, Holland and Belgium, and Bavaria with the new Austrian State, such movements might be permitted but should not be forced or

artificially stimulated as was the Rhineland Separatist movement after the last war. Prussia must in any event be separated into a series of political units and reduced to modest size to include Berlin, Pomerania, and West Prussia and such, if any, of East Prussia as remains. The tendency toward federalism in Germany may come naturally if the situation is skillfully handled and in drawing any lines of demarcation for military occupation, attention should be paid to the frontiers of the old German states prior to the days of Bismarck.

8. The Nazi Party with its various excrescences is today the sole organized institution in Germany with the single exception of the two churches, the Protestant and Roman Catholic. These churches still have an organization and a substantial following and in both churches there are courageous leaders (as well as back-sliders) who are now planning for the future and whose organizational facilities should be immediately availed of by the occupying authorities. This is important.

After the collapse in Germany, the Communist Party which now has a clandestine activity, and the Socialist and Labor groups will be among the first to attempt to resume organized activity. It seems to be true that the Communist Party in Germany has been instructed by Moscow to lie low until after the German collapse.

9. The future of German industry and economy should be determined only after a full survey has been made of the situation resulting from:

1) The bombing destruction; 2) The transfer of industries to new locations to escape bombing damage; 3) The particular needs of devastated France, Russia, Poland, etc. for manufactured goods and German manual labor; 4) The legitimate desires of the devastated countries to obtain material and labor; 5) The problem of reintegrating German labor into some types of useful work, to prevent social disorder, etc.; 6) The policy with respect to German industry which may be inaugurated by the Russians in the German zone under their occupation.

10. While the course of events in Germany is quite unpredictable, the internal collapse will probably come with the military collapse. and when the complete hopelessness of further military resistance is apparent; it is always possible, however, that there might be a coup d'état after the pattern of the July 20 attempt. If so, it would probably be led by Guderian who is ruthless and realistic. Among the other German Generals who might do something, it is worthwhile to mention General Model who is unscrupulous, vastly ambitious but without great personal force. He might make a deal with us if he felt it would advance his personal career, just as up to the present he has been a "yes" man for Hitler with the same selfish personal ends in view.

11. Upon the German collapse, hundreds of thousands of Nazis and SS will attempt to hide themselves in the German community. There are various conflicting stories as to the extent to which they are already preparing an underground organization. In any event, this is a danger which is sufficiently real to justify the most careful following and we should have in Germany competent secret police and CE forces to attempt to break this up at its inception. The younger generation of Germans are fanatical Nazis and will not change overnight. A long period of education

will be necessary and this education to be effective cannot be under a foreign imposed system. We will have to find the Germans who can re-educate their own people and this re-education may take years.

12. There are also reports, credible but not confirmed, and I believe on the whole unlikely, that the Nazis will create their own Maquis in the Bavarian Alps and the Vorarlberg and attempt to hold out there after resistance is broken in the rest of Germany. This possibility should be considered and studied even though it is in the realm of the improbable rather than the probable.

Document 4-88

Radiotelephone Transmission No. 229, October 23, 1944 (extracts)

[Dulles used his first evening telephone call upon return from consultations to discuss the situation in France and to urge that the Allies recognize General de Gaulle's Provisional Government immediately. He warned of the danger of Communist subversion in the absence of an effective government.]

General

I have just returned after a week spent in France, and this brief report embodies not only my impressions but the opinions gleaned in France and here in Switzerland from persons in whose judgments I have confidence.

The general impression is one of apprehension. The crisis is in the offing in France, and no one knows whether or how it will break. The FFI may have been incorporated into the regular army on paper, but in fact they are still behaving as if they were a state within a state. The CNR is negotiating with the Provisional Government on almost equal terms. The high military official who was charged by de Gaulle with incorporating the FFI and disarming the elements which would not agree to being incorporated finds his task almost impossible of accomplishment under his existing instructions. . . .

As for General de Gaulle, personally, he keeps his own counsel and it is believed that he is now learning a good deal about the France of today that he never thoroughly understood when he was in London and Algiers, where he was kept in the dark by many of his advisers. When he came to France, he apparently thought that France was either Communist or was Clerical-Radical, and that the old bourgeois Socialist Party was finished once and for all. He had not been long in France, however, before he realized his mistake, and recent conversations which he has had with leaders of these bourgeois parties, and reports coming from these leaders indicate that his political enlightenment has made considerable progress.

On one point there appears to be complete unanimity, except in the ranks of the Communists. The Provisional Government of de Gaulle should be recognized by the United States, Great Britain and Russia at the earliest possible moment, in order that it may have the strength and prestige to cope more effectively with the manifold problems which it has to face. Even de Gaulle's personal and political opponents, insofar as they are true Frenchmen, are united on this point. Today they consider the failure to recognize de Gaulle as a slight, not to de Gaulle, but to France, and as such they resent it.

We find ourselves in a vicious circle. If we say that we will not recognize that government, until there has been a formal approval by vote of the French people, we may deprive the Provisional Government of the prestige and authority necessary to proceed to any such consultation under the conditions permitting a true popular expression of opinion. The Provisional Government, if not strengthened, may not be able to meet the determined threat of the Communist minority, and elections held by a partially discredited unrecognized government might well lead to a Communist victory. There cannot be any real doubt today that the Provisional Government is the only body which conceivably could exercise governmental authority in France, unless such authority is exercised by the Communists, or unless France slips into a condition of anarchy, which many serious-minded people fear.

The problem is no longer solely a political one; it has its serious military implications. If we are obliged to ensure necessary order along essential lines of communications by our own military forces, and if we cannot rely on orderly French administration, we will be forced to divert troops which can better be employed at the fighting front. . . .

There seems to be general agreement that France is not Communist. In fact, the Communists, a remarkably small minority, are greatly concerned to prevent their numerical weakness from coming to light. . . .

However, all observers agree in their warning not to underestimate the danger that the Communists will contrive to gain control when the elections come by using their technique of infiltration. They have won their victories the world over by tricks put on by small but determined minorities, and the very fact that they know that they are sliding will make them willing to take big risks. They know well that this coming winter is a great opportunity. France is without transportation, practically without heat, without many of the important services, and without rapid intercommunication between the various parts of the country. This winter may well be a harder one in France than even the four preceding winters of German occupation. These next months are the great opportunity for the Communists. . . .

Document 4-89

Telegram 1498-1504, October 24, 1944

[In this message, Dulles deals with the complex issues of coordination created by the advance of Allied forces in France. It gives a snapshot view of the new situation. Number 399 is Gerhard Van Arkel of the OSS Labor Desk.]

110 for 105. I met Stoneborough and Gamble on my return trip to confer with them on future plans for liaison work, and in addition I talked with General Devers and the G-2 branches of the 6th and 7th Armies. All parties concurred in the opinion given by Bill Jackson and General Sibert, that they wished to continue to have direct contact with us for battle order information. I also looked into the present situation in Annemasse and Pontarlier and I should like to advance the following recommendations:

1. I advise that we establish a temporary liaison post in Pontarlier to afford improved communications with the 6th, and 12th Army Groups and the 7th Army. The refugees who have been moved from the Belfort region via Switzerland into France offer the Nazis good cover for infiltration of spies, saboteurs and the like, and because of this, General Devers is apprehensive about the situation on the Franco-Swiss border in the area of Pontarlier. Essentially this concerns the army, but a station at Pontarlier might secure valuable information and could be used to dispatch agents to and from Switzerland for German work as well. Gamble is willing to put Major Simon in the post at Pontarlier and he will soon send you a report on his findings there. This station at Pontarlier should probably be moved east to the region of Mulhouse and Belfort as the Allies press ahead into Alsace.

2. Annemasse has many uses, but the matter of responsibility should be settled. I feel that this place should be used mainly for penetration into Italy through France and to service Switzerland. It should also be employed for such penetration into the Reich as can be managed well from there, including that of 399 and of Henry Hyde.

3. Gamble was most willing to cooperate, but he naturally felt that he is not responsible for either Pontarlier or Annemasse. From a military supply standpoint, I suggest that both be directed from Paris. If you wish, I am agreeable to assuming responsibility for these posts in matters of overall policy directives and in working out arrangements on conflicting requests from different theaters and agents. Pontarlier is easily accessible by car and I have a direct phone connection with Annemasse.

4. I should very much like to transfer most of the Italian work from here to Campione and Annemasse. This has become a very ticklish problem and I do not want further to burn our situation and create any feeling that might be detrimental to the pursuit of our main job to the north. I have been informed that Major Cox has schemes in mind for the penetration of Italy via the Franco-Italian border. For these, the Annemasse post might prove useful to him. To some extent, this might help to solve the present troublesome job of supplying partisans in this sector by plane.

5. The efficiency of our messenger service with our armies and to Paris is a big factor in the ultimate value of our work here. The weekly Paris Embassy service is at our disposal, but I advise you to talk with Edward Clark at the Embassy to see if it is possible to make this service more frequent. I am also making use of 520's twice weekly service to the 7th Army. For the time being this could be utilized for communication with the 6th Army Group, but nothing has been worked out for

the 12th Army. Since I understand that the 12th Army rather than the 6th Army Group possibly is to be assigned to occupy the American Zone in Germany, it seems of special importance that the Sibert-Jackson initiative be pursued, and that we set up direct relations with them from here, unless you believe that Paris would be a better location from which to handle this.

6. Ted Ryan, now at Caserta or Bari, has been recommended by Gamble for reports officer here, especially for battle order work and for contact with our Army Groups. Jigsaw and 399 agree with Gamble's selection. Please rush Ryan's assignment for a clerk's job at the legation if this is possible and if Glavin approves.

Document 4-90

Telegram 4867-69, October 25, 1944

[Admiral Horthy, Regent of Hungary, delivered a broadcast on October 15 announcing that his nation was requesting an armistice. He was immediately replaced by the Germans. Horthy and other members of the former government were arrested the following day and deported to Germany. As Soviet forces advanced, Dulles, Royall Tyler (number 477), and U.S. Minister Harrison continued to take an interest in noncommunist Hungarian resistance elements.]

From 110. 477 tells me that the quotation given below is a translation of an open radio communication in Hungarian heard on the Moscow radio the 22nd of this month. "MFM advises their representative in Switzerland, Bakach Bessenyey, that the proper contacts have been made. They advise Tony in Geneva that he ought to be ready to go abroad because, should the need arise, he will be asked to afford the negotiations his expert help."

Tony is Baron Anthony Radvanssky, once the secretary-general of the Hungarian National Bank and an old friend of mine and of 477. He has been working here with Bakach Bessenyey, our 684, ever since the country was occupied by the Nazis last March, on Hungarian resistance activities. This resistance movement uses the name MFM. Radvanssky is ready to go to Moscow if he is asked.

The MFM, which includes a number of Hungarian ex-diplomats, represents the liberal anti-German circles but not the Communists. It is thought that the foregoing communication was sent by members of this group who had got through the Russian lines to Moscow. Since Moscow permitted the communication to be broadcast, it seems likely that the Russians intend to play with certain anti-Communist groups in Hungary for some ultimate aim as yet unknown to us. Tachauer and Bolgar, 2 Hungarians connected with MFM, are broadcasting on the Soviet-controlled Sofia radio twice a week.

Would appreciate your letting us know if you have had any news of this Hungarian resistance movement from Moscow or elsewhere.

Document 4-91

Telegram 4872, October 25, 1944

[Bombing results continued to be an important aspect of reportage from OSS Bern.]

A trustworthy source has introduced a Chinese engineer to us who says that not very long ago he was working at the Vereinigte Aluminium Werke Lautawerk near Dresden. He declared that the bombing of September 12 was especially successful because only a few days before the anti-aircraft guns had been taken out and shipped to the front. The engineer says that the greater part of the works was demolished and that in all likelihood the Germans will be unable to get them working again before the war is over. The electric transformer was utterly ruined. According to the source, the factory manufactured about 25 per cent of the aluminum put out in Germany.

Document 4-92

Telegram 10, October 29, 1944

[Dulles reports that German Ambassador von Rahn and General Wolff have attempted to reach a modus vivendi with Italian partisans. The same individuals would figure prominently in 1945 negotiations for the surrender of German forces in Italy.]

Chris service reports von Rahn and Wolff, representing, respectively, German diplomatic and Gestapo services North Italy, summoned 2 representatives Turin CLNAI, including Pasoni, Socialist member of Turin committee and proposed to them armistice for Piedmont under which partisans would agree to restrict their activities to certain mountain areas and under these conditions would be left unmolested by Germans. Reported this proposal rejected and as consequence Germans threatened immediate cleanup of Piedmont valleys and particularly said they knew all about contact with Swiss via Valtournache and Breuil in upper Aosta Valley and proposed to liquidate this resistance nest.

Document 4-93

Telegram 127, October 29, 1944

[Ironically, the opening of the French-Swiss frontier aggravated OSS Bern staff shortages.]

From 110. This is an SOS. Our very limited personnel now seriously depleted by loss of half of internee coding staff. View new demands on us from Armies and other quarters resulting from opening frontier and greatly increased incoming code traffic in new cipher we are now in situation where with present staff we can barely decode incoming messages and outgoing messages are delayed 2 to 3 days, 25 cables now awaiting despatch. Preparation of Battle Order and other material has practically come to a standstill. We have plenty of generals for the moment but no privates to get out the work. . . .

Document 4-94

Telegram 19, October 31, 1944

[Numerous reports of escape plans by Nazi leaders began to appear. Dulles relays one such item to General Donovan.]

For 109 from 110. Trusted intermediary who has rendered us recognized services over past two years has been informed via Zurich lawyer who has specialized in representing South and Central American countries that Goering and Ley are making plans to leave Germany via Suisse about middle November and are putting up very large sums in Swiss francs to buy passage and false passports of some South American country. Understand they will travel separately, one coming via Leichtensteil(?) and other via Friedrichshafen. Intermediary indicates Zurich lawyer prepared to work with us in order facilitate apprehension at convenient point. This may be fairy story even though person who brought news is completely trustworthy. Latter, however, may be misinformed. However, will follow matter closely and report developments. At moment no question of payment by us has been raised, as Zurich lawyer and his contacts apparently would have no scruples in taking the Nazis' money. My intermediary expressed surprise that Goering and Ley could not get plane for Spain trip. Zurich lawyer replied too closely guarded, but might be able get near Swiss frontier.

Document 4-95

Telegram 337, November 3, 1944

[This message concerns the trip of Italian partisan leader Ferruccio Parri and two colleagues from northern to southern Italy through France. They were captured by the Germans on the return trip, and were later released as part of the negotiations for the German surrender in Italy in the spring of 1945.]

From 110. Three representatives of CLNAI Milan, namely Parri, previously referred to as Attom, who is one of principal members of military section of Milan committee, Longhi, and Sogno are passing through here shortly enroute to southern Italy for consultations which understand requested by AFHQ there. Trip through here to Lyon is being arranged by my Zulu SOE colleague in full collaboration with me. I consider Parri's trip of great importance as he is probably best qualified person to advise fully regarding Italian partisan activity North Italy. Trust you will arrange to see him. Will report further after conference with him later this week.

Document 4-96

Telegram 387, November 3, 1944

[This message contains Dulles's account of a meeting with General Guisan, Swiss Army commander (number 839), at which Hitler's health and the accidental U.S. bombing of Swiss territory were discussed.]

In personal conversation yesterday with 839 he stated that information reached them from 2 trustworthy sources that Hitler was really ill. Reports indicate that while he quickly recovered from immediate effects of July 20 attack, he later had some sort of cerebral hemorrhage resulting from shock and has been in bed approximately 3 months. This accounts for his failure to deliver Volkssturm speech. Alleged public appearances of Hitler during this period were fictitious.

839, who is a good friend of ours, was obviously seriously disturbed at repetition of our bombing attacks on Swiss towns and villages. He indicated this was seriously affecting attitude Swiss people toward USA. While realizing mistakes are inevitable he could not understand low level attacks on Swiss territory. Personally I believe situation created by attacks makes it more difficult to get Swiss cooperation in our present task of penetrating Germany. Assume everything being done to prevent recurrence.

Document 4-97

Telegram 42, November 4, 1944

[Marshal Albert Kesselring became German Commander in Chief Southwest in the fall of 1943 and was commander of German troops in Italy. He played a role in the early stages of negotiations for the surrender of German forces there in early 1945. Dulles reported on his wounding in October 1944.]

Press report that Kesselring gravely injured confirmed by good source who states that occurred October 24th somewhere near front, when returning from General Staff meeting. Apparently circumstances of accident very similar to Rommel's. Question arises whether accident result bombing attack, partisan sabotage or SS attempt eliminate K. It is significant that on Monday following accident, K was scheduled conclude agreement with Fascist government, proposed by Italian industrialists in agreement with General Leyers, restricting further immediate export Italian industrial machinery to Germany, but providing plan whereby at last moment important parts this machinery would go Germany to cripple industry in event German evacuation. SS opposed agreement and advocated continued stripping Italian industry.

Document 4-98

Telegram 44, November 5, 1944

[This message concerns intelligence implications of Italian representation in Switzerland.]

Italian Minister received instructions from FO which in effect mean clean sweep Italian diplomatic and consular representatives with few exceptions. Also, certain consular offices closed. While I understand Italian desire for house cleaning and economy measures these instructions will remove certain individuals and close certain offices useful to us in operations. For example, understand consulates Chur and Sion to be closed. These are only official cover usable in these areas and with increasing importance of Stelvio pass route for German retreat we were considering building certain operations out of consulate Chur.

Realize this is delicate matter and naturally don't wish interfere in removal of personnel whom Italian Government considers tainted by Fascist connections. Could you discuss situation with Kirk and possibly see whether in certain cases there could be few months delay in closing certain offices especially Chur and Sion, and removing certain personnel who actively linked with us in present operations, particularly consulate Lausanne where we have no representation? In most cases changes merely effect substituting one functionary for another and new arrivals will be of little use to us for some time.

Document 4-99

Telegram 537, November 7, 1944

[Dulles continues to report on internal dissension in Germany.]

Source close to SS advises 476 that leading German industrialists together with certain Wehrmacht circles desire end war promptly to prevent complete destruction industrial plants by air raids and devastation incident fighting on German territory. However, these army and industrial groups feel they have insufficient power overthrow Hitler, Himmler regime and therefore necessary secure collaboration of certain less compromised but still influential SS members. Talks along these lines understood to be going on secretly. Our informant is close to Kauffmann, Gauleiter of Hamburg, one of abler and less compromised of Gauleiters. Informant also states that Brauchitsch indicated willingness accept command on East front provided Halder act as his chief of staff.

Schacht recently released from arrest but understand Hitler personally studying his dossier to determine possible July 20 complicity, since he was on plotters' list as Minister of Economics. Source states Goerdeler not executed, which tends to confirm Stockholm report your #005. Understand he being kept alive by Himmler to use in emergency for contact with Anglo-Saxons.

Document 4-100

Telegram 667, November 10, 1944

[Parri and other Italian resistance leaders traveled to Allied Headquarters at Caserta to establish liaison. Colonel Edward J. F. Glavin was head of the 2677th Regiment, the OSS headquarters for the Mediterranean theater at Caserta. General Raffaele Cadorna was sent by the Italian Government to take command of the resistance movement in the north.]

Mare now Communist member of Military Committee CLNAI is proceeding with Parri and others instead of Gallo. Met with them yesterday and they proceeding to Lyons from Geneva tomorrow. We are facilitating transportation to Lyons, but Zulu arranging papers and air transport to Italy.

For Glavin: Believe important you and others concerned see Parri during his stay. He generally familiar OSS work North Italy. Trust that Parri's visit will facilitate solution of financing CLNAI. We are extending no further aid now and ZULU is also holding up financial aid pending result this visit. Understand that CLNAI is in agreement that Cadorno [Cadorna] be military head North Italian resistance with Parri and Gallo as deputies.

Document 4-101

Telegram 677, November 10, 1944

[As the outcome of the war became obvious, Allied intelligence in Switzerland received various inquiries and peace feelers from German individuals. This message is another indication of imperfect coordination between Dulles and his British counterparts. Number 502 is Colonel Prince Alois Auersperg, Abwehr agent and Assistant Air Attaché in the German Consulate at Bern.]

Our 502 has been consulted on following matter by Neurath, German Consul Lugano and son of former German Foreign Minister. Neurath claims that Cable, Zulu Consul General, Zurich, approached him through Bishop of Lugano stating Cable desired establish contact with SS. Neurath desired some evidence Cable's intentions and was apparently shown copy of unsigned document indicating British interest in organization anti-Bolshevist front Germany and preservation Germanic race.

Neurath then got approval of Himmler to bring to Switzerland one important SS personality stationed at present in Italy. Bernardici, Papal Nuncio in Bern, well known to 140 knows of these feelers through Bishop of Lugano and proposed 110 should be introduced into any conversations between SS personality and Cable.

Understand this matter caused some excitement in SS quarters in Berlin. Cable is an expansive person and has not given impression here of being particularly discreet. Difficult for me to judge whether this is his own initiative as consider unlikely he would have been used for highly confidential task.

View possible capital Nazis could make out of this vis-à-vis Russians I have had nothing whatever to do with it, but I am considering putting cutout in direct touch with Neurath who undoubtedly has interesting contacts.

For Armour London: suggest no distribution whatever of this message unless instructed by Washington.

Document 4-102

Telegram 747, November 15, 1944

[With access to Switzerland restored, the Allies dispatched expert delegations to collect intelligence on the status of the German atomic energy development program, augmenting and partially supplanting the efforts of OSS Bern. A measure of redundancy and discord resulted. Those mentioned in this message include Samuel Goudsmit, scientific head of the Alsos Mission, and Morris "Moe" Berg.]

. . . Believe you should realize that if we put Wardenburg and Goudsmit in touch with Flute it will be difficult duplicate later with Chittick and Berg. If they are all here at the same time to make initial contact under our introduction we can later determine who is best qualified follow up on permanent basis. These contacts are particularly temperamental and in case of Flute heavily overworked and all approaches require greatest care and tact.

Document 4-103

Telegram 757, November 15, 1944

[This report that the Germans planned to evacuate northwestern Italy within a month is an example of increasing Swiss cooperation in intelligence matters.]

Learn confidentially from highest Swiss source that Kesselring has received orders to complete German withdrawal from northwest Italy by December 15th. Extent of withdrawal not indicated but supposition that it would be to Lake Garda-Adige area. Difficulty of transport, due to early snows, one of ostensible reasons for withdrawal.

Document 4-104

Telegram 867, November 19, 1944

[When General Donovan approached General Henry H. Arnold, Commanding General, Army Air Forces, concerning the bombing of Swiss towns, he was informed that the reports could not be confirmed and that perhaps the attacks were the work of Germans using captured American planes. Instructed to raise that possibility with the Swiss, Dulles responded with irritation. Number 520 is General Legge, the U.S. Military Attaché.]

109 from 110. In reference to your #0777. 520 and air attaché examined bomb craters near Eglisau which was latest attack and found fragment of American 1,000 pound bomb. Swiss observers state they clearly identified planes as American planes, reports indicate 14 to 15 involved. It will be hard to make Swiss believe that Germans had this number of American planes with American bombs assigned to apparent task of blowing up power plant in which Germans have joint interest with Swiss. Unfortunately evidence available 520 does not bear out thesis in your paragraph 1.

Document 4-105

Telegram 927, November 20, 1944

[OSS Bern relayed reports of the collapse of the German transportation system. From time to time, Dulles and other OSS officials considered fomenting strikes in Germany, despite the brutality of Nazi repression; this message relates to such strategy.]

From 110. Dr. Schnurre, leading German government economic expert just visited Switzerland. He stated to thoroughly trustworthy friend, who advised us, that German traffic problem approaching catastrophe and might lead to most serious crisis during next few weeks. According to Schnurre it is becoming impossible distribute food supplies adequately with result that for first time population cannot obtain food called for by ration cards and German organization for food distribution threatened with disruption. Schnurre stated that chief fear haunting Nazis was possibility of general strike in railways. Continuous raids on trains and transport facilities made RR men reluctant to work and further German labor felt that RR strike was type of action which would carry blow to heart of Nazi war machine and therefore offered better possibilities to end war than local strike in industrial plants. View source and character of this information, consider it carries real weight. Our other reports confirm increasing crisis in German transport problem.

Document 4-106

Telegram 969, November 20, 1944

["George Wood" continued to supply OSS Bern with information and documents obtained from the German Foreign Ministry. In response to OSS requirements, much of the material dealt with the Japanese target. KANOV connotes information received in November 1944.]

KAPPA. This is a Kanov message. Japan. Following is extract of more urgent Jap military information contained in Kanov:

1. German MA School Bangkok November 8th: learns from Nakamura that after rain period big English offensive expected direction Rangoon, Bangkok, Saigon mainly by land operations with air supply. Major landings expected west Rangoon subsidiary operations against Andaman Islands. Japs optimistic preparing counter measures. Marshal Terauchi's staff to be transferred soon from Manila to Saigon. In preparation Jap military police said to have just arrested 3,000 Gaullists but don't intend interfere Indo-China's independence for the moment.

2. MA Tokio Kretschmer November 11th: Japs expect middle November new American landings Philippines outside Leyte, perhaps Luzon southeast of Manila, confident as to defense possibilities. Jap landings Leyte have not yet restored balance but preparing counter attacks. Samar situation bad for Japan.

3. Ditto November 8th: increased riots and sabotage in whole Philippines especially Leyte and Samar. British commando raid near Akaab (sic) interpreted as preparation later landing. First Allied air attack on Jap naval bases Seletar (sic) and refineries Medan claimed unsuccessful believed to be flown from India but perhaps from southern China. While Burmese and Malayan populations safe, attitude certain Thailand sectors considered dangerous. Japs expect soon occupation Liuchow.

4. Niemoeller (with subsignature Kretschmer) Tokio November 9th Japs ask information about defense measures against V-1 as they expect possible American attacks with similar weapons. However, large defensive use of flak, aircraft or balloons as in England not feasible due shortages.

5. Grand memo unsigned reporting conversation with Jap Berlin Embassy Secretary Ushida October 27th. Jap attacks 13th to 16th October only Air Force, attack 17th October by combined fleet. Japs claimed smashing victory. (Wood commented on this as example of Jap lies to Germany.)

Document 4-107

Telegram 1037, November 22, 1944

[Despite his interest in psychological warfare, Dulles expressed doubts about proposals to expand activities of the OSS Morale Operations Branch in Switzerland. This position was consistent with his preference to manage psychological and informational programs out of Switzerland himself, with the cooperation of OWI representative Gerald Mayer.]

110 to Mann, MO . . . . Various proposals for MO work through Suisse directed chiefly against Germany have been made and believe desirable we have meeting Annemasse on date to be determined (I suggest December 10) with representatives interested parties to try to coordinate action and discuss: 1) MO work now being done from here. 2) Possibilities for extension and redirection this work. 3) Assignment of permanent or agent personnel Suisse. 4) Liaison personnel Annemasse or elsewhere.

I am frankly not over-optimistic that results MO work via Suisse will justify doing much more than now being attempted from here, but recognize I do not have entire picture. Clandestine passages via Suisse limited, as is personnel we can maintain here and I am apprehensive that time, personnel and clandestine passage can only be allocated to MO at expense other activities, especially SI and latter seems to me now of paramount importance as far as OSS Suisse concerned. Would appreciate your reaction above and view in reference to utility of proposed meeting.

Document 4-108

Telegram 917 to Caserta, November 23, 1944

[Dulles addresses the necessity for the Allies to assert control over the Italian resistance in the interests of military efficiency and postliberation civil order.]

Having worked past year close touch CLNAI, particularly with Longhi and Marri believe measures to strengthen CLNAI would solidify resistance and increase possibility maintain civil order, North Italy period immediately after German withdrawal. Certain this is only Italian organization which could perform any useful function this nature North Italy; unfortunately CLNAI tends confuse military and political objectives, and if [garble] support . . . accorded would seem wise that control military activities, presumably under Cadorna, subject Allied command, should be established. Re our own relations CLNAI, assume we will insist 50-50 participation with SOE. I appreciate your current information and wait final conclusions. If mission returns via Switzerland advise if I can facilitate trip through Annemasse or other.

Document 4-109

Radiotelephone Transmission No. 242, November 23, 1944
(extract)

[Dulles presents this overly optimistic view of the state of the war one month before the Nazi Ardennes offensive.]

Germany
In judging the German situation from this nearby vantage point, it is sometimes difficult not to be over-influenced by what has proved to be temporary military successes on our part, or by momentary but possibly passing military, economic or internal crises in Germany. However, with all due allowance, there is an accumulation of evidence indicating that Germany is now going through a particularly serious and what may prove to be a fateful crisis. They may be able to stand on the Rhine, and in the South and East, for a little time longer, but the next week may well prove decisive, unless weather conditions are so impossible as to stop the offensives which are rapidly closing in on Germany, or to prevent the bombardments which are wrecking industry and transportation.

As to the Western Front, the events of the last few days have been particularly alarming for Germany. The fact that we have reached the Rhine in Alsace would have an effect, insofar as anything can have effect, on the benumbed German people. The reaction of Berlin to the battles near Aachen are [is] somber. Despite the recently reinforced censorship over all dispatches of foreign correspondents in Germany, the Berlin correspondent of La Suisse was able to report today that the battle of Aachen is alarming Berlin, and that the operation of General Patton's army, if it succeeded, would be very important for the months to come, because it would mean the total occupation of the Ruhr, and that, in consequence, Berlin was considering the present battle, not only as a defensive battle for the Siegfried Line, but for the region of the Rhine and the Ruhr, and for the entire Reich. These are significant words to hear from Germany. . . .

Document 4-110

Telegram 957 to Caserta, November 24, 1944

[This telegram treats questions relating to relations with the Italian resistance, including establishment of control by the Allies via an Italian military officer, funding, parachute drops, and Anglo-American coordination.]

Have just conferred with Captain Pieri, General Cadorna's aide, who was sent here by latter to report: (1) Cadorna (hereinafter called by his nom de guerre, Valenti, for security reasons), acting for past 15 days as military chief North Italy but recognizes that his possibility of action depends upon closest consultation and accord with military representatives of five parties, on CLNAI, and particularly upon close collaboration with Parri and Gallo. Apparently Valenti does not ask that he be given anything approaching military dictatorship North Italy as effective action only possible if partisan leaders with their varying political affiliations go along willingly with him. Rather he feels situation must be handled by diplomacy rather than by military dictation. (2) Valenti's representative emphasizes that question of financing is urgent. He desires that funds for distribution to bands should be put at Valenti's disposition for distribution. In this manner his effective authority over bands can be reinforced. Meanwhile local representative CLNAI, who called on me with Valenti's envoy, urged earliest possible solution of financial problem . . . and asked whether I could help them meanwhile. I answered that I could do nothing pending determination of this whole matter which now being considered with CLNAI in Rome. (3) CLNAI committee Turin sent via Magistrati appeal for financial help and Magistrati received from Rome authorization addressed to Turin banks to advance fifty million to Turin committee against promise of reimbursement by Italian Government. Dugoni . . . , who leaving today for Annemasse to establish line into Turin, will pass on message via Chris service. (4) . . . , re parachutage. Pieri promises send me Valenti's suggestions shortly. Pieri does not consider massive daylight drops feasible at present time and for moment favors 5 to 6 plane droppings by night but hopes give me definite indications within week and believes something might shortly be arranged in Cuneo region. Need for explosives for sabotage, and winter clothing particularly acute. (5) Pieri emphasizes that partisan movement now undergoing serious crisis and I gather that much reorganization, and particularly coordination with our military authorities, urgently required. (6) Local representation of CLNAI may need some slight financial aid and I have advised them that I would assist up to 5,000 Swiss francs for November-December. (7) . . . I have just learned from local CLNAI representative that Zulu SOE here recently advanced additional 50,000,000 lira to CLNAI. This corresponds to our second payment of 50,000,000 and means that total advances of Zulu SOE to CLNAI from here have somewhat exceeded ours.

Document 4-111

Telegram 1217, November 25, 1944

[As the end approached for Germany, Japanese personnel sought sanctuary in neutral Switzerland.]

From 110 and DB/001. 472 reports: 1. Japanese Embassy Berlin evacuating certain services including intelligence and press to Suisse. 2. Japs advised Swiss of intention create consulate at Zurich and renting large villas here. 3. Domei agency reported opening offices Zurich and Geneva to which Berlin services being transferred. 4. Approximately 100 Japs apart from officials requested Swiss entry visas and 5 secretaries or attachés recently transferred Embassy Berlin to Bern.

Investigating this report and hope cable further details shortly.

Document 4-112

Telegram 1407, November 29, 1944

[OSS Bern gave further consideration to promoting a railway strike in Germany. Number 399 is Gerhard Van Arkel, formerly of the OSS Labor Desk in Algiers, who arrived in Bern in September 1944. Van Arkel gradually assumed day-to-day direction of labor/socialist-based intelligence and of special operations penetration of enemy territory from Switzerland.]

From 110 and 399. We have been studying possibility of attempting to organize general railway strike in western Germany as possibly most effective means of crippling German war effort. In discussion last night with Eclair and 328 they considered idea worth following up and are sending couriers north to contact railway workers to ascertain their views as to practicability of such measures and as to simultaneous and coordinated steps which might be taken on our side both from viewpoint of propaganda and possibly from viewpoint institution particular type of bombing campaign against RR objectives.

It is our idea that if we could persuade RR workers that after certain date they would be merely sacrificing their lives in order to prolong Nazi war by continuing to run trains, it would give added incentive to strike idea. Our plans are as yet quite tentative and we cannot underwrite probabilities of direct accomplishment, but consider this whole program is well worth considering and would be most interested to have SHAEF reaction. We still consider here that transportation is Germany's most vulnerable point and that over next weeks everything should be done to bring about breakdown transportation in western Germany.

For London. 399 considers that Hans Jahn might be extremely helpful in this connection and suggests Pratt or 922 discuss matter with him pending Eclair's return, when he will also go into matter with his friends.

In general connection foregoing, today's *National Zeitung-Bale* states German RR administration has called upon heavy industry to repair their own freight cars.

Document 4–113

Telegram 1467, November 30, 1944

[Dulles exercised a leadership role in reorganizing OSS operations in Europe in accordance with the evolving military situation.]

Baker arrived last night Annemasse and we had a very satisfactory meeting. Present were Baker, Mathieu, Hyde, Volpe, Mellon, 399 and 110. Matters affecting Hyde service discussed and understanding reached that Volpe would continue his work for Hyde but from administrative angle would keep Baker advised, it being understood that Baker should be kept acquainted with all activities in general Annemasse area. Discussed Italian work and use of base for penetration of Germany and quick liaison with Switzerland, Mellon acting as liaison officer, Geneva.

Document 4–114

Telegram 1687 to Paris, November 30, 1944

[This message concerns Dulles's relationship with Noel Field, an individual now known to have served as a Soviet agent at the State Department and the League of Nations in the 1930s.]

From 110. Noel Field, our 394 prior liberation of France, maintained close contact with anti-Nazi German group composed of German political refugees, deserters, etc. This group actively engaged since November 1942 in clandestine propaganda and sabotage with headquarters largely Marseille, later Paris. Thru Field, we furnished part of funds for financing this group's activities. From Field I understand group is now continuing active work in France under name "National Komitee Freies Deutschland fuer der Western." While group now working largely with FFI, Field understands they have some representatives working with our troops. Possible that group contains valuable personnel for German penetration and consider it urgent that Field discuss whole problem with you and put you in touch with certain of their leaders who are now in Paris and whom he knows personally.

Field's main task is director for Western Europe of Unitarian Service Committee and as such he has so far been refused SHAEF permit to proceed France although all French approvals given and understand French relief organization most anxious for him to come. Sam Reber, personal friend of Field, is fully informed of his relief work, but not with clandestine activity.

Would appreciate your discussion with SHAEF to ascertain whether permission for Field to go to France to establish contact with you in connection with above clandestine work can be quickly arranged. You can tell Reber that this is not an excuse to get around SHAEF apparent reluctance to permit American relief workers to come to France, and Field would be willing to come to France to see you and return to Suisse if this latter question is not settled favorably in meantime. Kindly investigate soonest and advise.

Document 4-115

Telegram 1607, December 2, 1944

[Dulles anticipated heading the OSS "German Unit," a mission that would enter the Reich immediately after the end of the war. Interdepartmental organizational arrangements proved troublesome, as indicated in this cable to Donovan.]

Action: 109 and Leo. Information: Armour, Bastedo and 105. Last sentences of phraseology tentatively worked out with Murphy as quoted London cable November 30, #92364 to Washington, #23124 to Paris, gives me real concern. In practical effect this would mean dual control by Military and State Department. Further, as we are primarily responsible to military authorities and submit all reports to them, we cannot control their transmission of such reports to Washington. Practical impossibility of defining what constitutes political reports might lead to endless misunderstandings. Any report on German conditions might be deemed to have political implications.

In view of complete uncertainty as to conditions under which we will work in Germany and whether physical location our headquarters will be Berlin or elsewhere, it seems to me unwise to commit ourselves on procedural matters at this stage. In any event we are in the hands of the higher governmental authorities to whom we are responsible and I have little doubt as to ability to reach agreement with Murphy when we know practical conditions under which we will respectively work. Until such conditions determined, I believe unwise to accept the wording of the last sentence of this draft.

Document 4-116

Telegram 1849 to Paris, December 2, 1944

[Switzerland remained a major listening post for information on the German atomic energy program.]

AZUSA. From 110 and 493 to 105 or Giblin for Major Furman. Information: 106, Washington. Isotope separation plant located Berlin has made big step forward by using following new process which gives increase in concentration up to 3% each time. Separation is carried out by solid electrolysis of crystals formed by a salt of uranium isotopes. Difference in electric charge to mass ration of each isotope salt gives different electrolysis velocity for each isotope according to its atomic weight. Flute's source did not know which uranium salt used. Hope to identify Flute's source and cable more soon. Weizsaecker lectured November 30 in Zurich on cosmology. In private he said he and other physicists [garble]schungsstelle E live in Hechingen.

Document 4-117

Letter to Colonel David Bruce, OSS Paris, December 2, 1944

[Dulles provided a channel of communication for Catholic Church authorities, who sought an agreement with the Germans specifying that the latter would not adopt a scorched earth policy when forced to retreat from northern Italy.]

Dear David:

I refer to my telegrams . . . , outlining the plan of the ecclesiastical authorities of North Italy for sparing North Italy from destruction upon the German withdrawal. Enclosed are three copies of a careful translation of the memorandum which was handed to me November 30 by the Secretary of Cardinal Schuster, Bicchierai. The important points of the conversation which my British SOE colleague and I had jointly with Bicchierai are summarized in my cable.

Bicchierai came here thoroughly authenticated and stayed with the Nuncio while in Bern. As stated in the cable, he impressed us with his sincerity and I have no doubt as to the authenticity of the document which he brought, which is undoubtedly, primarily, the work of Cardinal Schuster of Milan, but which he states was concurred in by the Cardinals of Genoa and Turin. The only other two Cardinals of North Italy, namely Venice and Bologna, were not brought into the matter, since Bologna is in the area of the present fighting and Venice would probably not be evacuated by the Germans at the present time in any event.

My British colleague and I were careful to make no commitment on the proposal. We expressed our understanding of the humanitarian objectives which the ecclesiastical authorities had in view and said we would submit the document to our respective military authorities.

As I reported, the document will be sent forward in due course by the Nuncio to Rome, and possibly a copy will go through the lines via an envoy named Frascati, who I understand has been sent by General Cadorna.

As I have no early means of sending this paper either to Washington or to Caserta, I would greatly appreciate it if you would send a copy forward to each place, with a copy of this letter.

Faithfully yours, Allen W. Dulles

Document 4-118

Telegram 1757, December 5, 1944

[Dulles reports to Donovan on additional efforts by Neurath, German Consul at Lugano, to establish contact.]

From 110 to 109 and 154. In reference to my #0677. N, mentioned 1st paragraph my cable has made several efforts to establish contact with me through 502. According to latter, N is acting as intermediary for SS Polizei Gen. Harster now North Italy, who said to have special mission from Himmler through subordinate in the SS hierarchy to Wolff. Unless I have evidence that concrete information of value could be obtained, I propose continue handle through cutout either 502 or 476. If you have any special views in reference to method of handling this type situation, please advise.

Document 4-119

Telegram 2027 to Paris, December 6, 1944

[OSS Switzerland conducted various operations designed to disrupt day-to-day life in enemy territory, including the distribution of bogus food-rationing cards in Germany. Colonel Edward Gamble was commander of the OSS forward detachment accompanying advancing U.S. forces in France.]

One of our chief agents in Basel area claims to have attempted successfully distribution German food cards, seized Alsace, in neighboring German territory east of Rhine. Claims it should be possible to obtain in Alsace ration cards of 70th period, which are valid from December 10th, and he has means of distribution. Also states has obtained few hundred kilos ration cards for 69th period, expiring December 10th, which distributed Grenzach and Lorrach, with result that at both places all food sold out by noon on 2 successive days. Suggest via Gamble we might obtain cards for 70th period. Kindly investigate.

Document 4-120

Letter to Joseph C. Grew, Under Secretary of State, December 6, 1944

[The Foreign Service connections established by Dulles from 1916 to 1926 and maintained thereafter provided him with a basic source of influence and support. Dulles had known Joseph Grew since they served together on the U.S. Delegation at the Paris Peace Conference of 1919.]

Dear Joe:

You cannot appreciate the pleasure and satisfaction it was to hear of your appointment as Under Secretary of State. We are going into the most critical period of American foreign policy when the greatest wisdom and foresight will be required if our diplomacy is to realize the maximum for the country from our magnificent successes in battle. It is certainly reassuring to know that you will have such a leading part in the formulation of policy.

Switzerland continues to be a fascinating point of observation. I only wish we could get more for you on the Far Eastern end of things. From various indications it seems that the Japanese have decided to make Switzerland their European observation point for the coming years. As I have cabled, members of the Japanese official and unofficial family in Berlin are coming here as they realize that their days in Germany are numbered and that when the German collapse comes, their position in Germany will be precarious—not only because we could seize them but also because they well might have their throats cut by an enraged German populace which is inclined to hold the German-Japanese alliance responsible for having brought the United States into the war against Germany.

I am trying to build up lines into Germany which both before and after the crash, will help us to get our hands on as much material about the Far East as is possible. Some of it is coming out now and I assume gets to you.

With love to Alice and my very best wishes.

Sincerely yours, A. W. Dulles

Document 4-121

Telegram 1937, December 9, 1944

[As in other countries, German official representation in Switzerland began to disintegrate as it became obvious that the war was lost. Dulles discouraged defections and resignations, because his sources in the German diplomatic and intelligence community were valuable only so long as they remained in place.]

1. OWI in New York open cable to Mayer OWI here queried report by Radio Atlantic that 2 members of the German Legation here, namely Federer and Walter Bayer, had resigned.

2. While realize difficulty of controlling Atlantic broadcasts, recommend they do not broadcast rumors regarding anti-Nazi activities here without some prior check. Federer and Bayer are both unimportant as far as news value goes, but former was useful to us and this usefulness probably blown without any corresponding advantage. Neither have resigned.

3. In accord with Wash and Broadway views, neither we nor Zulu have encouraged resignations by German officials here. Once resigned they are useless and a burden if we assume responsibility for them. No German official here except possibly Minister has such importance that his resignation would have any real effect in Germany. If you have means of doing so, without further compromising Federer, suggest you arrange for Atlantic to lay off this type of useless and potentially harmful propaganda.

4. For your information, Vice Consul Graf at Zurich has refused to return to Germany and has resigned. He is rather disreputable character. Kurt Heberlein of same Consulate reported to have disappeared but probably has now returned to Germany. Vice Consul Weber, Basel, reported to have resigned. As result of these incidents, Consul General Dienstmann of Zurich said to have tendered his resignation to Ribbentrop who declined to accept it. Dienstmann has long been anti-Nazi and has been moderately useful. Von Ilsemann, former military attaché here, who distrusted by Nazis, was recalled to Germany and reportedly offered job in munitions factory. He found excuse to return here to close his household and then apparently refused return Germany. More resignations could probably be had for the asking, but, as stated above, they seem to us pointless at this stage.

Document 4-122

Telegram 2067, December 13, 1944

[Reichsmarschall Hermann Goering, Commander in Chief of the Luftwaffe and President of the Council of Ministers for Defense of the Reich, was at one time regarded as Hitler's probable successor. Dulles described for Donovan the decline of Goering's influence.]

109 from 110. We have no direct first-hand intelligence as to Goering's present status and whereabouts but piecing together series of reports from good sources, following is our best size-up of situation:

1. Goering no longer participates in inner councils or decisions of Party. He is somewhat distrusted by Himmler, Goebbels, Bormann, who appear to be running affairs as Hitler's lieutenants.

2. Failure of Luftwaffe and ineffective resistance against bombing destruction has resulted in great loss of prestige, but he still has some hold over the people and for this reason Himmler et al. do not dare put him aside entirely.

3. Goering is accordingly used from time to time by Himmler et al., as it is considered important that his name appear in press occasionally, viz., recent report of his inspecting armament factories in Bodensee area. Impossible state whether this trip actually took place or mere propaganda.

4. Do not believe that Goering is actually under arrest but assume that Himmler has assigned certain Gestapo agents to him and doubt whether he has complete freedom of movement. Probably he is being watched against possibility of a second Hess trick.

5. Probable that Goering is still loyal to Hitler but his first interest and concern is preserving his own skin and property and if Hitler were effectively sidetracked by Himmler et al. and Goering could make getaway [garble] arrangement with part of Army, I believe he would do it. . . .

6. Believe no foundation to story Goering's wife in Switzerland. This story has been recurrent and each time checked and proved false. Occasionally wife of Goering's cousin has been here.

7. Will report soonest any new information.

Document 4-123

Telegram 2077, December 13, 1944

[Dulles relayed various reports that offered the potential for interdiction of enemy activities.]

Learn indirectly from alleged Abwehr agent Brandes recently here from Lisbon that German plane leaves Barcelona every midnight with 4 tons precious merchandise and 3 or 4 passengers. Route over Genoa, Brenner to Berlin. Flies at 3,000 to 4,000 meters in good weather, zero altitude in bad weather. Washington, see your file reference Brandes.

Document 4-124

Telegram 2087, December 13, 1944

[In this message, Dulles takes exception to OSS and State Department dissemination of untested British information.]

Legation has received mail dispatch from Secretary of State #2504, November 20th, quoting OSS communication to them dated November 1st containing information from "British sources" regarding Wolfgang Krauel and H. G. Retzel (presumably Ritzel is meant). I consider contents of reports regarding both men as bunk and regard it as unfortunate such information is circulated on untested British information without check here.

Document 4-125

Telegram 2099, December 13, 1944

[Marcel Pilet-Golaz, Chief of the Swiss Federal Political Department (equivalent of Foreign Minister), was regarded by the Allies as a wily defender of Swiss neutrality. He provided Dulles with an assessment of German internal relationships.]

109 and 154 from 110. In long personal conversation today with Pilet-Golaz, he outlined with great frankness his information on German situation as follows:

1. German internal situation even more critical than generally believed but Himmler is still hopeful of finding way out somewhat along following lines. Ribbentrop likely to be replaced shortly and among those being considered are Seyss-Inquart, Neubacher and Kesselring (last named is recovering from his injury). After this appointment, effort will be made to contact Western powers and if this fails, Himmler will start program of disclosure of Anglo-Saxon peace feelers to Germany with view breaking Anglo-Saxon Russian alliance. Hassell and Goerdeler neither of whom executed are being kept alive for this purpose.

2. Himmler is also expecting some sort of revolt in Ukraine and Vlasov expedition being prepared to go into Carpathians to facilitate this.

3. Hitler is now in Berlin in underground quarters at Reichskanzlei. His health is somewhat better and he has seen some foreign diplomats but he can only talk to visitors for very short periods. Himmler proposes to keep Hitler as sort of Hindenburg in the upper background but he will probably not have physical strength to exercise direct control of affairs.

4. Conduct of military affairs being left to Guderian and Rundstedt but political, diplomatic moves concentrated in Himmler's hands and being particularly worked on under Himmler by Obergruppenfuehrer Berger.

5. Goering has lost influence. Some honorific but innocuous post will be found

for him. He would like to leave the country but has not made any direct overtures to Switzerland. (From 110: In distribution of above, source must be deleted. Please advise whether such messages should be sent also Paris or London or whether you wish control distribution in Washington.)

Document 4-126

Telegram 2129 to London, December 14, 1944

[This message concerns planning for intelligence operations in postwar Germany.]

For Bastedo and Leo, . . . Referring our Annemasse conversation, it is important to secure as soon as possible information regarding section of Berlin which will be allocated American Forces as desire arrange now safe addresses here with agents inside Germany and arrange wherever possible to accumulate at safe points in this area records and documents. Suggest you cable general indication by districts and certain important bounding streets.

Document 4-127

Telegram 2207, December 16, 1944

[Although Germany successfully tested jet aircraft in 1939, it failed to reach full production. Few German jet fighters saw combat before the end of the war, but this formidable weapon was a matter of great concern for the Allies. Number 496 was Maurice Villars, a banker in Zurich.]

Difficult get accurate information regarding production jet-propelled aircraft. Report following which may be propaganda: "Brindlinger of Messerschmitt recently here and talked with Inter-Avia people. From latter our 496 heard that jet-propelled fighters will make their appearance in force soon against Allied bombers. Production rate of several thousand per month, but actual numbers available greatly reduced by high percentage of accidents due to pilots' inexperience in handling this type of plane. Speed about 900 kilometers and fighters can reach altitude of 10,000 meters within four to five minutes." Endeavoring secure more information this general subject.

Document 4-128

Radiotelephone Transmission No. 254, December 21, 1944
(extract)

[On December 16 three German armies launched a surprise counteroffensive against American forces in the Ardennes Forest area of Belgium and Luxembourg. Dulles believed that the Nazi leadership sought to restore morale at home and to exacerbate prevailing differences among the Allies. He seems to have underestimated Hitler's personal involvement.]

Germany

I. I have just returned a couple of hours ago from a very brief visit to Paris. On the way back, I passed through Luxembourg, Metz, Strasbourg, and reached Basle just after dusk tonight.

On my trip, I found that one of the chief subjects of interest was as to the real meaning of the German offensive. First, whether it was dictated solely by military considerations, and therefore sponsored and lead by Rundstedt, or, second, whether it was a Hitler move, and thus evidence that the Fuehrer had aroused himself and forced the hand of the generals, or, third, whether it was a political military move, probably with limited military objectives, with much hope for important political repercussions.

Personally, I am inclined to believe that this third alternative is the most likely. In the present German political situation, I doubt whether this move would have been made unless there had been some sort of agreement between the generals, particularly Rundstedt and probably Guderian, on the one hand, and the leading Nazi politicians, Himmler and Goebbels, on the other. Undoubtedly, Hitler was allowed to believe that it was his initiative which was the responsible driving factor.

As regards the attitude of the German generals, there is reason to believe that they feel it imperative to defend German territory west of the Rhine-Ruhr area. To retreat to the Rhine would mean the loss of the use of the Ruhr to a large extent, and the end of any possibility of German military initiative in the West. It would condemn the German generals to a hopeless defensive battle, with a major section of German industry within crippling range of our guns. If, on the other hand, they could succeed in threatening our line of communication from Antwerp, then they, the generals, would probably feel that considerable time might be saved during which the political leaders could work out some solution.

The political leaders, particularly Himmler and Goebbels, on their part, probably felt that the present was a precious moment to try to add a military success to the political asset which they consider has fallen into their lap during recent weeks. No doubt, the Germans believe that events in Italy and Greece have driven somewhat of a wedge between the USA and Britain, and events in Poland are causing serious rifts between the Anglo-Saxons and the Russians, and that the trend of events in Belgium, France, Greece, and elsewhere portend social disorders which will sap Allied strength and bring about war-weariness. Hence, the German politicians probably felt that now was the best possible time to try to show the Allies that Germany was also strong in a military way.

Whatever may be the motives, it seems clear that Germany is committing a large share of its military strength west of the Rhine, with consequences which might be serious if not fatal for Germany, if the offensive should prove to be a failure. . . .

Document 4-129

Telegram 2319, December 22, 1944

[In this Top Secret cable to Donovan, Magruder, and Shepardson, Dulles volunteered suggestions for OSS structure to deal with the German target and with postwar Germany. He discusses the Allied intelligence failure prior to the German Ardennes offensive, then in process, and indirectly criticizes top OSS management for having senior officers in the United States, rather than on site in Europe where they were needed badly.]

For 109, Magruder, and 154 from 110.

1. Returned here yesterday after conference Paris with 105 and with General Betts and others at SHAEF. On return trip stopped at 12 AG where saw General Bradley, Sibert, Kirkpatrick and his unit. Also saw Colonel Harrison, G-2, 6th AG, Colonel Quinn, G-2, 7th Army, and spent night with Wentworth and our unit with 7th Army.

2. Had full discussions with above persons regarding production and handling of intelligence from Switzerland and improving methods of getting intelligence to points where required.

3. Convinced we should do everything possible during the next few months to improve procurement and handling German intelligence, and that is primary service we can render. Emergency created by German offensive and our armies' lack of adequate intelligence which permit substantial German concentrations unknown to us, points up our immediate task. For example at 12 AG learned that Germans able concentrate for new offensives following divisions without our having adequate prior intelligence covering their movement: 5th Parachute from Holland, 276th from Dresden, 62 from inside Germany, 560 from Norway, 1st and 12 SS Panzer from reserve, possible 242 Panzer Lehr from 3rd Army front, 2nd Panzer from reserve, 3rd Parachute shifted southward.

4. Believe we should strengthen and encourage every way possible our forward units with 12 AG and 7th Army. Conversations with Sibert and Quinn respectively convince me they both anxious cooperate and that these units can render increasing service. In certain cases believe personnel of MO could be helpfully assigned at least temporarily to duty with SI units. Believe MO units can accomplish little now view lack of governmental policy on our part which appeals to German Army or public, publicity given to Allied plans compensate Poland at expense eastern Germany, and success of German propaganda that Germany faces hopeless fate in defeat and that condition of soldiers and workers is better today than it will be after collapse. Hence believe that any MO personnel trained in German and intelligence lines, for example several of Stacy Lloyd's men, should be integrated into forward intelligence units.

5. I urgently recommend in strongest terms that 105 return to Europe as shortly as possible, be relieved of all administrative burdens and made something corre-

sponding to overall head of European intelligence directed against Germany to supervise intelligence from here, from forward units with Army and all other sources, to see that intelligence gets quickly to proper Army heads and to deal on highest level with our Army officers and with heads of British, French and other Allied intelligence services. In my opinion no one can replace him in this work and that to assign him to a Washington Planning Board in this emergency would be a grave error. Here he could work with Hugh Wilson and Callisen and this could constitute overall intelligence team which would restore morale of those working in field which is affected by fact that senior men such as Bruce, Armour, Forgan and Gamble are all in the United States at this particular juncture. Despite their individual ability, junior ranking men cannot effectively handle relations with our senior army people or with foreign intelligence services.

6. Splendid record which organization made in French field can still be partially duplicated in German field and preparations can now be made which will both improve present intelligence on Germany and build groundwork for effective job upon Germany's collapse. In this connection, feel we should also concentrate on sending agents into Germany who would lie low in strategic points until Germany's collapse and then carry out previously assigned tasks as regards seizure documents, identification Nazis going underground, etc. This requires careful planning and trust that Wilson and Callisen will give it particular attention and help to carry out definite program of this character.

Document 4-130

Telegram 2349, December 23, 1944

[Dulles feared that several of his French sources had been compromised with General de Gaulle by indiscreet OSS Headquarters handling of certain reports.]

Personal for 109 from 110. 477 tells me that information in our cables #4345-7 and #4332-44, both of August 4, (and possibly some earlier Lorraine material) was given by you to Deuxieme Bureau man (possibly Passy), sent Deuxieme Bureau Paris, and has been injected into radical party politics France via politician named Bayet. 477 says situation seems rather serious for our 850, 802 and 492, all of whom rendered important services to us prior France's liberation. Report comes to 477 through highly reliable source who mentioned your name and Deuxieme Bureau man Wash. but did not identify latter. Realize this may be only fishing expedition by French politicians who may know of contacts in Switzerland of 850, 802 and of 492 work with us but would appreciate any background you could give.

Document 4-131

Telegram 2369, December 23, 1944

[This report on German atomic energy matters came from OSS agent Moe Berg.]

AZUSA. Berg to 106 and Dix only. Brought Flute deuterium for his cyclotron also latest English and French scientific books.

Timed entry Switzerland to attend Heisenberg lecture and discussion Dec. 18 Zurich University Physical Institute sitting behind Weiszacker, 20 present including Flute, Wenzel, Fierz.

Subject theoretical physics. Flute explained that: A. Heisenberg has now found frame for new theory of elementary particles in which relativity and quantum relations are coordinated to avoid quantities to infinity. B. The frame itself is not yet filled in. C. It is called ETA matrix theory.

Flute places following personnel in Hechingen with activities: Heisenberg-cosmic rays; Moliere—Heisenberg's pupil; Laue—electronic diffraction; Weiszacker—cosmogeny; Hahn there but not working on Azusa. Clusius in Switzerland three months ago told Flute separation U235 isotope absolutely hopeless after experiments Munich with U fluorite. However, at present Flute believes Clusius and Dickel are in Berlin area on Azusa. He repeated electrolysis story. German chemist, still unnamed, from Berlin told Flute U was used in solid crystals for this purpose.

Flute predicts at least two years probably ten for successful Azusa.

Heisenberg confided to Flute Hitler was seen by friend, healthy and working about Dec. 1 also said desperate Nazi Party control over German scientists who doubtful politically. Weiszacker remained in Switzerland until recently perhaps for surveillance Heisenberg.

More conferences with Flute Wednesday, the 27th. Complete pouch to follow.

Document 4-132

Telegram 2407, December 25, 1944

[This message concerned Frederick R. Loofbourow (number 493), who worked for OSS in Zurich.]

109, Cheston, Rhythm, and 154 from 110, . . . Pursuant arrangements worked out by John Hughes with SONJ, 493, to my great regret, will be leaving here about January 15. 493 has rendered outstanding services and his replacement most difficult. Important, if feasible, that 224 arrive here by January 10, but, if this is not possible, 493 could arrange see 224 in London between January 15 and 30. 493 has now received cable from Robert Price Russell via Secretary of State and Legation . . . asking him to act as special consultant to War Department for 6 weeks, reporting here on January 15 and followed by inspection trips France and Italy to make detailed study of effects aerial bombing on oil, rubber and chemical plants Germany. Consider 493 eminently qualified for this work, and, with your approval, he will carry out this mission, reporting London January 15. Suggest you advise Robert Price Russell. If, after completion this mission, arrangements could be reached with War Department and SONJ whereby 493 could be temporarily attached our German unit for carrying forward work in the above field, this would be highly gratifying to me, but do not wish to prejudice 493's future with his established connections.

Document 4-133

Telegram 2417, December 26, 1944

[Dulles reports that the Soviet Union sought to arrange for the purchase of small arms in Switzerland.]

From 110. Trusted local official advises us that Russian Ambassador Bogomiloff, Paris, instructed two business men in Switzerland to attempt to purchase from Swiss [garble] works machine pistols and other arms in total value 9,000,000 francs to be turned over to Partisans in Northern Italy. Arms were to be delivered at Campione. Swiss authorities who consulted by manufacturers refused to sanction transaction. Source who claims to have seen documents, should be carefully protected. This cable not repeated elsewhere. Very possibly this was merely Russian move to build up case against Swiss as latter's refusal foregone conclusion.

Document 4-134

Telegram 2487, December 26, 1944

[In this message, Dulles urged that the Swiss be encouraged to accept nonpolitical Germans possessing technical expertise who wanted to take refuge in Switzerland. The question foreshadowed East-West competition for German scientific and industrial know-how and personnel at the end of the war.]

Reliably informed that 2 important German industrialists, brothers, named Schmidt, one a director of munitions plant at Eisenach and the other, first name something like Eberhard, Director of Messerschmitt plant in Augsburg, endeavored pass clandestinely Switzerland with families. Both thrown back into Germany but minor children allowed remain. Latter said to have been in charge of building Messerschmitt plant Vienna and of Messerschmitt decentralization program. Both men reported to be nonpolitical with brilliant industrial records. Motive for attempted escape fear of Russians and of chaos and foreign workers when crash comes.

Swiss official who ordered rejection mentioned matter to our 476 as evidence of Swiss attitude reject all who had worked with Nazis and seemed to feel he had done us great favor. Obviously these men might have given invaluable information if allowed to come here.

Please advise whether you consider feasible attempt reach any understanding with Swiss for different treatment of non-political industrialist and technical men. Possibly such refugees would prefer to surrender to us, say at Annemasse, after they had taken refuge in Switzerland. While extremely delicate and problematical whether this could be arranged secretly with Swiss it might be worth trying if you approved.

Obviously if word gets around that German technical men cannot escape here, we will lose both for present and possibly for post-collapse period valuable sources of information. Swiss obviously frightened at being overrun by refugees from Germany and also of complications with USA and Britain if they accept any persons who worked for Nazis.

Document 4-135

Telegram 2519, December 26, 1944

[Significant German efforts to contact the Allies from northern Italy occurred in late 1944. These tentative initiatives constituted the beginning of the process that resulted in the separate German surrender in Italy in May 1945.]

From 110. Re previous cables re alleged German attempt to contact Allies from North Italy, . . . Neurath, German Consul Lugano, who is in touch with Kesselring, Wolff and Harster, has given my cutouts the following information: (1) Kesselring is one of the few remaining German Generals with independent mind and interest in political affairs. He had planned to work through General Speidel, formerly Paris and at one time member of Kesselring staff as he, Kesselring, desired remain in the background. Speidel, however, recently arrested by Gestapo. Kesselring has recovered and leaving for Germany shortly on 3 weeks leave. (2) Reattempted negotiations with ZULU, Cable their Consul General in Zurich has been called off but some other intermediary in Zurich was brought into the picture. Neurath alleges ZULU suggested that representative Wehrmacht be produced. (3) In view position Wolff and Harster, Neurath's view is impossible to do anything with Kesselring for OKW alone, but Neurath apparently feels that some Gestapo North Italy might work with Kesselring for OKW re program re use of German Army in Italy as separate unit to help liquidate Nazis or immediately preceding German collapse if they could save their own skins thereby.

From 110. This whole project seems rather fantastic but believe ZULU knows more than they tell me here. Possibly 109 could obtain some further clues during his forthcoming trip.

Document 4-136

Telegram 2527, December 26, 1944

[This messages illustrates the confusing state of contacts with German officials in Switzerland. Dulles assisted counterintelligence in distinguishing useful Nazis, those who provided information to the Allies, from those who remained loyal to the Führer.]

Your #0917 re Engelbrechten. Subject long attached German Consulate Geneva. Member of Abwehr and reported to us as associated with oppositional groups Abwehr such as our 502, 512, 670, and vouched for by them. Reported that SD agent operating here for Stuttgart SD office who apprehended by Swiss authorities had instructions to tell Swiss that he worked for subject. Also believed SD agent attempted use subject as channel transmission Swiss military information which agent picked up here. As result subject invited leave Switzerland some 6 months ago by local authorities, is now reported to be Berlin. Understand Swiss authorities who now know true facts prepared allow him return but SD unwilling permit this. Possible that intrigue against subject was for purpose creating Geneva vacancy into which Sonnenhohl, notorious German agent from Tangier, has now been inserted. Likely that Sonnenhohl will replace active head SD here, Daufeld, whom Swiss endeavoring eliminate.

Document 4-137

Radiotelephone Transmission No. 257, December 26, 1944 (extract)

[On December 26 the U.S. Fourth Armored Division broke through to Bastogne, turning the tide in the Battle of the Bulge. That evening, Dulles offered further thoughts on the significance of the German counteroffensive and prevailing German attitudes.]

Germany

1. The significance of the German offensive in the West is the subject uppermost in the press and in private conversations here. Undoubtedly Germany has shown a military force in the West which exceeded general expectations here, but most commentators, as well as most private well-informed individuals are inclined to feel that the offensive will fail to achieve vitally important strategic objectives.

The offensive shows that Germany does not yet consider that she is completely licked. It also shows, as I have previously suggested, that the morale in Germany, if one can call fatalistic resignation morale, does not have much effect on military operations. Germany is fighting as a cornered beast that sees no possible alternative. The impression is widespread and is growing, even in anti-Nazi circles, that general conditions in Germany would be worse after the collapse than during the period of combat. Recent pronouncements regarding Polish annexation plans in the East of Germany, and French economic designs on the Rhineland and Ruhr have helped to solidify this impression. The German soldiers at the front probably consider that they are better off now than they will be when they lay down their arms; that death is possibly preferable to the future they see in Germany after they stop fighting.

In effect, we have succeeded in building up a desperation complex in the German people, and we cannot expect any internal collapse except under the pressure of German military defeat or the breakdown of transportation and distribution of food, raw materials, and munitions.

It is possible, of course, that the German Wehrmacht is consciously or unconsciously committing a kind of hara-kiri. They may have realized that the grinding, defensive warfare to which they had been subjected in the West would only mean the gradual destruction of Germany, just as Aachen has been destroyed. The Wehrmacht possibly does not wish to bear the responsibility for this destruction for future generations. It is possible that they therefore prefer to make a last effort to transfer this destruction into Belgium, Luxembourg, and France, even if they perish in the attempt. At least then they would not be responsible for the destruction of German cities and of the industrial area of the Ruhr. If, as a result of their desperate move, they are trapped, then the war might end and some members of the Wehrmacht, at least, would have the honorable status of prisoners of war, which they might well prefer to returning to a Germany torn by civil war and possibly thrown into chaos by the breakdown of transportation and production, and ravaged by the millions of foreign laborers and prisoners, and by the desperate bombed-out population.

Such considerations may well have influenced the Wehrmacht in accepting and possibly even advocating this offensive move. It also possibly fits in with the plan of the leading Nazis. The latter have always had the mistaken view that, if only they could make the Americans and English bleed sufficiently, we would be ready for a compromise peace. The Nazis are also undoubtedly most anxious to reoccupy as much German-occupied territory as possible in order to mete out punishment to any Germans who may have collaborated with our forces of occupation and thus frighten Germans from any future collaboration in German territory we may occupy in the future. . . .

Document 4-138

Telegram 2617, December 27, 1944

[After almost two years of operation, the George Wood channel temporarily ran afoul of Swiss neutrality.]

KAPPA. 154 and Rhythm. Last batch Kappa dispatched Paris immediately, 1 copy developed photo plus original films; assume Paris can make reproductions quicker than we. Believe chief delay between Paris and Washington. At present most material comes in film not document form.

Very Secret. Unfortunate delay in securing more material. Wood planned come home for holidays but Swiss refused him visa and so far direct undisclosed intervention, which is all I dare risk, has been ineffective. Laudable but somewhat indiscriminating Swiss effort keep out Germans is serious handicap to SI activities.

Document 4-139

Telegram 2677, December 28, 1944

[The Safe Haven program was designed to prevent the enemy from transferring and hiding assets abroad, especially in neutral countries such as Switzerland. It presented problems for intelligence-gathering.]

See Callisen memorandum of November 30th re Safe Haven Project. Work on this project requires careful planning as it might defeat direct intelligence activities and close important channels for German SI if believed this one of our main objectives. Today we must fish in troubled waters and maintain contacts with persons suspected of working with Nazis on such matters. For example, see question H of attached memorandum which relates to our 496. Both 496 and X-2 here can be useful under cover but believe idea of working practically as agents of Commercial Attaché and Consul General, Zurich, on this project would be unwise. Further, to deal effectively with matter, it would require special staff with new cover. Possibly Mocarski would have special qualifications to develop organization for this work. At present we do not have adequate personnel to do effective job in this field and meet other demands.

Document 4-140

Telegram 2819, December 29, 1944

[OSS Bern frequently received Swiss reports on the situation in Germany. This information came from Foreign Minister Pilet-Golaz, number 518.]

Following from same source as my #2099, given our number 518. 1. Hitler had serious relapse and physicians refuse permit him travel. He is now in new headquarters some 50 kilometers southwest of Berlin. (From 110: Possibly this is Zossen, but latter is south of Berlin.)

2. Himmler had hoped to secure from Hitler, during recent period when his health had considerably improved, rearrangement of government whereby he, Himmler, would become in effect Premier, with Hitler remaining as Chief of Staff. Apparently this not put through, and now Hitler believed too ill to be approached on subject.

3. Regarding rumors of heavy concentrations of German troops on Swiss border, and of possible German attack via Switzerland (which SI Paris transmitted but said discounted by SHAEF), source believes no basis for such rumors, and Swiss military

authorities undisturbed. 2 additional Swiss divisions to be called up early January to replace other divisions, but latter will not be immediately dismissed, thus in effect substantially increasing Swiss standing army during early weeks of year.

4. Source views German offensive as having purely political objectives. He believes general German situation excludes possibility of major sustained offensive. (From 110; Please advise other offices identity our 518.)

Document 4-141

Radiotelephone Transmission No. 259, December 29, 1944 (extract)

[Dulles commented on the evolving political situation in Hungary and how it might be viewed in Germany with regard to an Eastern versus Western option.]

Germany

1. A report just received from Germany indicates that the Russian action in permitting the formation of a Hungarian government at Debrecen has caused a lot of astonishment in Germany. They were particularly surprised, and the Nazi leaders particularly disturbed, to note that the leading position in this Hungarian government is now held by a Hungarian general who has only recently been received and decorated by the Fuehrer. General Miklos, who presides over the new government, has the Ritterkreuz. And the report adds that he received this decoration from Hitler recently last November at the Fuehrer's Hauptquartier.

Undoubtedly, this Hungarian government was carefully planned with a view to its psychological effect on Germany. It will help to build up the impression which is already existing in certain German military circles that there may be hope for them on the Russian side, whereas they see no hope whatever from the West. Probably the question is going through the minds of many German generals that, if the Russians are ready to show such favor to Miklos, a general of the particularly hated Hungarian Army, why should not the Russians do the same for the generals of the Wehrmacht?

Document 4-142

Telegram 2847 to Caserta, December 31, 1944

[Dulles found himself in a position to obtain the diaries of Count Ciano, former Foreign Minister of Italy, from the Count's widow, Edda Mussolini Ciano, the Duce's daughter, who had taken refuge in Switzerland. The material promised to be of great value in understanding Axis diplomacy and for psychological warfare purposes.]

Action: Rodrigo. Information 106 and 154. From 110 . . .

2. Believe best line to take that Edda should desire make diaries available as generous gesture to help Allies and to present husband's memory in correct light to history. If she tries bargain, this impression will be defeated and any delay will deprive diaries of great part of value except as history.

3. Regarding your specific queries: (a) Giving photographic copies to us will leave her publication rights unaffected. (b) Unless Washington disapproves, prepared pay reasonable amount for diaries, had in mind something between $5,000 to $10,000. Hope arrange this payment through newspapers and ostensibly against future royalties to keep us out of financial picture. (c) Washington alone could pass on asylum question. This is what probably interests her most. All I propose say is that her position would be improved generally if diaries made available.

4. Have now enlisted aid of Magistrati, until recently Italian minister here, who married Ciano's deceased sister and also knows Benini well. Next few days particularly important, hence please expedite cable summary Benini letter.

For Washington. Would appreciate for my guidance any comments on Caserta's 21967 to you and on this cable.

CHAPTER

5

The Collapse of the Reich, the German Surrender in Italy, and Planning for Postwar Europe

January–May 1945

Document 5-1

Telegram 2227 to Caserta, January 2, 1945

[Dulles sought to maintain orderly procedures in an increasingly complex environment brought about by the opening of the Swiss-French border. He did not roll out the welcome mat for junkets to Switzerland.]

Jigsaw from 110. Information: Gadfly and Rhythm.

1. Unless there are compelling reasons, I do not favor casual short visits to Bern. Meetings to discuss particular problems can be arranged Annemasse. Every request

for visa for special visitor renders more difficult obtaining visas for badly needed permanent personnel. Persons coming here for short visits unacclimated to particular conditions of work are time consuming and affect security. . . .

3. Competent persons assigned here as members of staff to conduct serious operations after full study of local conditions, security and other problems are welcome. Mere visitors not wanted.

Document 5-2

Telegram 2909, January 2, 1945 (extracts)

[With the outcome of the war decided, the Allies were in a position to increase pressure on Switzerland to curtail the transit of German material through its territory. Dulles advises against heavy-handed tactics.]

Magruder only from 110.

1. This is highly controversial subject with thorny background of diplomatic correspondence. Following are my views based on general impressions rather than intimate knowledge of details.

2. Both factions cited are partly right. Traffic reduced because of changes in war situation and also as result of diplomatic and economic pressure. Latter has obtained some results because fear attack by Germany gone and because Swiss vitally need certain facilities from Anglo-Saxon side, particularly food and raw material imports. Also Swiss firmly convinced of, and in great majority desire, our victory and hope it will come soon.

3. It is mistake to ask Swiss to give up a principle, particularly one which they consider vital to their neutral status. Having experienced 2 wars in 25 years and seeing possibility of future wars, they are stubbornly attached to certain principles which rightly or wrongly they feel have twice helped save them from invasion. However, results can be achieved by asking concessions on specific points of interest to us. For example, far better to insist upon limitation transit traffic to point where unimportant militarily than to attempt force Swiss to abandon in principle all such traffic. . . .

7. We should also consider possibility that later, but before end of hostilities, we might wish to use transit through Switzerland if Germans evacuated western and central North Italy but held in Veneto or if German project for final stand in Bavarian Alps materializes.

8. See no objection to bombing attacks on Italian end of Gotthard Line and we might also help with SO operations.

9. I am undoubtedly influenced by fact that in my work, I constantly need from Swiss favors to which, under strict rules of neutrality, I am not entitled. As we now give Swiss little except dynamite and diplomatic demands, it is not easy to create best atmosphere for my work. Hence I do not favor pressing Swiss to wall for what

seems to me to be very small military advantages, particularly as it is a wall which Swiss may not jump.

Document 5-3

Telegram 3047, January 6, 1945

[Planning proceeded for the OSS German Unit, which was to enter Germany at the moment of victory and operate under the Allied occupation regime. Dulles discussed the subject with Donovan at Lyon on January 4.]

To Leo, information Bastedo and Canfield from 110.

1. Full discussion at Lyon with 109, Murphy and Canfield re German Unit. General program appears to be satisfactory to Murphy. Canfield will send report of conference to Leo and Bastedo.

2. Also discussed MO participation with Roller Baldwin in presence 109 and Murphy. Agreed MO to have 3 to 5 highly qualified men in initial German Unit names to be submitted to 110. These men would be divided between R&A and SI thus avoiding separate departmentalized MO staff. Understood other MO activities re Germany might be directed from outside Germany and that MO personnel attached to German Unit could be increased as circumstances and work justify. Exact formula to embody foregoing to be drafted by Canfield in consultation Roller Baldwin on basis memo prepared by 109 and agreed to by all concerned.

Document 5-4

Radiotelephone Transmission No. 263, January 6, 1945

[Dulles consistently advocated the bombing of Berlin and military and transportation targets within Germany. As the war progressed, he became more outspoken in opposition to city blasting, regarding it as ineffective and counterproductive.]

Many Germans, who normally might be expected to prefer to work with the Anglo-Saxons after the German collapse, are quite likely to surprise us by choosing to collaborate with the Russians. One of the leading German industrialists, whom I shall call Meyer, was here some weeks ago and so expressed himself to a German-Jewish refugee who some years ago had had himself a leading place in German industry. The refugee remarked to Meyer, who is not a Nazi, that he, Meyer, should be able to play an important role with the Americans and British, who would have need of such a man as he for the work of reconstruction. Meyer, as I hear, vindictively rejected the idea of working with those who had destroyed German cities by bombing. Meyer did not specifically say that he was ready to work with the Russians; this was implied in his reference to the fact that Russia had never bombed

German cities and had spared the industrial area of Silesia, even though it was in easy range. When the history of the war is written, I believe that the net military advantages gained by the bombing of cities will be rated relatively low. It has hardened and embittered the people; it has made them completely dependent on the State and the Nazi state machinery; it has rendered difficult, if not impossible, the organization of any civilian anti-Nazi work among the bourgeoisie of the great cities, where such oppositional work would naturally develop. Unfortunately, the bitterness caused by the bombing has not turned against the Nazis in the long run, as it seemed likely to do when the bombing started. It has, rather, aroused resentment and hatred against the West and, unfortunately, among the classes, that is to say, the small householder and worker where opposition to the Nazis might have been best cultivated. As our air supremacy over Germany increases, . . . [omission] be directed, as seems bound to be the case, against transportation and specific factories and other direct military targets. Such bombing will, of course, inevitably affect civilian as well as military objectives, but the resultant effect on war morale will be less hostile to us. Competent observers here do not believe that we will break German morale by seeking the destruction of a few more cities, but many of them do believe that we may wreck their war machine by causing a breakdown in transportation by the bombing.

Document 5-5

Telegram 3929 to London, January 12, 1945

[The zones of occupation of Germany and the division of Berlin were determined by the Allies' European Advisory Committee in London and approved by the Big Three at the Yalta Conference, February 4–11, 1945. Dulles asked that information on the condition of various sections of Berlin be taken into consideration in defining the sectors.]

Bastedo from 110. Information: Leo. Re map indicating division Berlin as between Great Britain, USSR and USA occupational forces. My reports indicate that large parts of Zehlendorf, Steglitz and Schonekera destroyed and that USA will occupy largely rubble here with inadequate working quarters. Just over borders of Berlin opposite our zone are Potsdam and Babelsberg which not greatly damaged with many admirable quarters for Army purposes. While possibly too late for reconsideration, suggest you mention this to military authorities in case Berlin occupation zone comes up for reconsideration.

Document 5-6

Telegram 3317, January 12, 1945

[Dulles continued to promote plans to obtain German industrialists and scientists for the West. This message was sent to SI in Washington and to London for William J.

Casey, then involved in operations for the penetration of Germany and later Director of Central Intelligence (1981–87).]

To 154. Information: Casey.

1. Personally considered unfeasible exfiltrate directly France due lack of training. Likelihood accompanied members of family and difficulty of waking prior contact to conclude arrangements. Doubt existence effective underground for such purposes.

2. Your suggestion indicates possible misunderstanding. My project contemplates that in normal course of events and without any prior contact with us but merely to escape pending chaos, important German industrialists, scientists, etc., will desire to find some haven, preferably Switzerland. If Switzerland is closed to them these men might possibly turn to Russia as only alternative.

3. Impossible make thorough prior appraisal of motives or value in individual cases. My idea that we would make no commitments as to treatment and if individual industrialists or scientists who surrendered to us, say at Annemasse after passage via Switzerland, proved recalcitrant or untrustworthy we could intern or imprison them. Of course we would only accept at Annemasse persons we consider of probable utility.

4. Discreet preliminary conversations indicate some hope of securing Swiss cooperation.

Document 5-7

Radiotelephone Transmission No. 265, January 15, 1945

[Dulles attempted to gauge whether the Germans intended an early withdrawal from northern Italy.]

Italy

There is considerable speculation here with regard to the future German movements in North Italy and the general belief here [is] that before many weeks the Germans will withdraw from the Piedmont, Lombardy and Liguria to a shortened line from the Adriatic to the Alps. . . .

The Germans have already done about as much looting in North Italy as they can do in view of the difficulty of transportation under winter conditions and the frequent interruptions by our bombings of the Brenner line.

The whole situation in North Italy is becoming very difficult, and the Germans are not in a position to do much about it without taking badly needed supplies from Germany itself. In fact, they are not considering any such solution, and are even taking some foodstuffs from North Italy to Germany, particularly rice.

As spring approaches, the problem of the industrial areas of North Italy will become more and more acute, and if the people are not fed and given work rioting and disorder are likely to break out, threatening German lines of communication.

The industrial capacity of North Italy is going down every day, as the supplies of coal and raw materials are dwindling. The continued supply of coal from Germany to North Italy is a substantial burden on the Germans, both from the point of view of their own coal supplies and from that of transportation. With both the Ruhr and Silesia now threatened, every ton of coal may be precious to Germany.

The actual military advantages gained from holding North Italy appear to be rather negligible from the German angle. Again it is a question of prestige, and it seems reasonable that the German military authorities are exerting pressure on Hitler to concede to a withdrawal, thereby making available on the hard-pressed Vienna front certain divisions which are now tied down in North Italy. If Germany waits too long, the way of escape for these divisions may be cut or so limited as to make it impossible for them to extricate their heavy equipment. Kesselring is supposed to be back in Germany now to discuss this situation, and he is said himself to favor a withdrawal.

As I have stated above, the foregoing is based more on deduction than on any evidence actually at hand, and we are carefully looking for signs to confirm or refute our deductions.

Document 5-8

Telegram 2637 to Caserta, January 16, 1945

[On his return trip from southern Italy, resistance leader Ferruccio Parri was captured by the Germans.]

From 110. Longhi in letter to me of January 9 gives following regarding Parri's arrest: Germans arrested P. by chance in Turin while actually looking for somebody else. Please report his arrest immediately to SACMED and to Commandante AAI. Longhi strongly advises have high German official who is our prisoner exchanged against P. even if latter should eventually be neutralized in Suisse. . . .

Document 5-9

Telegram 3657, January 18, 1945

[Dulles urges the Allies to take measures to spare Vienna from destruction.]

Fate of Budapest and influx Hungarian refugees has made deep impression on war-weary inhabitants of Vienna. Any move on Russian and our part to spare Vienna same fate might have strong effect on Vienna population. If, as seems likely, measures which we might propose were rejected by Germans this reaction might bring something approaching open revolt if these war-weary people can revolt. Further, it would stamp Allies as their friends and Nazis as their enemies. If Allies proposed spare Vienna from air bombardment and frontal attacks or treat as open city provided

Germans ceased transport troops and war material through Vienna and removed or ceased using Vienna armament factories and all military installations there this might accomplish psychological objective sought. As Vienna is essential military rail center, conditions would probably be impossible of acceptance by Germans. Realize this matter may now largely be in hands of Russia but fate of Vienna is matter of concern to us all.

Document 5-10

Radiotelephone Transmission No. 267, January 18, 1945

[Dulles speculates on the state of mind of the Nazi leadership and the possibility of a last stand in the Bavarian Alps.]

Germany
The Russian offensive has made a deep impression on Germany. Communiqués and reports of the German military critics have never been more somber. Apparently now, in contrast to some months ago, no real attempt is being made to hide from the German people the seriousness of the situation. Breaks in the line are frankly admitted. Also the German, rather than the Russian, communiqués are often the first to give the details of the depth of the Russian penetration and of the loss of important cities.

All this fits in with the line of propaganda for which Goebbels has been so carefully preparing the people. Now it is not a war for supremacy but a war for survival. It is a war against the invader at the frontier, and against an invader—or rather, three invaders—who, according to Goebbels, have vowed to destroy, partition, and enslave the German people. To whip the people up for such a war, Goebbels uses unsparingly bad news when it suits his purpose. He is no longer frightened of it. To a certain extent, it is grist to his new mill.

As the threat to Silesia and a part of Germany becomes acute in the East, the German military authorities must be asking themselves what fronts must be sacrificed in order to try to create a new stabilized line somewhere. Norway and Italy may well be the first theaters from which German withdrawals will start. Several divisions have reportedly gone from Italy towards Vienna already. But the forces in these theaters will not suffice, and soon the High Command will be forced to decide whether to try to hold the east or west front to the end. And the answer to this depends upon whether they would prefer to have the Russians or the Americans and British first occupy the country and impress their mark upon the occupation; whether they would prefer to fall into Russian or Anglo-Saxon hands. Here the views are likely to be differing. Old-line conservative Wehrmacht officers would probably prefer the West. The younger, more Nazi, officers would prefer the East as offering the greater likelihood of being able to continue in their profession. In the Party itself there is also some division. The radical wing would prefer Russia.

Others would prefer the West, probably on the theory that a trial by the easy-going and quick to forget Anglo-Saxons is preferable to the risks of quick liquidation at Russian hands.

While such speculation is probably going on, it seems likely that the men around Hitler and Himmler are preparing for the possibility of a last stand in the inner German fortress of the Bavarian and Austrian Alps, playing their last card, namely, that when the Russians and Anglo-Saxons actually meet somewhere in Germany there will be such dissension among them that the Nazis in the mountains, if they can hold out long enough, can still save something from the wreckage or at least choose to whom to deliver themselves.

This idea of a defense in a mountain fortress is in line with the Wagnerian complex of the whole National Socialist movement and the fanaticism of the Nazi youth. Hitler and his small band of brigands, who started in the beer-hall of Munich, may find their end not far away in the Bavarian Alps, after having laid most of Europe in ruins.

Document 5-11

Telegram 2769 to Caserta, January 19, 1945

[OSS Bern received peace feelers through Gottfried von Nostitz, German consul at Geneva.]

Glavin and Saint from 110. Information: 154. . . . Reference possibility of meeting K and Nostitz, . . . Understand that Nostitz recently received letter from K suggesting possibility of obtaining sick leave from Foreign Office for cure Switzerland. Nostitz doubts whether this feasible, but is proposing it to Berlin. Nostitz and our 670 consider early meeting with K most desirable and view doubt securing above permission wish him to consider possibility clandestine visit Annemasse. N and 670 consider that K visit might lay groundwork whereby his chief's influence could at appropriate time be brought to bear on conservative German generals to open front to our troops and avoid useless destruction of Germany. While this may be far cry, stakes are high and gamble may be worth it.

Document 5-12

Telegram 3689, January 19, 1945

[OSS Bern received additional reports on the situation in Germany, including news of continuing vengeance against opposition elements.]

476 reports from reliable source. Zulu also advised by 476.

1. Helmuth Moltke condemned to death. View important role he played in

Breakers circles, this will be serious loss. 476 suggesting to Zulu possibly considering some delaying action view Moltke's mother British or South African. While hope rather tenuous, our experience here that if some stir is created, Germans at this stage may consider person more valuable alive than dead.

2. State Secretary Planck, son of famous physicist, was condemned to death, but Oshima intervened on ground he had participated in concluding certain agreements with Japanese and that his execution would offend Jap dignity. Sentence commuted and Planck sent concentration camp.

3. Gersten Meyer, one of leading men Confessional Church, condemned 6 years penitentiary.

4. Same source who direct from important circles Berlin states deepest disappointment Germany at failure Ardenne offensive on which Germans had built highest hopes of taking Antwerp.

Document 5-13

Telegram 4107 to Paris, January 20, 1945

[Dulles discussed Noel Field's connection with CALPO in Paris, revealing knowledge of the organization's connection to the Soviet-sponsored Freies Deutschland group.]

For Major Black and Climax. Information: 154. Most interested your memorandum January 10th meeting re CALPO. Noel Field of Unitarian Service Committee is proceeding Paris next week. During period German occupation France, Field, who was at Marseille until November 1942, developed contact with nucleus which developed into CALPO. Through Field I assisted finance work to extent and under conditions he will explain. Suggest that Field, after preliminary talk with you, see his CALPO friends and advise you of his impressions. View his early contact with movement he might be useful in certain respects for liaison while he is in Paris. 284 can advise you of Field's relations with us Switzerland. Also following closely Freies Deutschland group here which is working with CALPO.

Document 5-14

Radiotelephone Transmission No. 269. January 20, 1945

[In this evening telephone message, Dulles sets forth his views on what might be done to energize the Austrian resistance and influence that nation's future.]

Austria

It is high time that something be done about Austria. The resistance there, both in Vienna and the Austrian Alps, appears to be beginning to take some shape. It is hard to appraise the extent of it, but at least there is some evidence of its existence.

Since the Moscow Declaration of over a year ago, little has been done to encourage the Austrian resistance movement. The absence of any outstanding Austrian patriots abroad has been some handicap. There has been no voice to speak for Austria in the United States. Great Britain and Russia have largely passed the matter over in silence, except to urge the Austrians to revolt at times and under conditions when revolt was impossible. With the Russian armies not far away, the situation is now altered. The Austrians are faced with the alternative of becoming a second Hungary and Vienna a second Budapest or of making it so uncomfortable for the Nazis that they will decide to draw their defense lines in the Austrian Alps to the west of the capital.

There are many difficulties in the way of securing action by the Austrians themselves: (1) they are by nature an easy going and not an heroic people; (2) the country has been purposely emptied of the men and many of the women who might form a resistance front. These are in the army or defense work, many far from their Austrian homes; (3) Austria, and in particular Vienna, is filled with a motley crowd of foreign workers and displaced people who have no particular feeling for an Austrian state and are unwilling to make sacrifices for it. In the country and mountain areas there are many bombed-out refugees from Germany who have no interest whatever in an independent Austria; (4) there is such physical and mental lassitude and depression among the people, at least in the cities, that the physical energy to react is largely gone.

However, with all these obstacles it still seems worthwhile to try to arouse the Austrians to more effective opposition but this will require some encouragement on our part.

Here are some ideas which occur to me: (1) the United States, Great Britain and Russia in the absence of any authoritative Austrian body which can as yet act for Austria might constitute themselves as joint trustees, assuming the obligations to carry out the Moscow Declaration and to constitute an independent Austria within boundaries and under arrangements with neighboring states which would give Austria a chance to work out a viable state; (2) something more should be done to impress the Austrians that every effort would be made by the Allies to save Vienna the fate of Budapest, if the Austrians themselves would take some steps to sabotage the war effort in and around Vienna and to make Vienna generally an unhealthy spot for the Nazis and Gestapo. If Vienna is to become a second Budapest, the responsibility for it should be placed squarely on the Nazis; (3) a study should be made of aid to be given to Austrian partisans in the mountains. In winter weather this is not easy, possibly impractical and we should not hold out false hopes. However, the end of the war is sufficiently near to make it possibly justifiable today to encourage Maquis activities in this area. We have a particular interest in this as it might help to discourage the Nazis from trying to make a last stand in a Maquis of their own based in the Austrian and Bavarian Alps.

The next few weeks may have a particular importance in determining whether we can secure some aid from Austria toward shortening the war and whether Austria can herself do something to help achieve her own freedom. This would have real political importance in building up the self respect and national consciousness necessary to justify and consolidate independent Austrian resistance. But Austrians cannot yet start in on this course alone. We must find a way to give them first some morale and then if a resistance starts to take shape, some material aid.

Document 5-15

Radiotelephone Transmission No. 270, January 22, 1945 (extracts)

[Dulles elaborates on the themes of Germany's "Eastern Option" and the possibility of an Alpine redoubt.]

Germany

The question is generally being asked here whether the Russian offensive will bring about the collapse of organized German resistance, or whether Germany will be able to organize for another stand. The loss of Silesia would certainly be a serious blow, but it is extremely difficult to understand German military dispositions except on the theory that the Germans still have confidence in their ability to halt the Russians well short of Berlin. . . .

It is most unlikely that the Germans now nourish any illusion that they can make a separate deal with Russia prior to German military collapse. On the other hand, many Nazis believe that there are similarities between the National Socialist and Communist movements; that the National Socialist movement can be shifted to the Left and communized; and that, after the collapse, they, the SS in particular, will find it easier individually to work out their future with the Russians than with the Anglo-Saxons. . . .

I do not mean to imply and do not believe that Hitler would be likely to surrender himself to the Russians under any circumstances. The information we get here locally seems to tend more and more to the theory of a final Nazi withdrawal into the Austrian and Bavarian Alps, with the idea of making a last stand there. This seems more likely than a dramatic attempt on the part of Hitler and the present Nazi leaders to escape by submarine or other modes of flight. Such flight might be attempted by the weaker characters of the Goering class. Hitler will probably seek a Wagnerian end, and Himmler et al. will presumably be with him. The smaller fry among the SS will probably be divided into two groups—those who might prefer to take a chance with the Russians, and the fanatical ones who will follow Hitler into a mountain retreat. This is all speculation and guesses made here are probably no better, and possibly not as good as those made from the perspective of Washington, and the end may not come for some months yet.

Document 5-16

Telegram 3037 to Caserta, January 24, 1945

[The appearance of Fritz Molden (number K-28), a young member of the Austrian opposition, offered Dulles a channel to the resistance and hope for finally exercising significant influence on Austrian affairs. After the war, Molden became Dulles's son-in-law. Gerry is Gerhard Van Arkel.]

Gerry from 110; Information Horton, 154 and SO. . . .

1. Long conference K-28 yesterday and I am now convinced that he represents best link to Austrian resistance which we have yet seen. Despite his youth he is extraordinarily mature and thoroughly indoctrinated in clandestine operations and procedure.

2. While willing to assist to utmost in SI, his primary desire is to serve as link to Austrian resistance and he therefore desires to work in accord with us, Zulu, French and Russians. View courtesies and encouragement shown him by the French, he expects to take radio operator to be furnished by them from Besancon, on early trip to Vienna. However, he realizes force of our statement to him that substantive aid to resistance and maquis can only come from Italian theater and he is willing to arrange facilities for team mentioned. . . . If so, he will probably locate French radio in Salzburg area and our team in Vienna.

3. For Gerry: pending report which Wood will bring back after scheduled conference today with 339, who familiar all details, suggest you tentatively arrange for your radio team to be ready go Annemasse to join K-28 on trip early February. K-28 leaving for Vienna 25th via Milan but expects return here within 2 weeks.

4. Again stress importance of maintaining absolute secrecy for names in 493's top secret memorandum of January 5th. K-28 much distressed at extent to which these names used in conversation with him at our Paris office as given us on condition they would not be passed on anywhere. I regret that I failed to stress this adequately in my covering memorandum. Suggest Paris mail copy 493 memorandum Washington subject above restrictive handling.

5. K-28 anxious to obtain publicity in Allied countries for statement regarding Austrian resistance and formation of provisional Austrian national committee dated January 3rd attached to above mentioned 493 memorandum. This has already had some publicity here. . . .

Document 5-17

Telegram 4039, January 24, 1945

[Hans Bernd Gisevius (number 512) made a miraculous escape from Germany six months after the July 20 plot of which he was a key participant. He traveled on forged documents prepared by the OSS and smuggled to him. Gisevius provided new details on the July 20 disaster and the state of the German resistance.]

512 has just escaped from Germany on last express train running from Berlin on papers prepared by C and D London (congratulations to London, particularly on Geheimstaats Polizei identification disk, which was particularly useful). He has been in hiding in Berlin since he left the Bendlerstrasse at 1830 hours July 20, 1/2 hour before the plotters were arrested. His friends' fate and 6 months hiding have shattered his nerves and it may take a few days to piece together his story, which will send soonest possible.

For 154. . . . It might have good psychological effect if you could give any encouraging reaction regarding manuscript.

Document 5-18

Telegram 3127 to Caserta, January 25, 1945

[By virtue of the efforts of Fritz Molden (number K-28), Dulles obtained far more substantial intelligence information on Austria than was previously available.]

Following miscellaneous intelligence, etc. from K-28, 1 or 2 items appeared in his recent written reports: (1) Widespread demand Austria for intensified use of leaflets, particularly bearing factual news. People thoroughly tired of propaganda or political jokes. Recommends planning for Austria with usual heading *Wiener Arbeiter Zeitung* and dropping at regular, say weekly intervals. (2) Salzburg area becoming concentration point for secret archives. Following places believed to be particular hideouts: (a) cellars and tunnels of old fortress Hohen Salzburg in Salzburg. Here secret Documents of OKW are stored. (b) Cellars and tunnels of Jonnberg in Salzburg. (c) Cellars of Moenchsberg in Salzburg. (3) Parts of German Foreign Office formerly in Krummhuegel area Silesia moved to Schloss Hellbrunn near Salzburg. (4) Head of Archiv-Kommission of German FO, Professor Jagow, recently instructed his staff to gather information for report on cruelties committed by Allied soldiers against German soldiers. Also on use of gas by Allied Armies. K-28 suggests this looks like preparing alibis. (5) Himmler reported to have established one of his Stabs-Feld-Hq. in Aigen-Glas near Salzburg located on railroad line Aigen-Glas to Hallein, one and a half kilometers from Aigen-Glas directly east of railroad. (6) Goering reported to have established one of his Hq. between Reichenhall and Freilassing in upper Bavaria. (7) According to captured secret Russian order major part of Russian offensive reserves have been moved to Baltic Polish theaters. So it is therefore safe to assume that strength of Russian Armies in Hungary considerably weakened and prospects favorable for German forces to advance via Stuhlweissenburg to Danube and to relieve Budapest. Lengthening of Russian southern flanks in Carpathians to be expected which offers opportunity for German offensive in this area after liquidation of Russian Armies west of Budapest. The defenders of Budapest must hold out under all circumstances and relief measures from air are under way. Accompanying order were instructions addressed to German Commander Vienna ordering discontinuation evacuation of military hospitals from Vienna and providing that arms intended for Vienna Volkssturm should be made available to Chief H. Ruest and RDE (date of order about January 7th). . . . (8) POW does not believe that Nazi Maquis can be effectively established Austrian Alps view hostility local population. Had heard particularly of 4 German centers for Maquis, viz. Berlin, Harz, Theringen and Berchtesgaden. They emphasize that experience Stalingrad, Warsaw etc. has shown that bombed and destroyed cities are best suited for last stand resistance.

Document 5-19

Telegram 4077, January 25, 1945

[As the war approached its final stages, Dulles continued to report on the attractiveness to certain German military leaders of an accommodation with the Soviet Union. He also reported on his efforts to establish contacts with the German generals Rundstedt and Kesselring.]

One item of news brought by 512 was that Stauffenberg who was the active element in July putsch had planned eastern solution if putsch successful and proposed initiate declaration of workers and peasants regime in Germany. Old line generals who participated in plot while not agreeing with this solution, did not oppose Stauffenberg as he was only one willing to risk his neck and also was only man who had facilities for placing bomb. Former hoped they could control developments later in more conservative sense.

Situation on Eastern Front and general drift of German situation leads me to conclude that eastern solution now more attractive to Germany as well as harmonizing with march of events. Not impossible we may find Germany maintaining stubborn resistance in west while Russians are deep in Germany, unless we find way of breaking resistance of Wehrmacht forces opposing us in west. Subtlety and psychology may help our military forces.

Endeavoring explore possibilities of secret line to Rundstedt and already have a line to Kesselring via contact who is seeing 476 today before proceeding to Italy to see Kesselring. Could anything along following lines be given discreetly to cut outs who have contacts in high Wehrmacht circles? (1) Unconditional surrender remains unaltered policy but problem for German military leaders to face is future of own country in face of inevitable and rapidly approaching military defeat. (2) In both west and east Germany faces the choice of making each German city an Aachen, Warsaw or Budapest, or of facilitating entry of the Allied forces and orderly transfer of authority to forces of occupation under conditions which would (a) spare unnecessary destruction, (b) facilitate distribution of food and raw materials so as to render possible an earlier resumption of economic life and, (c) render possible orderly evacuation of prisoners and foreign workers, (3) Officers of Wehrmacht who contribute to such constructive policy, assuming war criminals not involved, would be treated with consideration due their rank and in relation to the services they thus render in facilitating liquidation of the Nazi regime and those forces which have supported it.

This is merely rough outline of ideas, but some affirmative program along some such lines may help to drive a wedge into German Army and to facilitate American and British occupation of at least Western Germany before effects of Russian successes in east create situation of complete chaos throughout Germany. Even though Russia may not, and probably does not, desire to see a Bolshevized Germany, many Germans believe this would facilitate an understanding with Russia and are working in this direction aided by events, by the distress incident to the slowly creeping paralysis in German transportation and the suffering resulting from air bombardments and the presence in Germany of millions of undernourished and desperate prisoners of war, foreign workers and bombed out population.

Document 5-20

Telegram 4377, January 26, 1945

[In January 1945, Hans Bernd Gisevius made his escape from Germany, having eluded the Gestapo since the collapse of the July 20, 1944, plot against Hitler. This message contains his initial account of the failure of the assassination attempt and military takeover. Surprisingly, it was Gisevius's opinion, as summarized by Dulles, that some of the younger plotters, including Stauffenberg, intended to strike a deal with Russia rather than the West. Gisevius/Dulles attribute this preference within the German opposition for an Eastern option to the failure of the West to hold out any hope for the future of Germany beyond Unconditional Surrender.]

BREAKERS. Cheston and 154. 512's complete story will require time in preparing and will be sent by pouch. Believe he only person now in safety of those who met in War Ministry Bendlerstrasse on July 20. Goerdeler, who 512 believes still alive, had been sent away by Stauffenberg just prior to July 20. 512 had prominent part in plot. However, program had been formulated on strictly military lines prior to his arrival Berlin on July 11 and police aspects were largely neglected, which he feels was one of the causes of failure. Plotters depended upon military occupation of Government buildings rather than arrest of key individuals and when military plans were too slow in moving, Nazi police measures wrecked program.

2 prior coups had been planned, 1 failed on July 6 in Munich due to Hitler's sudden departure and further attempt on July 16 in East Prussia, failed when Stauffenberg's collaborator, General Stieff lost his nerve. On July 16 military forces which were to march on Berlin had been set in motion. When attempt failed this troop activity had to be passed off as exercise which could not be repeated on July 20

without arousing suspicion. Hence on July 20 troops only set in motion after bomb actually exploded and did not reach Bendlerstrasse in time to prevent Nazi countermeasures.

By July 20 nerves of Stauffenberg and other participants were at or beyond breaking point and some failed carry out their part, particularly General Feldgiebel, who was to destroy Central Information office including all communication installations of East Prussia Headquarters to prevent any communication, so that even if Hitler not killed, he would not be able to make this known until plotters had control of the situation.

Remer's defection which also described in press, also contributing factor in failure.

When Stauffenberg reached Berlin Airport, after placing bomb, he telephoned Bendlerstrasse that everything was okay and to go ahead. Thereupon, Olbricht set military forces into motion. When Stauffenberg arrived Bendlerstrasse, he admitted he was not certain Hitler was dead to which Beck replied that for us he is dead. About this time Keitel telephoned to Bendlerstrasse and to all military Commanders, not then knowing Olbricht and others were in plot, and gave news Hitler was alive.

512 was saved because he went on mission from Beck to Helldorf and Nebe at Police headquarters and actually passed through troops under Remer, which were coming to arrest Bendlerstrasse plotters, but which 512 then thought came to seize Bendlerstrasse for plotters. While with Helldorf, 512 learned of fiasco and also that Nebe had been asked to send his officials to East Prussia to start investigation. Helldorf and others not caught at Bendlerstrasse then took futile steps to create alibis, but 512 could not do this as his presence Berlin unauthorized. He found shelter in Berlin, where he stayed in practically solitary isolation until we managed to get false papers to him.

Failure also due in part to sudden total divergence of views among plotters. Stauffenberg and his immediate collaborators were determined on Eastern solution and opening front immediately to Russia without even trying to negotiate with them. Stauffenberg claimed he had been in touch with Seydlitz Committee and that he had from Seydlitz Committee through Kollantay assurances that Germany would have fair peace and that German Wehrmacht would not be completely disarmed. Also Trott, who apparently had tried to contact British in Stockholm and had received no encouragement, had himself gone over to Eastern solution and supported Stauffenberg. Hence, there was disunity as to whom should form new government and there were two states, conservative Western element headed by Goerdeler and Beck, while pro-Russian faction, though willing keep Beck as acting Chief of State wanted Leftist Prime Minister either Leuschner or preferably Leber.

Younger men, especially Stauffenberg, were real dynamic forces in plot, older went along, though disagreeing on policy, on theory that anything was better than Hitler. It is significant of situation in Germany then and today that younger men like Stauffenberg and Trott saw in Anglo-American policy or lack of policy no hope for Germany's future and therefore, were prepared to take their chances with Russia.

512 sees only chaos for Germany. He says Germans expect harsh but realistic policy from Russia, that Russia will need Germany's economic resources and therefore, will permit Eastern Germany to work, although it may be only for Russia's benefit, whereas Western powers have no interest in seeing any economic life rebuilt in Germany and hence, Germans feel little hope for Germans under American and British occupation. He believes that conditions in Germany which American and British occupying forces will have to meet will be so intolerable for persons used to western form of life and culture, that it will be next to impossible to maintain occupying forces there from point of view of morale and living conditions, not of course from point of view of any military opposition. Russians are hardened to such things and in any event, with exception of Berlin, cities in their zone will have suffered less bombing destruction.

Full story by pouch later.

Document 5-21

Telegram 4267, January 27, 1945

[Dulles here presents his views on propaganda lines to be directed at Austria. Typically, he criticizes proposals suggested by the OSS Morale Operations Branch.]

Bigelow from 110. . . .

1. Proposed statement re Dollfuss and Schuschnigg regimes would probably please socialists and Syndicalists and those who represent majority in resistance. It might not find same favorable reaction in right and Catholic resistance circles.

2. Believe our propaganda regarding Austria should be simple and direct and avoid references arousing any internal political faction or ism. Our program should be to get Nazi[c] and Prussians out of Austria and to restore political and social liberties and to abolish vestiges of all totalitarian regimes whether of Nazi or other origin. We should emphasize our interest in restoring free press, freedom of assembly, trade unions and independent political parties.

3. Believe foregoing would accomplish objectives sought without alienating anti-Nazi elements in previous regime even though they may be minority in present resistance movement. Remember that Dollfuss was murdered and Schuschnigg tortured by Nazis and while their totalitarian regimes have no appeal today to Austrian public, use of their names in proposed pronouncement might be unfortunate.

Document 5-22

Radiotelephone Transmission No. 272, January 29, 1945

[Dulles reports on the expectation that the Soviet Union would soon set up a German puppet government similar to the Polish Lublin Government, and on rumors of German peace feelers.]

Germany

1. Reports from Germany indicate that the Germans are expecting that the general pattern which the Russians have followed in Rumania, Bulgaria, and Hungary will be followed in Germany. They anticipate that the Russians, as soon as a substantial part of Germany has been occupied, will form a German government composed in part of generals, such as Paulus and Seydlitz and in part of Leftists from the territory occupied. If such an effort on the part of the Russians were blocked today by the Allies, the Germans feel that the Russians would still succeed later with it, just as they did with the Lublin Committee. Some of the German representatives here in Switzerland are wondering what they would do if they should be called on to repudiate the Nazi government and adhere to such a new German government. Most of them here would be glad to get out of their present job if they felt it would help their position to do so at this late date.

2. We have no evidence here that von Papen is either in Switzerland or Spain, as rumored. In fact, according to our latest report, he was in Germany when last heard from, but of course we don't know exactly where he may be today. If Germany makes any desperate peace feelers, it would probably be done by some one more trusted by Himmler than von Papen. According to reports reaching us, Himmler still feels that he might be able to do something at the last moment in the way of peace negotiations. There are reasons to believe that he is even now trying, but without success so far, to establish contact for this purpose with high Catholic authorities in North Italy.

Document 5-23

Telegram 5377 to London, January 30, 1945

[OSS established teams to enter major cities liberated from the enemy immediately behind combat forces. Dulles sought to accompany the unit entering Berlin, as well as to assume control of overall OSS operations in occupied Germany.]

Bastedo and Peters from 110. . . . Most interested your #3837 re Berlin T Force. We will probably wish 4 slots. View certain recent developments and prospects of securing important Documents through personal contacts, believe it is desirable I go with T Force, also 476 and possibly 512 if he willing, also Wood intermediary.

Attempting arrange now safe deposits for certain documents in American zone particularly those relating Far East and South American affairs. Assume that if Russians first reach Berlin as seems likely, they would occupy entire city as matter of military necessity and then later evacuate American-British zones. Have you any clue on this?

For Washington: Consider 512 would be most useful single individual for guiding us to Gestapo hideouts and old Abwehr records. In general consider that even trained Americans will be fairly helpless in ruins of Berlin and that use of trusted Germans essential for any successful penetration Nazi records.

Document 5-24

Telegram 4697, February 2, 1945

[OSS Bern became desperate for additional working-level personnel in early 1945. Dulles's irritation reflects that common disdain often felt by field commanders for the slow-moving central bureaucracy.]

Cheston and Rhythm from 110. Answer is yes. Please forget indoctrination. My need is immediate. Do you realize that not one single person has yet reached Bern from Washington since frontier opened in September? If you will get personnel to Annemasse I will get them in.

Document 5-25

Radiotelephone Transmission No. 273, February 2, 1944

[Dulles discusses a German Government propaganda statement designed to preempt possible Allied action at the Yalta Conference to qualify the doctrine of unconditional surrender.]

Germany

Today's statement by the Wilhelmstrasse to the German people seemed to me particularly significant. Its purpose, of course, was to counteract the effect of any possible statement which might be made at the Roosevelt-Churchill-Stalin conference. In particular, the Wilhelmstrasse wished to warn the German people that they should not be misled by any definition we might give to the term "unconditional surrender."

The statement was obviously dictated by fear—fear that we would at last say something to the German people which might give them a ray of hope for their future as individuals, that we would define what we meant by "unconditional surrender," not in terms of promises to Germany, which we neither should nor will give, but in terms of the kind of Europe we would hope to see once the Nazis and the militarists were crushed and eliminated.

The statement of the Wilhelmstrasse is cleverly drawn. It is probably the work of Goebbels, who is an extraordinary stylist and a master of the German language. But it shows the grave apprehension the Germans have that, at the eleventh hour, we might use the weapon of psychological warfare on a grand scale to deprive the Nazi leaders of their last desire, namely, to hold the people with them until the end, so that they can drag the German people with them into the common disaster.

Document 5-26

Radiotelephone Transmission No. 274, February 3, 1945

[This message summarizes reports from Germany and Bulgaria.]

Germany

A report from a recent arrival from Germany states that Himmler has the fixed idea that he can blackmail the Western Allies into a joint front against the Soviets. Here are further items from this report. Himmler hates Ribbentrop and reproaches him for his awkward simultaneous blackmail efforts with the West and the East by threatening each side that he would make a separate peace with the other. He was therefore prepared to replace Ribbentrop with a man of his own choosing as soon as his military plans had matured. It was his idea to reconquer Alsace-Lorraine by the end of January and for that purpose had accumulated large strategic reserves behind the Western Front. The Rundstedt offensive was intended to be only the first part of a move. Himmler had the idea that the Western Allies would negotiate after a serious reverse, which explains a good deal of his strange mentality. His whole plan was upset by the failure of the Rundstedt offensive and by the unexpected success of the Russian drive, which has forced a shifting of reserves from West to East.

According to this report, one of the most serious situations Germany is now facing is the coal shortage. Goebbels, for propaganda reasons, has been insisting upon priority distribution of coal to householders. As a result, industry now has low stocks and can only maintain activity thanks to the use of lignite.

In the German view, according to this report, Stalin is now so strong that, whatever arrangements are made among the Allies, he will keep not only eastern and southeastern Europe, but will infiltrate the whole of Germany, even the parts to be occupied by the Western Allies.

The generals of the Moscow Free German Committee are considered in Germany as far more efficient than any German political exiles in the western countries.

In the long run, the Germans feel, Stalin will also dispose of the nationalistic elements in the country, of many former Nazis, and the Communists. With these elements a reign of terror could be let loose in Germany which would eliminate any Germans who still had pro-Western orientations and disgust the Anglo-Saxons to a point where isolationism would revive.

The report states that Churchill's speech to the effect that the evacuated population of the East Prussian territory to be ceded to Poland would find sufficient "Lebensraum" in Germany, owing to the millions of dead, was distributed by Goebbels to the soldiers and has helped to discourage the Germans who had favored the western solution. Himmler, according to the report, feels that the general prospects of a Russian domination of Germany will eventually force the Western Powers to make common cause with him, and he apparently is nursing the hope that he will then be accepted as the only possible bulwark to protect Europe from the eastern menace.

Bulgaria
I have a long report here from a Bulgarian, a former official, and well known for his anti-German feelings, who expresses great bitterness at the results of the trials of the war criminals in Sofia. Here is a brief summary of the report, on which I do not feel competent to comment except to state that I believe that the writer is an honest man.

(Beginning of report) The sentences exceeded in rigor those demanded by the public prosecutor, who, in the cases of Groneff and Pomenoff, had only asked imprisonment. In the case of the members of the Mouravieff cabinet, the prosecutor had merely asked the court to render a verdict according to their consciences in view of the statement of witnesses that this cabinet had taken all possible political measures effectively to bring about a change of policy in favor of the Allies.

A manifestation of 15,000 people was timed to take place just as the verdicts were to be rendered and undoubtedly to exercise its influence on the tribunals. The tribunals themselves, ostensibly created for the purpose of catching war criminals, by lumping together the guilty and the innocent, the friends of the Axis and the friends of the Allies, totalitarians and democrats, have shown that they had quite different intentions. It has become obvious that they exist for the purpose of destroying the bases of democratic government and the monarchy in Bulgaria and with them the surviving foundations of national independence. By playing the Russian card, Bulgarian extremists seek to eliminate any Anglo-American influence in Bulgaria.

Document 5-27

Telegram 4837, February 4, 1945

["George Wood" obtained new information from Berlin for Dulles in January 1945. It was transmitted from Bern to Washington in the "Jakka" series of cables. This German report from China alleges that Japanese-Soviet contacts had occurred.]

JAKKA.

1. Woermann, Nanking to Grand, December 16 refers to unconfirmed rumor that Jap Commission including Marishuma visited Moscow at Soviet request to discuss use East Siberian Railroad for transport American supplies and brought back conditions under which Soviet willing mediate between Japan and USA.

2. Wagner, Hsingking, January 17 to Grand, reports information via agent that negotiations Jap Commission Moscow failed. Japan offered eternal peace. Russia

declared existing agreements would be kept for time being and new arrangements would only be possible after meeting Roosevelt, Churchill.

Document 5-28

Telegram 4827, February 5, 1945

[This cable reveals Dulles's concerns regarding difficulties in the processing and distribution of the Wood Traffic.]

JAKKA.

1. Have now practically completed brief survey Jap material to give you general idea of contents and most urgent BO. Originals should reach you next few days. . . .

3. Again emphasize that to get full value out of this material will require staff of workers thoroughly competent German, with some background Wood material, knowledge of personalities and German diplomatic procedure plus ability decipher crossword puzzles. Our telegrams have only scratched the surface. . . .

5. Would appreciate for my guidance some idea handling your end. Confidential. When in Washington I had some impression that antagonism of Bissel at G-2 and mysterious methods of Berle had result that this material handled as museum pieces and that full value operationally not obtained. (Also never thoroughly understood why this considered as X-2 matter since this is intelligence, not intercepts.) For example, Joe Grew, who close personal friend and then head of Far Eastern section apparently knew nothing of Far Eastern material. . . . Also . . . full clues given re provisioning German-Atlantic ports, yet under our noses Germans carried out very attempt Kappa cable described.

6. I appreciate your previous expressions of interest this material, but my efforts could be directed more intelligently, if I knew more about handling your end. Recent exchanges of cables with London not fully understood and am also not clear how much I should tell my British colleague 521 about contents of these cables.

Document 5-29

Telegram 4909, February 5, 1945

[This message concerns the political configuration of postwar Germany, and particularly the views of Dulles and Gisevius on the Soviet-sponsored Free German Committee.]

BREAKERS. Carib from 110. Information: Forgan and 140. . . . 512 is convinced that Russians will come to Germany with carefully assembled and thoroughly indoctrinated group of Germans probably including Paulus, Seydlitz et al. If they can succeed in putting this over as the government of Germany they will do so but more likely, in view of probably American and British opposition, they will at first merely use this in Russian zone. However, as this will be the only German organization and as it will profit from its long advertisement and prestige of Russian backing, it will more and more be looked to as the government of Germany since USA and Britain will have nothing comparable. It may, of course, be initially set up as a committee and procedure followed similar to that in case of Lublin Committee.

512 believes we have only 3 alternatives: 1) Accept Russian German committee; 2) Set up rival committee or probably 2 rival committees in respective Anglo-Saxon zones, or 3) Organize jointly with Russians some type of German committee which is subject to Allied occupation authorities and will assist in transacting current affairs as successor to German government on the understanding, of course, that final authority rests solely with military occupation. Such committee might be largely of technical men, experts in their respective fields such as finance, transportation, food rationing and distribution, public works, labor relations, police and the like but we would probably have to accept some of the Paulus, Seydlitz crowd.

512 feels, and I agree, that if we go into Germany without any plans along this 3rd line, something like the Seydlitz committee will eventually be imposed on us.

512 stresses importance, particularly from our viewpoint as regards South America, of controlling German Foreign representation. He believes that if this is properly handled we might be able to infiltrate and break up entire Nazi espionage ring in South America.

Certain German diplomats here who are not too compromised as Nazis are expecting early summons to adhere to Seydlitz committee or alternatively that Seydlitz committee will send its own people here and endeavor to infiltrate German diplomatic, consular establishment.

Some weeks ago 476, at the invitation of General Sibert, G-2, 12th AG, visited 12th AG and later London and SHAEF and with my backing presented plan for getting together small group of high anti-Nazi German officers, whom he interviewed in France and England, to advise on certain phases of German matters and methods of penetrating OKW. This group was not to have any political functions and was to work secretly. This plan which I consider constructive has apparently died in SHAEF, or, at least, I have heard nothing further about it, possibly owing to Gen. Betts' illness as he had matter in hand.

While agreeing that we should not set up German committee of political refugees such as Bruning, Wirth, Braun, Treviranus et al., I feel we should prepare quietly and without formality in Switzerland, France, and elsewhere certain individual Germans who have maintained close contact with Germany and who would be suitable to advise on certain phases German matters and possibly serve on technical administrative committees which any occupying authorities in Germany will find absolutely essential. I have several candidates here including 512 who was slated for high post if the July 20th affair had succeeded. If we do nothing of this nature, the ready made Russian German committee may monopolize the field.

Document 5-30

Radiotelephone Transmission No. 275, February 6, 1945 (extract)

[This message contains additional observations on Germany.]

. . . Germany

1. It is often useful to get the views of the less educated strata of German society as to what is going on in Germany. Here is the view of a German servant girl, Anna, working in Switzerland, but who has several brothers working in the German Army and one who died in the Crimea. Anna says that, if Field Marshal von Paulus can really succeed Hitler without the Russians installing Communism in Germany, everything will be just beautiful. This almost equivalent to the Germans' winning the war. It would show that the Russians also have had enough. Anna, so I am told, is radiant that such a "victory" might be obtained.

2. Reports of Saturday's [Feb. 3] bombing of Berlin indicate that it was the most devastating that the city has yet experienced. Telephone communication to here has been cut. No travelers have yet reached Switzerland since the raid, and only a few telegrams have yet come through. The actual facts are not so well known here. Apparently the center of the city experienced the worst beating it has yet received.

I'll probably have to be away for several days. I expect to be back possibly for Monday, certainly for Tuesday.

Document 5-31

Telegram 360 to Caserta, February 9, 1945

[Neurath, the German Consul in Lugano, served as a go-between for Dulles in tentative contacts with Generals Kesselring and Wolff and Ambassador Rahn in northern Italy. Neurath paid a visit to these wavering Nazi principals in early February.]

Neurath returned from meeting with Kesselring, Rahn and Wolf. He did not then get impression of plans for immediate withdrawal and apparently even high German officials in Italy are somewhat surprised that bulk of reinforcements for the Eastern Front are coming from west rather than from the south. He felt possible explanation German army in Italy being kept largely intact as eventual protection for southern flank of the German inner fortress based on Bavarian Austrian Alps. (From 110: K-28 reports do indicate certain withdrawals.) Kesselring saw Rundstedt recently and the two are on friendly terms but according to Neurath neither is yet ready to come over to us. Neurath discussed with Kesselring the Freies Deutschland Committee. Kesselring indicated Seydlitz had little prestige with army but on contrary if

Paulus agreed to form government this might have substantial effect on Wehrmacht. Neurath has contact with Westphal but was advised by Kesselring not to try to see him immediately view suspicion which such trip might occasion. Very secret: via Neurath we now have existing line to Kesselring and potential line to Westphal but this not useful for general BO as Neurath will not lend himself to that but might someday be useful in event of major developments.

Document 5-32

Telegram 6447 to London, February 13, 1945

[This message concerns plans for postwar intelligence penetration of Germany from external bases.]

For Forgan, Gamble and Bastedo. From 110. 140 and I discussed yesterday with Henry Hyde and Major Crosby certain plans in which they interested covering possible penetration Germany in post hostilities occupation period using Alsace-Lorraine as base and holding available for this purpose certain of their present personnel, American and agent. To realize this plan probably desirable that such personnel should not go into Germany with armies and OSS tie up as this might blow their future cover.

Both 140 and I consider these ideas interesting and deserving of future study. At our suggestion they preparing memo to submit to you and us and we can then in consultation decide as to method of implementing program which based on principles often followed by our cousins and French, viz, that base for penetration should be outside of country to be penetrated. In view of chaotic situation we likely find Germany, believe desirable we study application of this principle not only as regards operating in Germany from France but also from neighboring countries.

In connection with foregoing, Henry believes that French acquiescence contemplated procedure could be obtained in view his existing relationships provided appropriate moment our military authorities took up with French authorities.

Document 5-33

Radiotelephone Transmission No. 276, February 13, 1945

[The prospect of a Nazi last stand in a "reduit" and diehard guerrilla resistance gained currency in the European press as well as in Allied intelligence circles. Its likelihood was founded both in fragmentary reports and in historical precedent.

General Donovan sent this message to President Roosevelt, Secretary of the Treasury Henry Morgenthau, and Assistant Secretary of War John McCloy on February 14.]

Germany

1. When organized German military resistance collapses, there will probably be more than one "reduit" or inner fortress of Nazi resistance which may remain. It seems generally accepted now that a delayed defense fortress will lie in the Bavarian and Austrian Alps. Swiss sources have information which they consider reliable that substantial amounts of foodstuffs being collected here, and that some underground factories are being prepared to supply arms required for mountain warfare. The difficulty about these reports is that it is impossible to put your finger on the particular area where the foodstuffs are being collected, or where these underground factories are being prepared. In connection with the above, it is also reported that the Nazi authorities are taking careful measures to prevent the refugees from the evacuated areas and Berlin from going into the general area of southern Germany and the reduit. Apparently, these evacuees are being moved in a westerly rather than in a southerly direction.

In addition to the main reduit, people here believe that there will be other isolated centers of Nazi resistance; for example, in the area of Thueringen, around Weimar, and also in the Black Forest area, flanked by the northern frontier of Switzerland and the Rhine.

2. Here is a report from the *National Zeitung* of Basle of a few days ago, which gives clearer . . . picture of the German maquis plan. (Beginning of summary) The rapid advance of the Russians and the threatened collapse of the German Eastern Front have forced the German command, not only to concentrate its reserves in front of Berlin, but also to rush its preparations for the German maquis. The most important centers of resistance of this maquis are to be in Thueringen, south of Stuttgart, and in Middle Bavaria and Austria. There is plenty of protection there by mountains and hills, and many fortifications have been constructed. There is already an armament industry in operation, with picked workers available to run it, while it is reported that measures to evacuate the useless civilian population have been prepared.

The so-called ideals of National Socialism are nothing new. They are those of the old pan-Germanism developed to the most radical and utmost degree. Similarly, the idea of a maquis existed in 1918, although not anything like as complete as the plan which the Nazis are preparing to present the war-weary world in the last stages of the second world war. In 1918 and after, there was a "black" Reichswehr. There were Freikorps and secret . . . organizations. Great stores of arms were hidden away and never disclosed to the Allied Control Commission—all this with the idea of organizing and maintaining secret resistance until such time as a new international constellation, such as, perhaps, an agreement with Russia, would permit the movement to come out into the open. Even then, the watch-word was "Death to the traitors!" Only the prominent victims, such as Erzberger, Rathenau, Eisener, Landauer, Liebknecht, and Rosa Luxemburg, came to public notice. No one has yet told the whole tale of the many others who were murdered, especially those who betrayed plans and secret depots of arms to the Allies. Similar plans are now to be carried into effect by the Nazis, with their habitual thoroughness, and aided by their experiences with the resistance movement in occupied countries, such as Tito's guerrilla war. There are special schools for recruits taught by selected officers from the front. The establishment of huge underground ammunition plants and tremendous stores of ammunition and food serve the same purpose.

(This report is incomplete due to technical difficulties.)

Document 5-34

Telegram 5327, February 15, 1945

[Atomic energy intelligence continued to flow out of Bern. This message was addressed to Deputy Director Buxton.]

AZUSA. For 106 and Dix only. For 908 only for Calvert.

1. Max Planck, 86 year old originator quantum theory operated on for hernia Sauerbruch.
2. His non-physicist son Herman, age about 33 was condemned to death for alleged participation July 20 anti-Hitler plot.
3. Heisenberg terribly shocked by news, informed Flute last December.
4. Editor Zurich paper *Die Tat* recently informed Flute Himmler reprieved Planck's son.
5. Nils Bohr Copenhagen Institute saved from removal or destruction after Bohr departure when Heisenberg, although accompanied by Nazi, pledged no Bohr anti-Nazi activity.
6. Heisenberg cleared at Leipzig trial called at own request early in war for being "Wditetew" (sic), spiritual love for non-Nazi scientists such as Einstein.
7. Weiszaeker now definitely known to have been officially designated to accompany Heisenberg in Switzerland.

Document 5-35

Telegram 5407, February 16, 1945

[On February 10, General Donovan cabled Dulles that henceforth all Kappa and Breakers material should be sent to Washington only. In accordance with a general policy of increased centralization, Washington would determine action and dissemination. Dulles objected to this development; his observations constitute another in a series of outspoken reservations concerning the policies of the Director.]

KAPPA. 109 and 154 from 110.

1. Your 3327 disturbs me considerably. Long delay in getting material to Washington, processing and redistribution might have serious operational consequences.

2. London has been distributing selected material promptly to certain important contacts whose continued cooperation is vitally essential in developing our plans for Germany, for example Bob Murphy and certain top G-2 contacts.

3. Trained London staff has acquired competence and security in handling material.

4. If all flow to British via London terminates, this may affect certain established relationships with them here and in London.

5. Remember question now is of terminating midstream existing relationships. View chaotic situation Germany we may get no more Kappa prior collapse.

6. You have requested us to have Wood concentrate on Far Eastern material and we endeavored comply and gave transmission of this material absolute priority. I have no clue whatever whether this material proved of value to you.

7. Earnestly request your reconsideration at least as far as Jakka concerned since understood when in Paris that distribution this material already started. We can reconsider if new material received.

Document 5-36

Radiotelephone Transmission No. 278, February 17, 1945 (extract)

[Dulles now asserts that evidence was sufficiently strong to justify Allied planning against the eventuality of resistance by German irregular forces after the collapse of the Reich. He suggests elements of what in later times would be called a counterinsurgency program.]

. . . Germany

1. It is increasingly the impression here that, even after organized military resistance on the eastern, western and southern fronts of Germany has been broken, there will remain for a considerable period, not only a relatively large maquis in the south of Germany and Austria, but several other maquis organizations in various mountainous and forest areas, such as the Harz, Thueringen, and the Black Forest. Military experts here also believe that the Nazis will endeavor to make each large German city a center of resistance.

The Germans expect to apply, in their last stand resistance, not only the lessons of Stalingrad and Budapest, but also the lessons of the French and Yugoslav maquis. I believe that there is sufficient basis for these reports to justify our most serious consideration and the planning now of all appropriate measures to meet this problem.

In the case of the European maquis, the resistance forces have been successful because of the secret backing of the population in the areas where the maquis forces were concentrated, despite lack of arms and ammunition. The Germans expect to have no shortage of the type of military supplies needed for guerrilla warfare, and there is not much we can do at the moment to prevent them from assembling these supplies in the strategic areas they may select. What we can do, possibly, is to help create a situation where the local population will be hostile rather than helpful to the Nazi forces which will try to assemble in the respective maquis areas. It might well be worth considering the line of propaganda to tell the German people that those who aid in the organization of the maquis, those who give any support to it will be classed with the SS and Gestapo forces and with the Nazi criminals who will make up the bulk of the maquis forces. We must show the German people that the men of the German maquis are those who are preventing the restoration of peace, those who are thus responsible for the final and complete destruction of Germany. We must in this way induce the Germans themselves to track down the Nazis in their mountain and forest retreats. This will give anti-Nazis a last chance to show that there are some Germans who are willing to turn on their Nazi oppressors and to risk their lives to destroy vestiges of Nazi control in Germany. . . .

Document 5-37

Telegram 5527, February 19, 1945

[Spurred by concern over the Soviet-sponsored Free Germany Committee, Dulles encouraged German exiles in Switzerland to organize themselves clandestinely for the purpose of infiltrating the Nazi establishment in Switzerland. The implicit objective of this proposal was to enhance the ability of Germans with a Western orientation to compete with pro-Soviet elements in Switzerland and in postwar Germany. Individuals mentioned include Gisevius (512), Waetjen (670), and Prince Auersperg (502).]

BREAKERS. . . . For 109 and 154; Information: Forgan and 140. During 140's visit here we had some conversations with 512, 670 and 502 in reference to form of aid which anti-Nazi German ex-officials etc. here in Switzerland might be able to render. Their general impression was that in view of obvious reluctance of Anglo-Saxons to encourage organization of, or to extend any recognition to, any committee of Germans outside of Germany, such ex-officials should organize themselves clandestinely starting here in Switzerland. This form of organization appeals to individuals concerned as they fear consequences to members of families still in Germany from any public declaration. Also open activities directed from here against Germany by such a group would contravene Swiss ideas of neutrality.

The above mentioned persons, who have already been working with us for over 2 years in case of 512 and about 1 year in case of other 2 promise to constitute a secret group together with certain other ex-German officials and to secure secret adherents within German Legation and consulates, who would retain their positions and assist in obtaining information on following general points: (a) unofficial and secret Nazi agents; (b) Nazi press and 5th column activities; (c) secret Nazi funds; (d) location secret files and Documents; (e) activities of semi-official German organizations, such as German Purchase Commissions etc; (f) details in reference to German colony generally and German schools and so called philanthropic institutions; (g) Nazi links between Suisse and other countries particularly South America (group would contemplate acting as "Shadow Legation" working clandestinely within existing official Nazi organization. They are also willing, if agreeable to us, to facilitate organization of similar activities in other neutral countries or to establish contact with possible opposite numbers there to develop same type of work). I have encouraged idea of this type of clandestine activity and unless you see objection, propose to give it thorough trial. If by any chance you felt that time had come to endeavor secure wholesale public resignations (rather than to continue along clandestine line) we could try to develop such possibilities, but we have assumed here that it was wiser to avoid the responsibilities and complications which would inevitably follow from fostering public movement of secession to which undesirable characters would undoubtedly try to adhere. . . . While I recognize importance of taking no action which would give Russians any just ground for complaint, I feel it is important you should realize that unless we can show some interest in working along lines indicated above or adopt some other program to accomplish similar objective there is grave danger that anti-Nazi elements, who might render real service and who are oriented toward Western rather than Eastern culture and civilization, will find no practical alternative except to throw in their lot with Russians. I have reason to believe that Freies Deutschland Committee here which as yet has little influence in Suisse is becoming active and is trying to build up its own prestige by infiltrating German Legation and Consular personnel. I recognize that bulk of this personnel will probably be uninteresting for us or unwanted, but believe a few selected members could render substantial service.

Your general comments on proposed program would be appreciated as well as any suggestions as to measure of protection which can be held out to those who retain their official positions and render service to us.

Document 5-38

Telegram 6847 to London, February 19, 1945

[In this message, Dulles gives an indication of his thinking on the postwar organization of the OSS in Germany and of his own personal plans for the future.]

For Bastedo. . . . Information 109 and Cheston. . . . As indicated, I consider desirable to have a second in command in both Berlin and American Zone. As you know, I have always made it clear that for personal reasons I cannot undertake indefinite assignment Germany, and question as to who should be deputy to take my place upon my return to USA is matter for 109 to determine. Possibly there was some confusion in my cables through unclear use of terms Deputy and Executive Officer, but I had in mind that executive officer in each zone would act as my deputy during my absence from such zone, as my time might be divided between Berlin and American Zone. If deputy is used to mean my successor then, as indicated above, this decision lies with 109. Possibly fundamental changes of our whole ETO, MEDTO set-up after Germany collapses would make it desirable to defer naming of my successor. For 109: Bastedo and I have considered possibility of inducing Bill Jackson to work with us in Germany. If you agree, possibly you could help to influence him in this direction. He would be excellent head for German SI.

Document 5-39

Radiotelephone Transmission No. 279, February 19, 1945

[The reported founding by Mussolini of an Italian National Socialist Party drew the following comment from Dulles.]

Italy

The reports in the evening papers state that Mussolini has approved the founding of a new Italian party, namely, the National Socialist Party of Italy. The press report goes on to say that this will mean a split in the Neo-Fascist Party and that this is probably brought about at German instigation, as the Germans are not entirely satisfied with all the various elements which are included in the Neo-Fascist Party of today.

This report is also interpreted in the press as a step taken in preparation for a withdrawal into the maquis. Obviously, the Germans do not want to take a large number of Italian Fascists with them. On the other hand, they do not want to be entirely without some Italian representation there. Therefore, by forming a new party and by controlling admission to its ranks, the Germans can pick out the chosen few whom they will take with them into their last refuge. . . .

Document 5-40

Telegram 5617, February 20, 1945

[In February "George Wood" obtained new German Documents from the Foreign Ministry in Berlin. OSS Bern transmitted this material, which consisted of German reports on Japan and the Pacific war, in the "Kafeb" series of telegrams.]

KAPPA. For 109 and 154. Wood has unexpectedly succeeded in sending about 50 additional pieces. Processing today, will start cabling tomorrow. Will repeat London unless instructed to contrary but assume they will withhold action pending your advice.

Jap traffic indicates that preparations for defense Chinese coast proceeding slowly and that surprise landings might provoke crisis.

Document 5-41

Telegram 5727, February 23, 1945

[Dr. Wilhelm Abegg (number 836), a German émigré, supplied Dulles with information about General Kesselring's state of mind.]

Following from source #836. Official of German embassy North Italy, who is in Switzerland to turn into Swiss francs some marks belonging to members of Kesselring's staff, says Kesselring and Rahn are ready to quit, and even fight against Hitler, if we can offer them something to show for it. He says K is moved by the feeling that his ultimate destiny, as things are going now, is to wind up in the Alpen reduit, subordinate to SS officials, to die in the last resistance or be killed for not resisting. As long as he is still in Italy, he has power and is willing to use it by surrendering in return for some concession. It is not clear whether it is question of concessions to him and his staff or troops personally or whether it is a question of concession for Germany generally. He and his staff seem to want usable postwar funds.

Source did not disclose name of German Embassy official who is here, but will do so, and step out of the matter himself, if we are interested. Official is to come to him again to seek help in selling the free marks at good rate and source will string him along in order to delay him here for few days.

From 110. We do not rate this source very highly but we do have some independent reasons to believe that not impossible that K and R might be preparing for something like this. We are investigating rumor through more direct and reliable channels.

Document 5-42

Telegram 5839, February 23, 1945

[This message records indirect contact between OSS Bern and high-ranking German generals on the western front respecting the possibility of allowing Anglo-American forces to enter Germany unopposed.]

109 and 154. London for Forgan and 140 only from 110. Re my #5069 (IN-3740). London #6079.

1. Following conversation reported my above telegrams, Neurath visited his father near Stuttgart February 10. While there, Kesselring telephoned him and advised him to proceed to secret rendezvous.

2. At rendezvous night of February 10–11, Neurath found Westphal (whom he knew intimately from 2 years collaboration African campaign) and Blaskowitz whom he also knew personally but less well. In long conversation during which there was frank discussion of possibility of opening West Front to our forces, Westphal and Blaskowitz asked what was utility of doing this if they were merely to be judged as war criminals and lose all possibility usefulness to help work out orderly liquidation. They asked Neurath whether they would be considered as war criminals to which Neurath said unable to give reply.

3. Westphal and Blaskowitz said that it was increasingly difficult to organize any large scale move to open front not only on account of technical difficulties vis-à-vis SS, but also on account of state of mind of troops. Their armies have large elements of Germans from East Prussia and East Germany. Russian occupation this area has stiffened rather than weakened fighter qualities their German forces as troops now feel that they have no homes or families to which to return, have lost everything and consider it is better to stay on and fight. Westphal even said that sometimes HQ gives orders to retire which troops do not obey stating that as they are in good position and may not find as good ones in rear they prefer to fight it out.

4. While neither Westphal nor Blaskowitz made any definite suggestions, it seems that: A. They are working together with Kesselring. B. Whole program of opening Western and Italian fronts is uppermost in their minds. C. They are approaching frame of mind where they might talk under conditions of security, possibly here in Switzerland if they could get here, with USA Army officer on purely military lines, re methods of opening front provided they could receive some personal assurance re war criminal list and had some basis to justify their action, such as helping in orderly liquidation to prevent unnecessary destruction in Germany.

5. After having received, through intermediary, an outline of above, I saw Neurath personally last night and foregoing is summary of his statement. He is not brilliant but reasonably solid type with excellent relations to army view his long liaison work in Africa and as German Consul Lugano he has possibility of direct access to Kesselring without arousing suspicion though he must exercise greatest care. Since his own life is at stake and since he is not of Nazi background, I doubt whether he will be guilty of indiscretion. Also, as I had known his father reasonably well, he is inclined to go rather far in being frank with me.

6. Neurath proposes to contact Kesselring, report to him his conversation with Westphal and Blaskowitz and ascertain whether routine reason can be found for visit by Westphal to Kesselring. If this were arranged, and if these two could be induced to move simultaneously on West and Italian fronts, major military objectives might be achieved with minimum loss American lives.

7. While I cannot predict percentage chances of success, I evaluate them as sufficiently serious to justify most careful consideration by our military authorities.

8. No political strings or impairment of unconditional surrender principle in-

volved. Purely military meeting might take place on Swiss side of Italian frontier in Lugano area assuming Neurath's next contact with Kesselring shows progress.

9. Foregoing represents developments arising indirectly out of program which 476 and I discussed with General Sibert, G-2, 12 AG and others see penultimate paragraph our #4909 (IN3501) London #5979, if man of calibre Sibert could be delegated to explore pure military phase of matter, we would at least be in a position to take advantage of quickly moving events. If Westphal makes Italian trip he could probably only stay very short time without arousing suspicion. You will note that Kesselring is already object of press rumors which might result in his elimination by Himmler.

10. I realize extreme delicacy of this matter, but consider it my duty to follow up to extent indicated above pending your further instructions.

Document 5-43

Telegram 5997, February 26, 1945

[Communications intercepted by George Wood in Berlin included German attaché reports from the Far East. This material contained frequent indications of German-Japanese mutual mistrust and German suspicions of Japanese-Soviet collusion. The bracketed notations in this message were inserted by OSS Bern.]

KAPPA. KAFEB.

1. Stahler to Grand, February 5, transmitting Gronau report #29 re Jap anti-aircraft weapons. Jap rocket weapon for air targets not yet developed. Please advise whether Jap attachés, Berlin have advised that trials are going on in Tokyo or why you put these questions (obviously refers to Berlin queries). Neither IN or representatives of German Heereswaffenamt know of any development of rocket weapons against air targets which have yet been planned. In general, development of Jap rocket weapons are years behind Germany's. (From 110: Query how far Japs have kept Gronau in the dark as there is obvious mutual mistrust which resulted Jap desire have him replaced. . . .)

2. Kretschmer reports [date cut, apparently end January] with reserve confidential agents report via Polizei attachés Shanghai that on February 1 there was Jap-Russian agreement that each would reduce their Far Eastern strength: (a) Soviet to 10 divisions between Vladivostock and Novosibirsk. (b) Japan to 6 divisions and Manchurian Army. (c) Strength of each in inner Mongolia not affected.

Kretschmer says no confirmation of this reported agreement but substantial reduction of Jap forces in Manchuria. Soviet Far Eastern forces had undergone no change according views of Jap general staff middle December.

Polizei attaché Shanghai also reported January 16 re imports from America via Siberia.

Document 5-44

Letter to Robert D. Murphy, U.S. Political Adviser for Germany, February 26, 1945

[This message indicates that Dulles no longer considered a railroad strike in Germany to be a viable possibility. It is revealing as to the scope and nature of Dulles and OSS labor operations throughout the war.]

Dear Bob:

I was most interested to get your letter of February 12, 1945, concerning the possibility of organizing a railroad strike in Germany with the aid of the ITF. We have been working for some three years with the ITF and have a fairly accurate picture of their possibilities and connections. George Pratt in London has even closer contacts with them than we can have here. We have also been studying the chances of organizing a strike among German railwaymen and have some channels by which to judge their temper and possibilities. The following seems to be the situation:

(1) The ITF channels to German railwaymen, for some time past, have been rather tenuous. Here in Switzerland we are closer to the German railway workers than Oldenbroek, or his people.

(2) The ITF, and the former German Railwaymen's Union, retain a prestige among the older railway workers which is distinctly worth cultivating and which has been, and will be, of interest to us both militarily and in the post-hostilities period. The ITF performed some services for us in Italy, but it is possibly stretching a point to say that they were "notable"—not for lack of desire to help, but because they had few channels which can be turned over to our purposes.

(3) We recently asked one of our contacts in Germany, with fairly wide connections among railwaymen, about the possibility of organizing a strike. He replied that it was out of the question at this time for the following reasons:

(a) The great number of SD and Gestapo spies among railroad personnel made suicidal any effort at organizing more than a very few men for a common end.

(b) The remaining cadre of former trade unionists among the railway personnel is small and steadily dwindling. . . .

(c) The railwaymen and German workers generally—and this he considers the all-important obstacle—are without communications.

(d) He feels—and it seems to me clearly true—that an abortive strike would be harmful to the considerable aid which the railway workers are now lending the Allies, through sabotage, and so on. He has no doubt of the willingness of the vast majority of the railway workers to do anything feasible to defeat the Nazis, but they must see a chance of success in their activity. Almost as bad from a moral point of view as an unsuccessful strike is, in his judgment, Allied appeals to strike or otherwise resist (here he criticizes particularly the Russian demands for resistance) which are regarded for the moment as unrealistic. Confidence in Allied leadership is lost when the impossible is demanded. Again the readiness of individuals to risk their lives is not to be doubted, but the opposition does not wish to see its strength frittered away in pointless sporadic action.

Our other information makes me believe that the point of view here expressed is accurate and realistic. It seems to me that the best points of attack on the railway workers situation are the following:

(1) Continuance of the bombing and strafing attacks at their present tempo. They will frighten the timid among the workers, and give our friends the best chance to commit sabotage. Emphasis over the radio of the dangers involved to railway personnel in these attacks should be continued.

(2) Radio appeals to individual and unorganized sabotage. Everyone agrees that this is a feasible method for the average railway workers, and there seems reason to believe that its total quantity (not of course known even to the Gestapo) is important. We have (in connection with the ITF) done some work in laying the foundation for a clandestine leaflet campaign for sabotage and only await instructions from SHAEF before releasing it.

(3) Continuance of the present radio appeals to the railwaymen; again it would be well in my judgment if this could be on a more personal basis—or [for] instance through individual appeals to workers by Hans Jahn, former secretary of the German Railwaymen's Union, Koenig, former secretary of the Austrian railway workers union, and others similarly situated who command the continuing respect of the workers. The points to be continually emphasized, I suggest, are (a) that sabotage will hasten the end of the war, (b) that the workers will have their jobs after occupation (insofar as they are not compromised with the Nazis), (c) that the Allies have an interest in the reconstruction of Germany on a sound and democratic basis and are ready to support those elements of the population prepared to go forward for these ends. This is perhaps a somewhat trite repetition but it seems to me they still remain the most important objectives. The announcement by General Eisenhower that freedom of trade unions organization would be allowed has apparently had a very salutary effect.

With respect to sending Hans Jahn to Switzerland, I have already taken this question up with London at some length and await their reply. It seems to me that he could be more useful broadcasting regularly over the BBC, but I do not know whether that can be arranged or not. I do not know enough of the situation in Luxembourg to have a judgment in the matter.

On the whole problem, our people in London, particularly George Pratt, —who have been working very closely with the ITF for a considerable period of time—might profitably be consulted with respect to any steps that may be planned. We have already submitted some proposals from here. I understand they were passed on to SHAEF for their approval, and implementation if approved. The chief need at the moment is a feasible program, approved at the highest echelons, with clear directives to each branch of the services and non-military organizations which will allow a maximum weight to be brought to bear at one time here where Germany is now most vulnerable.

Sincerely yours, [Allen W. Dulles]

P.S. Many thanks for General Bedell Smith's acknowledgement of Dr. Jung's letter. The doctor will be delighted with this.

Document 5-45

Telegram 6097, February 28, 1945

[In early 1945, OSS Bern began receiving indirect soundings from Himmler and the Nazi Party security police and intelligence chief Ernst Kaltenbrunner via SS Sturmbannführer Wilhelm Hoettl. Hoettl would play a prominent role in Nazi efforts to avoid the consequences of defeat in the months to come. Number 503 was Fritz Weston, an Austrian industrialist.]

BREAKERS. 503 arrived from Austria February 25, having left Vienna about 18. 503 for several years acquainted with Hoettl one of Viennese SS chiefs who knew vaguely that 503 had indirect contacts with Americans Suisse. Prior 503's recent departure from Vienna for Suisse, Hoettl informed him that Kaltenbrunner, Chief of SD wanted to see him. Kaltenbrunner informed 503 that he and Himmler most anxious to end war and as first step were contemplating liquidation of "war mongers" within Nazi Party, especially Bormann. Himmler and Kaltenbrunner were most anxious to establish contact with British and Americans and asked 503 to make effort in this direction on his trip to Suisse and contemplated sending here high SS official to speak on their behalf provided contact could be established. 503 on own initiative suggested that Alfred Potocki, brother of former Polish Minister to Washington should be permitted to go to Suisse with him as he felt Potocki had first class contacts with British. Hoettl arranged immediate exit visa for Potocki and his mother. Potocki expected proceed first to Liechtenstein where has not yet arrived. While 503 is rather lightweight, consider above approach interesting as sign of increasing disintegration within Nazi Party and as indication antics of Himmler to prepare alibis. According 503, Himmler now organizing defense on Eastern Front and largely in command of this theater of war.

Document 5-46

Radiotelephone Transmission No. 282, February 28, 1945 (extract)

[Dulles reported that Germany continued to maintain a large measure of domestic cohesion despite the imminence of military defeat.]

Germany

1. Despite the fact that our forces and Russia's forces are fast closing in on Germany from East and West, there is as yet no real evidence of the breakdown of governmental authority or anything as yet approaching a general panic. Press reports to this effect which you may be receiving should be discounted.

Up to a few days ago, the date of our last authentic report, the great majority of government offices appeared to be still in Berlin. Government services were functioning after a fashion, and the control of the SS was still complete. Of course, civil transportation is now extremely difficult and slow, and the rationing of many of the severely bombed cities is getting more and more precarious. Mail delivery has been curtailed by new regulations and even such mail as is permitted is delivered with the greatest delays. The people of Germany are losing the facility of intercommunication, and what remains of transport and communications facilities are devoted largely to military, police, and Party purposes.

The refugees from eastern Germany constitute today one of the most serious problems. . . .

Document 5-47

Telegram 6149, March 1, 1945

[Dulles reported that General Eisenhower had been apprised of OSS Bern's contacts with German generals in the west, had cabled Washington on the matter, and wanted the channel kept open.]

Cheston from 110. . . . Reference my #5839. . . . In view of fact that developments described my above cable resulted from work which we had initiated in common with General Sibert, I gave Gen. Sibert's representative Col. Wies who was at Hegenheim February 25 strictly confidential summary of developments for Sibert personally. Wies was advised to tell Sibert that matter had been fully reported Washington and London for information appropriate authorities. Have just received message from Sibert stating that information in report had been placed before Supreme [Allied] Commander who had cabled Washington for guidance and indicating that he wished to have contact kept open and to be advised. It is going too far to designate this move as "peace feeler from German generals." It is fair to state however that certain German generals are considering among themselves how and under what conditions they could eventually terminate needless slaughter and destruction.

Document 5-48

Telegram 6209, March 2, 1945

[Dulles comments further on the recent approach from Himmler and Kaltenbrunner via Hoettl and Weston (number 503).]

BREAKERS. From 110. . . . Further conversations with 503 indicate that his SD contacts and information have more importance than I originally believed. Information received from other good sources tends to bear out indications brought by 503 that Himmler, Kaltenbrunner, and certain other high SS officials might not go along with die-hard fanatics and might try to gain some immunity by serving as "uebergangs" regime between Hitler and occupation forces. They might possibly prefer this to joining Hitler, Bormann, et al. in German reduit. Please note particularly significant statement my #6097 attributed to Kaltenbrunner that Himmler anxious to liquidate "warmongers such as Bormann."

Naturally, persons of Himmler, Kaltenbrunner type can gain no immunity from us, but as long as they believe this is possible it might give us opportunity to drive a wedge in SD and thus reduce effectiveness of German reduit plans. This seems to be a matter well worth handling by clandestine methods as I feel one need have no scruples in double crossing types such as Himmler, Kaltenbrunner et al. Through indirect channels we are arranging to have Hoettl come to Swiss frontier where trusted intermediary will see him.

It would be most interesting to know if you have any other clues bearing on this situation.

Document 5-49

Radiotelephone Transmission No. 283, March 3, 1945

[As the possibility of a Nazi last stand in Alpine regions became a matter of general public speculation, Dulles offers the view that such an eventuality might take the form of a last-minute decision rather than a carefully planned move to well-prepared positions.]

I am sorry to have had to cancel so many calls recently, but there has been a very heavy pressure of work recently.

Germany

I have reported several times about the alleged plans of the Germans to establish a maquis or a reduit, or possibly several of them. On the whole, I am inclined to believe in this possibility, but I must admit that a critical analysis of reliable data received so far does not indicate that the preparations have as yet progressed very far.

There are a number of newspaper articles on the subject, with maps indicating the boundaries of the reduit and generalities about great hidden stores of provisions, about the preparation of underground factories, and the like. Much of this is probably fiction or at least it is not proved as yet by reliable evidence. Quite naturally, some plants have been moved into the mountain or forest areas to be better protected from bombing. Hitler and other Nazi leaders have their castles in the Bavarian and Austrian Alps. Some preparations have undoubtedly been made, but not yet on the scale we have been led to believe.

If, as seems likely, the fanatical Nazis will fight it out to the bitter end, then something in the nature of a reduit is inevitable, and the mountains and forest areas will be the last centers of resistance. I doubt, however, whether there will be the extent of prior preparation in the way of fortifications and supplies which propaganda stories have indicated. Persons well acquainted with the Austrian Alps who have recently been here see no real signs of serious preparations going on there as yet.

The fact of the matter is that Hitler may not yet be ready to concede the need of a maquis. He still stubbornly defends Berlin and plans countermeasures. The Germans have never been good in planning what they would do in the face of defeat. Their strength lay in planning for conquest; thus, their administration for the British Isles was complete in all details, and the freight rates for the transport of the Baku oil were published. But when it came to preparing beforehand for the evacuation of Paris and Strasbourg, they failed dismally to think ahead of time or take even normal precautions.

Further, in their present situation in the west, east, north and south, they have neither the supplies, the transport or the men to spare [for] any great effort to fortify and stock a vast inner fortress. And, from the practical angle, the talk of building in the mountains great new underground factories is nonsense. It would take years. There are some tunnels, some abandoned mines, some quarries, and the like, which can be used or adapted. But new construction on a great scale during recent months has been out of the question.

This does not mean, as I have suggested above, that we will not have to fight the Nazis into mountain retreats. It is likely that we will have to do so. Nature itself, without much preparation, as the Italian campaign has shown, may make the going slow, difficult, and costly. I do not believe, however, that months of elaborate preparation have been devoted to fortifying, arming, and stocking a great German reduit. Much in the way of supplies and man-power may possibly be flung into this area at the last moment, unless our armies can cut off the Nazi retreat.

In connection with the German maquis, it is interesting to note that there are increasing signs that not all the leading Nazis are reconciled to sharing in this plan for last-ditch resistance. There may well come a split in the Nazi ranks before the end, and, if this goes deep enough, there might be only a relatively small number who would seek the maquis.

Document 5-50

Telegram 6329, March 5, 1945

[With this message, the two-month, on-again-off-again negotiations for the surrender of German forces in Italy began in earnest. The telegrams presented here on "Operation Sunrise" are part of the documentary base for Allen Dulles's published account, *The Secret Surrender* (1966).]

Cheston and 154 only. . . . From 110. No distribution.

1. Through 2 close friends in Swiss SI . . . we were advised that important Italian industrialist named Baron Parelli (not certain of spelling) desired to facilitate contact between important German officials North Italy and Allies with general view terminating German resistance North Italy. Baron P has been for many years Nash-Kelvinator representative Italy and claims to be well known in Detroit.

2. After a meeting between an intermediary and Baron P, it seemed desirable to follow up the matter and rather unexpectedly we were advised late March 2 by our Swiss SI friends that Standartenfuehrer Dollmann and Zimmer [garble] had arrived at Swiss frontier.

3. DB-001 who was proceeding Lugano on other business met Dollmann, Zimmer, Baron P and Swiss SI man at Lugano March 3.

4. Dollmann's background you probably know better than I. Our reports indicate that he was exceedingly influential Rome prior its liberation and he apparently claims credit for having saved Rome from destruction. Reputedly built up considerable fortune in connection ransoming important individuals and generally showed some sympathy for Italy though sometimes at a price.

5. To Swiss intermediary Dollmann apparently claimed that he represented Kesselring, Rahn, Wolff and Harster but never specifically so stated to DB-001. To latter he indicated only that he wished to establish channel of communication and that, subject to confirmation on March 6, he would return on Thursday, March 8, after consultation at Faseno with credentials and definite proposals. Nature of proposals not indicated but from other talks which intermediaries had, we assume they will bear upon future disposition of German forces in North Italy.

6. As an earnest of ability produce it was suggested to Dollmann that release of certain Italian patriots be promptly effected.

7. DB-001 gave no name and mere fact that he was presented by accredited intermediaries seemed to suffice. Presumably, however, intermediaries told Dollmann that he was associated with me.

8. It is not yet clear whether this move is separate from, or parallel to, Neurath negotiations, but I am inclined to believe they will merge insofar as North Italian situation concerned if Dollmann is in fact acting for persons mentioned in paragraph 5 above. Not knowing clearly his role, naturally no mention was made of Neurath line.

9. If Dollmann returns I shall arrange to ascertain what he has to say. If this should be of a nature to facilitate unconditional surrender of German forces North Italy it might be desirable to arrange that military contact take place on Swiss side of frontier.

10. In recent message from 148 at Caserta, he remarks that if Kesselring wishes to dispatch emissary with official message, he could find ways of doing it. It must be remembered, however, that elements with Kesselring who might wish to facilitate surrender may only act with greatest secrecy lest their movements be betrayed by fanatical Nazis in Kesselring's entourage. Thus normal procedure of sending aero-

plane or messenger to our lines might prove difficult. It is relatively easy, however, for high officials to come to Switzerland without arousing suspicion as they have been doing this continuously over long period.

11. I have confidence in Swiss through whom we are dealing. Also, all Swiss interests lie in facilitating peaceful surrender of Germans in North Italy.

Document 5-51

Telegram 6459, March 6, 1945

[As its ultimate defeat became apparent, Japan and Japanese individuals also attempted to make contact with the Allies in order to avoid total devastation or unconditional surrender. One such effort occurred in Switzerland; Dulles and the OSS, as well as other Allied diplomatic and intelligence entities, engaged in a complex series of indirect exchanges with the Japanese for the last six months of the Pacific war. Number 496 is Maurice Villars; 673 is Dr. Friedrich Hack, former Krupp representative in Japan.]

SAINT. To 154 and Saint from 110 and DB/001. Our 496 after consultation with us established discreetly contact with Kojiro Kitamura via 673. Kitamura is Director of Bank of International Settlements and also we believe representative here of Yokohama Specie Bank. He is reported to have been anti-militaristic and representative better elements in Japan. He expressed himself very pessimistically. Said Japan would have to surrender view heavy losses army and navy. Navy already incapable protecting communications. Believe Jap army in China will not continue fighting because military caste will disintegrate. Expects Japan will lose Manchukuo, Formosa and Korea. Modern elements his country counting on Grew and Ballantine to save their country from annihilation.

Recently Kitamura and Kan Yoshimura, latter financial expert attached to BIS, had long talk with Per Jacobsen, Swedish expert with Bank to obtain views as to possibility of clash between USA and Russia. When Jacobsen expressed view this possibility absolutely excluded, both Japs departed quite pleased much to Jacobsen's surprise. Jacobsen had impression that Japs here received instructions report on this subject and that his, Jacobsen's views conformed with what both Kitamura and Yoshimara had been personally reporting.

Our information indicates both these Japs belong to circle which had opposed war with USA and at appropriate time they might seek occasion to leave sinking ship.

Document 5-52

Telegram 6477, March 7, 1945

[Fritz Molden, number K-28, became Dulles's main channel to Austria. Through Molden, Dulles and the OSS sought to further intelligence-gathering, special operations, favorable internal political developments leading toward reaffirmation of national independence, and subversion of Nazi control via contacts with wavering individual officials.]

For Climax and Jolis from 110 and 399.

1. K-28 with whom we had long conversation last night leaving for Paris via Besançon, arriving probably Saturday evening. He promises to report immediately at our Paris office, and believe it of utmost importance that he be seen immediately and that we do what we can to further his mission. View Hofer's report, believe we can now accept K-28 as fully security checked and as representative of Austria resistance. Despite his youth he is man of striking ability and maturity and has extraordinary knowledge of situation.

2. Hofer proceeding with Antoine via Annemasse, also arriving Saturday the 10th. It might be well to arrange that K-28 (who will introduce himself under name of Wieser) should stay with Jolis and Hofer at St. Germain. K-28 expressed preference do this.

3. Pouching Friday three additional important K-28 reports covering political situation Austria, organization of resistance movement (known as 05) and report on economic situation Austria.

Document 5-53

Telegram 1146 to Caserta, March 8, 1945

[Dulles now reports SS General Karl Wolff's arrival at Lugano for preliminary conversations.]

Personal for Glavin. Info 109, Forgan. . . .

1. I am advised that Waffen SS General Karl Wolff, top SS officer North Italy together with OKW representative presumably from Kesselring staff plus Dollmann and Zimmer arrived Lugano this morning allegedly prepared to talk definitely. If this confirmed I shall see what Wolf and OKW man have to say.

2. . . . My intermediary told Dollmann to produce Parri here as evidence of good faith and ability to act. I am told they are doing so.

3. If 1 and 2 confirmed, suggest high SACMED authority be prepared to come here. I could arrange entry Switzerland in civilian clothes with absolute secrecy and we can be assured of secret cooperation local authorities. Nothing unusual in this as high military authorities from SHAEF come here constantly.

4. Potentialities of these developments so far-reaching that I think they justify immediate consideration highest quarters. If Wolff really working with Kesselring these two might pull off unconditional surrender provided absolute secrecy can be preserved.

5. Will endeavor report further tonight. Question is how much does Himmler know about this.

Document 5-54

Telegram 6647 to Paris, March 8, 1945

[Molden's reports on Austria give evidence of an emerging east-west political struggle, as in Germany. Dulles and Molden interested themselves in the emerging resistance group POEN as a focus for democratic national development and were concerned about the Soviet-supported Free Austrian Committee.]

Following oral information furnished by K-28:

1. POEN anxious about POW now in Allied hands named Brauer, one of their Paris representatives. He is prisoner at Compiegne, rendered valuable services to Austrian resistance before capture and has since organized many of 6,000 Austrians in this camp into pro-liberation group. Suggests efforts be made free him to work with POEN in Paris.

2. Free Austrian Committee set up by Russians at Debrecen includes only Communists, some disguised as Social Democrats or Christian Socialists. Among leaders are Fischer and Koplenik. To date little known in Austria, and where known commanding no confidence.

3. Estimated about 800 patriots executed Vienna monthly, among whom fall Social Democrat and former Landtags Abgeordneter of lower Austria, Major Eifler, Commander of Schutzbund and Social Democrat, both hung, Beno Kautsky burnt to death at Auschwitz, Paul Herbiger condemned to death but still alive.

4. Stalag 17A now located at Kaisersteinbruch in Leithagebirge.

Document 5-55

Telegram 6487, March 8, 1945

[Molden relayed a report that gave rise to the possibility that Hitler might have been considering escaping by air.]

Source K-28, report B-1839. In Pocking, lower Bavaria near Braunau between Zeithen and Schoenberg recognizable by 2 hangars and large runways is located part of "Flieger Staffel Adolph Hitler." Work going on actively in hangars. There is 1 4-motored JU 290 being luxuriously equipped with armored plates, bullet proof glass, guns fore and aft, etc. Capacity 20-22 persons. Delivery originally fixed for February 28 for Berchtesgaden now postponed to middle March. Hitler greatly disturbed over delay. Original plan called for 3 machines but, on account of material shortage, only 1 built. General Bauer, air pilot of Fuehrer, personally supervising reconstruction together with assembly man Zintel. Bauer also practicing handling of airplane.

Document 5-56

Telegram 6679, March 9, 1945

[In this message, Dulles reported on his initial meeting with General Wolff.]

For Glavin. Info 109, Forgan.

1. Wolff indicated willingness try develop program to take North Italy out of conflict. He considers mere military surrender difficult and prefers that capitulation be preceded by statement to German people from German leaders North Italy that struggle hopeless, merely causing needless German bloodshed, destruction and so forth. Kesselring not yet won over and his adherence essential. Wolff states Rahn in accord with him.
2. Wolff proceeding immediately to Kesselring to endeavor sell program to him and will keep in touch with us.
3. He inquired regarding alleged British agent Captain Dulker/Ducher who was recently turned over to him by Graziani and released to return to SACMED via Suisse. Wolff uncertain whether this real contact, mere intelligence mission or mystification. Please advise.
4. Parri was delivered to me in Zurich unconditionally and even prior any indication I would see Wolff. Saw him last night in good health. Does not know how released and important this be kept secret. Propose hint that this was an exchange when his presence here becomes known.
5. Wolff claims Himmler unaware his activities. This may or may not be correct.
6. Wolff apparently controls all police and border forces on entire Swiss-Italian frontier and believe we now have means of quick contact with top German personalities North Italy.
7. 476 having further meeting with Wolff today ninth and cabling full report by regular channels shortly.

Document 5-57

Telegram 6689, March 9, 1945

[Dulles elaborated on his initial meeting with General Wolff. This Top Secret report on contacts with the Germans in Italy, as well as most others in the series, was sent to Washington, London, Paris, and Caserta, for the attention of General Donovan, Glavin, and Forgan.]

Referring to my previous messages re SS General Ogruf Wolff.

1. Wolff accompanied to Zurich by Dollmann, Sturmbannfuehrer Wenner his military expert, Zimmer and Italian go-between Baron Parilli. I only consented to see Wolff who came to my apartment evening 8th with Swiss intermediary. 476 and I then talked to Wolff alone. 476 later saw Wolff and Dollmann.

2. Wolff is distinctive personality, our reports and impressions indicate he represents more moderate element in Waffen SS, with mixture of romanticism. Probably most dynamic personality North Italy and most powerful after Kesselring.

3. Wolff stated that time had come when some German with power to act should lead Germany out of war to end useless material and human destruction that he was willing to act and felt he could persuade Kesselring to join, that together with Kesselring they controlled situation in Northern Italy, and as far as SS concerned he likewise controlled Western Austria, as his authority included Vorarlberg, Tyrol, and Brenner Pass with both northern and southern approaches. He felt that in case of joint action with Kesselring, Hitler and Himmler would be powerless to take effective counter measures, thus distinguishing situation from that of July 20. He also felt that their joint action would have vital repercussion on German Army, particularly Western Front, as many generals waiting for some one to take lead.

Wolff made no request re personal safety or privileged treatment from war criminal viewpoint.

4. To bring about action Wolff envisaged following procedure:

a. He will meet Kesselring this weekend to obtain from him definite commitment to joint action. He says he has had closest personal relations with Kesselring for several years. He indicated Kesselring's problem was to reconcile action with oath of allegiance. Kesselring insisted that throughout long military career he had always kept oath and too old to change, but Wolff believes he can be won over to senselessness of struggle and that his duty to German people above that to Fuehrer.

b. Draft with Kesselring appeal, to be signed by them, Rahn, and others, setting forth uselessness of struggle, their responsibility toward German people to terminate it and calling upon military commanders and others generally to disassociate themselves from Himmler-Hitler control, plus statement that hostilities North Italy would be terminated by Germans.

c. Prepare radio and leaflet action to get message over to German people and commanders.

d. Provided Kesselring won over, Wolff believes he, Kesselring would come clandestinely Switzerland within week to meet our military men to coordinate purely military surrender measures with above appeal. Apparently no one on Kesselring immediate staff particularly suited to do this for him. His Chief of Staff PZ General Roettiger not yet acquainted with project.

5. As evidence of his ability to act, in addition to release of Parri (reported separately), Wolff prepared:

a. To discontinue active warfare against partisans merely keeping up necessary pretense pending execution of plan.

b. Release to Switzerland several hundred Jews interned at Bozen. He claims he has refused any ransom money offered this connection and possibly already swallowed up by intermediaries.

c. Assume full responsibility for safety and treatment of 350 British and American prisoners Mantua of whom 150 in hospital and 200 on southern outskirts. Claims this is all British-American prisoners held Northern Italy as they had been currently transferred to Germany.

d. If he can be found, release to Switzerland Sogno Franci, well known patriot working with CLNAI and British whose release particularly desired by Parri.

e. Facilitate to extent possible return North Italy of Italian officers presently held Germany who might be useful in post hostilities period.

6. Re previous cables re Neurath contacts Wolff welcomes Neurath's help as he felt Neurath had considerable influence on Kesselring. Will invite Neurath to join him Italy, Saturday, 10th.

7. Claims Himmler knows nothing of his present activities. Saw Himmler and Hitler early February and advised them of general hopelessness of North Italian situation but received no definite instructions from them.

8. While necessary withhold final judgment until results Wolff Kesselring talk are known I believe this may present very unique opportunity to shorten war and to permit occupation of North Italy and possibly even penetration Austria under most favorable conditions. Also this might wreck German plans for establishment of maquis.

9. Re your #614, I trust that SACMED will be prepared send appropriate military man here if we get word that Kesselring or other high military authority is coming here with power to act on military matters. We know of no particularly close relations between Kesselring and Himmler.

10. Wish it clearly understood I have engaged in no negotiations, merely listened to his presentation and stated, with no refutation Wolff's part, that unconditional surrender only possible course.

Document 5-58

Telegram 6709, March 9, 1945

[In this message, Dulles discusses the release of Italian resistance leader Ferruccio Parri as part of ongoing negotiations for a German surrender in Italy.]

Glavin . . . , 109, and Forgan. . . . At meeting described . . . , we had asked immediate release of Parri and Major Usmiani, latter ran one of our SI chains Milan, former imprisoned Verona, latter Milan. Both were delivered to me unconditionally at Zurich with cooperation 511. Wolff fully realized Parri's importance and remarked to my intermediary that he was giving up his most important hostage. Both men when taken out by SS assumed they being led to execution and neither yet knows, and should not know, why released. Request early advice re disposition Parri. He desires return North Italy but personally believe this unwise for next few weeks because if re-arrested this would prejudice our ability secure release other personalities. Consider Parri should be held available proceed North Italy to be on spot when break comes and to assist in keeping in hand political situation there. Working with Swiss on conditions his residence here or alternatively to secure permission for him to proceed to Annemasse from where he could go SACMED if you desire. Please instruct soonest. May desire also send Usmiani south. Zulu SOE advised of release but not of means by which effected.

Document 5-59

Radiotelephone Transmission No. 285, March 9, 1945

[The oath to Hitler sworn by German officers was viewed by Dulles as a decisive factor in the Wehrmacht's failure to take action against the Nazis as defeat approached.]

Germany
One of the chief reasons today for the continuing stubborn resistance of the German Army and Officer Corps is the oath of allegiance to the Fuehrer. The German sense of discipline and obedience is controlling. The old-line officers, most of whom are not Nazis and whom we should expect to find in revolt today against the needless continuation of the struggle, are often the most difficult to win over. The Prussian military tradition dies hard, and at the core of that tradition is that breaking the military oath is the most heinous of crimes.

One of the reasons for the brutal form of the execution of the generals after the July 20 affair was the desire of the Nazis to emphasize the character of the crime committed, namely, what the Germans call "Eidbruch"—breaking the oath. The Nazis realize that once the sanctity of the oath to Hitler falls, then the break between the Party and the Army would be complete and the end of military resistance would come. This is also the reason why it is essential for the Nazis to keep Hitler in evidence, to bring him out from time to time, to show that he is still alive and acting. Himmler may exercise the real power, but it is only because Hitler is there that he can do so. If Hitler disappeared, then the struggle of conscience, which many Wehrmacht officers have today would be ended. They would no longer be bound by their oath, and revolt would be general.

Document 5-60

Telegram 6969 to Paris, March 12, 1945

[Movement toward the surrender of German forces in Italy received a setback when General Kesselring, the commanding officer thought to be sympathetic, was recalled to Germany. This message from Dulles to Donovan via Paris kept the OSS Director abreast of developments. "Sunrise" is the code indicator for telegrams relating to the series of talks.]

SUNRISE. To 109 only . . . from 110.

1. Parrilli has just returned from Wolff. He states that when Wolff reached Fasano [garble] he telephoned Kesselring headquarters and found that Kesselring had been summoned by Hitler and had just gone to Fuehrer headquarters. Wolff expects him back in 3 days but there is a chance that he may never come back.

2. Meeting, therefore, postponed pending word from Kesselring but suggest AFHQ consider whether they would be interested in contact with Wolff assuming of course, he had a plan of action . . . , when we saw Wolff on 8th he said he would come here any time.

3. We suggested to Parrilli that Wolff indicate: A. What he proposes to do if Kesselring does not return. B. What he would do if he likewise ordered to report to Fuehrer. C. If he refuses to report, what is his plan and what forces does he dispose of to carry it out. D. What areas could he temporarily control for possible contact with our forces if principal army commanders do not cooperate.

4. More to follow in few hours by regular channels.

5. I surmise that Kesselring's visit may foreshadow attempted evacuation of North Italy and that if Kesselring does not make Hitler, Himmler believe that he will cooperate he will be given new command or prison.

Document 5-61

Telegram 6829, March 12, 1945

[The negotiations with General Wolff now became endangered by entanglement with the peace feelers from SD head Kaltenbrunner, Wolff's desire for financial gain, and the possible repatriation of Italian prisoners of war held in Germany. This message is a continuation of Dulles's report on information just received from Baron Parilli, the Italian industrialist serving as a go-between.]

SUNRISE. Glavin from 110. Information 109, Forgan, Armour. . . .

1. Upon his return to Italy Wolff received telegram from Kaltenbrunner advising him to avoid establishing contact Switzerland as it would disturb his Kaltenbrunner's plans and might mean catastrophe. Upon investigation Wolff discovered that Harster, high SS man, at time of first Dollmann trip had telegraphed to Kaltenbrunner advising him that an attempt might be made to make contacts in Switzerland. According Parilli, Wolff feels that this was sent to cover Dollmann's tracks and that Harster is dependable. I consider this explanation possible but difficult verify.

2. View information that Musso had obtained Spanish consent entry and was preparing flee Spain, he has been placed under guard.

3. Wolff considers that Obersturmbannfuhrer and Eichenlaubtrager Wuensche, wounded and taken prisoner Normandy and now believed hospitalized France as PW, would be useful to further his plans. He was adjutant to Hitler but had a row with Fuehrer and was sent to troops as commander of a PZ regiment to *Leibstandarte Adolf Hitler.* For Forgan: please ascertain location Wuensche. Advise whether he USA PW and whether he could be made available and how soon. Also what do you know about his sentiments and eventual reliability.

4. Wolff is having some difficulty explaining to underlings the disappearance of Parri and might wish to dress him up as an exchange. If so, Wuensche, if available and you consider likely to be trustworthy, could be used to kill two birds with one stone.

5. Wolff says he has three milliard (sic) . . . shares Italian companies under his control and asks whether we have any requests regarding disposition. . . . I suggested that if possible he make available to us list giving numbers and names where registered securities involved and meanwhile do what he can to protect certificates from being sent Germany.

6. Wolff again inquired whether we had any requests regarding point five (E) my 482, Washington 668 [see 6689, March 9]. . . . Approximately 10,000 officers involved. I replied was checking but suggested no action to complicate an already involved situation or bring his activities to Führer's attention.

Document 5-62

Radiotelephone Transmission No. 286, March 12, 1945

[The likelihood of the Nazi final defense of a national mountain redoubt and last-ditch guerrilla warfare was not universally accepted, as indicated in this report.]

Germany

A German official, who arrived here very recently from Berlin after a 24-hour trip by auto, gave us his impressions as follows:

He said he did not believe in the efficacy of the reduit and did not think that the German population would give sufficient support to guerrilla warfare to make it worthwhile. The mass of the population, he is convinced, is worn out and has only the wish that the war should come to an end. He remarked that a few weeks ago the Government's policy of evacuation of populations has been changed. In the West, these populations will be left behind the retreating troops, while in the East, the evacuations will continue. This change has been made because there is no place to accommodate populations from both fronts. Already the center of Germany is crowded to the breaking point. In the East, efforts will continue to be made to evacuate populations because of the Russian deportation policy and because there have been a number of instances of mishandling of civilians.

He stated that, along the lines of this policy, civilian administrative officers, insofar as they are not conspicuous Nazis, will remain with the civilian population in the West. He expressed the opinion that the attitude of these people will be correct and cooperative insofar as maintaining order and routine existence requirements are concerned.

He also stated that, while plans have been made to move administrative organizations of the German Government from Berlin to Central Germany, very few offices, except parts of the Air Ministry and War Ministry, have as yet left. The Foreign Office is still at the Wilhelmstrasse. In spite of bombings, recent attacks have been largely towards the East of the city, the local transportation system functions, and Berlin is still distinctly the center of the country.

Document 5-63

Telegram 6897 to Caserta, March 13, 1945

[Dulles and the Allies generally were alert to the danger that the resistance in northern Italy would seek to establish a separate government not answerable to authorities in Rome.]

Ryan . . . from 110. Your #4097 re possible indication CLNAI intentions setting up government distinct from present Italian Government. Parri has just given me most positive assurance that there is no such intention and he claimed he could also give that assurance in behalf of his CLNAI colleagues. I believe Parri is sincere and that there is no present intention on part of CLNAI to set up separate government. However, in politics rapid changes are possible and probability exists that North Italy will be farther to left than present Rome government. I discount any present plan but agree this is a matter to watch and I shall report any indications. If North Italy, including CLNAI, when liberated promptly secures adequate representation in Rome government, I should doubt whether movement for separate government would make much headway, particularly as they will be absolutely dependent on us for food, raw materials, coal etc.

Document 5-64

Telegram 6909, March 14, 1945

[This message contains additional information on contacts with the Germans.]

From 110. . . . Plans have been under way for some little time for meeting between Carl Burckhardt and Himmler to discuss refugee and possibly PW questions. Burckhardt, who now resigned from International Red Cross, is acting solely in private capacity. While have no definite news, believe meeting scheduled to take place very shortly, probably in neighborhood Feldkirch, and possibly Kaltenbrunner will also be there. Believe our WRB has some interest in refugee angle this meeting and possibly may have additional information.

I surmise that Himmler may endeavor use this occasion, if it is presented, for peace feelers. Also advised that Fusto Pancini, old friend of Mussolini, recently arrived here with letters from Musso to Edda Ciano and Papal Nuncio. He indicated to Edda that Himmler wished Nuncio to advise Vatican that Germans wished peace, disposed let Americans and British in but did not want Russians. Pancini quoted Musso as commenting on Himmler's plans, "The fools; they should have done this 3 years ago."

Document 5-65

Radiotelephone Transmission No. 287, March 14, 1945

[Dulles discusses the possibility of a final German "peace offensive" using hostages, refugees, and prisoners of war as bargaining chips.]

Germany
I think we should be prepared for a final German peace offensive, at least if Himmler can persuade Hitler to let him put it on.

It seems clear that Himmler is trying to find points of contact with the Western Powers. For this purpose he has been making use of refugee and prisoners of war matters and is now beginning to evidence a softer policy in this direction.

The German peace offensive may be based on the problem involved in the ten million-odd prisoners of war, foreign workers and deportees, and hostages. Himmler, or Hitler, if he makes the appeal, will probably say that, under existing conditions and in view of the bombings, the Nazis can no longer assume responsibility for the safeguard of these people and can no longer assure their supplies of food, etc. They will say that the fate of these people now rests with the Allies and not with Germany. They might even propose a truce while these prisoners and refugees were evacuated, or make some other seeming "humanitarian" gesture, in the hope that, in the interval, some way of entering into negotiations could be found under the cover of negotiating the evacuation of prisoners, refugees, deportees, etc. Presumably, conditions would be included by Himmler which would render the proposal impracticable of fulfillment.

It is possible that the appeal would be addressed only to the western powers and exclude Russian prisoners or workers in hope of thus driving a wedge between us and the Russians.

Possibly coupled with this gesture, which the Nazis might hope would appeal to wide circles of people in the West, the Nazis might also indicate that, unless their proposals were accepted, the new secret weapons, gas, etc., would be launched on the world.

The above is all speculation and may never take place, but there are some straws in the wind which seem to point in this direction. At any rate, it would do no harm to consider the implications of such a move in order to be ready to meet it, in case it should come.

Document 5-66

Telegram 7037, March 15, 1945

[OSS Bern's Kaltenbrunner-Hoettl-Weston (number 503) channel remained open as a source of intelligence information.]

503 recently had contact with Obersturmbannfuehrer Hoettl who intimate friend Kaltenbrunner and operates Vienna. Previously represented Kaltenbrunner in Hungary to supervise activities Vessen Mayer. Recently given task by Kaltenbrunner of establishing contact with opposition groups in Austria. Alleges that within SS there is so-called Austrian opposition represented by Kaltenbrunner, Neubacher, himself and others, and that they have been responsible for saving many people from SS persecution, including Count Bercherm and Amster, of Abwehr. Marognia, Chief of Abwehr in Vienna, participated July 20 and executed. Hoettl also claims he responsible for transfer of Seitz from concentration camp Silesia to Bavaria, and hopes shortly to free Seitz.

Document 5-67

Radiotelephone Transmission No. 288, March 16, 1945

[Here Dulles presents a pessimistic assessment of possibilities for the period leading to the final collapse of German resistance. He relays press comments envisioning a national redoubt, the slaughter of Allied prisoners, gas warfare, and a Wagnerian cataclysm brought on by the gangster leaders of a people now in a state beyond despair.]

Germany

1. The stubbornness of the German resistance in the neighborhood of Lake Balaton and Danube, while the defenses are crumbling in the seemingly more vital areas in the East and West, has caused a good deal of comment. We have sought views of several experts on the subject, particularly some recent arrivals from Austria, and the following seems to be the explanation:

The Germans realize that it is now completely impossible for them to hold the relatively flat country in the North of Germany from the Ruhr to Berlin. They are therefore reconciled to the inevitability of losing this. Their struggle in this area they conceive as a delaying action to gain time to regroup their forces towards the South and to complete their preparations for the defense of the reduit.

As I suggested some days ago, the actual evidence we had up to that time did not indicate that the Germans had really made very serious progress in the fortifications of the reduit area or in collecting there any vast amount of supplies. Over the last several weeks, some evidence of this, however, has been coming in. Whether the reduit will become a reality, I cannot predict, but their present military strategy seems to be built around the idea of a reduit.

Actually, top Nazis look upon this not merely as a method of saving their lives for a few months longer. They have more far-reaching plans. They have followed with close attention the social unrest and upheavals in the Balkans. They believe that it is towards the Southeast and in the general Balkan area that their best chances lie. Taking the reduit as a base, they are possibly planning to organize guerrilla bands in the mountains of Croatia and Serbia, Greece, Bulgaria and elsewhere. To facilitate this plan, it is important for them that the reduit extend as far as possible towards the Balkans, and this is apparently the reason for the strong concentration of German forces in the area east of Vienna.

The Germans apparently recognize that the American and British forces will meet the Russian forces somewhere in the North German plain. They hope then to be safely entrenched in their reduit. Then, if there is friction between the Anglo-Saxons and the Russians, they hope to be in a position to pour oil on the flames by stirring up all kinds of mischief in the Balkan areas.

They have seen how Tito defied their best efforts over several years. They believe they can play the game of several Titos, primarily in the main reduit, which will serve as a basis for supplies and for the despatch of parachutists and agents to foment trouble in minor nets of resistance to be scattered far and wide in Southeastern Europe. This may well be the basic plan that they are now preparing the reduit to serve as an arsenal of manpower and material to give it effect. In particular, preparations are reported to have been made to assure the possibility of manufacturing light, defensive arms and anti-tank guns in the reduit.

2. Here is an interesting editorial that appeared in the *Weltwoche* last night. The Allied leaders, especially Churchill, appear to think that one decisive Allied victory will be sufficient to break all German resistance. We hope this optimism is justified, but we do not quite believe it. We fear that, between the moment through which we are now passing and the moment of the end of the war, seemingly so near, terrible things will happen, namely, the destruction of the Allied prisoners in Germany, unless an amnesty is granted to the Nazi leaders.

What we are reporting is not based on definitive knowledge, but rather on familiarity with the Third Reich and the Nazi mentality, concerning which we have rarely been deceived. Unfortunately, we do not dare hope that the Nazi leaders will be deterred from the most terrible action by the consideration that the blood which they shed must fall back on the German people and signify their doom. On the contrary, we fear that any such considerations will only strengthen them in their dire determination. Hitler himself once said that, if the German people lost the war, it would have failed in its historic mission and would deserve only annihilation.

National Socialism arose as an anti-social movement from the ashes of the corrupt bourgeois world which remained after the last war. It was an outbreak from reality, it was a bloody and cruel world of Wagner's operas and the Germanic heroic sagas. At the same time, it was an outbreak into the world of gangsters. In so doing, the Nazis made themselves outlaws of the bourgeois world and, on top of that, they have been officially banned from this world by the Allies.

They now feel themselves as beyond the law and outside the old world, relying solely on their own resources in the fight for their bare existence in a hopeless struggle. We know that no fighters are more dangerous than those who fight with the energy of despair. They shrink from nothing and no one, for they have nothing more to lose. There is much thought in this connection of new miracle weapons, especially in the use of gas, to which they might resort at the moment of complete despair. For our part, we do not believe that any such miracle weapon exists, for if they existed they would have been used before now.

It is possible that Hitler may still occupy himself with such things, but, more than all that, we fear the supreme threat which would confront the Allied statesmen with the awful alternative of either renouncing punishment of the Nazi leaders, or jeopardizing the lives of millions of decent human beings.

3. Here is a brief item from the Berlin correspondent of the *Neue Zuercher Zeitung* which appeared today. The whole German press quotes a Reuters report from Washington to the effect that the President intimated in a press conference that Great Britain and the USA had agreed in the Yalta Conference that, after the overthrow of Germany, the German prisoners of war would be employed in the reparation of war damage caused in Russia. This report obviously gives rise to grave concern in Germany and affords fresh material for German propaganda aimed at the improvement of the fighting morale of the German people. The press calls the Anglo-Americans "slave-drivers for Siberia" and claims that Roosevelt is selling German soldiers to the Kremlin. Deportation to Siberia is featured in the Berlin papers to show the public what they must expect if they give up determined resistance. It goes without saying that the German press seizes on every utterance from the Allied camp which tends to show that dire disaster awaits the German people if they are finally defeated.

Document 5-68

Telegram 7199, March 17, 1945

[Dulles kept Donovan apprised on Operation Sunrise.]

SUNRISE. Personal for Forgan only from 110; Washington 109 only.

Sunrise matter still in very tentative state and do not consider that any action required at moment at your end. Representatives from south are here including Glavin and at this stage, matter being handled by AFHQ. Believe latter have clearly in mind SHAEF interest if any progress made but until we have something more definite, silence seems best policy. Would naturally welcome your visit here at any time and hope your proposed return London does not mean this indefinitely delayed.

Document 5-69

Telegram 7329, March 20, 1945

[After weeks of preliminary soundings, Dulles met with SS General Karl Wolff, commander of Nazi SS forces in Italy, concerning the surrender of the German Army in Italy. Matters were confounded by the sudden replacement of General Kesselring (thought amenable) as Wehrmacht commander in Italy by General von Vietinghoff, an unknown quantity. Critic stands for Wolff, and Emperor for Kesselring. Field Marshal Sir Harold Alexander was Supreme Allied Commander in the Mediterranean Theater. His representatives sent to Switzerland to participate in the talks were U.S. General Lyman L. Lemnitzer and British Major General Terrence S. Airey (Alexander's chief intelligence officer). Number 476 is Gaevernitz; his estate at Ascona provided the site for the meeting. Colonel Edward Glavin was OSS chief at Caserta. 511 indicates Swiss intelligence.]

SUNRISE. Personal for 109. Information Forgan, Armour and Gamble. From 110.

1. Any distribution should be most carefully controlled. Name key given separately corresponding to AFHQ designations.

2. Matters dealt with below are being covered by direct radio to AFHQ from representatives here of Field Marshal Alexander and may reach SHAEF and JCS through AFHQ and CCS. Military contacts with Critic are being carried on here by CCS. This and subsequent Sunrise messages from 110 will, therefore, not be sent Caserta, and are being sent to Washington and ETO to make available there any pertinent intelligence, and for information on such other matters as may pertain to Washington and SHAEF. Before adopting this method of reporting I have consulted with Marshal Alexander's representatives here who concur.

3. Pursuant arrangements previously made, meeting with Critic took place near Locarno March 19. 110 and 476 had long preliminary talk with Critic, after which Glavin met him under assumed name, and later Marshal Alexander's representatives met him briefly, no name or ranks being given, as 110's military advisors.

4. Critic stated he prepared proceed with program to bring about surrender German armies Italy as clear duty to his country. Emperor's absence had, however, forced change in procedure and what he should do next depended upon time which he had for action. If he had practically no time, he would be forced to see what he could do alone. If less than week available, he would deal directly with von Vietinghoff. If he had 7 days or more he would go immediately to Emperor whom he considered more than ever key to situation both Italy and west front.

5. Emperor was assuming Rundstedt's command and had not been allowed by Fuehrer's headquarters even to return to Italy to pack up his effects. Hence, Critic had had no opportunity to see him since his first meeting here 10 days ago.

6. Vietinghoff who had gone Germany on leave middle January, after Emperor returned upon recovery from injury, had subsequently exercised brief command in Kurland. After short conference Fuehrer's headquarters, he was now returning to take Emperor's command as OBHSW and probably reached his Italian HQ on 19.

7. If Critic forced act alone, he had only following forces at his disposal which were heterogeneous and equipped only with light arms and few old tanks: in his capacity as Hoechster SS und Polizeifuehrer which post had held since September 1943, he commanded approximately 15,000 Germans, 20,000 Russians mostly cossacks, Don Kubans and Turkmans, 10,000 Serbs, 10,000 Slovenes, 5,000 Czechs, an Indian legion, 100,000 Italians including the X Mas. As Bevollmaechtigter General der Deutschen Wehrmacht, a post he had occupied since July putsch, he directly commanded 10,000 Germans, and had under his tactical command 55,000 German service of supply and similar troops, north of Po. Critic frankly admitted his forces other than German were not very dependable, and that if he endeavored initiate isolated action without prior coordination with OKW, he would probably be caught between German armies to north and south.

8. As regards prospects from direct approach to Vietinghoff he said that latter was non-political soldier who would be unprepared to take political action without support from others in Wehrmacht. Critic said his relations with Vietinghoff were excellent, but he had not prepared the ground with him as he had in the case of Emperor.

9. Hence Critic proposed proceed immediately to Emperor's headquarters and endeavor get Emperor and Westphal, whom he highly regarded, to join in common action, in which case he felt sure Vietinghoff would go along. If he was successful, he hoped to bring back with him within a week qualified military representatives from both Emperor and Vietinghoff's headquarters to discuss details of military surrender.

10. Critic stated that he realized fast developing military situation left him little time for action, and that as matter of fact German headquarters Italy expected an offensive before end of month. (To our 511 contact Critic mentioned that they were expecting attack about March 25th.)

11. Critic crossed back into Italy evening March 19th with expressed intention proceeding immediately to Emperor by car since for technical reasons flying excluded. He seemed determined to do utmost to get action started.

12. I report Critic's statements as made to us, without attempting predict whether he can realize his plan. He gave impression of being determined, and those who have had closer contact with him since his first approach 10 days ago are inclined to believe he is sincere in his desire to effect immediate German surrender. He particularly emphasized that it would be a crime against German people if the German

reduit plan was realized as it would merely cause untold additional useless destruction and slaughter.

Document 5-70

Telegram 7337, March 21, 1945

[This report from Maurice Villars, an important source in Zurich, was part of the flow of information on Japan obtained by OSS Bern. Kitamura, a Japanese financial expert in Switzerland, was regarded as a political moderate.]

154 and Saint from 110 and DB-001. Following is report by 496 of interview with Kitamura: 1. Jap ambassador to Moscow was summoned to Tokyo to discuss technical details of renewal of Russo-Japanese non-aggression pact. He left Moscow with firm conviction Russia would renew. Kase, Jap minister to Bern and source of foregoing, added that he sees recent improvement in Russo-Japanese relations. 2. There will be no big naval engagement because 1/3 Jap fleet is sunk and other 1/3 is undergoing very slow repairs. Jap air force insufficient to protect remainder. 3. Crack army divisions are in Manchukuo and China, still untouched. 4. Food situation in Japan serious. Fish rationed, rice unrationed but hard to obtain. He does not expect decline in efficiency as result of under-nourishment. 5. Bombardment by incendiaries more damaging than explosives. Osaka and Nagoya badly damaged because unlike Tokyo, they lack fire breaks. 6. Japs have few assets in Suisse. Have enough for their legation needs.

Document 5-71

Telegram 7387, March 21, 1945

[This message records a conversation between the Director of the Reichsbank and Thomas H. McKittrick (number 644), the American head of the Bank of International Settlements in Basel.]

From 110. Puhl, Director of Reichsbank, has just arrived to see what financial arrangements he can make with Switzerland to cover German official expenses here in light of recent Swiss arrangements with Allies. In talk with 644 he stated:

Reichsbank still at Berlin and Puhl gave no hint of any plans to leave. However, some of Reichsbank gold has been moved to Constance, amount not specified, but may be considerable.

He said that the jig was up but that Nazis had made careful plans to go underground, that every essential figure had his designated place, that Nazis would not end with military defeat as Hitler and his fanatical followers would no more change their philosophy than would Socrates or Mohammed, that these men were just as convinced of their cause as ever and carried a great body of people with them. He emphasized that Naziism was like a religion not merely a political regime.

In reply to 644's inquiry as to whether he, Puhl, would assume any responsibility under occupying forces if asked to do so he replied that this presented serious problem, that it would be both physically and politically dangerous to collaborate with Allies at first and that choice of proper moment to do this without losing confidence of German public opinion would be a most difficult problem, that men who collaborated too soon would be sacrificing their subsequent utility and that useful men should wait until the public they seek to influence is prepared to accept loyal collaboration with the democracies. Puhl remarked that it was surprising how well the Bank was able to work in the bombed out quarters without any facilities they had previously considered essential.

Document 5-72

Radiotelephone Transmission No. 289, March 21, 1945

[This message contains information on Russian administration of occupied German territory. The German source believes that the Soviet policies are more effective than those likely to be pursued by Western occupation authorities.]

Germany

A German businessman, who has just arrived from Berlin, gives the following picture of the Russian behavior in occupied German territories in the East. The Russians are treating the Germans in the occupied territory on the whole very fairly. The Russian policy is to let the occupied territory go on working, leaving it in the condition in which it is found and saying that it must produce the same quantities as before. Later, a workers' committee is set up in each plant to see which executives should be got rid of. Of those to be discharged, those whose conduct was otherwise all right are given a pension, and those whose conduct was hostile are shot. The Russians recognize the value of engineering personnel. They are following a clear line. They are shooting the Nazis, but are being good to the workers, engineers, and those whom they need. The German people are cooperating with the Russians in the occupied area up to a certain point. They feel more secure than under the Nazis. The large estates are being divided up and given to the farmers, with notice, however, that the farmers may have to join a Russian cooperative.

The Germans feel that the Russians are making a success of their occupation, and there is a growing feeling that they will make a greater success than the English and Americans will of theirs. For one thing, the Russians never bombed workers' quarters, and the Germans feel that they committed less willful destruction. The Russians do not strafe fleeing German civilians but instead assist them to get out of the districts the Russians are about to capture. The German businessman making the foregoing comment feels that the Americans, with their stand-off policy towards the ordinary

German on the one hand, and with the likelihood that they will not shoot many Nazis, on the other, will probably blunder in their occupation methods.

Document 5-73

Telegram 7427, March 22, 1945

[OSS Bern continued to forward odds and ends relating to Japan and Japanese personnel in Europe.]

Informant with close contact Jap legation here reports that of some 650 Japs in Germany, including officials and private businessmen, etc., some 600 propose to hide themselves in eastern part of Germany and to be overrun by Russians hoping that Russians will then permit them work their way back via Siberia. Members Jap legation here including their MA and commercial attaché reported to be spreading reports that Hitler determined start gas and bacteriological warfare which will cause epidemics throughout Europe including Switzerland. They say Japs backing up Hitler in this determination but he meeting opposition in military and some party circles.

Document 5-74

Telegram 7569, March 23, 1945

[Among the various Nazi elements seeking to cut a last-minute deal was a conservative/Catholic faction centered on General von Epp in Bavaria. Dulles entertained the possibility of using this dubious entity to further undermine Nazi and SS cohesiveness.]

Heinze, Berlin Foreign Office man press department recently arrived here and reported as follows to 502.

When in Munich he was entertained by General von Epp, Reichsstatthalter of Bavaria who had been Statthalter prior to Hitler and who stayed on thereafter as Reichsstatthalter, but as practical matter subordinate to Gauleiter. Von Epp stated he had arranged with General Kriegel [Kriebel] OKW to take over power in Bavaria at time of collapse, that he was in touch with Faulhaber and had tried to contact Vatican through him but Faulhaber unable to do this safely as Gestapo man in his entourage. Von Epp apparently desired to know whether his appearance at head of Bavarian anti-Hitler movement would tend to prejudice movement view his Nazi background and retaining office under Hitler. He probably also has monarchical and strongly anti-communist ideas.

Heinze reported to be friend of von Haeften, executed after July 20, and 502 considers him reliable. Heinze will return Bavaria within week.

I have full information Epp's bad record but would appreciate anything you may have on Heinze or Kriegl [Kriebel]. Also your views on question of policy whether should encourage even rascals to fight Hitler Himmler in order weaken home front and in this case prejudice possibility of German reduit, or whether man like Epp is beyond pale.

Document 5-75

Telegram 7589, March 24, 1945

[Nazi figures Hoettl, Kaltenbrunner, and possibly Himmler himself intensified their efforts to strike some sort of a deal with the West via contacts in Switzerland. Dulles saw the possibility of using this high-level subversion to destroy Nazi plans for a last stand in Bavaria and Austria.]

. . . Hoettl made 2nd trip here from Vienna and on this occasion we arranged put our 502 in contact with him. Hoettl who I am convinced is righthand man of Kaltenbrunner gave following picture of situation Vienna:

Within ranks of Austrian SS the majority, who mostly Austrian nationals, desires liquidate party and arrange orderly transfer of administration to Western powers. This plan involves elimination of SS elements favoring continuation of war, particularly Bormann supporters and a number of Gauleiters.

This viewpoint was also confirmed to us by 503 who has also been here again and who saw Kaltenbrunner between Hoettl's first and second trip and who advised us that second trip was at Kaltenbrunner's special request. According to Hoettl Kaltenbrunner had entrusted him with task of establishing contact with Austrian opposition circles with view of supporting anti-communist elements. Because of his Catholicism and fact his father social democratic school reformer Hoettl deemed qualified for this task which facilitated by anti-communist leanings of Austrian workers. Hoettl claimed contact with anti-Nazi worker leaders Steirmark, Wiener Neustadt and Vienna and also with Catholic opposition groups and cited name of Catholic leader Rudolph as opposition leader. (From 110. This name checks with K-28 report.) Claimed he knew other leaders only under their cover names. Hoettl promised return here with certain opposition leaders and hinted even at possibility of bringing out Seitz as well as representatives of workers and Catholic opposition.

This program was subject of discussion in Salzburg attended by Kaltenbrunner, Neubacher, Glaise-Horstenau, Neustadter-Stuermer, and Hoettl upon latter's return to Austria after second trip.

Re general situation Hoettl declared Nazis expected wave of anti-Nazi communism in Balkan area, that in Rumania Iron Guard strengthened and present party of Maniu opposed to communism. Similar developments in Jugoslavia. He gave these developments as reason why at present time in spite of unfavorable situation on east and west fronts, SS divs among them *Leibstandarte* remained on Plattensee front while von Weich's army in Croatia remained there and relatively inactive. He said Alpine reduit would be finished and stocked in about 3 months, that Steyrwerke is already underground and producing particularly such defensive weapons as panzer faeuste. It is intended that Wehrmacht units as well as SS be taken into reduit including families of fighting men.

As regards situation within Nazi Party, Hoettl stated that split between West and East oriented persons becoming more apparent. Ley and Arbeitsfront plus Bormann and many Gauleiters go with latter. Kaltenbrunner and his followers belong to Western oriented group. He predicted sort of Tauroggen movement with the uncovering of Western front and march toward the East leaving government of Germany to Western allies while continuing to fight as Free Corps band.

From 110. The above is well within range of possibility. As you know there are other indications that certain SS elements are trying to save their skins by turning to West, dropping their attacks against local anti-Nazi movements or even favoring them and preparing to follow line which will obviate necessity of their joining diehards in last ditch struggle in reduit.

Elements of similarity in movements of von Epp in Bavaria, Kaltenbrunner in Austria and our contacts in Italy are striking. It seems to me that these trends offer possibility of checkmating any effective organization of German reduit. Interesting question whether Himmler is pulling strings behind these varying movements and possibly preparing himself to desert the diehards.

Document 5-76

Radiotelephone Transmission No. 290. March 27, 1945

[Dulles updated his views on the German redoubt concept.]

Germany

With the Western Front rapidly disintegrating, the time remaining for the Germans to gather together the last remnants of their forces and retire to the reduit is now becoming short. There seems to be no alternative for them now. The question remains as to how many will follow the fanatical Nazi leaders and how effective the resistance in the reduit will prove to be.

We now have considerable evidence on the reduit. It does not tend to prove that any vast-scale preparations have as yet been made. The Germans are never very effective in preparing for defeat or reverses. From the point of view of the effects on the home front, it is not easy for any country to proceed too openly with measures which, if advertised widely, would themselves tend to show a hopeless military situation. In Germany, with their theories of the Superman, it is particularly difficult to admit that they are reduced to the status of guerrilla fighters. Further, Hitler is not the type of man who, at this stage in his career, would be good at planning to play the role of Robin Hood.

These various intangible factors, plus the lack of convincing evidence of really large-scale preparations, lead me to the conclusion that the German reduit will be a less well-prepared affair than newspaper reports would lead us to believe.

However, some sort of reduit seems inevitable from the force of circumstances, and some stocking of this reduit has been carried out. Elaborate fortifications are not in themselves necessary to make a mountain area, such as the Tyrol and Bavarian Alps, a formidable fortress if defended by resolute men with training in mountain warfare. Very possibly, the Nazis can still find and pull together in the Alps enough of these troops, plus some determined and fanatical SS divisions, such, for example, as those commanded by Sepp Dietrich, to make a determined stand. The German divisions in Italy still remain intact and are possibly ready to fall back into the Alps and defend the southern flank of the reduit. Some of the best German troops are still fighting the Russians east of Vienna. The pattern of the last German defense tends to take shape. The forces which are defending the Rhine and Berlin are very possibly being sacrificed to gain a few weeks more for the gathering together of the chosen forces in the reduit.

It is not yet clear whether the SS will act as a unit in accepting the idea of retiring to the reduit. There may well be a split in their ranks. The same is true of the Wehrmacht. Some of the latter would obey any order from Hitler, but others may well try to find other methods of preserving their lives for some time longer.

Document 5-77

Telegram 7699 to London, March 28, 1945

[For Dulles, the Sunrise negotiations represented an opportunity to derail Nazi plans to establish a national redoubt in the Alps.]

SUNRISE. To Forgan, London . . . from 110. Information: Gamble, Armour, and 109. . . . No further word received Monday night from Critic. His associate Zimmer, however, reported that both Ambassador Rahn and Harster had been recalled to Germany for conference in FHQ. Harster is prominent SS man who probably has some knowledge of Critic's activities.

It is becoming more and more apparent that it is Hitler's intent to use bulk of German army Italy for defense of German reduit. Interesting feature of the Critic negotiation is possibility it might offer to defeat this project.

Document 5-78

Telegram 7737, March 28, 1945

[Dulles here reports on the location of Kesselring's headquarters on the Western Front.]

511 has a report that Kesselring's HQ is, or was, at Zeigenberg, near Bad Nauheim where are large underground installations dating from 1940, when used by Hitler as FHQ during France invasion. (From 110: View our rapid advance, this information may be outdated.)

Reliable source reports that German officers and SS are now being officially apprised of secret Himmler order, and forced to acknowledge it, whereby entire family of officer is rendered directly answerable for his failure to perform his duty. The German word for this is "Sippensuehne."

It is interesting to note that according to our reports, Kesselring has no immediate family.

Document 5-79

Telegram 585 to Caserta, March 29, 1945

[OSS Bern continued to exercise a role in liaison with resistance leaders in northern Italy.]

SUNRISE. To Newhouse from 110. Parri and Cadorna . . . crossed frontier to Annemasse today and proceeding immediately Lyons. SOE had Cadorna in their custody and cooperated with us in connection frontier passage. I believe that trip of these men can be most useful in coordination plans for handling North Italian situation upon collapse and sincerely hope that it will be used for this purpose. Both men went with some reluctance as they considered that they should be at post of duty North Italy. We assured them that every effort would be made to return them North Italy presumably via Switzerland at earliest possible moment so that they can be on the spot to prepare for liberation North Italy.

Document 5-80

Telegram 9119 to London, April 1, 1945

[In this message, Dulles provides an account of the debate over the Sunrise negotiations among the Germans, as related by Zimmer, aide to General Wolff. Critic is Wolff; Emperor is Kesselring; Glazier is Vietinghoff.]

SUNRISE. Forgan, Armour, Gamble only from 110. Information: 109. . . . Following is summary of information received 31, AFHQ representatives reporting direct. Zimmer gave us the following report:

1. Critic arrived Fasano Friday morning [March 30] and immediately summoned Parilli and Zimmer to Fasano where they spent Friday afternoon together. Zimmer was then sent here by Critic, Parilli remaining Fasano.

2. Critic endeavored contact Vietinghoff before he went to see Emperor, but was unable to reach him.

3. Trip to Emperor most difficult and when he reached Emperor's headquarters, hell had already broken loose. First conversation took place only 15 km. from our advancing forces. Critic presented his plan for Italian surrender and Emperor advised him to go through with it. He, Emperor, regretted he was not also in Italy.

4. In a second conversation with Emperor, latter again expressed his agreement with Critic's plan and that he should so advise Vietinghoff, but said that on his front he could not go along (mitmachen). Emperor found himself largely surrounded by strangers whom he did not trust. Zimmer gained impression from Critic Emperor was half a prisoner (from 110: No mention made of Westphal).

5. Immediately on his return, Critic had tried to reach Glazier but he was on an inspection trip at the front and was returning to his headquarters only night of 31. Critic proposed to see him immediately and would spend Sunday with him. Critic gave this message to Zimmer for 110: I am ready to come to a final conversation in order to arrange matters. I hope to come with Rahn, Dollman and either Vietinghoff or a staff officer.

6. Rahn had been called back to Germany but avoided the trip by alleging serious strike conditions North Italy which he had to handle. Harster did return Germany, but apparently on account of a row with Gauleiter Hofer of the Tyrol. Neither summons believed to be connected with Sunrise.

7. While in Germany and one of reasons for delay, Critic was summoned by Himmler, who asked him to explain his surrender of British agent Tucker. Critic replied that he was arranging an exchange and he wanted to give the Fuehrer Wuensche as birthday present. Himmler also accused him of having been in Switzerland and asked the reasons. Critic answered that he had a contact in Milan who promised to bring him in touch with Allies and that he was acting pursuant Fuehrer's recent secret order to seek any possible contact with Allies. Critic had heard that many efforts had failed and wanted to see what he could do. Himmler ordered Critic to wait around for a couple of days as he wanted to think the matter over. However, Himmler was suddenly called urgently to Hungary and referred Critic to Kaltenbrunner. Himmler told him that he should not leave Italy and particularly that he should not go to Switzerland. Critic did not see Kaltenbrunner but left for Italy.

8. In his conversation with Emperor, latter said to Critic our situation is desperate, nobody dares tell truth to Fuehrer who surrounded by small group of advisers who still believe in a last specific secret weapon which they call "Verzweiflunge" weapon. Emperor believed this weapon can prolong war but not decide it, but might cause terrible blood bath on both sides. Emperor said if Fuehrer gave him order to use weapon he would surrender his command. End of Zimmer report.

9. Under foregoing program and assuming no further delays which may be inherent in situation, Critic should come to a meeting sometime Monday or early Tuesday. Any action by Kesselring via Critic seems excluded. Whether Critic will

win over Vietinghoff is still matter of conjecture, despite Critic's apparent optimism. Zimmer understands Critic has support of one of Vietinghoff's chief subordinates.

Document 5-81

Telegram 9169 to London, April 3, 1945

[The German side of the Sunrise negotiations now threatened to unravel, as Wolff ("Critic") came under intense suspicion from Himmler. The latter, of course, was concurrently attempting to make his own bargain with the Allies, in Switzerland and elsewhere.]

SUNRISE. Personal for Forgan, Armour . . . Gamble . . . only from 110. Information 109. Following is substance of information received today by AFHQ representative here, 110 and 476. AFHQ being advised directly.

1. Parrilli who had spent last 3 days at Critic's headquarters at Fasano came over frontier today and reported following:

2. On April 1 Himmler who had apparently returned to his headquarters in Germany peremptorily ordered Critic by telephone that under no conditions should he leave North Italy and that he, Himmler would telephone him periodically. Himmler chided Critic for having removed his family to point near Brenner and said that he could take better care of them and had sent them back immediately to St. Wolfgang near Salzburg.

3. Critic stated that if he now made false move and left his headquarters for Switzerland whole project would probably collapse and that as corpse he would be helpful neither to German people nor Allies. He believed Himmler had given special instructions that he be watched. Accordingly impossible for him to come Switzerland now.

4. Critic reported that he had talked with Ambassador Rahn who was in full agreement with his program.

5. Critic had conference with Vietinghoff and latter's chief of staff Roettiger night of April 1. He claimed that both were in agreement with him and that Vietinghoff remarked it was nonsense to go on fighting. According to Critic, Vietinghoff had received instructions in case of general Allied attack to withdraw to Alps fighting (kaempfend abzugetzen) destroying as they went. Critic gave Vietinghoff full report of his conference with Emperor including Emperor's judgment that fighting on his front might last 10 or 15 days longer, but Germany was facing catastrophe. Critic asked Parilli to give message to 110 that if they could be given 10 days more they could hand over North Italy on silver platter. End of Parilli report.

6. Parilli returns tomorrow to Fasano and channel of contact via 110 here is being maintained.

7. Parilli took back message to Critic acknowledging receipt of information that Vietinghoff and Rahn had been won over to plan, stating that if military surrender

is to be effected, it must be done quickly and could be effected by sending parliamentarians thru lines at points and times which could be communicated via 110.

8. With approval of AFHQ representatives, Parilli also bore further message to Critic from 110 reminding him of previous messages that it was vital that he and Vietinghoff should prevent carrying out of Hitler-Himmler instructions regarding destruction North Italy and also reminding him of previous promise to restrain action against partisans and to protect Allied and partisan prisoners and hostages in his hands. Critic was finally reminded that he and his friends now had final opportunity for action and only action counted.

9. Note from 110 and 476. We judge that Critic and his associates including probably Vietinghoff desire to wait in hope that complete chaos in Germany will permit them to act in Italy without serious risks to themselves and their families. We warned Parilli for Wolff that Himmler from possible German reduit might increasingly exercise terroristic influence and that delay was no answer and might even complicate picture. We believe that threat to Wolff may well be real as it is more than likely with time that has passed, number of meetings held and persons in know that some inklings of plot have reached Himmler's ears. Whether action will be taken by Critic and Vietinghoff we cannot predict, but we feel that AFHQ representatives and we have done everything possible to bring home to them realities of situation and need to act now.

Document 5-82

Telegram 8099, April 4, 1945

[After eighteen months as one of World War II's most effective agents in place, Fritz Kolbe made his escape to Switzerland. Even on his last trip he brought valuable documents and information from the German Foreign Office in Berlin.]

KAPPA. From 110. #9199 to London. Wood arrived last night after laborious trip from Berlin, which he left about March 16. He reports that Foreign Office no longer has importance as regards current developments and that office of his boss, Ritter, which served as contact between FO and OKW, is to be liquidated and it seems probable that Wood would be sent to Volkssturm if he returned. He has 5 day visa for Suisse and pending its expiration I must determine his future activity and probably shall either keep him here or, if it can be done with reasonable safety, send him to area where he could be helpful in reporting on German reduit. Would welcome your suggestions, but would wish to reserve final decision in light of what seems practicable and reasonably safe, view his future usefulness.

As previously, he brought many photographs and some documents which I promise send immediately via 244 as special courier. Sending Wood's impressions and other information separately.

Document 5-83

Telegram 8139, April 5, 1945

[By the end of the war, Walter Schellenberg of the Nazi SD had become the preeminent figure in German intelligence. He too sought an accommodation with the Allies, attempting to establish contact through Swiss intelligence, with which he had an ongoing arrangement for the exchange of information.]

From 110. Masson, head of Swiss intelligence, again inquired whether I had any interest in making contact with Schellenberg of German SD. I replied our interest was unconditional surrender of German forces and that any contact Schellenberg seemed quite futile. Schellenberg's idea was apparently time-worn one of opening west front but holding east front. I told Masson west front was already opened up without Schellenberg help.

Masson had information that Kesselring has already abandoned his command as hopeless and Ghali of *Chicago Daily News* has information from Swiss intelligence source of intercepted message from FHQ to German generals on west front to act on their own responsibility as they might not be able receive orders from HQ for several days. Maybe they are moving to the reduit?

Schellenberg is obviously attempting to buy immunity as he has just delivered Gen. Giraud's family to Masson, who repatriated them to France, and is apparently prepared to release further women and children.

Document 5-84

Telegram 8179, April 5, 1945

[This message contains "George Wood's" final observations on the situation in Berlin, and in particular the status of the Foreign Ministry.]

KAPPA. Following information given by Wood mostly dated middle March when he left Berlin.

1. Hitler headquarters at Stolpe near Dannenwalde on Berlin-Stralsund RR. With him were staff of Reichskanzlei and Bormann. Hitler never sleeps twice in same place.

2. With Hitler's consent, Ribbentrop sent persons to Bern and Stockholm to try to make contacts, von Schmieden sent to Bern, Hesse to Stockholm to contact Russians. If nothing comes of these peace feelers, Ribbentrop likely to be dismissed. (From 110: Nothing known of Schmieden here.)

3. Foreign Office Headquarters still Berlin, but with various scattered sections elsewhere. Part of Kulturabteilung under Windecker is at Constance. Another part

this section is at Ravensburg in Württemberg. Also at Constance are various removed German diplomats, including Hoyningen-Huene, Dieckhoff, Stoirer, Wiehl.

4. Archivabteilung of Foreign Office is located in the Harz near Quedlinburg and archives distributed in old salt mines. Current files were still Berlin middle March.

5. Burning of archives proceeding on large scale and instructions to this effect have been given to every government office in case of danger of enemy occupation. Unfortunately material which Wood had put in his office safe was burned during his last absence from Berlin.

6. Ausweichsstelle located between Weimar and Erfurt has been prepared for Foriegn Office personnel. 300 to 400 of Foreign Office personnel still Berlin middle March, of these all except 80 constituting Fuehrungsstab here shortly to move above Ausweichstelle but doubtful whether this plan carried out in view rapidity military developments.

Document 5-85

Radiotelephone Transmission No. 291, April 5, 1945

[Dulles reports that as Allied armies sweep through Germany, Hitler remains in Berlin, as do most government bureaus.]

Germany

According to reports received today from excellent sources, Hitler is still at or near Berlin with Bormann and his chief advisers. He is said to be endeavoring to reach a final decision, whether to make a last stand with his troops at Berlin, or to leave for the German reduit.

It seems fairly clear that the Germans have abandoned as hopeless any organized defense in the West, but are still hopeful of holding off the Russians for some little time longer. It is easier to induce the German soldier to keep up a hopeless fight against the Russians than it is against the Americans and British. The idea seems to be fairly prevalent in Germany that for the soldiers taken prisoner by the Russians years of labor in Russia or Siberia may be their fate. On the other hand, it is generally believed that, if one becomes a prisoner of the Americans or British, then after a brief period of captivity under comfortable conditions, there is a prospect of early return to Germany.

Strange as it may seem, there is no conclusive evidence of a general and wholesale evacuation of government bureaus from Berlin. Most departments of the government still have their chief administrative centers there as yet, but not very much to do. Each department has one or more places of retreat already chosen and with some personnel already shifted to these retreats. However, the movement away from Berlin by government personnel has been thrown into some confusion by the rapid advance of our forces in the West, with the result that many places chosen as safe refuges for government departments are now threatened with being overrun by our forces. No general movement of government offices to the reduit has as yet been established, but a great many high Nazi officials have apparently moved their families there.

Document 5-86

Telegram 8277, April 6, 1945

[The Safehaven program was one of the main concerns of OSS Bern in the last weeks of the war and after VE-Day. Switzerland was a prime location for attempts by Germans and other enemy nationals to secrete assets. The Dulles organization cooperated with the U.S. Safehaven program's mission in Switzerland, but also clashed with it over the activities of Germans who had been cooperative with the OSS. Number 441 is OSS staff member Valerian Lada-Mocarski.]

From 110 and 441. Following information furnished 441. Ostrow requests copy be given to Harry White at Treasury: Thomas De Pechy, Managing Director Hungarian small arms and ammunition factory recently arrived Zurich from Vienna with trunk weighing 250 pounds containing securities. De Pechy works closely with SS Obergruppenfuehrer Becher of Vienna, who arranged his trip to Switzerland. Becher one of biggest "fixers" in Nazi Party, suspected of being charged with providing safe haven for Nazi funds. De Pechy is also reported to be negotiating the sale to the Swiss of German copper for 3,000,000 Swiss francs payable outside clearing account. Copper is stored in Regensburg in Bavaria where it has been earmarked by Becher as Swiss property.

Intelligence secured by 441 independently corroborates in part above statements. Suggest investigation of reported copper stocks when Regensburg occupied.

Document 5-87

Telegram 8349, April 6, 1945

[This message to General Donovan contains unambiguous evidence that Dulles considered German plans for a last stand in an Alpine redoubt a reality that had to be taken into account in Allied planning.]

109 from 110. Re your #5149 (OUT 8175).

1. Trust that memo sent via 244 can be added to your McCloy report when it reaches Washington.

2. Assume you have several score of our reports on reduit already submitted.

3. While we believe that press has somewhat exaggerated extent of German preparations and probable territorial extent of reduit, there is evidence that considerable activity has recently developed, particularly since failure of Rundstedt's offensive,

and that sufficient supplies and weapons have been stored in inner reduit to equip with light arms and feed approximately 25,000 men for period of year. Work on defense of important passes into reduit and on certain underground plants for light arms and on hidden depots has also been pushed.

4. Inner reduit lies to the southwest of Salzburg around Berchtesgaden. There is also evidence of a further inner reduit in area Bregenz, Bregenz Erwald, Dornbirn, Feldkirch area based on Swiss frontier. Undoubtedly plans exist for connecting these 2 areas which would be the chief arsenals for reduit.

5. In addition, there is probably an outer reduit to be held temporarily but as long as possible stretching from near Vienna in the east, including parts of lower Austria, Carinthia Steiermark and possibly parts of North Italy and running westward to Swiss frontier southwest of Munich.

6. As reported earlier today Hitler apparently had not yet retired to reduit or finally decided whether to make last stand there or around Berlin where he still located. Undoubtedly many high Nazis have already decided in favor of reduit as evidenced by movement of their families to this area, probably including families of Himmler, Bormann, Ley, Goering, Ribbentrop, Goebbels, Wolff, etc.

Document 5-88

Telegram 8399, April 7, 1945

[The last documents from Fritz Kolbe / George Wood, those brought with him when he defected from Germany, dealt in large part with the Far East. They were based on reports from German diplomats and military attachés in Japan and elsewhere in Asia. The bracketed notations to this summary cable were supplied by OSS Bern as a key to microform copies of the full documents, which were being sent by pouch. "Aprilka" indicates Wood, or Kappa, material received in April.]

APRILKA. . . . Military information items summarized from Kretschmer's reports.

1. February 9th indicates Jap intention to resist in northern Luzon notwithstanding our overwhelming air superiority and increased Philippine Partisan activity. Japs hope to hold out there until end April despite increasing supply difficulties [print B21].

2. February 28th "though Jap supply line to Luzon reduced to submarines as result increasing air raids against Formosa Jap General Staff estimates resistance will last for longer period than it did early February" [print B22].

3. February 9th confirms Jap intention to hold southern half of Burma. Kretschmer considers USA especially interested in improving equipment Chungking Chinese Divisions as USA intend land southern China. [print B21].

4. February 28th refers to air raid of February 25th when mainly airdromes, ports and ships were hit: also some railways, factories and . . . dwelling quarters around Tokyo, Hamamatsu and Nagoya. As raid no surprise allegedly only 40 Jap planes

destroyed on ground and ship losses small, damage to factories more important. In Tokyo over 20,000 houses destroyed. [print B22].

5. Kretschmer learned from Jap General Staff February 10th: last Jap courier to Moscow observed transports of recruits and some hospital trains eastward, many new planes westward. Jap MA observes increasing anti-American sentiments of Russian officers especially those returning from Bulgaria or Rumania. [print B21].

Document 5-89

Telegram 8759 to Paris, April 7, 1945

[Dulles considered that it was "a good gamble" to deal with the right-wing von Epp group in hope that Bavaria could be detached from Nazi control. This message describes efforts to establish contact.]

Forgan, Gamble from 110 and 476. Information: 154. See our previous cables re von Epp-Heintze matter. . . .

1. Trusted messenger who working with Heintze returned from Munich April 6, having made contact with von Epp group. He confirms reports that von Epp with several other high ranking officers in Bavaria are prepared to do everything in their power to cut short war in Bavaria to prevent unnecessary destruction and if possible to make establishment of reduit impossible. He states important men in this group in addition to von Epp are: (a) Wehrkreis commandant of Wehrkreis Munich, General Kriebel; (b) Luftgau commandant of Munich, General Lt. Vorwald who said to control military ground personnel of large airfields especially Schlesissheim and Riehm near Munich, and Reichenhall near Salzburg; (c) local SS commander of Nurnberg, Martin. Group further includes several younger officers and government officials.

2. Group is prepared receive immediately radio operator near Murnau in southern Bavaria. Following are pin points: Germany 1 to 100,000. Center of reception field Y-5 at Y 653047. Boundaries of field Y 651–655.046–7. Safe house at Guglhor about 700 meters due west of field at Y 645045. This field is about 5 kilometers east of Murnau and about 500 meters north of river Loisach. For security reasons operator to be dropped should be either Austrian or German.

3. Dropping can take place any time on or after April 12, and BBC signal should be arranged immediately. Following signal has been agreed on: Die (blank) Bucher Haben (blank) Siegel. Number of books indicates date and number of seals indicates time of operation in local German time. Call word introducing and identifying message is Christian.

4. On word from you that operation feasible we will send special messenger to Munich to give hour and program of BBC broadcast and to arrange reception and ground signals. Please instruct on this point. Our operator will be received by von

Mutius, right hand man of von Epp and Heinz Heintze, German FO man and our original contact for this operation.

5. While we cannot predict that above mentioned group will be able to take effective action against SS machine in Bavaria, we consider operation is good gamble and in any event useful military information should be obtained.

6. Following information brought from group by our messenger: Reduit becoming a reality. Large quantities of supplies are being accumulated in Salzburg area and local population being evacuated. Further indications are that OKW is being transferred from Bendlerstrasse, Berlin to Reichenhall and parts of FO being transferred to Badgastein. Number of troops now in reduit still small and it is estimated that in Berchtesgaden Salzburg area there are now only 6,000 SS troops. Wehrkre is commandant of Nurnberg. Weissenberger is ardent Nazi and must be expected to fight to end. Local SS chief of Munich Koppe, formerly on staff of German Governor of Poland, Frank is Nazi of the worst type, having committed many crimes Poland and elsewhere. No cooperation of any kind can be expected from him. Prominent hostages being taken to reduit.

Document 5-90

Telegram 8787 to Paris, April 7, 1945

[To the very end, Hitler and his entourage continued to hope for salvation by means of a revolutionary new weapon.]

Horton from 110. Information: Peters and 154. Sending by today's pouch copy Hitler order dated 31 January 1945 establishing German emergency armament program together with secret list of 16 priorities which are to rank equally. Report #B-2391. Item 16 on this list is "Die Fuhrer Gewalt Aktionen Mistel, EZ 42, Steuersender, Elefant." Source of this information is 511, who assures me of authenticity of documents.

Document 5-91

Telegram 8499, April 9, 1945

[The German generals in Italy were now amenable to surrender in principle, but complex administrative matters remained to be resolved. Further, General von Vietinghoff wanted to capitulate in such a way that would preserve his military honor.]

For 109, Forgan, Armour, Gamble only, from 110. Information Magruder.

1. Sunrise matter has revived and I communicated last night via Glavin to Lemnitzer at AFHQ comprehensive report based on information just received from Critic, Vietinghoff and his Chief of Staff, Roettinger. Substance of information is

that they desire text of our surrender formula, but have included certain conditions relating to preservation "military honor" and handling of surrender armies which will presumably be unacceptable to us. According to Critic who had long conferences Thursday [Apr. 5] and Saturday with Vietinghoff and Roettinger, principle of unconditional surrender not questioned provided it can be honorable surrender.

2. They all recognize that with march of events German armies in Italy will soon be isolated unit and as such justified in acting on own initiative.

3. Subject to solving military honor problem, they have proposed point on front lines for passage parliamentarians and have confirmed that they will do everything possible to prevent destruction, limit warfare against partisans, and protect prisoners and hostages. They state, however, that Admiral Doenitz has ordered marine destruction and they doubt whether they can effectively prevent this.

4. Critic recognizes futility and uselessness of further fighting, but his report indicates that Vietinghoff is old line soldier and insists that surrender be dressed up so as to be compatible with his "military honor" and not place him in position of being traitor.

5. Development still problematical and difficult to tell whether they playing for time or have serious intentions to surrender. However, matter has such potentialities that it may be extremely difficult for me to leave here unless there is week-end lull due to period required send messages from here to Fasano, Critic's headquarters, and back.

Document 5-92

Telegram 6689 to Caserta, April 11, 1945

[Dulles informs General Lemnitzer at Caserta that Gaevernitz (476) wanted to meet with the German leaders to work out the final details of the surrender in Italy.]

Sunrise Crossword. Glavin for Nicholson from 110. Re point 4 our 662. Your Ascona host is sincerely convinced that if allowed to make trip he could have real influence in persuading Glazier of necessity of immediate and complete capitulation. His arguments are impressive and whether or not he succeeds in that particular task intelligence obtained might be valuable. There are obviously certain risks but at this concluding stage of war danger is more from accident than premeditated plot. View his knowledge of German psychology and of method of approach to men of type Critic Glazier his arguments have impressed me and I wish therefore to supplement somewhat casual reference made to this matter in para 4 above message.

I believe you can count on his discretion and idea that at this stage and with Germans thoroughly beaten we would stoop to negotiations is in itself ludicrous and hence any attempt to exploit his trip from this angle not likely to have any repercussions.

Document 5-93

Radiotelephone Transmission No. 292, April 11, 1945

[As the end approached for Nazi Germany, foreign diplomatic missions left Berlin, the will to resist weakened even on the Eastern Front, and the Gestapo lost the means to enforce its regime of terror.]

Germany

1. The press this evening announces that, following the departure from Berlin of several foreign embassies and legations to places in southern Germany, a part of the Swiss Legation together with the Minister has been removed to Tegernsee in southern Bavaria. A part of the Swiss Legation personnel is remaining in Berlin.

It is interesting to note that the place selected is not really in the German reduit, but on the outer fringes of it, and this rather leaves open the question as to whether a Swiss representative is being sent into the reduit. However, Tegernsee is only about sixty miles from Berchtesgaden as the crow flies.

2. The relatively quick surrender of the fortress of Koenigsberg is one of the most interesting developments of the past few days. The will to fight, even on the Russian front, is waning. One of the reasons for this is the disappearing threat for the families of the German generals and soldiers who give themselves up. With such a large part of Germany occupied, the families of many are now safely in Allied hands and beyond the reach of the Gestapo. Further, the soldiers know well that, except in special cases of prominent military leaders, the Gestapo no longer has the time to run down and wreak revenge on individual families. Hence, one of the great deterrent weapons is slipping from the hands of the Nazis.

What is going on in the inner circle of the Nazi Party is still a mystery. We have lurid stories in the press from various Allied and neutral capitals. But there is as yet no evidence here that Hitler has left the Berlin area or that there has been any break in the inner Nazi ring. It is reported on reasonably good authority that Kaltenbrunner is gaining in power and is often seen with Hitler, who is supposed to have offered him Ribbentrop's job. Since it is hard to tell whether and where there is any Foreign Office really functioning, it is unlikely that he will accept even if the job were offered to him.

Document 5-94

Telegram 6719 to Caserta, April 12, 1945

[Dulles's correspondence with General Lemnitzer ("Nicholson") at AFHQ regarding Sunrise/Crossword indicates concern about press reports that could tip off the Nazis, and doubts about General Wolff's sincerity.]

Glavin from 110 for Nicholson.

(1) Your 626 received. Nothing in writing has been or will be given.

(2) I realize we must play our cards close to our chest and will act accordingly.

(3) Swiss newspaper item is similar to rumors which appeared long prior Crossword about alleged Kesselring negotiations. As Parri release now known many people it could have reached newspapers from variety of sources including source you mentioned.

(4) If there is satisfactory evidence that Critic did not visit Emperor this would naturally throw grave suspicion on entire Crossword. It would be helpful to know whether your doubt is based on evidence or deduction.

(5) Six months ago I would have considered that Critic was merely maneuvering. Today I consider at least 50 percent chance it is genuine but agree sufficient margin of doubt to make every precaution necessary. Swiss SI have rarely been fooled by Nazis in such matters.

(6) As I may be required proceed urgently Paris for two or three days April 13 to 15, I should like to show your 626 to 476 for his guidance but await your advice.

(7) Barnes thoroughly briefed will handle with 476 if I am absent. I will not leave if Crossword becomes active before departure and will return immediately if activated during absence.

Document 5-95

Telegram 8567, April 12, 1945

[Anti-Nazi Germans in Switzerland, including associates of Dulles, stepped up their activities in the last month of the war.]

Committee is being formed here apparently with tacit Swiss approval entitled "Das Demokratische Deutschland." It includes particularly Socialists, Protestants, and Catholics among its members. Prominent members of group are: Dr. Hoegener, Baron Godin, Dr. Wirth, Ritzel, Otto Braun, and Kindt Kiefer, all of whom are well known to us.

Group is reported to have acquired newspaper of German colony called "Deutsche Zeitung in Der Schweiz." Paper will now turn complete somersault.

Document 5-96

Telegram 8577, April 12, 1945

[OSS Bern was contacted by the Zurich correspondents of the Japanese newspaper *Asahi* with regard to the appropriate "peace procedure."]

SAINT. Saint and SI from 110 and DB/001. . . . New contact in office of Jiro Taguchi and Shunji Sasamoto, Zurich correspondents for *Asahi*, reports their disappointment at composition new cabinet. It is neither pro or anti-militarist, has "no strong line." They apparently had expected Konoye to be Minister without Portfolio. Dissatisfied at choice of Hirose, Kiabe the Communist baiter, Ota notorious reactionary. Claim it contains no strong militarist save Anami, a second-rater. Okada described as Suzuki type. Matsuoka bureaucrat and unimportant. Taguchi and Sasamoto are representative intelligent, liberal element. They know war is lost, are interested in peace which first they had hoped would be negotiated through good offices Russia, now believe will come about either through Jap Government proclamation stating people war weary and willing make concessions, or through secret negotiations in Sweden or Suisse. They stated that big industrialists having obtained economic objectives are very anti-militarist today; smaller industrialists still favor militarism. They asked contact to ascertain US reaction to new ministry and what US believed would be "the peace procedure," apparently completely ignoring unconditional surrender.

Document 5-97

Telegram 6859 to Caserta, April 13, 1945

[One of the more incredible aspects of Operation Sunrise was that Dulles placed a radio operator, the Czech Vaclav Hradecky (Walter, "Little Wally") in SS Headquarters in northern Italy. This arrangement provided instant communications with General Wolff.]

Urgent. Glavin from 110. Sunrise. We have borrowed from Henry Hyde Bari-trained radio operator Walter Czech origin fluent German. He should arrive Milan early 13 April where he will maintain contact Sunrise group and communicate directly with you via Bari. He has Bari pad and will contact under his Bari plan.

Important to keep in mind that any message from him will be material received from Critic, Parilli, Zimmer etc. and all messages must therefore be carefully scrutinized as possible plants or double-cross. As chief purpose is to provide quick means of communication in event they wish send parliamentarians or advise us re sending couriers here, kindly advise if contact established and give us repeats of anything Walter may send. Walter was told nothing about Sunrise by us and he is solely to send what he is given.

Document 5-98

Telegram 8619, April 13, 1945

[Dulles continued to explore contacts with Nazi leader Wilhelm Hoettl. He acknowledged OSS London's warning that Hoettl was regarded as an extremist and that Himmler might be using both Hoettl and Kaltenbrunner to embroil the Western powers in negotiations likely to become known.]

The following information obtained from Hoettl, hereafter called Alpberg, who arrive Suisse April 9:

1. Alpberg's relations with Kaltenbrunner now somewhat strained as Kaltenbrunner drawn into Hitler camp and spending much time with him. Hitler offered Kaltenbrunner post of foreign secretary.

2. Alpberg stated he and his friends wish to work with us to prevent establishment of reduit and that if established despite their efforts they would go into reduit and work underground with us.

3. Alpberg brought with him to Feldkirch alleged member of Austrian resistance movement named Winkler who carrying letter from Cardinal Innitzer of Vienna. (From 110: In view of Innitzer's earlier record this is not much of a recommendation.) Winkler now at Feldkirch awaiting arrangements for entry Suisse.

4. Alpberg in contact with Glais Horstenau/Orstenau who at Ajuchenwall (Reichenhall?) advising OKW on political problems of southeastern Europe particularly Croatia. He confirms our #875 to Paris that sections of OKW moved Reichenhall. Alpberg also in contact with General Loehr whose HQ at Agram. Among Loehr's forces many Austrians and Alpberg trying win Loehr over to sabotage any efforts to establish reduit.

5. Alpberg now has HQ in South Tyrol where he controls certain radio facilities. In cooperation with 511 we have arranged for him to establish radio link here and we will get all info.

6. Alpberg confirms that reduit rapidly becoming reality with mountain troops being increasingly concentrated there. General manager of Steyrwerke is close friend of his and this organization is to become background for reduit armament industry with major part of work underground. Alpberg endeavoring arrange for general manager of Steyrwerke to come Suisse.

7. Alpberg stated one of top Nazis in Hitler inner circle claims powerful secret weapon to be applied in next few days. Alpberg believes that unless this happens within next week we can write it off as mere bluff of Hitler's to keep waning fighting spirit of Nazis.

8. London's #710 and #747 carefully noted. Agree this type of source requires utmost caution and am handling exclusively through cutout.

Document 5-99

Telegram 8717, April 14, 1945

[Swiss intelligence reported the location of a key German radio transmitter in Bavaria.]

Report B-2448, source 511, B-2, April 8. German central radio station servicing transmitters of German foreign agents camouflaged under name of Havel Institute, now located in Bamberg, Bavaria. Quartz crystals used. Capture of Bamburg transmitter would make it impossible to provide foreign agents with new modulation and crystals, thereby paralyzing communications with German foreign agents.

Document 5-100

Telegram 8787, April 17, 1945

[OSS Bern continued to relay reports on the situation in the Balkans.]

Following via 477 from source whole [who was?] at Zagreb about week ago.

Miura, Jap chargé at Zagreb, has been working for Russians. He was slated for Bratislava last year but Tiso Government refused exequatur having some knowledge of his activities.

2. Micko, formerly in Tiso's Slovakian diplomatic service, has arrived Suisse to join staff of Kopecky, long Czech representative here and now appointed Czech Minister to Suisse. Micko claims to have long been working for Slovak resistance and for Kopecky while holding post under Tiso.

3. Pavelic endeavoring curry favor with Macek by protecting him against Germans in the hope future protection from Macek.

4. Source confirms Russian intentions to reach Trieste first; they plan to pass through Carinthia, Slovenia, north of Zagreb in order to isolate Croatia from West and to avoid misunderstanding with Tito possibly incident to Russian occupation of Croatian territory.

Document 5-101

Telegram 710 to Caserta, April 18, 1945

[This telegram indicates Dulles's position with regard to Operation Sunrise in the context of U.S.-Soviet relations.

He also urged that the Sunrise negotiations be continued even if Wolff's sincerity was not above question. One objective cited was the elimination of a German reduit strategy by neutralizing the divisions in Italy.]

Glavin from 110 for Nicholson, info 109, Gamble.

1. I found your 663 [633?] when I returned from Paris. 476 fully understands viewpoint expressed your para 3. Subsequent developments also render his trip quite out of question.

2. While Critic's trip north will make us doubly circumspect in any Crossword

contacts, there still remains interesting intelligence possibilities. Also suggest you give consideration following points.

3. It seems obvious and from their viewpoint natural that Russians should do everything possible to block realization of Crossword. Its success would mean that our forces Italy would probably be first to occupy Trieste, which from various indications received here now constitutes an even more important objective for Russians than Berlin. If Crossword or something like it fails and German retreat fighting to Adige line, then in all probability Russians will reach Trieste ahead of us. In my opinion this largely explains Russian susceptibility re Crossword about which I obtained additional info when in Paris.

While I realize we will deal openly and fairly with our Russian allies, this should not preclude us from doing everything possible to bring about quick surrender which would save the lives of our troops and bring us into the heart of German reduit.

Whatever may be game which Critic is playing and whether this be with full connivance Hitler, Himmler, should we not still work to effect unconditional surrender of Germans in North Italy, keeping our eyes open to all pitfalls incident to having any contact with man who comes from Hitler, Himmler HQ.

German forces North Italy will shortly be faced with alternative of surrender to our forces or to Russians possibly scrambling back into reduit if transportation still exists. Majority of these forces will probably prefer to surrender to us rather than accept either of other alternatives.

4. Now that Germany is cut in two and assuming as our reports indicate that Emperor is commanding forces in southern Germany it seems not entirely excluded that there might be common action by Emperor or Glazier Critic combination which would help checkmate any reduit possibilities. Our previous report, if true, that Emperor had recently telephoned Critic may throw some light on this.

5. Any comments you may have on foregoing for my guidance would be greatly appreciated.

Document 5-102

Telegram 8887, April 18, 1945

[Various German civilian agencies of government also contemplated separate surrender. Dulles was willing to make contact, as in the case of the German foreign radio broadcast monitoring unit.]

From 110. B-2536. From source Shaedler with whom we have been working for some time learn that Sonderdienst Seehaus (German unit for monitoring foreign broadcast) which formerly at Wannsee was evacuated on a special train and on 15 April was on siding near Kaufbauren southwest of Munich. Personnel of train divided whether to drive to meet advancing American forces and surrender or take train into reduit with view establishing from there clandestine contact with us. Our contact claims to be in direct touch with Albrecht, head of Sonderdienst Seehaus, and went to Feldkirch to meet him.

We are following up and endeavoring to arrange direct radio contact with train. Please advise whether you have anything on Albrecht or Sonderdienst Seehaus.

Albrecht stated that he was in contact with Minister Ruehle, Chief of Ueberrundfunk Politische Abteilung of German Foreign Office who evacuated to Lauterbach and is potential member of opposition.

Document 5-103

Telegram 22949 from London, April 18, 1945

[This message was a composite of two telegrams from Bern on Sunrise developments. It was relayed to Washington at the request of General Donovan.]

"SUNRISE. Glavin from 110. Crossword for Nicholson, information 109. . . . Parrilli's report follows:

1. Critic's letter to Himmler was read by Parilli and then dispatched by Sturmbannfuehrer Sayle . . . who flew in Fieseler Storch from Sirmione to Bolzano thence by fighter to Munich and from there by larger plane to Berlin. He reached Berlin 1700 hours 15th and delivered letter as confirmed by phone. Parilli then returned Milan. Both Hitler, Himmler at or near Berlin.

2. 0700 hours 16th Rauff called Parilli to Fasano where Wenner told him that after receipt of Critic's letter, Himmler had called Critic several times and Critic had left for Berlin via Munich. Last news confirmed its arrival Munich 1000 hours 16th. No confirmation arrival Berlin.

3. Wenner was given message by Critic for 110 via Parilli that he Critic was going as he thought there was chance do something for entire German people. He expected return 17th.

4. Critic ordered Zimmer to await news at Chiasso frontier and check periodically at Fasano Hq.

5. From 110: It appears that Himmler may now either eliminate Critic or attempt to use him to help Himmler himself establish some contact. I shall naturally refuse to have anything to do with latter alternative. Possibility that Critic might still be used to help effect general or Italian theater capitulation not completely excluded."

"SUNRISE. Glavin from 110. Information: 109. More regarding . . . Sunday conference with Waibel, Husmann, Zimmer. Zimmer reported.

1. Glazier Hq. at Recoaro situated in small emplacement just east of hotel which at southwest corner of town.

2. Rauff second in command of SS under Critic in Italy now wholly in know and with Critic.

3. Order within last week by High Command Germany took territory east of Isonzo River from command Glazier, Critic and gave to Gen. Loehr. Pohl has placed all Luftwaffe personnel west of Isonzo and subsequent Critic letter to Himmler has blocked Brenner with flak to protect against entry from east. Zimmer claims only danger to surrender plan might be entrance of Loehr on Glazier flank in Isonzo area.

4. Walter Secunde living in Zimmer's house, Via Cimarosa 22. Has all necessary technical equipment. Bombings in immediate vicinity Piazza Po making life and transmission difficult.

5. Please give Nicholson copy of above. . . .

Document 5-104

Radiotelephone Transmission No. 293, April 18, 1945

[Dulles now doubted that the German reduit would be defended by any significant number of troops, or that Hitler would personally participate in an Alpine last stand.]

Germany

With the collapse of the German Western Front and with the Russian offensive in the East, there remain only a few military problems between the Allies and the end of the war in Europe. One of these is the so-called German redoubt in the Austrian Alps. I continue to feel that there is, as yet, no conclusive evidence that the redoubt will develop into a very serious military problem. This will depend upon several factors, the chief factor being whether the Germans are able to get into the redoubt an adequate number of first-class fighting troops with any fighting morale left.

As yet, there is little to indicate any large troop concentrations in the redoubt area; in fact, most of our evidence is to the contrary. There are three German forces which might fall back into the redoubt. Of these, the most considerable and the most compact is the unit of twenty or more German divisions in North Italy. The question is, first, whether this army is able to get back into the redoubt and, second, whether it desires to do so. There is in northern Italy a dramatic shortage both of gasoline and of coal required to transport over 200,000 fighting men and an almost equal number of rear-echelon supply troops, etc., from their present positions over the mountains into the redoubt. The mountain passes, such as the Stelvio, are still snow-bound, and passage is impossible. The Brenner rail and road is open from time to time only in view of our bombing attacks. The more easterly routes, particularly the Tarvisio, are precarious and likely to be shortly threatened by Russian and Tito forces. It is probable that only a fraction of the fighting forces in northern Italy could safely disengage themselves and make their way into the redoubt. There is also some question whether, in view of the news reaching them from Germany, they will be at all unanimous in their desire to make a last stand in the Austrian mountains, even if they could get there. They realize that an attempted retreat by the eastern route might mean that they would merely become prisoners of the Russians rather than of the American and British Armies. Faced with this alternative, they would greatly prefer to fall into Anglo-Saxon hands. In fact, I venture the prediction that only a small fraction of the German armies in Italy will turn out as defenders of the German redoubt.

A second possible defensive force for the redoubt are the armies which have been fighting in Hungary and defending Vienna. They are badly battered, as is evidenced by their inability to make a strong stand for Vienna. Sepp Dietrich is undoubtedly a die-hard, and he might succeed in getting some remnants of his SS Panzer divisions back from Linz into the mountain area north of Salzburg, as the relatively narrow Danube Valley will furnish good terrain for a delaying action.

Presumably Kesselring has some remnants of an army in Bavaria covering Munich and the upper Danube. These forces too could probably fall back into the redoubt if they move in time. The fighting quality of the troops left in Bavaria, however, is certainly questionable. The total of forces which might reach the redoubt from Italy, Austria, and Bavaria is probably numerically sufficient to hold this difficult mountain area for some time, assuming, as we believe to be the case, that a reasonable supply of munitions and other military supplies and food have been collected there. However, the utter hopelessness of the enterprise is so apparent that it can appeal to only the most fanatical of Nazis. Furthermore, it is likely that the Nazi leaders who look forward to forming a future underground Nazi movement throughout Germany and in the Balkans will wish to avoid having their most incorrigible members and, hence, the best elements for an underground caught in a mountain slaughterhouse where in the long run no escape will be possible. Finally, the local population in the Austrian Alps will be hostile to the Nazi invaders of their mountain and valley homes, and no maquis movement can last long without the support of the local population. The latest reports from the most excellent sources indicate that Hitler and Himmler are still in the neighborhood of Berlin. It would seem more in line with Hitler's mad psychology and Wagnerian complex to prefer to wage his last fight against the Russians on Prussian soil, rather than permit himself to be hunted down in a cave in the mountains. Hence, there seems to be a possibility that Hitler, himself, may not go to the redoubt, but will leave that retreat for certain of his followers. In this case, the military significance of the redoubt may not prove very serious.

Document 5-105

Telegram 8927, April 19, 1945

[OSS in Switzerland was concerned about the danger of a German scorched-earth policy. Donald Jones, OSS representative in Lugano (number 809), reported on local arrangements designed to head off last-minute destruction of utilities.]

809 understands that there was a conference Switzerland last week between SOE and Italian electrical interests re protection electrical installations in various Italian valleys. He reports understanding reached that CLNAI should make no accords with Germans but that private companies could do so promising some protection in cases where installations preserved and CLNAI was to respect these private deals. Have you any information on foregoing and any suggestions as to our policy?

Document 5-106

Telegram 9067, April 20, 1945

[Dulles reports another indication that the days of the Third Reich are numbered.]

For the first time since Hitler accession to power, swastika flag was not flown today over German Legation to celebrate his birthday.

Document 5-107

Telegram 9099, April 21, 1945

[The impending collapse of Nazi Germany precipitated the appearance of alleged opposition elements in Austria. This report from Hoettl and Winkler was forwarded with caution. It mentions various Austrian personalities and badly overestimates the potential of the German national redoubt.]

Report B-2551 from 110. Obersturmbannfuehrer Dr. Wilhelm Hoettl and von Winkler (latter represented to us as member of Austrian right wing resistance) have supplied following information through cutout. . . .

Hoettl's record as SD man and collaborator Kaltenbrunner is of course bad and information supplied by him to be viewed with caution, but I believe he desires to save his skin and therefore may be useful. Von Winkler made good impression but his statements to be accepted with reserve pending further check.

1. Winkler resistance group includes: Dr. Theodor Veiter, Christian Socialist; Dr. Roman Haeldmayr, Socialist, reformed Nazi, 5 years in concentration camp; Prof. Schreyvogel, left wing Christian Socialist; Dr. Rafael Spann, Nazi prior 1934, subsequently arrested for anti-Nazi activities; Dr. Walter Heinrich, National Democrat, Nazi prior 1934, subsequently arrested for anti-Nazi activities; Obersturmbannfuehrer Goettsch, Nazi until 1938 but remained in SD allegedly to assist anti-Nazi movement; Gesandschaftsrat Dr. Theodor Blahut, Conservative, in German FO. Men of foregoing group are individually in touch with various other resistance groups particularly leading men among clandestine Socialist, Social Democrat, National Democrat, Communist, and military circles. Thus Winkler himself works with Loehr, Loos, Resseguer, while Goettsch and Hoettl are in touch with Glaise-

Horstenau, Neubacher and Kaltenbrunner. Goettsch has secured safe house to shelter resistance leaders which called "Rodelhuette" located on Vomperberg opposite Schwaz in Inn Valley.

Group also worked with Cardinal Innitzer who remained Vienna and Prelat Podolf; with economic circles including Meindl of Steyrwerke which transferred to underground reduit factories. It is planned bring Meindl to Switzerland. Other important economic contacts are Werner Schicht of German Unilever, Urban, Schoeller.

2. Hoettl claims his chief concern now is to undermine reduit by: (a) coordinating resistance groups Austria, (b) contacting western Allies through Switzerland, (c) placing trusted agents in each Gau, (d) securing military information from Glaise-Horstenau, (e) establishing radio contact between reduit and Switzerland, (from 110: arrangements already completed for this), (f) sending liaison man to Gen. Loehr with radio, (g) sending liaison men to Adriatic zone, (h) organizing propaganda to undermine reduit, (i) winning over staff of Army Group Weichs.

3. Nazi Party is taking over power even from SS. This facilitated by fact that SS sent fighting front. Gauleiters under recent law become "Reichsverteidigungskommissaere," and hence take over from Wehrkreis commanders.

Bormann becoming even more powerful than Himmler. Gauleiters arranging for party members to take over arms from Wehrmacht, Waffen SS and police troops for use in reduit. Winkler remarked that his papers bearing signature of high SS official were treated with contempt by Gauleiters' men. Hence reduit will be controlled by Party not by SS. This likely to lead to conflict between Wehrmacht and SS on one hand and Gauleiters and party on other, but fact that Gauleiters are also Reichsverteidigungskommissaere means that average SS accept their orders.

4. Werewolf organization for reduit based upon SS Jagddivision Brandenburg and other SS Jagdverbaende. Chief of organization Prutzmann, military chief Skorzeny who rescued Mussolini, aided by Major Benes. Skorzeny has some 100,000 SS and reliable Wehrmacht men under his command and Hitler has ordered Skorzeny take them into reduit.

Political organization of Werewolf includes Neubacher, now at Kitzbuehl, Vessenmeyer and Altenburg, all of FO, plus various exile Quislings, Degrele, De Brinon, Mussert, Vlasov.

5. Social Democrats constitute best organized resistance movement Austria and out of this grew "05" program, but did not have time to get really organized and riddled with Gestapo agents. Catholic opposition group second most important which is growing as result of marked revival of religious feeling. Communists were unimportant, but gaining greatly in prestige as result of Russians arriving first. Austrian masses entirely apathetic, want only peace and food and will support any regime assuring these.

6. Reduit is to be taken seriously but will contain so many unreliable elements that will not hold out for long and original Nazi plans entirely upset by rapid military developments. According original plan only reliable SS, police troops and party lead-

ers were to go to reduit. This plan abandoned and strong military reduit now planned including Wehrmacht units, particularly troops North Italy, although doubtful if they can ever get there. Gen. Loehr's men Croatia are more likely to get there, plus certain Balkan groups with strong anti-Bolshevist tendencies (Mihailovich et al.), but haste such that large number of unreliable elements will get in. In general, military preparations within reduit feverishly but ineffectively prepared, with food supplies not well organized. Once reduit established, valley accesses to outside world will be blown up.

High Wehrmacht officers originally destined for reduit include: Keitel, Schoerner, Kesselring, Model, Loehr, Rendulic (Loehr and Rendulic are potential oppositional elements).

Reduit Gauleiters are: Aigruber (Upper Austria), Hofer (Tirol), Uiberreiter (Styria), Giessler (Bavaria), Schael (Salzburg) Raener (Carinthia). First 4 are radical Nazi fanatics, last 2 more reasonable. King Leopold near Salzburg and Petain on his way there.

7. Winkler reports that army group under Loehr, viz. 12 to 15 divisions and situated in triangle Agram, Esseck, Sarajevo, are looking for directives from Allies as to best way to bring war to speedy conclusion. Panzer divisions this army not serious view lack of fuel. Cossack divisions under General Panwitz are hodge-podge of refugee Russians and recruited war prisoners. Average strength of divisions not above 7,000 to 8,000. German speaking divisions 70% Austrian. Loehr realizes subversive movement in his army group, but is ignoring it and believed to be open to persuasion. Main preoccupation of army is not to fall into hands of Tito, and would prefer to fall into Anglo-Saxon hands, but may have no alternative to giving up to Russians.

Document 5-108

Telegram 9119, April 21, 1945

[On April 20, OSS Washington cabled Dulles that the Joint Chiefs of Staff had directed him to break off all contacts with German emissaries. The JCS determined that the German commander did not intend to surrender on acceptable terms, and cited "complications which have arisen with Russians." The matter was to be regarded as closed.]

SUNRISE CROSSWORD. 106 and Cheston only from 110.

1. Am taking immediate steps to carry out instructions your #5429 (OUT 9333), but here are my problems.

2. Yesterday we received message indicating final conclusions in this matter were then being reached Fasano, and Parilli who is not German emissary but anti-Fascist Italian intermediary is now on way here to advise us of results. As I have no way of stopping his journey and probably will not receive your further instructions prior

his arrival, I see no recourse but to use my judgment as to whether to receive and transmit to AFHQ and you his report which may or may not contain vitally important intelligence. In any event he is only available channel through which to communicate that contact is to be broken.

3. We have radio operator in Milan who is not an American and who knows nothing about Sunrise Crossword, but who was used to transmit intelligence from Sunrise sources and to advise movement of parties concerned. I have responsibility of extricating him and must do what is possible in accomplishing this. Abrupt break might result in complications here but will do my best to work out.

4. While it is my personal opinion that we are breaking this contact a couple of days too soon and just at moment when we could judge whether or not something can be achieved, I realize orders are orders and those who have broad overall picture must decide.

5. This contact, originally initiated for intelligence purposes, was largely developed through outstanding, competent and Allied friendly Swiss officer who has charge of Swiss intelligence work directed toward Germany, and who is rendering us vital services in matters affecting reduit. I have task of effecting break in manner not to alienate this contact which is potentially the most useful and important we have for developing work directed against reduit.

6. I shall endeavor meet foregoing problems strictly within scope of orders of JCS. As yet have received no instructions from AFHQ to modify those contained in Caserta-Bern #667 quoted in my #9109 (IN 10958).

7. Am not relaying this message to 109 or Caserta. Will leave any repetition to you if you think wise. 109 has my Bern-Caserta #710, but not Caserta reply #667.

8. In my #9109 Glazier is Vietinghoff, Nicholson is Lemnitzer.

Document 5-109

Telegram 7419 to Caserta, April 22, 1945

[Dulles informs OSS Caserta and Allied Force Headquarters (AFHQ) of his compliance with JCS instructions to terminate Operation Sunrise.]

Glavin from 110 for Nicholson . . . Information 106 and Cheston. . . .

1. Substance your point A received directly from Washington and I am taking immediate steps for full compliance. At present have no contact with Crossword personalities and Parilli only arrives tomorrow. He will be immediately informed.

2. As you know, I have never indicated that this matter was being dealt with in high quarters and have no information that others know identity of my "military advisers." I believe matter should be kept on this level and I shall advise Parilli that I have no further time to give to matter which now has dragged beyond all bounds and has failed to effect only objective we had in mind, viz., immediate unconditional surrender.

3. Swiss intelligence for their own purposes will probably desire to retain contact with Parilli et al., but over this I have no control and it is solely their concern.

4. I am taking immediate steps to endeavor to extricate radio operator from Milan. If these measures fail, we shall have to consider with you whether or not to cut off reception from him.

5. I again express my deep appreciation for your reference to our associated efforts. It has been sincere pleasure to have worked with you and McNeely on this matter, inter Armis, Silent, Critic, and Glazier, et al.

Document 5-110

Telegram 9209 to Caserta, April 23, 1945

[Operation Sunrise proved to have a momentum of its own, as German emissaries came to Switzerland before Dulles could break off contact in accordance with JCS orders. Clearly, Dulles walked a narrow line bordering on insubordination in not discouraging Swiss and Italian intermediaries, and his own assistant, Gaevernitz, from treating with General Wolff and his colleagues. Dulles also continued to report on developments in German circles, a vital and legitimate intelligence function that preserved the flickering flame of the possibility of a surrender in Italy.]

SUNRISE. To Glavin for Nicholson from 110. Information: 109, Forgan, London; 106 and Cheston, Washington. . . .

1. As reported my Bern-Caserta #7419 . . . I received and am complying with JCS and CCS instructions. I pointed out, however, that no contact existed at moment and that Parrilli was on way here.

2. I am now informed (but have not yet directly confirmed) that Parrilli arrived early this morning with news that Critic and Roettiger, Glazier's chief of staff, were arriving at frontier about 1300 hours our time with Powers. They contemplate proceeding Lucerne. I had no means of stopping this arrival or of communicating information that matter was being dropped.

3. Pending your instructions, I shall decline see Critic or Roettiger, assuming they arrive safely, but will receive and communicate to you and Washington, as intelligence, any information they may pass via our Swiss intermediaries.

4. Kindly instruct soonest.

Document 5-111

Telegram 7569 to Caserta, April 24, 1945

[Dulles now "broke off" the Sunrise negotiations, but simultaneously informed AFHQ that Wolff and an officer empowered by Vietinghoff to surrender wanted to come to Caserta to capitulate. In one stroke Dulles thus "ended" the negotiations and propelled them forward.]

SUNRISE. Glavin from 110 for Nicholson. Information 109, Forgan, London . . . ; 106 and Cheston, Washington. . . .

1. Critic, Lt. Col. Victor Von Schweinitz and Wenner, Critic's adjutant, are in Lucerne at house of Weibel.

2. Tonight, April 23, I advised Parilli in presence of Weibel and Husmann that on basis of information before us matter was no longer of interest to us and I was taking this first opportunity I had to communicate this fact to him.

3. Parrilli, whose statements were supported by Weibel and Husmann, stated that Critic and Schweinitz were prepared to proceed to our headquarters in southern Italy to conclude matters, that when they started out they believed that this was 1 of 2 alternative procedures for surrender suggested to them, other being to pass through lines but latter had been discarded as likely to lead to premature disclosure or accident, particularly in present unsettled condition of front. Weibel stated that Schweinitz had impressed him as capable staff officer who I understand had been on Kesselring's staff in Italy.

4. German text of Schweinitz powers on official stationery reads "Der Oberbefehlshaber suedwest und Oberbefehlshaber der Heeres Gruppe C Hq, den 22. April 1945. Der Oberstleutnant I. G. von Schweinitz ist von mir bevollmaechtigt Verhandlungen zu fuehren und im Rahmen der ihm von mir erteilten Weisungen fuer mich bindende zu sagen zu machen. Von Vietinghoff." Critic clearly has full powers as to SS and other troops under his command.

5. It is difficult to see clearly in this complicated matter and I only ventured to listen to their story after advising of decision in paragraph 2 because that decision was apparently predicated upon evidence then available that Germans had no intention of surrendering under terms acceptable to us. I can give no guarantee that they are now prepared to do so, but if in fact Critic and Schweinitz are ready to go to southern Italy to work out unconditional surrender this could not fail seriously to undermine German morale in Italy even if immediate surrender is not effected. Naturally, I cannot guarantee that they will go, in absence of their direct assurance, but Weibel's statement carries much weight with me as their willingness to do so. We must not overlook possibility that in view approaching crisis North Italy, Critic may want to substitute Venner as his representative with full powers.

6. I await instructions. If negative, kindly advise so that I may merely confirm that break is final and that there is no interest in having above emissaries go south.

Document 5-112

Telegram 7589 to Caserta, April 24, 1945

[This message concerns SS General Wolff's visit to Berlin the previous week and provides new information on the German side of the Sunrise negotiations and on the state of affairs in Hitler's inner circle.]

Glavin . . . from 110 for Nicholson. Information 109, Forgan . . . , 106, and Cheston. The following information given by Critic to Weibel and Husmann April 23.

1. Critic, on first day of his visit to Berlin April 18 saw first, Himmler alone, thereafter Himmler and Kaltenbrunner. Both meetings lasting many hours. Kaltenbrunner appeared well informed on Critic's 2 visits to Switzerland for which K attacked Critic furiously. As to Hitler's and his own personal future, Himmler spoke of 3 possibilities. (a) Fight it out in Berlin. (b) Retreat to northern redoubt. (c) Retreat by plane to Berchtesgaden. As to last possibility Himmler added that Hitler now did not like to fly, but might do so in emergency.

2. On second day of visit, Critic saw Hitler in a bunker about 2 hours motor ride from center of Berlin. Hitler seemed in low spirits, but not hopeless and stated substantially "We must fight on to gain time. In 2 more months the break between Anglo Saxons and Russians will come about and then I shall join party which approaches me first, it makes no difference which." Critic tried to put in a word about senselessness of further destruction in Italy to which Hitler did not react.

3. Hope to piece out this rather sketchy account of Berlin trip. Critic returned to Fasano April 19, about noon.

4. On 20th, Parilli came to see Critic at Fasano but could make little progress due to Critic's physical and mental exhaustion from journey to north.

5. On 21st Critic visited Glazier and Gauleiter Hofer to assure their following in any action he might take.

6. On evening of 22nd Critic had final talk with Parilli, as result of which British [Critic] decided to go to Suisse together with authorized representative of Glazier. During night written power for Schweinitz . . . was obtained from Glazier.

7. On 23rd Critic, Venner and Schweinitz crossed border into Suisse as previously reported.

8. Critic told Swiss that he is firmly convinced some one of inner circle of Sunrise participants is passing on information to Kaltenbrunner as otherwise K accurate knowledge of details of Sunrise cannot be explained.

9. According to information received late last night from Fasano, Mussolini is leaving Milan and will not return to his former headquarters, but take up new headquarters at Sondrio, not far from Swiss border.

Document 5-113

Telegram 767 to Caserta, April 25, 1945

[Dulles relays a report from Donald Jones, OSS representative in Lugano (number 809), of a German attempt to surrender to Americans on the local level.]

From 110. 809 advised by contact man in Como that Wehrmacht there willing to surrender at moment of collapse but wish to make surrender to us, not to partisans. Group interested in surrender claim they could introduce American officer clandestinely for purpose. They have asked 809 to meet with them to work out method of accomplishing this.

I have advised 809 to take no action pending word from you as this probably typical of many situations where Germans will endeavor induce us intervene to save them from partisans.

Document 5-114

Telegram 10137 to Paris, April 25, 1945

[This cryptic last-minute report seems to provide evidence that a Nazi redoubt was approaching reality.]

B-2612. April 20th. K-1. OKW, Himmler ordered northern reduit front be held approximately line passing through Pfaender, Lingen, Sulzberg, Hochgrat, Hoher, Ifen, Hochvogel. Field fortifications under construction along this front and in Vorarlberg, Rhine valley. German occupation of Liechtenstein principality seriously indicated. Rhine bridges along Vorarlberg Swiss frontier and approach roads from Vorarlberg to Liechtenstein principality mined on German side.

Document 5-115

Telegram 9389, April 26, 1945

[Dulles reported that, although surrender negotiations had been suspended, General Wolff was behaving in a cooperative manner and that some sort of unilateral German suspension of hostilities in Italy was a possibility.]

SUNRISE. Glavin from 110 for Nicholson, 109, Forgan, London; Cheston, Washington. . . . Weibel reports following:

1. As result of my refusal to have contact with Critic, latter returned northern Italy late evening April 25th. His return further motivated by Critic's belief that his presence northern Italy essential to control situation there, especially to be certain that his personal orders to SS forces to protect political prisoners and to avoid destruction Italian factories, power plants, etc. are complied with, according to promise given to me in March. Critic also stated to Weibel that he is facing possibility of Hitler and or Himmler suddenly arriving by air in his territory with attempt to take over command for which event he had to prepare countermeasures.

2. Schweinitz and Wenner remain at Weibel's house in Lucerne. Prior to departure Critic left for Wenner full powers written on official stationery to act and sign on his behalf. Both Schweinitz and Wenner are prepared to proceed immediately to AFHQ with powers if desired by you. They expect to remain Lucerne one or two more days before returning Italy.

3. Critic upon return will propose to Glazier issuance of joint proclamation to German forces northern Italy and South Tyrol announcing that Italian theater now

separated from German high command, that therefore independent action will be taken to end fighting, to avoid useless bloodshed, destruction and futile mountain warfare in redoubt. Proclamation to be signed by Glazier, Critic, Rahn and Gauleiter Hofer.

4. Critic will further urge Glazier to send parliamentarians across lines in spite uncertainties involved, using password Nuernberg as previously discussed. For your information, Weibel does not favor this alternative as he thinks Schweinitz particularly suited for task to go to AFHQ.

5. According to reports received by Weibel directly from Italy late last night Mussolini just had three hours conference with Cardinal Schuster of Milan re evacuation of city. Thereafter Schuster tried to contact Critic but could not find him as latter was in Switzerland.

Document 5-116

Telegram 9399, April 26, 1945

[Dulles relayed Swiss reports on the situation in Italy.]

Weibel further reports:

1. Critic reached Como this morning. Further progress impossible as all roads cut by partisans and also road from Como back to Chiasso.

2. 809 reports from Lugano that Mussolini and other high Fascist officials are trapped in Como which is still held by Fascists, but with surrounding territory in hands of partisans. As yet unable confirm independently Mussolini's presence Como.

Document 5-117

Radiotelephone Transmission No. 294, April 26, 1945

[On almost 300 evenings from the fall of 1943 to the spring of 1945, Dulles offered his observations to a growing audience of officials in the United States. This final transmission describes the scene on the eve of Allied victory in Europe.]

Germany

The last remnants of Nazi and Fascist power still cling to their link with Switzerland as the last land outlet to the outside world. The areas of contact are becoming hourly narrower and narrower. Today the valleys leading from southern Switzerland and to Italy are almost entirely controlled by Partisans, and even the main railway link, that from Chiasso to Como and Milan, is now cut. Como is still said to be defended by Fascist forces, but their position is hopeless, as they are cut off, both on the Swiss and Milan sides, by Partisans. Como is also reported to be the place of refuge of many high Fascists, and rumors have it that Mussolini is there. However, since he suddenly left Milan a couple of days ago, there is no clear evidence as to his whereabouts. In any event, Fascist Italy is fast dying, and it seems doubtful whether it will even be able to pull together her last stand in the eastern corner of the Veneto. This depends upon whether Vietinghoff's beaten forces can rally on the Adige, now that the Po is well past. This seems unlikely, as the Germans have lost the will to fight, and they prefer Anglo-Saxon prisoner camps to the alternative of falling into the hands of Tito or the Russians. Not many of the Germans appear to have any interest in joining the hodge-podge of armies that are drifting back into the reduit.

On the Swiss frontier with Germany, there only remains a part of the lake of Constance and the narrow area to the south, where one railway runs to Munich and the other through the Vorarlberg to Innsbruck. Here, in and about Bregenz, is a motley gathering of refugees of all nationalities, many of whom would like to cross the frontier into Switzerland. Laval is reported to have tried to come over and been refused. The problem of separating the wheat from the chaff among those pressing at the Swiss frontier is not easy. It is fair to say, however, that an honest effort is being made here to keep out those who are not worthy of asylum.

The case of Petain is of particular interest. If he had asked asylum here it would have presented a difficult problem for the Swiss. However, since he only asked the privilege of crossing to face trial, there was no issue. The old man had quite an enthusiastic reception from the people in the streets as he passed through Switzerland today to the French frontier to give himself up.

The whereabouts of Hitler and Himmler are still a mystery. A few days ago they were both in or near Berlin. Have they remained there, to go down in ruins, or have they got away by plane? This is a question we can't answer. With the sky patrol of Anglo-American and Russian planes in this area, the retreat by air during recent days would have been a hazardous job. It is conceivable that Hitler will just disappear and that we will never know definitely what has happened to him. This will give his fanatical followers the possibility of continuing to use his name to keep alive the underground movement.

Document 5-118

Telegram 9419, April 27, 1945

[By April 26, the Joint Chiefs of Staff had reversed their policy and decided that arrangements should be made for SS General Wolff and an associate to go to AFHQ. Donovan was instructed to tell Dulles that the Germans must depart immediately or the deal was off, and that there could be no conferences in Switzerland. The Russians had been told that the capitulation was being effected at German request and that a Russian would attend the surrender meeting. Donovan again cautioned Dulles to carry out his instructions literally.]

SUNRISE. 109 only from 110.

1. Taking immediate steps comply your #5589 (OUT 77855) and also 3 corresponding messages received from AFHQ.

2. AFHQ messages instructed send only Schweinitz and Wenner to Caserta possible because of information I gave that Critic blocked at Como. Subsequently Critic extricated himself and is now proceeding via Suisse, Buchs, Feldkirch to his new headquarters at Bolzano where Glazier is also established.

[3.] Schweinitz and Wenner here also enroute Buchs when your and AFHQ messages received. We hope to intercept them and send Schweinitz and Wenner Caserta leaving probably Saturday morning.

4. Have carefully noted your instructions. There will be no conferences here.

Document 5-119

Telegram 9497, April 29, 1945

[Jones, OSS agent in Lugano, reported the end of Mussolini.]

809 reports that Mussolini was shot at Como yesterday, strung up for populace to see and today sent Milan for similar exhibition. Among others reported shot this area Pavolini, Buffarini, Starace and Farinacci. Graziani first surrendered to one of 809's Italian employees who was en route to Milan.

Document 5-120

Telegram 7937 to Caserta, April 29, 1945

[As Fascist and German control evaporated in northern Italy, Dulles sought to put his contacts with the resistance at the disposal of OSS generally.]

Glavin and Suhling . . . from 110. Information: 109 and 154.

1. With rapid progress toward liberation North Italy consider desirable we make available to you any of our useful Italian contacts. In particular, close association we have had with CLNAI have resulted in establishing particular relationship between Committee and our service here and I myself have several good friends on Committee. They also have feeling of personal gratitude as we here were among the first to give them support, beginning 18 months ago. Naturally Parri while still ignorant of circumstances has not forgotten his liberation from Verona.

2. I would appreciate word from you re your plans for Milan, and if feasible 809 or I could meet your representative there and make available to him any personal contacts we have.

Document 5-121

Telegram 9519, April 29, 1945

[As negotiations for the surrender of German forces in Italy neared their successful culmination, OSS Bern received information from the untrustworthy Nazi Hoettl that a surrender might also be arranged for Austria. Allegedly, Kaltenbrunner, head of the Nazi security forces and intelligence, was prepared to turn on Hitler and Himmler in order to arrange the capitulation. Whatever the extent of Kaltenbrunner's intrigue, it failed to deflect Allied retribution. He was hanged as a war criminal in 1946.]

Glavin from 110. Information: Forgan, Gamble, 109 and 154.

1. View interest following may have in connection Sunrise, kindly give copy Nicholson, McNeely with information on previous Hoettl cables pointing out that this contact handled very discreetly through cut-out.

2. Hoettl has returned Feldkirch and reported to our Swiss intermediary as indicated in paragraphs 3 and 4 below.

3. Using Glaise-Horstenau and Muehlmann to assist him, Hoettl contacted following persons: Kesselring, Vietinghoff, Rendulic, Loehr and Gauleiters Hofer, Schael and Rainer. Certain of foregoing seen individually, others at recent general meeting Innsbruck which also attended by Rahn. All above mentioned persons ready for capitulation (Hoettl remarked possibly Vietinghoff will have already capitulated). Kaltenbrunner, who is most powerful figure in this area, has taken over leadership in this capitulation move and desires come to Swiss frontier to discuss matter.

4. Hoettl also stated that Kaltenbrunner had arrested Goering on Hitler's orders and that if Himmler should attempt to come into reduit Kaltenbrunner would liquidate him.

5. Apparently Kaltenbrunner is now attempting to save his skin by playing the Austrian card and wants to work out an Austrian capitulation, allegedly to prevent establishment of a reduit.

6. Swiss intermediary who extremely well informed on this area, states that Hungarian Staat-Schatz on 26 railway trucks is in Vorarlberg including much looted goods, and believes it might be possible to have this run into Switzerland for safe keeping.

Document 5-122

Telegram 9537, April 30, 1945

[The new Austrian provisional government was viewed with favor by the Austrian émigrés in Switzerland with whom Dulles had close relations.]

110 and 399 to Horton for Lamber. . . . POEN Committee here asks following be transmitted by any available means to Vienna. "To Bundeskanzler Dr. Renner, namens des oesterreichischen Komitees in der Schweiz und persoenlich als die hiessengen zertreter des Provisorischen oesterreichischen National Komitees an glueckwuenschen wir Sie und Ihre Regierungs-Kollegen herzlich zur Bildung der ersten oesterreichischen Regierung nach der Befreiung vom Nazi Joch. Wir unterstellen uns Ihren Weisungen und bitten um Instruktionen duerch die Schweiz. Der Kampf in den noch nicht befreiten Gebieten Oesterreichs geht weiter. From Anton Lindner, Doktor Kurt Grimm, Ludwig Klein, Gerhard Wieser Molden."

R&A for Horton only: Members of new government personally known to Committee which feels no better selection could have been made. 3 POEN members included and is thought new government is thoroughly representative and democratic.

Document 5-123

Telegram 9569, April 30, 1945

[This message is another indication of OSS Bern's involvement in American efforts to obtain German technology and expert personnel as the war drew to a close.]

496 advised by Air Attaché German Legation here that Professor Messerschmitt and his associate Brindlinger, latter well known to 496, are both at Bregenz and are prepared come over to us with complete plans of jet propulsion plane experimental engine and their entire experience. Understand 2 or 3 engineers with them.

As practically no time to get instructions, I am making preliminary investigations with view to passing them through here to us, assuming above information confirmed. If we do not act immediately, they will presumably fall under French control. If you see objection or have any suggestions, please advise immediately.

Document 5-124

Telegram 9649, May 1, 1949

[Even after General Wolff and Vietinghoff agreed to the surrender of German forces in Italy, the situation remained uncertain amid frantic communications between Switzerland, Caserta, German headquarters at Bolzano, and southern Germany. Only at 4:00 A.M. May 2, after the death of Hitler, did General Kesselring, Vietinghoff's superior, authorize the surrender. German forces began laying down their arms at 2:00 P.M. that day.]

SUNRISE. 109 only from 110. After every possible vicissitude, Sunrise appears again to be on the tracks with some prospect of results within next 48 hours or less.

We have been in almost hourly contact with AFHQ on all details and have had vital part in keeping up essential lines of communications, etc. We succeeded in getting Schweinitz and Wenner back to Bolzano with surrender terms signed by them and it now depends upon final acceptance and execution by Glazier, Critic, et al.

Document 5-125

Telegram 9717, May 2, 1945

[Dulles continued the process of turning over contacts and sources in northern Italy to OSS in Caserta.]

109 from 110.

1. I have sent the following cable to Glavin, "Glavin from 110. Kindly advise us soonest regarding your personnel and any city or other teams in general Piedmont-Lombardy area. We have many contacts and agents this area which should be turned over to you or dismissed if you do not want them. Also there are many other pending matters to straighten out in this area in connection our work there over many months past.

Reports from 809 indicate that CIC units in Milan etc. have been proceeding widespread arrests including certain of our trusted agents. Pending establishment your units here, 809 and his people should be authenticated with appropriate Army Command to protect our agents and work we have been doing. Please arrange this for 809 and he will take care of any of his co-workers."

2. For over 2 years we have been working North Italian field actively and have closest and most intimate contacts there in highest Italian resistance circles including Cadorna, Parri, Longhi, et al. However, we have no recent information from MEDTO regarding their plans and have been unable therefore to coordinate our work with theirs or to make plans to turn over to them our experience or agents. Our access to Milan and other adjacent points has been easy and rapid and both 809 and 441 visited there recently. Having originated, developed, and initially financed our relations with CLNAI, having rescued Parri from his Verona dungeon and having closest personal relations with Milan committee, we have influence there which it seems unfortunate not to use. Purpose of message quoted above was to ascertain MEDTO's plans so that we may better coordinate with them in order to make available for the general benefit such assets and experience as we may have here.

Document 5-126

Telegram 8237 to Caserta, May 3, 1945

[Further information on the Austrian provisional government came from Kurt Grimm, a prominent émigré lawyer who collaborated with Dulles for much of the war.]

110 to Chapin. . . . Following are Grimm's comments on provisional Austrian government. Renner is old but highly experienced and although he once believed in a Germanized Austria he has plainly changed his views as evidenced by fact Nazis had him in concentration camp for 2 years. Renner has been in touch with resistance through Sherf who is POEN socialist. Sherf was parliamentary secretary until 1934 and engineered cooperation between all resistance elements which culminated in POEN. Buchinger is old popular peasant leader who was often minister before '38; expert parliamentarian and agriculturist. Heinl served frequently as Minister of Economics and Transport; his age and conservatism are largely offset by his popularity especially in Christian Socialist circles. Boehm is popular Viennese union leader never before in politics who was jailed until recently. Winterer is believed to have been leader of workers sports program and if so is entirely sound and good organizer. Gen. Koerner was leader of Republican Schutzbund, the army socialist organization, and is absolutely reliable. Kunschak is very popular left wing Christian Socialist who understands new trends despite age. Raab was president of Gewerbebund which should qualify him for important responsibilities as Christian Socialist and POEN member. Koplenik, Fischer and Steinhardt all were in Moscow for some years and have full confidence of Russians.

Document 5-127

Telegram 9769, May 3, 1945

[With the ink scarcely dry on the Sunrise agreement, Dulles informed Donovan that he was now considering steps to induce the surrender of German forces in Austria.]

109 from 110. Expect proceed Caserta today with 476, returning Bern or Paris from Caserta probably within 48 hours, unless further work develops from Caserta trip. Have in mind as possible important objective Army Group Loehr and believe that through Sunrise contacts we might do something here. Russian angle renders matter complicated and of course will take no action unless under instructions approved by AFHQ.

Document 5-128

Telegram 15389 from Paris, May 6, 1945

[Dulles reported to Donovan on the conclusion of Operation Sunrise (Crossword).]

1. 476 and I arrived Paris last night after 36 hours Caserta where we received most enthusiastic reception from the Field Marshal and Generals McNarney, Morgan, Lemnitzer and Airey, and thanks to organization for successful carrying through of Sunrise Crossword. We also advised with them on certain final steps incident to

effort being made by Kesselring to get on same bandwagon and to arrange contact with Eisenhower through channels which we had set up for Crossword.

2. Believe Crossword now can be considered as completed. As this is a rather unique example of type of services which OSS can supply and results which can be achieved thereby, 476 and I propose prepare and send you detailed history from inception of this project over 2 months ago. This will include certain details which heretofore not included in any cabled or written reports.

3. Substantial share of credit this operation goes to ex-PW young Czech W/T operator borrowed from Henry Hyde whom we infiltrated first Milan and then Bolzano and who kept up under most difficult conditions direct radio contact from Wolff Vietinghoff headquarters to Alexander headquarters via OSS headquarters Caserta. Latest messages this little fellow sent through these channels were addressed "to Eisenhower through Alexander from Kesselring" in addition to almost hourly messages from Wolff to Alexander, etc.

4. Solely for the record, following is text of cable which I received from AFHQ signed Lemnitzer dated 2 May just before our departure for Caserta. The statements therein should be attributed to the organization rather than to particular individuals. "Heartiest congratulations results Crossword. Has been complete and tremendous success. You and your associates may well be proud of splendid part you all played in epoch-making events which occurred today. My admiration for your loyalty and devotion to duty during these recent difficult weeks equalled only by pride which is mine for having privilege and pleasure of participation with you in this operation which spells end of Nazi domination in Europe."

5. Following telephone conversation with General Bedell Smith this morning 476 and I shall report to SHAEF forward tomorrow morning. O'Malley will accompany us and I shall take advantage this opportunity to expedite certain matters in connection German unit and try secure definite approval location our first headquarters in Germany. From SHAEF will proceed Switzerland via Heidelberg as General Harrison, G-2 6th Army Group, has asked to see me.

Document 5-129

Telegram 9857, May 8, 1945

[As the war in Europe ended, Dulles prepared to turn over his Bern position to Robert Joyce and proceed to Germany to head OSS operations under the occupation regime. Two months would pass before his new assignment came into effect.]

109 and 154 from 110.

1. Returned Bern today after conferences Paris with Forgan, Gamble and various members German unit, particularly Wisner and his SI colleagues. I feel that SI unit under Wisner direction is moving forward very satisfactorily and personally am delighted with Wisner.

2. Yesterday at SHAEF Forward Forgan, O'Malley and I had satisfactory talk with General Clay which Forgan will follow up in Paris.

3. Also at SHAEF Forward had follow up discussion with one of McSherry's deputies, and last night Heidelberg with Colonel Parkman, G-5 of 7th Army and made arrangements to send personnel from here to G-5, particularly Munich area.

4. I plan shortly take week's vacation during which will write up Sunrise and then turn over to Joyce and proceed Germany in about 2 weeks. Had satisfactory conferences Paris with both Joyce and Hyde about future work here.

Epilogue

Following the end of hostilities in Europe, Dulles visited Italy in regard to the aftermath of Sunrise and sought in vain for remnants of the Ciano diaries. Press reports concerning Sunrise, some relatively accurate, began to appear within days. They were a matter of concern for Dulles and the OSS because they threatened to compromise Swiss sources and in one case gave undue credit to the British. Dulles and Gaevernitz completed their classified report on the operation on May 22.

On June 23, 1945, the OSS sent two similar, highly favorable reports summarizing the wartime activities of Dulles and OSS Bern—one to President Truman and the other to the Joint Chiefs of Staff. Commissioned by Donovan and based in part on testimony from Dulles, these reports were intended to portray the organization at its best in a period when it was fighting for its postwar institutional life. The reports are filed in Entry 99, Box 18.

Dulles expected to head an OSS German Unit going into occupied territory immediately but was required to remain in Switzerland until July, when he became head of the OSS mission in Germany. The reasons for the delay are unclear, but problems with the U.S. Army, the Red Army, or the OSS bureaucracy and General Donovan could have been involved. Robert Joyce took over day-to-day management of OSS Bern in early June. Dulles busied himself with loose ends and matters of intelligence transition to a peacetime footing. This included personnel questions concerning those who had served under him and were now leaving Switzerland, and the transferring or terminating of agents in such areas as northern Italy.

From May to August 1945, while Dulles remained in Bern and after he moved to Germany, a series of significant negotiations occurred in Switzerland involving

Japanese representatives and the OSS. The talks originated through contacts between Friedrich Hack, an expatriate German with extensive ties in Tokyo, and Gero Gaevernitz, Dulles's top aide, and were followed by communications through Japanese naval channels in which Japanese representatives in Switzerland sounded out high authorities at home about surrender terms. The peace-minded Japanese in Europe were particularly interested in dealing with Dulles because they were aware of his role in the surrender of the German armies in Italy. Extensive discussions occurred between the Japanese and Per Jacobsson of the Bank of International Settlements in Basel. The Swedish official informed Robert Shea, OSS officer on the scene, about the progress of the talks. By July, "Palladium Project" had evolved to the point where the local Japanese Minister, Military Attaché, and top banker were corresponding with high officials in Tokyo on the possibility of surrender. The Americans made no promises, but under instruction from Washington, Dulles visited the Potsdam Conference to report to Secretary of War Stimson on the contacts. He indicated that the Japanese wanted to surrender if they could retain the Emperor and their constitution to maintain order. Events, of course, intervened. The United States used the atomic bomb, and the Soviet Union declared war against Japan. On August 10, Dulles cabled Headquarters that the "elimination of Moscow as contact point . . . may enhance importance of Swiss group as a channel of communication if Japs decide to accept unconditional surrender. Russian action plus atomic bomb should also have result in bringing some early action unless Japs decide to commit national harikiri as is possible" (Tel. 154 from Berlin, Entry 88, Box 151). As it turned out, the Swiss channel had no role in the surrender process, but could have assumed enormous importance had events in the Far East evolved differently.

While still at Bern, Dulles continued to devote attention to the role of OSS in the occupation of Germany. He sought to recruit U.S. scientists and other specialists who could help gather intelligence. Dulles and OSS identified Germans with good records who could serve under the occupation regime. He supported Gaevernitz and other wartime contacts that he knew had served the Allied cause. Some of his assistants, particularly Gisevius, later testified for the prosecution at the Nuremberg war crimes trials. OSS Bern transferred a number of anti-Nazi Germans who had aided Allied intelligence to OSS in Munich in June. Such individuals were known by the generic term "crown jewels." They included Wilhelm Hoegner, Baron Michel Godin, Fritz Leibrecht, Philip Keller, and Eduard Waetjen.

On June 29, Dulles informed Washington that he planned to take Mildred Gasser, his personal secretary, with him to his new assignment in Germany. He signed over to Robert Joyce on July 6, and was in Germany the following day. Gerhard Van Arkel, his wife Ruth, and his secretary, Erika Glaser (Noel Field's adopted daughter), transferred from Switzerland with Dulles. During July, August and September, Dulles served first at the headquarters for the American Zone in Germany (AMZON) in Wiesbaden and then in Berlin.

Documentation on Dulles's activities as Chief of the OSS Mission in Germany is fragmentary, but cable traffic indicates that he continued to concern himself with matters of transition, budget, and the organization of peacetime intelligence; identification of individuals, documentation, and resources useful for intelligence-gathering in Europe; and at least some collection of intelligence in the Soviet zone and Poland. He apparently had oversight responsibility for intelligence activities in Austria, Czechoslovakia, and Switzerland, as well as Germany. He made side trips to Czechoslovakia in August and London in September.

The incomplete record of the period seems to indicate that the OSS in Europe made Soviet activities a new primary intelligence target almost instinctively, without any comprehensive directive from above. Stations in AMZON and Berlin reported on Soviet excesses and their capture of sources and materials coveted by the Western services. Although Dulles does not appear to have been operationally involved, networks were established to the east. The Hoettl network into the Balkans was not incorporated into Allied intelligence. Rather, the United States, with the concurrence of Donovan and Dulles, helped the Soviets roll it up.

Dulles's colleagues during this period included Frank G. Wisner, head of SI in Germany; Lieutenant Commander Richard M. Helms, who coordinated SI production in Berlin; William D. Suhling who succeeeded Dulles as head of the German mission; Harry Rositzke; and former Bern hands Gaevernitz and Stalder. From Germany, Dulles interested himself in the postwar affairs of many of his Bern contacts, including Josef Wirth, Vaclav Hradecky (the Czech radio operator in Italy), Fritz Kolbe, General Wolff's family, Eduard Schulte, the von Hassel family, Struenk, Gisevius, Gafencu, Visser 't Hooft, Walter Bauer, and Max Waibel, among others. Kolbe ("George Wood") was in a serious auto accident in Berlin on August 8. Dulles arranged for his recuperation in Switzerland at U.S. expense.

President Truman abolished OSS on September 20, 1945, effective October 1. Headquarters informed missions still active that they would henceforth be part of the War Department under Assistant Secretary John McCloy (Circular tel. 12335, September 27, 1945, Entry 134, Box 192). On October 3, Dulles cabled General Donovan and General Magruder, who became chief of the Strategic Services Unit (SSU), the successor to the operational elements of OSS, that he was doing everything possible to hold together a working nucleus to carry forward intelligence activities (Tel. 3717 from Berlin, Entry 90, Box 4). Dulles left Germany on October 10, and after spending two weeks in Bern returned to the United States.

Back in Washington, Dulles assisted General Magruder in setting up the SSU and lobbied for the establishment of a permanent national central intelligence organization. He cabled principal missions in Europe on November 21: "Since my arrival here week ago I have been working with General Magruder and consulting with key persons State War Navy Departments regarding organization of Central Intelligence Agency. Real progress is being made and urgency of matter is generally appreciated. Program now being worked out by an interdepartmental committee on which majority of members favor general set up along the lines General Magruder is advocating. It is not possible as yet to predict final outcome or whether conclusion will be reached prior year end but some solution prior January 1 is a reasonable possibility" (Tel. 35757, Entry 134, Out Bern, D-27). Hopes for intelligence unification faded, however, and the influence of the military prevailed. In January 1946, President Truman created a weaker, decentralized system built around the coordinating mechanisms of the National Intelligence Authority and the Central Intelligence Group. The Central Intelligence Agency, for which Dulles campaigned, did not emerge until 1947.

On December 10, 1945, just before resigning from the U.S. Government, Dulles wrote Gaevernitz who was still in Switzerland. "I hope this letter will reach you before Christmas and bring my remembrances," he stated. "This will be my first Christmas in the last four out of Switzerland and I remember particularly our first Christmas together in December 1942. . . . It is my present intention to return to private life and law practice on January 1. Several opportunities in other directions were presented but the sands were too shifting to offer any firm foundation or assurance of ability to do constructive useful work. . . . The future of the Central Intelligence Agency is problematical. I have faith that it will eventually be established but I am less optimistic as to whether it can get going properly within the next two months. . . . Meanwhile, however, I am toying with the idea of writing a comprehensive report or possibly even a book on July 20" (Allen Dulles Papers, Box 21). The result was *Germany's Underground*, published in 1947, the same year the Central Intelligence Agency, with Dulles's input, came into existence.

On July 18, 1946, President Truman awarded Dulles a Medal for Merit. The accompanying citation read in part as follows: "Allen W. Dulles for exceptionally meritorius conduct in the performance of outstanding services as chief of the foremost under-cover operations conducted by the Office of Strategic Services. . . . Mr. Dulles . . . effectively built up an intelligence network employing hundreds of informants and operatives, reaching into Germany, Yugoslavia, Czechoslovakia, Bulgaria, Hungary, Spain, Portugal, and North Africa, and completely covering France, Italy, and Austria. He assisted in the formation of various Maquis groups in France and supported the Italian partisan groups both financially and by pinpointing airdrops for supplies. The exceptional worth of his reports on bombing targets and troop movements . . . was recognized. . . . Mr. Dulles by his superior diplomacy . . . built up for the United States enormous prestige among leading figures of occupied nations taking refuge in Switzerland. . . . His courage, rare initiative, exceptional abilities, and wisdom provided an inspiration for those who worked with him and materially furthered the war effort of the United Nations" (Allen Dulles Papers, Box 19).

Abbreviations, Acronyms, Code Names, Cover Names

AA	Auswärtiges Amt, German Foreign Ministry
AAI	Allied Armies in Italy
Abwehr	German military intelligence
Acropole	Executive Committee of the Lorraine Group
AFHQ	Allied Force Headquarters (Caserta)
AG	Army Group
Agnes	Patio
Alden	Hungary
Alessandri, General	Trabucchi
Allad	Japan's Ambassador to Moscow
Alpberg	Wilhelm Hoettl
Alpha	Leobe; also Parodi
Ames	A paid agent
AMGOT	Allied Military Government of Occupied Territories
AMZON	American Zone of Germany
Anatole	Franc Snoj
Anderson	Royall Tyler
Angus	Yugoslavia
Anna	Nazi cover name for Hitler's headquarters
Ante, Anty	OSS labor contact in New York (Luigi Antonini?)
Antoine	French labor/resistance leader
Antoinette	Captain Marcel Pichon
Apotheme	Agent in French/British SOE operations
Apple	Otto Abetz, German ambassador in France
Aprilka (APRILKA)	Indicator for Kappa messages transmitted April 1945
Aramis	General Stephen Ujszaszy
Argus	OSS representative in Spain
Arias (Arius)	Bulgaria

AS	Armée Secrète (French resistance)
Attom	Ferruccio Parri, aka General Maurizio
Axe	A German businessman
Azur (Asur)	French CER delegation in London
Azusa (AZUSA)	Designation for atomic energy intelligence material
Baker Street	SOE headquarters in London
Bakus	Indicator for a category of information on Germany, 1943
Balagny	Pierre de Leusse
Barres	Pierre Guillain de Benouville, number 642, aka Lahire, Duroc, and Maroyer
Barry	Source on Hungary, Italy. Number 646, aka Clive (Leopold Baranyai)
BBC	British Broadcasting Corporation
BCRA	Bureau Central des Renseignements et d'Action; intelligence and sabotage arm of the Free French movement
Bearcat	Wolf Heinrich Graf von Helldorf (aka Bobcat); also Willard J. Beaulac
Behr, Mr.	Ignazio Silone, number 475, aka Frost, Len, Tulio
Beki	Number 663
Ben	Maximilian Hohenlohe, number 515; also Buroff, number 504
Bertrand	Colonel Marcel Descour
Beta	Colonel Georges Revers
Bin	Number 661
Birds	OSS infiltration missions—Sparrow, Redbird, etc.
BIS	Bank of International Settlements
Black Series	Kappa messages dealing with the Balkans (1944); also bogus reports from the Vatican
Blew	Frederick R. Loofbourow
Blue	Sweden in 1943 Kappa messages
Blue-White	Indicator for messages dealing with certain German resistance elements
BO	Battle order (order of battle)
Boatman	René Charron (number 492)
Bobcat	Helldorf, the Police Chief of Berlin (aka Bearcat)
Bones	Swiss Intelligence (number 511)
Bonty	Kappa indicator for Lisbon
Boston Series	Mimeographed intelligence reports based on George Wood / Kappa information
Brake	Henri Frenay (number 517)

Breakers (BREAKERS)	German opposition group involved in July 20, 1944, attempt on Hitler's life; indicator for telegrams on the German opposition
Brine	Code name for reports from Rhine bargemen
Broadway	British intelligence in London (MI-6 headquarters)
Brown	Indicator for Kappa cables on Spain
Bujce	Thomas Cassady (number 930, aka Climax)
Bureau Ha	Semi-official Swiss intelligence service headed by Captain Hans Hausamann
Burns	Allen W. Dulles, 1942–43
CALPO	Comité de l'Allemagne Libre pour l'Ouest, the Paris branch of the Soviet-sponsored Free Germany Committee
Cantab	W. Arthur Roseborough (number 235)
CAPS	An intelligence network in Geneva reporting to OSS
Carib	F. L. Mayer
Carte	André Girard, aka Trump
Cassia	Anti-Nazi underground group in Vienna
Castle	Indicator for messages dealing with the German threat to Switzerland
CCS	Combined Chiefs of Staff (U.S.-U.K.)
C&D (CD)	OSS Censorship and Documents Branch
CE	Counterespionage
Cello	Josef Deniffel
CER	Paris Executive Committee of the French resistance
CFLN	Comité Français de Libération Nationale
CGT	Confédération Générale du Travail
Cheval	Georges Rebattet
China	A source reporting to OSS in Basel
Chris (Cris Cross)	A messenger service between Switzerland and northern Italy
CIA	Central Intelligence Agency
CIC	Counter Intelligence Corps (U.S. Army)
Cicero	Elyeza Banza, a German spy in the British Embassy in Turkey
Climax	Thomas Cassady (number 930, aka Bujce)
Clive	Important Hungarian, number 646, aka Barry (Leopold Baranyai)
CLNAI	Committee of National Liberation for Northern Italy
CN	Comité National
CNL	Committee of National Liberation
CNR	Conseil National de la Résistance
Coachman	Ernst Kaltenbrunner

Coffee	Number 87
Cok	Aka Mice
Como	A source in northern Italy
Cornet	Forest master in Oberammergau area
Cousins	The British, "our cousins"
Cris Cross	An intelligence network / messenger service in northern Italy
Crispin	A German socialist residing in Bern
Critic	SS General Karl Wolff
Crossword	British designation for Operation Sunrise, negotiations for the German surrender in Italy
Crown Jewels	Germans deemed to be important for postwar purposes
The Cub	Hans Bernd Gisevius, number 512
Culber	Hans Bernd Gisevius, number 512
Curate	Daniel McCarthy
DAF	Deutsche Arbeitsfront, Nazi labor organization
Dafoe	France
Dan	Massimo Magistrati, Italian Minister in Bern; number 812
David	Didier, French resistance member
DCA	Antiaircraft artillery
Della	Sardelli
Delta	Colonel Navarre
Demerest	General Oberst Loehr
D'Etat	Indicator for certain telegrams sent via State Department channels
Deuxième Bureau	French Intelligence Service
DF	Direction finding
Diana	Franz Josef Messner
Diane	Dolbeare
DNB	Official German news agency
DOC	A category of Kappa material indicating documentary source
Dogwood	Alfred Schwarz
Drum	An indicator for certain OSS messages from Bern, 1942–43
Drumbee, Harold	Pseudonym of an Italian opposition figure; number 638
Dulac	An Austrian with ties to railway workers
Dumont	Aka Doru; number 650
Dunoyer	General Davet, number 516, aka René
Duroc	*See* Barres
Dusty	Maria Oitana
Ecdar (ECDAR)	Indicator for telegrams concerning Edda Ciano and the Ciano diaries

Eclair	French resistance figure
Elmer	Elmer Davis, Director of the Office of War Information
Emperor	Field Marshal Albert Kesselring
Epaminondas	An independent intelligence service made up of former French intelligence officers
Epsi	Senator Pierre de Chambrun
Eta	General Friedrich Olbricht
ETNA	An OSS-Navy psychological warfare program to exploit bomb psychosis in Germany
ETO	European Theater of Operations
ETOUSA	European Theater of Operations, United States Army
Eureka	A category of intelligence material concerning bombing targets
Eva	New York correspondent with French resistance figures in Switzerland
Fat Boy	Reichsmarschall Hermann Goering
Feltre	Viteliano Paduzzi, resistance figure in northern Italy and OSS source; also an intelligence network
FER	A CER service
FFI	Forces Françaises de l'Intérieur
FHQ	Führer Headquarters
FIDES	OSS field detachment headquarters in Paris, 1944–45
Flash	Allen Dulles evening radiotelephone transmission
Flora	A source of atomic energy intelligence
Flute	Professor Paul Scherrer
FN	Foreign Nationalities Branch of OSS
FO	Foreign Office
Foi	Frederic Brown, aka Tommy
Forestier	François Morin, French resistance leader
Forking	German exile in Switzerland; number 662
Fres	French resistance
Friends	British, "our friends"
Fritz	Frederick J. Stalder, number 244
Frost	*See* Behr
FTP	Francs-tireurs et Partisans
FRUS	*Foreign Relations of the United States* series
G-2	U.S. Army intelligence
G-5	Civil Affairs division of SHAEF
Gadfly	B. Homer Hall, number 949
Gamma	Dr. Walter Bauer
Garbo	War Refugee Board

Gates	Number 591
Genesis	Direct Rome-Bern communication system for Operation Sunrise
Georges, Commandant	French resistance representative in Switzerland
Gerplan	General Donovan's plan for infiltration of Germany in 1944
Gestapo	Geheime Staatspolizei; German Secret State Police
GHQ (U)	General Headquarters
Gilbert	Sunzio Weissman
Gisel	An OSS Bern agent in France
Glazier	General Heinrich von Vietinghoff
Glore	Glaise Horstenau
Gobey	Gregoire Gafencu, number 495
Goose	Via Sidoli
Gorter	Eduard Waetjen, number 670
Grand	German Foreign Ministry or German government in Berlin (Kappa series indicator)
Gray	A Kappa indicator signifying Finland
Green	A Kappa indicator signifying Italy; also an Italian opposition figure, number 664
Gregory	OSS chief in Lisbon
Grimm	Germany
Grinka	Hans Netal
Guide	Maquis
Gussy	Schoeni
Hal	Number 665
Ham	Hungarian official; number 658
Hansom	Robert D. Shea
Harem	Sukru Saracoglu (Kappa designation)
Harry	Pasteur Alexandre Simovec
Harvard Plan	A German-language propaganda periodical produced in Washington and distributed by OSS Stockholm
Hawkins	A German woman in Switzerland; number 494
Hazel	Kappa indicator for Hungary
Hearn	Emilio Q. Daddario
Hermann	Otto von Hapsburg (aka Niklaus)
Hugbear	System for transmittal of unclassified press material from Bern to New York
Iceland	A category of material transmitted between Bern and Italy in 1944

ICRC	International Committee of the Red Cross
IDC	Interdepartmental Committee for Acquisition of Foreign Publications
Indigo	A French resistance contact
Iris	Delegation of the French CER resistance in Geneva; also General Davet
ISK	Militant Socialist International
Isolde	Emmy C. Rado
Itchy	Robert Bratschi
ITF	International Federation of Transport Workers
Ivan	Ivan Pavelic; number 501
Jack and Jill	A German opposition group associated with Breakers
Jackpot	Whitney H. Shepardson, head of the OSS Special Intelligence Branch
Jackson	Vladimir Miselj
Jadwin Mission	An operation designed to achieve the withdrawal of Bulgaria from the war
Jake	A source on France, number 404
Jakka (JAKKA)	Indicator for certain 1945 Kappa material
Janni	Italian source; former editor of Corriere Della Sera
JCS	Joint Chiefs of Staff
Jean Jacques	Jean Jacques Dreyfus, number 667
Jeb	A British intelligence officer in Switzerland
Jennings, Charles Baker	Fictitious name of Washington recipient of Dulles evening radiotelephone transmissions
Jerome	Michel Brault, number 296
Jerry	An Italian general
Jigsaw	Robert Wauchope
Johnston, Bertram L.	Allen Dulles when making evening radiotelephone transmissions
Jones series	Concerns military deception
Jonny	A left-wing resistance movement in Vienna
K (Kay)	An OSS contact in 1944; possibly the banker Kuyumjiiski
K	Prefix for numbers of joint U.S.-U.K. sources (Unison sources)
Kafeb (KAFEB)	Indicator for Kappa messages transmitted in February 1945
Kagust (KAGUST)	Indicator for Kappa messages transmitted in August 1944

Kam	Helped in Dutch escapes
Kamay (KAMAY)	Indicator for Kappa messages transmitted in May 1944
Kappa (KAPPA)	Indicator for messages containing information and documents obtained from the German Foreign Ministry by Fritz Kolbe ("George Wood")
Kapril (KAPRIL)	Indicator for Kappa messages transmitted in April 1944
Katya	William L. Mellon
Keller, Philip	An OSS agent who penetrated Germany from Switzerland in 1945
Kiss	Gheorghi Kiosseivanov, Bulgarian Minister in Bern; number 491
Kobler	Hans Broga
Kolog	Karl Ludwig Guttenberg
Kreuz, Leo	An anti-Nazi German banker
KWI	Kaiser Wilhelm Institute
Ladder	General Franz Halder
Lahire	*See* Barres
Lake Service	A Lausanne-Turin message network
Lamballe	André Enfière
Lando	Antonio Milano
Lapin	Indicator for certain Hugbear material
Latte	A Kappa indicator for Budapest
Lavender	A Kappa indicator signifying China
Leman	Maurice Fatio
Len	*See* Behr
Leo	An OSS officer in Washington; also George Richter, number 817; also William Hoegner
Leper	Dr. Carl Goerdeler; aka Lester
Lester	*See* Leper
Lever	Count Carlo Sforza, number 510
Lili	Member of French resistance
Lizzy	Sofia Bergamin
Longhi, Pietro	Dr. Alfredo Pizzoni
Lorraine	French opposition group based on inter-war parliamentary political parties; also Laurent Eynac
Luber	Hans Bernd Gisevius, number 512
Lucy Ring	Soviet spy ring in Lucerne
Luke	Otto John
Lulli	Paris (in December 1943 Kappa cables)

Lummy	Indicator for certain messages to and from London
Lunter	Stehle
MA	Military Attaché
MacGregor Mission	An OSS operation in Italy
Madame V	Number 666
Magro	Kappa indicator for Lorenzo Marques
Mariet	Britain
Marcus	Bloch Laine
Mare (Marri)	Communist member of the Military Committee of CLNAI
Marie	A series of Allen Dulles reports on France, beginning in December 1943
Marion	S, number 649
Maroyer	*See* Barres
Martel	Philippe Monod, number 405
Mathieu	Jacques Lecompte-Boinet, French resistance leader
Maurizio, General	Ferruccio Parri, aka Attom
Max	Iuliu Maniu; also Max Egon Hohenlohe von Lagensberg; also Jean Moulin
McNeely	Major General Terrence S. Airey, during Operation Sunrise
MEDTO	Mediterranean Theater of Operations
Medusa	A large OSS intelligence-gathering operation targeting France from Spain
Mel	A source on Germany, number 648
MEW	Ministry of Economic Warfare
Mezard	Captain Ojetti, a partisan commander in Italy
MFM	A centrist Hungarian opposition group
MI	Military Intelligence
MID	Military Intelligence Division
Midas	John C. Hughes
Mike	Max Shoop, number 284
Milit	German Ambassador in Turkey, in December 1943 Kappa messages
Mimo	An Italian partisan source
MIS	Military Intelligence Service
MLN	Mouvement de Libération Nationale
MNPGD	Mouvement National des Prisonniers de Guerre et Déportes
MO	Morale Operations Branch of OSS
Moe	Robert Bratschi, number 508
Moffet	An indicator for certain cables to and from Bern in 1942–43
Mondo	An Italian opposition figure
Monte, Monty	Vanni Montana

Motta	Milan Committee of National Liberation
Motto	OSS Morale Operations in London
MUR	Mouvements Unifiés de la Résistance (French resistance)
Mutt	Raymond A. Schuhl ("Robert Salambier")
Nabors	The Germans ("neighbors" to the Swiss)
NAC	Renato C. Senise
National Gallery	The Bern master cryptonym list
NATO	North Africa Theater of Operations
Nelli	Signifies Paris in December 1943 Kappa messages
Nemo	Leon Nemanoff
Nicholson	General Lyman Lemnitzer during Operation Sunrise
Nicod	Signifies an Italian consul in Kappa cables
OBHSW	German military command for southwestern Europe
OG	Operational Group
OKH	Oberkommando des Heeres (High Command of the German Army)
OKL	Oberkommando der Luftwaffe (High Command of the German Air Force)
OKM	Oberkommando der Kriegsmarine (High Command of the German Navy)
Okrad	German General Headquarters in East Prussia
OKW	Oberkommando der Wehrmacht (High Command of the German Armed Forces)
Old	J. H. Oldenbroek
OPC	Office of Policy Coordination, CIA
Orange	A Kappa indicator signifying Bulgaria
Orlan	Antonescu
OSS	Office of Strategic Services
OT	Organization Todt
OWI	Office of War Information
Paca (PACA)	An indicator for certain Kappa messages, February 1944
Packy	Lanning MacFarland, OSS representative in Turkey; number 550
PAKBO	Anti-Fascist freelance intelligence service based in Switzerland
Pam	Micha Perez, number 401; also Nicholas Kallay
Paradise	Call name for certain Kappa cables involving the penetration of Germany
Parkel	Danilo Zelen

Passy, Colonel	Colonel André de Wavrin
Pater	MUR
PBKLY	Indicator for a series of Kappa cables, July 1944
Pedro	A partisan leader in northwestern Italy
Pegasus	Weekly confidential reports from SNCF, the French railroad system
Penni, Penny	Stands for Numan Menemencioglu, the Turkish Foreign Minister, in Kappa messages
Pente	Indicator for requests for battle order information for MID
Peslier	François Bondy
Pestalozzi	Jean Rufenacht
Mrs. Pestalozzi	Mary Bancroft
Pesterlloyd	A category of press reports
Peter	Joseph Modigliani
Phillips, Carr	An Italian opposition representative; number 639
Piano	A German patent attorney in Switzerland
Picasso	Prince Auersperg
Pink	A Kappa indicator signifying Tangiers
Plato	Edoardo Amaldi
POEN	Provisorische Oesterreichische Nationalkomitee (Austrian resistance organization)
Poppy	Indicator for certain cables to Paris
Porto	Signifies German diplomatic post in Kappa cables
Prado	Signifies Madrid in Kappa cables
Pro Deo	An anti-Axis Christian information organization operated by European exiles in the United States
Pupin	Brigadier General Barnwell Legge, U.S. Military Attaché in Switzerland; number 520
Purple	An indicator for certain Kappa cables
PW	Prisoner of war
PWD	Psychological Warfare Division
PWE	Political Warfare Executive (British)
PWS	Psychological Warfare Staff
PZ	Panzer (armor)
Quail	OSS operation to liberate the enclave of Campione
Quint	Nicholas Kallay; number 655
R&A	Research and Analysis Branch of OSS
Rag	Robert Grimm
Ragon	Signifies Istanbul in December 1943 Kappa cables
Ralph	Erwin Respondek

Randy	Rheinhaben
Ratier	A French intelligence officer in Switzerland who worked closely with OSS
Raz	A source in Basel
Red	Signifies France in December 1943 Kappa messages
Redbird	An OSS plan to establish contact with the Austrian resistance
Regis	Reginald Foster
Remus	Morris "Moe" Berg
René	General Davet; number 516
RF	SOE section dealing with the Free French movement
Rhythm	William A. Kimbel; number 116
Rick	Giovanoli
Ringer	Field Marshal Maximilian Freiherr von Weichs
Risler	General Friedrich Fromm
Robin	Vittorio Emanuela
Rocky	A person involved in Breakers
RR	Railroad
RSHA	Reichsicherheitshauptamt, a German intelligence service; absorbed the Abwehr in April 1944
Rudi	Bauer-Katz
SACMED	Supreme Allied Commander Mediterranean
Saint (SAINT)	OSS indicator for messages concerning security and counterintelligence
Sanders	Evert Smits; number 843
Sandy	An OSS official in London
Santu	Aka Jouglu
Scarlet	Signifies Japan in Kappa cables, January 1944
Schubert, Shubert	An indicator for a category of messages to and from Bern, 1942–43. *See also* Moffet and Drum
Scotti	Donald Jones, OSS representative in Lugano
SD	Sicherheitsdienst
Sedgwick	Dr. Ernst ("Putzi") Hanfstangl
SF	Swiss francs
Shaedler	A source on Germany
SHAEF	Supreme Headquarters Allied Expeditionary Force
SI	Secret Intelligence Branch
SIM	Servizio Informazioni Militare, the Italian military intelligence service
Simmons	Indicator for certain cables on German guided bomb program
Simpson	A Czech or Polish source; number 498
SIS	Secret Intelligence Service (British)

Smith	A source reporting to the U.S. Consulate in Basel
SKL	Seekriegsleitung, German Naval Ministry
Smokey, Smoky	Alan Sciafe
Snafu	Indicator for certain messages on military matters
SNCF	Société Nationale des Chemins-de-Fer Français, French national railroad organization
SO	Special Operations Branch, OSS
SOE	Special Operations Executive (British)
SONJ	Standard Oil of New Jersey
Sorel	Slovakia
Sparrow (SPARROW)	OSS operation for the penetration of Hungary
Spinster	A French source in Geneva; number 284-H
Spirit	Geneva
SR	Service de Renseignements, the prewar French intelligence service
SS	Schutzstaffel armed wing of the Nazi Party
SSU	Strategic Services Unit
Stanislas	Number 499
Steel	Constantin Vulcan; number 636
Steve	Steigmeier
Stork	Gerhard Van Arkel
Sunrise (SUNRISE)	Negotiations for the surrender of German forces in Italy
T Force	OSS unit organized to enter Berlin upon its liberation
Tab	Abbé Journet, professor of theology at the Grand Séminaire de Fribourg
Tavernier	Henri Frenay
Taylor, Willard	OSS representative in Stockholm
Teba (TEBA)	Indicator for Kappa messages based on a letter received from George Wood, March 1944
Ted	Eduard Schulte
Tertius	A senior OSS officer in London involved in special operations
Theta	General Adolf Heusinger
Tiflis	An OSS official in London concerned with Breakers
Toledo (TOLEDO)	Indicator for messages dealing with chemical and biological warfare intelligence
Tommy	Frederic Brown; aka Foi
Tony	Baron Anthony Radvanssky
Top	Zurich
Topper	Major Valla Lada Macorski

Tosar	Signifies Sofia in December 1943 Kappa messages
Trick	C. Tracy Barnes
Trude	Signifies Hungarian Lieutenant Colonel Hatz in December 1943 Kappa messages
Trump	*See* Carte
Tucky	Gen. Ludwig Beck
Tulio	*See* Behr
Turtle	Count Thurn
2677th Regiment	OSS Mediterranean Command
Ultra	German wireless messages intercepted and decoded by the U.K. and the U.S.
Uncolored	Signifies Denmark in Kappa messages
Unison	Indicator for sources used jointly by the U.S. and the U.K.
UNRRA	United Nations Relief and Rehabilitation Administration
USTRAVIC	Indicator for and recipient of many OSS messages to London
Valenti	General Raffaele Cadorna
Vessel	Indicator for a series of reports from a spurious source in the Vatican
Victor	An OSS transmitting and receiving station in England
Vinta	A Kappa indicator in October 1943 messages standing for German Foreign Minister Ribbentrop
Waldo	Signifies a German consul in Kappa messages
Wally	Vaclav Hradecky, Czech radio operator who assisted OSS in Operation Sunrise
Waner	Captain Ludwig Gehre
WD	War Department
Werewolves	Nazi organization trained to wage guerrilla warfare after the defeat of German regular forces
White	Signifies Switzerland in Kappa messages, January 1944
Wieser, Gerhard	Fritz Molden
Winter, George	Fritz Kolbe, aka George Wood
Wood, George	Fritz Kolbe, OSS agent in the German Foreign Ministry; number 674
Wood Traffic	Material received from George Wood and messages generated by it
WRB	War Refugee Board
WT, W/T	Wireless telegrapy, wireless transmitter
Wynn, Wyn	Captain Artturo F. Matthieu
X-2	SS Counterespionage Branch

Y, Mr.	Otto von Hapsburg
Yodel	A duke of Bavaria; brother of Elizabeth of Belgium
Zaccone	A source in Italy
Zeta	General Kurt Zeitzler
Zucca	An Italian partisan group and courier service
Zulu	The British

OSS Code Number Identifications

OSS numbers were assigned to more than 1,000 individuals, including OSS officials, foreign sources, institutions, contacts, outright spies, and well-known persons best not mentioned by name in cable traffic. Assignment of an OSS number did not necessarily indicate that the individual was an agent controlled by OSS.

87	Coffee
101	Baker
104	Ferdinand Lammot Belin
105	Colonel David K. E. Bruce
106	Colonel G. Edward Buxton
109	William J. Donovan
110	Allen W. Dulles
111	Thomas G. Early
112	Henry Field
113	M. Preston Goodfellow
114	Harold Guinsburg
115	M
116	William A. Kimbel (Rhythm)
117	William L. Langer
119	Captain Stacy Lloyd
120	James R. Murphy
124	Spencer Phenix
125	DeWitt Poole
128	Lane Rehm
130	Atherton Richards
131	T. S. Ryan
132	Robert E. Sherwood
133	James Warburg
136	John C. Wiley
140	Hugh R. Wilson

146	Fisher Howe
148	William B. Maddox Jr.
154	Whitney H. Shepardson (Jackpot)
158	John D. Wilson
180	Francis Burke
224	Russell D'Oench
226	Pierre Dupont
227	Charles B. Dyar
235	W. Arthur Roseborough (Cantab)
240	John A. Bross
244	Frederick J. Stalder
251	Arthur Raymond Lewis
257	Robert P. Joyce (also 1090)
284	Max Shoop (Mike)
284-A	A source with French contacts
284-B	A French network headed by an army officer
284-C	A source that headed a network in northern France
284-D	A source with contacts in France
284-E	A network in southeastern France
284-F	A network of French officers with contacts in France
284-G	The 284 network's liaison with Swiss intelligence
284-H	A source in Geneva (Spinster)
296	Michel Brault (Jerome)
300	Colonel Ellery Huntington
304	George Pratt
305	Arthur Goldberg
308	George K. Bowden
313	A source on communist and Soviet affairs
321	Evert Smits (Sanders; also 843)
328	A German, French, or Alsatian source in Switzerland with a labor/socialist background; key contact with French exiles in New York (possibly known as Antoine or René; possibly Berthelot)
331	A Swiss source
334	William A. Eddy
339	A source on Austria
356, 357, 358	William A. Eddy
387	Donald Downes
394	Noel H. Field
399	Gerhard Van Arkel
399-A	A network reporting to Van Arkel from Belfort
399-B	Certain German and Austrian internees in Switzerland
399-D	An Austrian socialist group
399-E	A counterespionage source

399-F	A counterespionage source
399-G	German socialists
399-H	A Swiss businessman
399-I	A Hungarian group
399-J	An Austrian source
399-K	A railway union source
399-N	German social democrat with German railway worker contacts
401	Micha Perez (Pam)
402	Reported on Holland in 1943
403	Reported on France in 1943
404	Reported on France in 1943
405	Philippe Monod (Martel)
406	Reported on Greece in 1943
407	Count Henri Marone
408	Reported on France in 1943
409	Mike's lady friend, L., and her group
409-B	Reported on Germany, Austria, and Alsace in 1943
410	Reported on France in 1943
411	Source on Germany and the Balkans
412	Reported to OSS in Geneva
433	Lieutenant A. Doster Jr
441	Major Valerian Lada-Mocarski
442	Captain Otto C. Doering
445	Kenneth H. Baker
450	Lieutenant Colonel B. A. C. Sweet-Escott
452	Robert D. Murphy
470	A source involved in French prisoner-of-war relief
472	Elements of prewar French intelligence located in Switzerland; sometimes used to refer to an individual
473	A French source
474	Dr. W. A. Visser 't Hooft
475	Ignazio Silone (Frost, Len, Tulio, Mr. Behr)
476	Gero von Schulze Gaevernitz
477	Royall Tyler (Anderson)
478	Josef Wirth
479	Robert Chi
480	Hans Klein
481	Louis Cruvilier
482	A source on Germany
483	A female source with an Airedale named Durban; number reassigned to an expert on Italy in 1943
484	A source reporting on Italy
485	Baron Michael Goden

486	Walter Bringolf
487	Dr. Hans Opracht
488	Dr. Carl Jung
489	Romanescu; also Donald Lowrie
490	Walter Bovari
491	Gheorghi Kiosseivanov
492	René Charron (Boatman)
492-A	A source who interviewed persons at refugee camps in Switzerland
493	Frederick R. Loofbourow (Blew)
494	A German woman in Switzerland (Hawkins)
495	Gregoire Gafencu (Gobey)
496	Maurice Villars
497	A Polish source; possibly Captain Szczesny Chojnacki, intelligence officer, Polish legation in Bern
498	An unofficial representative of the Czech government in Switzerland (Simpson)
499	A French resistance figure (Stanislas)
500	Franz Boergler
501	Ivan Pavelic
502	Prince Alois von Auersperg, German Assistant Air Attaché
503	King Boris of Bulgaria. Number reassigned to Fritz Weston, Austrian industrialist
504	Buroff, former foreign minister of Bulgaria (Ben)
505	AJ
506	Egidio Reale (Drumbee)
507	AC
508	Robert Bratschi (Itchy, Moe)
510	Count Carlo Sforza
511	The Swiss intelligence service; General Masson, chief of Swiss intelligence (Bones)
512	Hans Bernd Gisevius
513	A Polish source
514	François Bondy
515	Maximilian Egon Hohenlohe von Lagensberg
516	General Davet (René, Iris)
517	Henri Frenay (Brake, Tavernier)
518	Marcel Pilet-Golaz
519	George Barcza
520	Brigadier General Barnwell Legge
521	British intelligence in Switzerland
523	Henry Hyde
540	Lieutenant Graveson (USNR)
550	Lanning MacFarland (Packy)

555	Reported on Italy in 1944
557	Sidney E. Clark
558	John C. Hughes
591	Gates
604	Russell J. Livermore
620	A source on Germany
621	Head of British SIS in Switzerland
625	Possibly Baron Anthony Radvanssky
636	Constantin Vulcan
638	A representative of the Italian Partito d'Azione (Drumbee)
639	A representative of the Italian Partito d'Azione (Carr Phillips)
642	Pierre Guillain de Benouville (Lahire, Barres, Duroc, Maroyer)
643	Eduard Schulte
644	Thomas H. McKittrick
645	British Special Operations Executive (SOE) in Switzerland; John McCaffrey, SOE chief in Switzerland
646	Leopold Baranyai (Clive, Barry)
648	A source on Germany (Mel)
649	Marion, S
650	Dumont, a French source (Doru, M.D.)
651	Roger Auboin
652	Rist, a German source
653	Karl Weigl, a German or Austrian source
655	Nicholas Kallay (Quint)
656	Anton Krier
657	Don Juan of Spain
658	Ham
659	Admiral Wilhelm Canaris
660	Adriano Olivetti
661	Bin
662	Forking, a German source. Also assigned number K-7
663	Beki
664	Green, a well-known leader of the Italian opposition
665	Hal, a prominent German Protestant clergyman associated with the Fellowship of Reconciliation
666	Madame V
667	Jean-Jacques Dreyfus
668	Jacques La Grange (aka Jacques Vernier)
669	E.P., a reliable American source
670	Eduard Waetjen
673	Dr. Friedrich Hack
674	Fritz Kolbe (George Wood); also assigned number 805
675	A contact of 643, Eduard Schulte, in Switzerland

676	Another Schulte contact in Switzerland
677	Employed by OSS in Switzerland
678	Gerald Mayer
679	C. Tracy Barnes
680	Josef Johan
681	M. Z. D. Dragoutinovitch
682	A representative of the Partito d'Azione who came to Switzerland from Italy in September 1943
683	Another representative of the Partito d'Azione who came to Switzerland from Italy in September 1943
684	Baron George Bakach-Bessenyey
685	An Italian opposition figure who had left the cabinet for exile in the 1920s
686	Raoul Bossy
690	Ignazio Silone (also 475)
691	Reported on Nazi/Croat forces in 1943
706	An OSS officer at Bern
738	Reported on France in 1944
759	Reginald C. Foster (Regis)
760	Colonel Edward J. F. Glavin
774	Emilio Q. Daddario (Hearn)
800	Adam von Trott zu Solz
801	A prominent German Catholic
802	Devignat, French source
803	M, a backdoor channel to Swiss intelligence
804	Bombassei
805	Fritz Kolbe (George Wood); also assigned number 674
809	Donald Jones
812	Count Massimo Magistrati (Dan)
813	Jacini
814	Don Sturzo
815	Professor V. F. Wagner
816	Donald Downes
817	George Richter
820	Joseph Modigliani
821	A prominent German Catholic
822	Richard Quant
824	Professor Mooser
826	Damiani, representative in Switzerland of the Italian resistance movement Motta
827	Professor Paul Scherrer (Flute)
828	Klaus Wittig
829	John Madonne

830	Otto Braun
831	W.D., a German labor leader
832	V.B., a German labor leader
833	G.R., a German labor leader
834	Linder, an Austrian source
835	Weigl
836	Dr. Wilhelm Abegg
837	Johannes Schwartzenberg
838	Krauel, the German Consul General in Geneva
839	General Henri Guisan
840	Franz Josef Messner (Diana, Oysters)
842	Westrick
843	Evert Smits (Sanders, also 321)
844	Rakolczai, Hungarian Military Attaché in Bern
845	Jaksekovic
848	Reported on German troop movements in 1944
849	Nerdrum, Norwegian press attaché in Bern
850	Former physician to French Premier Daladier
901	Rodrigo
913	Daniel McCarthy
930	Lieutenant Commander Thomas Cassady (Climax)
945	Reported on Italy in 1945
949	Homer Hall (Gadfly)
971	Dr. Walter C. Langsam
1004	An OSS staff member in Geneva in 1945
1049	Emmy C. Rado
1090	Robert P. Joyce (also 257)
K-1	K numbers were assigned to Unison sources, sources shared with the British to avoid duplicate reporting; a French intelligence officer in Switzerland
K-2	A French intelligence officer in Switzerland; reported on Italy
K-3	A Swiss intelligence officer who provided the U.S. Military Attaché in Switzerland with battle order information
K-6	An Austrian contact
K-7	Same as 662
K-13	SIM (Italian Intelligence Service)
K-23	Headquarters of the CNL resistance movement in Milan
K-24	A German source
K-27	A category of reports from the U.S. Military Attaché's office in Bern
K-28	Fritz Molden, an Austrian source (Gerhard Weiser)
K-29	Source Navik of Basel

Certain Persons Residing in or Visiting Switzerland, 1942–1945

*Indicates U.S. government official

Abegg, Lilian (Lili)	Writer-journalist in Zurich suspected of being a Nazi spy.
Abegg, Dr. Wilhelm	Former Home Secretary of the State of Prussia; provided information to the U.S. Consulate in Zurich.
Airey, Major General Terence S.	Intelligence Chief, Allied Forces in the Mediterranean; British; visited Switzerland during Operation Sunrise.
Alessandrini	Counselor of the Italian Legation in Bern.
Alfieri, Dino	Italian Ambassador to Germany, 1939–43; fled to Switzerland in October 1943; interned at Lugano.
*Altaffer, Maurice W.	American Consul, Zurich.
Anastasiu	First Secretary of the Rumanian Legation in Bern.
Antoine [code name]	A French resistance representative; corresponded with Eva (code name) in the United States.
Auboin, Roger	General Manager, Bank of International Settlements, Basel.
Bachman, Gustave	Suspected Nazi spy.
Backes, Gert	Employee of the German Legation in Bern.
Baechtold, Paul	Chief of the Swiss Police Bureau for foreigners.
Bakach-Bessenyey, Baron George	Hungarian Minister in Bern, 1943–45.
Bally, Ernest	Cousin of Max Bally.
Bally, Max	A Swiss shoe manufacturer; corresponded with Dulles.
Bancroft, Mary	American socialite married to Jean Rufenacht, a Swiss; friend and associate of Allen Dulles; helped to translate Gisevius manuscript; resident of Zurich; aka Mrs. Pestalozzi.

Baranyai, Leopold	Governor of the National Bank of Hungary; visited Switzerland.
Barcza, George	Former Hungarian Minister in London.
*Barnes, C. Tracy	Staff member, OSS Bern, 1945.
Barth, Dr. Karl	Professor of theology at the University of Basel.
Basseches, Nikolaus	Austrian journalist, émigré.
Bauer, Leo	Left-wing German émigré.
Bauer-Katz	Left-wing émigré. Code name Rudi.
*Bell, James C.	American Vice-Consul at Lugano.
Bellia, Franco	Italian Consul in Lausanne; previously served in Ciano's personal office; helped Dulles obtain the Ciano diaries in 1945.
*Berg, Morris (Moe)	OSS officer who visited Switzerland in 1945 to gather intelligence on the German atomic energy program.
Berio, Alberto	Official in the Italian Legation, Bern.
Bernardici	Papal Nuncio in Bern.
Berruti, Dr. Luigi	Italian businessman.
Bezzola, Richard	A director of the Crédit Suisse, Zurich.
Bianchi	Italian Military Attaché in Bern.
Bielefeld	German diplomat gathering information on U.S. domestic politics.
*Bigelow, Don	First Secretary, U.S. Legation in Bern.
Bishop [cover name]	A source on German military matters.
*Bland, T. F.	An OSS funds officer in Bern, 1945.
Blattner, Doris	Associated with Minerva-Institute, Zurich; applied for employment with OSS in 1944 but not hired.
*Blum, Paul C.	Staff member, OSS Bern, 1944–45; previously served with OSS in Paris; made first contacts for Operation Sunrise.
Boergler, Franz	A German social democrat and labor leader.
Bondy, François	A French freelance journalist.
Bovari, Walter	A German businessman; a source on German military production.
*Bradford	U.S. Vice-Consul at Bern.
Bratschi, Robert	A trade union leader.
Braun, Otto	A German socialist.
Briner, Mary	An American married to a Swiss; friend of Mary Bancroft; helped to translate Gisevius manuscript; reported to Dulles on local news and personalities.
*Brown, Walter D., Jr.	Staff member, OSS Bern, 1945.
Burckhardt, Carl J.	President of the International Red Cross; former High Commissioner of Danzig.

Caracciolo di Castagnetto, Princess Margaret	U.S. citizen married to a member of the Buonomi Government in Italy.
Carlier, Father	Head of Pro Deo organization in Geneva.
Cartwright, Colonel Henry	British Military Attaché in Bern.
*Carver, Lieutenant Thomas	Downed U.S. flier. Served with OSS Bern 1943–44.
Casagrande	Anti-Fascist figure.
Castelbarco, Countess Wally Toscanini	Daughter of conductor Arturo Toscanini; acquaintance of Allen Dulles.
Charron, René	French source in Geneva; former Director of the Economic Section of the League of Nations.
*Chase, Warren M.	Second Secretary, U.S. Legation; drafted summary telegrams based on intelligence reports from U.S. consulates and other sources.
Chi, Robert	Economic Attaché, Chinese Legation in Bern.
Chojnacki, Szczesny	A Pole who served as Allied agent; served as an initial intermediary between Eduard Schulte and Dulles; cover name Jacek Lubiewa.
Ciano, Edda	Widow of Count Ciano, daughter of Mussolini; provided Ciano diaries to Allen Dulles.
*Clark, Corporal John	Staff member, OSS Bern, 1944–45.
*Coleman, Frederick S.	Staff member, OSS Bern.
*Cowan, Bob	Assistant to F. L. Loofbourow, U.S. Commercial Attaché in Zurich.
*Crittenden, Charles V.	Staff member, OSS Bern.
*Daddario, Emilio Q.	OSS officer dealing with Italian affairs from Switzerland late in the war.
Damiani	Representative of the Milan Committee of National Liberation.
Daufeldt	Resident of Lausanne suspected of being a Nazi.
Davet, General	Representative of the French resistance.
*Daymont, L. J.	Financial officer, U.S. Legation, Bern.
De Chollet, Mme. Louis	An American married to a Swiss; helped Dulles obtain the Ciano diaries from Edda Ciano in January 1945.
De Leusse, Pierre	Former French consul at Lugano; informal representative of General de Gaulle from April 1943.
*Demian, Vivian	Staff member, OSS Bern, 1945.
De Nobili, Rino	An acquaintance of Dulles.
Di Angelis, Admiral	Former Italian Naval Attaché in Berlin.
Dittman, Wilhelm	German socialist refugee in Zurich.

*Dodson, Cordelia	Staff member, OSS Bern, 1944–45.
*D'Oench, Russell	OSS staff member at Zurich; U.S. Vice-Consul at Zurich from February 1945.
Doerner, Max	A German banker.
Dollmann, Colonel Eugen	A German staff officer involved in Operation Sunrise.
Dragoutinovitch, M. Z. D.	Counselor of the Yugoslav Legation in Bern.
*Drum [code name]	Presumably an OSS staff member at Bern and point of contact for "Drum" messages early in the war.
Drumbee, Harold [cover name]	An Italian opposition figure.
*Dulles, Allen W.	Chief of the OSS mission in Switzerland.
*Dyar, Charles B.	Financial officer, OSS Bern.
Einaudi, Giulio	Member of prominent Italian liberal family; interned.
Einaudi, Luigi	Italian figure residing in Basel and Lucerne.
*Elting, Howard, Jr.	U.S. Vice-Consul at Geneva.
Field, Noel	Assisted OSS Bern in refugee affairs; relief worker, former State Department and League of Nations official; sometime Soviet agent; confidant of Dulles.
Forking [code name]	German Jew residing in Ascona; a source for Allied intelligence.
*Free, Captain Lloyd	Assistant to the U.S. Military Attaché in Bern with psychological warfare responsibilities.
Frobe-Kapteyn, Olga	Head of Eranos-Tagung, a study group in Zurich.
Fujimura, Yoshiro	Japanese Naval Attaché; key figure in peace feelers in Switzerland in 1945.
Gaevernitz, Gero von Schultze	German-American businessman; top assistant to Allen Dulles.
Gafencu, Gregoire	A Rumanian source for OSS; former foreign minister.
Garland	British consul in Lausanne.
*Gasser, Mildred	OSS staff member in Bern; personal secretary to Allen Dulles late in the war.
Gautier, Christine	A resident of Geneva who corresponded with Allen Dulles.
Georges, Commandant	French intelligence official; representative of General Koenig.
Ghali, Paul	Correspondent for the *Chicago Daily News;* involved in the procurement and publication of the Ciano diaries.
Gisevius, Hans Bernd	German Consul in Zurich, Abwehr agent, and member of the opposition to Hitler; author of a manuscript on the German resistance.
Glaser, Erika	Foster daughter of Noel and Herta Field; Communist

	connections; hired as Gerhard Van Arkel's secretary in early 1945 and went with him to Germany.
Gordon, Winifred	A resident of Lausanne who corresponded with Allen Dulles.
Grandjean, Dr. H.	General Manager of the Crédit Suisse, Zurich.
*Greco, Elinor	Staff member, OSS Bern, 1945.
*Greer, Donald	Staff member, OSS Bern, 1945.
Grimm, Kurt	Austrian expatriate lawyer.
Grimm, Robert	Prominent member of Swiss Social Democratic Party.
Guillain de Benouville, Pierre	French resistance leader who visited Switzerland.
Guillon, Pasteur Ch.	Geneva clergyman active in international relief organizations.
Guisan, General Henri	Commander of the Swiss Army.
*Gunther, Jean	Staff member, U.S. Legation in Bern; sister of author John Gunther.
Gut, Hans (Dr. Guth)	Swiss involved in negotiations with Germans who wanted to enter Switzerland in 1945; resident of Zurich.
Hack, Dr. Friedrich Wilhelm	Anti-Nazi German living in Bern; former Krupp representative in Japan.
*Harrison, Landreth M.	Second Secretary, U.S. legation; had intelligence responsibilities.
*Harrison, Leland	U.S. Minister in Bern.
Hausamann, Major Hans	Swiss intelligence officer; headed Bureau Ha, a semi-official Swiss service.
Hawkins	Associated Press correspondent.
Hawkins [code name]	A female German informant.
Hermann, Gisela	Employee of the Red Cross in Geneva.
*Hill	Staff member, OSS Bern.
Hoegner, Dr. Wilhelm	A Bavarian socialist leader in Zurich.
Hofer, Dr. Rudolf	A resident of Zurich who corresponded with Allen Dulles.
Hohenlohe, Maximilian Egon von	Sudeten German aristocrat with access both to Nazi leaders and to Allied intelligence; met with Dulles in Switzerland.
Hollitscher, Dr. Hans	A former Austrian official residing in Zurich.
*Hood, William J.	Staff member, OSS Bern, 1945.
Horn, General von	Military Attaché, German Legation in Bern.
*Hubbard, Phil H.	U.S. Consul at Zurich.
Huber, Max	President of the International Red Cross Committee, Geneva, in 1945.
*Huddle, J. Klahr	Counselor of the U.S. Legation.

Husmann, Professor Max	A Swiss intermediary in Operation Sunrise.
*Hyde, Henry	Staff member, OSS Bern, 1945; number 523.
Jacobsson, Per	An official of the Bank of International Settlements; involved in transmittal of Japanese peace feelers to Allen Dulles in 1945.
Jaksekovic, Dr.	A Croatian source in Zurich.
Jardin, Jean	Former official in the Laval Government.
Jeb [code name]	A British intelligence officer.
*Johnston, Bertram L. [cover name]	Name used to place Allen Dulles evening radiotelephone calls.
*Jones, Donald [Donald Price-Jones, Donald Pryce-Jones]	OSS representative at Lugano.
*Joyce, Robert P.	Staff member, OSS Bern, 1945; succeeded Dulles as chief of the mission.
Jung, Carl Gustav	Eminent Swiss psychologist; resident of Zurich; acquaintance of Allen Dulles.
Jungk, Bob	Czech-born, Berlin-raised freelance journalist. Provided information on Germany to Dulles and Mary Bancroft.
Jurisic, Moncilo	Yugoslav ambassador in Bern.
*Katsainos, Captain Charles	Assistant to General Legge, U.S. Military Attaché.
Keller, Philip [probably a cover name]	Agent who penetrated Germany from Switzerland in 1945.
Kiosseivanov, Gheorghi	Bulgarian Minister in Bern.
Kirschbaum, Dr. Jozef	Slovak Minister in Bern.
Kitamura, Kojiro	A director of the Bank of International Settlements; involved in late-war Japanese peace feelers.
Kocher, Otto	German Minister in Bern.
Kocherthaler, Dr. Ernesto	Assisted Allen Dulles; a go-between for George Wood / Fritz Kolbe.
Kolbe, Fritz	OSS agent in the German Foreign Ministry who brought and transmitted documents to Dulles in Switzerland; code name George Wood.
Krashevski, Stefan H.	Polish refugee.
Krauel, Wolfgang	Former German consul general in Geneva.
Krier, Anton	European labor leader.
*Kronthal, James Speyer	Staff member, OSS Bern, from mid-1945; involved in recovery of looted art; knew Allen Dulles from Sullivan & Cromwell.
Kruse	Former Danish Commercial Attaché in Berlin.
Kullman	Swiss with a connection with Noel Field.

*Lada-Mocarski, Major Valerian "Valla"	Staff member, OSS Bern.
Laracy, Darina	Secretary to Ignazio Silone.
*Legendre, Gertrude	Captured OSS officer who escaped from Germany through Switzerland in 1945.
*Legge, Brigadier General Barnwell R.	U.S. Military Attaché in Bern.
*Lemnitzer, Major General Lyman L.	Deputy Chief of Staff, Allied Forces in the Mediterranean; visited Switzerland during Operation Sunrise.
*Leslie, E. M.	Assistant to Gerald Mayer, OWI representative in Bern.
*Leslie, Nancy (Mrs. Edgewood Leslie)	Secretary to Gero Gaevernitz.
Levi, Mrs. Doro	Wife of a Princeton professor.
Lienert, Hauptmann Dr.	Police and intelligence officer of Canton St. Gallen.
Lipski [code name]	A frequent U.S. Legation source of intelligence on Germany.
*Loofbourow, Frederick R.	U.S. Commercial Attaché at Zurich and OSS officer; on leave from Standard Oil.
Lowrie, Dr. Donald A.	World YMCA representative in Geneva; frequent source of intelligence for OSS and the U.S. Legation on relief matters and the Nazi persecution of the Jews.
*Ludwig, Helen	Staff member, U.S. Consulate in Geneva.
MacKillop, Douglas	Counselor, British Legation in Bern.
*Madonne, John	U.S. Consul in Bern.
Maggi	Former leader of the Fascist Party in Milan; fled to Switzerland in October 1943.
Magistrati, Count Massimo	Italian Minister in Bern; provided information to OSS and the U.S. Legation.
Mallaby, Lieutenant	British SOE officer.
Manfredi	A communist friend of Ross McClelland.
Manuel, Bruno	An escapee from Germany.
Marieni, Alessandro	In the Italian Consulate at Chur.
Marone, Count Henri	OSS contact with Cris Cross service in northern Italy.
Marras, General	Former Italian Military Attaché in Berlin.
*Marsching, John H.	Staff member, OSS Bern, 1945.
Masson, Brigadier General Roger	Head of Swiss military intelligence.
*Mayer, Gerald	OWI representative in Bern; close associate of Dulles.
Mazé, Dr.	Secretary of the Radical Socialist Party.
McCaffrey, John	Head of British SOE in Switzerland; Assistant Press Attaché, British Legation.
*McCarthy, Daniel	Staff member, OSS Bern, 1945.

McClelland, Ross	Quaker relief and refugee worker; performed similar duties at U.S. Legation.
*McCollum, Lieutenant	Downed U.S. pilot.
McKittrick, Thomas H.	President of the Bank for International Settlements, Basel.
Meissner	Head Abwehr official in Switzerland.
*Mellon, William L., Jr.	Staff member, U.S. Consulate in Geneva, with OSS duties, 1944–45.
Meyer, Dr. Karl	Professor of European history at the University of Zurich.
Meyer, Mrs. Otto	Jewish wife of a Nazi businessman.
Modigliani, Joseph	Former Vice-President of the Italian Socialist Party; brother of the artist.
Molden, Fritz	Austrian resistance leader and Dulles contact; visited Switzerland frequently late in the war.
Monod, Philippe	French source reporting to OSS in Geneva; former member of the Paris office of Sullivan & Cromwell.
Mooser, Professor	Consultant to the Swiss General Staff and professor at the Hygiene Institute at Zurich University.
Morand, Paul	Ambassador of Vichy France in Bern.
Mottu, Philippe	Swiss official concerned with postwar planning; visited the United States in 1944.
Nerdrum	Official at the Norwegian Embassy.
Neurath, Baron Alexander Constantin von	German Consul at Lugano.
Neyrac, Paul	Chief of the Press Section, Vichy French Embassy in Bern.
Norton	British Minister in Bern.
Nostitz, Gottfried von	German Consul at Geneva.
Novak, Henry Vincent	Associated Press correspondent in Zurich; informant for the U.S. Consul-General.
Novak, Vladimir	Vichy French official.
Olivetti, Adriano	Italian typewriter-manufacturing executive; met with Dulles in Switzerland.
Opracht, Dr. Hans	Leader of the Socialist group in the Nationalrat.
Oprecht, Dr. Emil [Opi]	Prominent publisher in Zurich; member of the Swiss National Council.
Oprecht, Emmi	Wife of Emil Oprecht; corresponded with Dulles.
Orlovitch, Colonel	A Yugoslav leader.
Paillard	Former French Counselor of Embassy in Moscow.
Parilli, Baron Luigi	An Italian businessman who served as an intermediary in Operation Sunrise.

*Parsons, Elizabeth C.	Personal secretary to Allen Dulles for most of the war.
Pavelic, Ivan	Assisted OSS Bern on Croatian matters.
*Peiss, Reuben	Staff member, OSS Bern, 1945.
Pelenyi	Former Hungarian Minister in Washington.
Perez, Micha	A source in Geneva.
Phelps, Livingston	An American living in Geneva.
Phenix, Elizabeth	Staff member, OSS Bern, 1945.
Phillips, Carr [cover name]	An Italian opposition figure.
Piano [code name]	A patent attorney of German origin.
Piercy, Countess	An Italian married to an Englishman.
Pilet-Golaz, Marcel	Chief of the Swiss Federal Political Department (Swiss foreign minister).
Popper	United Press correspondent.
Pourchot, Gaston	Important source for OSS within the Vichy French Embassy.
*Rado, Mrs. Emmy C.	Staff member, OSS Bern, 1945; Swiss-American.
Radvanssky, Baron Anthony	Former Secretary-General of the Hungarian National Bank.
Rakolczai, Colonel	Hungarian Military Attaché; number 844.
Rappard, Professor William	Corresponded with Allen Dulles.
Raz [code name]	A Swiss source in Basel.
*Reagan, Daniel J.	Commercial Attaché, U.S. Legation in Bern.
Reale, Egidio	An Italian opposition figure.
Repond, Dr. A.	Psychoanalyst treating Edda Ciano.
*Rexford, Lieutenant Dean	Assistant U.S. Military Attaché.
Reynolds, Devereaux	An American woman aided by OSS Bern in leaving Europe.
Richter, George	German trade union official.
Riedel, Mrs.	Suspected Nazi agent.
Riegner, Gerhart	German Jew émigré in Geneva; associated with the World Jewish Congress; had contact with Eduard Schulte and other Dulles associates.
Roberts	Staff member, OSS Bern.
Roepke	A prominent German author in Geneva.
Rosenstein	Swiss banker.
Rufenacht, Jean	Swiss businessman, OSS contact; code name Pestalozzi; husband of Mary Bancroft.
Sanford	Staff member, OSS Bern, 1945.
Scherrer, Professor Paul	Prominent physicist in Zurich; important source for OSS on the German atomic energy program.

Schindler, Professor Dietrich	Resident of Zurich; nephew of Max Huber.
Schmid, Professor	Protestant figure at Basel.
Schuhl, Raymond A.	An Alsatian businessman in Geneva; aka Robert Salambier; aka Mutt.
Schulte, Eduard	German industrialist; provided information on Germany, including warning of the extermination of the Jews.
Schwartzenberg, Johannes	Official of the International Red Cross; dual Austrian-Swiss nationality.
Scott-Montagu, Elizabeth	British citizen, cousin of Lord Lothian; helped Mary Bancroft with translation of Gisevius manuscript.
Seiler, Dr.	Husband of daughter of Allen Dulles; friend from his 1916–17 Vienna posting.
Shaedler	A source on German affairs.
*Shea, Robert D.	OSS staff member; U.S. Vice-Consul at Basel.
*Sholes, Walter H.	U.S. Consul General at Basel; source of frequent intelligence reports for the Legation in Bern.
Siemsen, Anna	German socialist intellectual.
Silianoff	High-ranking Bulgarian Legation official.
Silone, Ignazio	Italian literary figure and member of the Socialist Party; aka Frost, Len, Tulio, and Mr. Behr.
Simons, Professor Hellmuth	German-Jewish biologist employed by the Zurich Polytechnic Institute.
Simpson [code name]	An unofficial representative of the Czech government.
Singer	*New York Times* correspondent in Zurich.
Smits, Evert	Source Sanders; publicity manager for Fokker.
Soutou	Member of the French resistance delegation in Geneva.
"The Spider"	Man of Moorish extraction who passed mail to Lisbon for OSS Bern.
Spinster [code name]	Important source on France in Geneva.
*Squire, Paul C.	U.S. Consul in Geneva.
*Stalder, Frederick J.	Staff member, OSS Bern; number 244.
Stampfli, Walter	Swiss Federal Councilor and head of the Department of Economic Affairs.
Stoppani, Dr. Pietro	Former Director of the Economic Section of the League of Nations.
Stucki, Walter	Head of the Foreign Affairs Division of the Swiss Federal Political Department.
*Tait, George	First Secretary, U.S. Legation.
Tyler, Royall	Former expert in the Economic, Financial, and Transit Department of the League of Nations; U.S. citizen; a

	top assistant to Allen Dulles and adviser to the U.S. Legation; authority on Hungary.
Urach, Prince Albrecht von	Head of the Press Section, German Legation in Bern.
*Van Arkel, Gerhard	Staff member, OSS Bern; specialized in labor-based penetration operations against Germany.
Vanden Heuval, Frederick	British SIS Chief in Switzerland; postwar friend of Allen Dulles.
Vergé, Jean	French Chargé d'Affaires in Bern, 1944–45.
Villars, Maurice	General Director of the Electro-Bank in Zurich; important source for OSS.
Visser 't Hooft, Dr. W. A.	Secretary of the World Council of Churches, Geneva.
Von Auersperg, Prince Alois	German Assistant Air Attaché.
Von Biber	German Chargé d'Affaires at the Consulate in Zurich until May 1943; suspected of intelligence activities.
Von Straempes	Nazi agent collecting data on the United States.
Vulcan, Constantin	Rumanian Cultural Attaché in Bern.
Waetjen, Eduard	Important German resistance figure; lawyer and Abwehr agent; reached Switzerland in January 1944.
Wagner, Professor V. F.	Professor at University of Basel; expert on the Danubian nations.
Waibel, Major Max	Swiss intelligence officer; close contact of Allen Dulles; role in Operation Sunrise.
Wenner, Major Eugen	German staff officer involved in Operation Sunrise.
*Williamson, David	Information officer, U.S. Legation in Bern; OSS MO Branch.
Wirth, Josef	Former Chancellor of Germany.
Wiskemann, Elizabeth	British scholar.
Wittig, Klaus	German émigré.
Wolff, General Karl	German SS commander who visited Dulles in Switzerland to launch negotiations for the surrender of German forces in Italy.
*Woods, Sam E.	U.S. Consul General at Zurich; source of frequent intelligence reports for the Legation in Bern.
Yoshimura, Kan	Financial expert at the Bank of International Settlements; involved in 1945 Japanese peace overtures.
Zimmer, Captain Guido	A German staff officer involved in Operation Sunrise.

Notes

[All citations to box numbers refer to containers in RG 226, Entry 134, unless otherwise indicated. The chronological arrangement of cable files permits document identification within boxes.]

Introduction

The Allen Dulles Papers at Princeton University constitute the most important source on his career before World War II. This material contains extensive information on his early life, education, diplomatic service, and law career with Sullivan & Cromwell. Letters and other personal papers document Dulles's accumulation of friends and contacts. State Department records at the National Archives (RG 59 and RG 84) contain some documents pertaining to his diplomatic service from 1916 to 1926 and to his service as an adviser in the 1930s. Regarding the Dulles family, see Eleanor Lansing Dulles, *Chances of a Lifetime: A Memoir* (Englewood Cliffs, N.J.: Prentice-Hall, 1980). Leonard Mosley's *Dulles: A Biography of Eleanor, Allen, and John Foster Dulles and Their Family Network* (New York: Dial/Wade, 1978) is an important source but should be used with caution. *A Law Unto Itself: The Untold Story of the Law Firm of Sullivan and Cromwell,* by Nancy Lisagor and Frank Lipsius (New York: Morrow, 1988), is revealing on the role of the Dulles brothers.

Chapter 1: An Island in Occupied Europe, November 1942–August 1943

Doc. 1-1, Tel. 5098, Nov. 10, 1942, Box 307. Dulles's arrival in Switzerland is reported in Tel. 52 from Bern, Nov. 12, 1942 (Box 171). Dulles had a harrowing trip to his post via Lisbon and Barcelona, including a border encounter with the Gestapo. He saw his tasks in Bern as gathering information about the enemy and rendering support and encouragement to resistance forces in neighboring countries (Allen W. Dulles, *The Secret Surrender* [New York: Harper & Row, 1966], chap. 2, "Mission in Switzerland"). Anthony Cave Brown also gives an overview of the Bern operation in *The Last Hero: Wild Bill Donovan* (New York: Times Books, 1982), chap. 18, "The Dulles Organization." Brown's account is useful and provocative but not uniformly reliable. A similar treatment appears in Burton Hersh, *The Old Boys: The American Elite and the Origins of the CIA* (New York: Scribners, 1992). Bradley Smith presents a brief but more balanced account in *The Shadow Warriors: OSS and the Origins of the CIA* (New York: Basic Books, 1983). R. Harris Smith, *OSS: The Secret History of America's First Central Intelligence Agency* (Berkeley and Los Angeles: University of California Press, 1972), is also helpful.

Evidence of an OSS presence in Switzerland before the arrival of Dulles is found in cables in Boxes 171, 307, 339. These existing sources or channels are designated "Drum" and "Moffet." The designations "Schubert" and "Michael" also appear in telegrams of 1942 and early 1943. The office of the Military Attaché, Gen. Barnwell Legge, conducted intelligence operations before November 1942, as reflected in documents in RG 319. State Department post files for Switzerland show pre-Dulles intelligence activity and networks into enemy-controlled territory. The legation and consulates ran sources, including "Ralph" from Zurich, where Consul General Sam E. Woods was involved in intelligence matters (RG 84, Zurich Post Files). "Ralph" appears to have been Erwin Respondek, a German economist, politician and opponent of Hitler whom Woods had met at his previous assignment in Berlin. The Woods-Respondek connection is treated in *Two Against Hitler: Stealing the Nazis' Best-Kept Secrets,* by John Dippel (New York: Praeger, 1992). Thus, Dulles hardly started from scratch. In addition, OSS headquarters sent Dulles a list of twelve potential sources on Dec. 4, 1942. This compilation, called "Wayne's List," included individuals of various nationalities who apparently resided in Switzerland or were frequent visitors. Their identities cannot be determined from sanitized documents (Tels. 6-8 and 98-102, received from the Central Intelligence Agency under the Freedom of Information Act, hereafter cited CIA/FOIA). Tels. 111-13 (Moffet 10–12), Dec. 19; 133–135 to Drum (Moffet 29–31), Jan. 14, 1943; and Moffet 33–35, Jan. 19, 1943, added twenty-six more potential sources to "Wayne's List" (CIA/FOIA). Throughout the war, Washington provided Dulles with similar suggestions for sources that might be developed.

With the Allied invasion of North Africa, German forces occupied southern France over the objections of the Petain government. On Nov. 14, Dulles reported that personnel in the Vichy Embassy in Switzerland were vacillating and that excellent opportunities for opening new channels into France via pro-Allied French individuals in Bern now existed (Tel. 5192, Box 171).

Doc. 1-2, Tel. 60-65, Nov. 21, 1942, Box 171. Gen. Donovan had sent the following message to Dulles on Nov. 17: "Glad to hear you arrived. I want now to give you full charge of all activities of OSS. This will include direction of special propaganda. All facilities including printing etc. will have to be set up. Would you want Ed Stanley there to help on this if we can get him? Please keep us fully informed on everything" (Tel. 71, Box 171). Dulles received the following additional guidance on Nov. 24: "Although this message does not reflect anything specific we nevertheless suggest that you do not approach the frontier of any enemy country closely and that you take all reasonable precautions for your own personal safety" (Tel. 78, Box 165).

Funding for OSS Bern's operations was arranged by OSS purchase of Swiss francs in the United States and their transmittal to Switzerland via U.S. banking channels. For example, headquarters informed Dulles on Mar. 8, 1943, that a purchase of $1,400,000 in Swiss francs was being made for his use by means of a complicated process involving blocked dollars and a buy-back provision (Tel. 70-78, CIA/FOIA).

Doc. 1-3, Tel. 6-10, Nov. 24, 1942, Box 171. Important sources on the French resistance movement include M. R. D. Foot, *SOE in France: An Account of the Work of the British Special Operations Executive, 1940–1944* (Frederick, Md.: University Publications of America, 1986), and David Schoenbrun, *Soldiers of the Night: The Story of the French Resistance* (New York: Dutton, 1980). Sources of particular value on the role of the OSS in France and on Dulles's connections include Fabrizio Calvi, *OSS: La Guerre Secrète en France, 1942–1945* (Paris: Hachette, 1990), and Henri Frenay, *The Night Will End,* trans. Dan Hofstadter (New York: McGraw-Hill, 1976). The Gestapo head at Lyons was the notorious Klaus Barbie. Dulles's aggressive support for resistance movements generated both cooperation and controversy with "Zulu," the British. The OSS had been given a subversive warfare role subordinate to that of the SOE under an agreement concluded with the British in June 1942 (Smith, *Shadow Warriors,* 170–71).

Doc. 1-4, Tel. 5688, Dec. 6, 1942, Box 171.

Doc. 1-5, Tel. 5792, Dec. 10, 1942, Box 171.

Doc. 1-6, Tel. 5861, Dec. 14, 1942, Box 171. For a useful account of U.S. policy toward Italy during and after the war, see James Edward Miller, *The United States and Italy, 1940–1950: The Politics and Diplomacy of Stabilization* (Chapel Hill: University of North Carolina Press, 1986).

Doc. 1-7, Tel. 5913, Dec. 16, 1942, Box 307. Regarding the complex situation in Hungary, see Nicholas Kallay, Premier and Foreign Minister from March 1942 to March 1944, *Hungarian Premier: A Personal*

Account of a Nation's Struggle in the Second World War (New York: Columbia University Press, 1954). Count Stephen Bethlen was Premier of Hungary from 1921 to 1931; Count Maurice Eszterhazy was Premier during World War I; Leopold Baranyai was president of the Hungarian national bank.

Doc. 1-8, Tel. 6103, Dec. 24, 1942, RG 226, Office Director's Files, Microfilm, Reel 16A. James Grafton Rogers was director of the OSS Planning Group. This body, which devoted much of its efforts to psychological warfare, included Hugh Wilson, former Ambassador to Germany and Switzerland, a personal friend of Dulles. Rogers stated in his diary that Dulles was "a geyser of psych. warfare news and suggestions" (Thomas F. Troy, ed., *Wartime Washington: The Secret OSS Journal of James Grafton Rogers, 1942–1943* [Frederick, Md.: University Publications of America, 1987], 95).

Doc. 1-9, Tel. 17180, Dec. 27, 1942, Box 171. London added in Tel. 20140, Dec. 20, that the Free French had approved the proposal in principle. Although they had no funds of their own and needed British and American financial help, they expected to have control over expenditures.

Doc. 1-10, Tel. 127-128, Jan. 6, 1943, Box 307.

Doc. 1-11, Tel. 278, Jan. 12, 1943, Box 171. The pro-German Gen. Ion Antonescu had become dictator of Rumania in September 1940 with the abdication of King Carol II. On Jan. 24, 1943, Dulles reported that Antonescu had refused Hitler's demand for an additional 100,000 troops and had unsuccessfully tried to resign (Tel. 28, Box 171).

Gero von Schultze Gaevernitz, Dulles's inseparable right-hand man, was the son of a leading German economist, professor, and liberal politician who had fled to Switzerland. His father was a Quaker and his mother was Jewish. Gero journeyed to the United States in 1924, pursued business interests, and became an American citizen. His sister married Edmund Stinnes, a Haverford professor who was the son of German Ruhr industrialist Hugo Stinnes. Gaevernitz went to Switzerland at the beginning of World War II and soon began to assist Allied intelligence. Items of postwar Dulles-Gaevernitz correspondence are in the Allen Dulles Papers, Boxes 21 and 25.

As was the case with many of Dulles's German sources, the British were not impressed by Gaevernitz. On Feb. 23, 1943, the U.S. Embassy in London informed Dulles that the British had found Gaevernitz's information to be of little value because he was German in outlook and influenced by persons close to Air Marshal Goering. The telegram suggested that Gaevernitz be told that unless he rendered genuine service his citizenship might be in jeopardy (RG 84, classified Bern Post Files, Box 24).

Number 474 is Dr. W. A. Visser 't Hooft, Secretary of the World Council of Churches in Geneva and head of the European branch of the YMCA. Visser 't Hooft had extensive international connections and was well acquainted with anti-Nazi Germans, including the aristocratic intellectual/diplomat Adam von Trott zu Solz, who would participate in the July 20, 1944, attempt on Hitler's life. Dulles maintained close ties with Visser 't Hooft throughout the war. A portion of their correspondence is in RG 226, Entry 125, Box 5. Visser 't Hooft's *Memoirs* (London: SCM Press, 1973) describes his ties with the Dutch resistance and German dissident elements, including the Confessional Church, but mentions Dulles only in passing.

Doc. 1-12, Tel. 314, Jan. 14, 1943, Box 171. The best study on the internal opposition to Hitler is Peter Hoffmann, *The History of the German Resistance* (Cambridge, Mass.: MIT Press, 1977). Other important sources include Allen W. Dulles, *Germany's Underground* (New York: Macmillan, 1947); Hans Bernd Gisevius, *To the Bitter End* (London: Jonathan Cape, 1948); Fabian von Schlabrendorff, *They Almost Killed Hitler,* ed. Gero von Gaevernitz (New York: Macmillan, 1947); and Hans von Herwarth von Bittenfeld, *Against Two Evils* (New York: Rawson, Wade, 1981). The Dulles Papers at Princeton contain substantial documentation on the subject in the form of book drafts and notes, and postwar correspondence.

The person cited as a member of the German opposition in the first paragraph is Adam von Trott zu Solz (Tel. 13-14 from Bern, Jan. 15, 1943, CIA/FOIA). Trott was an aristocrat, intellectual, and government official who was motivated by strong Christian beliefs. His efforts to undermine Hitler through his many contacts in the West and the resistance activities that resulted in his death are described in Giles MacDonough, *A Good German: Adam von Trott zu Solz* (Woodstock, N.Y.: Overlook Press, 1992).

Doc. 1-13, Tel. 18155, Jan. 18, 1943, Box 171.

Doc. 1-14, Tel. 528, Jan. 23, 1943, Box 171. The stylistic inelegance of this telegram, typical of OSS cables sent through State Department channels, is attributable to paraphrasing of the original for security purposes. Copies of many Dulles messages from 1942 to 1945, as received at the State Department, are filed in RG 59, 103.918.

Doc. 1-15, Tel. 30-32, Jan. 24, 1943, Box 171. Tel. 139, Jan. 20, 1943, read as follows: "I wish you would try, as the OSS head in Switzerland, to devise a plan for penetrating the Axis countries. There is a very active underground movement in Alsace-Lorraine, according to reports received here" (Box 165). The last sentence of Tel. 74-75, Dec. 2, 1942, reads as follows: "Instructions have been given the French Embassy here to end all military naval services including the Deuxième Bureau [intelligence.] Any useful personnel remaining here will be taken over by us" (Box 171).

Among the refugees arriving from France about this time was a young American woman, Devereaux Reynolds, who had lived in Europe before the war and served as an ambulance driver in its early stages. She apparently was willing to join Allied intelligence and came to the attention of Dulles. However, after buying her new clothes and lending her $600 (later repaid), he found her unsuitable for OSS purposes. She then made her way to Iberia and on to London, where later in the war she joined British SOE. Documents on the Reynolds case are in Entry 190, Box 26. Her memoirs, published as Devereaux Rochester, *Full Moon to France* (New York: Harper & Row, 1977), indicate that she was captured in Paris in 1944 but eventually transferred from prison to the Vittel internment camp for Allied civilians.

Doc. 1-16, Tel. 723, Jan. 31, 1943, Box 171. In Tel. 147-48, Jan. 29, OSS Washington requested information on the reaction to the Casablanca Conference and the doctrine of "unconditional surrender" (Box 165). Regarding the origins, promulgation, and consequences of this doctrine, see *FRUS, The Conferences at Washington, 1941–1942, and Casablanca, 1943* (Washington, D.C.: GPO, 1968); Anne Armstrong, *Unconditional Surrender: The Impact of the Casablanca Policy upon World War II* (New Brunswick, N.J.: Rutgers University Press, 1961); and John P. Glennon, " 'This Time Germany Is a Defeated Nation': The Doctrine of Unconditional Surrender and Some Unsuccessful Attempts to Alter It, 1943-1944," in Gerald N. Grob, ed., *Statesmen and Statecraft of the Modern West: Essays in Honor of Dwight E. Lee and H. Donaldson Jordan* (Barre, Mass.: Barre Publishers, 1967).

Doc. 1-17, Tel. 729, Feb. 1, 1943, Box 171. Among the persons mentioned are Field Marshal Pietro Badoglio, who resigned as Chief of Staff in 1940 in opposition to Mussolini's policies; Prince Umberto of Savoy; Count Galeazzo Ciano, Mussolini's Foreign Minister and son-in-law; Dino Grandi, Fascist leader; and Count Carlo Sforza, a descendant of the prominent Renaissance family, who was forced into exile by Mussolini in 1926 and continued to oppose him from a liberal/democratic position. On Jan. 9, Dulles had reported that Ignazio Silone, playwright and Italian Socialist Party leader in exile in Switzerland, had received feelers from a group including Badoglio and Umberto asking the attitude of the Socialists should they arrange for a separate peace. Silone (code name Len, OSS identification number 475) had offered Socialist support provided the Italian people could decide on the form of government later. Silone also asked for funds from the United States for the Italian Socialist Party, but that to keep the record clean, they come from socialist labor unions. He mentioned (Luigi) Antonini, New York labor leader (Tel. 191, Jan. 9, 1943, Entry 180, Donovan microfilm, roll 126A; copy also from CIA/FOIA).

Doc. 1-18, Tel. 41-43, Feb. 3, 1943, Box 171. Dulles met Dr. Carl Jung in 1936 and conferred with him on a number of occasions during the war. "Paul M." refers to Paul Mellon, the philanthropist, who knew Jung well and later served with the OSS in Europe. He treats these subjects in his memoirs, *Reflections in a Silver Spoon* (New York: Morrow, 1992). Mrs. Olga Frobe-Kapteyn, an associate of Jung and founder of the Eranos research and conference center in Ascona, which studied the psychology of religious experience, corresponded with Dulles (Entry 190, Box 28). Additional information on Dulles's interest in Jung and his circle appears in Mary Bancroft, *Autobiography of a Spy* (New York: Morrow, 1983). Bancroft, an American socialite married to a Swiss, knew Jung in Zurich and performed various tasks for Dulles. (This book is eccentric, but it contains substantial information on OSS Bern operations.) Dulles wrote to Mellon on Feb. 17, 1950, indicating that during the war he had had long conversations with Jung on political developments and vigorously refuted rumors that the doctor had pro-Nazi sympathies (Allen Dulles Papers, Box 46).

Doc. 1-19, Tel. 827, Feb. 4, 1943, Box 307. Tel. 528, Jan. 23, 1943, appears here as Doc. 1-14.

Doc. 1-20, Tel. 44-45, Feb. 5, 1943, Box 171. Allied intelligence uncovered evidence of the German V-1 rocket bomb program and launch sites in France by 1943. Consequently, British bombers struck the Peenemünde development center on Aug. 17, 1943, inflicting heavy damage. The raid and subsequent raids prevented the Germans from using V-1s against London until June 13, 1944, and V-2s until September. This intelligence success is described in R. V. Jones, *The Wizard War: British Scientific Intelligence, 1939–1945* (New York: Coward, McCann & Georghegan, 1978), and in Jozef Garlinski, *Hitler's Last Weapons: The Underground War Against the V1 and V2* (London: Julian Friedmann, 1978). For the German side, see *V-2,* by Walter Dornberger, commander of the Peenemünde Rocket Research Institute (New York: Viking, 1954). Michel Hollard headed an espionage network within France that provided critical information on German rockets to the British in Switzerland, as described in George Martelli, *Agent Extraordinary: The Story of Michel Hollard* (London: Collins, 1960). In his *Of Spies and Stratagems* (Englewood Cliffs, N.J.: Prentice-Hall, 1963), Stanley P. Lovell, Chief of the OSS Research and Development Branch, recalls that a fragmentary report from Dulles helped identify Peenemünde as a bombing target. The extent to which OSS Bern contributed to overall Allied knowledge is uncertain, but numerous reports were submitted from 1943 to 1945. Field reports on the subject exist in Entry 108, Boxes 1, 3 and 5; Entry 125, Box 6; Entry 190, Box 26; and Bern Post Files, RG 84, Box 15.

Doc. 1-21, Tel. 898, Feb. 9, 1943, Box 307. Royall Tyler, OSS number 477, code name "Anderson," was a top aide to Dulles, particularly with regard to Hungary and the Balkans. He also cooperated closely with Minister Leland Harrison, as indicated in Bern Post Files, RG 84, Box 15, and in Geneva Post Files, Box 2. An American expatriate in Europe, Tyler was a scholar who studied under Unamuno, served as Keeper of the Public Records in Britain, and worked on royal family correspondence of the sixteenth century in Paris. In 1917 he volunteered for the U.S. Army and served on General Pershing's staff interrogating prisoners. At the Paris Peace Conference, he served on a U.S. Delegation intelligence committee that focused on Germany with the Dulles brothers and A. A. Berle. He then became a member of a commission that monitored the German payment of reparations. Sent to Hungary by the League of Nations in connection with a reconstruction loan, he became a financial adviser to the Hungarian government, learned the language, and formed many contacts. When the Germans overran France in 1940, Tyler went to League headquarters in Geneva, where he served with U.S. authorities but never received payments from the OSS. After the war, Tyler joined UNRRA and continued scholarly writing. With the assistance of Allen Dulles, he established the Free University at Strasbourg as a center for intellectuals from behind the Iron Curtain, funded by the CIA (interview with Ambassador William Tyler). Limited Dulles-Tyler postwar correspondence is located in the Allen Dulles Papers, Boxes 22 and 27.

Doc. 1-22, Tel. 933, Feb. 10, 1943, Box 171.

Doc. 1-23, Tel. 934, Feb. 10, 1943, Box 171. Tel. 729, Feb. 1, 1943, appears here as Doc. 1-17.

Doc. 1-24, Tel. 967, Feb. 11, 1943, Box 307.

Doc. 1-25, Tel. 57-59, Feb. 13, 1943, Box 307.

Doc. 1-26, Tel. 1050, Feb. 15, 1943, Box 171. Dulles forwarded further ideas on fragmenting the German leadership in Tel. 286-287 to Donovan on April 22: "It is too early yet to drive a wedge among Hitler, Goebbels, Bormann and Himmler, because . . . they are closely bound together . . . .It is feasible, however, to drive a wedge between this group and Goering or Ribbentrop. Inasmuch as Goering is probably the only high Nazi who has the confidence of OKW, it might help towards a crisis between the Party and the military if we could further weaken him. As for Ribbentrop, I consider him unimportant and probably an asset to us because he is generally discredited and hated" (Box 307). In Tel. 11-12, Apr. 26, OSS headquarters agreed with Dulles in principle but added: "In attempting to drive wedge between members of the Nazi Party, our only caution is to insure that no encouragement is given to the idea that the military group or the Party could expect anything short of an unconditional surrender" (Box 165).

Dulles reported in May that according to reliable sources Hitler's inner circle consisted of Ruppen, Oberg, Ley, Speer, Bormann, Wolff, Goebbels, and Goering. Wolff was more important than generally recognized. Speer was so unpolitical that he would construct a new Communist Party headquarters if so instructed. Goering was oblivious to the seriousness of the military situation. The most corrupt and influential member of the inner circle was Bormann (Tel. 3115, May 21, 1943, Box 307).

Doc. 1-27, Tel. 1051, Feb. 15, 1943, Box 307.

Doc. 1-28, Tel. 75-77, Feb. 23, 1943, Box 307.

Doc. 1-29, Tel. 183-85, Feb. 25, 1943, Box 307. Dan, Mary, and Jerry are identified in Tel. 78-80, Feb. 25 (Box 307).

Throughout 1943, OSS Bern received numerous inquiries from individuals in Germany, Italy, and the Axis satellite states of Hungary, Rumania, and Bulgaria concerning the postwar settlements. Most of these contacts fell short of being "peace feelers," but some were quite significant. Regarding approaches received by the Allies throughout Europe, see the compilation on "Peace Feelers from the Axis Nations," in *FRUS*, 1943 (Washington, D.C.: GPO, 1963), 1:484–512.

Doc. 1-30, Tel. 188-189, Feb. 27, 1943, Box 307.

Doc. 1-31, Tel. 1381, Feb. 27, 1943, Box 307. Mary, Tom, and Jones were identified in Tel. 95-96, Feb. 27 (Box 307). Regarding the Bulgarian situation, see Stephane Groueff's *Crown of Thorns* (Lanham, Md.: Madison Books, 1987), which describes the reign of King Boris III, 1918–43. René Charron (number 492), whom Dulles designated "Boatman," was former League of Nations envoy to Bulgaria and Director of the League's Economic Section. Located in Geneva, he gathered information for OSS from sources throughout the Balkans and was a key operative in providing aid to the French resistance. In a memorandum to Annemasse station on Oct. 23, 1944, Dulles referred to Charron as "one of my closest friends and a man who has rendered extraordinary services to the common cause" (Entry 190, Box 30). After the war he entered the tobacco business in Switzerland. His postwar correspondence with Dulles is in the Allen Dulles Papers, Box 24.

Tel. 48-52 from Bern, Feb. 10, reads in part as follows: "The identity of Ben is Buroff. He was formerly foreign minister of Bulgaria. Balkan circles in Bern, including Kiosseivanov [Bulgarian Minister], indicated that they would like to establish contact. I am aware that this region is being handled through Ankara, but I would welcome any directions since information which may prove useful may be brought to light here. Charron states that Buroff might be more valuable to us than anyone else in helping rally Bulgarian opinion, especially if possible to get him to Turkey from Bulgaria. According to Charron, Buroff is thoroughly trustworthy and has been consistently opposed to the Axis. I suggest that you see Cannon at the State Department concerning Kiosseivanov" (Box 307).

In Tel. 202–3, Apr. 7, OSS headquarters informed Dulles that the Bulgarian question had been referred to the State Department. Under Secretary Sumner Welles had requested that he report all contacts from groups in enemy territories to Minister Harrison (Box 165).

Doc. 1-32, Tel. 1425, Mar. 2, 1943, Box 307. Max Shoop, OSS number 284 ("Mike"), was an expatriate American lawyer who had worked in the Paris office of Sullivan & Cromwell, Dulles's firm. With the outbreak of war he escaped to Geneva, where he began working with Allied intelligence. In late 1942 one of his former French law office subordinates, Philippe Monod (number 405, "Martel"), now with the resistance in the Lyons area, made contact with him. It was through this law office network that Dulles established one connection with the French resistance that rewarded him with a steady stream of intelligence information. This matter is treated in memoirs by the resistance figures Henri Frenay, *The*

Night Will End, trans. Dan Hofstadter (New York: McGraw-Hill, 1976), and by Pierre Guillain de Benouville, *The Unknown Warriors: A Personal Account of the French Resistance*, introduction by Allen Dulles (New York: Simon & Schuster, 1949), and in Lisagor and Lipsius, *A Law Unto Itself*. A collection of reports from 284, who remained in Geneva until November 1944, exists in Entry 125, Box 10.

According to an assistant to General Legge, the U.S. military attaché, his office had a source in the hotel that housed German headquarters in Paris. The information thus obtained was shared with Dulles, providing him with an additional source on events in France (Interviews).

Doc. 1-33, Tel. 1432, Mar. 2, 1943, Box 307. In Tel. 193-97 to Donovan, Mar. 3, Dulles identified "Pam" as PM, Prime Minister Kallay, and stated that the Hungarians were ready to hold nonbinding talks in Switzerland. He and Tyler were convinced of the authenticity of this approach but recognized possible policy difficulties, particularly with regard to Russia (Box 307). Headquarters responded on Mar. 10 that "in reference to the R[ussian] situation, your discussions and contacts have been brought to [Assistant Secretary of State] Adolph [Berle]'s attention. Adolph is taking them across the street [to the White House]. Hence, at present, the matter is temporarily suspended" (Tel. 79-80, Box 165). Tel. 187 to Bern, Mar. 15, added the following: "It is suggested by Adolph that although we are not ready to enter discussions, we are still interested in information about the line of thought. He adds that of course we are Russia's loyal allies, and without that in mind we could do nothing" (Box 165). Berle had known Dulles since the Paris Peace Conference of 1919 and was an intimate of President Roosevelt. Indeed, he addressed some of his letters to the President in the 1930s "Dear Caesar." (FDR/PSF/94/State Dept. A. A. Berle Jr.).

Dulles pursued the matter in Tel. 164–65, Apr. 9, asking permission to keep the Hungarian channel open by at least expressing willingness to listen (Box 307). On Apr. 13, Shepardson gave headquarters' approval for Dulles to do whatever he saw fit, contingent on adherence to previous instructions (Tel. 10-11, Box 165).

Doc. 1-34, Tel. 1496, Mar. 4, 1943, Box 307. Number 478, Dr. Josef Wirth, was Chancellor of Germany, 1921–22, and Minister of the Interior in the Bruning government, 1930–32. This prominent émigré in Switzerland was strongly Catholic and had belonged to the German Center Party.

On Jan. 19, Dulles had reported the following: "Have been working on chemical warfare, but the secret of the details is carefully guarded. According to a good German source, Germany is believed to be well prepared offensively, but there is opposition on the part of military leaders because German civilian population is not adequately equipped with gas masks in order to meet retaliation. This is due to the rubber shortage. It is my opinion that the most advisable technique to adopt in this field for psychological warfare would be to continue to place emphasis on the fact that gas warfare will never be started by us, but that if Hitler uses it, we are fully prepared to deluge Germany with gas" (Tel. 443, Box 307).

Doc. 1-35, Tel. 1527, Mar. 5, 1943, Box 307. A summary of this telegram was one of an initial selection based on cables from Bern sent by Gen. John Magruder, Deputy Director of OSS, to the White House Map Room on March 10. Magruder transmitted additional batches of summaries of Dulles messages in 1943 and 1944 (FDR Library, Map Room Files, Boxes 72–73). Later in 1943, and especially in 1944, Gen. Donovan sent Dulles cables directly to the President on a regular basis. Reports from Bern reaching the White House through the two separate sources far exceeded those from other OSS posts.

Doc. 1-36, Tel. 1529, Mar. 6, 1943, Box 171. On Mar. 8, Dulles reported that Rumanian centrist politicians Constantin Bratianu and Iuliu Maniu had written to Gen. Ion Antonescu, the pro-Axis dictator, demanding that the country change its policy lest it go down to defeat with the Germans and lose all (Tel. 1578, Box 307).

Doc. 1-37, Tel. 1534, Mar. 6, 1943, Box 307. Dulles had informed Gen. Donovan on Feb. 25 of reports indicating the existence in certain cities of cells of officers with allegiance to Gen. Giraud. He also cited reports that Laval's Milice National had been organized "partly to have something in hand to bring us when the last rats try to leave the ship and partly as a personal bodyguard" (Tel. 83-85, Box 307). On Mar. 6 and 10, Dulles provided additional information on resistance forces in the mountains of southeastern France. He reported that according to Max Shoop some 12,000 men were gathering there (Tel. 1543, Mar. 6, Box 171; Tel. 1616, Mar. 10, 1943, Box 171).

OSS headquarters responded as follows on Mar. 16: "Give financial aid at your discretion to the French Resistance Groups and maintain a contact with them. In order to prepare them for the day when they can be of most use, help them in any other ways to subsist and grow strong. Any action which might lend to the dissolution or destruction of the groups should be discouraged but normal guerrilla activity and sabotage should be encouraged" (Tel. 92–93, Box 165).

Doc. 1-38, Tel. 1544, Mar. 6, 1943, Box 171.

Doc. 1-39, Tel. 107–8, Mar. 8, 1943, Box 307.

Doc. 1-40, Tel. 1597, Mar. 10, 1943, Box 171. A summary of this telegram was sent to the White House Map Room by S. Everett Gleason, an assistant to Gen. Magruder, along with other Bern material in May 1943 (FDR Library, Map Room Files, Box 72). This message is one of the few in which Dulles reported on the extermination of the Jews, notwithstanding the numerous accounts received by Allied authorities in Switzerland from the International Red Cross, the YMCA, the World Jewish Congress, and other Jewish organizations. The Bern Legation and Geneva Consulate files contain numerous horrifying reports received by U.S. diplomats beginning in 1942 (RG 84, Bern unclassified Box 103 and classified Boxes 6, 13, 15, and 18; and Geneva classified Box 2). Military attaché files contain similar material (RG 319, Bern, Boxes 621, 622, and 624–28). There are also occasional items on the subject in OSS files, including a report from the Geneva office of the Ecumenical World Council of Churches, Mar. 19, 1943 (RG 226, Entry 125, Box 5) Walter Laqueur discusses the extensive knowledge of the situation possessed by Allied intelligence in Switzerland in *The Terrible Secret* (London: Weidenfeld & Nicolson, 1980) and in "Hitler's Holocaust: Who Knew What, When & How?" *Encounter* 55 (July 1980); 6–25. In *Breaking the Silence* (New York: Simon & Schuster, 1986), Laqueur and Richard Breitman reveal more of what the Allies in Switzerland knew, while telling the story of Eduard Schulte (OSS number 643), a German industrialist who brought early word of the Holocaust. He worked closely with Dulles on various matters. The scholarly literature of the Holocaust considering world reaction and Allied policy includes Martin Gilbert, *The Holocaust: The Jewish Tragedy* (London: Collins, 1986); Lucy S. Dawidowicz *The War Against the Jews, 1933–1945* (New York: Holt, Rinehart & Winston, 1975); and David S. Wyman, *The Abandonment of the Jews: America and the Holocaust, 1941–1945* (New York: Pantheon Books, 1984).

Why did Dulles choose not to emphasize the Holocaust in his reports to Washington? Given the range of his contacts, associates, and friends, one must assume that he was neither ignorant of nor insensitive to the fate of the Jews. Perhaps he believed that in view of German and European anti-Semitism, highest priority denunciation of the Holocaust would be counterproductive for the purposes of Western psychological warfare. Perhaps he feared that the flight of new refugees to Switzerland would interfere with his espionage activities. Whatever the reasoning, his reticence on this subject is among the most controversial and least understandable aspects of his performance in Bern.

Doc. 1-41, Tel. 1593, Mar. 12, 1943, Box 307. Silone was also known at times as Mr. Behr, Tulio, and Frost. A folder of material concerning his contacts with OSS Bern is in RG 226, Entry 125, Box 8.

Doc. 1-42, Tel. 212–14, Mar. 15, 1943, Box 307.

Doc. 1-43, Tel. 515, Mar. 21, 1943, Box 171. OSS headquarters cabled Dulles its approval of the proposed program on Mar. 26 but hoped that OSS Bern could fund it with resources on hand (Tel. 107-11, Box 165).

Doc. 1-44, Tel. 516, Mar. 21, 1943, Box 171.

Doc. 1-45, Tel. 126-30, Mar. 23, 1943, Box 307.

Doc. 1-46, Tel. 1926, Mar. 26, 1943, Box 307. Number 472 was the designation for the remnants of pre-war French intelligence in Switzerland, which was essential to OSS Bern operations. The cable files (RG 226, Entry 134) contain hundreds of reports on order of battle information from all over Europe processed by "472." In a memorandum of Jan. 8, 1945, to Captain Henry R. Macy concerning OSS liaison with advancing U.S. forces in France, Dulles stated the following: "The French Deuxième Bureau had . . . one of the best . . . intelligence services in Switzerland when the war broke out in 1939. After the collapse of France this service continued and reported to certain persons in Vichy who were trusted as anti-German. Our Military Attaché, General Legge, was in close touch with this service during this period. . . . After the occupation of Southern France, the Deuxième Bureau was supposedly abolished and all financial aid to the French officer in the Embassy in Bern who ran the service was terminated. At that time, in agreement with General Legge, we agreed to finance the French service and they passed to us all of their reports. Their information, particularly on the German forces in France, proved invaluable during the period of German occupation. They also had a well developed service in North Italy and in Germany. When the Algiers government was established, I served as the medium for the transmission by cable of the French Deuxième Bureau reports from here to Algiers but continued to make direct use of them with Washington and London. . . . These reports go out under the number 472, also with the additional label K-1 and K-2, the latter two being symbols used in common with our British friends" (CIA/FOIA). In *OSS: La Guerre Secrète en France, 1942–1945,* Fabrizio Calvi describes contacts between Dulles and French intelligence in Switzerland. Gaston Pourchot in the Vichy Embassy was particularly helpful to the Allies.

Doc. 1-47, Tel. 2181, Apr. 7, 1943, Box 171. Hohenlohe was assigned OSS number 515 and was also known as "Ben." Because of this aristocrat's dubious reputation and connections with high-ranking Nazis, Dulles has been criticized for meeting with him several times during the war. Soviet postwar propaganda alleged that Dulles sought to conclude a separate peace through this individual. The case is made in Bob Edwards and Kenneth Dunne, *Study of a Master Spy* (London: Housmans, 1961), a work that many experts believe was Soviet-inspired.

On Apr. 6, 1943, Dulles reported the additional information obtained from Hohenlohe: "Hitler . . . is not really sick, but close associates find that he is of a less confident nature. He is a great deal more anti-American than anti-British. Hitler's prestige . . . has been shaken with certain important members of the Nazi Party; talk of his 'elimination' is not rare. Expectation of our landing in France is prevalent. . . . Among generals, Manstein, Guderian and Bock are the most influential today. The Army now has Hitler somewhat under control. If anything 'happened' to Hitler, Himmler, being the one with real power, would . . . take over, though probably behind a military facade. . . . No illusions on the power of the Germans to continue resistance should be entertained, for the country's power to do so is still unbroken. There is in Germany some fear . . . that Japan might attempt to make a separate negotiation with America and run out on the Nazis" (RG 226, Entry 134, Box 307).

Doc. 1-48, Tel. 32-35, Apr. 9, 1943, Box 307. Dulles added the following in Tel. 36, Apr. 9: "The Soviet Union has been strengthening its position in Bulgaria by claiming that it will be able to help Bulgaria retain enlarged frontiers. Kiss is of the opinion that the Prime Minister personally engineered the declaration of war on the United States when Germany insisted on this move. When he asked King Boris and leading personalities for the reason, however, he could not get a coherent answer from anybody" (CIA/FOIA). Bulgaria had declared war on the United States on Dec. 13, 1941.

Doc. 1-49, Tel. 173-74, Apr. 10, 1943, Box 307. Gisevius, a lawyer and a conservative, had become disillusioned with the Hitler regime at an early stage but served in the Gestapo before finding refuge in Adm. Canaris's Abwehr. He was assigned to Zurich as an intelligence officer under the cover of Vice-Consul. In *Germany's Underground* (New York: Macmillan, 1947), Dulles describes his close ties with Gisevius, number 512, as a source of information, and in connection with his prominent role in the July 20, 1944, plot against Hitler. Mary Bancroft discusses him in *Autobiography of a Spy.* While in Switzerland, Gisevius continued writing and had translated into English a memoir on his experience in the German resistance. It was published after the war as *To the Bitter End* (1948). Gisevius testified for the prosecution at the Nuremberg war crimes trials but played no role in postwar German politics.

Doc. 1-50, Tel. 60-66, Apr. 14, 1943, Box 307. Reference is made to a U.S.-sponsored congress of anti-Fascist Italians at Montevideo, Uruguay in mid-1942, which issued a declaration supporting the democratic aims of the United Nations.

Sforza had sent a message to Italian resistance leaders in Switzerland on March 17, which read in part as follows: "I hope to receive from you news and useful reports. Am glad you realize how high-minded our friend 110 is. . . . The full American support for complete Italian democracy should be communicated to our friends in Italy" (Tel. 86-87, Box 165).

Dulles transmitted an additional appeal for support to Count Sforza from the Action Party Executive Committee ("Drumbee," "Carr Phillips," and "Harold Taylor") in Tel. 293-96, Apr. 28, 1943 (Box 307). In Tel. 100-102, Apr. 29, Dulles stated that the Action Party was of increasing importance, but should look for leadership from anti-Fascist elements within Italy rather than from Sforza (Box 307). Donovan provided Dulles with the following guidance on Apr. 23: "It is necessary to synchronize the activities in your area with other areas that deal with the same policies and factions. To determine our policy we have been holding conferences with Monty [Italian-American labor leader Vanni Montana] and his associates, and will report to you soon in later cables how the matter is progressing" (Tel. 29, Box 165). On May 8, OSS headquarters sought further to restrain Dulles with guidance on U.S. policy toward Italy: the Italian people were offered the provisions of the Atlantic Charter, including the restoration of a full and free national life, but the terms for peace were unconditional surrender. Dulles was admonished to cooperate with Washington, which was in touch with the principal Italian leaders (Tel. 53-55, Box 165).

Doc. 1-51, Tel. 260-64, Apr. 15, 1943, Box 307. "Barry," number 646, was Leopold Baranyai, an influential supporter of Kallay.

Doc. 1-52, Tel. 2360, Apr. 16, 1943, Box 307.

Doc. 1-53, Tel. 2483, Apr. 21, 1943, Box 307.

Doc. 1-54, Tel. 2635, Apr. 28, 1943, Box 307. Also on Apr. 28, Dulles received a discouraging message indicating that "All news from Bern these days is being discounted 100% by the War Department," since Switzerland was an ideal location for plants, tendentious intelligence, peace feelers, and the like. OSS headquarters expressed its continuing confidence in Dulles's judgment, however (Tel. 8-9, Box 165).

Doc. 1-55, Tel. 27-30, May 4, 1943, Box 307. Reference telegram 1381 appears here as Doc. 1-31. On June 11, OSS headquarters sent Bern a message, resulting from talks with the State Department, that was to be delivered to the Bulgarian Government via Minister Kiosseivanov. The communication deplored Bulgaria's collaboration with Germany and persecution of the Jews. The Allies would not bargain for terms. Bulgaria should realize that what it contributes to the fall of the Axis would determine its final treatment (Tel. 214-16, Box 341).

Doc. 1-56, Tel. 32-33, May 5, 1943, Box 307. On Apr. 10, Dulles had reported a meeting he had held with Philip Monod and other French resistance leaders. They wished to send Henri Frenay to Algiers to cement liaison with non-Gaullist elements. Dulles stated that the resistance leaders in this group wanted to cooperate with de Gaulle but avoid being dominated by the French National Committee (Tel. 166-73).

The head of the British SOE mission in Switzerland was John McCaffery. He operated under the cover of Assistant Press Attaché in Bern.

Doc. 1-57, Tel. 45-50, May 7, 1943, Box 307. In Tel. 34-35, May 4, 1943, OSS Washington had requested a more complete picture of the French underground (RG 226, Entry 134, Box 165). Dulles reported further on May 10 that Henri Frenay now planned to go to London on behalf of the MUR resistance to reach agreement with De Gaulle and the French National Committee. MUR, Davet, Monod, Frenay, and de Benouville—resistance elements with whom Dulles consorted in Switzerland—reportedly sought cooperation with de Gaulle but rejected domination and attempts to designate individuals in France who would direct the entire resistance on behalf of the London Free French (Tel. 63-75, Box 307).

Doc. 1-58, Tel. 56-62, May 8, 1943, Box 307. Dulles received an unfavorable response from headquarters on May 18: "The State Department feels that recent conferences have progressed too far for such suggestions to be useful. They also feel that Winston would object" (Tel. 80-81, Box 165).

Dulles had known Minister Leland Harrison since their service together at the Paris Peace Conference of 1919. This personal relationship furthered effective cooperation between the Legation and OSS operations. Assistant Secretary of State Berle had also served on the U.S. Peace Conference delegation. During World War II, he was the State Department's point of contact on intelligence matters.

On Apr. 10, Donovan had instructed OSS Bern to spread a number of rumors affecting Italy, including reports that the Swiss had refused to deal with Mussolini, the Americans now had a weapon that could destroy any tank, and that Italian troops would be sacrificed to cover the German evacuation of North Africa (Tel. 204-7, Box 165).

Doc. 1-59, Tel. 8-9, May 17, 1943, Box 307.

Doc. 1-60, Tel. 3025, May 17, 1943, Box 307. The reference in paragraph 2 is to the massacre of thousands of Polish officers in the Katyn Forest near Smolensk in the spring of 1940. The Germans announced finding the gravesite in Apr. 1943 and accused the Soviet Union of the atrocity. When the London-based Polish government protested to Moscow, the Soviet Union severed relations and thereafter claimed that the Germans had murdered the Polish officers. Investigations since the war have established beyond doubt that this crime was committed by the NKVD under orders from Stalin.

Doc. 1-61, Tel. 103-8, May 18, 1943, Box 307. In reference Tel. 58-59, OSS Washington instructed Dulles to keep up all contacts with the French underground (Box 165). The OSS London office sought to restrain Dulles in Tel. 23-25 of May 19, contending (1) that it was not advisable for a representative of the French resistance to direct operations from Switzerland, (2) that the operational headquarters for resistance movements was in London, and (3) that support for resistance groups was a joint U.S.-U.K. operation coordinated in London (Box 165). The SI Branch in Washington cabled its views to Bern on May 22. It made the distinction between intelligence-gathering and special operations while recognizing that various French groups did not. Dulles was commended for fostering French resistance groups but was enjoined to maintain his intelligence contacts independently of SO and British SOE interests and activities (Tel. 93-96, Box 165). Dulles pleaded innocence on May 22, promising to untangle any difficulties. But in the same cable, he repeated the request for permission to give generous support for resistance elements fighting in the French Alps (Tel. 141-45, Box 307).

Doc. 1-62, Tel. 3079, May 19, 1943, Box 307. On May 18, Dulles informed Washington that his sources reported some twenty German divisions near the Pyrenees and the Bay of Biscay. He believed that this force was insufficient for an invasion of Spain but did not entirely discount the possibility of a desperate German attempt to close the Mediterranean by such a move (Tel. 113-14, Box 307).

Doc. 1-63, Tel. 3080, May 20, 1943, Box 307. Dulles established contact with various factions in Yugoslavia. On Mar. 6, 1943, he had transmitted a message from the Executive Committee of the Croatian Peasant Party of Vladko Machek stating that Croatians looked to the United States with hope, asked that radio broadcasts from Croatian-Americans be transmitted into the country, and that battalions of Croatian-Americans be formed for service in the Near East (Tel. 1537, Box 307). Kirk Ford Jr. provides information on OSS policy and missions to the area in *OSS and the Yugoslav Resistance, 1943–1945* (College Station: Texas A&M University Press, 1992).

Doc. 1-64, Tel. 3101, May 20, 1943, Box 307.

Doc. 1-65, Tel. 15-17, June 1, 1943, Box 307. Guillain de Benouville, who crossed the French-Swiss border on numerous occasions to meet with Dulles and other Allied officials, presents a detailed account of French resistance and its Swiss back door in *The Unknown Warriors*. On June 5, 1943, OSS in London cabled Bern that British SOE agreed to financial support being given to French Maquis in the Haute Savoie (Tel. 101-3, Box 339). However, OSS London determined, in consultation with SOE, that no arms could be delivered by parachute at least until August when the nights were longer (Tel. 111-13, June 11, 1943, Box 339).

Doc. 1-66, Tel. 212-16, June 1, 1943, Box 307. Gerald Mayer was born in Berlin of American parents and attended high school in Germany and Switzerland. He graduated from the University of California and studied law at Stanford and Harvard. He worked as a newspaper man in the 1930s and was part owner of the family publishing business (Leland Harrison Papers, Box 31). As OWI representative in Bern, he cooperated intimately with Dulles, who recommended him for a commendation after the war. OWI/OSS Bern sent more than 6,000,000 leaflets, pamphlets, newspapers, brochures and forged documents and tickets into enemy-controlled territory. A printing plant was maintained within Fascist Italy. Mayer had close contact with the French resistance elements and supplied them with all manner of propaganda material and bogus documents such as identification papers. He smuggled his material into Germany itself by means of ties with Socialist railroad workers, and facilitated penetration operations late in the war. Mayer also planted stories favorable to the Allied cause in the Swiss press. His role was essential in developing contact with Fritz Kolbe ("George Wood"), an agent for Dulles within the German Foreign Ministry (Mayer to Dulles, Mar. 24, 1947; Dulles to Donovan, Apr. 25, 1947, Allen Dulles Papers, Box 31).

Doc. 1-67, Tel. 235, June 4, 1943, Box 307. A notation on the source text reads: "MO is considering this. Example of ticket has been requested." Tel. 234 from Bern, June 4, described the new commuter railroad ticket system being put into effect in Germany (Box 307)

Doc. 1-68, Tel. 254-258, June 7, 1943, Box 307. "The Marshal" Henri-Philippe Pétain, Chief of State of the Vichy government. Adm. William D. Leahy, Chief of Staff to President Roosevelt, had been Ambassador to Vichy 1941–42. Ménétrel ("M") presumably is Dr. Ménétrel, Pétain's physician and confidant. On June 10, OSS headquarters responded as follows: "At the present time, it is felt that any communication with Marshal would be undesirable. Will contact you again should there be any change" (Tel. 173, Box 341).

Doc. 1-69, Tel. 3651, June 19, 1943, Box 307. Paraphrase; sent through State Department channels.

Doc. 1-70, Tel. 3545, June 12, 1943, Box 307. Paraphrase; sent through State Department channels. Allied forces captured Tunis and Bizerte on May 7. The Allies sunk some 28 German U-boats in the North Atlantic during the month, known as "Black May" in the German Navy. Henceforth, the Allied lifeline to Europe was secure. Bela Imredy was the pro-German former premier of Hungary (1938–39); he was executed after the war.

On May 27, Dulles had transmitted two other significant reports based on information from Gisevius. Mussolini was said to be disillusioned with Hitler for lack of military support in Italy, and over the German occupation of Croatia. Hitler would remain on the defensive in Russia. Hitler was under pressure from Mussolini as well as from the Japanese to undertake separate peace negotiations with Russia. Hitler did not contemplate an attack on Spain, and had been informed by Franco that he would resist an attack from any quarter. President Inonu had assured German ambassador von Papen that Turkey would not go to war against Germany. Hitler was thoroughly disgusted with his Hungarian ally. Japan was attempting to promote a Japanese-Chinese-Russian understanding (Tel. 3229, Box 307) Germany was reeling from air attacks and food shortages. Hitler was increasingly isolated. His inner circle was comprised of Keitel, Zeitzler, Bormann, Lammers, Buhler, and Himmler (Tel. 3241, Box 307).

Doc. 1-71, Tel. 305-14, June 16, 1943, Box 307. In Tel. 225-27 of June 22, OSS headquarters informed Dulles that Whitney Shepardson and F. L. Mayer of the SI Branch, and Hugh Wilson of the Planning Group were considering the best means of exploiting contacts such as those described in this message. They had not yet decided if Dulles should turn over such information to Minister Harrison for transmittal to the State Department, or whether A. A. Berle and other ranking State Department officers could avail themselves of the information as transmitted from OSS to State in Washington (Box 341).

Doc. 1-72, Tel. 317-18, June 17, 1943, Box 307.

Doc. 1-73, Tel. 331-32, June 23, 1943, Box 307.

Doc. 1-74, Tel. 333-34, June 23, 1943, Box 307.

Doc. 1-75, Tel. 338-342, June 24, 1943, Box 307. In Tel. 186-188 of May 29, Dulles had relayed information received from Gisevius indicating that the Germans were experimenting with a long-range gun that the military hoped would be useful for the bombardment of London (Box 307). In another area of German weapons production, Bern reported on June 4 that 100 to 120 Tiger tanks were being built monthly for assignment to SS divisions. Another tank, the 70-ton Panther armed with a 150 mm. cannon was also reportedly being produced (Tel. 242-43, Box 307).

Doc. 1-76, Tel. 349-50, June 25, 1943, Box 307.

Doc. 1-77, Tel. 38-42, June 28, 1943, Box 307. General Davet, number 516, became head of the French resistance delegation in Switzerland. According to Frenay (*The Night Will End,* 253), Davet was an airman and a former member of Action Française.

Dulles's reference to Tel. 179 concerned tentative instructions to Bern concerning OSS-SOE coordination of contacts with the French resistance. Under existing bilateral agreements concluded in June and October 1942, OSS had been accorded a junior partnership role in special operations and support for resistance elements in Europe (see Kermit Roosevelt, *The War Report of the OSS*, vol. 2, *The Overseas Targets* [New York: Walker, 1976] 3–7; Smith, *Shadow Warriors,* 170ff.; R. Harris Smith, *OSS,* 165ff.; and Foot, *SOE in France*, 31ff. In Tel. 179-83 of June 14, 1943, OSS headquarters transmitted proposed guidelines instructing Dulles to send all messages dealing with SO (Special Operations) matters to London for action, with information copies to Washington. SO relations with French resistance groups through existing London channels were to be encouraged to avoid confusion, and in the interests of U.S.-U.K. relations. However, Washington deemed it desirable that Bern retain SO contacts in France consistent with those objectives. It was also considered permissible that Dulles extend some minimal financial support to French resistance elements (Box 165).

On June 26, 1943, OSS Bern transmitted a message from the labor leader 328 to "Eva" in New York. Expressing appreciation for New York labor's help, he stated that he was now in a position to expand Syndicalist propaganda in France, and cited various underground publications. He also noted a newly created organization among French deported prisoners which offered opportunities for sabotage and propaganda within Germany (Tel. 352-57, Box 307).

Doc. 1-78, Tel. 3894, June 30, 1943, Box 307. Walther Funk was German Minister of Economic Affairs and President of the Reichsbank.

Doc. 1-79, Tel. 48-52, July 3, 1943, Box 307. Roseborough had practiced law in the New York and Paris offices of Sullivan & Cromwell from 1929 to 1940.

"Max," Jean Moulin, was sent by de Gaulle to France to centralize the resistance and assert the authority of the General's exile government over it. Some Maquis elements opposed Moulin's mission. He was arrested by the Gestapo in June 1943, apparently as the result of treachery. The resistance figure René Hardy became the principal suspect in a complex story of intrigue. In Tel. 44-45 to London, July 3, unidentified French resistance sources informed Henri Frenay of Moulin's arrest: "The Gestapo has arrested Max Thomas at Aubrac; . . . Max had arranged a general reunion A.S. for Monday, June 21, to prepare reorganization necessitated by Vidal's arrest. Bardot, who had opened fire, is still detained by French police. I beg you to obtain at once a military chief named by you. Likewise arrange for immediate remittance of funds via COCCOZ. We are completely unfurnished with ammunition and cut off from sources of money. Everybody is at his post" (Box 307).

On July 3, 1943, Dulles sent a telegram to Washington regarding another tragedy in France. This message may have been totally realistic, but it also appears to reflect an astounding lack of compassion. General Donovan had cabled Dulles on June 18, with regard to a report from Donald Lowrie of the YMCA that "4000 children ranging from the ages of two to 14 were being sent without adult escort via Paris in box cars destined for some unknown points." Donovan asked for suggestions as to how the children could be aided (Tel. 217-18, Entry 160, Box 2). Dulles replied: "Unless our Government is willing to give consideration to a broad program whereunder in reciprocation for temporary asylum here, guarantee the issuance of visas after the war and the granting of transportation to the United States or elsewhere and possibility some assurance with respect to supplementary shipments of food in order to provide for the care of children here, I do not see that much can be done in regard to this type of situation. A problem of this type hardly come within the scope of my activities here and since similar conditions exist in virtually all the countries which are under German domination, its ramifications are broad" (Tel. 3942, Box 307).

Doc. 1-80, Tel. 396-400, July 7, 1943, Box 307.

Doc. 1-81, Tel. 401-3, July 7, 1943, Box 273. In Tel. 247, June 29, Washington informed Bern that OWI policy was directed toward splitting Italy from Germany, rather than fomenting internal rivalries (Box 341).

Doc. 1-82, Tel. 4017, July 8, 1943, Box 273. Count Stephen Bethlen had been Premier of Hungary from 1921 to 1931. Dulles added in Tel. 407-10, July 8, that Baranyai was a very influential contact. He proposed, however, to tell the Hungarians that since Allied victory was certain, no conditions would be considered. Hungary would be judged according to the extent that it severed relations with Germany and denied it support (Box 273).

Doc. 1-83, Tel. 4018, July 8, 1943, Box 273. Mussolini and Hitler had met at Salzburg from April 7 to April 10. The day-by-day development of Axis relations is set forth in F. W. Deakin, *The Brutal Friendship: Mussolini, Hitler, and the Fall of Italian Fascism* (New York: Harper & Row, 1962).

Doc. 1-84, Tel. 428-31, July 12, 1943, Box 273.

Doc. 1-85, Tel. 4158, July 14, 1943, Box 273.

Doc. 1-86, Tel. 35-37, July 15, 1943, Box 273. Funds from American labor continued to flow to French labor through the OSS Bern channel. On July 13, 328 cabled Eva: "I appreciate the financial aid which enables the Socialist Party to decentralize propaganda work which is of utmost importance. . . . We have transmitted the money for CGT and the Socialist Party. . . . The work of organization and propaganda for French workers in the Reich is progressing. Thanks to your financial aid, Syndicalist work is also progressing well. We have just put out an 8 page pamphlet of excellent material and documentation for militants" (Box 273).

Doc. 1-87, Tel. 3-5, July 19, 1943, Box 273.

Doc. 1-88, Tel. 449-56, July 19, 1943, Box 273. In Tel. 288-96 to Bern, July 10, Shepardson and Mayer in OSS headquarters expressed concern over Dulles's perceived role in the politics of the Italian resistance, the type of activities "which the State Department has previously said were none of our business." Dulles was instructed to maintain his connections, but that he should channel political messages through the Legation (Box 165). Telegram 174-78, June 11, from General Donovan to Dulles, stressed the necessity of abiding by agreements between OSS/SO and British SOE, which gave the latter predominant responsibility for organization and support of European resistance elements. Donovan defined SO operations as sabotage, conduct of guerrilla warfare, and contact and support of the resistance. He added, however, that "nothing of the above-mentioned, is to be construed in any manner as limiting the development, maintenance and establishment of intelligence networks" (Box 165). This issue remained the subject OSS cable traffic for months. On Aug. 23, Shepardson of SI informed Dulles that it was understood in Washington that he was free to contact any French groups he wished for the purpose of obtaining intelligence, without reference to London (Tel. 482-83, Box 341).

Doc. 1-89, Tel. 460-64, July 20, 1943, Box 273. Count Massimo Magistrati, Italian Minister in Bern, was known to be well disposed toward the Anglo-Americans from contacts he made at previous posts. Magistrati, assigned source number 812, cooperated with OSS Bern and the American Legation throughout the war. He had married the sister of Count Ciano, Mussolini's foreign minister. Correspondence with Magistrati is located in RG 226, Entry 125, Box 7; RG 226, Entry 190, Box 32; and RG 59, Classified Bern Post Files, Boxes 12 and 18.

Doc. 1-90, Tel. 4323, July 21, 1943, Box 273. OSS Bern reported on the location and strength of German submarine bases in France in Tel. 189-91, May 28, 1943 (Box 171); Tel. 219-22, June 2, 1943 (Box 339); and other cables.

Doc. 1-91, Tel. 4357, July 22, 1943, Box 273. Hitler and Mussolini met at Feltre, in the province of Venice, on July 19 to discuss the declining military situation.

Doc. 1-92, Tel. 4417, July 24, 1943, Box 273.

Doc. 1-93, Tel. 4446, July 25, 1943, Box 273.

Doc. 1-94, Tel. 490-91, July 26, 1943, Box 273. Reference Tel. 305-14, June 16, is printed here as Doc. 1-71.

Doc. 1-95, Tel. 12-13, July 27, 1943, Box 273.

Doc. 1-96, Tel. 492-94, July 27, 1943, Box 273. Dulles described Vulcan as his first contact with the Rumanian Legation, and considered him thoroughly anti-Nazi while maintaining a realistic attitude on his country's position vis-à-vis Russia. He had once been a Rockefeller Foundation scholar. With the surrender of Rumania, Vulcan was dismissed by the new government (Dulles to Jigsaw—Lt. Robert Wauchope, Dec. 8, 1944, Entry 190, Box 22). Dulles-Vulcan correspondence is located in Entry 125, Box 10. After the war, Dulles supported Vulcan in his attempt to find employment (Allen Dulles Papers, Box 27).

Doc. 1-97, Tel. 497-500, July 27, 1943, Box 273.

Doc. 1-98, Tel. 510-13, July 27, 1943, Box 273. Telegram 387-88, July 31, read as follows: "Would appreciate your paying 8000 francs to 475 and, at the same time give him the following message which is signed, Antonini. Another installment of $2000 is being sent to you by the Italian-American Labor Council. The Italian Socialist Party is to be assigned $5000 of this sum, and the Italian Confederation of Labor is to be allotted the balance of this sum which will amount to $1500. Regarding the new situation, we are awaiting information anxiously" (Box 341).

Doc. 1-99, Tel. 4491, July 27, 1943, Box 273.

Doc. 1-100, Tel. 4513, July 28, 1943, Box 273.

Doc. 1-101, Tel. 4544, July 28, 1943, Box 273.

Doc. 1-102, Tel. 515-16, July 29, 1943, Box 273. The rumor regarding former Fascist Party Secretary Carlo Scorza was untrue. Reference is to Roberto Farinacci, a senior Fascist official.

Dulles added the following on the Italian situation on Aug. 3: "It would seem that the Nazis are still undecided whether to reinforce their positions in North Italy, with the intention of defending the line of the Apennines, or to withdraw. This is indicated not only by the reports which have reached us, but also by the absence of palpable evidence that unusual movements of troops and equipment, either to or from Italy, have taken place recently. Even should the Nazis decide to withdraw, it is suggested by reports that they would try to defend the Trieste-Brenner line" (Tel. 537-38, Box 273).

Doc. 1-103, Tel. 534-36, Aug. 2, 1943, Box 273.

Doc. 1-104, Tel. 4639, Aug. 2, 1943, Box 273.

Doc. 1-105, Tel. 530-533, Aug. 2, 1943, Box 273. With regard to morale and psychological operations, Dulles informed Morale Operations on July 21 that OSS Bern had not been active in spreading the rumors sent periodically. He stated that personnel was lacking and the danger existed of compromising SI work by engaging in the dissemination of rumors. He reported, however, that he and local MO and OWI personnel regularly sent out propaganda leaflets (Tel. 471-73, Box 273).

Doc. 1-106, Tel. 544-48, Aug. 3, 1943, Box 273. In Tel. 342-46, OSS headquarters (Shepardson, F. L. Mayer, Hugh Wilson and others) stated agreement with Dulles's view that dealing with resistance groups was a very important aspect of OSS activities and should not be done through diplomatic channels. It was policy to work with any patriotic groups who could help the United Nations. OSS's interest was said to be nonpolitical, attempting as a military organization to support military programs rather than promoting political doctrines. "In maintaining your cooperation with anti-Fascist groups in Italy and with resistance elements in other countries you are practicing the right policy" (Box 341).

The section in this cable on Hungary, especially the proposal to send radio operators, foreshadows the tragic "Sparrow" mission of March 1944. The ongoing relationship between anti-Nazi Hungarian elements are traced in Kallay's *Hungarian Premier.*

General Draja Mihailovich, leader of the noncommunist Serbian resistance, is mentioned here. Dulles maintained contact with various Yugoslav resistance elements, Serb and Croatian individuals, and with certain of the thousands of Yugoslav refugees in Switzerland.

Doc. 1-107, Tel. 125-26, Aug. 4, 1943, Box 273. Tel. 487-88 reported that the Nazis in Paris were recruiting pro-Nazi French aviators to travel to London via Spain, join the Royal Air Force, and perform espionage on behalf of Germany (Box 171).

Doc. 1-108, Tel. 541-43, Aug. 4, 1943, Box 273.

Doc. 1-109, Tel. 552-53, Aug. 4, 1943, Box 273. Also on Aug. 4, Dulles transmitted a message from Silone on behalf of the Italian Socialist Party to Assistant Secretary of State Berle requesting that the United States adopt a position in favor of the liquidation of the Monarchy (Tel. 4716, Box 273). Donovan admonished Dulles on Aug. 8 that such messages should be sent through State Department channels to avoid giving the impression that OSS was carrying on activities of a political nature (Tel. 414-16, Box 165).

Doc. 1-110, Tel. 4721, Aug. 4, 1943, Box 273.

Doc. 1-111, Tel. 142, Aug. 7, 1943, Box 273. Dulles provided additional information in Tel. 581-82. The source for Tel. 142 was actually a Swiss businessman. The source added that there had been some comment in Bucharest about the fact that the Romana Americana refinery owned by Standard Oil of New Jersey had not been bombed (Box 339).

Doc. 1-112, Tel. 583-87, Aug. 10, 1943, Box 273. Mario Badoglio was the son of the marshal.

Doc. 1-113, Tel. 4877, Aug. 11, 1943, Box 273.

Doc. 1-114, Tel. 4883, Aug. 11, 1943, Box 273.

Doc. 1-115, Tel. 610-12, Aug. 16, 1943, Box 273. Tel. 428-29 to Bern, Aug. 10, reads in part as follows: "Please give the following message from Dominique with 50,000 francs to Robert. '$3,000 for the Christian Unionists and $6,500 for CGT from New York Unions and $3,000 to the Socialist Party from the Jewish Labor Committee is being sent herewith by Dominique. Dominique and Joseph would like to have the money for the Christian Unionists distributed by the Lyon Committee of Coordination' " (Box 341).

Doc. 1-116, Tel. 5003, Aug. 16, 1943, Box 273. Dr. Reale became Italian Minister in Bern after the war.

Doc. 1-117, Tel. 616-18, Aug. 17, 1943, Box 273. Reports transmitted from Bern on German-Japanese relations and in particular on Japanese promotion of a German-Soviet settlement complemented the intelligence gained through "Magic," the interception and deciphering of Japanese coded radio messages. From 1941, Anglo-American cryptanalysts were privy to the communications from Hiroshi Oshima, the Japanese Ambassador in Berlin, to Tokyo. This extraordinary source is examined in detail by Carl Boyd in a series of five articles in *Intelligence and National Security* (Jan. 1987, Apr. 1987, Oct. 1988, Jan. 1989, and July 1989).

Reference is to Adm. Kichisaburo Nomura, who was Japanese ambassador in Washington at the time of the attack on Pearl Harbor.

Doc. 1-118, Tel. 5014, Aug. 17, 1943, Box 273. In Tel. 408, Aug. 5, headquarters, on behalf of antisubmarine command, asked Bern to gather information on the effect of high mortality rates among submarine crews on the submarine service, the German navy, and the German people (Box 341).

Bern provided many reports relating to submarine personnel, production and deployment throughout the war. Headquarters sent numerous specific taskings and emphasized the eagerness of military authorities to receive this information (Tels. 445-46, Aug. 12, and 450, Aug. 14, 1943, Box 341).

Doc. 1-119, Tel. 621-22, Aug. 19, 1943, Box 273. Reference is apparently to Dr. Paul Vignaux, a former professor at the Sorbonne who worked on French matters in the OSS New York office during the war. Certain of his correspondence and a report on Christian Syndicalism in France are in Entry 115, Box 32. As part of the transatlantic correspondence among French religious and intellectual elements via the OSS Bern channel, Jacques Maritain in New York directed the following to his compatriots in Europe on Aug. 9: "When the horror will have been swept away, it is you and your companions who will create the future. Our hope is in you, and in the French people. . . . We hope for a strong and free citizenry, where democratic and evangelical inspiration will go hand in hand. We hope too for an international order which will be not only continental, but also global and where France, supported by the friendship of America, will help the Anglo-Saxon and Russian worlds understand one another. I salute our persecuted Jewish brothers. May you who struggle and suffer for France and for the spirit of Jesus Christ be blessed by divine guidance and protection" (Tel. 419-21 to Bern, Aug. 9, 1943, Box 341).

Doc. 1-120, Tel. 623-27, Aug. 19, 1943, Box 273. On Aug. 21, F. L. Mayer of SI cabled Dulles as follows: "Greatly appreciate your fine #623. Have sent it on to 109, who is now in a certain place where it can be used. It is not yet possible to get any opinion from the State Department about action on Italian and Hungarian political questions mentioned in your cables. We are, however, in steady personal communication with State" (Tel. 479, Box 341).

Doc. 1-121, Tel. 628, Aug. 20, 1943, Box 273. The source was Fritz Kolbe; see Doc. 1-123.

Doc. 1-122, Tel. 629-30, Aug. 20, 1943, Box 273. OSS headquarters transmitted this cable to the State Department which determined that no response should be made (*FRUS, The Conferences at Washington and Quebec, 1943* (Washington, D.C.: GPO, 1970), 1087) On Aug. 23, Donovan informed Dulles that "the highest place, to which your [Tel. 629-30] was delivered, welcomed it as a confirmation of other things. It did not seem advisable to employ your channels, too, considering conversations via other channels. For intelligence purposes, however, kindly keep up your relations, and do not let the relationship cool off. When anything further develops, we will let you know" (Tel. 484-85, Box 165; Tel. 486, Aug. 24, Box 341).

Doc. 1-123, Tel. 164-66, Aug. 21, 1943, Box 339. Fritz Kolbe, assistant to Karl Ritter, the Foreign Ministry official in charge of liaison with the military, was the most important single source for Dulles, and perhaps for the OSS as a whole. Kolbe first contacted the OSS in Bern on Aug. 17, 1943, through Dr. Ernesto Kocherthaler, a German-born Spanish citizen living in Switzerland. Kocherthaler knew Paul Dreyfus, a banker in Basel, who was able to arrange for Kolbe to meet Gerald Mayer, Dulles's OWI colleague in Bern. Kocherthaler was Kolbe's intermediary with OSS from the beginning and conduit for all subsequent "George Wood" reports (Tel. 2577 from Bern, Dec. 27, 1944, CIA/FOIA).

The Dulles telegrams that transmitted intelligence obtained from Kolbe to Washington and London are interfiled in Bern cable files, Entry 134. Separate collections of Bern cables based on Wood information exist in Entries 121 and 138. In Washington, OSS reorganized material from Kolbe's reports according to subject. The resulting documents, labeled the "Boston Series," were circulated within OSS and elsewhere. On Jan. 10, 1944, Acting OSS Director Buxton transmitted the first in the series to the White House under the cover of a memorandum to the President that read in part as follows: "We have secured through secret intelligence channels a series of what purport to be authentic reports, transmitted by various German diplomatic, consular, military and intelligence sources to their headquarters. The source and material are being checked as to probable authenticity both here and in London. We shall submit later a considered opinion on the point. It is possible that contact with this source furnishes the first important penetration into a responsible German agency. . . . We have labeled these reports the 'Boston Series' and append hereto the first fourteen. Copies of the material are being made available to the State, War and Navy Departments" (Entry 162, Box 7).

In due course, the authenticity of the Wood/Kolbe reports was established beyond doubt. Among those tasked with verification were F. L. Mayer in OSS and Kim Philby in British SIS. (See Philby, *My Silent War* [New York: Grove Press, 1968]. Sets of the Boston Series exist in RG 226 at the National Archives and in the William J. Donovan Papers at the U.S. Army Military History Institute, Carlisle Barracks, Pa.) Kolbe's role was described in "The Spy the Nazis Missed," by Edward P. Morgan in *True* (July 1950), reprinted in Allen W. Dulles, ed., *Great True Spy Stories* (New York: Harper & Row, 1968). Anthony Cave Brown presents detailed coverage of Kolbe's exploits in *Wild Bill Donovan.* His motivation is treated in Mother Mary Alice Gallin, *The Ethical and Religious Factors in the German Resistance to Hitler* (Washington, D.C.: Catholic University of America, 1955). An important account of Kolbe's contribution appeared in CIA's classified publication *Studies in Intelligence* 10:1 (winter 1966), 69–90: "Alias George Wood," by Anthony Quibble. It has been declassified and is available under FOIA. Another significant article appeared in *Die Zeit,* no. 19, May 9, 1986, "Der Mann, der den Krieg verkurzen wollte" (The man who wanted to shorten the war").

Doc. 1-124, Tel. 5150, Aug. 22, 1943, Box 273.

Doc. 1-125, Tel. 5163, Aug. 23, 1943, Box 273. The negotiations leading to the Italian surrender are documented in *FRUS,* 1943, vol. 2 (Washington, D.C.: GPO, 1964). Francis D. G. Osborne was the British minister to the Holy See. Number 645 is John McCaffrey, head of British SOE in Switzerland. In Tel. 639-41 of Aug. 24, Dulles added the following: "This is in reference to Italy and especially to my #5163 through the Secretary of State. My Zulu colleague sent a corresponding cable which went to the War Office. In this type contact the War office consults F [Foreign Office?] to the extent required. As a result of his ability to receive prompt directives, Zulu is ahead of us every time. A situation like this, where important contacts such as 639 have to look to Zulu alone for their directives, does not appeal to me. Particularly in view of Eisenhower's position, it seems to me that this should be more of a partnership arrangement. I would not like to disturb the effective work of 645 by bringing out our own problems of action and coordination, as I realize that the above is very delicate" (Box 273).

Doc. 1-126, Tel. 651-53, Aug. 25, 1943, Box 273. Edward Lawler, now an attorney in Memphis, served in X-2 (OSS counterintelligence) in London, and had access to the George Wood material. He recalls that he never liked his British counterpart, Philby, who also participated in the evaluation of this critical source as the sole UK channel, because he asked too many questions. Lawler is writing an account of his experiences for publication (Interview).

On another counterintelligence matter, Kolbe was able to warn Dulles that the Germans were aware that the U.S. military attaché in Ankara was attempting to establish a Balkan espionage ring (Tel. 847 from Bern, Oct. 9, 1943, CIA/FOIA).

Doc. 1-127, Tel. 5223, Aug. 25, 1943, Box 273. Paul C. Squire was U.S. Consul in Geneva, 1941–45. Reference Tel. 5222 does not identify the intermediaries (Box 273).

Doc. 1-128, Tel. 654-657, Aug. 26, 1943, Box 339. In a cable of the same day, Dulles relayed Kolbe's minutely detailed description of the location of the East Prussian German General Headquarters, including the exact position of Foreign Minister Ribbentrop's offices and Hitler's bombproof hideout (Tel. 644-48, Aug. 26, 1943, Box 273).

Doc. 1-129, Tel. 658-60, Aug. 26, 1943, Box 273.

Doc. 1-130, Tel. 5240, Aug. 26, 1943, Box 273.

Doc. 1-131, Tel. 5269, Aug. 26, 1943, Box 273.

Doc. 1-132, Tel. 666-68, Aug. 28, 1943, Box 273. On Aug. 31, OSS headquarters approved the proposal that intelligence from Dulles's French sources be provided to the Fighting French in London and Algiers (Tel. 513, Box 341).

In Tel. 167-68, Aug. 24, Dulles had indicated that he was providing funds to the maquis through Gen. Davet, head of the French resistance delegation in Switzerland. He reported that the maquis were ready to carry out definite operations as directed by the Allies (Box 165).

Doc. 1-133, Tel. 5313, Aug. 28, 1943, Box 273. On Sept. 11, 1943, OSS headquarters informed Dulles that "the Army gives our Bern information the following relatively high rating: 40% definitely valuable; 40% secondary valuable, 20% casual, and 0% worthless" (Tel. 580, Box 341). This estimation contrasted sharply with the military's low evaluation of Bern material earlier in the war.

Doc. 1-134, Tel. 5317, Aug. 28, 1943, Box 273.

Doc. 1-135, Tel. 5341, Aug. 29, 1943, Box 339. In Tel. 669-71, Aug. 29, Dulles reported that according to "Kiss" King Boris might have taken an overdose of his customary sleeping drugs following a brow-beating by Hitler. The ambassador also said that the new regime would be a German instrument (CIA/FOIA).

In *Crown of Thorns*, Stephane Groueff writes the following on the basis of conversations with Kiossei-vanov: "Some secret contacts already had been established with the Allies in Switzerland, the operational base for Allen Dulles, the American OSS representative. The American intelligence officer had been in touch with the former League of Nations' envoy to Bulgaria, René Charron, a good friend of the country and admirer of King Boris. During the war, Charron, a Frenchman, resided in Switzerland and was on close terms with Kiosseivanov. Early in 1943, Dulles asked Charron to transmit a memorandum to King Boris in which, after asserting that Germany was about to lose the war, the American suggested that the king indicate in some way that Bulgaria intended to withdraw gradually from the Axis. The memorandum did not insist on an immediate break, only advised that Bulgaria signal its willingness to change policies at the first opportune moment. The memorandum further recommended that the exist-ing anti-Jewish measures should, if possible, be annulled. The message concluded that if Bulgaria did not indicate its intention to withdraw from her alliance with Germany, the Allies would be forced to con-tinue military action, even onto Bulgarian soil. Charron transmitted Dulles's message to Kiosseivanov, who brought it to King Boris. During his short stay in Bulgaria, Kiosseivanov had three audiences with the king, who was very interested in the memorandum and its recommendations. But when Kiosseivanov returned to this post, he had no concrete answer to bring back to Charron and Allen Dulles" (351–52).

Reference is to Bogdan Filov, Prime Minister of Bulgaria. Telegrams 214 and 669 have not been found. George V. Earle, Assistant Naval Attaché in Istanbul, was a confidant of President Roosevelt and former Ambassador to Bulgaria. He was relieved from his free-lancing responsibilities in 1944 after numerous controversies and security lapses. (See Barry Rubin, *Istanbul Intrigues* [New York: McGraw-Hill, 1989].)

Doc. 1-136, Tel. 676, Aug. 31, 1943, Box 273. Of the cited cables, the following are printed above: Doc. 1-114, Doc. 1-125, Doc. 1-112, Doc. 1-131.

Chapter 2: The Invasion of Italy, Resistance Movements, and Balkan Intrigues, September 1943–January 1944

Doc. 2-1, Tel. 682-83, Sept. 1, 1943, Box 273.

Doc. 2-2, Tel. 182-84, Sept. 2, 1943, Box 340. Reference is to Edgar Faure, a resistance leader who became director of legislative services for the de Gaulle exile committee. He became a fixture in French governments after the war, twice serving as Premier.

Doc. 2-3, Tel. 5453, Sept. 3, 1943, Box 340. Baron Georges Bakach Bessenyey became one of Dulles's leading sources. He was a career diplomat of pro-Western sentiments who had been political director of the Hungarian foreign ministry in the 1930s. After the war, Dulles corresponded with him and supported his fortunes as an exile (Allen Dulles Papers, Box 23). Adm. Nicholas Horthy served as Regent of

Hungary from 1920 to 1944, pending a restoration of the Hungarian monarchy that never occurred. He allied Hungary with Germany in order to regain territory lost in World War I, but also sought to limit German influence.

Doc. 2-4, Tel. 693-97, Sept. 7, 1943, Box 340. Tel. 516-18 to Bern, Aug. 30, 1943, stated that in response to a request from high military quarters, Dulles should describe the current situation and ultimate possibilities of resistance groups particularly east of the Rhone and in France generally (Box 165). A.S. stands for Armée Secrète, the unified military forces of the French resistance.

Doc. 2-5, Tel. 5548, Sept. 8, 1943, Box 340. Olivetti, of the typewriter manufacturing family, sometimes contacted Dulles when in Switzerland on business.

Doc. 2-6, Tel. 5565, Sept. 8, 1943, Box 340.

Doc. 2-7, Tel. 703-5, Sept. 9, 1943, Box 340. Reference is to the British bombing of Peenemünde on Aug. 17, 1943.

Doc. 2-8, Tel. 710, Sept. 10, 1943, Box 340.

Doc. 2-9, Tel. 711-12, Sept. 10, 1943, Box 340.

Doc. 2-10, Tel. 713-17, Sept. 11, 1943, Box 273. Tel. 552-56 stated that OSS Morale Operations now wanted to establish a branch office in Bern. This was to be accomplished by assigning additional duties to someone already on hand, since it was not possible to get MO agents into Switzerland. The following definition of MO functions was provided: "All types of subversive morale operations other than physical. This includes bribery, rumors, fifth column activities, poison pen letters, false freedom radio stations, misleading or false printed matter spread directly or through agents, forged documents, or any other media that may be used to undermine morale, [and] create division and confusion among the enemy and governments, groups, and individuals who are collaborating with them" (Box 165).

Doc. 2-11, Tel. 718-21, Sept. 11, 1943, Box 273. Dulles provided additional information on the French resistance "secret army" in Tel. 932-37, Oct. 27. Based on recent discussions with de Benouville and other resistance leaders in Geneva, he reported that the A.S. had some 70,000 men, and if properly armed could cut off France from Italy, isolate Marseille and Bordeaux, and hold bases in remote areas. It intended to completely paralyze transportation throughout the country on D-Day (CIA/FOIA).

On Sept. 20, George Sharp, head of the West Europe branch of the OSS Special Operations (SO) branch in Washington, sent a cable to Dulles reading as follows: "Exactly the type of information I needed was contained in your #718-721. Accept my thanks" (Box 165). Before the war, Sharp was a senior partner of Sullivan & Cromwell.

Doc. 2-12, Tel. 5674, Sept. 12, 1943, Box 340. Marshal Ion Antonescu was named Premier of Rumania in 1940. He established a military dictatorship in league with Nazi Germany in 1941. Michael Antonescu was Deputy Premier and Foreign Minister. Both were executed for war crimes by the pro-Soviet successor regime in 1946. Iuliu Maniu and Constantin Bratianu were important noncommunist, non-Fascist political leaders.

Doc. 2-13, Tel. 726-29, Sept. 13, 1943, Box 273. Tel. 4357 is printed as Doc. 1-91; Tel. 629 is printed as Doc. 1-122. Number 475 is Ignazio Silone; 638 is a representative of the Action Party; and 639 is "Carr Phillips," another Italian contact. In Tel. 615, Sept. 18, OSS Assistant Director Buxton informed Dulles on behalf of Donovan that the building up of resistance units behind German lines in Italy was of the utmost importance (Box 165).

Doc. 2-14, Tel. 734-35, Sept. 14, 1943, Box 340.

Doc. 2-15-16, Tel. 5752, Sept. 15, 1943, Box 340. Gen. Hans Jeschonnek, Chief of the Luftwaffe General Staff, did commit suicide.

Doc. 2-17, Tel. 5781, Sept. 16, 1943, Box 340.

Doc. 2-18, Tel. 5829, Sept. 18, 1943, Box 340.

Doc. 2-19, Tel. 763-67, Sept. 21, 1943, Box 273.

Doc. 2-20, Tel. 5876, Sept. 21, 1943, Box 340. Tel. 5781 is printed here as Doc. 2-17.

Doc. 2-21, Tel. 777-79, Sept. 22, 1943, Box 340. Adm. Karl Doenitz was commander of the German Navy. Informant 496 was Maurice Villars, Director of the Electro-Bank in Zurich.

Doc. 2-22, Tel. 783-84, Sept. 24, 1943, Box 273.

Doc. 2-23, Tel. 5971, Sept. 24, 1943, Box 273. In July 1943, the Free Germany Committee was established in Moscow under Soviet auspices, followed in September by a Union of German Officers, including the captured generals Walther von Seydlitz-Kurzbach and Freiherr Alexander von Daniels. The latter body appealed to the German Army to follow the traditional policy of friendship toward Russia advanced by Bismarck and Seeckt and cease the struggle against the Red Army.

Doc. 2-24, Tel. 5974, Sept. 25, 1943, Box 340. Acting Director Buxton's letter to Secretary of State Hull is in RG 59, file 103.918/1754. Tel. 5876 is printed here as Doc. 2-20. Tel. 599-603 from OSS headquarters to Dulles, Sept. 13, 1943, read in part as follows: "1. We are prepared and anxious to carry on in Hungary the SO program suggested by 646 [Baranyai—see Doc. 1-82 and 1-85], for JCS has at last sent us orders. 2. . . . The time is ripe, JCS concurs, to expand into Hungary, Rumania and Bulgaria, our subversive activities in the Balkans, subject to continuing coordination with SOE and the permission of the Theater Commander involved. The Soviet Government ought to be advised of the activities planned for the countries mentioned, JCS directs. . . . The State Dept. must be kept informed. The exclusive purpose of the program must be victory over the Axis nations and it cannot be allowed to entail any commitment by this country. Preferment will be shown those resistance groups or candidate successor governments in proportion to their desire to overlook their political platforms or distinctions in doctrine and to engage in full coordination." (Box 165)

In Tel. 2499, Oct. 12, Dulles received State Department guidance on responding to Rumanian contacts: the only proposal that would be given serious consideration would be unconditional surrender. However, OSS Bern remained willing to listen. Meanwhile, the Allies continued to note that Rumania was still fighting against the Soviet Union, persecuting the Jews, generally supporting the cause of Germany (Box 165) The following day, he was further informed that Assistant Secretary of State Berle had decided that the Rumanian situation as described by Dulles could not be exploited for the present (Tel. 717-19, Oct. 13, 1943, Box 341).

Doc. 2-25, Tel. 5985, Sept. 25, 1943, Box 273.

Doc. 2-26, Tel. 794-97, Sept. 28, 1943, Box 340.

Doc. 2-27, Tel. 58-61, Sept 29, 1943, Box 340. In Tel. 314-15 from London to Bern, Oct. 19, Dulles was informed that Donovan had confirmed London OSS/SO responsibility for coordination of SO activities, and that he should operate in close consultation with SOE in Switzerland (Box 157).

Doc. 2-28, Tel. 799-801, Sept. 30, 1943, Box 340.

Doc. 2-29, Tel. 805-6, Oct. 1, 1943, Box 273. Randolfo Pacciardi was an exiled Italian anti-Fascist and anticommunist political leader.

Doc. 2-30, Tel. 809-10, Oct. 1, 1943, Box 273. Schulte, a prominent German industrialist was secretly opposed to Hitler and from early in the war passed information on the situation in Germany to the Allies in Switzerland. His reports treated German armaments production and secret weapons, and the persecution of the Jews. He knew the anti-Nazi Abwehr officials Gisevius and Waetjen and frequently traveled to Switzerland where he finally took refuge in December 1943. He continued to be an important source for Dulles as an exile. Certain papers prepared by Schulte and correspondence concerning him are in Entry 125, Box 10. Documentation on postwar efforts by Dulles to assist Schulte are in the Allen Dulles

Papers, Box 26. Schulte's accomplishments are the subject of *Breaking the Silence*, by Walter Laqueur and Richard Breitman.

Doc. 2-31, Tel. 6137, Oct. 1, 1943, Box 273.

Doc. 2-32, Tel. 811-20, Oct. 2, 1943, Box 273. Tel. 637-38, Sept. 24, informed Bern that the Military Intelligence Service of the U.S. Army had great interest in Hungary as a transit area for German troops being redeployed from Russia to areas including Italy. Dulles was urged to upgrade on-site coverage of railway bridges and stations in Hungary (Box 341) The present telegram presages the ill-fated Sparrow Project. Number 646 is Baranyai. Number 655 is Hungarian Prime Minister Kallay.

Doc. 2-33, Tel. 840, Oct. 8, 1943, Box 273. Kolbe, who had first approached OSS Bern in August with a collection of German foreign ministry documents, supplied an additional consignment of some two hundred items in early October.

Doc. 2-34, Tel. 843-44, Oct. 9, 1943, Box 273. The code words were identified in Tel. 842 from Bern, Oct. 8, 1943 (Box 274).

Doc. 2-35, Tel. 850-51, Oct. 11, 1943, Box 273. Reference is to Dr. Rudolf Rahn, German Ambassador to the Mussolini regime.

Doc. 2-36, Tel. 852-53, Oct. 11, 1943, Box 273. Many of the code words used by Dulles in transmitting Kolbe/George Wood material are set forth in Tel. 854, Oct. 11; 868, Oct. 13; and 879, Oct. 16, from Bern (CIA/FOIA).

Doc. 2-37, Tel. 869-71, Oct. 14, 1943, Box 273. Carte (André Girard) was a loose-cannon French resistance leader whose organization attracted the attention of British SOE in 1942 and 1943, but proved to be a security liability. Carte's activities are described in Foote, *SOE in France*, and Pierre Guillain de Benouville, *The Unknown Warriors*. In Tel. 688-90, Oct. 4, Shepardson and Foster informed Dulles that Girard was in Washington lobbying for his organization, and spreading the word that the resistance elements adhering to de Gaulle were anti-American. Bern was requested to evaluate the status of Carte's organization and sort out French resistance politics, without consulting the British, who opposed Carte (Box 341).

Doc. 2-38, Tel. 880-87, Oct. 16, 1943, Box 273. A list of code words used in the Wood Traffic is in Entry 97, Box 40. From October 18 to 30, 1943, Secretary of State Hull and British Foreign Secretary Eden met with Soviet Foreign Minister Molotov in Moscow to discuss the timing of the Allied invasion of Europe and to begin the process of determining postwar arrangements.

Baron Anthony Radvanssky, code name Tompus, knew Dulles and Royall Tyler from before the war when he was Secretary-General of the Hungarian National Bank. Residing in Switzerland during the war, he served as a source of information on his homeland for OSS Bern (Entry 125, Box 7; Entry 190, Box 32).

Reference is to Armindo Monteiro, Portuguese Ambassador in London, who was more favorably disposed toward the Allies than was Premier Salazar.

Doc. 2-39, Tel. 6600, Oct. 21, 1943, Box 273. This was a State Department cable. "Y," also known as number 495, was Gregoire Gafencu, former Rumanian Foreign Minister (1938–40), now residing in Switzerland. Attempts by Dulles to assist him after the war are documented in the Allen Dulles Papers, Box 30. Iuliu Maniu was a leading opponent of both the Nazis and Soviets in Rumania.

Doc. 2-40, Tel. 245, Oct. 22, 1943, Box 273.

Doc. 2-41, Tel. 76-77, Oct. 25, 1943, Box 273.

Doc. 2-42, Tel. 919-21, Oct. 25, 1943, Box 273.

Doc. 2-43, Tel. 924-25, Oct. 25, 1943, Box 273.

Doc. 2-44, Tel. 78-79, Oct 26, 1943, Box 273. René Massigli was Commissioner for Foreign Affairs under General de Gaulle. Jean Monnet was Commissioner of Armaments, Supplies, and Reconstruction. Pierre De Leusse was de Gaulle's chief representative in Switzerland, based in Geneva. In Tel. 826, Nov. 10, Washington authorized Dulles to pay De Leusse 100,000 Swiss francs for French refugee relief (Box 341).

Doc. 2-45, Tel. 927-29, Oct. 26, 1943, Box 273. Tel. 778 to Bern, Nov. 1, 1943, read as follows: "With reference to your 927-929. Concerning the contradictory recommendations received by the group with Kallay, JCS have authorized specifically an attempt to break away the satellite nations, including H, from the Axis powers at once. This is for your exclusive information. Adolph knows that this has been decided and he is telling his boys. Your attitude should be ruled by the JCS directive" (Box 341). "Adolph" is Assistant Secretary of State A. A. Berle, who was the Department's point of contact on many intelligence matters.

Doc. 2-46, Tel. 83-84, Oct. 27, 1943, Box 273. Dulles further reported in Tel. 87-90 to Algiers, Oct. 29, that a Lieutenant Thomas Carver had reached Switzerland after being shot down in northern Italy and was willing to return to join partisans he had encountered. This group, Dulles suggested, could make good use of assistance delivered by parachute (Box 273). He added in Tel. 258-60 to London that the head of SOE in Switzerland was incapacitated by illness and that in any event "giving Zulu entire control over support for the maquis groups in Italy would have an unfortunate outcome" (Box 273).

Doc. 2-47, Tel. 930-31, Oct. 27, 1943, Box 273.

Doc. 2-48, Tel. 946-47, Oct. 29, 1943, Box 273.

Doc. 2-49, Tel. 6761, Oct. 29, 1943, Box 273.

Doc. 2-50, Tel. 962-63, Nov. 1, 1943, Box 170. Source 670 was Eduard Waetjen, an Abwehr officer and lawyer who played an important role in the German resistance to Hitler. Number 670 was also assigned at one time to Max Doerner, a German banker in Switzerland. On Nov. 6, headquarters replied as follows: "Your message #962-963 is of much interest to us. As it is very unlikely a rumor of this nature would have started if the Germans had really broken the code, this would appear to be a sign that our codes remain secure" (Box 341).

The security of U.S. codes in Bern was a matter of concern throughout the war. Apparently, a security lapse in the office of the military attaché compromised certain codes for a time. Also, Washington was most concerned that Dulles's efforts to obtain information on German codes would trigger an investigation by the Nazis that could uncover Ultra. For example, on Nov. 22, 1943, Dulles reported on information he had received via Max Shoop's network in France identifying possible call signals used in coded navy and air force communications (Tel. 1114-15, Box 170) Washington responded as follows on Nov. 24: "Kindly drop all interest in this subject until you receive word to the contrary from here, due to policy considerations involving inter-departmental arrangements" (Tel. 887, Box 165). Washington explained the policy and chastened Dulles on Dec. 6. In September, headquarters said, instructions were sent worldwide stating that unless explicitly authorized by Donovan, field missions should refrain from efforts at acquiring cryptographic material or codes. "Evidently you did not receive these instructions." The above orders had been issued to keep any information already possessed from being endangered by positive efforts to increase our knowledge of ciphers and codes. "An indifferent attitude on your part, if this is the case, might make them [the enemy] suspect that their system has already been broken" (Tel. 941-43, Box 274).

Doc. 2-51, Tel. 965, Nov. 2, 1943, Box 341. Walter Schellenberg's memoirs, *The Labyrinth* (New York: Harper, 1956), are suspect and self-serving. They describe purported German success in confounding Allied intelligence in Switzerland and generally throughout the war.

Doc. 2-52, Trans. no. 30, Nov. 2, 1943, Box 169. The records of the Moscow Foreign Ministers Conference of October 1943 are published in *Foreign Relations of the United States,* 1943, vol. 1.

OSS headquarters confirmed the radiotelephone hookup in Tel. 502-4 to Bern, Aug. 27, 1943. It stressed to Dulles that the method was not secure, and that no material harmful to the Allied cause if learned by the enemy should be transmitted (Box 341). The phone call process received a favorable response. Tel. 730, Oct. 16, read as follows: "All of us appreciate the effort which goes into preparing your flash reports and hope that you feel compensated by their enormous assistance to us. An enthusiastic vote of thanks from Carib, Regis, Leman, 109, 140 and 154" (Box 341).

Doc. 2-53, Tel. 967-70, Nov. 3, 1943, Box 341. Numbers 683 and 638 were representatives of the Partito d'Azione; 638 was also known as "Drumbee." Also on Nov. 3, Dulles relayed a message from "Reale, Tino, De Nobili and their associates" to Count Sforza, urging that he assume personal leadership of all anti-Fascist groups. They said that they were in touch with the Liberation Committee for Northern Italy and with the National Liberation Committee at Rome (Tel. 99-100, Box 166).

Doc. 2-54, Tel. 971-974, Nov. 3, 1943, Box 341. In Tel. 764-65, OSS headquarters asked Dulles to suggest people in Switzerland who could be helpful in Germany should the Hitler regime collapse on short notice (Box 165).

Doc. 2-55, Tel. 985-88, Nov. 4, 1943, Box 341. In Tel. 824-25 to Bern, Nov. 10, the Chiefs of the SO and SI branches responded to Dulles as follows: "Last year's SO/SOE agreement is still operative but specifically stipulates that if there is an invasion under American command the region would be assigned to American SO with the British in the cooperating role. Contact with General Headquarters and general direction over support in Northern Italy for activist work and Maquis groups should therefore be focused in yourself and your activities to be directed by Algiers with information London and Washington. General Headquarters is now using all of our men in Italy to do whatever the situation dictates. This is an interesting commentary on the effect of battle on agreements" (Box 341).

On Nov. 17, Dulles reported to Algiers that OSS agent Donald Downes had established contact with a strong Italian resistance group near the northern end of Lake Como. Contending that this force could provide valuable intelligence, Dulles urged that it be supplied with arms and munitions by air (Tel. 122-24, Box 166).

Doc. 2-56, Tel. 994-95, Nov. 4, 1943, Box 341. In Tel. 801, Nov. 5, OSS headquarters approved the position taken by Dulles, and promised additional instructions after the U.S. delegation had returned from the Moscow Conference (Box 165).

Doc. 2-57, Tel. 1012-16, Nov. 8, 1943, Box 341. Dulles told OSS Algiers, London and Washington on Dec. 6 that "I join with SOE and Zulu in recommending that we do all we can to give some definite help to Motta at once. It would be extremely hard, at a later date, to reorganize Italian resistance in the north, should their attempt to build up resistance meet with failure because of our inability to help" (Tel. 150-52, Box 274). On Jan. 5, 1944, Dulles reported that he and the British had had discussions with Damiani (number 826), the representative of Motta in Switzerland, and believed that Motta was worthy of all assistance that it was possible to render. Dulles also urged that full publicity be given to mounting Fascist atrocities in northern Italy (Tel. 203-4 to Algiers, Box 274).

Doc. 2-58, Tel. 1018-20, Nov. 8, 1943, Box 170. OSS headquarters transmitted the questions in Tel. 784-88, Nov. 1, 1943 (Box 341).

Doc. 2-59, Tel. 105, Nov. 9, 1943, Box 166.

Doc. 2-60, Tel. 1023-28, Nov. 9, 1943, Box 341. In Tel. 853, Nov. 18, OSS headquarters warned that Hohenlohe was not to be trusted. Carlton Hayes, U.S. Ambassador to Spain, which Hohenlohe had recently visited, had described him as "utterly without scruples, lying to anyone without hesitation, including his German chiefs" (Box 165). Dulles reassured Washington in Tel. 1108, Nov. 21, in the following terms: "Agree Max is a tough man and that it will be necessary to use an unusual degree of caution in dealing with him. There is a high degree of possibility that Himmler might use Max for feelers of major importance. On the opposite side of the picture, he can be of use to us if certain kinds of information are disregarded. His property interests will be his main concern. He is aware that these interests will be better guarded if he plays with our side than if he is too closely identified with the Nazis. I only pass on chosen pieces of information from the whole mass which is supplied, although I have received several useful clues from him" (Box 341).

Doc. 2-61, Trans. no. 34, Nov. 9, 1943, Box 169.

Doc. 2-62. Tel. 1054-55, Nov. 12, 1943, Box 341.

Doc. 2-63, Trans. no. 37, Nov. 13, 1943, Box 169.

Doc. 2-64, Tel. 115-21, Nov. 15, 1943, Box 341. Col. Gaston Pourchot, a World War I hero and veteran of French intelligence between the wars, was assigned to Switzerland in 1939. After the fall of France in 1940, he maintained contact with pro-Allied Vichy intelligence officers in his homeland, such as Col. Louis Rivet. (Rivet fled to Algiers when the Germans occupied all of France in November 1942 and joined the Allied cause.) Pourchot established close ties with Gen. Barnwell Legge, the U.S. Military Attaché in Bern, and with Dulles when he arrived in late 1942. Arrangements were concluded for the Americans to subsidize the operations of Pourchot and other stranded French intelligence officers in exchange for access to their information. The U.S. Legation also transmitted the Pourchot group's messages to the Free French in Algiers on the basis of copies also being sent to Washington. Pourchot ran lines into France, and one particularly active agent/courier, Albert Meyer, provided invaluable information on the German Atlantic Wall defenses. Pourchot's contribution to Allied intelligence is described in *OSS: La Guerre Secrète en France,* by Calvi. See also Calvi's "The OSS in France," in *The Secrets War: The Office of Strategic Services in World War II,* ed. George C. Chalou (Washington, D.C.: National Archives and Records Administration, 1992). In Tel. 115 from Bern to Algiers, Nov. 18, 1943, Dulles stated that Pourchot's organization, which he began financing shortly after the suppression of the Deuxième Bureau by Vichy, was "an information source of inestimable value" (Entry 97, Box 40).

Doc. 2-65, Tel. 1085-87, Nov. 17, 1943, Box 341. Arthur Goldberg, head of the OSS Labor Desk, informed Dulles on Nov. 24 that the frequent transmittal of funds from American trade union sources to number 328 in Bern was causing refugee circle gossip and other security problems. OSS would continue to send the funds, however, as long as Dulles believed it helpful to his activities (Tel. 885-86, Box 341).

Doc. 2-66, Tel. 1093-95, Nov. 18, 1943, Box 341. Tel. 783 to Bern, Nov. 2, read in part as follows: "According to information received from our office in Madrid, . . . Poles and Czechs make up most of the 62nd and 25th Infantry Regiments which are located at Ste. Etienne. If 498 and Harry [Pasteur Alexandre Simovec] have means of getting in touch with these men, have them suggest that the soldiers escape to Barcelona, reporting there to the American Consul" (Box 165).

Doc. 2-67, Tel. 1096-98, Nov. 19, 1943. Box 341. Dulles in effect identifies his principal sources on German forces in France as being former French intelligence agents in contact with the resistance with some help from Swiss intelligence, and networks run into France from Geneva by Max Shoop. Tel. 1342-44, Dec. 16, provides some detail on various French sources centered on Geneva. 284-A was an individual with personal contacts in France and with Swiss intelligence. 284-B represented a network headed by a French Army officer. 284-C operated a network in northern France. 284-D stood for information from Philippe Monod and Gen. Davet. 284-E included several units in southern and Alpine France. 284-F represented French officers covering all but northeastern France. 284-G stood for contacts with Swiss intelligence in Geneva (Box 274).

Dulles received periodic guidance for reporting and mixed evaluations of his product. On Oct. 1, Washington stated that the most important task of the SI Branch was now the positive penetration of Germany (Tel. 676-78, Box 341). On Oct. 14, Dulles was forced to defend his battle order reporting and point out that he was dependent on a long chain of people, many of whom never visited Switzerland and were out of reach (Tel. 873-74, Box 273). On the 16th, headquarters praised Dulles for certain BO reports and stated that the MIS found his cooperation extremely useful (Tel. 727, Box 341). Washington informed Bern on Oct. 30 that "although you are to remember that reports on battle order and similar topics are still needed by the armed forces as much as possible, nevertheless different government agencies are becoming growingly interested in political intelligence" (Tel. 779-80, Box 341). Tel. 844 to Bern, Nov. 16, asserted that a recent cable from Bern was so inaccurate that its source was either planting information or was grossly misinformed (Box 341).

Washington stated on Dec. 8 that "the obstacles confronting you are understood . . . and we wish you to know that most of your BO reports are of high value. MID Washington wishes to go on receiving all data, despite any possible undependability in the contents" (Tel. 954-56, Box 274) On Dec. 21, 1943, Dulles was informed that his recent BO reports had been splendid and were shared regularly with Army MIS, even though the latter did not reciprocate by providing attaché reports (Tel. 1016, Box 274). In another reversal, headquarters notified Dulles on Jan. 22, 1944, that there had been a sudden degeneration of his BO information which was now given a lower rating than other sources (Tel. 1148-49, Box 274). On Mar. 8, 1944, headquarters informed Dulles that MID and the OSS reporting board agreed that Bern's messages in late January were much more accurate than those of the previous November (Tel. 1317, Box 307).

Doc. 2-68, Tel. 1128-30, Nov. 23, 1943, Box 170. Tel. 617, Sep 22, 1943, contained praise from Magruder and Buxton (Box 165). Tel. 863, Nov. 19, extended the good wishes of the SI Branch (Box 165). Dulles sent salutations to Washington on Dec. 23: "From 110 to Jackpot. Kindly transmit the season's greetings and my deep appreciation of your ever-present support in the preceding year to the Chief, Regis, Carib, 140 and others, Eleanor included" (Tel. 1418, Box 274). He also received a holiday acknowledgment: "From Regis, Carib, Jackpot, 140 and everyone. Everyone here sends you greetings. Your accomplishments during the past year have been outstanding, and have been a source of inspiration to all of us" (Tel. 1030, Dec. 24, 1943, Box 274).

Doc. 2-69, Tel. 1140-45, Nov. 24, 1943, Box 341. On Nov. 20, Washington provided Dulles with the following news: "It was just made known to us that the British infiltrated 2 agents into southwestern Hungary about 3 weeks ago. This information came to us from an extremely reliable and confidential source, and is interesting in the light of our H. ideas. This infiltration was made contrary to H's wishes and recommendation. Ninety-four natives who had been in contact with the agents were compromised; furthermore, both agents were captured" (Tel. 864, Box 165).

Doc. 2-70, Tel. 1151-53, Nov. 26, 1943, Box 341.

Doc. 2-71, Tel. 1157-58, Nov. 27, 1943, Box 341. Useful information on Canaris may be found in André Brissaud, *Canaris* (London: Weidenfeld & Nicolson, 1979); Ian Colvin, *Chief of Intelligence* (London: Victor Gollancz, 1951): and David Kahn, *Hitler's Spies* (New York: Macmillan, 1978). Dulles followed closely developments concerning the Abwehr, German military intelligence headed by Canaris. In April 1943 he had reported accurately that two top assistants to Canaris, Gen. Hans Oster and Hans von Dohnanyi, had been dismissed, possibly as part of an attempt by Himmler and the SS to take over all intelligence functions (Tel. 67-70, Apr. 17, 1943, and Tel. 284-85, Apr. 22, 1943, Box 307). The Abwehr was finally absorbed by SS intelligence in February 1944. Canaris, Oster, and Dohnanyi were all ultimately compromised by their ties to the resistance and the July 1944 attempt on Hitler's life. They were executed just before the end of the war.

In Tel. 1052-53, Nov. 12, 1943, Dulles reported that Canaris was expected to visit Switzerland at the end of the week. He probably simply intended to iron out some troubles in the local Abwehr, but the trip might signify something more (Box 341).

Doc. 2-72, Tel. 1159-61, Nov. 27, 1943, Box 341. Dulles offered another psychological warfare suggestion on Nov. 18: "Even though we were not set up in such a way that we could do worthwhile work from here in disseminating MO rumors, we feel that we could be of use in planting false military information every now and then in regard to landing plans, movements of troops, or other like subjects, in a few circles which would be carefully chosen. Such false information could be of a specific and even technical nature" (Tel. 1092, Box 341).

Doc. 2-73, Tel. 1162-68, Nov. 29, 1943, Box 341. With regard to the existence of German elements that could cooperate with the Allies following the collapse of the Hitler regime, OSS Washington informed Dulles on Dec. 7, that a German POW had said that he was a member of a secret anti-Nazi cell in Berlin made up largely of former diplomats. He identified his leader as "Dr. Rispondek" [Respondek], a retired official of the German Foreign Office. He also stated that Respondek was formerly in contact with Sam Woods, U.S. Consul General at Zurich. Respondek had asked the POW, when he learned that he planned to desert, to convey the following message to Woods: "I am still working and all is prepared in Lichterfelds-Ost. All you have to do is come" (Tel. 963-64, Box 165). Dulles replied on Dec. 16 that Woods knew Respondek, and that Breckinridge Long at the State Department had the details. Dulles urged that the utmost discretion be exercised to protect Respondek (Tel. 1345-46, Box 274). The Respondek-Woods connection is described in *Two Against Hitler*, by John Dippel.

Doc. 2-74, Tel. 7520, Nov. 30, 1943, Box 170. This cable further reported that according to the source, Archbishop Stepanac of Zagreb had been detained by the Gestapo for preaching a sermon against totalitarianism. Further, the Croatian Peasant Party was negotiating with the communist-leaning partisans of Tito in the attempt to slow their drift toward communism.

Doc. 2-75, Tel. 1183-85, Dec. 1, 1943, Box 274. In Tel. 931-33 to Bern, Dec. 3, Dulles's old friend Hugh Wilson of the OSS Planning Group and F. L. Mayer of SI stated that an American observer recently returned from Yugoslavia contended that Mihailovich was completely compromised by his cooperation with the Nazis and that his forces were small compared to those of the partisans. Wilson and Mayer accepted this assessment (Box 374). Responding in Tel. 1236-37, Dec. 8, Dulles stated that OSS Bern also agreed in general, but added, "We do caution, however, against the possible tendency to underestimate Mihailovitch and even Neditch the collaborationist who may in due time take part usefully, and the reverse tendency to overestimate the Partisans. This hinges partly on whether the Balkan invasion is to be Anglo-Saxon, or Russian or Allied" (Box 274). As a matter of additional perspective on Dulles's views on Yugoslavia, a member of the Bern Military Attaché office recalls that Dulles was very well informed on the subject and definitely favored the Chetniks over the Partisans. The British scholar Elizabeth Wiskemann, who served with the Political Warfare Executive in Switzerland during the war, also states that Dulles favored Mihailovich over Tito (*The Europe I Saw* [London: Collins, 1968], 171).

Doc. 2-76, Tel. 7535, Dec. 1, 1943, Box 274.

Doc. 2-77, Tel. 1187-88, Dec. 2, 1943, Box 274. The tangled career of Noel Field is traced in an expert manner by Flora Lewis in *Red Pawn: The Story of Noel Field* (Garden City, N.Y.: Doubleday, 1965).

Doc. 2-78, Trans. no. 43, Dec. 3, 1943, Box 273.

Doc. 2-79, Tel. 1212-15, Dec. 4, 1943, Box 274. Field Marshal Jan Christian Smuts, Prime Minister of the Union of South Africa, gave a widely noticed address in London on Oct. 25, 1943. He said that the old European power structure had disappeared and that after the war Russia would stride the continent like a Colossus.

Doc. 2-80, Tel. 7607, Dec. 4, 1943, Box 274.

Doc. 2-81, Tel. 1220-25, Dec. 6, 1943, Box 170. Reference is to Cavendish W. Cannon of the Division of European Affairs, Department of State.

Doc. 2-82, Trans. no. 44, Dec. 6, 1943, Box 273.

Doc. 2-83, Tel. 1244-45, Dec. 8, 1943, Box 274. In Tel. 1022, Dec. 23, headquarters emphasized to Dulles the importance of reporting in the chemical/biological warfare field, to which the code name "Toledo" was being assigned (Box 274). A separate file of Toledo messages exists in Entry 134, Box 216.

Doc. 2-84, Tel. 1246-47, Dec. 8, 1943, Box 274. Headquarters expressed interest in this report, particularly in connection with existing plans for penetration of Austria from Partisan-held areas of Yugoslavia (Tel. 973-74, Dec. 10, 1943, Box 274) In Tel. 1284-87, Dec. 11, Dulles reported that two envoys from a purported Austrian resistance central committee had arrived at Zurich. They requested a radio transmitter and would eventually need financial assistance (CIA/FOIA).

Doc. 2-85, Tel. 7708, Dec. 8, 1943, RG 59 103.918/1912.

Doc. 2-86, Tel. 1248-50, Dec. 9, 1943, Box 274. Headquarters replied on Dec. 10 that this type of information was useful in preparing Black radio material, and should be sent to MO in Washington and London (Tel. 969, Box 274).

Doc. 2-87, Tel. 1257-61, Dec. 9, 1943, Box 274.

Doc. 2-88, Tel. 1266-67, Dec. 10, 1943, Box 274.

Doc. 2-89, Tel. 1272-73, Dec. 11, 1943, Box 274. Of the OSS officers and sources cited, 809 is Donald Jones, representative in Lugano; 244 is Frederick Stalder; and 284 is Max Shoop. Jones, an American OSS agent, had been established in Lugano by Oct. 1943, working under the cover of the Bern Legation press section (Tel. 855-58, Oct. 12, 1943, CIA/FOIA). He had numerous contacts with the Action Party and other Italian resistance elements. He played a critical role in Dulles's operations in Italy for the duration of the war.

In addition to problems with Swiss authorities, OSS Bern had to deal with obtaining funds to support its various activities. Dulles reported on Dec. 13 that he projected a budget of 2,580,000 Swiss francs (about $600,000 U.S.) for fiscal year 1944–45, but warned that if the Italian resistance came to be funded on the same level as the French, another million francs would be consumed. He warned that his funds might soon need replenishment (Tel. 1301-3, CIA/FOIA).

Doc. 2-90, Tel. 1274-75, Dec. 11, 1943, Box 274.

Doc. 2-91, Tel. 7789, Dec. 11, 1943, RG 59 103.918/1688.

Doc. 2-92, Tel. 1305-6, Dec. 13, 1943, Box 274. In Tel. 1448, Dec. 27, 1943, OSS Bern reported that Machek was living in Zagreb. The Germans were seeking his favor in hopes of stopping the Croat Peasant Party from joining forces with Tito. Dulles thought that Machek's influence was the one slight hope of reconciling the Croats and the Serbs (Box 274).

Doc. 2-93, Tel. 1309-11, Dec. 14, 1943, Box 274. The plan discussed in this cable appears to be an antecedent of the abortive Sparrow mission carried out through the OSS mission in Istanbul in March 1944. In Tel. 192-94 to Algiers, Dec. 27, 1943, Dulles discussed certain aspects of the plan and urged its immediate approval (Box 166).

Doc. 2-94, Trans. no. 49, Dec. 14, 1943, Box 273. In his radiotelephone transmission of Jan. 8, 1944, Dulles again elaborated on the theme that many Europeans now believed that Russia would play the dominating role on the continent after the war. The Soviet Union was believed to have planned carefully to gain control of Poland, Central Europe, and the Balkans, while the Western Allies had failed to project either the power or idealism to prevent it (Trans. no. 64, Box 273). On Jan. 24, Washington informed Dulles that the JCS had given wide distribution to the Flash of Jan. 8 (Tel. 1151, Box 274). It was sent to the White House Map Room by OSS on January 11 (FDR Library, Map Room Files, Box 73).

Doc. 2-95, Trans. no. 51, Dec. 16, 1943, Box 273.

Doc. 2-96, Tel. 1347-1350, Dec. 17, 1943, Box 274. Dulles transmitted this message to Assistant Director Buxton in response to Tel. 978, Dec. 13, which read as follows: "109 informed the JCS of a contact with Hungary when he was in Cairo. The contact was given approbation by the Joint Chiefs and they again stated their interest in the possibility that Hungary might be detached. They stress, in addition, their wish for information regarding this possibility at frequent intervals" (Box 274). Gen. Donovan (109) attended portions of the US-UK conferences at Cairo, Nov. 22–26 and Dec. 2–7, 1943. The conference records are published in U.S. Dept. of State, *Foreign Relations of the United States: The Conferences at Cairo and Tehran, 1943* (Washington, D.C.: GPO, 1961).

The referenced "flash" of Dec. 14 is printed here as Doc. 2-94. Tel. 1309-11, Dec. 14, is printed as Doc. 2-93. Tel. 834-38, Nov. 10, requested detailed order of battle information on behalf of the Military Intelligence Division, U.S. Army (Box 341).

Doc. 2-97, Trans. no. 53, Dec. 18, 1943, Box 273. For the records of the Teheran Conference, see *FRUS: The Conferences at Cairo and Tehran, 1943.*

On Jan. 8, 1944, Shepardson informed Dulles that his radiotelephone transmissions were much prized in Washington and constituted a real contribution. He was admonished, however, to avoid including classified information when using this insecure channel (Tel. 1081, Box 274).

Doc. 2-98, Tel. 1280, Dec. 20, 1943, Box 274. Sherman is Irving J. Sherman of the OSS New York office; Carib is F. L. Mayer; and Jackpot is Shepardson. "Top" refers to Zurich. Number 497 is a Polish source.

Doc. 2-99, Tel. 311-15, Dec. 22, 1943, Box 274. Number 284, Max Shoop, formerly of the Paris office of Sullivan & Cromwell, operated out of Geneva and received intelligence from a number of networks in France. Regarding the Geneva networks reporting to Dulles through Shoop, see the endnote to Doc. 2-67.

Doc. 2-100, Tel. 1443-47, Dec. 27, 1943, Box 274.

Doc. 2-101, Tel. 1466-76, Dec. 29, 1943, Box 274. Messages based on documents obtained by Fritz Kolbe ("George Wood") were slugged "KAPPA." Certain code name identities were provided in Tel. 1482 from Bern, Dec. 29: "Harem is Saracoglu; Bulgarian . . . is Orange; Penni is Numan; Tosar is Sofia; Yellow is Turkey; Ragon is Istanbul; Trude is Hungarian Lieutenant Colonel Hatz" (Box 274). "Cicero" was Elyeza Bazna, the Albanian valet of Sir Hughe Knatchbull-Hugessen, the British Ambassador to Turkey. He worked as a paid German spy from October 1943 to April 1944, rifling the Ambassador's safe and procuring valuable information on subjects including, apparently, the code word for the Normandy invasion and related information. The Germans apparently ignored or misused much of the intelligence supplied by Cicero and rewarded him with counterfeit currency. The Allies became aware of the Cicero penetration through a number of sources, including Dulles's Wood traffic and Ultra intercepts. Sensing that he had been detected, Bazna resigned his position with the Ambassador. In *The Secret Surrender* (24–25), Dulles describes the episode as follows: "Of direct practical value of the very highest kind among Wood's contributions was a copy of a cable in which the German Ambassador in Turkey, von Papen, proudly reported to Berlin (in November, 1943) the acquisition of top-secret documents from the British Embassy in Ankara through 'an important German agent.' This was, of course, the famous Cicero, the valet of the British Ambassador who had managed to procure the keys to the Ambassador's private safe and to photograph its contents. I immediately passed word of this to my British colleagues, and a couple of British security inspectors immediately went over the British Embassy in Ankara and changed the safes and their combinations, thus putting Cicero out of business. Neither the Germans nor Cicero ever knew what was behind the security visit, which was, of course, made to appear routine and normal. Thus our rifling of the German Foreign Office safes in Berlin through an agent reporting to the Americans in Switzerland, put an end to the rifling of the British Ambassador's safe by a German agent in Turkey." This was achieved even though Kolbe himself was ignorant of Cicero's identity (Tel. 335-36 from Bern to London, Jan. 10, 1944, CIA/FOIA).

Bazna describes his experiences in *I Was Cicero* (New York: Harper & Row, 1962). His German handler, L. C. Moyzisch, provides his account in *Operation Cicero* (London: Wingate, 1952). Other sources on the case include Schellenberg's *Labyrinth*, Kahn's *Hitler's Spies*, Anthony Cave Brown's *Bodyguard of Lies* (New York: Harper & Row, 1975), and Fitzroy Maclean's *Take Nine Spies* (London: Weidenfeld & Nicolson, 1978).

Doc. 2-102, Tel. 1477-79, Dec. 29, 1943, Box 274. In code word designations used by Dulles in transmitting the George Wood traffic, Waldos and Portos are German embassies and legations, Grand is the

German Foreign Ministry, and Vinta is Foreign Minister Ribbentrop. Reference cable 868 of Oct. 13, 1943, contained certain other code words (Box 273).

The material received from Kolbe in late 1943 was transmitted in a series of over 75 cables during December, January, and February. These messages were slugged "KAPPA" and contained translations of actual German documents, designated "D"; descriptions of documents; and information provided orally by Kolbe. Dulles provided an overview of the series in Tel. 1729-31, Jan. 13, 1944, and indicated a country color code which was used in the Kappa cables: Hazel, Hungary; Purple, miscellaneous outgoing German messages; Black, Balkans; Scarlet, Japan; Red, France; Lavender, China; Yellow, Turkey; Gray, Finland; White, Switzerland; Brown, Spain; Uncolored, Denmark; Pink, Tangiers; Blue, Portugal; and Green, Italy. The series covered reports from German diplomats in all of the above countries (CIA/FOIA).

Doc. 2-103, Tel. 1484, Dec. 29, 1943, Box 274. In Tel. 1480-81, Dec. 29, Bern relayed other particularly sensitive information from Kolbe. German Ambassador von Papen in Turkey had reported to the German Foreign Ministry on the 13th that the American Military Attaché had attempted to bribe the Rumanian Military Attaché to establish a transmitter with the Rumanian General Staff, but had failed. Further, the Spanish Minister had told von Papen that Lawrence Steinhardt, U.S. Ambassador in Turkey, had indicated to him that "a propos of any arrangement with Stalin concerning Spain . . . everything would be done to effect a change of government in Spain, but that it is intended that retirement in an honorable manner be guaranteed to Franco" (CIA/FOIA).

Doc. 2-104, Tel. 1486-93, Dec. 30, 1943, Box 274. Leitner was a minister in the German Foreign Office.

Doc. 2-105, Tel. 1496-97, Dec. 30, 1943, Box 274.

Doc. 2-106, Tel. 1498-99, Dec. 31, 1943, Box 274. Tel. 1496-97, Dec. 30, 1943, is printed here as Doc. 2-105.

Doc. 2-107, Tel. 1500-1502, Dec. 31, 1943, Box 274.

Doc. 2-108, Tel. 1503-5, Jan. 1, 1944, CIA/FOIA.

Doc. 2-109, Tel. 1534-38, Jan. 2, 1944, CIA/FOIA. In Tel. 335-36 to London, Jan. 10, 1944, Dulles reported that according to additional Wood information, the Germans were not "over-certain" of the loyalty of Trude (Col. Hatz) (CIA/FOIA).

Documentation on various Allied contacts with elements in Axis satellite nations during 1944 is presented in *FRUS, 1944*, vol. 1, *General* (Washington, D.C.: GPO, 1966), 580–613.

Doc. 2-110, Tel. 1555-56, Jan. 3, 1944, Box 274. In Tel. 1037-38, Dec. 28, 1943, F. L. Mayer (Carib) requested specific information on the Nazi labor organization, and whether it could be modified to serve a useful purpose in the postwar occupation (Box 274). In Tel. 1051-53, Mayer and Shepardson requested Dulles's views on methods for sending agents into Germany (Box 341).

Doc. 2-111, Tel. 1604-12, Jan. 5, 1944, Box 274. Tel. 1509-11, Jan. 1, 1944, reads in part as follows: "KAPPA. White. To Jackpot. The following is based on D sources. Included in the communications is a wire to Grand from Lomax, number 3119 of November 12th. It is 4 1/2 pages long. The wire says that reports from Grunn made on the basis of discussions with VP HW have been viewed by the German intelligence. The report then lists what is alleged to be detailed observations on the Moscow Conference. The substance of the report is not especially injurious, even though it presents the conclusion of VP HW that England and the United States alone must win World War II, possibly even against the Soviet Union, that the Soviet Union has already realized a great measure of success in carrying out its clear purpose of gaining control of entire Europe, and that the possibility exists that grave judgments will soon be required of United States Government. . . . I have possessed evidence for some time that there are leaks . . . northward. I trust that you will be able to notify me before any steps at all are taken which might endanger the Wood source or cause an explosion here" (CIA/FOIA). Tel. 1051 to Bern, Jan. 4, asked for more information on the subject as a matter of high priority (Box 274).

President Roosevelt confronted Vice President Wallace with evidence of his indiscretion, remarking that "the only thing for us to do is to remember that the Germans seem to be taking your name in vain." Wallace replied that the incident only indicated that the keystone of German policy was to drive a wedge between Russia and the US/UK, and that the report was possibly a German plant (Wallace letter to Roosevelt, Jan. 17, 1944, FDR Library, Map Room Files, Box 169, A16/Germany).

Doc. 2-112, Tel. 205-7, Jan. 6, 1944, Box 166. Reference is to Robert Pflieger, head of the SO Branch in Algiers. Tel. 1309-11, Dec. 14, is printed as Doc. 2-93.

Doc. 2-113, Tel. 1633-35, Jan. 6, 1944, CIA/FOIA. Pursuant to an Anglo-Portuguese agreement imposed on Salazar on Aug. 17, 1943, British forces arrived in the Azores in October, soon followed by American units. The U.S.-U.K. negotiations with Portugal are documented in *FRUS, 1943*, vol. 2.

Doc. 2-114, Tel. 190, Jan. 8, 1944, Box 274.

Doc. 2-115, Tel. 1655-57, Jan. 8, 1944, CIA/FOIA.

Doc. 2-116, Tel. 1671-73, Jan. 8, 1944, Box 274.

Doc. 2-117, Tel. 190, Jan. 9, 1944, Box 170.

Doc. 2-118, Tel. 1684-85, Jan. 9, 1944, Box 274. Dulles believed that Oprecht had an intimate knowledge of the German situation. Correspondence involving Oprecht and his wife is in Entry 190, Box 24.

Doc. 2-119, Tel. 230, Jan. 10, 1944, Box 170.

Doc. 2-120, Tel. 1692-93, Jan. 10, 1944, Box 274. In Tel. 1336-38, Dec. 16, 1943, OSS Bern provided sketchy information on the competence and political outlook of various German and European scientists. The telegram was slugged "AZUSA," indicating scientific and particularly atomic energy information. The message indicated that "Flute is the designation given to S. . . . The greater part of the above was provided by Flute, to whom I have an excellent line. It seems to me that he would agree to help as much as he can in the field, and considering the things the members of the Azusa club have in common, I imagine this will be of interest to you" (Box 228, Azusa). "S" is Dr. Paul Scherrer, a prominent Swiss physicist. The Box 228 Azusa file contains dozens of rather cryptic messages to and from Bern for 1943–1945 dealing with atomic energy and related matters.

Heisenberg's War: The Secret History of the German Bomb (New York: Knopf, 1993), by Thomas Powers is largely an account of the attempts of the Allies to evaluate the German atomic energy development program directed by the eminent physicist Werner Heisenberg. Dulles and OSS Bern provided one source of information.

On Dec. 20, 1943, OSS Bern reported indications that Germany was developing biological weapons. Information came from Scherrer (number 827); a Professor Mooser (824); and Gaevernitz (Tel. 1381-85, Box 274).

Doc. 2-121, Tel. 1705-08, Jan. 12, 1944, Box 170.

Doc. 2-122, Tel. 349, Jan. 13, 1944, Box 274.

Doc. 2-123, Tel. 1746-50, Jan. 14, 1944, Box 274. Dulles's comments on German expectations respecting an invasion of France was part of continuous reporting on the subject, including detailed coverage of troops dispositions and coast defenses. In Tel. 792-93 to Bern, Nov. 3, 1943, OSS Headquarters had requested on behalf of the Military Intelligence Division of the U.S. Army "all the material which can be obtained on the extent and geographical situation of defense lines on and behind the Channel coast . . . from Amsterdam to Brest. . . Info wanted includes all which gives any indication whether we may expect the principal defense to be some distance inland or on the coast" (Box 341).

The item concerning Hitler's attitude in radiotelephone message 66, Jan. 12, 1944, read as follows:

"Reports from Germany indicate that Hitler, in extremis, would prefer to have the dam break on the Russian front than in the West, as being a sort of justification of his preaching to the German people about the reality of the Russian menace" (Box 273).

Doc. 2-124, Tel. 1754-56, Jan. 15, 1944, Box 170.

Doc. 2-125, Tel. 367-69, Jan. 17, 1944, Box 274. This message originated with Benouville (Barres) of the French resistance, through the resistance delegation in Switzerland, to its leadership in London. Gen. Davet was chief resistance delegate in Switzerland. Tel. 242-44 from Bern to London, Oct. 21, 1943, identified the following symbols to be used in messages: CER was the Executive Committee of the French resistance in Paris, Asur (Azur) was the CER Delegation in London, and Iris was the CER Delegation in Geneva (CIA/FOIA).

In Oct. 1943, a large group of French resistance leaders met in Switzerland with a view toward achieving political cohesion and a master plan for military action (Tel. 932-37 from Bern, Oct. 28, 1943, Entry 97, Box 40). Dulles felt compelled to cable London on Oct. 29 to deny that he had arranged this conclave, which had occurred beyond the reach of OSS London, the British, and Gen. de Gaulle (Tel. 256-57, Box 273). In a draft cable to David Bruce, dated Jan. 19, Dulles further protested that he was doing nothing in his relations with the resistance to create sentiments against de Gaulle or the French communists, apparently in response to ruffled feathers in London (Entry 165, Box 14).

Doc. 2-126, Tel. 1807, Jan. 19, 1944, Box 107. On Jan. 11, 1944, Mussolini's remnant Fascist government executed Count Ciano and other leaders involved in the Duce's overthrow of July 1943. Edda Ciano fled to Switzerland in possession of the late count's diaries, which promised to be an intelligence and propaganda windfall for the Allies. The saga of the Ciano diaries is described in Howard M. Smyth, *Secrets of the Fascist Era: How Uncle Sam Obtained Some of the Top-level Documents of Mussolini's Period* (Carbondale: Southern Illinois University Press, 1975).

Doc. 2-127, Tel. 1811, Jan. 19, 1944, Box 274.

Doc. 2-128, Tel. 1841-43, Jan. 24, 1944, Box 274. In Tel. 1944–52, Feb. 3, Dulles relayed further information from Devignat (802), an associate of the politician Henri Queuille, that a National Committee of Resistance was being formed under leaders loyal to Gen. de Gaulle and representing the principal French political groups, including possibly the communists (Box 275).

Doc. 2-129, Tel. 1875-78, Jan. 26, 1944, Box 274. OSS headquarters informed Dulles on Feb. 3 that this message had been sent to the Joint Chiefs of Staff and the State Department (Tel. 1191 to Bern, Box 275). In Tel. 1173, Jan. 25, Washington confirmed that "Sparrow" should be used as the indicator for all messages on this subject to ensure limited distribution (Box 274).

Doc. 2-130, Tel. 403-5, Jan. 27, 1944, Box 274.

Doc. 2-131, Tel. 406-8, Jan. 27, 1944, Box 274. Number 328 corresponded frequently with labor elements in Allied-controlled European areas and the United States using OSS Bern channels of communication. J. H. Oldenbroek was Secretary of the International Federation of Transport Workers in London.

In Tel. 2014-15, Feb. 9, Dulles reported on further information from the barge men. They stressed the vital degree to which river and canal traffic was replacing railroad traffic for the Germans, and suggested particular targets for bombing and sabotage (Box 170).

Doc. 2-132, Tel. 409-10, Jan. 27, 1944, Box 274. On Feb. 3, OSS transmitted a message from the Italian-American labor leader Vanni Montana to Silone and Modigliani in Bern stating that if all Italian democratic parties would break their relationship with the Communist Party, American labor and public opinion would come out more strongly in support of Italian democratic aims (Tel. 1192, Box 274).

Doc. 2-133, Tel. 1888-89, Jan. 27, 1944, Box 274. Hereafter, Dulles frequently slugged cables dealing with the German resistance "Breakers." Such telegrams are found in Bern chronological cable files, and in a Breakers folder in Box 228. His ability to identify and describe this anti-Nazi group well in advance of its attempt on Hitler's life contributed immeasurably to his standing in Washington and career reputation.

Reference is to Otto John, then a Lufthansa lawyer with Abwehr connections who worked with British intelligence in London later in the war. In 1954, as a West German intelligence officer, he either defected or was kidnapped in Berlin. He returned to the West the next year and was jailed for espionage. John describes his strange career in *Twice Through the Lines* (New York: Harper & Row, 1969). Willard Beaulac was Counselor of the U.S. Embassy in Madrid. Sir Ronald Campbell was the British Ambassador in Lisbon.

OSS headquarters transmitted a composite of this message and Tel. 1913-14 (Doc. 2-136) to the State Department. On Feb. 2, 1944, Assistant Secretary A. A. Berle, State's focal point for intelligence matters, sent a memorandum to the Secretary of State expressing concern. "OSS, of course, is not following up in any way and has no desire to, which is in line with the consistent policy of the Department. . . . My fear is that attempts will be made by German intelligence groups to create some situation which they can later represent to the Soviets as preliminary steps to a separate peace. This would be in line with their present known strategy of endeavoring to find ways and means of dividing the three powers. . . . You may also wish to consider informing the Soviet representatives. . . . OSS officials have told me that the cable has been suppressed and that they have no further interest other than to lay it before the Department for its information" (*FRUS, 1944,* 1:496–98). Documentation on efforts of German opposition groups to contact the Allies during 1944 appears in the compilation "Consideration of the application of 'unconditional surrender' terms to Germany; unofficial peace feelers from Germany," ibid., 484–579. See in particular the memorandum from OSS Deputy Director Magruder to Berle, May 17, 1944, summarizing early Breakers cables from Dulles (ibid. 510–13).

One particular German resistance initiative came from Count von Moltke in the form of an approach to the OSS in Istanbul in late December 1943. It offered cooperation with the Western allies, accepting total military defeat and occupation, provided Germany was allowed to maintain the Eastern Front. After four months of consideration, the OSS decided to attempt to keep the channel open, but not pursue the matter with the State Department and the Joint Chiefs of Staff. (See Jürgen Heideking and Christof Mauch, eds., "Das Herman-Dossier: Helmuth Graf von Moltke, die deutsche Emigration in Istanbul und der amerikanische Geheimdienst OSS," in *Vierteljahrshefte für Zeitgeschichte* 4 [1992]: 567–623.)

For important additional articles by German scholars on Breakers and other aspects of OSS operations with respect to Nazi Germany, see Jürgen Heideking and Christof Mauch, eds. *Geheimdienstkrieg gegen Deutschland: Subversion, Propaganda und politische Planungen des amerikanischen Geheimdienstes im Zweiten Weltkrieg* (Göttingen: Vandenhoeck & Ruprecht, 1993). The same editors also published *USA und Deutscher Widerstand: Analysen und Operationen des amerikanischen Geheimdienstes im Zweiten Weltkrieg* (Tübingen: Francke, 1993). This outstanding selection of documents from OSS records at the U.S. National Archives (RG 226) in German-language translation includes about eighteen messages from Dulles concerning the German resistance, most of which are printed in English language in this volume.

Doc. 2-134, Tel. 1890-93, Jan. 27, 1944, Entry 138, Box 2. Headquarters advised Dulles on Feb. 2 that Assistant Secretary of State Berle had "expressed his extreme antagonism toward any steps which might help Germany . . . to promote dissension among the Allies" (Tel. 1137-38, Box 228).

Doc. 2-135, Tel. 415-17, Jan. 28, 1944, Box 274. Some observers, including John Bross, a key OSS officer in London involved with British SOE in French operations, believed that support for the resistance enabling it to interfere seriously with the Germans' capability to reinforce their troops opposing the Allied landing after D-Day, was the most significant OSS contribution of the war (Interview).

Doc. 2-136, Tel. 1913-14, Jan. 29, 1944, Box 228. "Fat Boy" is Hermann Goering, the discredited commander of the Luftwaffe, who had previously been the second most powerful man in Germany.

Doc. 2-137, Tel. 1920-22, Jan. 29, 1944, Box 170. Dulles discusses the anti-Fascist coup in Campione in *The Secret Surrender,* 18–19.

Doc. 2-138, Tel. 425-27, Jan. 31, 1944, Box 274.

Doc. 2-139, Tel. 1923-24, Jan. 31, 1944, Box 274.

Chapter 3: Prelude to D-Day; the Rise of the German Opposition, February–June 1944

Doc. 3-1, Tel. 1937-38, Feb. 1, 1944, Box 275.

Doc. 3-2, Tel. 1945-46, Feb. 3, 1944, Box 275. Fritz Sauckel was German Plenipotentiary-General for Labor Mobilization. Responsible for the deportation of some five million persons to Germany for slave labor, he was hanged as a war criminal in 1946. Albert Speer was Reich Minister for Armaments and War Production. He served twenty years in prison for his part in Nazi aggression.

Doc. 3-3, Tel. 1963, Feb. 4, 1944, Box 275. On Feb. 5, OSS headquarters informed Bern that additional information had been received on this new type of bomb, justifying further investigation (Tel. 1197, Box 165).

Doc. 3-4, Tel. 1965-66, Feb. 4, 1944, Box 228. The individuals mentioned here, Wilhelm Leuschner, Hans Oster, and Carl Goerdeler, were indeed prominent members of the anti-Hitler movement.

Doc. 3-5, Tel. 1992-94, Feb. 5, 1944, Box 275. Motta was the resistance committee in Milan; 826 was Damiani, an Action Party representative in Switzerland; and 510 was Sforza. Adolfo Tino was an antimonarchist organizer in Milan.

Doc. 3-6, Tel. 450-53, Feb. 8, 1944, Box 275. Iris is the French resistance delegation in Switzerland, or its chief, Gen. Davet. Azur is the French CER delegation in London. Indigo, Zeus, Hercule, and Ulysses are French resistance connections. Barres is Benouville. The "Smuts incident" apparently refers to the South African leader's Oct. 25, 1943, London speech in which he said Russia would dominate Europe after the war.

Doc. 3-7, Tel. 2026-30, Feb. 11, 1944, Box 170. Jean Jardin was reportedly a former cabinet director for the Pierre Laval, the collaborationist premier of France. 492 is René Charron, a close associate of Dulles. Maurice Couve de Murville was a foreign affairs adviser to de Gaulle.

Dulles reported the following information on Feb. 23, based on German documents provided by Fritz Kolbe. "The following is taken from a wire dated January 22, from Porto, at Paris, to Grand. Jardin, who became a member of the French Embassy at Berne a short time ago, was advised by a 3rd person that 110 discussed relations between America and the Soviet Union (All statements attributed to me are wholly untrue. —110.) and that at different times 110 had attempted to get in touch with Jardin (This, too, is entirely untrue, for I abruptly declined to meet him. —110.) If the Nazis were willing for him to do so, Jardin was ready to establish contact with 110. The wire also states that this contact might be valuable for obtaining information. At the end of January, Berlin answered Porto at Paris by stating that it was not advisable for Jardin to be in contact with 110. This position was based on data which Berlin had received regarding 110" (Tel. 2161-64, CIA/FOIA).

Doc. 3-8, Tel. 242-44, Feb. 11, 1944, Box 275.

Doc. 3-9, Trans. no. 85, Feb. 12, 1944, Box 273. This comment on the educational reforms instituted by Allied Military Government for Allied Territories in Italy reflected the importance that Dulles attached to intellectual concerns as part of political warfare.

Doc. 3-10, Trans. no. 86, Feb. 14, 1944, Box 273. Dulles here manifests his general view that the fate of postwar Europe would be determined by the outcome of a struggle between democratic socialism and Communism.

Doc. 3-11, Tel. 482, Feb. 15, 1944, Box 275. Gisevius provides only fragmentary information on his relations with Dulles in *To the Bitter End*. In *Autobiography of a Spy*, Mary Bancroft, an American living in Switzerland, recalls that on instructions from Dulles she assisted Gisevius in the translation of his manuscript on the German resistance. According to her account, she also saw to the general care and feeding of this intense giant of a man who was living three lives—German lawyer/diplomat, Abwehr agent, and source for Allied intelligence.

Doc. 3-12, Tel. 483, Feb. 15, 1944, Box 275. Iris was the French resistance delegation in Switzerland. Indigo represented certain resistance elements within France. "Tertius" was a ranking OSS officer in London concerned with special operations and liaison with British SOE.

Doc. 3-13, Tel. 2054-56, Feb. 15, 1944, Box 170. In Trans. no. 71, Jan. 20, Dulles discussed the Nazi labor organization DAF, and German labor in general (Box 273). He further reported on Jan. 21 that Gaevernitz had obtained the information in Trans. no. 71 from German trade union officials in Switzerland: George Richter, Valentin Bauer, and Wilhelm Dittman (Tel. 1825-26, Box 274). In No. 72, Jan. 21, Dulles analyzed the German and Austrian police (Box 273), based on information from exiles Wilhelm Abegg and Otto Braun (Tel. 1828, Jan. 22, 1944, Box 274). On Feb. 1, OSS Headquarters asked for additional information on individuals who would be useful during the postwar occupation (Tel. 1181-83, Box 275).

Doc. 3-14, Tel. 2057-61, Feb. 15, 1944, Box 170. Paragraph 4 of Tel. 1183 asked for the names of German publishers. Paragraph 3 concerned teachers, educators, and clergy.

Doc. 3-15, Tel. 2068-73, Feb. 15, 1944, Box 275.

Doc. 3-16, Tel. 252-53, Feb. 16, 1944, Box 275.

Doc. 3-17, Tel. 2083-84, Feb. 16, 1944, Box 170.

Doc. 3-18, Tel. 2086-87, Feb. 16, 1944, Box 170. Gen. Donovan replied as follows on Mar. 1: "Saint from 109. In further reference to your #2086-7 and related cables. It is imperative to be extremely careful about causing any open breach of allegiance on the part of German agents. Every case should be closely scrutinized and you should be entirely persuaded in your own mind that the defection will be more valuable than harmful. In some cases, desertion will be the only course of action open to the agent. On the other hand, our main concern is to effect contacts inside the enemy's espionage system without letting it be known. If this course is not followed, we will lose our sources of information and our work will be permanently damaged. Moreover, it is necessary to prevent publicity no matter what the cost" (Tel. 1289 to Bern, Box 307). Dulles responded in Tel. 2317 of Mar. 6: "Appreciate your directive. Agree unwise encourage defection of any agent so long as he has possible utility. However, regarding your last sentence if defection results believe widest publicity then desirable to create impression in Germany that people are beginning to leave sinking ship. Naturally any preliminary negotiations prior open defection should be guarded with utmost secrecy. Do you agree?" (Entry 165, Box 14).

Doc. 3-19, Tel. 484, Feb. 17, 1944, Box 275.

Doc. 3-20, Tel. 2089-94, Feb. 17, 1944, Box 275.

Doc. 3-21, Tel. 1026, Feb. 18, 1944, 103.918/2078. A paraphrase of this cable was sent through State Department channels as Tel. 1026 (Box 170). Dulles added on Mar. 4 that von Straempes reportedly considered the election in the United States a matter of primary interest. The German saw little possibility of actually changing U.S. policy, but believed something had to be contrived to cheer up Hitler. He planned to continue to collect intelligence on U.S. matters through sources in Switzerland, including a Mrs. Riedel in Davos (Tel. 1323, Box 307).

On Feb. 18, Donovan cabled Dulles from London regarding the danger of German penetration: "We have been informed by certain visitors from Sweden who know nothing of your association with OSS that Nazi sources in that country credit you with being head of United States intelligence in Switzerland, that they are cognizant of all your activities and that you confer with all agents they send you. I am informing you of this to caution you against taking anything for granted so far as security is concerned" (Tel. 530, Box 274).

Doc. 3-22, Tel. 498-99, 501-2, Feb. 19, 1944, Box 275.

Doc. 3-23, Trans. no. 89, Feb. 19, 1944, Box 273.

Doc. 3-24, Tel. 2137-42, Feb. 21, 1944, Box 275.

Doc. 3-25, Tel. 503-4, Feb. 22, 1944, Box 275.

Doc. 3-26, Tel. 2143-45, Feb. 22, 1944, Box 275. "Paca" signified information from a particular 8-page document smuggled out of Germany by Kolbe in February (Tel. 2126-27, Feb. 21, 1944, Box 275). Gen. Eugen Ott was German Ambassador in Tokyo. Japanese pressure on Germany to seek a separate peace with the Soviet Union was a recurring theme in Wood traffic reports on East Asia.

Doc. 3-27, Tel. 2160, Feb. 22, 1944, Box 275. "Hazel" connotes Hungary.

Doc. 3-28, Tel. 2173-75, Feb. 24, 1944, Box 274. Canaris was dismissed and the Abwehr incorporated into SD intelligence under Walter Schellenberg in Feb. 1944. Two events contributed to this development. Dr. Erich Vermehren, an Abwehr operative, defected to the British in Istanbul. (Point 4 of Tel. 2139, cited here, concerned the Vermehren defection.) Also, Argentina, yielding to U.S. pressure, broke relations with Germany on Jan. 26, 1944, and proceeded to arrest a large number of Nazi spies. Col. Georg Hansen, who succeeded Canaris as head of the Abwehr under Schellenberg, was also sympathetic to the German resistance movement, and allowed the organization to continue to be a refuge for anti-Nazi elements, including sources for Allied intelligence. Field Marshal Wilhelm Keitel was Chief of Staff of the German High Command (OKW). Tel. 2086 is printed as Doc. 3-18. In Tel. 1247 to Bern, Feb. 21, Headquarters had agreed with Dulles that it was inadvisable to try to induce German Abwehr defections in Switzerland at the present time (Box 275). Number 512 is Hans Bernd Gisevius. Gorter is Eduard Waetjen.

Doc. 3-29, Tel. 2183-85, Feb. 24, 1944, Box 170.

Doc. 3-30, Tel. 2188, Feb. 24, 1944, Box 275. In Tel. 1251, Feb. 21, Headquarters had stated that "since it is not improbable that there will be Allied zones of occupation in Germany, we should like to warn you against thinking too exclusively of Germany as a whole" (Box 275).

Doc. 3-31, Tel. 2189-93, Feb. 24, 1944, Box 275. At the Moscow Foreign Ministers Conference of October 1943, the Allies agreed that Austria would be independent and separate from Germany after the war. The Austrian people were called upon to accept responsibility for their part in the war, and to help in expelling the Germans from their country.

Doc. 3-32, Tel. 1191, Feb. 28, 1944, Box 170. Field Marshal Erich von Manstein was the highly competent commander of the southeastern front. He was dismissed by Hitler in March 1944 for opposition to the Führer's inflexible no-retreat strategy. Field Marshal Georg von Kuechler was commander of Army Group North.

Doc. 3-33, Tel. 2226-28, Feb. 28, 1944, Box 170. Tel. 1264-65, Feb. 25, contained a message from Vanni Montana, a prominent Italian-American labor leader, that read in part as follows: "The democratic cause in Italy will benefit if democratic groups in that country shun association with dictatorial parties such as the Communists. The present United Front of Socialist and other democratic groups with Communism is imperiling Italian democracy and playing into monarchist hands. Furthermore, it alienates the support of the American people" (Box 274).

Doc. 3-34, Tel. 2242-43, Feb. 29, 1944, Box 275. Number 642 was Pierre Guillain de Benouville. Dulles's radiotelephone transmission of Feb. 28 dealt with the attitude of the French resistance, based on a long memorandum from resistance leaders. Principal points included the following. U.S.-U.K. prestige had suffered during the war. The resistance resented Allied reluctance to accept Gen. de Gaulle as the French leader, while promoting Darlan and Giraud. At the same time, the resistance fighters in France rejected the attempt of French politicians in exile to restore the old France. The resistance wanted a transformed nation based on social justice, a new regime opposed to both capitalism and communism. The resistance also reproached the Allies for failing to arm them, bombing civilians, and waging a prolonged war of attrition rather than seeking early liberation. In conclusion, the resistance appeal, as represented by Dulles, called for a statement by President Roosevelt recognizing de Gaulle as leader of the French nation and guaranteeing that France would be allowed to determine its own destiny after the war (Box 273).

Doc. 3-35, Tel. 2263, Mar. 1, 1944, Box 191.

Doc. 3-36, Tel. 2282-85, Mar. 3, 1944, Box 191. Field Marshal Albert Kesselring was commander of German forces in Italy from 1943 to Mar. 1945.

Doc. 3-37, Tel. 2288-92, Mar. 3, 1944, Box 307. In Tel. 2293, Mar. 4, Dulles informed Donovan that Sparrow mission preparations had now been firmed up with Algiers, and all that was now needed was his general encouragement of the operation (Box 307). On Mar. 8, Dulles informed Brewster in Algiers that he was in agreement with pin-points selected as the location of the drop and was notifying Bakach-Bessenyey, the Hungarian Minister in Bern that all details had been arranged (Tel. 307, Box 307). Other cables dealing with the operational details of mission include Tel. 279-81 from Bern to Algiers, Feb. 28; Tel. 293-97 from Bern to Washington, Mar. 3; and Tel. 2467-68 from Bern to Washington, Mar. 15 (CIA/FOIA). Tel. 2335-38, Mar. 9, reported that Kallay had had some success in placing men he could depend on in vital spots in the general staff and war ministry (Box 307).

The three-man Sparrow mission, headed by Lt. Col. Florimond Duke, was dropped into Hungarian territory on the night of Mar. 15, 1944, and succeeded in reaching its principal intended point of contact, Gen. Stephen Ujszaszy, the chief of Hungarian military intelligence. The mission met with disaster when the Germans took military control of the country on Mar. 19-20. Duke and his team were turned over to the Germans on Mar. 25, and numerous pro-Western Hungarians were arrested or executed. The Sparrow team spent the rest of the war in captivity, as described in Duke's *Name, Rank, and Serial Number* (New York: Meredith Press, 1969). The Sparrow mission and other Allied efforts to contact anti-Nazi elements in Hungary contributed to the German decision to invade. In *Hungarian Premier,* Nicholas Kallay asserts that the Germans were aware of Sparrow mission through the breaking of U.S. codes.

In addition to telegrams in the Bern cable files in Entry 134, documentation on Sparrow mission is located in Entry 134, Box 214, and Entry 97, Box 35. This material underlines the confusion that was inevitable given that OSS units in Istanbul, Algiers, Bern, and Washington each had a role in planning. It also demonstrates that the United States attempted to conceal the operation from its British Allies, who in turn were receiving messages from within Hungary that they did not share with Washington. Informed of British objections to Sparrow mission, Generals Donovan and Magruder cabled OSS in Algiers on Mar. 24 that "we have the approval of all authorized American authorities and we are empowered by the JCS to set up intelligence networks and carry out intelligence operations in any country occupied by the enemy or in enemy countries themselves. We need no authorization from any other government or its agencies, nor are we required to notify them of any action we may take." Donovan and Magruder described Sparrow as an effort to secure military intelligence, not a mission authorized to conduct peace negotiations or act in political matters (Tel. 3203[4], Entry 97, Box 35).

Doc. 3-38, Tel. 2301, Mar. 4, 1944, Box 191. On Feb. 24, 1944, Dulles had defended Gaevernitz as follows: "I should like to rectify any unfairness which may have been shown to 476, and verify the fact that for over a year he has been working for us on virtually a full-time basis. He has been a tremendous help to us with respect to the Breakers and Bakus connections, and in this sphere generally. Among other things, he has acted in such capacities as go-between with 478, 830, 817, and others. I would be grateful for word from you as to what Stinnes is engaged in at the present time. It is possible that he could provide you with valuable clues on which 476 could work" (Tel. 2182, CIA/FOIA).

In Tel. 1281, Feb. 28, headquarters informed Dulles that efforts to enlist Gero Gaevernitz's brother-in-law, Edmund Stinnes, in anti-Nazi propaganda activities, had been unsuccessful. The telegram described Stinnes, a Haverford professor from the German industrialist family, as having far-right affiliations

(Box 165). Gaevernitz, who had served Allied intelligence since 1940, came under suspicion after the war for allegedly having had pro-Nazi sympathies and engaging in corrupt business practices. Dulles and Gen. Legge for whom he had also worked, defended him vigorously. Pertinent correspondence is located in the Allen Dulles Papers, Box 21.

Doc. 3-39, Tel. 2307-11, Mar. 5, 1944, Box 228.

Doc. 3-40, Tel. 2318, Mar. 6, 1944, Box 191. In Tel. 2216, Feb. 26, Dulles reported that Krauel had failed to return to Germany when he was replaced, and was known to have written a letter advocating a pro-Western military coup in Germany to save the country from Bolshevism (Box 274). Replying on Feb. 28, F. L. Mayer stated that he had known Krauel prior to the war and regarded him as a patriotic, high-minded individual (Tel. 1278, Box 275).

Doc. 3-41, Tel. 2321-22, Mar. 6, 1944, Box 307.

Doc. 3-42, Tel. 2327-28, Mar. 7, 1944, Box 191.

Doc. 3-43, Tel. 2341, Mar. 9, 1944, Box 191.

Doc. 3-44, Tel. 2355, Mar. 9, 1944, Box 191. Bern further reported on March 28 that the Germans had turned the guns of the Maginot Line toward France and that the defense works now housed arms factories and repair shops (Tel. 2618-20, Entry 139, Box 26).

Doc. 3-45, Tel. 2381, Mar. 11, 1944, CIA/FOIA. Teba indicated information based on letter received from Fritz Kolbe in March 1944.

Doc. 3-46, Tel. 2408-11, Mar. 13, 1944, CIA/FOIA. In Tel. 2412-16, Mar. 13, Dulles reported that number 840 (Messner in Vienna) was able to hear radio transmissions from OSS in Istanbul. He also discussed operational details of a projected parchute drop of agents, either Sparrow mission or a related plan, Redbird (Box 307). On Mar. 24, Goldberg and Shepardson in Washington sent a "Redbird" cable to Van Arkel and Rodrigo in Algiers as follows: "1. The arrangements effected by you and Packy for sending 840 a unit of 2 men from SI Algiers has our endorsement in principle. 2. Such a team does not have authorization to carry on political transactions, but is sent out for the sole purpose of performing intelligence work. . . . 3. 109 has prepared . . . instructions for the Sparrow. . . . These instructions should be duplicated in general for Redbird unit. . . . 5. Both Bern and Istanbul are concerned in the Redbird project, and it is therefore essential that not only Washington but 110 and 550 be kept informed of the action continuously" (Tel. 1403-5, Box 307). Redbird was already overtaken by events. With the German occupation of Hungary, Allied contacts in Vienna as well as in Budapest were eliminated by the Nazis.

Doc. 3-47, Tel. 2435-39, Mar. 14, 1944, Box 191. Tel. 529-31 from Bern to London, Mar. 7, had also contained information on German rocket projectile specifications and deployment (Box 307).

Doc. 3-48, Tel. 2460-64, Mar. 15, 1944, CIA/FOIA. Dulles informed Donovan on Mar. 20 that he was scheduled to meet with Gen. Guisan on Mar. 25 and requested further instructions (Tel. 2524, Box 307). On Mar. 21, Donovan and Shepardson advised Dulles not to confer with Guisan in any manner that might require him to reveal his sources (Tel. 1382-83, Box 307).

On a related subject, Dulles reported on Mar. 14 that a number of Swiss officers had been arrested for espionage on behalf of Germany, and a Major Pfister had been sentenced to death. Conversely, a number of junior Swiss intelligence officers believed to be too close to the OSS in Lausanne and Geneva had been arrested. Swiss intelligence officers generally had been forbidden to have contact with aliens (Tel. 2440-41, Box 191). Regarding the complexities of Swiss wartime neutrality, see Jozef Garlinski, *The Swiss Corridor: Espionage Networks in Switzerland During World War II* (London: Dent, 1981); Jon Kimche, *Spying for Peace: General Guisan and Swiss Neutrality* (New York: Roy Publishers, 1961); and Schellenberg, *The Labyrinth*.

Doc. 3-49, Tel. 2465-66, Mar. 15, 1944, Box 307. In Tel. 1341, Mar. 13, OSS Headquarters asked for clarification of conflicting reports on the extent to which German morale had been affected by the bombing of Berlin (Box 307). Dulles makes reference to the week-long Allied bombing assault on Hamburg in August 1943.

Doc. 3-50, Tel. 2469-72, Mar. 16, 1944, Box 307. Source 819 has not been identified. Gen. Edmund von Glaise-Horstenau, an Austrian, was German Consul General in Zagreb. On Mar. 17, headquarters informed Dulles that this report was contradicted by other sources and had every indication of being propaganda (Tel. 1361, Box 307). Dulles defended his report on Mar. 21, stating that the information on Mihailovich had originated with the Hungarian Consul General at Belgrade, who had twenty-five years of intimate experience with Yugoslavia. "We are of the opinion," Dulles stated, ". . . that just as we underestimated the Partisans and Tito during the initial stages . . . , at the present time our tendency may be to place too much importance on this movement as compared with other factions including Matchek and Mihailovich" (Tel. 2531-32, CIA/FOIA).

Doc. 3-51, Tel. 2473-76, Mar. 16, 1944, Box 342. Prince Barbu Stirbey, a former Rumanian high court figure, was in Cairo attempting to arrange an accommodation with the Allies as the Red Army approached the frontier. Eduard Benes, head of the Czech government in exile, visited Moscow in Dec. 1943 and signed a Czech-Soviet Treaty of Alliance.

Doc. 3-52, Tel. 540-41, Mar. 17, 1944, Box 307.

Doc. 3-53, Tel. 2501, Mar. 17, 1944, Box 191. Dulles's apprehension concerning increasing Soviet influence in Europe apparently did not prevent him from interacting with the local chapter of "Freies Deutschland." Tel. 2319-20, Mar. 6, reads in part as follows: "Pamphlet 'Freies Deutschland' is clandestinely mimeographed here by so-called Swiss Section of Moscow Committee and has some circulation in Germany. Also recently 678 [Mayer] and I arranged print booklet which we considered excellent general propaganda for dissemination via Freies Deutschland channels among workers and soldiers Germany. Through cutout we have good contact with this group which is excellent channel to get clandestine material northward" (Entry 165, Box 14).

Doc. 3-54, Trans. no. 106, Mar. 17, 1944, Box 273. Tel. 1348 to Bern, Mar. 14, read as follows: "From the beginning your flashes have been extremely helpful. They are now being read by a rapidly growing number of people. As we would like to ask head man to listen in when you have an especially interesting conversation piece, please advise us several days beforehand when something of this character is coming up" (Box 307).

Doc. 3-55, Tel. 317, Mar. 20, 1944, Box 307. Giuseppe Saragat was a prominent socialist opponent of both Fascism and communism. He headed the assembly that drew up the postwar constitution and later served as foreign minister and President of Italy.

Doc. 3-56, Tel. 319-21, Mar. 20, 1944, Box 166.

Doc. 3-57, Tel. 2518-22, Mar. 20, 1944, Box 191. The War Refugee Board, established by Executive Order on Jan. 26, 1944, was charged with taking all possible measures "to rescue the victims of enemy oppression who are in imminent danger of death and otherwise to afford such victims all possible relief and assistance consistent with the successful prosecution of the war." In Tel. 2492-93, Mar. 17, Dulles stated that he did not want to get too deeply involved in refugee work and proposed that Washington work through Ross McClelland, the Quaker representative in Switzerland, who was about to assume War Refugee Board responsibilities for the Legation (Box 342). This issue provides additional support to the argument that Dulles was inadequately sensitive to the reality of the Holocaust.

Reference is made to Noel Field, Robert Dexter, and Charles Joy of the Unitarian Refugee Committee. Field was Dulles's contact in Switzerland on refugee matters.

Doc. 3-58, Tel. 2523, Mar. 20, 1944, Box 191. Wally Toscanini refers to the world-famous violinists Yehudi Menuhin and Jascha Heifetz. Headquarters replied as follows on Apr. 1: "Since Toscanini recently dispatched $5,000 to the Unitarians and a like sum to the Quakers for similar purposes, he is a trifle startled by Wally's request. He would be grateful if the message below were delivered to Wally: 'I advised 3 American organizations already active in Switzerland as soon as I received your request. These organizations will get in touch with you and I also recommend that you contact Noel Field of the Unitarian Service Committee at 52 Quai Wilson, Geneva. . . .' If necessary, Toscanini is ready to raise more money which would be sent through the services of the bank" (CIA/FOIA).

Doc. 3-59, Tel. 324-25, Mar. 21, 1944, Box 307. Dulles reported on McCollum's arrival in Tel. 310-12 (Box 307).

Doc. 3-60, Tel. 2526, Mar. 21, 1944, Box 191. The Dulles evening radiotelephone transmission of Mar. 20 reported that all communication with Hungary had been cut and it seemed likely that the Germans were taking control (Box 273). In *Hungarian Premier,* Nicholas Kallay recounts the tragic days leading to the German occupation and subsequent deportation of thousands of Hungarian Jews to death camps. Hitler summoned Horthy to Austria on Mar. 18 and informed him that German troops were already on the move due to Hungary's faithlessness. With the Regent out of the country, the Premier and the military didn't even attempt to mount token opposition. Kallay took refuge in the Turkish legation and survived the war. He attributes the German coup to numerous motives, reaction to Sparrow and other Hungarian contacts with the West among them. The anti-Nazi, anticommunist geopolitical outlook expressed in his memoirs bears a striking resemblance to that of Allen Dulles.

Doc. 3-61, Tel. 2541-43, Mar. 22, 1944, Box 191. Tel. 1363 from Arthur Goldberg of the OSS Labor Desk to Dulles, March 18, read as follows: "Kindly deliver to 328 the message below, which is sent by Dominique and Eva: 'Labor in the United States will regularly transmit large sums of money which are to be expended for the relief of French labor. Kindly supply us with the name and address of an individual to whom the funds can be sent on license, for we would like to avoid overloading your account' " (Box 165). Shepardson (SI) advised Dulles on Mar. 27 that Washington consented to his paying 328 within reasonable limits to the extent warranted by the worth of the information he supplied (Tel. 1416, Box 342).

Doc. 3-62, Tel. 2544-47, Mar. 22, 1944, CIA/FOIA. Among the persons mentioned are Nikola Momtchilov, former Bulgarian minister in London with close ties to the British government; Damian Veltchev, former Prime Minister Kimon Gheorghiev, and Peter Todorov, leaders of the Zveno antimonarchist political group; Gen. Konstantin Loukash; Prince Kyril, brother of the deceased King Boris III and member of the three-man regency governing the country; Princess Evdokia, sister of Boris and Kyril; and Prime Minister Dobri Bojilov.

On Apr. 7, Dulles reported that Kiosseivanov's trip had been delayed by the situation in Hungary, but that he remained anxious to return to Bulgaria to strengthen the opposition and to work out an accommodation between Bulgarian elements and the Allies (CIA/FOIA). He reportedly departed on Apr. 11. Dulles recommended that bombing of Sofia therefore be suspended for a few days (Tel. 2804, Apr. 12, 1944, Box 307). On Apr. 21, Dulles reported that Kiss had reached Sofia and intended to return to Bern soon. Dulles proposed to establish direct contact in a discreet manner (Tel. 3122, Box 307).

When Kiss returned to Bern in early May, he stated that Bulgaria was under tight German control and subject to increasing pressure from the Soviet Union. He had been approached by centrist politicians about heading a new government, but had rejected the proposal on the grounds that he did not wish to be his nation's Kerensky. He believed a Soviet-dominated government was inevitable (Tel. 3451-59, May 11, 1944, CIA/FOIA).

Doc. 3-63, Tel. 2548-49, Mar. 22, 1944, Box 191.

Doc. 3-64, Tel. 2557-58, Mar. 23, 1944, Box 191.

Doc. 3-65, Tel. 2563-67, Mar. 23, 1944, Box 191. In Tel. 1328, Mar. 10, OSS headquarters instructed Dulles to take charge of planning for "occupation penetration" of defeated Germany. He was to determine which agents should be introduced into what points in Germany and to define their missions (Box 307). Tel. 1162-68, Nov. 29, 1943, is printed as Doc. 2-73.

Doc. 3-66, Tel. 2569-71, Mar. 23, 1944, Box 191. Tel. 1195 contained a message from Hermann and Elspeth Weichmann to Dr. Braun by OSS on behalf of the German Labor Group in the United States (Box 275). On Mar. 27, F. L. Mayer in OSS headquarters cabled Dulles as follows: "I have sent forward the personal sections of the above message [2569]. Did not deliver the section containing the political observations, which I found to be of interest and assistance, because, . . . in my opinion it is not wise to allow our facilities to be employed for controversial views of this type" (Box 342).

Doc. 3-67, Tel. 548-49, Mar. 24, 1944, Box 342. Some sources that were employed by both U.S. and British intelligence were given K numbers (K-2, etc.) to avoid duplication. Information from such sources were transmitted as "Unison" messages intended for the use of both services. K-2 was a French source in Switzerland. K-13 was the SIM service, an Italian resistance source. Source 472 is a remnant of prewar French intelligence in Switzerland; 521 connotes British SIS (MI-6) in Switzerland. Broadway stands for SIS headquarters in London; 520 is the U.S. Military Attaché office in Bern. Zulu means British.

On May 5, 1944, Dulles cabled: "We have entirely harmonious relations with 521 and he is sending continuously increasing material which we employ to prevent duplication and as a check only. Trust that unison system is satisfactory to both London and Washington as it is working satisfactorily here." Dulles now even planned to share most George Wood material with his British counterpart (Tel. 3351-53, Box 275).

Doc. 3-68, Tel. 2576-81, Mar. 24, 1944, Box 228. On Mar. 28, Shepardson responded as follows from Washington: "You and your helpers are to be highly praised for the extremely usable intelligence contained in your #2576-2581. We are deeply grateful for your exceptional efforts" (Tel. 1415, Box 307). Allied intelligence efforts targeting the German atomic energy program are expertly described in *Heisenberg's War*, by Thomas Powers. Source 493 is Frederick Loofbourow who played an important part in OSS scientific intelligence activities in Switzerland. KW stands for Kaiser Wilhelm [Institute]. OSS Bern transmitted additional AZUSA messages on Apr. 3 (2697-98, Box 307), Apr. 24 (3146-47, Box 307), Apr. 29 (3240, Box 307), and May 11 (3396-99, Box 275). In the latter, one point made by Flute was that if the renowned Danish physicist Niels Bohr was brought to Germany, Werner Heisenberg, the director of the German program, was too proud of his own fame to work under him.

Doc. 3-69, Tel. 2600, Mar. 26, 1944, Box 191. This text reflects corrections transmitted in Tel. 2568, Mar. 24 (Box 191). Headquarters informed Dulles on Mar. 24 that OSS in Stockholm had confirmed the removal of Canaris. He had reportedly gone to Switzerland at the end of February and then had been ordered to Istanbul to solve the case of the Gestapo deserters. He was removed when he failed to do so, and might have been liquidated (Tel. 1397-98, Box 307).

Doc. 3-70, Tel. 2612-17, Mar. 28, 1944, Box 342. In Tel. 1360, Mar. 16, Shepardson requested information on the number of Bern's staff officers, agents, and subagents, with their locations, for an SI "order of battle" (Box 342).

Doc. 3-71, Tel. 339-42, Mar. 29, 1944, Box 166. Allied forces had landed at Anzio south of Rome on Jan. 22, 1944, but were unable to make rapid progress against determined German resistance.

Doc. 3-72, Tel. 336-37, Mar. 29, 1944, Box 307.

Doc. 3-73, Tel. 2627-28, Mar. 29, 1944, Box 191.

Doc. 3-74, Tel. 2630-31, Mar. 29, 1944, Box 307. In Tel. 1382-83, Mar. 21, Donovan and Shepardson instructed Dulles not to confer with Gen. Guisan about Swiss leaks to the Germans in any way that might compromise sources (Box 307).

Doc. 3-75, Tel. 2633, Mar. 29, 1944, Box 307. The Bureau Ribbentrop was a Nazi Party agency headed by Foreign Minister Joachim von Ribbentrop that provided independent foreign policy advice to Hitler. Alfred Rosenberg, an architect of Nazi ideology, was Minister for Occupied Eastern Territories. Martin Luther, a top Ribbentrop aid, failed in an Apr. 1943 coup against his superior and spent the remainder of the war in prison.

Doc. 3-76, Tel. 2634, Mar. 29, 1944, Box 191.

Doc. 3-77, Tel. 2651-53, Mar. 30, 1944, Box 191. Francis Deak was an American citizen of Hungarian origins who was sent to Lisbon to provide a possible link to authorities in his homeland. Tel. 1335, Mar. 11, made brief reference to Deak's travels. Tibor Eckhardt, a former leader of the Smallholders Party, represented Hungarian interests in the United States while Kallay was premier.

Doc. 3-78, Tel. 2659-67, Mar. 31, 1944, Box 191. A partial paraphrase of this telegram was sent by Gen. Magruder to James Clement Dunn, Director of the Office of European Affairs at the State Department on Apr. 5 (*FRUS, 1944*, 1:505–7). In Tel. 1406-10, Mar. 25, Donovan instructed Dulles to use his sources to obtain answers to three questions with respect to German public opinion, which may be summarized as follows: (1) Were Germans aware of the inevitability of defeat? (2) Could German civilians be made to believe that "unconditional surrender" was not synonymous with total disaster for them as individuals? (3) Did Germans believe that it was possible that the Nazi government could be overthrown by some minority group? Unison source K-24 was deemed qualified for circulating such a questionnaire (Box 307). Dulles's radiotelephone transmission of Jan. 31, 1944 dealt with German morale, which he believed had stiffened recently despite military reverses. This was due in part to Gestapo terror and to failure of the Anglo-American powers to offer anything but a fight to the end. "When Germany cracks," he stated, "it will probably come suddenly. . . . This crack might be brought about by a successful invasion of the continent, the disappearance of Hitler, or a new catastrophe on the Russian front. Otherwise, I do not expect that the inner front will crack until the military front . . . cracks. . . . It might be fair to say that Germany has impetus rather than morale. It is a machine rather than an aggregate of normal human beings. When the efficiency of the machine is reduced below a certain point, the crack will come, both on the fighting and on the home fronts" (Box 273).

Donovan replied to Dulles on Apr. 2 as follows: "To 110 from 109. Reference your #2659-67. 1. By the full treatment it gives to the questions formulated, your cable in my opinion exactly satisfies the situation which was submitted to us, and I thank you for it. Unless you receive additional queries from me, you need take no further action in this matter. I concur fully with the purport of your paragraph 7, and the Joint Chiefs of Staff are now in possession of my proposal as to how the phrase to which you refer could be handled. 2. I am departing from here for the Headquarters of General MacArthur, but, as I have arranged for your cables to be sent on to me, I shall continue to receive them with extreme interest" (Tel. 1444-45, Box 307).

Doc. 3-79, Tel. 2674-75, Mar. 31, 1944, Box 191.

Doc. 3-80, Tel. 355-56, Apr. 3, 1944, Box 307. Dulles further discussed establishing contacts with the Italian resistance in Tel. 376-78 to Algiers, Apr. 14. Emphasizing difficulties in coordination with the British, he observed that "the Sulu SOE person here [McCaffrey] is very competent but he is not especially cooperative except following regular crackdowns by me, which are wasteful of time and energy" (CIA/FOIA).

Doc. 3-81, Tel. 2724-26, Apr. 6, 1944, Box 307.

Doc. 3-82, Tel. 2714-16, Apr. 6, 1944, Box 228. Gorter is Eduard Waetjen; 512 is Hans Bernd Gisevius. Tucky is Gen. Ludwig Beck, Chief of Staff of the German Armed Forces from 1935 to 1938. An opponent of Hitler's policies, he had been involved in various unsuccessful anti-Nazi plots and activities. Lester is Carl Goerdeler, Mayor of Leipzig from 1930 to 1937 and a long-time opponent of the Nazis. Tel. 1965-66, Feb. 4, is printed as Doc. 3-4.

On Mar. 17, OSS headquarters answered a query from the London office with the following definition: "The term 'Breakers' refers to a German resistance organization which is made up of liberal and educated persons from special governmental and military circles; however, its organizational structure is loose. It is reported that they would like to see drastic social changes based on a western rather than eastern orientation but that they fear that circumstances are forcing Germany toward an eastern influence" (Tel. 30394, Box 228).

Doc. 3-83, Tel. 2709-10, Apr. 6, 1944, Box 191. The Dulles radiotelephone transmission of Apr. 3 included an account of the German occupation of Hungary and the Hitler-Horthy meeting that preceded it (Box 191).

Doc. 3-84, Tel. 2712-13, Apr. 6, 1944, Box 191. Tel. 1438-39, Apr. 1, requested Dulles's evaluation of short-wave broadcasts to Czechoslovakia, Germany, Switzerland, Belgium, Austria, and France (Box 307).

Doc. 3-85, Tel. 367, Apr. 7, 1944, Box 307.

Doc. 3-86, Tel. 2718-22, Apr. 7, 1944, Box 228. On Apr. 19, Dulles added the following views on dealing with the Breakers group: "It is worthwhile to give them, as a possible agitating element, some quiet encouragement, while employing the greatest discretion and not committing ourselves. I am quite dubious of practical possibilities, since I am not certain in my own mind whether it is desirable to do away with the principal devils before collapse. Furthermore, I suspect that the Gestapo is thoroughly familiar with most of the names listed among those prepared to join" (Tel. 3045-46, Box 228).

OSS headquarters responded as follows on Apr. 29: "From last sentence of your #3046, we assume that you believe it improbable that a group so large and of such a nature could exist in the Reich clandestinely. It would be most unwise to liquidate and uncover a large conspiracy implicating prominent personages just prior to an invasion or coincident with it. We are in complete agreement with the sort of bolstering you propose. However, the intelligence return is not worth the risk of anything beyond this" (Tel. 1537-38, Box 228).

As part of his ongoing practice of sending summaries of Dulles messages to the White House Map Room, OSS Deputy Director Magruder transmitted a report based on the Bern telegrams of Apr. 6–7 on contact with the German resistance group (Cover memo, Apr. 12, 1944, FDR Library, Map Room Files, Box 73). OSS continued to supply the Map Room with "Breakers" reports in the months that followed.

Doc. 3-87, Tel. 2729, Apr. 7, 1944, Box 191.

Doc. 3-88, Tel. 2732, Apr. 8, 1944, Box 191. OSS in Algiers cabled the following to Dulles on Apr. 18: "Tito has sent us this message, via Bari, replying to #2732 from Berne: 'Consent to the coming to our territory of Hungarian troops on condition that they bring with them as many arms as they can, and that they join us in fighting the Nazis. The Allies ought to give certain guarantees for such troops' " (Tel. 30887 [301 to Bern], Entry 90, Box 6).

Doc. 3-89, Tel. 2751, Apr. 9, 1944, Box 191. In Tel. 1421, Mar. 28, Shepardson had requested that Dulles seek secret intelligence on Japan, and also obtain important Japanese periodicals (Box 342).

Doc. 3-90, Tel. 568-69, Apr. 10, 1944, Box 342. Tel. 1437, Apr. 1, indicated that London proposed that additional funds be put at the disposal of the Maquis, and authorized Dulles to grant the increase if he believed it was justified (Box 165).

Doc. 3-91, Tel. 2787-92, Apr. 12, 1944, Box 307. Buxton's memorandum of transmittal recommended that the report receive the President's immediate attention, and read in part as follows: "As is customary with material of such special character these enclosures are also being delivered personally to the Secretary of State, General Marshall, Admiral King, General Eisenhower and the Secretary of the Joint Chiefs of Staff. Under existing arrangements on this particular contact the British will see this cable and, as in the past, will doubtless show it to their highest officials." In addition to the text of Tel. 2787-92, Buxton sent a memorandum describing Dulles's credentials as an expert on Europe since 1915, and his personal involvement in the Kappa/Boston material from Kolbe's first appearance in 1943 (FDR Library, Map Room Files, Naval Aide Files A/82, Box 163).

Doc. 3-92, Tel. 572, Apr. 17, 1944, Box 307. Hitler and Mussolini did meet at Klessheim, Apr. 22–23. The Duce accepted total subordination, agreeing to the ongoing exploitation of Italian manpower by the Germans.

Doc. 3-93, Tel. 2966-69, Apr. 17, 1944, Box 307. Buxton's memorandum to the President is in FDR Library, Map Room Files, Naval Aide, Box 171, President's File.

Doc. 3-94, Apr. 18, 1944, CIA/FOIA. On Apr. 20, Dulles reported that a contact in the Rumanian Legation had indicated that the Minister wholeheartedly approved of efforts to communicate with officials in Bucharest, and offered to help in any way possible (Tel. 3115, CIA/FOIA).

Doc. 3-95, Tel. 387-88, Apr. 20, 1944, Box 307. In Tel. 310-12 to Algiers, Mar. 15, Dulles had reported the arrival of downed airmen from Italy, where they had had contact with the resistance (Box 307).

Doc. 3-96, Tel. 2543, Apr. 21, 1944, Box 191.

Doc. 3-97, Tel. 2560, Apr. 21, 1944, Box 191.

Doc. 3-98, Tel. 3152-53, Apr. 25, 1944, Box 307. Bern transmitted an additional "Toledo" message concerning possible German biological warfare research on Apr. 28 (Tel. 3215, Box 307).

Doc. 3-99, Tel. 3163-65, Apr. 26, 1944, Entry 121, Box 19.

Doc. 3-100, Tel. 3167-69, Apr. 26, 1944, Entry 121, Box 19. Kappa Tel. 2643-46, Mar. 29, contained information obtained by Kolbe on German activities in Ireland. The German Minister, Hempel, had asked for instructions on how to deal with the possibility that the government of Prime Minister Eamon De Valera might yield to Allied pressure and call for the Germans to turn over their transmitter capable of sending secret messages on military matters (CIA/FOIA). Kappa Tel. 2778-86, Apr. 12, summarized additional intercepts from the German legation, which reported on the capture of German-trained parachutists and advocated German military aid to Ireland should the Allies invade that country (CIA/FOIA). Joseph P. Walshe was an official of the Irish Ministry of External Affairs.

Doc. 3-101, Tel. 405, Apr. 27, 1944, Box 307.

Doc. 3-102, Tel. 586-87, Apr. 28, 1944, Box 342. Pietro Nenni was leader of the pro-Soviet faction of the Italian Socialist Party.

Doc. 3-103, Tel. 3228-29, Apr. 28, 1944, Box 191.

Doc. 3-104, Tel. 3238-39, Apr. 29, 1944, Box 191.

Doc. 3-105, Tel. 590-96, May 1, 1944, Box 275.

Doc. 3-106, Tel. 3256-59, May 1, 1944, Box 275.

Doc. 3-107, Tel. 589, May 2, 1944, Box 192.

Doc. 3-108, Tel. 3261-68, May 2, 1944, Box 275.

Doc. 3-109, Tel. 3274-76, May 2, 1944, Box 192.

Doc. 3-110, Tel. 3278, May 2, 1944, Box 275. Number 331 was a Swiss source; 227 was Charles Dyar, U.S. financial officer in Switzerland.

Doc. 3-111, Tel. 3297-98, May 3, 1944, Box 275.

Doc. 3-112, Tel. 3282-91, May 4, 1944, Box 275. On Feb. 15, 1944, Allied bombing largely destroyed the monastery at Monte Cassino which was part of German defensive positions. Despite additional controversial air and artillery attacks on the historic abbey, it did not fall until May 18.

Doc. 3-113, Tel. 3301-9, May 4, 1944, Box 275. Prime Minister Pibul Songgram, whose pro-Japanese sympathies waned with the course of the war, was forced from power in July 1944. The regent Pridi Phanomyong continued the policy of neutrality, but secretly cooperated with OSS and British SOE in the interest of enhancing Thailand's postwar position.

Doc. 3-114, Tel. 3320, May 4, 1944, Box 275. Tel. 3279, May 2, read as follows: "Information that Aramis, head of G-2 Hungary had been shot by the Nazis has just been received from a very good Hungarian source. Katharine Karady, an Hungarian actress, is also reported to have been seized in connection with reported meetings of Aramis and British parachutists in Karady's home. (Perhaps they were Sparrow: this from 110.) The new War Minister, Voros, has offered Rakolozai, Hungarian MA here, the position of head of G-2. Rakolozai has been given the number 844 by us" (Entry 139, Box 26). The fate of Ujszaszy is uncertain. Former Prime Minister Kallay writes that he was taken off by the Russians after a period of German captivity. Florimond Duke, writing in 1969, stated that although his friends thought he was an unwilling prisoner of the Russians, affidavits by Ujszaszy supporting Soviet claims were presented at the Nuremberg trials and he was heard broadcasting the same line from Moscow. He was never again seen in the West. Cave Brown asserts in *Wild Bill Donovan* that he was shot immediately by the Germans in Mar. 1944.

On May 13, Dulles sent a "Kappa" message based on information from Fritz Kolbe on the aftermath of Sparrow Mission. It read in part as follows: "On April 20th, the [German] Legation in Budapest sent the following report concerning the examination of the officers who had been taken into custody: It seems that negotiations were carried on between Americans and the Hungarian representative at Bern. As a consequence of these negotiations, a US colonel and 2 colleagues were parachuted into Hungary on March 16. They had a transmitting set with them. Ujszaszy secretly took care of them in Hungary. Szent Miklosy prepared the plan. Hungary was to quit the war. The progress of the plot was halted by the German occupation of Hungary. The documents were destroyed. The US agents were apprehended and are in Berlin. (The following is from 110: I assume that the foregoing represents not only the wire from the Legation at Budapest but in addition all the data which Wood could obtain on the matter"[)] (Tel. 3440-42, CIA/FOIA).

Doc. 3-115, Tel. 3321, May 4, 1944, Box 192. Reference is to Col. Georg Hansen, director of the Abwehr since the dismissal of Adm. Canaris in February.

Doc. 3-116, Tel. 3327-33, May 5, 1944, Box 275.

Doc. 3-117, Tel. 3343-44, May 5, 1944, Box 192.

Doc. 3-118, Tel. 3345, May 5, 1944, Box 192.

Doc. 3-119, Tel. 3377-79, May 8, 1944, Box 275. Tel. 1582 to Bern, May 2, stated that Lanning McFarland, OSS chief in Istanbul, held 840 in full trust (Box 275). Tel. 3300 from Bern, May 3, reads as follows: "A laconic message which we received from a friend of 840 leads us to believe that in view of the fact the evidence against them is not conclusive he and his associate are not now in danger of death. They will probably be held for quite a while, however" (Box 275).

Doc. 3-120, Tel. 609-10, May 10, 1944, Box 342.

Doc. 3-121, Tel. 611-16, May 11, 1944, Box 157. In a draft of this telegram found in Entry 139, Box 26, David is identified as Didier and Bertrand as Major Desnour/Descour [Col. Marcel Descour]. This is confirmed in Doc. 3-122. On May 19, OSS in London informed Dulles that Bertrand was known to them locally, and added, "Your proposals are all right in theory, but no action should be taken without specific orders from the Allied Command which is the sole authority for choosing regions of strategic importance." He was also advised that resistance operations were not under the supervision of the British alone, but rather came under an Anglo-American agency that reported to the Supreme Allied Commander (Tel. 46157, Box 157).

Doc. 3-122, Tel. 3401, May 11, 1944, Box 192. Pierre Mendes France was a financial adviser to General de Gaulle and future Premier of France.

Doc. 3-123, Tel. 3423-31, May 13, 1944, Box 228. Tel. 2718-22, Apr. 7, is printed as Doc. 3-86. Field Marshal Erwin Rommel, legendary German commander in North Africa, was presently Inspector of Coastal Defenses in northern France and commander of an army group. In Tel. 160-31, May 17, F. L. Mayer and Shepardson informed Dulles that they concurred completely with his thinking and his statements to Gisevius and Waetjen, which had been relayed to the highest military and civilian authorities in Washington (Box 228).

Doc. 3-124, Tel. 3443-46, May 13, 1944, Box 192. Other Bern reports on the enemy order of battle in France prior to the Normandy invasion, all filed in Box 192 of Entry 134, include Tel. 3292-96, May 3; Tel. 3334-39, May 5; Tel. 3492-94, May 16; Tel. 3498-99, May 16; Tel. 3520-21, May 18; Tel. 3522-24, May 18; Tel. 35-45-48, May 20; Tel. 3572-75, May 23; Tel. 3591-94, May 25; Tel. 3625-29, May 27; Tel. 3630-33, May 27; and Tel. 3644-48, May 31.

Tel. 647-58 to London, May 22, listed the location of all German divisions throughout Europe as known by OSS Bern (Box 157). In Tel. 675-77 to London, May 30, Dulles responded to messages from London and Washington indicating that some of the information in the cable of May 22 had been highly inaccurate. He said that the original report had been received from a source in Swiss intelligence and sent forward without evaluation (Box 342).

Tel. 3515 from Bern, May 17, read as follows: "I have been advised by one of 802's [Devignat] agents that only a minor portion of the actual troop movements during the last 6 weeks in France revealed in railroad figures. The Nazis are aware of the fact that it takes little time to learn of movements by rail and they are consequently trying to make important transfers by road. In order to conceal the true destination, when movements are being made by rail, they frequently have trains make detours" (Box 192).

Doc. 3-125, Tel. 3464, May 14, 1944, Box 275.

Doc. 3-126, Tel. 3460-63, May 15, 1944, Box 275. Apparently L. C. Moyzisch, the German intelligence officer who handled "Cicero," continued to operate in Turkey after his most famous spy was uncovered in late 1943.

Doc. 3-127, Tel. 3484-91, May 15, 1944, Box 192. Number 802 was M. Devignat, an assistant of Henri Queuille, a prewar politician who was active in the resistance. Queuille was premier of France on several occasions after the war. "Lorraine" was Laurent Eynac. Dulles added on May 16 that Devignat was an entirely reliable individual. "There is no doubt," he cabled, "that a great many of the French authorities who have stuck to their guns and kept up the proper attitude could give valuable aid to the invasion units, and as the matter of whether prompt and complete support could be procured by the Algiers committee alone is open to question . . . the agency described by 802 . . . may be helpful for this purpose. It must be observed, however, that the committee of which 802 speaks extends complete cooperation to de Gaulle's party. . . . I anticipate a visit from 802 here presently, and would like to know what you think about the contact which the Comité National wants set up with Allied forces. . . . Recommend that, until we can determine more definitely what procedure will be considered advisable, neither Algiers nor London discuss with any French groups my #3484 and this message" (Tel. 3495-97, Box 192). On June 1, OSS in London advised Dulles that his messages in Tels. 3484-91 and 3495-97 had been given to Allied Headquarters, and "because of the complex nature of the French situation, and the fact that public announcements on the central topic have been made already, Headquarters refuses to answer 802 officially" (Tel. 49517 from London to Bern, Box 157).

Doc. 3-128, Tel. 456, May 16, 1944, Box 275.

Doc. 3-129, Tel. 630-31, May 16, 1944, Box 275.

Doc. 3-130, Tel. 3518-19, May 18, 1944, Box 192. Tel. 1984-85 to Dulles from the OSS MO Branch in Washington, May 5, suggested that the effort be made to undermine Adm. Horthy, Regent of Hungary, by promoting the idea that he intended to sell out to the United Nations. This would encourage pro-Allied elements and discourage collaborationism within the country (Box 275) Count Stephen Bethlen was a former Premier of Hungary and a pro-Allied supporter of deposed Premier Kallay.

Doc. 3-131, Tel. 3565-66, May 23, 1944, Box 192.

Doc. 3-132, Tel. 665, May 24, 1944, Box 157.

Doc. 3-133, Tel. 3589-90, May 25, 1944, Box 192.

Doc. 3-134, Tel. 3595-97, May 25, 1944, Box 192. Dulles submitted additional information on Rumania on May 26. It was based on a conversation with a recently arrived Rumanian Foreign Office courier, who reported that the Germans gave no evidence of planning to make a vigorous defense of Rumania against the advancing Red Army. The source saw no hope for the country since the government would be seized by Russian-supported Rumanian communists. There could be no resistance by the bourgeoisie without considerable help from the Anglo-Saxons, an unlikely prospect (Tel. 3604-7, Box 192).

Doc. 3-135, Tel. 3650-56, May 31, 1944, Box 192. Kurt Freiherr von Hammerstein-Equord was chief of the German Army Command from 1930 to 1934. An anti-Nazi, he was dismissed, but then recalled to head an army group in the west in 1939. Again removed as unreliable, he became involved in resistance activities, but accomplished little prior to his death in 1943.

Doc. 3-136, Tel. 3674-83, June 2, 1944, Box 192. For Tel. 3484-91, May 15, and Tel. 3495-97, May 16, see Doc. 3-127 and the notes thereto. Tel. 3684-94, transmitted from Bern on June 3, contained part 2 of the Lorraine series. It consisted of a précis of a study by Devignat, endorsed by the Lorraine organization, analyzing the situation in France. It made the case that the prewar parliamentarians represented by the Lorraine group were gaining public support as Frenchmen increasingly turned away from the totalitarian extremes of collaboration with the Nazis and communism. Moderate democrats, i.e. the Lorraine group parliamentarians, were said to be willing to cooperate with General de Gaulle provided the terms of an alliance with him respected the democratic heritage of France (Box 192). Bern sent part 3 of the Lorraine series in Tel. 3668-73, June 3. It consisted of the opinions of "Beta," a resistance commander in southwestern France. Apparently, "Beta" was Col. Georges Revers, former Chief of Staff to Admiral Darlan. Beta protested that the Free French office of Col. Passy in London did not pay enough attention to him. Dulles noted parenthetically that he had never heard of Beta, but that Devignat and the Lorraine group had extreme confidence in him and believed that he had the approval of de Gaulle. The telegram contained a summary of a recent memorandum from Beta to de Gaulle concerning the peril attendant upon the infiltration of the resistance movement by communists (Box 192).

Doc. 3-137, Tel. 3702-7, June 3, 1944, Box 192. On June 6, OSS Headquarters informed Dulles that the State Department was being kept apprised of his Lorraine messages, which were of extreme interest (Tel. 1695-97, Box 165). Two days later, OSS in London informed Dulles that Gen. Eisenhower had designated Gen. Pierre Koenig, one of de Gaulle's top assistants and commander of French forces within the Allied invasion force, head of the French resistance as well. Therefore, U.S. and U.K. Services on the Continent should not aid any organization in France independent of Gen. Koenig. Davet, the French resistance delegation leader in Switzerland, had no independent authority. Dulles was asked to refrain from transmitting "additional messages of either a propagandist or a political nature" from Devignat (Tel. 51227 from London, June 8, 1944, Box 157). However, OSS headquarters informed Dulles on June 10 that it still wanted to receive political information from Devignat, although it was in full accord with military centralization of control (Tel. 1706, June 10, 1944, Box 276).

Doc. 3-138, Tel. 688-89, June 5, 1944, Box 157.

Doc. 3-139, Trans. no. 151, June 5, 1944, Box 273.

Doc. 3-140, Tel. 3722-26, June 6, 1944, Box 192.

Doc. 3-141, Trans. no. 152, June 6, 1944, Box 273.

Doc. 3-142, Tel. 3747-48, June 7, 1944, Box 192.

Doc. 3-143, Tel. 3749, June 7, 1944, Box 192. OSS Headquarters replied as follows on June 13: "Because Remarque feels that his dog, cat, and valuable books might not be safe, he does not wish to make his Locarno residence available to us" (Tel. 1721 to Bern, Box 276).

Doc. 3-144, Tel. 3750-51, June 7, 1944, Box 192. Other funds for European labor and resistance elements were being channeled through Bern during this time period. Tel. 1669-70 from OSS headquarters to Dulles, June 7, read in part as follows: "The message below is from Oldenbroek and Peter Krier to 656 [Anton Krier, labor official in Bern]: An agreement has been made by the CIO and AFL to remit $200,000 through the American Legation in Bern, Switzerland, to be used for the assistance of underground movements and Nazi persecution victims. The money is to be allocated: $20,000 for Luxembourg, $90,000 for Holland and the same sum for Belgium" (Box 165). On June 12, John Hughes and Arthur Goldberg in OSS Headquarters relayed information from Paul Vignaux, a former professor in France who worked with the OSS office in New York, that the National War Fund had allocated $50,000 to U.S. labor for the relief work among Christian trade unionists. The funds would be transmitted incrementally to Bern (Tel. 1710-11, CIA/FOIA).

Doc. 3-145, Tel. 3758-59, June 9, 1944, Box 192.

Doc. 3-146, Tel. 3787-91, June 10, 1944, Box 228. OSS Headquarters responded as follows on June 6: "In the future, kindly forward an information copy of all Breakers cables to London for 109's [Donovan] attention. When this request from 109 was acknowledged, he was informed of your recommendation not to discuss Breakers with Zulu [the British]. We suggest you either send direct confirmation of this to 109 with repeat here or show whatever change may have taken place in this attitude since the beginning of the year" (Tel. 1703, Entry 138, Box 2). Dulles cabled Donovan in London on June 12, acknowledging that recent Breakers telegrams should have been directed to him. Dulles added, "If you should deem it advisable to utilize the material contained in the Breakers cables in your conversations with Zulu, I see no reason why you should not do so. I have not revealed the contents of these cables to Zulu at this end, and at this extremely tentative phase of this somewhat indefinite matter, I do not feel that I should now; particularly, since Zulu here does not give us any information of their activists operations within the Reich" (Box 228).

Doc. 3-147, Trans. no. 155, June 10, 1944, Box 273. In his radiotelephone transmission of Dec. 23, 1943, Dulles noted the appearance in Switzerland of a German postage stamp bearing the face of Reichsführer Heinrich Himmler, Minister of the Interior and second most powerful man in Germany. Dulles was unable to determine the source of the stamp or confirm that it was genuine. (Box 273) On Dec. 29, Headquarters asked Dulles for additional information on the Himmler stamp since it had provoked considerable interest in Washington (Tel. 1036, Box 274). Headquarters further cabled on Feb. 3, 1944 that "the President would undoubtedly be glad to have the Himmler postage stamp for his album. Would it be possible to secure it without any unnecessary expenditure, bother or risk?" (Tel. 1189, Box 275). Dulles reported on June 12, 1944, that after a great deal of searching, he had found a Himmler stamp which could be purchased for about 1,000 Swiss francs, but without a guarantee of its authenticity (Tel. 3795, Box 276). General Donovan authorized Dulles to buy the stamp on June 16 (Tel. 1794 to Bern, Box 193). On Oct. 24, 1944, Donovan transmitted the Himmler stamp (and a copy of the bogus *Frankfurter Zeitung* that Dulles and Gerald Mayer of OWI had been producing in Switzerland) to Grace Tully, Roosevelt's Secretary, for the President (Roosevelt Library, PSF, Box 169). Donovan sent other items to the White House for Roosevelt's collection, including stamps printed in the mountains of Yugoslavia by Mihailovic's Chetniks (Memorandum for the President, Oct. 5, 1944, and thank-you note from FDR to Bill, Oct. 9, 1944, PSF, Box 169).

After the war, Dulles informed Donovan, who had received queries on the Himmler stamp, that he had no further information on the subject, adding, "These stamp collectors are the most insistent people I know. Several have been on my trail" (Letters of July 23 and 24, 1946, Allen Dulles Papers, Box 24). It has since been revealed that the Himmler stamp was the creation of Sefton Delmer of Britain's Political Warfare Executive. Its purpose to stir dissension between Hitler and Himmler, the unauthorized stamp was introduced into the German mails through Stockholm (L. N. Williams, "Black Propaganda Stamp," *Linn's Stamp News*, May 11, 1992, 13).

Another famous Allied stamp gambit was the Hitler death's-head issue produced by OSS Morale Operations. Mimicking the standard German regular issue Hitler-head inscribed "Deutsches Reich," the OSS stamp portrayed a Hitler skull bearing the inscription "Futsches Reich" (Collapsed state). (See Richard B. Graham, "WWII Spy Stamps and Undercover Addresses," *Linn's Stamp News*, July 26, 1993, 30.) In a letter to Donovan of May 13, 1946, concerning the Himmler stamps and other propaganda items, Dulles mentions "a so-called Hitler stamp showing him as a death's head with skull and cross-bones, which Gerry Mayer and I got out as black propaganda and smuggled into Germany in as many copies as we could get over the frontier" (Allen Dulles Papers, Box 24). Large numbers of forged and propaganda postage stamps also were dropped into Germany in 1945 as part of OSS "Operation Cornflakes" for the airborne dissemination of psychological warfare materials. (See Werner M. Bohne, " 'Cornflakes' Numbers Now Known," *American Philatelist*, May, 1989, 434-37.)

Other aspects of the use of postage stamps for intelligence and propaganda purposes during the war include the Allied production of French stamps with minute identifying marks that were used by the French resistance to ensure security of its communications (see Herman Herst Jr., "The Story of WWII French Spy Forgeries," *Linn's Stamp News*, Feb. 18, 1991, 42); issues printed by the Germans for use in India once it had been occupied; German satirical stamps replacing crowns on British issues with small Stars of David and hammer-and-sickles; and commemoratives released in German-occupied nations publicizing puppet forces fighting on the Eastern Front. After the enclave of Campione was liberated from the Fascists, it eased its economic problems by philatelic means. Dulles recalls in *The Secret Surrender* (19): "With our help they arranged to issue a special set of stamps to commemorate the union of the enclave with the Kingdom of Italy. The stamps naturally became collectors' items throughout the world. Enough were sold to carry more mail than Campione would send for generations and enough money was realized to meet the budget deficit. Residents of Campione were gainfully employed writing letters to addresses in many nations, since collectors were anxious to have the stamps on postmarked envelopes." For additional information on the general subject, see L. N. Williams and Maurice Williams, *Forged Stamps of the Two World Wars: The Postal Forgeries and Propaganda Issues of the Belligerents, 1914–1918, 1939–1945* (London: Authors, 1954).

Doc. 3-148, Tel. 3793-94, June 12, 1944, Box 192.

Doc. 3-149, Tel. 3800-3806, June 12, 1944, Box 192. Source number identifications may be found in "OSS Code Number Identifications," pages 543–49 of this volume. On June 17, Gen. Donovan informed Dulles that he was in full agreement with para. 3 and that the contacts cited in para. 4 should be encouraged. "The feeling here is that when Germany collapses, but prior to Allied occupation, you must be all ready to move in at once, letting events determine the length of your stay. The connection described in the first paragraph . . . would appear to constitute a fine cover for this, while the initial work which you propose to have done ought to render this cover even better than it first appears to be. In all likelihood, the renascent anti-Nazi groups will look upon you as their first demi-official contact with America. . . . It is true that so far as our occupational plans are concerned, we are still in need of a definitive decision on military areas of occupation. However, such a mission as you suggest would, at the start, come outside the field of those plans, thereby furnishing our SI occupational groups and the civil administrations people the most useful kind of intelligence, [i.e.] . . . the rapid location of important papers. . . . Go ahead in accordance with the scheme outlined in the fifth paragraph. . . . In the meantime, as the situation develops and more detailed plans can be made, we shall see that you are kept posted. It is quite possible that your contemplated mission might be greatly assisted by the services of some of the individuals whom you mention in your cable (Tel. 1735-37 to Bern, June 17, 1944, Box 165).

Doc. 3-150, Tel. 3818-22, June 14, 1944, Box 192.

Doc. 3-151, Tel. 724-25, June 15, 1944, Box 157. On May 24, Prime Minister Churchill told the House of Commons that the United States and Great Britain had not recognized the French Committee because they were not certain that it truly represented the French nation. Allied bombing of occupied France prior to D-Day exacted a terrible toll on civilians. For example, more than 700 were killed in the attack on Lyon of May 26, and more than 1,000 at Saint-Lô on the eve of the Allied landings.

Doc. 3-152, Tel. 3825-29, June 15, 1944, Box 192.

Doc. 3-153, Tel. 734-35, June 16, 1944, Box 157.

Doc. 3-154, Tel. 736-37, June 16, 1944, Box 157.

Doc. 3-155, Tel. 738-44, June 17, 1944, Box 157.

Doc. 3-156, Tel. 3854-55, June 19, 1944, Box 192.

Doc. 3-157, Tel. 3866-68, June 20, 1944, Box 192.

Doc. 3-158, Tel. 3878-79, June 21, 1944, Box 192. In Tel. 689-90 to Bern, May 26 (Box 234), OSS in London informed Bern that the German order of battle information contained in Bern's Tel. 647-58, May 22, was inaccurate in the extreme (Box 342).

Doc. 3-159, Tel. 602-3, June 25, 1944, Box 276. Alexandre Parodi was an official of the prewar French government who had become one of de Gaulle's top assistants charged with bringing various resistance factions to heel. After the war, he became a prominent career diplomat.

Doc. 3-160, Tel. 3908-15, June 26, 1944, Box 192.

Doc. 3-161, Tel. 770-72, June 27, 1944, Box 157.

Doc. 3-162, Tel. 3918-20, June 28, 1944, Box 192.

Chapter 4: The Failed July 20 Plot Against Hitler; the Liberation of Western Europe, July–December 1944

Doc. 4-1, Tel. 775-77, July 1, 1944, Box 157.

Doc. 4-2, Tel. 3966-68, July 4, 1944, CIA/FOIA.

Doc. 4-3, Tel. 3988-90, July 5, 1944, CIA/FOIA.

Doc. 4-4, Tel. 3991-97, July 6, 1944, CIA/FOIA.

Doc. 4-5, Tel. 4001-3, July 6, 1944, Box 191.

Doc. 4-6, Trans. no. 171, July 6, 1944, Box 273. In Tel. 4373, July 10, Dulles transmitted a detailed account of the Oradour massacre of June 10. He reported that a village of 85 houses had been destroyed and 800–1,000 men, women, and children killed by an SS detachment belonging to the *Das Reich* Division (Box 191).

Doc. 4-7, Tel. 4019-25, July 7, 1944, CIA/FOIA.

Doc. 4-8, Tel. 4029-32, July 7, 1944, CIA/FOIA. Sukru Saracoglu was Prime Minister of Turkey; Laurence A. Steinhardt was U.S. Ambassador in Turkey; Salim Sarper was Turkish Press Director (later Ambassador to the Soviet Union).

Doc. 4-9, Tel. 4033-36, July 8, 1944, Box 276. Dr. Bernard Ménétrel was Marshal Pétain's personal physician. Donovan transmitted a copy of this cable, and seven other Bern messages, to President Roosevelt on July 10 (FDR Library, PSF, Box 168).

Doc. 4-10, Tel. 4045-46, July 10, 1944, Box 191.

Doc. 4-11, Trans. no. 173, July 10, 1944, Box 273.

Doc. 4-12, Tel. 4067-68, July 11, 1944, Box 191. Donovan's reply of July 23 is printed in the endnote to Doc. 4-37, July 26.

Doc. 4-13, Tel. 804-7, July 12, 1944, Box 157. In Tel. 1769, June 29, Headquarters requested confirmation from Dulles on a report published by the writer Paul Winkler in Stockholm that 2,300 separatists had been arrested in Hannover (Box 276).

Doc. 4-14, Tel. 4085, July 12, 1944, Box 228. Tucky is Gen. Ludwig Beck, Chief of Staff of the German armed forces from 1935 to 1938. Unable to rally senior officers against Hitler's policies which he saw leading toward a disastrous war, Beck had resigned and thereafter participated in various plots against the regime. In Tel. 1782-83, July 4, Headquarters informed Dulles that Adam von Trott zu Solz had visited Stockholm in March and June and had sought to determine Soviet intentions toward Germany through an intermediary named Kollantay. Trott's group reportedly resembled Breakers and was projecting a coup. Washington asked if any of Dulles's associates were connected to this enterprise (Box 276). Wolf Heinrich Graf von Helldorf, Berlin police chief since 1935, was a World War I and Freikorps veteran. General Friedrich Fromm was commander of the Reserve Army, a position that made him an invaluable participant in any coup attempt.

Doc. 4-15, Tel. 4110-14, July 13, 1944, Box 228. Risler is Gen. Fromm. Eta is Gen. Friedrich Olbricht, Deputy Commander of the Reserve Army. Zeta is Gen. Kurt Zeitzler, Army Chief of Staff since 1942, who was disillusioned by Hitler's refusal to extricate the 6th Army from Stalingrad.

On July 24, Headquarters informed OSS in London that tel. 4110 and certain earlier Breakers cables had been disseminated to the Joint Chiefs of Staff, the Joint Intelligence Survey, the Secretary of State, Fletcher Warren (assistant to Assistant Secretary of State Berle who managed liaison with OSS), and the White House Map Room. A summary report was being disseminated to the same customers plus President Roosevelt and General Marshall (Tel. 57744, Entry 138, Box 2). The report, dated July 18, reprinted from OSS Research and Analysis Summaries in RG 226, appears in Hoffmann, *The History of the German Resistance,* 749.

Doc. 4-16, Trans. no. 175, July 13, 1944, Box 273. Donovan memorandum to Roosevelt, July 15, 1944, FDR Library, PSF, Box 168.

Doc. 4-17, Tel. 818-21, July 15, 1944, Box 157. Transmitted by Donovan to Roosevelt, July 21, 1944, FDR Library, PSF, Box 168. Edouard Herriot, leader of the Radical Party, had resisted the Vichy regime and was imprisoned by the Germans from 1942 to 1945. Louis Marin was a conservative politician. In his radiotelephone transmission of July 14, Dulles relayed reports on the internal politics of the Laval regime and on Herriot's attitude toward de Gaulle, which was said to be conditional and dependent upon the general's willingness to restore true democracy (No. 176, Box 273).

Doc. 4-18, Tel. 4111-12, July 15, 1944, Box 228. Reference is to Clement Attlee, leader of the Labour Party and Deputy Prime Minister in Britain's wartime coalition government.

Doc. 4-19, Tel. 4148, July 15, 1944, Box 191.

Doc. 4-20, Tel. 4154, July 15, 1944, Box 191.

Doc. 4-21, Tel. 774-76, July 18, 1944, Box 166. In Tel. 767-69 to Algiers, July 17, Dulles stated that "there is no understanding between Zulu and myself other than that SI and SO data sent here by Motta is shared by us. Zulu SOE has tried to secure all of Motta's SO work for themselves. I unqualifiedly declined to agree to this. Motta backed me without reserve in this position. As a matter of fact, I feel that Attom [CNL leader Ferrucio Parri] prefers to work with us provided it is possible for us to extend aid to him. However, lacking any indications regarding Motta's financing from this end, the real state of affairs at this time is that Zulu here is extending them greater financial backing than we are" (Box 166).

Doc. 4-22, Trans. no. 178, July 18, 1944, Box 273.

Doc. 4-23, Tel. 847-48, July 21, 1944, Box 157. Among the more important accounts of the July 20 attempt on Hitler's life are those found in Hoffmann, *History of the German Resistance*; Dulles, *The German Resistance*; Gisevius, *To the Bitter End*; Schlabrendorff, *They Almost Killed Hitler*; Wheeler-Bennett, *The Nemesis of Power*; and William L. Shirer, *The Rise and Fall of the Third Reich* (New York: Simon & Schuster, 1960).

On July 28, Dulles identified "Leo Kreuz" as a banker from Frankfurt who was aquainted with Nerdrum, a press attaché at the Norwegian legation. Nerdrum indicated that Kreuz had been working against the Nazis since before 1933 and had sent him reports out of Germany from time to time. The true identity of Kreuz was not known to his correspondent (Tel. 886-88 to London, Box 157). Although the Kreuz message may have been a Nazi ruse rather than a genuine communication from resistance elements, the requested broadcast was made from London on July 23 (Tel. 62567 from London to Bern, July 23, 1944, Box 157).

Doc. 4-24, Trans. no. 180, July 21, 1944, Box 273. Copy sent by Donovan to Roosevelt, July 22, 1944, FDR Library, PSF, Box 168. Ray S. Cline was a young OSS officer serving under Gen. John Magruder, Deputy Director for Intelligence, in the Washington headquarters. Cline helped to select the most valuable incoming cables for transmittal to Magruder and his top assistants. He recalls that Dulles's success in providing warning of the coup attempt of July 20 established him as a credible and valued source (Interview with Ray S. Cline, Jan. 13, 1989). Thereafter, his telegrams and evening phone reports were frequently transmitted to the White House.

Doc. 4-25, Tel. 4199-4202, July 22, 1944, Box 228. Reference telegram 4110-14, July 13, printed here as Doc. 4-15. Theta is Gen. Heusinger. Claus Schenk Graf von Stauffenberg, Chief of Staff to the Commander of the Reserve Army, planted the bomb under the table at Hitler's staff meeting in Rastenburg, East Prussia. A German nationalist and devout Catholic, Stauffenberg became disillusioned by Nazi atrocities and the disastrous war policies. He became active in the resistance in 1943 and, unlike most of the other conspirators, espoused socialist politics.

Tel. 2307-11, Mar. 5, 1944, is printed here as Doc. 3-39. Lester is Carl Goerdeler. Tel. 4085, July 12, is printed as Doc. 4-14. C is Culber (i.e. Hans Bernd Gisevius). Luber also stands for Gisevius. 670 is Waetjen. Trans. no. 175, July 13, is printed here as Doc. 4-16.

Doc. 4-26, Tel. 4204, July 22, 1944, Box 276.

Doc. 4-27, Trans. 181, July 22, 1944, Box 273. Extract sent by Donovan to Roosevelt, July 24, 1944, FDR Library, PSF, Box 168. Gen. Beck attempted suicide and was then shot after the failure of the coup on July 20. Gen. Zeitzler, Army Chief of Staff, stepped down for reasons of health after the coup, and was dismissed from the army by Hitler in January 1945. He survived the war. Gen. Wilhelm Keitel, Chief of Staff of the Armed Forces, remained loyal to Hitler and was executed as a war criminal in 1946. General Erich von Manstein, one of Germany's most competent commanders, was dismissed in Mar. 1944 for questioning Hitler's inflexible strategy on the Eastern Front. He served time as a war criminal after the war. Gen. Walter von Seydlitz, captured at Stalingrad, headed a pro-Soviet group of German officers. The ungrateful Russians held him prisoner for ten years after the war. The Moscow Declaration issued by the Allied Foreign Ministers in October 1943 stipulated that Austria would be independent after the war, but its exact status would be determined in part by its contribution to the defeat of Germany.

On July 22, OSS Headquarters sent an analysis of the attempted coup d'état, based on the reports received from Dulles over the previous several months, to the White House Map Room, the State Department, the JCS and Army Chief of Staff Marshall. The report, reprinted from R & A Summaries in Rg 226, appears in Hoffmann, *History of the German Resistance*, 750–53. A copy sent by Donovan to the President is in FDR Library, PSF, Box 168.

Doc. 4-28, Tel. 851-55, July 23, 1944, Box 228. The persons cited by code name or number in this report are identified in "OSS Code Number Identifications," pages 543–49 of this volume. Tel. 1861 to Bern, July 22, read as follows: "We still want to know who Luber is. The answer is affirmative: you are to send information copies describing Zulu's circumstances to London for 105" (Box 193). Tel. 4085, July 12, is printed here as Doc. 4-14.

Doc. 4-29, Tel. 859, July 24, 1944, Box 157.

Doc. 4-30, Tel. 860-61, July 24, 1944, Box 228. Neither OSS in London, nor MI-6 headquarters ("Broadway") were well informed on Breakers matters. OSS in London cabled Dulles as follows on July 23: "We wish to extend our congratulations on the fine scoop you scored with your Breakers information. We secured the data contained in your #4110 [Doc. 4-15] and your related wires to Washington only following our requests for them. The resulting loss of time caused us difficulty at this end. In the future, please be sure to send us information copies of every dissemination of intelligence" (Tel. 823, Entry 138, Box 2). Similarly, British intelligence did not share everything it knew about German anti-Hitler elements with the Americans. In Tel. 63417 from London to Bern, July 26, OSS London transmitted fragmentary information on the roles of Gisevius and Waetjen in the attempt on Hitler's life, and that MI-6 in Switzerland had not received data that it had expected from Gaevernitz (Box 228). In Tel. 63664 to Bern, July 27, OSS London repeated warnings received from MI-6 in 1943 about the unreliability of Gisevius (Box 228). On July 28, Dulles informed OSS London that certain British information on the subject was inaccurate, as was their understanding on arrangements for exchange of data (Tel. 884-85 to London, Box 228). On Aug. 20, OSS London informed Dulles that secret Breakers messages given to Assistant Secretary of State Berle in Washington had been made available by him to Lord Halifax, the British Ambassador (Tel. 69094, Box 228).

Hjalmar Schacht, leading German financial planner between the wars and an acquaintance of Dulles, fell from favor in 1939 and was incarcerated after the attempt on Hitler's life for suspected sympathy with the resistance. He served several years in prison after the war for helping to organize Germany for aggression. Constantin Freiherr von Neurath, German Foreign Minister from 1932 to 1938, fell from favor and held ceremonial positions until the end of the war. He spent eight years in Spandau for helping to plot German aggression as foreign minister.

Doc. 4-31, Tel. 4214-19, July 24, 1944, Box 191.

Doc. 4-32, Trans. no. 182, July 24, 1944, Box 273. On July 25, Whitney Shepardson, head of the OSS SI Branch, sent the following message to Dulles: "Your results are sensational. We are giving your reports the very finest dissemination feasible here, including Secretary Hull, the President, General Marshall and Admiral Leahy." (Tel. 1870, Box 193).

Shepardson cabled Dulles on July 26 concerning possible allegations that he had exceeded his authority in dealing with the German resistance and had not kept the British informed. "All your Breakers communications have been turned over to State Department, complete, as soon as received. Your jobs have all involved merely the passive acceptance of intelligence regarding the desire of Breakers to find some way out. You have done no bargaining of any kind. You are aware of all these facts and there is no blemish on the record. It is possible that the little Zulus may raise little stinkos but I do not feel that this will occur" (Tel. 1875, Entry 138, Box 2).

Doc. 4-33, Tel. 4222-24, July 25, 1944, Box 228. In Tel. 1857, OSS Headquarters requested more particulars on individuals involved in the plot (Box 276) Tel. 4199-4202, July 22, is printed as Doc. 4-25.

Doc. 4-34, Tel. 4229-32, July 25, 1944, Box 191. Marcel Déat, Jean Bichelonne, and Bonnard were members of the Vichy government. Léon Blum headed the Popular Front government, 1936–38, and survived Nazi imprisonment. Paul Reynaud served as Premier in the months before the fall of France and was a prominent political leader after the war. Georges Mandel, Minister of the Interior in 1940, was murdered by Vichy militia as reported in this cable.

Doc. 4-35, Tel. 866-67, July 26, 1944, Box 228. On July 26, OSS London informed Headquarters that "as yet [Ambassador John] Winant has not wired the State Department about the Russian aspect of Breakers. He will not do so, in the light of 110's views. Therefore, we will leave in Washington's hands, any decision about the advisability of making a report to the Russians" (Tel. 63407, Box 228) Tel. 851-55 to London, July 23, is printed here as Doc. 4-28. On July 28, Donovan stated the following in a telegram to David Bruce, OSS chief in London: "We will by no means let the Russians see the Breakers correspondence. It can be easily seen from cable #2714-6 from Bern of April 6, 1944 [Doc. 3-82], that Bern did not feel that there was any possibility of our helping Breakers, but instead said most emphatically that we would inform the Russians of any action we might take.

"This is precisely the answer I gave through Turkish channels when, about a year ago, a group much like the Breakers, or possibly the Breakers themselves, said they were ready to help us in the West as a means of keeping Russia out. Simultaneously, it was reported that a similar group was inclined towards the Soviet. I took up this proposition with the British, and we concluded that it would be wiser not to inform the Soviet, (1) because it might arouse their suspicions of us rather than impress them with our desire to be helpful, and (2) because there was some evidence that the eastern-oriented group had already approached them with their proposals.

"I think events have already demonstrated the advisability of avoiding involvement in this matter, and I consider that, if the Germans battle it out inside Germany without help from us, it will be of more benefit to humanity" (Tel. 58807 to London, Entry 138, Box 2). Bruce reported to Donovan on July 31 that Winant had agreed not to send information on "the Russian angle" to the State Department (Tel. 64314 from London to Washington, Entry 138, Box 2). This exchange should be viewed with the knowledge that Kim Philby, the Soviet spy in MI-6, had access to Breakers as well as Wood material (Lawler interview).

Doc. 4-36, Tel. 4233-36, July 26, 1944, Box 191.

Doc. 4-37, Tel. 4247, July 26, 1944, Box 191. Tel. 1862, July 23, reads as follows: "109 to 110. With reference to your #4067-68 [see Doc. 4-12, July 11]. This will serve as your authority to transfer 50,000,000 Lira to Attom of CNL as you asked in the above cable. I am desirous of having you increase your resources in Italy regardless of action that may be taken on this situation in other regions. I will stand back of your judgment in the plan you adopt in equalling or over-bidding other offers. In a separate message, I have given you instructions on attendant action which you can take care of from your station" (Box 193).

Doc. 4-38, Tel. 4270-72, July 28, 1944, Box 191. Gen. Ernst von Busch, a commander on the Eastern Front, survived the war, but died in Allied captivity in 1945.

Doc. 4-39, Tel. 844-50, July 29, 1944, Box 276. While the principal OSS base in Italy was located at Allied Headquarters in Caserta, its main strategic infiltration operation was established at Brindisi. Poorly defined areas of responsibility resulted in tension between various OSS units and resentment of Dulles's attempt to orchestrate support of the Italian resistance from Bern. Max Corvo provides a detailed participant account in *The OSS in Italy, 1942-1945* (New York: Praeger, 1990).

Dulles reported on July 31 that he had now learned it was the CLN's understanding that the British had sole jurisdiction in the Val d'Aosta region. He said that he had concluded no such arrangement with British intelligence in Switzerland and continued to assume that the region remained open for U.S. operations (Tel. 851-53 to Algiers, Box 276). OSS in Algiers replied as follows on Aug. 8: "You are right. Must crush any idea that Zulu should have complete control over Val d'Aosta. Our own activities there are essential" (Tel. 558, Box 166).

Doc. 4-40, Tel. 892-93, July 30, 1944, Box 157. Niveau was a liaison officer with the resistance in Savoie and Haute Savoie. On July 13, Dulles reported that OSS Bern representatives had met with Niveau in Geneva and intended to remain in contact (Tel. 747 from Bern to Algiers, Box 166).

Doc. 4-41, Tel. 4300-4303, July 30, 1944, Box 191. Tel. 4286-93, July 30, is filed in Box 191.

Doc. 4-42, Tel. 4305-7, Aug. 1, 1944, Box 228. In his evening radiotelephone transmission of July 29, Dulles contended that the Soviet Union and the German communists had not been involved in the plot against Hitler and hence those Germans who wanted an "eastern solution were being spared the worst of the post-coup attempt crack-down. The Russian-sponsored Seydlitz committee and left-wing elements within Germany who wanted a revolution from below were now the greatest threat to the regime" (No. 186, Box 273). Tel. 4270-72, July 28, is printed here as Doc. 4-38. "Bearcat" was Count Helldorf, Berlin Police Chief and one of the plotters. He was arrested and hanged in August. "Luber" was Gisevius.

Hardly in step with Dulles, Morale Operations in Washington cabled on July 26 that he should attempt to give to the SS the names of all German officers and Nazis known to him, indicating that they had been involved in the putsch. This would confuse the SS and effect the liquidation of the persons implicated (Tel. 1879 to Bern, Box 276).

Doc. 4-43, Tel. 4314-18, Aug. 2, 1944, Box 231. On Aug. 5, Donovan cabled authorization for continued monthly payments of 50,000,000 lire to the resistance until liberation (Tel. 1924-26, Box 193). Dulles responded as follows on Aug. 10: "Thanks for your approval on continuing our monthly contributions. CNL's financial adviser in Milan has just departed for northern Italy. I shall notify you at once of any lire repayment guarantees which are made within the limits of your approval, so that you may furnish cover in accordance with your cabled suggestions. I shall try to avoid the necessity of a guarantee by Lloyd's" (Tel. 4422, Box 191).

Doc. 4-44, Tel. 4348-49, Aug. 4, 1944, Box 191. Turkey broke relations with Germany on Aug. 2, 1944.

Doc. 4-45, Tel. 4332-44, Aug. 5, 1944, Box 231. Number 850 was the physician of former French Premier Daladier. In Tel. 3696, June 5, "Alpha" is identified as Alexandre Parodi, an important assistant to General de Gaulle (Box 192).

Doc. 4-46, Tel. 4361, Aug. 5, 1944, Box 231. The fate of Arthur Nebe, an SS general and head of the criminal police, is uncertain. Reportedly, he was arrested by the Nazis and executed in Mar. 1945. By other accounts, he survived the war and went into hiding abroad.

Doc. 4-47, Tel. 896-99, Aug. 7, 1944, Box 276. Howard Chapin and Robert Joyce were OSS officers involved in agent penetration of central Europe and the Balkans.

Doc. 4-48, Tel. 4382-83, Aug. 7, 1944, Box 277. In Tel. 1915, Aug. 3, Donovan notified Dulles that War Department permission was not required to buy the items that they had been discussing (Box 193).

Doc. 4-49, Tel. 935-37, Aug. 8, 1944, Box 228. In Tel. 65787-88 to Bern, OSS in London stated that PWD (psychological warfare) had misinterpreted Dulles's Flash of July 22 (Doc. 4-27) and hence had made recommendations to BBC that included mentioning Count Helldorf (Box 228). Tel. 4361, Aug. 5, is printed here as Doc. 4-46.

Dulles reported further on the crackdown in Germany on Aug. 10, stating that source 620 had felt that the killing of Werner von Haeften and Peter Yorck von Wartenburg was important, since both of these young Breakers members would have been useful for future work. It was feared that the arrest of these two would lead the Gestapo to other resistance members in labor, the church movement, and the government (Tel. 4433-35, Box 228).

Doc. 4-50, Tel. 4394-95, Aug. 9, 1944, Box 231. Plotters in Paris under the Military Governor of France, Gen. Karl Heinrich von Stuelpnagel, moved against the Gestapo on July 20, but were crushed when it was learned Hitler had survived the bomb attack. Stuelpnagel was hanged in Berlin in August.

Doc. 4-51, Tel. 4396-4400, Aug. 9, 1944, Box 231. In Tel. 1899-1905, Aug. 2, Donovan discussed plans for SO guerrilla operations in Germany and Austria, acknowledging that there would be little support from the local population. He asked Dulles's opinion on prospects and stated that Dulles would have heavy responsibility for direction of such operation. He concluded as follows: "Please give this every consideration on a table stake plane and let me know the conclusions you reach. I am most grateful for the vast assistance you are rendering me" (Box 277). On Aug. 12, the OSS deputy director cabled, "Your provocative and valuable #4396-4400 and subsequent communications have been relayed to 109 who has departed for the Mediterranean. It is our desire to make arrangements to assist you at the earliest possible date. The heads of the various branches are in conference to evolve a feasible schedule. . . . We have started . . . to organize for SO work against Central Europe. This will emanate from bases both in Italy and Western Europe. Your ideas concerning regions of penetration are consistent with our own" (Tel. 1942-45, Box 277).

Doc. 4-52, Tel. 4401-6, Aug. 9, 1944, Box 231. Regarding OSS attempts to penetrate Germany, see Kermit Roosevelt, *War Report of the OSS,* vol. 2, *The Overseas Target;* Joseph E. Persico, *Piercing the Reich* (New York: Viking, 1979); and William Casey, *The Secret War Against Hitler* (Washington, D.C.: Regnery Gateway, 1988).

Doc. 4-53, Tel. 4111-15, Aug. 9, 1944, Box 231.

Doc. 4-54, Tel. 909-10, Aug. 10, 1944, Entry 139, Box 27.

Doc. 4-55, Tel. 943-45, Aug. 10, 1944, Box 276.

Doc. 4-56, Tel. 950-51, Aug. 10, 1944, Box 277.

Doc. 4-57, Tel. 912, Aug. 11, 1944, Box 276. Col. Edward J. Glavin was commander of OSS's 2677th Regiment in Italy and ranking OSS officer in the Mediterranean Theater. Gen. H. H. Arnold was commander of the US Army Air Force.

Doc. 4-58, Tel. 4443-46, Aug. 11, 1944, Box 231. Donovan's Tel. 69084 from London is in Box 228. Hans Oster, former deputy to Adm. Canaris, head of the Abwehr, was actually not killed by the Nazis until April 1945. Stauffenberg's family survived the war.

On Aug. 20, Donovan in London informed Headquarters that "it is important that the information contained in the second paragraph of Bern cable 4443-46 be sent to Marshall, and the President as coming from me abroad." A notation on the file copy indicates that according to Gen. Magruder, dissemination had already been made as requested (Tel. 69084 from London, Entry 99, Box 14).

Doc. 4-59, Tel. 4438-39, Aug. 12, 1944, Box 191. Headquarters stated on Aug. 17, "We have no desire to become a part of 495's plan. . . . This matter should be handled by him with his own people" (Tel. 1958, Box 231) Undeterred, Dulles added the following on Aug. 22: "495 is one of the most promising factors for Rumania's future, has been of considerable assistance to me and we ought to treat him courteously at least. It is probably advisable now, because of recent military events, to have him wait until the frontier is opened before departing. As soon as this takes place, however, I urgently recommend that he be permitted to proceed to some place where he will still be able to keep in touch with the British, Russians and ourselves" (Tel. 4619-20, Box 191).

On Aug. 20, the Soviets launched a major offensive in Rumania. Guerrillas overthrew the Antonescu government on the twenty-third. On the twenty-fourth, OSS Headquarters cabled, "The complete reversal of Rumania makes it necessary for us to know in detail how we can assist you in getting 495 to where his services will be of greatest benefit to the cause of the United Nations" (Tel. 1980, Box 193).

Doc. 4-60, Tel. 4471-73, Aug. 12, 1944, Box 191. Tel. 1939 to Bern, Aug. 10, read as follows: "The JCS have asked the State Department for data concerning the Nazis' schemes for going underground. Any and all pertinent material on this ought to be dispatched to us without delay" (Box 193). In Dulles's Radiotelephone Transmission no. 192, Aug. 10, he stated that some of his sources felt that it was unlikely that a German maquis would be the last line of resistance for the SS and Nazi leaders. However, he added, "Others differ on this point, and believe that preparations are now being made by the SS for the last stand in a German reduit, based on the Bavarian, Upper Austrian, and Vorarlberg Alps, and that the increasing concentration of government offices in the Salzburg area is, in part, a preparation for this. Those who sponsor this theory feel that this would be in line with Hitler's mad mysticism and Wagnerian complex, and that the chief criminals of the SS would have nothing to lose and a few months of life to gain by such a maneuver. If it came to such a solution, I would not expect to see the luxury-loving members of the Party, such as Goering, follow, and the final Party split would then come. As yet, however, there is no real evidence for this subject, and the idea of a German maquis is largely in the realm of speculation" (Box 273). Dulles and Allied intelligence continued to collect evidence on the possible emergence of a Nazi Alpine redoubt for the remainder of the war. This subject is treated by Rodney G. Minott in *The Fortress That Never Was: The Myth of Hitler's Bavarian Stronghold* (New York: Holt, Rinehart & Winston, 1964), and in Persico, *Piercing the Reich.*

Doc. 4-61, Tel. 966-68, Aug. 15, 1944, Box 228. Tel. 867-70 from London to Bern, was based on a report received from SIS. Paragraph 6 concerned alleged contact between the Seydlitz committee in Moscow and the German resistance (Box 228).

Doc. 4-62, Tel. 4478-79, Aug. 15, 1944, Box 191. Reference is to Fiorello La Guardia, Mayor of New York from 1933 to 1945.

Doc. 4-63, Tel. 4489-92, Aug. 15, 1944, Box 191. The remainder of the list of alleged spies was transmitted in Tel. 4647-55, Aug. 23 (Box 191).

Doc. 4-64, Tel. 4498-4500, Aug. 16, 1944, Box 231. Radiotelephone Transmission No. 194, August 14, is in Box 273. "Sherman" is Irving Sherman of the OSS New York office. On Sept. 9, F. L. Mayer cabled Bern from headquarters that the Morale Operations Branch agreed that no person who might later prove to be of value to the Allies should be harmed, but "that it would be advantageous to do away with a few, very fervent Nazi members." MO provided a list of twelve names (Tel. 2030-32, Box 193). At the time of receipt of this bizarre message, Dulles had left Bern for the United States. What follow-up occurred, if any, has not been determined.

Doc. 4-65, Tel. 4511-14, Aug. 17, 1944, Box 277. Tel. 1932-33, Aug. 8, requested additional information on how money provided by U.S. labor would be used (Box 193).

Doc. 4-66, Tel. 4532-34, Aug. 18, 1944, Box 231. Tel. 1955, Aug. 15, to Bern from Shepardson ("Jackpot"), read as follows: "Do you give any credence to the declaration made by 512 [Gisevius, reported in Doc. 4-58] in regard to the serious last minute break in regard to the East vs. West solution? How was it possible for such an enormous conspiracy to make so much progress without an unvarying and unified attitude in support of either solution, perhaps the Western to the uncompromising exclusion of the alternative?" (Entry 138, Box 2). Tel. 3423-31, May 13, 1944, is printed as Doc. 3-123.

Doc. 4-67, Tel. 4335-36, Aug. 19, 1944, Box 231.

Doc. 4-68, Tel. 4551-54, Aug. 18, 1944, Box 231.

Doc. 4-69, Tel. 4537-42, Aug. 19, 1944, Box 231.

Doc. 4-70, Tel. 4568-72, Aug. 19, 1944, Box 231. Acting OSS Director Cheston included the text of this message in a memorandum to the President of Aug. 25 (FDR Library, PSF, Box 168). Although Dulles was not a primary player in Yugoslav matters, he had many Yugoslav sources of various ethnic and political persuasions, as revealed by documents located in Entry 90, Box 8; Entry 125, Boxes 4 and 12; Entry 190, Boxes 24 and 26; and State Department Bern Post Files, Box 17. The author also received miscellaneous Bern intelligence reports on Yugoslavia under FOIA in 1992. (Regarding Dulles and Yugoslavia, see also the endnote to Doc. 2-75.)

On Sept. 19, 1944, General Donovan sent the following message to Col. Glavin, head of OSS Mediterranean and Balkan operations at Caserta, and asked him to transmit it to Gen. Ira Eaker, Commander of Allied Air Forces in the area: "As I told you and General [Jacob] Devers [Deputy Allied Commander in the Mediterranean] on the flight from France I have issued orders for the withdrawal from Mihailovich area, of our intelligence units including air rescue parties. This was done at the direction of the President on objection by the British. . . . For your information, dispatches to Department of State from Caserta show that Brigadier [Fitzroy] Maclean of British Mission was in Mihailovich territory sending out reports. . . . I regret that in view of British action we cannot continue to help you in evacuating your pilots from the Mihailovich area" (Entry 90, Box 8). Message #C 094 from Donovan to Glavin, Sept. 19, transmitted the text of a detailed memorandum filed by OSS with the JCS on Sept. 11 that indicated displeasure with the policy decision (Entry 90, Box 8). Regarding U.S. intelligence and the decision to support Tito, see also Ford, *OSS and the Yugoslav Resistance, 1943–1945.*

Doc. 4-71, Trans. no. 198, Aug. 19, 1944, Box 273.

Doc. 4-72, Tel. 4573-79, Aug. 20, 1944, Box 231.

Doc. 4-73, Tel. 4602-5, Aug. 22, 1944, Box 231. Reference is to Dr. Markus Timmler, a top official in Germany's radio propaganda operation.

Doc. 4-74, Tel. 4608-9, Aug. 22, 1944, Box 191.

Doc. 4-75, Tel. 4610-11, Aug. 22, 1944, Entry 139, Box 26.

Doc. 4-76, Tel. 4616-18, Aug. 22, 1944, Entry 139, Box 26. Tel. 4612-13, Aug. 22, concerned details of payments to the Italian resistance (Box 231). On Aug. 27, Dulles cabled Donovan to acknowledge that he saw nothing wrong with the Milan Committee of National Liberation (Motta) transmitting intelligence through the British to the Allies in the south. However, he added, "It is my candid opinion that the arrangements for Italian partisan activity between Zulu and our organization have been rather haphazard. I think that Motta does not want Zulu to have any exclusive rights and Motta agents here have always faithfully carried out their agreements with us" (Box 276). On Aug. 25, 1944, Donovan cabled the following to Dulles from London with reference to Tel. 4616-18: "This matter has been called to General [Colin] Gubbins [of SOE] attention by me. I requested him to take steps on it at once and he has already initiated action. In addition, I have wired Glavin to contact the Italians to inform them that we will not put up with any more of this" (Tel. 69987, Box 157). OSS in Caserta sent the following to Dulles on Aug. 30: "Through our direct channel, we have forwarded the following message to Motta today: At approximately the end of last month, tonnages and airplanes for American and English parachutages were placed on an equal footing. Therefore, the American and British results must of necessity be the same. The Commanding Officer of this theater OSS requires that in consideration of the above plan, and our financing of Motta, the Americans have the same representation as the English" (Tel. 628 from Caserta to Bern via Algiers, Box 276).

Doc. 4-77, Tel. 1018-20, Aug. 23, 1944, Entry 139, Box 27. In Tel. 894 from London to Bern, Donovan informed Dulles that recruiting was under way in Washington to augment the Bern staff. He proposed parachuting the new men into regions bordering Switzerland who would then cross the border (Box 157).

Doc. 4-78, Tel. 1047-48, Aug. 25, 1944, Box 276.

Doc. 4-79, Tel., 4673, Aug. 25, 1944, Box 231. Trott zu Solz was executed on Aug. 26. Goerdeler was tried and sentenced to death in Sept. and hanged in Feb. 1945.

Doc. 4-80, Tel. 1069-70, Aug. 27, 1944, Entry 139, Box 27. On August 31, Dulles reported that the Italian mission had successfully established contact with the resistance in southeastern France and had returned to Bern (Tel. 1092-93, Box 157).

Doc. 4-81, Tel. 4697-98, Aug. 31, 1944, Box 191.

Doc. 4-82, Tel. 1100-1101, Sept. 2, 1944, Box 157.

Doc. 4-83, Tel. 4699, Sept. 3, 1944, Box 191.

Doc. 4-84, Tel. 1135, Sept. 5, 1944, Box 157.

Doc. 4-85, Trans. no. 206, Sept. 5, 1944, Box 273. On Sept. 5, Headquarters informed Dulles that although the circumstances of the war had changed and the Swiss border was now open, the form of his evening transmission should remain unchanged, "since it is the most useful daily report which we get here" (Tel. 2006-7, Box 193). The suggestion regarding Austria originated with Johannes Schwartzenberg, number 837 (Tel. 4714 from Bern, Sept. 6, 1944, Box 191).

Dulles had discussed the German "total war" mentality in his previous flash, No. 205 of Sept. 1 (Box 273). OSS Acting Director Cheston transmitted an extract of that message to President Roosevelt in a memorandum of Sept. 4 (FDR Library, PSF, Box 167)

Doc. 4-86, Editorial Note, Sept. 6, 1944. An account of Dulles's trip from Bern to the United States via France and London appears in Richard Dunlop, *Donovan: America's Master Spy* (Chicago: Rand McNally, 1982), 453–54. It seems to have been based on interviews with Dulles and Hubert Will, an aide to Donovan who traveled with the group. Dunlop indicates that during the trip Donovan rejected the possibility of Dulles becoming head of European operations, but instead sent him back to Switzerland. From this point forward, messages from Dulles to his chief sometimes contained subtle and not too subtle indications of impatience or irritation. Correspondence in both the Dulles and Donovan Papers from before and after the war suggest that the two men were never close, although as Director of Central Intelligence Dulles did extend honors and kindnesses to the dying Donovan in 1959.

Dulles corresponded with Bern from Washington from Sept. 16 to Oct. 2, dealing with various policy matters and possibilities of augmenting the staff in Switzerland. He then visited New York and the New York OSS office. On his return trip, Dulles arrived in London on Oct. 9 and had lunch there on Oct. 11 with Eduard Benes, President of Czechoslovakia (Tels. 81054 and 81624 from London to Washington, Oct. 9, and 11, Entry 90, Box 5). He apparently was in Paris on Oct. 16 and reported that he had returned to Bern in Tel. 4848, Oct. 21, 1944 (Box 278).

Doc. 4-87, memorandum from Dulles to Donovan, Oct. 7, 1944, with attachments, Entry 180, Reel 81.

Doc. 4-88, Trans. no. 229, Oct. 23, 1944, Box 273.

Doc. 4-89, Tel. 1498-1504, Oct. 24, 1944, Box 157. Thomas H. W. Stonborough was OSS liaison officer with G-2 of the 6th Army Group. Col. Edward W. Gamble Jr. was commander of the OSS forward detachment in France. Gen. Jacob L. Devers was commander of the 6th Army Group, which had landed in the south of France and advanced northward to the Swiss border. Brig. Gen. Edwin L. Sibert was G-2 for the 12th Army. William H. Jackson was an OSS officer who served as an assistant to Gen. Omar N. Bradley. Henry Hyde was an OSS officer who had been active in France and would join Dulles in Switzerland late in the war.

On Oct. 25, Donovan cabled the following to David Bruce in Paris: "I agree with suggestions made by 110 in his #1498-1504 that you delegate him responsibility for general direction of bases at Pontarlier and Annemasse and that he have authority from you to resolve any conflicting requests from different agents and Theatres that arise at these bases. Personnel to staff a small base at Pontarlier should be available from surplus now in ETO" (Tel. 77767 to London, 107 to Paris, Box 194).

Documentation on liaison between OSS Bern and US Army intelligence is filed in Entry 190, Boxes 25, 26, and 32 (Bern Field Files) and in Entry 108, Box 1. Correspondence between Dulles and Gen. Sibert for this period can be obtained under CIA/FOIA. This material indicates that Dulles was keenly interested in the matter, and treats subjects including the establishment and mission of the OSS bases at Annemasse and Pontarlier.

With the opening of the French/Swiss border, OSS in Switzerland began transmitting many intelligence reports by pouch to both U.S. military forces and OSS offices in Paris, Washington, and London. One file location of such material is Entry 108, Boxes 2 and 7.

Doc. 4-90, Tel. 4867-69, Oct. 25, 1944, Box 191.

Doc. 4-91, Tel. 4872, Oct. 25, 1944, Box 191.

Doc. 4-92, Tel. 10, Oct. 29, 1944, Box 193. In a letter to Thomas Stonborough, OSS liaison at Sixth Army Group headquarters reported that the Germans had begun an operation to eliminate partisans in the Val d'Aosta (Entry 190, Box 25).

Doc. 4-93, Tel. 127, Oct. 29, 1944, Box 193.

Doc. 4-94, Tel. 19, Oct. 31, 1944, Box 277.

Doc. 4-95, Tel. 337, Nov. 3, 1944, Box 193. Pietro Longhi was a cover name for Dr. Alfredo Pizzoni, President of the Credito Italiano after the war. Eddy Sogno was an Italian officer who worked closely with British SOE.

Doc. 4-96, Tel. 387, Nov. 3, 1944, Box 193. Allied bombers mistakenly attacked targets in Swiss territory on a number of occasions. The most serious incident occurred at Schaffhausen on Apr. 1, 1944, when 100 Swiss citizens were killed or wounded. The United States quickly provided Switzerland with funds for the relief of the victims and paid a substantial indemnity after the war.

Doc. 4-97, Tel. 42, Nov. 4, 1944, Box 193.

Doc. 4-98, Tel. 44, Nov. 5, 1944, Box 193. Alexander C. Kirk was U.S. Political Adviser at Allied Force Headquarters in Caserta.

Doc. 4-99, Tel. 537, Nov. 7, 1944, Box 277. Gen. Walter von Brauchitsch had been Commander in Chief of the German Army from 1938 to 1941. He had been retired due to incompetence and illness. General Franz Halder had been Chief of the Army General Staff from 1938 until dismissed by Hitler in Sept. 1942. Karl Kaufmann served time in prison after the war for his role as Gauleiter of Hamburg.

Doc. 4-100, Tel. 667, Nov. 10, 1944, Box 193.

Doc. 4-101, Tel. 677, Nov. 10, 1944, Box 277. Consul Alexander Constantin von Neurath was the son of Baron Constantin von Neurath, German foreign minister from 1932 to 1938. Dulles describes this contact in *The Secret Surrender,* 44ff. OSS headquarters transmitted a survey of SS efforts to contact the Allies as reported by Bern to the White House on Dec. 13 (FDR Library, Map Room, Box 73). Lester Armour was assigned to the OSS SI Branch in London.

Doc. 4-102, Tel. 747, Nov. 15, 1944, Box 277. Flute was Dr. Paul Scherrer, a prominent Swiss physicist. Moe Berg was one of the most talented and fascinating figures in the history of espionage. A genius in linguistics and former professional baseball player, Berg performed a number of secret missions for OSS and predecessor intelligence organizations. Sent to Europe in 1944, one of his assignments was to gather information on the German atomic energy program. His exploits are described in Louis Kaufman et al., *Moe Berg: Athlete, Scholar, Spy* (Boston: Little, Brown, 1974); Nicholas Dawidoff, "Scholar, Lawyer, Catcher, Spy," *Sports Illustrated,* Mar. 23, 1992; and Powers, *Heisenberg's War.* The major U.S. intelligence operation targeting the German atomic program was Alsos mission, organized under the Manhattan Project. It was headed by Boris Pash, with Dr. Samuel Goudsmit serving as chief scientific adviser. See Pash, *The Alsos Mission* (New York: Award House, 1969), and Goudsmit, *Alsos* (New York: Henry Schurman, 1947). Martin Chittick and Fred Wardenberg were experts working for the Alsos mission.

Doc. 4-103, Tel. 757, Nov. 15, 1944, Box 277.

Doc. 4-104, Tel. 867, Nov. 19, 1944, Box 277. Donovan's message to Dulles was transmitted in Tel. 0777 to Bern, Nov. 16, 1944 (Entry 88, Box 589) On Christmas Day 1944, OSS Bern reported yet another bombing incident. On this occasion, the Swiss shot down an American plane (Tel. 2507 from Bern, Dec. 25, 1944, Box 193).

Doc. 4-105, Tel. 927, Nov. 20, 1944, Box 193. Reference is to Dr. Julius Schnurre.

Doc. 4-106, Tel. 969, Nov. 20, 1944, Entry 90, Box 7.

Doc. 4-107, Tel. 1037, Nov. 22, 1944, Box 162. Col. K. D. Mann headed OSS Morale Operations.

Doc. 4-108, Tel. 917, Nov. 23, 1944, Box 162. On Dec. 5, Dulles cabled William Maddox, head of the OSS SI branch in the Mediterranean theater at Caserta, that the Germans might know of the presence of the partisan delegation in South Italy. He urged that their return to the north via Switzerland be handled with all secrecy (Tel. 1357 from Bern to Caserta, Box 157).

Doc. 4-109, Trans. no. 242, Nov. 23, 1944, Box 273. Dulles provided another encouraging assessment by cable on Nov. 23: "While I desire avoid over-optimism, evidence accumulating here points to increasingly rapid disintegration in Germany. Transport conditions are becoming chaotic, dislocation of population due bombing and evacuation incident invasions in west and east has passed saturation point. Volkssturm is mere political gesture with no real military significance, mystery regarding Hitler leaves overall political leadership uncertain. Germany appears to be going through one of her sinking spells such as Reich had after fall of Mussolini and after collapse of southeastern front last April. With each sinking spell however, reserve power gets less and less and while Germany may still pull herself together for last fight on the Rhine, Danube and Vistula, possibility of collapse in next couple of months is not to be excluded" (Tel. 1097 from Dulles to Donovan, CIA/FOIA).

Doc. 4-110, Tel. 957, Nov. 24, 1944, Box 162. Dr. Eugenio Dugoni was a CLN representative. Arrangements were made for funding of the resistance in north Italy when partisan leaders visited Allied Headquarters in Caserta in November. Details are provided in Corvo, *The OSS in Italy, 1942–1945*. The continuing role of Bern in providing funds to the partisans is discussed in Tel. 1669 from Washington to Bern, Dec. 20 (Entry 90, Box 7) and Tel. 21459 from Caserta to Washington and Bern (1489), Dec. 24 (Entry 90, Box 8).

Doc. 4-111, Tel. 1217, Nov. 25, 1944, Box 193. Domei was the official Japanese news agency. On Dec. 11, Dulles sent more detailed information on the subject by pouch to Thomas Stonborough, OSS liaison with the 6th Army Group, Washington, and Paris (Entry 108, Box 2).

Doc. 4-112, Tel. 1407, Nov. 29, 1944, Box 193. Gerhard Van Arkel had been General Counsel of the National Labor Relations Board before the war. He served in the Labor Branch of OSS in New York, Washington, and North Africa before being transferred to Switzerland. George Pratt was head of the OSS Labor Desk in London. Hans Jahn was a former leader of the German railway workers union.

Doc. 4-113, Tel. 1467, Nov. 30, 1944, Box 193. Individuals mentioned include Lt. Col. Kenneth H. Baker, OSS Base Commander at Annecy and later Annemasse; Capt. Artturo F. Matthieu, who later commanded at Annemasse; Henry Hyde, a key OSS agent in France who joined Dulles in Bern late in the war; William L. Mellon, grandnephew of the financier, who took over for Max Shoop as Dulles's man in Geneva; and Gerhard Van Arkel (399).

Doc. 4-114, Tel. 1687, Nov. 30, 1944, Box 278. Allen Dulles's relationship with Noel Field, an individual now known to have served as a Soviet agent at the State Department and the League of Nations in the 1930s, is one of the great mysteries of his service in Bern. Dulles used Field as liaison to communist organizations and also to legitimate relief organizations including the Unitarians for whom Field worked, the Quakers, and the YMCA. Dulles is on record as testifying to Field's nonpolitical outlook. The CALPO group mentioned in this message, which Dulles urged be supported through Field, was a Soviet front organization. It is unclear whether Dulles was deceived by Field and his friends, or whether he was manipulating them. Field's adopted daughter, Erica Glaser, was known to be a communist in Switzerland during the war. In 1945, she accompanied OSS officer Gerhard Van Arkel to Germany as his secretary. Her memoirs, *Light at Midnight* (Garden City, N.Y.: Doubleday, 1967), deal largely with the horror of her imprisonment in the Soviet Union after the war and say little about the World War II period.

Field, who lived in eastern Europe after the war, was used by Stalin to purge national communist leaders of the region. They were accused of collaboration with American intelligence and Allen Dulles through Field. In *Operation Splinter Factor* (Philadelphia: Lippincott, 1974), British journalist Stewart Steven sets forth the dubious theory that Dulles orchestrated the East European purges by setting up Field. Flora Lewis presents a sounder account that admits that much about the matter may never be known in *Red Pawn: The Story of Noel Field*.

On Dec. 3, the OSS office in Paris informed Dulles that discussion at SHAEF and with Sam Reber, a U.S. Foreign Service Officer, indicated opposition to any official contact with, or support of, CALPO (Box 278).

Doc. 4-115, Tel. 1607, Dec. 2, 1944, Box 277. Those mentioned include Donovan (109); Lester Armour of SI in London; and David Bruce (105), head of the OSS London office. Lt. Philip Bastedo served as a key planner for the German Unit in 1944–45. Robert Murphy was the State Department's Political Representative for Germany and former Dulles Foreign Service associate.

While in New York in Sept., Dulles had addressed a memorandum to Donovan outlining the functions of an OSS unit in Germany after the war. He recommended use of Germans and German Swiss with whom OSS Bern had developed relationships; the seizure of records and documents; and the penetration of German government agencies, labor unions, and church movements. He recommended that this unit be staffed by his own people, presumably under his personal direction, for operations outside of the military occupation chain of command (Memorandum from Dulles to Donovan, Sept. 23, 1944, RG 226, Donovan Microfilm, Reel 81). It is understandable that Donovan, the military, and the State Department had difficulty accepting this concept. For example, on Nov. 3, 1944, State's Robert Murphy transmitted a cable from London insisting that the OSS German Unit be responsible to him, and be subject to State Department policy guidance (Draft tel. 9555, Box 349) Records on the planning for the German Unit are located in Entry 190, Boxes 22, 25, and 32.

Doc. 4-116, Tel. 1849, Dec. 2, 1944, Entry 90, Box 7. Number 106 is Col. Buxton, Deputy Director of OSS. Maj. Robert R. Furman was a member of the Alsos Mission. Flute is Professor Paul Scherrer. Carl Friedrich von Weizsacker was a prominent German physicist and son of Ernst von Weizsacker, a high-ranking diplomat.

Doc. 4-117, letter, Dec. 2, 1944, Entry 190, Box 32. The enclosure does not accompany the source text. Dulles describes this contact with the Reverend Dr. Don Giuseppe Bicchierai, the secretary of Idelfonso Schuster, Cardinal of Milan, in *The Secret Surrender,* 45ff. The CLNAI, which was planning a general uprising against the Germans, rejected the proposal out of hand. Gen. Donovan apprised President Roosevelt of the proposals from ecclesiastical authorities in Milan in memorandums dated Dec. 1, 2, 5, 7, and 8 (FDR Library, PSF, Box 170).

Doc. 4-118, Tel. 1757, Dec. 5, 1944, Box 277. Tel. 677, Nov. 10, is printed as Doc. 4-101. Gen. Wilhelm Harster was commander of German SS security police in Italy. General Karl Wolff was Himmler's personal representative and commander of all SS forces in Italy.

OSS treatment of peace feelers was influenced by a memorandum from President Roosevelt to Gen. Donovan on Dec. 18, 1944, which read as follows: "I do not believe that we should offer any guarantees of protection in the post-hostilities period to Germans who are working for your organization. I think that the carrying out of any such guarantees would be difficult and probably widely misunderstood both in this country and abroad. We may expect that the number of Germans who are anxious to save their skins and property by coming over to the side of the United Nations at the last moment will rapidly increase. Among them may be some who should properly be tried for war crimes or at least arrested for active participation in Nazi activities. Even with the necessary controls you mention I am not prepared to authorize the giving of guarantees" (OSS Records, Office Director Microfilm, Reel 81).

Doc. 4-119, Tel. 2027, Dec. 6, 1944, Box 193.

Doc. 4-120, letter, Dec. 6, 1944, Entry 190, Box 28. In his evening radiotelephone transmission of Dec. 12, Dulles expanded on the strains in relations between Germany and Japan. He observed that the German people blamed Japan for bringing the United States into the war and felt betrayed by Japan's failure to attack the Soviet Union. The Japanese, meanwhile, had great contempt for Hitler's conduct of the war (Trans. no. 252, Dec. 12, 1944, Box 273).

Doc. 4-121, Tel. 1937, Dec. 9, 1944, Box 278. On Dec. 13, Dulles reported that Schroeder, chief of personnel in the German Foreign Office, had recently visited Switzerland to round up dissident diplomats and bolster the shaky legation edifice (Tel. 2057, Box 193).

Doc. 4-122, Tel. 2067, Dec. 13, 1944, Entry 90, Box 7. On May 10, 1941, Rudolf Hess, Deputy Leader of the Nazi Party, had parachuted into England on an absurd, self-appointed peace mission.

Doc. 4-123, Tel. 2077, Dec. 13, 1944, Box 193.

Doc. 4-124, Tel. 2087, Dec. 13, 1944, Box 193.

Doc. 4-125, Tel. 2099, Dec. 13, 1944, Entry 90, Box 7. Among those mentioned, Arthur Seyss-Inquart was Reich Commissioner in the Netherlands. He was executed for war crimes after the war. Andrei A. Vlasov, a Soviet general captured by the Germans, led a Russian "liberation army" made up of prisoners of war and anti-Stalinist refugees against the Red Army. He was executed after the war. Gottlob Berger was administrative head of the SS and was convicted of war crimes in 1949.

On Dec. 16, Headquarters informed Dulles that the contents of this cable had been sent to London for British intelligence and to Paris for SHAEF (Tel. 1537, Entry 88, Box 589).

Doc. 4-126, Tel. 2129, Dec. 14, 1944, Entry 90, Box 7.

Doc. 4-127, Tel. 2207, Dec. 16, 1944, Box 193.

Doc. 4-128, Trans. no. 254, Dec. 21, 1944, Box 273. *A Time for Trumpets: The Untold Story of the Battle of the Bulge* (New York: William Morrow, 1985), by Charles B. MacDonald, and *Eisenhower: At War, 1943–1945* (New York: Random House, 1986), by David Eisenhower, contain accounts of the Ardennes offensive, including intelligence aspects.

Doc. 4-129, Tel. 2319, Dec. 22, 1944, Entry 90, Box 7. Those mentioned include Brig. Gen. T. J. Betts, deputy G-2 of SHAEF; Col. William W. Quinn, who recalls his service in *Buffalo Bill Remembers* (Fowlerville, Mich.: Wilderness Adventure Books, 1991); Capt. Stacy Lloyd, an OSS MO officer based in London for most of the war; and Dr. Stirling Callisen.

On Dec. 23, Dulles complained to Washington that the entire courier system from Switzerland to Italy and France was inadequate, causing intelligence to pile up. He urged establishment of a regular service to a central point such as Lyons (Tel. 2337, Box 157).

Doc. 4-130, Tel. 2349, Dec. 23, 1944, Entry 90, Box 7. Tel. 4332-44, Aug. 5, 1944, is printed in part as Doc. 4-45. "Colonel Passy" (Andre Dewavrin) was chief of intelligence for General de Gaulle. Number 477 was Dulles's aide Royall Tyler; 492 was René Charron; 802 was Devignat; 850 had been the physician of former Premier Daladier. On Dec. 24, Donovan replied that he had not even seen the cables in question and was confident that no one in OSS had provided Lorraine material to French intelligence (Tel. 1759, Entry 90, Box 7).

Doc. 4-131, Tel. 2369, Dec. 23, 1944, Entry 90, Box 7. Number 106 is Col. Edward Buxton, Deputy Director of OSS. Lt. Col. Howard Dix was head of the Technical Section of OSS's SI Branch. Flute was Prof. Paul Scherrer. According to Thomas Powers in *Heisenberg's War*, Berg was authorized to kidnap or assassinate Heisenberg, the dean of German nuclear physicists if it was apparent that he was developing the atomic bomb for Hitler. Berg had close contact with the target in Switzerland during this period, but did not act.

On Dec. 26, Dulles cabled Donovan recommending that the scientific component of the postwar intelligence mission to Germany be organized by OSS in Switzerland (Tel. 2547, Dec. 26, 1944, Box 277).

Headquarters informed Dulles and Berg on Dec. 29 that Tel. 2369 had been very helpful. Other reports from Berg on the German atomic energy program included Tel. 2867, Dec. 30, and Tel. 2877, Dec. 31 (Box 277).

Doc. 4-132, Tel. 2407, Dec. 25, 1944, Box 193. Number 493, Frederick R. Loofbourow, had been employed by Standard Oil of New Jersey before the war. Sent to Switzerland in 1942 by the Board of Economic Warfare to report on German petroleum production, he served as senior economic analyst at the U.S. Consulate General in Zurich but worked in large part for Dulles. He officially transferred to OSS on Sept. 1, 1944 (Tel. 3016 to Bern, Sept. 1, 1944, Box 193). Rhythm was William A. Kimbel (number 116), a businessman recruited early in the war by General Donovan to conduct OSS liaison with other agencies. Number 224 was Russell D'Oench of the SI Branch, previously stationed in London. He was grandson of the founder of Grace shipping.

The OSS force in Switzerland was augmented in late 1944 and early 1945 with the arrival of Gerhard Van Arkel, Robert Shea, Cordelia Dodson, Valerian Lada-Mocarski, Daniel McCarthy, Emmy Rado, Emilio Daddario, Paul Blum, Tracy Barnes, Henry Hyde, and Robert Joyce and others. Loofbourow, Max Shoop, and Charles Dyer were among those who departed.

Doc. 4-133, Tel. 2417, Dec. 26, 1944, Box 277. Alexander Y. Bogomolov was Soviet Ambassador to Vichy France, and later to the de Gaulle organization in London and Paris.

Doc. 4-134, Tel. 2487, Dec. 26, 1944, Box 193. In his evening radiotelephone transmission of Dec. 11, Dulles had related how the Swiss had turned back German soldiers who had wished to surrender anonymously in order to protect their families at home (Trans. no. 251, Box 273).

On Dec. 28, William Casey who was engaged in effecting agent penetration of Germany from the OSS London office, cabled Washington that he felt strongly that Dulles should be authorized to negotiate an agreement with the Swiss. If necessary, Casey said a holding area in France could be provided for those fleeing Germany (Tel. 98294 from London, Box 133).

Doc. 4-135, Tel. 2519, Dec. 26, 1944, Entry 90, Box 7. Gen. Hans Speidel, Chief of Staff to Gen. Rommel in France earlier in the war, had been involved in the July 20th plot against Hitler. He was able to convince the Gestapo of his innocence, survived the war, and rose to the highest ranks in the defense establishment of the Federal Republic of Germany.

Doc. 4-136, Tel. 2527, Dec. 26, 1944, Box 277.

Doc. 4-137, Trans. no. 257, Dec. 26, 1944, Box 273.

Doc. 4-138, Tel. 2617, Dec. 27, 1944, Box 277. Tel. 3129 from Bern, Jan. 7, 1945, indicates that at this point Kolbe was making photographs of documents, which were smuggled to Switzerland. OSS Bern passed the film and documentary material to Paris and London as received. This was in addition to telegraphic transmittal of key information to Washington in the Kappa series (Entry 90, Box 7).

Doc. 4-139, Tel. 2677, Dec. 28, 1944, Box 277. Documentation on Swiss aspects of the Safehaven program is located in *FRUS, 1945,* 5:765ff. The memorandum under reference has not been identified. Major Valerian Lada-Mocarski, a Russian émigré and international businessman employed by OSS, arrived in Switzerland about this time to join Dulles's staff.

On Dec. 30, Magruder and Shepardson responded to Dulles as follows: "You are right in your #2677. Your positive intelligence activities this juncture war are of paramount importance and you alone can judge whether they would be impaired by Safe Haven efforts" (Tel. 1927, Box 277).

Doc. 4-140, Tel. 2819, Dec. 29, 1944, Entry 90, Box 7.

Doc. 4-141, Trans. no. 259, Dec. 29, 1944, Box 273. During the last months of 1944, the German puppet government of Ferenc Szalasi conducted massive repression in Hungary and assisted the Nazis in exterminating the country's Jews. Some Hungarian troops went over to the Red Army. Hungarian general Bela Dalnoki Miklos headed a pro-Soviet government at Debrecen, until Budapest fell to the Red Army in February 1945.

Doc. 4-142, Tel. 2847, Dec. 31, 1944, Box 277. Col. Joseph Rodrigo was OSS Theater Intelligence Officer at Allied Headquarters in Caserta. Edda Mussolini Ciano, daughter of the Duce and widow of the Italian Foreign Minister whom her father had had shot for treason, escaped from Italy to Switzerland in January 1944 with her husband's diaries covering the years 1939–1943. Swiss authorities interned Edda in a mental hospital, but Dulles got on the trail of the diaries with the help of Paul Ghali of the *Chicago Daily News* who sought them for commercial purposes. The considerable cable traffic associated with this enterprise was slugged "Ecdar," and is filed in Box 215.

On Dec. 15, 1944, Dulles reported that according to Emilio Pucci, Edda's intimate friend who later became a famous fashion designer, five volumes of the diary were hidden in Switzerland. Dulles said that

Edda was a psychopathic case who one day promised the diaries as a goodwill gesture and the next asked for a large monetary payment. He suggested that Zenone Benini, a lifelong friend of Ciano, be enlisted to send a letter to Edda urging her to turn over the diaries (Tel. 2157 from Bern for Donovan, and to Caserta for Glavin, Dec. 5, 1944, Box 215). Donovan replied on Dec. 19, "Greatly interested in your 2157 and hope you will be successful" (Tel. 1607 to Bern, Entry 88, Box 589). In early Jan. 1945, Dulles succeeded in obtaining Edda's permission to make photocopies of the five volumes, which were sent to Washington (Tel. 3279 from Bern, Jan. 11, 1945; Dulles memorandum to Shepardson, Jan. 19, 1945, CIA/FOIA). In May 1945, he also sought to recover additional Ciano papers that had been hidden in Italy by Edda prior to her flight to Switzerland. These efforts failed. Apparently the Germans had discovered and removed the collection.

The story of the Ciano diaries is told in Howard M. Smyth, *Secrets of the Fascist Era: How Uncle Sam Obtained Some of the Top-Level Documents of Mussolini's Period* (Carbondale: Southern Illinois University Press, 1975). Also see Paul Ghali, "Dulles Got Secrets from Il Duce's Daughter," *Cincinnati Enquirer*, Feb. 23, 1969 (copy in Allen Dulles Papers, Box 24). The diaries were published after the war in French and Italian editions, and in the United States as Galeazzo Ciano, *The Ciano Diaries, 1939–1943* (Garden City, N.Y.: Doubleday, 1946).

Chapter 5: The Collapse of the Reich, the German Surrender in Italy, and Planning for Postwar Europe, January–May 1945

Doc. 5-1, Tel. 2227, Jan. 2, 1945, Box 162. Jigsaw is Lt. Robert Wauchope, head of the OSS Swiss/MEDTO Desk at AFHQ in Caserta. Gadfly is B. Homer Hall also of the OSS Swiss Desk in Caserta. Until August 1944, he had served on the Swiss Desk in Washington and processed many incoming reports from Dulles, including the radiotelephone transmissions. Rhythm, William A. Kimbel, had replaced Hall in that capacity at Headquarters. Dulles had also discouraged all but essential travel to Switzerland in a letter to Col. Edward Glavin, OSS Mediterranean commander at Caserta, dated Nov. 18, 1944 (Entry 190, Box 127).

Doc. 5-2, Tel. 2909, Jan. 2, 1945, Entry 90, Box 7. In Tel. 1869, Dec. 29, 1944, Gen. Magruder had asked Dulles's opinion on whether Switzerland should be pressured to curtail the traffic of German supplies between the homeland and Italy (Entry 90, Box 7). The issue of Swiss economic relations with Germany in the final stages of the war is documented in *FRUS, 1945,* 5:765ff.

Doc. 5-3, Tel. 3047, Jan. 6, 1945, Box 192. Lt. Philip Bastedo helped organize the German Unit from London. Lt. Col. Franklin Canfield was an OSS liaison officer with SHAEF. Robert D. Murphy was U.S. Political Adviser for Germany. At the meeting of Jan. 4, Donovan had said that CALPO-supplied German refugees in France could be used for penetration missions in Germany, but would be kept from any direct contact with OSS under the assumption that they were politically unreliable in the postwar period. There was discussion of intelligence gathering in Germany after the war. Dulles requested secretarial help and an additional officer who was an expert on Italy. He urged the establishment of a biweekly courier service between Bern and Paris and Caserta. He also argued against establishment of a "black" program fabricating appeals from captured German generals to the people in the Reich, and reported on the situation in Italy (unsigned notes on meeting of Jan. 4, 1945, CIA/FOIA).

Doc. 5-4, Trans. no. 263, Jan. 6, 1945, Entry 160, Box 1. In the final stages of the war, OSS Bern continued to transmit information on potential bombing targets. For instance, Tel. 4637 of Feb. 1, 1945, contained intelligence from a Swiss source on unbombed German factories producing parts for trucks, autos, tanks, and railroad cars (Box 192). Regarding the effects of the bombing of Germany, see U.S. Strategic Bombing Survey, *Summary Report (European War)* (Washington, D.C.: GPO, 1945), and David MacIsaac, ed., *The United States Strategic Bombing Survey*, 10 vols. (New York: Garland, 1976).

Doc. 5-5, Tel. 3929, Jan. 12, 1945, Entry 90, Box 7. Allied decisions on occupation zones for Germany are documented in *FRUS, The Conferences at Malta and Yalta, 1945* (Washington, D.C.: GPO, 1955), and Herbert Feis, *Churchill, Roosevelt, Stalin: The War They Waged and the Peace They Sought* (Princeton, N.J.: Princeton University Press, 1957).

Doc. 5-6, Tel. 3317, Jan. 12, 1945, Box 192. This cable cited a number of references, including Bern Tel. 2487, Dec. 26, 1944 (Doc. 4-134). In Tel. 2137 to Bern, Jan. 4, 1945, OSS Headquarters agreed that Dulles should negotiate with the Swiss to effect their acceptance of certain valuable German defectors, subject to clearance by Gen. Donovan, then in Europe (Entry 88, Box 589).

Contacts with German industrialists for any purpose was unpopular in high places. Eleanor Roosevelt addressed the following note to her husband: "Memo for the President: Allen Dulles who is in charge of Bill Donovan's outfit in Paris has been counsel, closely tied up with the Schroeder bank. That is likely to be the representative of the underground Nazi interests after the war. There seem to be in Paris a great many people who are pretty close to the big business side!" On Feb. 26, 1945, the President referred the note to his assistant, Harry Hopkins, with the notation "Will you run this down and do the necessary" (FDR Library, PSF, Hopkins folder) No record of follow-up has been found.

Doc. 5-7, Trans. no. 265, Jan. 15, 1945, Entry 160, Box 1.

Doc. 5-8, Tel. 2637, Jan. 16, 1945, Box 162. Longhi is Alfredo Pizzoni, leader of the CLNAI.

Doc. 5-9, Tel. 3657, Jan. 18, 1945, Box 192. Budapest suffered severe damage during the Red Army's capture of the city from the Germans in Jan. and Feb. 1945. Vienna largely escaped a similar fate, although Allied bombing destroyed the State Opera House. OSS Deputy Director Magruder transmitted the text of this telegram to the White House Map Room in a memorandum of Jan. 22 (FDR Library, PSF, Box 170)

Doc. 5-10, Trans. no. 267, Jan. 18, 1945, Entry 160, Box 1. On Jan. 12, 1945, Red Army forces under Marshal Zhukov launched a massive offensive in Poland and East Prussia. Western intelligence on a possible Nazi last stand in the Alps is described in Minott, *The Fortress that Never Was*.

Doc. 5-11, Tel. 2769, Jan. 19, 1945, Entry 90, Box 7.

Doc. 5-12, Tel. 3689, Jan. 19, 1945, Entry 138, Box 2. Erwin Planck, son of the physicist Max Planck, was executed despite whatever objections were raised by Japanese Ambassador Oshima.

Doc. 5-13, Tel. 4107, Jan. 20, 1945, Box 278. Those mentioned include Whitney Shepardson (154), head of SI in Washington; Thomas G. Cassady (Climax) and Edwin F. Black, OSS officers in Paris; and Max Shoop (284), in Paris en route to the United States after his long service in Switzerland.

The proposal for OSS to assist CALPO met with resistance at the Paris office. According to Flora Lewis in *Red Pawn* (172–73), Arthur Schlesinger Jr. and Bert Jolis, who served with OSS in Paris, led the opposition. Messages from headquarters on Mar. 26 and 28 informed Paris that the State Department was not favorably disposed toward CALPO or Field (Tels. 4757 and 5227, Entry 88, Box 590). His contacts with Noel Field and other left-of-center individuals placed Dulles under suspicion in some quarters. An unsigned memorandum prepared for Air Force Chief of Staff Hoyt Vandenberg (former Director of Central Intelligence) on May 4, 1948, titled "Penetration and Compromise of OSS in Switzerland and Western Europe (Allan [*sic*] Dulles)," is critical of the CALPO incident and the Dulles relationships with Field, Erika Glaser, and other leftists as part of his intelligence gathering operations (Hoyt Vandenberg Papers, Library of Congress Manuscript Division)

Doc. 5-14, Trans. no. 269, Jan. 20, 1945, Entry 160, Box 1.

Doc. 5-15, Trans. no. 270, Jan. 22, 1945, Entry 160, Box 1.

Doc. 5-16, Tel. 3037, Jan. 24, 1945, Entry 90, Box 7. Fritz Molden relates his wartime experiences in *Exploding Star: A Young Austrian Against Hitler* (London: Weidenfeld & Nicolson, 1978) and *Fires in the Night: The Sacrifices and Significance of the Austrian Resistance, 1938–1945* (Boulder, Colo.: Westview,

1989). Philip Horton was Chief of the Reports Board, OSS Headquarters Detachment, ETO Forward in Paris. Reports written by source 339, mainly on Austria, are filed in Entry 125, Box 11.

Doc. 5-17, Tel. 4039, Jan. 24, 1945, Entry 90, Box 7. Gisevius describes his escape from Germany in *To the Bitter End*, a personal account of the German resistance and the July 20, 1944, plot against Hitler, published in 1947. Gisevius finished writing and translating the manuscript in Switzerland with the support of OSS. Regarding it an important source of intelligence, OSS Bern transmitted it to Washington in Jan. 1945. In Tel. 2747 to Bern, Jan. 25, Headquarters stated the following: "Please tell him [Gisevius] that manuscript already proved of greatest value. . . . You are authorized to pay him $1,000 for valuable intelligence obtained from it. As you can appreciate believe it inappropriate to make arrangements with publisher to have it published now" (Entry 138, Box 2).

Doc. 5-18, Tel. 3127, Jan. 25, 1945, Box 192.

Doc. 5-19, Tel. 4077, Jan. 25, 1945, Entry 138, Box 2. Acting OSS Director Cheston transmitted a summary of this message to President Roosevelt in a memorandum of Jan. 27 (FDR Library, PSF, Box 170).

Doc. 5-20, Tel. 4377, Jan. 26, 1945, Box 228. Maj. Gen. Helmuth Stieff, a participant in several plots against Hitler, was hanged in August 1944. General Erich Fellgiebel was also executed. Major Otto Ernst Remer, commander of the Berlin Guard Battalion, spoke to Hitler by phone soon after the bomb attack and played a key role in defeating the coup in Berlin.

Dulles presented a similar account of the July 20 plot and the current German choice between East and West in his evening radiotelephone transmission of Jan. 26 (No. 271, Entry 160, Box 1). In a memorandum to the President dated Feb. 1, Acting OSS Director Cheston summarized the new information provided by Dulles on the failed coup against Hitler, relying mainly on Tel. 4377 (FDR Library, PSF, Box 171).

On Feb. 19, Dulles pouched a report on the background and effects of the July 20th coup to Washington, Paris, and London. It was written by an OSS agent on the basis of information supplied by Gisevius and was reviewed by him. Although there was some overlap, this report constituted a different document from the Gisevius manuscript that was ultimately published as *To the Bitter End* (Entry 190, Box 311). Shepardson sent it to Donovan on Mar. 26 (Entry 99, Box 14).

Doc. 5-21, Tel. 4267, Jan. 27, 1945, Box 278. Reference is to Edward L. Bigelow in OSS Headquarters in Washington. In Tel. 2737, Jan. 24, Headquarters asked Dulles and Glavin (Caserta) to estimate the effect on the Austrian resistance of a possible Allied announcement that not only would all Nazi laws be abolished, but also all vestiges of the Dollfuss and Schuschnigg regimes (Entry 88, Box 589) Englebert Dollfuss, was Chancellor of Austria from 1932 until assassinated in an attempted Nazi coup in 1934. The successor of Dollfuss, Kurt von Schuschnigg, was imprisoned by the Germans when they took over Austria in 1938.

Doc. 5-22, Trans. no. 272, Jan. 29, 1945, Entry 160, Box 1. Franz von Papen, Chancellor of Germany in 1932 and Hitler's Vice-Chancellor in 1933–34, served as German Ambassador to Turkey from 1939 to 1944. He was imprisoned after the war for his complicity with the Nazis.

Doc. 5-23, Tel. 5377, Jan. 30, 1945, Entry 90, Box 6. Documentation on OSS planning for operations in Germany after the war is filed in Entry 190, Boxes 25 and 32. OSS Major C. B. Peters contributed to this effort in London. Tel. 3837 from London to Bern, relayed to Washington on Jan. 31 as Tel. 6824, informed Dulles that the Berlin "T" force had been instructed to stand by on 72-hour notice. He was invited to nominate individuals including his assistants to be included. He was also invited to name candidates, including himself, for the first OSS plane to Berlin following the T Force mission (Entry 90, Box 6). Dulles received a sobering follow-up message from OSS in London on Feb. 2, stating that it was uncertain whether the Russians would actually allow Western personnel into Berlin, or the other parts of Germany that they occupied (Tel. 7524, Entry 90, Box 6).

Doc. 5-24, Tel. 4697, Feb. 2, 1945, Box 192. Dulles sent this cable in response to Tel. 4697 from Washington, Feb. 2, which asked if he wanted Ruth Van Arkel, wife of Gerhard Van Arkel, assigned to Bern even though her planned job description left little time for SI work (Box 192).

Doc. 5-25, Trans. no. 273, Feb. 2, 1945, Entry 160, Box 1. The Big Three met at Yalta from Feb. 4 to 11, 1945. They made no change in the policy of unconditional surrender.

Doc. 5-26, Trans. no. 274, Feb. 3, 1945, Entry 160, Box 1. On Feb. 1, 1945, the communist-dominated government of Bulgaria shot the three former regents, Prince Kyril, Bogdan Filov, and General Nikola Mihov. Also executed were a large number of former cabinet ministers and noncommunist political figures, including Pavel Grouev and Svetoslav Pomenov. Konstantin Mouraviev was sentenced to prison. In his transmission of Feb. 6, Dulles continued his discussion of Bulgarian matters, noting that a number of noncommunists remained in the cabinet, but would be eliminated in due course (Trans. no. 275, Feb. 6, 1945, Entry 160, Box 1; for other extracts, see Doc. 5-30). On Feb. 7, Dulles sent by pouch to Washington, Paris, London, and Caserta a lengthy memorandum by an ex-Bulgarian diplomat expressing outrage over the communist takeover of his country. Dulles noted that his Bulgarian contacts saw the purge as an attempt not only to punish those guilty of collaboration with the Axis, but to eliminate liberal and democratic elements who might have favored a western orientation for the country (CIA/FOIA).

Doc. 5-27, Tel. 4837, Feb. 4, 1945, Entry 138, Box 2. On Jan. 28, Dulles transmitted the following: "Wood has now returned here with large consignment hot material. Developing films today, keeping print here and sending films Paris by special courier, leaving 30th. Will cable certain items and send analysis shortly. Please arrange with Gamble and Forgan remaking prints and distribution in ETO and to Zulu and provide for earliest possible courier to bring films and/or prints to Washington. Will label series Jakka" (Tel. 4297, CIA/FOIA). The Jakka series included the following items. On Feb. 1, OSS Bern transmitted a six-page report on the overall status and disposition of Japanese forces as sent by German officials in Tokyo to the Foreign Ministry in Berlin, and intercepted by George Wood. It stated the following as to Japanese morale: "Combativity, spirit of sacrifice, discipline and sobriety of Jap Army in all theaters, especially in desperate situations, undiminished and compensate largely for numerical and material inferiority" (Tel. 4587). Tel. 4657, Feb. 1, contained an overall order of battle summary on Japanese air forces. Tel. 4707, Feb. 2, submitted a Japanese analysis of the Soviet Far Eastern Army also as intercepted by Wood from German dispatches from Tokyo. Tel. 4667, Feb. 3, transmitted German intelligence on the Japanese aircraft production industry. Tel. 4737, Feb. 3, contained German reports on the results of American bombing of Japan and Japanese air defenses, which reportedly included sending unarmed planes up to ram bombers. Tels. 4757, Feb. 3, and 4797, Feb. 5, provided additional information on U.S. bombing of targets in Japan and in Japanese-occupied territory. The German Ambassador also reported that the battle for the Philippines was of critical political importance in that if the Japanese lost, they would face stiffer resistance from the Chinese and more political and economic pressure from the Soviet Union (Tel. 4747, Feb. 3). (All filed in Entry 138, Box 2.)

Doc. 5-28, Tel. 4827, Feb. 5, 1945, Entry 138, Box 2. Gen. Clayton L. Bissell was Assistant Chief of Staff for Intelligence, U.S. Army (G-2). X-2 was the OSS Counterintelligence branch. On Feb. 8, Headquarters responded to Dulles's concerns over the use and security of Kappa material. Tel. 3247 read in part as follows: "Messages subject most rigid security restrictions. Be assured highest officials both in Washington and several theaters get material under appropriate safeguards and credit to OSS. If direct action does not result from this information, one reason is because action less vital than continuity of cryptographic sources which action might imperil" (CIA/FOIA). The last sentence raises the question of whether OSS had more knowledge of Ultra than is generally believed.

Doc. 5-29, Tel. 4909, Feb. 5, 1945, Entry 90, Box 7. Gen. Donovan summarized this message in a memorandum to President Roosevelt dated Feb. 7 (FDR Library, PSF, Box 171).

Doc. 5-30, Trans. no. 275, Feb. 6, 1945, Entry 160, Box 1.

Doc. 5-31, Tel. 360, Feb. 9, 1945, Entry 139, Box 60. Gen. Siegfried Westphal was Gen. Kesselring's chief of staff. Gen. Donovan sent a summary of this message to the President in a memorandum of the same date (FDR Library, PSF, Box 171).

Doc. 5-32, Tel. 6447, Feb. 13, 1945, Box 162. Number 140 is Hugh Wilson of the OSS Planning Group, an old friend of Dulles. Henry Hyde, former head of the OSS French Desk in Algiers, was now serving in France and later came to Switzerland. Major Richard Crosby was an OSS liaison officer with the military.

Doc. 5-33, Trans. no. 276, Feb. 13, 1945, Entry 160, Box 1. Dulles relayed the balance of the summary of the article in his radiotelephone transmission of Feb. 14 (Trans. no. 277, Entry 160, Box 1). On Feb. 16, he cabled a report received from French intelligence (source 472) that one thousand mountain-trained German troops had arrived in Austria from Denmark to organize the reduit (Tel. 5387, Box 192).

Doc. 5-34, Tel. 5327, Feb. 15, 1945, Box 228. Maj. Horace K. Calvert was a member of Alsos, Manhattan Project's arm for gathering intelligence, personnel, and equipment from the German atomic energy program.

Doc. 5-35, Tel. 5407, Feb. 16, 1945, Entry 138, Box 2. Tel. 3327 to Bern, Feb. 10, 1945, is filed in Entry 138, Box 2. Tel. 3327, Feb. 10, reads as follows: "Questions raised in last paragraph of your #4827 [Doc. 5-28] considered in relation basic policies involved. Changing circumstances and foreseeable developments make it essential that OSS Washington be increasingly controlling center for all similar activities and relations. In line with this policy Kappa and Breakers material will be centered in Washington. All cables and documentary material in these categories to be sent Washington only. Control of action and dissemination will remain in OSS Washington. Information essential to London, Paris, British or others will be determined and transmitted by OSS Washington" (CIA/FOIA). On Feb. 22, Donovan notified Dulles that the plan for centralized handling of Kappa and Breakers material would go into effect, with the exception that London would continue to receive the present Jakka series directly from Bern (Tel. 3797, Entry 138, Box 2).

Doc. 5-36, Trans. no. 278, Feb. 17, 1945, Entry 160, Box 1.

Doc. 5-37, Tel. 5527, Feb. 19, 1945, Box 228. On Feb. 27, OSS Headquarters informed Dulles that his proposals for the use of former German officials were approved. However, the approval was circumscribed by reference to President Roosevelt's position that no guarantees of protection could be given to Germans who cooperated with the Allies. Gen. Julius C. Holmes, Assistant Secretary of State for Administration and former head of the Joint Army and Navy Intelligence Committee did indicate to OSS that Germans wishing to be of service could be told that their actions would be taken into account after the war. Headquarters said nothing should be put in writing, nor should activities by German nationals be allowed to assume a political nature, but should rather be confined to intelligence gathering (Tel. 3887 to Bern, Feb. 27, 1945, Entry 138, Box 2). This outcome was consistent with the recommendations of Gen. Magruder to Gen. Donovan on Feb. 24, which opposed the creation of a western Free Germany Committee, but backed the concept of enlisting the adherence of German officials in place without offering any firm quid pro quo to them (Office Director's Microfilm, Reel 81).

Doc. 5-38, Tel. 6847, Feb. 19, 1945, Box 278. William H. Jackson served with OSS in Europe in 1944 and 1945. After the war, he collaborated with Dulles and others in setting up a permanent national intelligence organization and was Deputy Director of CIA in 1950–51. Donovan cabled Bastedo and Dulles on Feb. 22 that he had never doubted that in view of Dulles's desire to be in a position to resign as chief of mission in Germany that he would have a deputy. Donovan said he would consider candidates suggested by Dulles to the fullest degree (Tel. 3697 to Bern, Entry 88, Box 589).

Doc. 5-39, Trans. no. 279, Feb. 19, 1945, Entry 160, Box 1.

Doc. 5-40, Tel. 5617, Feb. 20, 1945, Entry 138, Box 2. Among the Kafeb reports on Japanese operations transmitted by OSS Bern were Tel. 5657, Feb. 20, 1945, and Tel. 5747, Feb. 22, 1945. Tel. 5737, Feb.

23, reported considerable bombing damage in Tokyo. Tel. 5767, Feb. 23, stated that Kafeb film was being transmitted to Paris by pouch (Entry 138, Box 2).

Doc. 5-41, Tel. 5727, Feb. 23, 1945, Box 192. OSS in Caserta reacted as follows on Feb. 25: "AFHQ is definitely interested in getting positive and authentic information to support this alleged disposition of Kesselring. Story repeatedly crops up but there has never been proof of its accuracy. If Kesselring wishes to dispatch emissary with official message he could find ways of doing it. Meanwhile AFHQ would certainly not recommend to combined chiefs any modification unconditional surrender such as would be involved in promises, commitments or bargaining. Indeed we believe it extremely doubtful that any modifications would be made although undoubtedly Kesselring would be given customary privileges his rank as prisoner of war" (Tel. 1876 from Caserta to Bern, Feb. 25, 1945, Entry 121, Box 19). On Feb. 24, Acting OSS Director Cheston sent President Roosevelt a summary of Tel. 5727 (FDR Library, PSF, Box 171). Throughout the negotiations that culminated in the surrender of the German army in Italy on May 2, OSS provided the White House with timely and detailed information as received from Dulles.

Doc. 5-42, Tel. 5839, Feb. 23, 1945, Entry 90, Box 7. Acting OSS Director Cheston sent a summary of this message to President Roosevelt by memorandum of Feb. 26 (FDR Library, PSF, Box 171). Gen. Johannes Blaskowitz, who had been removed as military governor of Poland for protesting SS excesses, served as a commander on the Western Front in 1944–45. Tel. 4909, Feb. 5, is printed here as Doc. 5-29. Dulles brought this contact to the attention of Gen. Sibert at the 12th Army Group, who in turn informed Gen. Eisenhower, the Supreme Allied Commander. Eisenhower cabled Washington for guidance, but indicated that he was unable to discuss anything beyond military matters and could make no commitments. He wanted the channel kept open, however (Tel. 655 from Paris to Bern, Feb. 28, 1945, Entry 121, Box 19). On Feb. 28, OSS headquarters informed Dulles that the British Chiefs of Staff and the U.S. Joint Chiefs of Staff were most interested in the contact (Tel. 3899 to Bern, Feb. 28, Entry 90, Box 7).

Doc. 5-43, Tel. 5997, Feb. 26, 1945, Entry 138, Box 2.

Doc. 5-44, letter, Feb. 26, 1945, Entry 190, Box 28. The reference letter from Murphy is in Entry 190, Box 28. Dulles remained in touch with Carl Jung, the eminent Swiss psychiatrist, during the war. Documents on efforts of the OSS Labor Branch to penetrate Germany, including reports from Gerhard Van Arkel in Switzerland to George Pratt in London, are in Entry 190, Boxes 32 and 306.

Doc. 5-45, Tel. 6097, Feb. 28, 1945, Box 228. Hoettl presents an unreliable and self-serving account of Nazi wartime intelligence in *The Secret Front: The Story of Nazi Political Espionage* (London: Weidenfeld & Nicolson, 1953).

Doc. 5-46, Trans. no. 282, Feb. 28, 1945, Entry 160, Box 1.

Doc. 5-47, Tel. 6149, Mar. 1, 1945, Entry 90, Box 7. Tel. 5839, Feb. 23, is printed here as Doc. 5-42. Lt. Col. Carl H. Wies served with the 12th Army Group.

On Mar. 3, Headquarters informed Dulles as follows: "The message of the Supreme Commander to the Combined Chiefs of Staff has been seen here and is believed to put the situation described in your #5839 in its proper light. It has not been felt necessary to transmit to the Joint Chiefs the caution suggested at the end of your #6149. Both the Supreme Commander's radio and our report to the Joint Chiefs make it clear that this a possible approach by individual Generals for purposes of their own and not peace-feelers from an organized group which the Combined Chiefs might not entertain" (Entry 90, Box 7).

Doc. 5-48, Tel. 6209, Mar. 2, 1945, Entry 90, Box 6. Tel. 6097, Feb. 28, is printed here as Doc. 5-45.

Doc. 5-49, Trans. no. 283, Mar. 3, 1945, Entry 160, Box 1.

Doc. 5-50, Tel. 6329, Mar. 5, 1945, Entry 90, Box 6. Baron Luigi Parilli was an Italian businessman. The intermediary was Swiss professor Max Husmann, to whom Parilli had indirect access. DB-001 was presumably Paul Blum, an OSS officer who had recently been reassigned from Paris to Switzerland. The

Swiss intelligence officers under reference included Major Max Waibel. SS Col. Eugen Dollmann, a Renaissance scholar who had translated at Hitler-Mussolini meetings earlier in the war was now an agent in Italy for SS chief Heinrich Himmler. Having played an important role in the surrender of the German army in Italy, he wrote memoirs that focused on the postwar ingratitude of the Americans (*Call Me Coward* [London: William Kimber, 1956]). Capt. Guido Zimmer was an SS counterespionage officer acquainted with Baron Parilli. Number 148 was Lt. Col. William Maddox, OSS SI MEDTO chief.

On Mar. 8, AFHQ, through OSS Caserta, recommended to Dulles that pending instructions from Washington and London, he meet with the Germans and intermediaries without entering into any negotiations and without promising further talks, securing whatever information could be obtained (Tel. 419 from Caserta to Bern, Entry 139, Box 60).

In addition to Dulles's *Secret Surrender*, see *Operation Sunrise* by Bradley Smith and Elena Agarossi for another day-by-day account of the Sunrise contacts. Extensive Sunrise documentation is filed in Entry 110, Box 1, including a narrative account based on Bern-Caserta telegraphic correspondence, personal statements by Gens. Wolff and Vietinghoff, and photographs. The 70-page after-action report written by Dulles and Gaevernitz is filed in Entry 110, Box 2, with much other pertinent material. Other Sunrise material focusing on the OSS office in Caserta is in Entry 139, Box 60. The Allen Dulles Papers at Princeton contain rich documentation on Sunrise/Crossword, especially Boxes 22, 210, 211, and 214. *FRUS, 1945*, vol. 3, *European Advisory Commission; Austria; Germany* (Washington, D.C.: GPO, 1968), 717ff., documents various threads of the negotiations that led to the final German general surrender, including Sunrise. This collection presents the top policy view, including Roosevelt-Stalin correspondence and papers setting forth the positions of the Joint and Combined Chiefs of Staff and the State Department.

Doc. 5-51, Tel. 6459, Mar. 6, 1945, Entry 90, Box 7. Contacts between Japanese representatives in Switzerland and the OSS continued for the duration of the war and were particularly frequent in July 1945. Extensive documentation on the subject exists in Boxes 21 and 167 of the Allen Dulles Papers at Princeton. Of particular interest is a copy of the publication *The Per Jacobsson Mediation*, edited by Erin E. Jucker-Fleetwood (Basle Centre for Economic and Financial Research, Series C, No. 4, c. 1967), which consists of notes by the late Jacobsson himself. The Swede, whom Dulles had known before the war, served as Managing Director of the International Monetary Fund from 1956 to 1963. Other notable items in Box 21 are a draft chapter 22, "The Dulles Operation," from an unidentified manuscript titled "A History of the End of the War," and a 1965 draft by Gero Gaevernitz titled "Was the Atom Bomb Really Necessary?: Secret Contacts of American, German and Japanese Agents in Switzerland—Three Months Prior to Hiroshima."

Doc. 5-52, Tel. 6477, Mar. 7, 1945, Box 192. Albert (Bert) Jolis, a naturalized American with connections in the European diamond market and with noncommunist unions, served with the OSS Labor Desk in Paris and helped to infiltrate left-wing agents into Germany. Reference is presumably to Dr. Josef Hofer, a resistance figure in upper Austria.

Doc. 5-53, Tel. 1146, Mar. 8, 1945, Entry 110, Box 2. Donovan sent a summary of this message to the President on Mar. 8 (FDR Library, PSF, Box 171). Extensive documentation on Operation Sunrise is located in Entry 110, Box 2, and in Entry 90, Boxes 6–7. This material includes cable traffic from Bern, Caserta, Washington, London and other OSS posts involved in this episode.

In Paris, Gen. Walter Bedell Smith, Gen. Eisenhower's Chief of Staff, asked to be advised directly of all developments (Tel. 15439 from London, Mar. 9, 1945, Entry 90, Box 6).

Doc. 5-54, Tel. 6647, Mar. 8, 1945, Box 192. Robert Fischer and Johann Koplenig were leading Austrian communists.

Doc. 5-55, Tel. 6487, Mar. 8, 1945, Box 278.

Doc. 5-56, Tel. 6679, Mar. 9, 1945, Entry 110, Box 2. Gen. Donovan sent a summary of this message to the President on Mar. 9 (FDR Library, PSF, Box 171). Gen. Rodolfo Graziani was Defense Minister in Mussolini's puppet fascist government in North Italy. Later on Mar. 9, Col. Glavin, OSS chief in Caserta, cabled Dulles that Tel. 6679 had been given to AFHQ. Field Marshal Harold Alexander, Allied Commander in the Mediterranean, had outlined to Sir Alan Brooke, Chief of the Imperial General Staff a plan for two senior staff officers to go to Switzerland via Annemasse to meet with the German representatives. Brooke directed OSS to make the arrangements, including transportation and communications. Dulles was asked to select a safe meeting place and to arrange transportation from Annemasse base to that location. Glavin's cable indicated that the operation had been given the code name "Sunrise" (Tel. 424 from Caserta to Bern, Entry 110, Box 2). In Anglo-American channels, Operation Sunrise was often referred to as Crossword. On Mar. 10, General Donovan in Washington instructed Dulles as follows: "We are depending upon you to inform Paris and Caserta, as you are now doing, respecting all negotiations with German individuals. . . . In this way Washington, SHAEF, and AFHQ will all be informed. The information is thus available to the British where it can best be used. London should be furnished a copy for information only, but in order to avoid possible confusion should not be disseminated locally. Information on these promising approaches is being furnished promptly to appropriate sources in Washington" (Tel. 2757(9) to Bern, March 10, Entry 110, Box 2). Although most OSS secret correspondence during the war bore the security classification "secret," many Sunrise documents, including those cited in this note, were labeled "Top Secret."

Doc. 5-57, Tel. 6689, Mar. 9, 1945, Entry 90, Box 7. Major Eugen Wenner was present at many of the meetings leading to the surrender of German forces in Italy. Gen. Hans Roettinger also played a significant role. According to a footnote in the source text, message 614 had not been identified. On Mar. 10, Donovan transmitted a memorandum to President Roosevelt containing the contents of this telegram and informing him of AFHQ's plan to send two senior staff officers to Switzerland (FDR Library, PSF, Box 171) In addition to regular reports on Sunrise from Donovan, the White House received considerable information from the War Department, including copies of messages between AFHQ and Washington. This material is on file in FDR Library, Map Room Records, Boxes 23 and 35.

Doc. 5-58, Tel. 6709, Mar. 9, 1945, Entry 90, Box 7. Antonio Usmiani had performed intelligence work for Dulles in northern Italy earlier in the war.

Doc. 5-59, Trans. no. 285, Mar. 9, 1945, Entry 160, Box 1.

Doc. 5-60, Tel. 6969, Mar. 12, 1945, Entry 90, Box 6. On March 12, Donovan informed President Roosevelt that, in accordance with AFHQ instructions, OSS was going ahead with plans to meet with German representatives to discuss taking German forces in North Italy out of the war. He summarized tel. 6969 in another memorandum to the White House on Mar. 13, and on the same day sent the President a résumé of contacts since Feb. 8 (FDR Library, PSF, Box 171). Operation Sunrise was considered at the highest policy level and became the subject of Anglo-American disagreement with Moscow. The Combined Chiefs of Staff approved AFHQ's plan to send representatives to Switzerland, provided the Soviet Union was informed in advance. Consequently, on Mar. 11 the State Department instructed W. Averell Harriman, the U.S. Ambassador in Moscow, to broach the proposed conversations with Soviet authorities. Harriman reported the next day that Foreign Minister Molotov requested that Soviet officers be present. Both Harriman and Gen. John R. Deane, head of the Military Mission to the Soviet Union, expressed the opinion that there was no justification for the Soviet request since this was a matter of a purely military surrender in an Anglo-American theater. They were aware that the Soviets had not permitted Allied observers to be present in similar situations in their area of control. The U.S. JCS agreed, but the British Chiefs suggested that the Russians be invited to attend the final surrender discussion, which was to occur at AFHQ in Caserta should the talks in Switzerland bear fruit. Therefore, the Soviet Government was told that it would not be represented in Switzerland, but that Field Marshal Alexander was being instructed to make arrangements for the presence of Soviet representatives at AFHQ. On Mar. 16, Molotov wrote Harriman and British Ambassador Sir Archibald Clark Kerr that the U.S.-U.K. refusal "to admit participation of the Soviet Representatives in the negotiations in Bern for the Soviet Government utterly unexpected and incomprehensible from the viewpoint of Allied relations. . . . The Soviet Government considers it impossible to give agreement to the negotiations . . . in Bern and insists that the negotiations be broken off. The Soviet Government, furthermore, insists that also from now on all possibility of the conduct of separate negotiations by one or two of the Allied Powers with German Representatives without the participation of the third Allied Power be ruled out." Ambassador Harriman's reaction, expressed in a cable to Washington on Mar. 17, was that the Soviet leaders had come to believe they could force their will on the West. "They have," he stated, "arbitrarily and in disregard of the facts, placed their own interpretation on the Yalta agreements regarding Poland, liberated areas as applied to Rumania and liberated prisoners of war. In the present case Molotov again bases his position on a distortion of the facts. . . . The arrogant language of Molotov's letter . . . brings out in the open a domineering attitude toward the United States which we have before only suspected. . . . I . . . recommend that we face the issue now by adhering to the reasonable and generous position we have taken and by advising the Soviet Government in firm, but friendly, terms to that effect" (*FRUS, 1945*, 3:722–33).

Doc. 5-61, Tel. 6829, Mar. 12, 1945, Entry 90, Box 6. Major Max Wuensche, commander of an SS armored regiment, had been captured on Aug. 8, 1944.

Doc. 5-62, Trans. no. 286, Mar. 12, 1945, Entry 160, Box 1.

Doc. 5-63, Tel. 6897, Mar. 13, 1945, Box 192. Ted Ryan was a senior OSS officer at Caserta.

Doc. 5-64, Tel. 6909. Mar. 14, 1945, Entry 90, Box 7. Prof. Carl J. Burckhardt was President of the International Committee of the Red Cross for most of the war and a source of information for the Allies.

Doc. 5-65, Trans. no. 287, Mar. 14, 1945, Entry 160, Box 1.

Doc. 5-66, Tel. 7037, Mar. 15, 1945, Box 162. Those mentioned include Col. Rudolf Graf von Marogna-Redwitz and Col. Otto Armster, plotters against Hitler in Austria, and Karl Seitz, former Burgomaster of Vienna.

Doc. 5-67, Trans. no. 288, Mar. 16, 1945, Entry 160, Box 1. Reinforcing the notion of a possible Alpine last stand, Dulles cabled on Mar. 16 that the families of Nazi leaders had moved to the reduit area, and that local Austrian commanders were being replaced by Germans loyal to the Hitler regime (Tel. 7057, Box 192).

Doc. 5-68, Tel. 7199, Mar. 17, 1945, Entry 90, Box 6. Russell Forgan, whom Dulles had known before the war, was serving at Paris as OSS chief in the ETO.

Doc. 5-69, Tel. 7329, Mar. 20, 1945, Entry 90, Box 6. Donovan summarized this message in a memorandum for the President dated March 21 (FDR Library, PSF, Box 171) For purposes of Sunrise, Gens. Lemnitzer and Airey assumed the names of two OSS radio operators at Annemasse Base: T/4 Guy H. Nicholson and T/4 William D. McNeely. In addition to his role in Sunrise, Gen. von Vietinghoff performed a humanitarian act in the last days of the war by countermanding, as chief of the German Southwest Command, orders for the SS in Austria to murder the families of the July 20 plotters and other special prisoners.

Meanwhile, the East-West disagreement over Sunrise intensified. On Mar. 20, Washington instructed Ambassador Harriman to deliver a message to the Soviets that rejected their objections to the Bern conversation and expressed surprise at the tenor of their previous communication. Undeterred, Foreign Minister Molotov replied on March 22 that the talks in Switzerland were being carried out "behind the back of the Soviet Government which has been carrying on the main burden of the war against Germany" and must be terminated. At this point, President Roosevelt weighed in with Chairman Stalin. His message of the 24th contended that surely the facts had not been correctly presented to the Soviet leader. The discussions simply involved a surrender of enemy forces in the field, had no political implications, and did not violate the principle of unconditional surrender. They would not be suspended. In his reply of March 29, Stalin held his ground on objecting to the talks and asserted that the Germans had used them to transfer three divisions from Italy to the Eastern Front. Field Marshal Alexander had not bound the troops of the enemy in place as required by Yalta decisions. This was "irritating to the Soviet Command and creates ground for distrust," Stalin wrote. If the Germans in Italy, who were not facing immediate annihilation, were willing to discuss surrender, they must have an ulterior motive, he stated (*FRUS, 1945*, 3:735–40).

Doc. 5-70, Tel. 7337, Mar. 21, 1945, Box 192. Donovan sent a summary of this cable to President Roosevelt on March 23 (FDR Library, PSF, Box 171).

Doc. 5-71, Tel. 7387, Mar. 21, 1945, Box 192. In a memorandum to the President of Mar. 26, Donovan transmitted a summary of this message (FDR Library, PSF, Box 171).

Doc. 5-72, Trans. no. 289, Mar. 21, 1945, Entry 160, Box 1.

Doc. 5-73, Tel. 7427, Mar. 22, 1945, Box 192.

Doc. 5-74, Tel. 7569, Mar. 23, 1945, Entry 90, Box 6. Gen. Franz Ritter von Epp was a conservative official who had helped the Nazis to rise to prominence in Bavaria. He became governor when Hitler came to power, but had little influence in the hierarchy of the Reich after the mid-1930s. He died in an American internment camp after the war. Number 502 was Prince Auersperg, German Assistant Air Attaché in Bern. Others mentioned include Heinz Adolf Heinze, Hans-Bernd von Haeften, and Cardinal Faulhaber. Gen. Kriebel was a commander of reserve troops in Bavaria. On Mar. 26, Dulles reported that Gaevernitz had met again with Heinze, and had learned more about Gen. von Epp's plans to take over Bavaria when central German government authority collapsed. Dulles noted that "this group obviously represents conservative right wing elements and whether they will have sufficient energy and determination to carry out their plans seems somewhat doubtful. However, we are endeavoring to establish clandestine line of communication to group in order to follow developments" (Tel. 7639, Entry 190, Box 6).

Doc. 5-75, Tel. 7589, Mar. 24, 1945, Entry 90, Box 7. Those mentioned include Dr. Karl Rudolf and Field Marshal Freiherr Maximilian von Weichs. Gen. Glaise-Horstenau was an Austrian officer who was formerly German commander in Croatia, with a long history of double-dealing. Dr. Neubacher was a former Austrian officer who had also served the Nazis in Yugoslavia. Under the Convention of Tauroggen, the Prussian Army had switched sides, joining Russia to bring down Napoleon. Gen. Donovan sent a memorandum to the President on Mar. 27 that summarized this message and included supplementary information prepared by OSS headquarters on the Austrian situation, von Epp, and Kaltenbrunner (FDR Library, PSF, Box 171).

Doc. 5-76, Trans. no. 290, Mar. 27, 1945, Entry 160, Box 1. Sepp Dietrich, a veteran Nazi, was a commander on the Western Front. His troops were responsible for the Malmedy massacre of American POWs during the Battle of the Bulge.

Doc. 5-77, Tel. 7699, Mar. 28, 1945, Entry 90, Box 6.

Doc. 5-78, Tel. 7737, Mar. 28, 1945, Box 192. *Sippensuehne* translates "family atonement."

Doc. 5-79, Tel. 585, Mar. 29, 1945, Entry 110, Box 2. Donovan informed Roosevelt of this message by memorandum of Mar. 29 (FDR Library, PSF, Box 171). Major Norman Newhouse was a senior OSS officer at Caserta. Ferruccio Parri and Gen. Raffaele Cadorna were, respectively, a ranking partisan leader in North Italy and the chief military representative of the Rome government in that region.

Doc. 5-80, Tel. 9119, Apr. 1, 1945, Entry 90, Box 6. Gen. Donovan sent the text of this message to the President in a memorandum dated Apr. 1 (FDR Library, PSF, Box 171). Friday was Mar. 30. Franz Hofer was Gauleiter of the Tyrol, with administrative control over South Tyrol in Italy and portions of lower Austria. A Capt. Tucker had been captured by the Italian Fascists in the fall of 1944, apparently bearing messages from the British to Marshal Graziani, head of Mussolini's armed forces. He was turned over to the Germans in Feb. 1945. Gen. Wolff sent him back to the Allies in early March, apparently as another effort to establish communications designed to hasten the cessation of hostilities. The "desperation weapon" Hitler's advisers might have been referring to may have been a guided missile. German atomic weapons were not even under development.

Doc. 5-81, Tel. 9169, Apr. 3, 1945, Entry 90, Box 6. Donovan apprised Roosevelt of the contents of this message in a memorandum of Apr. 4 (FDR Library, PSF, Box 171). Also on Apr. 4, Dulles cabled Donovan as follows: "Generals Lemnitzer and Airey left today for Caserta together with Glavin, Weil, and Crockett. Generals requested me to follow SUNRISE developments and arranged detailed program for sending envoy south in event Critic-Vietinghoff negotiations develop. They also indicated they would be prepared return here if necessary. We expect next message from Critic April 6" (Tel. 8089, Entry 190, Box 6).

Attempting to placate the Soviets, Roosevelt had written Stalin on Apr. 1, noting that "the matter now stands in an atmosphere of regrettable apprehension and mistrust." He assured the Soviet dictator that "no negotiations for surrender have been entered into, and if there should be any negotiations they will be conducted at Caserta with your representatives present throughout." He repeated that the meeting in Switzerland was for the sole purpose of establishing contact, and that when actual negotiations began at Caserta they would be on the basis of unconditional surrender. Stalin only became more abusive. In a rude and abrupt letter to Roosevelt of Apr. 3, he accused the western Allies of having concluded an agreement with Gen. Kesselring to open the front to permit full concentration of German forces against the Red Army. He claimed that in fact the Germans had stopped fighting British and American forces. Roosevelt replied immediately that he "had read with astonishment" the message of Apr. 3. He repeated the U.S. position on the Sunrise discussions and concluded as follows: "It would be one of the great tragedies of history if at the very moment of the victory, now within our grasp, such distrust, such lack of faith should prejudice the entire undertaking after the colossal losses of life, materiel and treasure involved. Frankly I cannot avoid a feeling of bitter resentment toward your informers, whoever they are, for such vile misrepresentations of my actions or those of my subordinates." Churchill associated HMG with Roosevelt's reply, and stated that he was "astounded that Stalin should have addressed to you a message so insulting to the honour of the United States and also of Great Britain." He urged a firm and blunt stand—and an effort to meet the Russian armies as far to the east as possible (*FRUS, 1945*, 3:740–47).

Doc. 5-82, Tel. 8099, Apr. 4, 1945, Entry 90, Box 7. Number 244, Frederick Stalder, a Swiss who had served on Dulles's staff since 1942, was slated to leave for Paris on Apr. 6 with Wood documents and film, a memorandum summarizing information on the reduit, and a report on the recent trip by agent "Philip Keller" to Munich (Tel. 8199 from Bern, Apr. 5, 1945, Entry 90, Box 7). The nineteen-page Keller report contained detailed information on conditions in southern Germany and a harrowing personal account of capture and escape (Entry 125, Box 7).

Doc. 5-83, Tel. 8139, Apr. 5, 1945, Entry 110, Box 2. Paul Ghali of the *Chicago Daily News* cooperated with Dulles on the Ciano diaries case and in other matters. German attempts to contact Dulles through Swiss intelligence came early and often. In Tel. 4769, Feb. 4, 1945, Dulles reported that Masson had been approached by an envoy from Schellenberg who had wished to see him, suggesting that unless the "unconditional surrender" policy were modified, Germany might open the door to Russia. Suspecting an attempt to cause trouble among the Allies, Dulles refused to see the envoy (CIA/FOIA; Allen Dulles Papers, Box 22). Schellenberg gave his version of attempted deals with the Allies in his memoir, *Labyrinth*. After the war, he spent most of his time in court or in prison before dying young in 1952.

Doc. 5-84, Tel. 8179, Apr. 5, 1945, Entry 90, Box 7.

Doc. 5-85, Trans. no. 291, Apr. 5, 1945, Entry 160, Box 1.

Doc. 5-86, Tel. 8277, Apr. 6, 1945, Box 193. Harry Dexter White served as Assistant Secretary of the Treasury under Henry Morgenthau. He helped to design the Morgenthau Plan, which would have reduced Germany to an agricultural nation, and the Bretton Woods plans for postwar monetary affairs.

When he died in 1948, he was under the cloud of having been accused before the House Un-American Activities Committee of being a communist sympathizer or operative.

Doc. 5-87, Tel. 8349, Apr. 6, 1945, Entry 90, Box 7. In Tel. 5149 to Bern, Apr. 6, Donovan indicated that he was about to send a report on the reduit possibility to John J. McCloy, Assistant Secretary of War, and requested any additional information (Entry 90, Box 7). Dulles's estimate of the extent of preparation for a final defense far exceeded reality. The reduit was either a plan never put into practice or an outright German deception.

Doc. 5-88, Tel. 8399, Apr. 7, 1945, Entry 90, Box 7. Another Kappa cable, dated Apr. 6, reported the view of German observers in Tokyo that a Japanese government crisis was at hand due to the cabinet's inability to deal with internal divisions as well as military defeat. The Germans expressed admiration for the valiant Japanese people, as opposed to the bickering politicians (Tel. 8259, Entry 90, Box 7).

Doc. 5-89, Tel. 8759, Apr. 7, 1945, Entry 90, Box 7. Acting OSS Director Buxton summarized this message in a memorandum to the President dated Apr. 9.

Doc. 5-90, Tel. 8787, Apr. 7, 1945, Box 232.

Doc. 5-91, Tel. 8499, Apr. 9, 1945, Entry 90, Box 7. Acting OSS Director Buxton sent a summary of this message to the President on Apr. 10 (FDR Library, PSF, Box 167). U.S. Maj. Gen. Lyman L. Lemnitzer was deputy chief of staff to Field Marshal Alexander, Allied commander in the Mediterranean theater. Thursday was Apr. 5. Adm. Karl Doenitz was commander of the German navy. Following Hitler's suicide, Doenitz became chancellor of Germany for the final week of the war.

Also on Apr. 9, Dulles cabled Gen. Wolff's ("Critic") statement in which he described Gen. von Vietinghoff's ("Glazier") position that out of "a sense of primary responsibility to the German people as a whole" he would draw appropriate conclusions from the military situation provided German troops could depart from Italy with military honors, and that a large part of them be maintained as a future instrument of order inside Germany (Tel. 646 from Bern to Caserta, Entry 110, Box 2). Dulles also transmitted an account based on information from Baron Parilli who had again returned to Switzerland describing the tortured discussions among the German leaders during the past week. Wolff had apparently instructed troops under his command not to engage in wanton destruction, and thought that Vietinghoff's sense of honor could be satisfied by such measures as promising that German troops could stand at attention while surrendering and could take their belts and bayonets home with them (Tel. 647 from Bern to Caserta, Apr. 9, 1945, Entry 110, Box 2). Further, Dulles informed Caserta that Wolff, in addition to limiting destruction, also acknowledged that time was short and negotiations had to proceed rapidly. He also wanted the Allies to return some German prisoner or at least make a gesture so that he could prove to Himmler's group that the release of Parri and Usiami had not been a unilateral concession (Tel. 648 from Bern to Caserta, Apr. 9, 1945, Entry 110, Box 2). On Apr. 11, Gen. Lemnitzer, Deputy Commander of Allied Forces in MEDTO at Caserta (AFHQ), warned Dulles not to give Wolff anything in writing. Lemnitzer and Gen. Airey, AFHQ intelligence chief, were highly suspicious that the whole gambit was simply an effort by Himmler to divide the Western Allies from the Soviets (Tel. 626(9) from Caserta to Bern, Entry 110, Box 2).

Meanwhile, inter-Allied rancor over Sunrise at the highest level continued unabated. On Apr. 7, Stalin wrote Roosevelt denying that he had ever questioned the honesty and dependability of the President and Prime Minister Churchill, but renewing the outrageous charge that the negotiations in Switzerland were related to alleged German nonresistance in the West and ferocious resistance in the East. The tone of the letter was insulting and hostile. Stalin addressed similar communications to Churchill during this period (*FRUS, 1945*, 3:749–53). Roosevelt sought to let the issue cool down, as it appeared that disarray on the German side would preclude the consummation of surrender negotiations. He cabled Churchill as follows on Apr. 11 as follows: "I would minimize the general Soviet problem as much as possible because these problems, in one form or another, seem to arise every day and most of them straighten out as in the case of the Bern meeting. We must be firm, however, and our course thus far is correct" (FDR Library, Map Room Files, Box 23). The President died the next day at Warm Springs, Georgia. The last message he sent abroad was to Stalin and read as follows: "Thank you for your frank explanation of the Soviet point of view of the Bern incident which now appears to have faded into the past without having accomplished any useful purpose. There must not, in any event, be mutual distrust and minor misunderstandings of this character should not arise in the future. I feel sure that when our armies make contact in Germany and join in a fully coordinated offensive the Nazi Armies will disintegrate" (*FRUS, 1945*, 3:756).

Doc. 5-92, Tel. 6689, Apr. 11, 1945, Entry 110, Box 2. Point 4 of Tel. 662(9), Apr. 10, indicated that Gaevernitz was willing to take the risk of going to German headquarters in Fasano to help Wolff win over von Vietinghoff (Entry 110, Box 2). Gaevernitz was deeply involved in various phases of the talks in Switzerland and later at Caserta, but did not go behind enemy lines to Fasano.

Doc. 5-93, Trans. no. 292, Apr. 11, 1945, Entry 160, Box 1.

Doc. 5-94, Tel. 6719, Apr. 12, 1945, Entry 110, Box 2. Regarding Tel. 626(9), see the note to Doc. 5-91. British Gen. Airey, head of AFHQ intelligence ("McNeely" who had visited Dulles in Switzerland) was skeptical of German intentions. On Apr. 14, he cabled the view that the Germans "intend to consider surrender only when rest of Germany has disintegrated and therefore safe for them to do so. Meanwhile they intend fighting withdrawal to Adige, if necessary. Critic hopes to have it both ways in that meanwhile he and other Crossword personalities feel they are insuring themselves and helping general German policy of arousing Russian suspicion of Anglo-American intentions" (Tel. 640(9) from Caserta to Bern, Entry 139, Box 60).

Doc. 5-95, Tel. 8567, Apr. 12, 1945, Box 162.

Doc. 5-96, Tel. 8577, Apr. 12, 1945, Box 193.

Doc. 5-97, Tel. 6859, Apr. 13, 1945, Entry 110, Box 2.

Doc. 5-98, Tel. 8619, Apr. 13, 1945, Entry 110, Box 2. Tel. 875(9) to Paris, Apr. 7, is printed here as Doc. 5-89. Gen. Alexander von Loehr was German commander in the Balkans. Tel. 710(7) from London to Bern, Apr. 7, urged caution in dealing with Hoettl, who was deemed an extremist. It was probable that Himmler was using both Kaltenbrunner and Hoettl to embroil the Western Allies in negotiations that would become known (Entry 110, Box 2).

Doc. 5-99, Tel. 8717, Apr. 14, 1945, Box 193.

Doc. 5-100, Tel. 8787, Apr. 17, 1945, Box 232. Father Jozef Tiso was President of the Slovak Republic, a Nazi satellite regime. He was executed for war crimes in 1947.

Doc. 5-101, Tel. 710, Apr. 18, 1945, Entry 139, Box 60. In Tel. 633(9) from Caserta to Bern, Apr. 13, Gen. Lemnitzer indicated to Dulles that sending Gaevernitz to German headquarters at Fasano was too risky, but that his offer to go showed great initiative and courage (Entry 139, Box 60).

On Apr. 13, Himmler ordered Gen. Wolff to Berlin. When they met on the 18th, the SS chief ordered Wolff to remain in Italy after his return and to cease contacts with the Allies. Wolff headed back to Italy the same day (Tel. 711 from Bern to Caserta, Apr. 18, 1945, Entry 110, Box 2).

Replying to Dulles in Tel. 667 from Caserta, Apr. 18, Lemnitzer stated that efforts should be continued to bring about the quickest possible unconditional surrender of German forces in Italy by maintaining contacts with Vietinghoff and Wolff (Entry 90, Box 7).

Doc. 5-102, Tel. 8887, Apr. 18, 1945, Box 193.

Doc. 5-103, Tel. 22949, Apr. 18, 1945, Entry 90, Box 6. Col. Walter Rauff was SS Chief Inspector in Italy. Gen. Max Ritter von Pohl was commander of the German Air Force in Italy. "Walter" refers to Vaclav Hradecky, the Allied radio operator communicating between SS headquarters and AFHQ in Caserta.

Also on Apr. 18, OSS Bern reported to Paris and Caserta that Guido Zimmer, an SS counterespionage officer known by Parilli, had come to Lugano with a letter from Wolff to Dulles that expressed regret at the death of President Roosevelt on April 12 and reiterated Wolff's determination to go through with plans for a German surrender in Italy (Tel. 9339 from Bern to Paris, Entry 190, Box 6).

Meanwhile, Donovan in London instructed OSS Headquarters to prepare a memorandum for President Truman summarizing Bern messages that provided background on the state of the Sunrise talks (Tel. 22919 from London, Apr. 18, 1945, Entry 190, Box 6).

Doc. 5-104, Trans. no. 293, Apr. 18, 1945, Entry 160, Box 1.

Doc. 5-105, Tel. 8927, Apr. 19, 1945, Box 193. On Apr. 12, OSS Bern had reported that according to Swiss intelligence, the Germans were preparing to blow up the Italian end of the Simplon Tunnel between Italy and Switzerland (Tel. 8597 from Bern, Box 193).

Doc. 5-106, Tel. 9067, Apr. 20, 1945, Box 193.

Doc. 5-107, Tel. 9099, Apr. 21, 1945, Box 193. In *The Secret Front*, his memoirs, Hoettl claims that the Germans focused their contacts with Dulles on the redoubt issue with the hope of extracting concessions in exchange for eliminating the possibility of a last battle in the Alps (281ff.).

Doc. 5-108, Tel. 9119, Apr. 21, 1945, Entry 90, Box 7. Tel. 5429 to Bern and London, Apr. 20, reads as follows: "106 and Cheston to 109 and 110 only. 1. By letter today JCS directs that OSS break off all contact with German emissaries at once. 110 is therefore instructed to discontinue immediately all such contacts. 2. Letter also states CCS have approved message to SACMED stating that it is clear from NAF 916 (apparently message from SACMED) German COMINCH Italy does not intend to surrender his forces at this time on acceptable terms. Message continues: Accordingly, especially in view of complications which have arisen with Russians, the US and British governments have decided OSS should break off contacts; that JCS are so instructing OSS; that whole matter is to be regarded as closed and that Russians be informed through Archer and Deane" (Entry 190, Box 6). Gen. John R. Deane and Adm. Ernest R. Archer were, respectively, heads of the U.S. and British military missions in Moscow.

The Anglo-American decision to break off the Sunrise contacts apparently was the result of a British initiative. The British Embassy had delivered an aide-mémoire to the Department of State on Apr. 14 urging that in view of AFHQ's pessimistic estimate of the chances of success and Soviet sensibilities, the discussions with the Germans regarding a surrender in Italy should be curtailed (*FRUS, 1945*, 3:757–58) In his memoirs, President Truman recalls that the talks were dropped at Churchill's urging (Harry S. Truman, *Year of Decisions* [New York: Doubleday, 1958], 200–201). British documents cited by Smith and Agarossi, *Operation Sunrise* (130–31), support his account.

Gen. Lemnitzer repeated the JCS instructions in a cable to Dulles from AFHQ on April 21. He added the following: "For my part I hope that the vast expenditure of effort on this project will one day bear fruit and hasten the surrender of German forces in North Italy which must inevitably take place. If the effort so expended results in saving a single Allied life it will not have been in vain. . . . It was a privilege and a pleasure to have worked with you and your associates. I shall always cherish the memory of the three most interesting and pleasant weeks spent with you all" (Tel. 681 from Caserta to Bern, Entry 139, Box 60).

Dulles also acknowledged receipt of the instructions to break off contacts in Tel. 9109 to Washington, Apr. 21. In that message, he repeated the texts of Tel. 710 to Caserta, Apr. 18 (Doc. 5-101) and Tel. 667 from Caserta, Apr. 18 (See note to Doc. 5-101) to establish that he had not been acting without high military support. The message also contained the following significant expression of his views on inter-Allied matters: "It seems obvious and from their viewpoint natural that the Russians should do everything possible to block realization of Crossword. Its success would mean that our forces Italy would probably be first to occupy Trieste, which from various indications received here now constitutes an even more important objective for Russians than Berlin. If Crossword, or something like it, fails and Germans retreat fighting to the Adige Line, then in all probability Russians will reach Trieste ahead of us. In my opinion, this largely explains Russians' susceptibility re Crossword about which I obtained additional information in Paris. While I realize we will deal openly and fairly with our Russian allies, this should not preclude us from doing everything possible to bring about quick surrender which would save the lives of our troops and bring us into the heart of German reduit." Dulles closed Tel. 9109 as follows: "This message not repeated 109 [who was in Europe]. View high regard I have for Lemnitzer and his attitude of complete cooperation, please do not use in any way which could embarrass him" (Entry 90, Box 7).

The acting OSS Director sent the following to Dulles on Apr. 22: "Many thanks for your #9109 and 9119. You must be fully aware of our admiration for the way you have handled Sunrise matter. Appreciate your problems, but as you say, orders are orders. You should know that no criticism on part JCS the way you have handled negotiations, but protest from one of our Allies for not being brought into the negotiations in the beginning brought about the decision. I know that you will meet the problems in such a way as to fully comply with the JCS directive to us" (Tel. 5529, Entry 90, Box 6).

Doc. 5-109, Tel. 7419, Apr. 22, 1945, Entry 90, Box 7. "Point A" refers to the portion of Caserta's 681, Apr. 21, instructing Dulles to break off contacts with the Germans.

Doc. 5-110, Tel. 9209, Apr. 23, 1945, Entry 90, Box 6. Tel. 7419, Apr. 22, is printed here as Doc. 5-109. Acting OSS Director Cheston responded to Dulles as follows on Apr. 23: "Action suggested in par. 3 your #9209 might be construed as continuation of Sunrise negotiations and should not be pursued. We assume your reference to Swiss intermediaries relates to the past and not to any continuing relationship on this question, but it is important that you confirm this assumption. If, however, . . . the Swiss are acting completely on their own and not as your intermediaries, any approaches by Sunrise personalities to Swiss is a Swiss affair. Information coming to you from Swiss, acting wholly in their own interests, and without instigation by you, direct or indirect, should properly be transmitted" (Tel. 5549, Entry 90, Box 6). Gen. Lemnitzer added the following from Caserta on the 23rd: "Instructions from CCS to break off contact with Critic are quite clear and you should continue strict compliance with them. . . . SACMED is sending message to CCS recommending that you be authorized to contact German officers who appear as parliamentaires in Switzerland if these officers appear to be genuine and have documentary evidence proving that they have full powers to act in effecting the capitulation of German forces in North Italy" (Tel. 691 from Caserta to Bern, Entry 139, Box 60). The next day, Lemnitzer suggested the Swiss intermediaries stall for time with the German emissaries until the CCS could give permission for Dulles to lift the restrictions on Dulles's contacts with them. The SACMED deputy added that Allied forces had decisively defeated German forces south of the Po and the end was near (Tel. 698 from Caserta to Bern, Apr. 24, 1945, Entry 139, Box 60).

On Apr. 24, Donovan cabled the following to Dulles from London: "I rely on your discretion and judgment and I am fully aware that you would permit no dangling strings to remain in your contacts. However, in your own interests it must never be said by your superior officers that you continued a contact after you were ordered to cut it. Since higher command has taken responsibility it is our duty to conform in the strictest manner" (Entry 190, Box 6).

Doc. 5-111, Tel. 7569, Apr. 24, 1945, Entry 90, Box 6. In English, Schweinitz's delegated powers were as follows: "Lieutenant Colonel in the General Staff von Schweinitz has been authorized by me to conduct negotiations within the frame of the instructions given by me and to make binding commitments on my behalf. v. Vietinghoff."

Doc. 5-112, Tel. 7589, Apr. 24, 1945, Entry 90, Box 6.

Doc. 5-113, Tel. 767, Apr. 25, 1945, Entry 110, Box 2.

Doc. 5-114, Tel. 10137, Apr. 25, 1945, Box 232.

Doc. 5-115, Tel. 9389, Apr. 26, 1945, Entry 90, Box 6.

Doc. 5-116, Tel. 9399, Apr. 26, 1945, Entry 90, Box 7.

Doc. 5-117, Trans. no. 294, Apr. 26, 1945, Entry 160, Box 1. Dulles had cabled the following to Headquarters on Apr. 19: "Under present conditions, with more frequent absences from Bern inevitable as well as probable early departure for Germany, I believe we should plan to terminate flash arrangement at end of month or whenever our contract permits" (Tel. 8937, Box 193).

Doc. 5-118, Tel. 9419, Apr. 27, 1945, Entry 90, Box 6. Saturday was Apr. 29. Tel. 5589 from Donovan in Washington to Dulles in Bern, Apr. 26, read as follows: "About an hour ago JCS dispatched cable to SACMED directing him to instruct us to inform P that arrangements will be made for Critic and his companion to go to AFHQ immediately.

"We were called in to insure there would be no conference or discussion in Suisse. Critic and companion must go AFHQ at once or deal is off. Russians have been told fact that this is done on request of Germany, and SACMED has been instructed to invite a Russian representative to meeting.

This is to inform you of situation so you can be ready when message comes. You understand we must carry out these instructions literally. Best of luck to you and keep us advised" (Entry 90, Box 6).

On Apr. 28, Lemnitzer at AFHQ informed Dulles that the German official party had reached Caserta and conferences were about to begin (Tel. 722 from Caserta, Entry 129, Box 60).

Doc. 5-119, Tel. 9497, Apr. 29, 1945, Box 193.

Doc. 5-120, Tel. 7937, Apr. 29, 1945, Box 232. Capt. William Suhling was a ranking officer at the OSS Siena station.

Doc. 5-121, Tel. 9519, Apr. 29, 1945, Entry 90, Box 7. Gen. Lothar Rendulic was the new commander of German forces defending Austria.

Doc. 5-122, Tel. 9537, Apr. 30, 1945, Box 193. Number 399 was Van Arkel. Philip Horton was an OSS officer serving in Paris. In 1947, he became CIA station chief. "Lamber" may be Robert Lambert, a French-born OSS officer. Karl Renner, leader of the Austrian Social Democratic Party became the first postwar President of Austria. Anton Linder and Ludwig Klein were Austrian Social Democrats in exile in Switzerland. Dr. Kurt Grimm, an Austrian living in Zurich, was a conduit between OSS Bern and his homeland for much of the war. Fritz Molden ("Weiser") was Dulles's chief Austrian contact in 1945.

Doc. 5-123, Tel. 9569, Apr. 30, 1945, Entry 90, Box 7. Number 496 was Maurice Villars. The famous German aircraft designer Willy Messerschmitt fell into the hands of the Western allies. By the 1950s, his company was again in production.

On May 7, Brindlinger, a former Messerschmitt test pilot, reported through Tracy Barnes of OSS Bern that the Germans had sold Japan plans for an advanced aircraft. The plans and technical experts purportedly left by submarine in mid-March (Tel. 9837, Box 193).

Doc. 5-124, Tel. 9649, May 1, 1945, Entry 90, Box 6. The surrender was signed by the German emissaries in Caserta on April 29, but it was not put into effect until May 2 due to the time taken by the emissaries' return trip to German headquarters at Bolzano via Switzerland, and by intense bickering and intrigue among the top German generals. Dulles describes the final events in *The Secret Surrender*, 219ff. On May 2, Donovan cabled Dulles: "Congratulations on the fine work you have done. The surrender means the saving of many American lives. Please send me a comprehensive report" (Tel. 5747, Entry 88, Box 590). OSS Deputy Director Magruder added the following: "Countless thousands of parents would bless you were they privileged to know what you have done. As one of them privileged to know, and with a boy in the mountain division, I do bless. Heartiest congratulations to you and your staff." (Tel. 5757, May 3, 1945, Entry 90, Box 6). Dulles also received telegraphic congratulations from Lemnitzer (May 2) and Glavin (May 3) (Entry 139, Box 60).

Doc. 5-125, Tel. 9717, May 2, 1945, Box 232. Number 441 was Maj. Valla Lada Mocarski.

Doc. 5-126, Tel. 8237, May 3, 1945, Box 232. Howard Chapin was a ranking OSS officer charged with Central European affairs. Among those mentioned are Adolf Scharf, Theodor Koerner, Johann Koplenig, Robert Fischer, and Julius Raab (Chancellor of Austria in the 1950s).

Tel. 9747, a continuation of Tel. 8237, read as follows: "Add Grimm comments: Geroe thoroughly reliable, is former Staatsanwalt whose opposition to Nazis exiled him to Hungary and Yugoslavia. Zimmerman independent, is honest former finance minister who may be short on international affairs but this is offset by unusual technical abilities. Horner is Vienna communist who as interior minister controls police, believed never in Moscow" (May 3, 1945, Box 193).

The official U.S. Government attitude toward the provisional government was set forth in a memorandum from the Department of State to the British Embassy on Apr. 20, 1945, which read in part as follows: "While the Department of State does not, at least at this stage, regard the evidence as conclusive regarding either the character or the existence of POEN, or wish to take any steps to assist in the development of POEN, or to aid the activities or movements of other Austrian individuals or groups, it does consider that it would be desirable to refrain from placing any obstacles in the way of the development of such a resistance organization by the Austrians themselves" (*FRUS, 1945*, 3:564–65).

Doc. 5-127, Tel. 9769, May 3, 1945, Entry 90, Box 7. On May 7, Wally cabled Dulles that Gen. Wolff requested a German-English grammar for beginners, cigarettes, Chanel toilet water, and books including "The Story of a Gentleman" (Tel. 54, Entry 139, Box 60). By the end of the month, Wolff was under arrest and listed as a war criminal. He was held in custody for four years as a witness at war crimes trials, but was never tried himself by the Nuremberg tribunal. However, in 1964, a German court sentenced him to 15 years for complicity in Nazi criminality.

Doc. 5-128, Tel. 15389 from Paris, May 6, 1945, Entry 90, Box 7.

Doc. 5-129, Tel. 9857, May 8, 1945, Box 232. Robert P. Joyce was an important figure in the transition from OSS to CIA and in integrating intelligence operations into national policy. A career foreign service officer, Joyce joined OSS and became Gen. Donovan's political officer at Caserta late in the war. He succeeded Dulles as head of OSS Bern in July 1945. He rejoined State in 1948 and became liaison between the Policy Planning Staff of George Kennan and CIA's first political action unit, the Office of Policy Coordination. Frank G. Wisner had a similar role, performing covert operations for OSS in Turkey and Rumania. He served in Germany for OSS and its successor, the Strategic Services Unit in 1945–46. In 1948, he transferred to CIA to head OPC, and later the Directorate of Plans. Gen. Lucius D. Clay became deputy military governor of Germany from 1945 to 1947 and later commander of U.S. Forces in Europe. Gen. Frank J. McSherry was Deputy Assistant Chief of Staff, Civil Affairs, at SHAEF. Henry Hyde, an OSS officer who dealt with French matters for most of the war, was assigned to Bern in 1945.

Dulles's report "Sunrise—Crossword Operation, Feb. 25–May 2, 1945," written with Gero von Gaevernitz and dated Bern, May 22, 1945, is filed in Entry 110, Box 2, and provided the basis for his *Secret Surrender*, published in 1966.

According to Thomas Powers in *The Man Who Kept the Secrets: Richard Helms and the CIA* (New York: Knopf, 1979), VE-Day found Dulles at Allied headquarters at Rheims in the company of Helms and Gen. Walter Bedell Smith, Gen. Eisenhower's Chief of Staff. All three eventually held the position of Director of Central Intelligence.

Epilogue

Cable traffic and other documentation relating to Dulles's activities in Switzerland and Germany from May to Oct. 1945 is in Entry 88, Boxes 151–152; Entry 90, Boxes 2–7; Entry 108, Boxes 8 and 11; Entry 134, Boxes 193 and 232; and Entry 139, Box 60. A set of Bern mission monthly reports for May–Sept. 1945 is in Entry 99, Boxes 7 and 8. Boxes 21 and 167 of the Allen Dulles Papers at Princeton contain key material on Japanese peace feelers through Switzerland.

Selected Bibliography

Archival Sources

OSS Operational Archives: Record Group (RG) 226, National Archives, Washington, D.C. [The primary source for documents in this volume, this collection totals over 3,000 cubic feet of records, most of which were declassified and opened to the public in the 1980s.]

Entries 1–86. Records of the Research and Analysis Branch. Reports comprise hundreds of feet of space and are accessible only through a card index.

Entry 88. Cable files. Includes Bern material.

Entry 90. Includes cables on Operation Sunrise.

Entry 99. OSS History Office Files. Material on Bern operations, Breakers, resistance groups.

Entry 106. Includes material on the New York office.

Entry 108. Includes reports sent from Bern by pouch after the border was opened in 1944.

Entry 110. Contains important files on Operation Sunrise.

Entry 115. London Field Files. Documentation on Germany and other subjects of concern to OSS Bern.

Entry 121. Includes material on the George Wood operation.

Entry 125. Includes Bern field files—raw agent reports.

Entry 134. Cable files. Basic source for Allen Dulles messages from Bern. Confusing organization, overlapping sets, but the mother lode on operations at Bern and other OSS posts.

Entry 138. Washington X-2 Records. Includes George Wood and Breakers documentation.

Entry 139. Washington / Field Station Files. Contains Caserta records relating to Operation Sunrise.

Entry 160. New York Office records. Set of Dulles radiotelephone "flash" transmissions.

Entry 162. Donovan records. Includes chronological files of items sent to other agencies.

Entry 180. William J. Donovan Microfilm (193 rolls). Copied by Donovan upon his departure from OSS. Obtained by Anthony Cave Brown from Donovan's law firm in the late 1970s and used by him in his books, listed below. Ultimately retrieved by the CIA, subjected to security review, and provided to the National Archives and the U.S. Army Military History Institute, Carlisle Barracks, Pa. Largely duplicated in other parts of RG 226.

Entry 190. Director's records and field files. Considerable Bern-related material, including reports from France and Italy and local contacts.

OSS Washington Director's Office Records (Microfilm: M1642, 132 rolls). Contains many documents relating to Bern and Dulles.

Franklin D. Roosevelt Library, Hyde Park, New York.

Map Room Files. Contains copies of numerous messages from Dulles transmitted to the White House by OSS.

President's Secretary's Files. Contains OSS documents sent by General Donovan to the President, including Dulles reports.

Naval Aide Files.

Allen Dulles Papers, Seeley G. Mudd Manuscript Library, Princeton University, Princeton, New Jersey.

Consists of 264 boxes, especially strong on pre–World War II background, private correspondence, and his own publications. Few official documents or firsthand information on the Bern period.

Department of State Records, National Archives, Washington, D.C.

Decimal files, RG 59. Contains some OSS and Dulles-related documents scattered through European War (EW) files.

Post files, RG 84, Suitland, Maryland. Bern, Geneva, Basel, Lugano, and Zurich collections contain pertinent material.

Military Attaché Records, RG 319, Entries 47 and 57. Washington National Records Center, Suitland, Maryland.

Contains messages received by the War Department from Bern; rather thin for 1943–44.

William J. Donovan Papers, U.S. Army Military History Institute, Carlisle Barracks, Pa.

Contains considerable material of interest, including sets of the Donovan microfilm mentioned above and the "Boston Series," subject reports based on the documents provided Dulles by Fritz Kolbe.

Leland Harrison Papers, Library of Congress.

Harrison was U.S. wartime Minister to Switzerland; some items pertain to Dulles.

Central Intelligence Agency, Freedom of Information Act.

Documents received by the author from the CIA between 1989 and 1993 under FOIA. Mainly documents that had been withheld when the OSS records were first reviewed for declassification. Cited as CIA/FOIA.

Interviews

John A. Bross, July 23, 1989. Former intelligence officer; served with OSS in London.

Ray S. Cline, January 13, 1989. Former intelligence officer with OSS, CIA, and the State Department; helped to process incoming messages from Bern during World War II; a top aide to Dulles at CIA.

George C. Constantinides, January 16, 1989. Intelligence bibliographer, former intelligence officer.

Robert T. Crowley, May 31, 1989. Former military, naval, and CIA intelligence officer.

Eleanor Lansing Dulles, July 13 and 18, 1989. Sister of Allen Dulles, expert on Germany, former State Department official.

Amb. Richard M. Helms, July 1991 (brief conversation). Former director of central intelligence; in OSS, helped process incoming Bern cables in Washington.

Edward J. Lawler, July 1991 (lunch). As an OSS X-2 officer in London, saw George Wood, Breakers, and Sunrise material.

William D. McNeely, July 1991 (lunch). OSS radio operator in Italy and Annemasse base. British General Airey used his name for cover in Operation Sunrise.

Amb. William Tyler, October 16, 1989. Son of Royall Tyler, aide to Dulles at Bern.

U.S. military intelligence officer in Bern during the war who does not want to be identified, October 27, 1989.

Former OSS and CIA counterintelligence officer who does not want to be identified, May 23, 1990.

Books: Memoirs

Bancroft, Mary. *Autobiography of a Spy.* New York: Morrow, 1983. An American married to a Swiss; performed minor tasks for the OSS in Switzerland and claims to have had a personal as well as professional relationship with Dulles.

Casey, William J. *The Secret War Against Hitler.* Washington, D.C.: Regnery Gateway, 1988. Head of OSS efforts in London to introduce agents into Nazi Germany; some information on efforts based in Switzerland.

Corvo, Max. *The OSS in Italy, 1942–1945.* New York: Praeger, 1990. An OSS officer in Italy; had some contact with Dulles operations in Switzerland and was not favorably impressed.

Dollmann, Eugen. *Call Me Coward.* London: Kimber, 1956. Sardonic recollections of an SS staff officer involved in Operation Sunrise.

Duke, Florimond, with Charles Swaart. *Name, Rank, and Serial Number.* New York: Meredith Press, 1969. An account of the Sparrow mission to Hungary by the team chief.

Dulles, Allen W. *The Craft of Intelligence.* New York: Harper & Row, 1963. References to Dulles experiences in World War II.

———. *Germany's Underground.* New York: Macmillan, 1947. A favorable account of the German resistance to Hitler; some references to Dulles's personal experiences.

———. *The Secret Surrender.* New York: Harper & Row, 1966. A detailed account of Dulles's negotiations leading to the surrender of German forces in Italy; stands up well against the original OSS records. Provides information on other aspects of Dulles's service in Bern.

Dulles, Eleanor Lansing. *Chances of a Lifetime: A Memoir.* Englewood Cliffs, N.J.: Prentice-Hall, 1980. Dulles's sister provides useful information on family history and her brother's early life.

Frenay, Henri. *The Night Will End.* Translated by Dan Hofstadter. New York: McGraw-Hill, 1976. Wartime memoirs of a French resistance leader who cooperated closely with the OSS in Switzerland.

Gisevius, Hans Bernd. *To the Bitter End.* London: Jonathan Cape, 1948. An account of the German resistance by a major participant and Dulles's most important link to the movement.

Guillain de Benouville, Pierre. *The Unknown Warriors: A Personal Account of the French Resistance.* Introduction by Allen Dulles. New York: Simon & Schuster, 1949. Recollections of a French resistance leader who had close ties to Dulles.

Hoettl, Wilhelm. *The Secret Front: The Story of Nazi Political Espionage.* New York: Praeger, 1954. The self-serving memoirs of a Nazi intelligence officer who sought to deal with the OSS in 1945.

Kallay, Nicholas. *Hungarian Premier: A Personal Account of a Nation's Struggle in the Second World War.* New York: Columbia University Press, 1954. Useful information on Hungarian policy and politics by a leader with whom the OSS was in contact.

Lankford, Nelson D., ed. *OSS Against the Reich: The World War II Diaries of Colonel David K. E. Bruce.* Kent, Ohio: Kent State University Press, 1991. Head of the OSS office in London; thin on substance.

Legendre, Gertrude Sanford. *The Time of My Life.* Charleston, S.C.: Wyrick, 1987. The author, who served with the OSS in France, describes her capture and imprisonment by the Germans and her escape through Switzerland, where she met Dulles.

Lovell, Stanley P. *Of Spies and Stratagems*. Englewood Cliffs, N.J.: Prentice-Hall, 1963. Colorful and partially fanciful memoirs of the OSS Research and Development Branch chief.

Molden, Fritz. *Exploding Star: A Young Austrian Against Hitler*. London: Weidenfeld & Nicolson, 1978. An account of an Austrian resistance figure who cooperated with Dulles and later became his son-in-law.

———. *Fires in the Night: The Sacrifices and Significance of the Austrian Resistance, 1938–1945*. Boulder, Colo.: Westview, 1989. Augments Molden's previous book.

Philby, Kim. *My Silent War*. New York: Grove Press, 1968. The Soviet master spy's unreliable account includes coverage of World War II and some matters relating to OSS operations in Switzerland.

Rochester, Devereaux. *Full Moon to France*. New York: Harper & Row, 1977. Memoirs of an American refugee who encountered Dulles in Switzerland.

Schellenberg, Walter. *The Labyrinth: Memoirs of Walter Schellenberg*. New York: Harper, 1956. Suspect account by the head of SS intelligence late in the war.

Schlabrendorff, Fabian von. *They Almost Killed Hitler*. Edited by Gero von Gaevernitz. New York: Macmillan, 1947.

Troy, Thomas F., ed. *Wartime Washington: The Secret OSS Journal of James Grafton Rogers, 1942–1943*. Frederick, Md.: University Publications of America, 1987. Head of the OSS Planning Group.

Visser 't Hooft, W. A. *Memoirs*. London: SCM Press, 1973. Recollections of a Dutch international church leader resident in Switzerland during the war.

Wiskemann, Elizabeth. *The Europe I Saw*. London: Collins, 1968. Recollections of a British scholar who served in Switzerland with the Political Warfare Executive.

Books: Secondary Sources

Armstrong, Anne. *Unconditional Surrender: The Impact of the Casablanca Policy upon World War II*. New Brunswick, N.J.: Rutgers University Press, 1961.

Baudot, Marcel, et al., eds. *The Historical Encyclopedia of World War II*. New York: Facts on File, 1989.

Calvi, Fabrizio. *OSS: La Guerre Secrète en France, 1942–1945*. Paris: Hachette, 1990. Important coverage of the links between OSS Bern and the French resistance.

Cave Brown, Anthony. *Bodyguard of Lies*. New York: Harper & Row, 1975.

———. *"C": The Secret Life of Sir Stewart Graham Menzies, Spymaster to Winston Churchill*. New York: Macmillan, 1987.

———. *The Last Hero: Wild Bill Donovan*. New York: Times Books, 1982. Based in part on special access to Donovan's private and official papers provided by his law firm after his death. Valuable information on Dulles as well as on Donovan and the OSS, but as with all three Cave Brown books, to be used with caution.

Chalou, George C., ed. *The Secrets War: The Office of Strategic Services in World War II*. Washington, D.C.: National Archives and Records Administration, 1992. Collected lectures delivered by twenty-four experts at a 1991 conference.

Constantinides, George C. *Intelligence and Espionage: An Analytical Bibliography*. Boulder, Colo.: Westview, 1983. Includes thoughtful, accurate reviews of numerous books pertinent to intelligence in World War II.

Deakin, F. W. *The Brutal Friendship: Mussolini, Hitler, and the Fall of Italian Fascism*. New York: Harper & Row, 1962. A meticulous scholarly account of German-Italian relations from 1942 to 1945.

Dippel, John V. H. *Two Against Hitler: Stealing the Nazis' Best-Kept Secrets*. New York: Praeger,

1992. Describes the contact between Erwin Respondek, a German opponent of Hitler, and Sam Woods, the U.S. consul general in Zurich, which proved to be an important source of intelligence.

Edwards, Bob, and Kenneth Dunne. *Study of a Master Spy*. London: Housmans, 1961. A critical account of Dulles's wartime record, claiming that he collaborated with the Nazis; believed by many experts to have been Soviet-inspired.

Foot, M.R.D. *SOE in France: An Account of the Work of the British Special Operations Executive in France, 1940–1944*. Frederick, Md.: University Publications of America, 1986. Reprint of a 1966 British official history. An essential study of the SOE and the French resistance, but offering minimal coverage of the OSS role.

Ford, Kirk, Jr. *OSS and the Yugoslav Resistance, 1943–1945*. College Station: Texas A&M University Press, 1992. Treatment of various OSS missions to Yugoslavia, based largely on the records in RG 226.

Gallin, Mother Mary Alice. *The Ethical and Religious Factors in the German Resistance to Hitler*. Washington, D.C.: Catholic University of America, 1955. Treatment of Fritz Kolbe / George Wood.

Garlinski, Jozef. *The Swiss Corridor: Espionage Networks in Switzerland During World War II*. London: Dent, 1981.

Groueff, Stephane. *Crown of Thorns*. Lanham, Md.: Madison Books, 1987. Treats the reign of King Boris III of Bulgaria, 1918–43. Good coverage of wartime political situation.

Heideking, Jürgen, and Christof Mauch, eds. *Geheimdienstkrieg gegen Deutschland: Subversion, Propaganda und politische Planungen des amerikanischen Geheimdienstes im Zweiten Weltkrieg*. Göttingen: Vandenhoeck & Ruprecht, 1993. Important articles on various aspects of OSS operations with respect to Germany. Based on OSS records and other documentary sources.

Hersh, Burton. *The Old Boys: The American Elite and the Origins of the CIA*. New York: Scribners, 1992. Unsympathetic and not entirely reliable coverage of Dulles operations in Bern. Brings together secondary accounts, especially Mosley and Cave Brown, augmented by some original research and interviews.

Hoffmann, Peter. *The History of the German Resistance*. Cambridge, Mass.: MIT Press, 1977. The best and most complete scholarly account of German opposition to Hitler.

Hymoff, Edward. *The OSS in World War II*. New York: Richardson & Steirman, 1986.

Kahn, David. *The Codebreakers: The Story of Secret Writing*. London: Weidenfeld & Nicolson, 1967. Offers still-valuable treatment of World War II codebreaking, including limited coverage of Dulles's code security problems.

———. *Hitler's Spies: German Military Intelligence in World War II*. New York: Macmillan, 1978. The best account of the subject, but contains limited information on OSS operations in Switzerland.

Kaufman, Louis, Barbara Fitzgerald, and Tom Sewell. *Moe Berg: Athlete, Scholar, Spy*. Boston: Little, Brown, 1974. Includes treatment of Berg's atomic energy intelligence work in Switzerland; the limited available OSS records on the subject supply some substantiation.

Kimche, Jon. *Spying for Peace: General Guisan and Swiss Neutrality*. New York: Roy Publishers, 1961.

Laqueur, Walter. *The Terrible Secret*. London: Weidenfeld & Nicolson, 1980. Discusses what Allied intelligence knew about the Holocaust.

Laqueur, Walter, and Richard Breitman. *Breaking the Silence*. New York: Simon & Schuster, 1986. The story of Eduard Schulte, a German industrialist who provided early information on the Holocaust and cooperated with Dulles in Switzerland.

Lewis, Flora. *Red Pawn: The Story of Noel Field*. Garden City, N.Y.: Doubleday, 1965. An excellent account of the ambiguous career of a practitioner of humanitarian assistance and Soviet espionage. In Switzerland, he was a close collaborator with Dulles on relief matters and apparently his liaison with the far left.

Lisagor, Nancy, and Frank Lipsius. *A Law unto Itself: The Untold Story of the Law Firm of Sullivan and Cromwell.* New York: Morrow, 1988. Important coverage of Dulles's career between the wars and his use of his law firm's European network while at Bern.

MacDonogh, Giles. *A Good German: Adam von Trott zu Solz.* Woodstock, N.Y.: Overlook Press, 1992. Coverage of this disaffected German diplomat/intellectual's contacts with Allied intelligence in Switzerland and elsewhere.

Miller, James Edward. *The United States and Italy, 1940–1950: The Politics and Diplomacy of Stabilization.* Chapel Hill: University of North Carolina Press, 1986. Important source on U.S. policy toward Italy and Italian domestic politics.

Minott, Rodney G. *The Fortress That Never Was: The Myth of Hitler's Bavarian Stronghold.* New York: Holt, Rinehart & Winston, 1964. Remains a significant study of Allied intelligence on the elusive "National Redoubt."

Mosley, Leonard. *Dulles: A Biography of Eleanor, Allen, and John Foster Dulles and Their Family Network.* New York: Dial/Wade, 1978. Considerable information on Dulles family history and OSS Bern, but sometimes inaccurate.

O'Toole, G. J. A. *The Encyclopedia of American Intelligence and Espionage.* New York: Facts on File, 1988.

Persico, Joseph E. *Casey: From OSS to the CIA.* New York: Viking, 1990.

———. *Piercing the Reich: The Penetration of Nazi Germany by American Secret Agents During World War II.* New York: Viking, 1979. Includes useful information on penetration efforts from Switzerland.

Powers, Thomas. *Heisenberg's War: The Secret History of the German Bomb.* New York: Knopf, 1993. A meticulous account of Allied intelligence on German nuclear activities, including the role of OSS and other agents in Switzerland.

Read, Anthony, and David Fisher. *Colonel Z: The Secret Life of a Master of Spies.* New York: Viking, 1985. This book concerns the career of Colonel Claude Dansey of British SIS who had wartime responsibilities with respect to Switzerland.

Rubin, Barry. *Istanbul Intrigues.* New York: McGraw-Hill, 1989. The author describes international espionage in the Turkish capital during World War II, including matters of concern to Dulles.

Schoenbrun, David. *Soldiers of the Night: The Story of the French Resistance.* New York: Dutton, 1980. A comprehensive treatment.

Shirer, William L. *Rise and Fall of the Third Reich.* New York: Simon & Schuster, 1960.

Smith, Bradley. *The Shadow Warriors: OSS and the Origins of the CIA.* New York: Basic Books, 1983. A valuable account of the OSS, with significant coverage of Bern operations.

Smith, Bradley F., and Elena Agarossi. *Operation Sunrise: The Secret Surrender.* New York: Basic Books, 1979.

Smith, R. Harris. *OSS: The Secret History of America's First Central Intelligence Agency.* Berkeley and Los Angeles: University of California Press, 1972. An important early study that includes coverage of the Bern operations.

Smyth, Howard M. *Secrets of the Fascist Era: How Uncle Sam Obtained Some of the Top-Level Documents of Mussolini's Period.* Carbondale: Southern Illinois University Press, 1975. Contains coverage of Dulles and the Ciano diaries.

Troy, Thomas F. *Donovan and the CIA: A History of the Establishment of the Central Intelligence Agency.* Frederick, Md.: University Publications of America, 1981. Especially important as an administrative history.

Vernoff, Edward, and Rima Shore. *The International Dictionary of 20th Century Biography.* New York: NAL Books, 1987.

Wistrich, Robert. *Who's Who in Nazi Germany.* New York: Bonanza Books, 1982.

Articles

Boyd, Carl. "Significance of MAGIC and the Japanese Ambassador to Berlin." *Intelligence and National Security* 2:1 (1987), 150–69; 2:2 (1987), 302–19; 3:4 (1988), 83–102; 4:1 (1989), 86–107; and 4:3 (1989), 461–81. Analysis of intercepts of Japanese diplomatic traffic from Berlin, which covered subjects reported in the George Wood traffic and other Dulles sources.

Calvi, Fabrizio. "The OSS in France." In George C. Chalou, ed. *The Secrets War: The Office of Strategic Services in World War II*, 247–72. Washington, D.C.: National Archives and Records Service, 1992.

Glennon, John P. " 'This Time Germany Is a Defeated Nation': The Doctrine of Unconditional Surrender and Some Unsuccessful Attempts to Alter It, 1943–1944." In Gerald N. Grob, ed., *Statesmen and Statecraft of the Modern West: Essays in Honor of Dwight E. Lee and H. Donaldson Jordan*, 111–51. Barre, Mass.: Barre Publishers, 1967.

Hood, William. "Eduard Schulte's Story." *Foreign Intelligence Literary Scene* 6:1 (1987), 8–10. An anti-Nazi German industrialist and a source for OSS Bern.

"Der Mann, der den Krieg verkurzen wollte." *Die Zeit*, May 9, 1986. An account of Fritz Kolbe's espionage for the OSS.

Morgan, Edward P. "The Spy the Nazis Missed." *True*, July 1950. Also printed in Allen Dulles, *Great True Spy Stories* (New York: Harper & Row, 1968). The exploits of Fritz Kolbe / George Wood.

Petersen, Neal H. "From Hitler's Doorstep: Allen Dulles and the Penetration of Nazi Germany." In George C. Chalou, ed., *The Secrets War: The Office of Strategic Services in World War II*, 273–94. Washington, D.C.: National Archives and Records Service, 1992.

Quibble, Anthony. "Alias George Wood." *Studies in Intelligence* 10:1 (1966), 69–90. A now-declassified study in CIA's in-house scholarly journal.

Published Documents

Cave Brown, Anthony, ed. *The Secret War Report of the OSS*. New York: Berkeley, 1976. The official account with commentary by the editor.

Heideking, Jürgen, and Christof Mauch, eds. *USA und deutscher Widerstand: Analysen und Operationen des amerikanischen Geheimdienstes im Zweiten Weltkrieg*. Tübingen: Francke Verlag, 1993. An outstanding collection of documents from OSS records at the U.S. National Archives (RG 226) in German-language translation. The Heideking/Mauch volume includes some eighteen messages from Dulles, most of which are printed here in the original English.

Kimball, Warren F., ed. *Churchill and Roosevelt: The Complete Correspondence*. 3 vols. Princeton: Princeton University Press, 1984.

Roosevelt, Kermit. *The War Report of the OSS*. New York: Walker, 1976. Official published account of OSS activities in Washington.

———. *The Overseas Targets: War Report of the OSS*. Volume 2. New York: Walker, 1976. Contains coverage of Bern operations and other European activities in which Dulles played a part.

U.S. Department of State. *Foreign Relations of the United States [FRUS], 1942*. Volume 3: *Europe*. Washington, D.C.: GPO, 1961. U.S. concern regarding Swiss trade with Germany.

———. Foreign Relations of the United States: The Conferences at Washington, 1941–

1942, and Casablanca, 1943. Washington, D.C.: GPO, 1968. Unconditional surrender.

———. *Foreign Relations of the United States, 1943*. Volume 1: *General*. Washington, D.C.: GPO, 1963. Axis peace feelers.

———. *Foreign Relations of the United States, 1943*. Volume 2: *Europe*. Washington, D.C.: GPO, 1964. France, Italy, Portugal, Switzerland.

———. *Foreign Relations of the United States: The Conferences at Cairo and Tehran, 1943*. Washington, D.C.: GPO, 1961. Grand strategy, postwar settlements.

———. *Foreign Relations of the United States: The Conferences at Washington and Quebec, 1943*. Washington, D.C.: GPO, 1970. Peace feelers, European matters.

———. *Foreign Relations of the United States, 1944*. Volume 1: *General*. Washington, D.C.: GPO, 1966. German resistance, unconditional surrender, peace feelers.

———. *Foreign Relations of the United States, 1944*. Volume 3: *The British Commonwealth and Europe*. Washington, D.C.: GPO, 1965. Bulgaria, France, Hungary, Italy.

———. *Foreign Relations of the United States, 1944*. Volume 4: *Europe*. Washington, D.C.: GPO, 1966. Rumania, Switzerland, USSR, Yugoslavia.

———. *Foreign Relations of the United States, 1945*. Volume 2: *General: Political and Economic Matters*. Washington, D.C.: GPO, 1967. Safehaven, refugees.

———. *Foreign Relations of the United States, 1945*. Volume 3: *European Advisory Commission, Austria, Germany*. Washington, D.C.: GPO, 1968. Peace feelers, Operation Sunrise, general surrender of Germany.

———. *Foreign Relations of the United States, 1945*. Volume 4: *Europe*. Washington, D.C.: GPO, 1968. Bulgaria, France, Hungary, Italy.

———. *Foreign Relations of the United States, 1945*. Volume 5: *Europe*. Washington, D.C.: GPO, 1967. Rumania, Switzerland, USSR, Yugoslavia.

———. *Foreign Relations of the United States: The Conferences at Malta and Yalta, 1945*. Washington, D.C.: GPO, 1955. Grand strategy, postwar settlements.

Index

(The lists on pages 527–61 are not covered by this index but should be used with it to associate code names, source numbers, and abbreviations with entries appearing below.)

www.ingramcontent.com/pod-product-compliance
Lightning Source LLC
Chambersburg PA
CBHW031537300426
44111CB00006BA/88
9780271028040